Poverty and Policy in Post-Apartheid South Africa

Edited by Haroon Bhorat and Ravi Kanbur

HSRC PRESS

Published by HSRC Press
Private Bag X9182, Cape Town, 8000, South Africa
www.hsrcpress.ac.za

© 2006 Human Sciences Research Council

First published 2006

ISBN 0-7969-2122-9

Copy editing by Karen Press
Typeset by Robin Taylor and Jenny Wheeldon
Cover design by Farm Design
Print management by comPress

Distributed in Africa by Blue Weaver
PO Box 30370, Tokai, Cape Town, 7966, South Africa
Tel: +27 (0) 21 701 4477
Fax: +27 (0) 21 701 7302
email: orders@blueweaver.co.za
www.oneworldbooks.com

Distributed in Europe and the United Kingdom by Eurospan Distribution Services (EDS)
3 Henrietta Street, Covent Garden, London, WC2E 8LU, United Kingdom
Tel: +44 (0) 20 7240 0856
Fax: +44 (0) 20 7379 0609
email: orders@edspubs.co.uk
www.eurospangroup.com/bookstore

Distributed in North America by Independent Publishers Group (IPG)
Order Department, 814 North Franklin Street, Chicago, IL 60610, USA
Call toll-free: (800) 888 4741
All other enquiries: +1 (312) 337 0747
Fax: +1 (312) 337 5985
email: frontdesk@ipgbook.com
www.ipgbook.com

Contents

List of tables

List of figures

Foreword

The end of apartheid, though not as bloody as many feared, was nothing less than a revolution. The downtrodden majority, oppressed for nearly five decades by apartheid and for three-and-a-half centuries by colonial racism won justice, but there was little time to celebrate. Democracy had to be built quickly to ensure that the country wouldn't relapse into conflict or dictatorship. This required the economy to be rebuilt.

The economy was not in good shape – it was shrinking. Between 1984 and 1993 per capita income fell by about 15%. Economic decline accelerated in the years leading to the transition.

Moreover, South Africa was not just politically unequal – inequalities of income and wealth matched the worst measured anywhere. In 1993 the poorest 10% of the country's population received 1.1 percent of income while the richest 10% received 45% of income. The formerly politically oppressed majority expected urgent economic redress.

At the heart of redress is the reduction of poverty and inequality. This volume assembles twelve essays by top researchers who ask how well South Africa has addressed these challenges. This is not simply an academic exercise – it is about the ability of the democratic state to build sound foundations for the long-term future of democracy in South Africa.

As the essays show, at this relatively early stage the answer to the question 'How well have we done?' is still subject to debate. While the economy is now growing strongly, there are different views on how well the battle against poverty and inequality has been fought. The debates are reflected within essays and between essays.

What is key is that the quality of the research underlying the essays is sound. The editors Ravi Kanbur and Haroon Bhorat are, respectively, one of the world's top experts on poverty and economic development and one of South Africa's premier economists, who specialises in labour market and poverty analysis. They have ensured that the quality of evidence presented is such that readers will learn a great deal about the most important South African challenges, and will be able to begin to form their own opinions.

Alan Hirsch
Chief Director: Economic Sector
Policy Coordination and Advisory Services
The Presidency
South Africa

Acknowledgements

This book arose out of a series of conversations between the two editors over eighteen months, and was ultimately inspired by South Africa's completion of a decade of democratic rule. However, these discussions, and their ultimate manifestation in the form of this volume, would not have been possible without the involvement of a number of institutions and individuals. These include, in the first instance, the US Agency for International Development (USAID) for its support of this project through its collaborative agreement with Cornell University, Strategies and Analysis for Growth and Access (SAGA). In addition, at a time when academic publishing has become a dying art, we would like to acknowledge the role played by the HSRC Press – in particular Garry Rosenberg and John Daniels, who facilitated the acceptance of this volume for publication. We also acknowledge the contribution to the project of Inga Norenius and her editorial team at the HSRC Press, whose professional advice and commitment to this volume have been a pleasure. To the authors, many of whom have extremely busy schedules, we express our gratitude for their patience and efficiency throughout this process. Finally, Haroon Bhorat would like to thank his wife Najma for enduring much beyond this book, and for her support and encouragement while simultaneously caring for Taahir, Aliya and Samiya.

Abbreviations and acronyms

ANC	African National Congress
ASSA	Actuarial Society of South Africa
ASYCUDA	Automated System for Customs Data
AVE	*ad valorem* equivalents
BCEA	Basic Conditions of Employment Act
BIG	Basic Income Grant
BTP	Benefit Transfer Programmes
CASASP	Centre for the Analysis of South African Social Policy
CCMA	Commission for Conciliation, Mediation and Arbitration
CDF	cumulative distribution functions
CMA	Cape Metropolitan Area
CPI	Consumer Price Index
CPIX	CPI excluding interest rates on mortgage bonds
CSG	child support grant
CSP	community, social and personal (services)
CTUA	Cape Town Urban Area
DPLG	Department of Provincial and Local Government
DSD	Department of Social Development
EA	Enumerator Area
EAP	economically active population
EAR	employment absorption rate
EPR/ERP	effective protection rates
EPRI	Economic Policy Research Institute
EPWP	Expanded Public Works Programme
ERP	effective rates of protection
EU	European Union
FFC	Financial and Fiscal Commission
FGT	Foster-Greer-Thorbecke
GATT	General Agreement on Tariffs and Trade
GDP	Gross Domestic Product
GDS	Growth and Development Summit
GEAR	Growth, Employment and Redistribution
GEIS	General Export Incentive Scheme
GHS	General Household Survey
GIC	growth incidence curve
GVA	gross value added
HOS	Heckscher-Ohlin-Samuelson
HS	Harmonised System
HSL	Household Subsistence Level
HSRC	Human Sciences Research Council
IDC	Industrial Development Corporation

IES	Income and Expenditure Survey
KIDS	KwaZulu-Natal Income Dynamics Survey
LFPR	labour force participation rate
LFS	Labour Force Survey
LRA	Labour Relations Act
LSMS	Living Standards Measurement Survey
MDG	Millennium Development Goal
MFN	most favoured nation
MLU	mature livestock units
MPS	Manpower Survey
Nedlac	National Economic Development and Labour Council
NES	natural, engineering and mathematical sciences
OHS	October Household Survey
OLS	ordinary least squares
PCAS	Policy Coordination and Advisory Services
PPP	purchasing power parity
PSLSD	Project for Statistics on Living Standards and Development
R&D	research and development
RDP	Reconstruction and Development Programme
RSC	Regional Service Council
SACU	Southern African Customs Union
SADC	Southern African Development Community
SAIHS	South Africa Integrated Household Survey, 1993
SALDRU	Southern African Labour and Development Research Unit
SAM	Social Accounting Matrix
SA-PPA	South African Participatory Poverty Assessment
SAPS	South African Police Service
SEE	Survey of Employment and Earnings
SMME	small and medium enterprise
SS	Stolper-Samuelson
SSA	Statistics South Africa
TFP	total factor productivity
TGR	target growth rate
TIPS	Trade and Industry Policy Strategies
TRAINS	Trade Analysis and Information System
UK	United Kingdom
USA	United States of America
VCS	Victims of Crime Survey
WTO	World Trade Organisation

Introduction

Poverty and well-being in post-apartheid South Africa

Haroon Bhorat and Ravi Kanbur

Introduction

The end of the first decade of democracy in South Africa naturally resulted in a wide-ranging set of political events to mark this date. South Africa's formal baptism as a democracy in April 1994 received international acclaim and recognition – and to this day serves as a model for other countries undergoing difficult and protracted political transitions. However, perhaps the greater struggle since the early post-apartheid days has been the attempt to undo the economic vestiges of the system of racial exclusivity. Alongside the political evaluation and praise, therefore, there has been a vigorous local research programme broadly aimed at measuring the changes in well-being that occurred during this ten-year period. In addition, a number of studies have also concentrated on measuring the performance of the government in meeting its stated objectives of reducing poverty, inequality and unemployment. This volume brings together some of the core pieces of academic research that have been prominent in this ten-year review, focusing on poverty and policy in post-apartheid South Africa.[1]

The 'headlines' and 'sound bites' of the ten-year review are by now well known – the first ten years have seen rising unemployment, rising income poverty, and rising income inequality, all in the context of a lacklustre performance in economic growth. The chapters in this volume present the detailed and nuanced analysis that underlies these headlines. In this overview we highlight three key aspects of the picture that the detailed research paints. Firstly, data quality and comparability have been a constant issue in arriving at a consensus among analysts on the outcomes for households and individuals in post-apartheid South Africa. Secondly, while the outcomes on unemployment, poverty and inequality are indeed bad, the outcomes on social indicators and access to public services are much more encouraging. Thirdly, the prospects for rapid and sustained economic growth, without which poverty and well-being cannot be addressed in the long run, are themselves negatively affected by increasing inequality, poverty and unemployment. The following three sections take up each of these points in turn, and the last section provides a conclusion to the discussion.

Data and debate

The most obvious starting point for a ten-year review research programme would be to ascertain the nature of the shifts in a composite set of key welfare indicators. While the key contributions within this arena are captured in this volume, underlying these outputs are critical issues related to the choice of data, data quality and data coverage. Collectively, these are important for scholarly purposes, as we expand on below, but they are also critical as accurate inputs into the policy formulation process in South Africa.

The World Bank-sponsored 1993 Living Standards Measurement Survey (LSMS) for South Africa, undertaken by a local research unit,[2] provided the first nationally representative micro-data set for South Africa on the cusp of its new democracy. Since 1995, however, there has been a steady flow of micro-data sets, differing in focus and coverage. These data sets range from household surveys (1995–99) and censuses (1996, 2001) to income and expenditure surveys (1995, 2000) and biannual labour force surveys (2000 onwards), all of which are nationally representative and are run under the auspices of the national statistical agency – Statistics South Africa (SSA). These data sets have served as the bedrock for undertaking much of the analytical work around welfare shifts in the post-apartheid period. In this sense, these data will continue to be an important source of reference for any re-examination of the country's first ten years of democratic rule.

Given the political impact of any analytical work directly or indirectly assessing South Africa's performance since 1994, the role of data quality and the need to ensure that the data were not contaminated in any form took on a particular relevance. This indeed has been the undertone of much of the research, and consequent debate, that has ensued around the income poverty and inequality shifts reported for the post-apartheid period (Meth 2006). The two key pieces in this literature have been extremely careful and transparent concerning data problems (Hoogeveen and Özler 2006 and Leibbrandt et al. 2006).

The two sets of data available for measuring poverty and inequality shifts since 1994 are the Income and Expenditure Surveys (IESs) of 1995 and 2000 and the Census of 1996 and 2001. Both are equally valid sources of data, but implicitly allow for some semblance of a corroboration of results. In both sets issues of data quality have loomed large (see Cronje and Budlender 2004; Simkins 2003; Meth 2006). These issues have included, with regard to the IESs, the lack of price data, the exclusion of home-grown products in consumption and significant problems with sampling weights. The census data are particularly problematic, for example with regard to large numbers of zero and missing income variables. The latter, in turn, was reported in bands, making a comparison over time a fraught exercise.

Perhaps the most vivid example of the importance of data quality lies in the national debate around 'jobless growth' (Bhorat 2004; Bhorat and Oosthuizen 2006; Casale, Muller and Posel 2004; Meth 2006). It was widely held in political, public sector and media debates that the South African economy had steadily shed jobs, despite positive economic growth, since 1994. The catchphrase for this claim was 'jobless growth' and it became a powerful epithet for reflecting on the general inability of the domestic economy to create jobs. Closer analysis, however, revealed that this notion of jobless growth was reliant on a single and, as it turns out, wholly incomplete, data set (Bhorat and Oosthuizen 2006). The data set, the Standardised Employment and Earnings (SEE) series, excludes large swathes of economic activity, and in so doing misrepresents aggregate employment in South Africa. As a consequence, reliance on this data revealed a steady decline in employment from the mid-1990s in South Africa. This result, when tested against the more reliable household and labour force survey data, has since been shown to be fundamentally flawed – with employment in fact expanding in the post-1994 period.

Whilst many of these issues and their resolutions are now common knowledge in the literature, there are a number of important lessons that arise from these various data decontamination exercises. Firstly, the data-cleaning exercise during this ten-year review process brings into sharp relief the importance of 'getting the numbers right'. For a national and international community intensely interested in how the country has fared in its first decade of democracy, accurate figures on poverty, inequality and unemployment hold a particular policy relevance. Incorrect results, for example as was the case with the 'jobless growth' numbers, can have significant political ramifications. Secondly, it needs to be accepted that the income poverty and inequality shifts, undertaken within the spirit of the ten-year review process, are not in fact a representation of the first decade of democracy. In covering the period 1995–2000 or 1996–2001, depending on the data sets used, these results obviously cover an incomplete time period. The non-availability of more recent data sets of course forced this time-period choice. What this reflects, however, is the importance of trading off imperfect data against the prevalent government policy imperatives. These imperatives were clearly to gain, as best as was possible, an understanding of welfare shifts in the post-apartheid period. Thirdly, the problems the research community has experienced with data delivered by the national statistical agency, whilst resulting in often fractious engagements, has opened up a portal of information-sharing. In so doing, the research community is able to feed back its concerns around data to the national statistical body – and this alone means that the process of data verification remains policy-relevant. Fourthly, South Africa has also, since 1994, seen the proliferation of a number of smaller, regional and unofficial surveys. These include most notably the KwaZulu-Natal Income Dynamics Survey (KIDS), which is a panel tracking households in this province (May 2006) and, more recently, the Cape Area Panel Survey. These data sets should remain an important source for corroborating national results and, furthermore, should serve as a tool for extracting more nuanced information on poverty, inequality and labour market issues in South Africa.

Outcomes: Incomes, unemployment and social indicators

Mindful of the hard questions that have been asked of the data, and of course of the fact that data availability in most instances prevents an analysis of trends that is true to the full decade of democracy – what, then, are some of the more important shifts we have witnessed under the guidance of the new government?

There is overwhelming evidence to suggest that income poverty has increased. The headcount index increased nationally from 32 to 34 per cent between 1995 and 2000 or, using a different data set, from 26 to 28 per cent between 1996 and 2001 on a $2-a-day poverty line (Hoogeveen and Özler 2006; Leibbrandt, Levinsohn and McCrary 2005; Leibbrandt et al. 2006). The increase is still seen when measured using the broader FGT class of poverty measures (Foster, Greer and Thorbecke 1984), which give weight to the depth of poverty as well as to the number of the poor. Hence, over the 1995–2000 period, we find that for any realistic poverty line, the headcount index and the poverty gap measure show significant increases nationally (Hoogeveen and Özler 2006). For example, on a poverty line of $2-a-day, the mean poor household earned 11 per cent below this line in 1995 and by 2000 this had increased to 13 per cent.

The data by race are particularly revealing. Between 1995 and 2000, absolute and relative poverty levels amongst African-headed households increased, while for non-African households they either remained stagnant or declined. While the inter-censal analysis also reveals an overall increase in the headcount and poverty gap measures, this result is not restricted to African-headed households. Hence the 1996–2001 Census data analysis suggests that both absolute and relative poverty levels increased for African, coloured and (at the higher poverty line) Asian/Indian households. Indeed, while coloured headcount poverty declines from 20 to 12 per cent in the 1995–2000 comparison, it increases from 10 to 13 per cent in the inter-censal comparison. The availability of future data sets would ensure a test of both these results for the coloured population (Hoogeveen and Özler 2006; Leibbrandt et al. 2006).

One of the more important results within this exercise lies in the spatial dimensions of poverty. Both a 1995–2000 and an inter-censal comparison indicate a rise in rural and urban household poverty. For example, the proportion of urban (rural) households classified as poor increased from 13 (45) per cent to 16 (46) per cent, on a $2-a-day poverty line, between 1996 and 2001 (Leibbrandt et al. 2006). Importantly, however, the share of the rural poor in overall poverty is declining; thus, while the rural poor accounted for 62 per cent of all poor households in 1996, five years later this had declined to 56 per cent. This suggests a rapid process of urban migration that could in the future reshape the spatial nature of poverty in South Africa. Indeed, more specific numbers on migrant workers indicate that the incidence of migrant (or sending) households in rural areas increased from about 1.2 to 1.5 million households (Posel and Casale 2006). This role of space in reinforcing or potentially overcoming South Africa's welfare challenges is likely to feature increasingly in future policy debates. The process of fairly rapid urbanisation from poorer to richer provinces is now beginning to be documented (Oosthuizen and Naidoo 2004) – and it is evident that this presents new challenges for wealthier provinces and their cities. One very specific example of these challenges is a study on recent migrants to the city of Cape Town. Results here show that, controlling for individual and household characteristics, recent rural migrants to the city stand a lower probability of finding employment in the city, relative to non-migrants (Rospabe and Selod 2006).

Income inequality has also increased, with the Gini coefficient rising from 0.565 to 0.577 between 1995 and 2000, while on a 1996 and 2001 comparison the Gini rose from 0.68 to 0.73 (Hoogeveen and Özler 2006; Leibbrandt, Levinsohn and McCrary 2005; Leibbrandt et al. 2006). Aside from the national Gini coefficients increasing in both sets of data, there is also Lorenz-dominance in the time comparisons, ensuring that this increase is unambiguous (Leibbrandt et al. 2006). The Gini coefficient has risen consistently across all race groups in the inter-censal comparison, although it declines noticeably for Asians/Indians and whites when using the IES data. Urban and rural inequality has also risen. Also interesting are the measures of between-group and within-group inequality, using the sub-group decomposable Theil index. It has always been argued that between-group inequality has been a key facet of understanding income inequality in South Africa. Hence, the contribution of between-group inequality to overall inequality in South Africa stood at about 60 per cent in the 1970s (Whiteford and van Seventer 2000). In 1996, using the census estimates, the share of between-group inequality had declined to 43 per cent, and by 2001 this figure was 40 per cent. Put differently, while the key fault-line in income inequality terms, that of the African-white income differential, was being eroded, this was being replaced by a significant growth in within-group income inequality. This share of within-group inequality has increased by some 20 percentage points over the last three decades in South Africa. Specifically, the overall driver of income inequality in post-apartheid South Africa continues to be the rising inequality amongst African households.

Whilst these national data sets are extremely useful for static comparative exercises, the one significant disadvantage is that they are unable to reflect on patterns of income mobility. The KIDS data set is a panel and hence allows for fairly nuanced, albeit geographically restricted, analysis of income mobility. Applying transition matrices to this data, results indicate that about one-third of those households that were poor in 1993 were non-poor in 1998, thus representing those in transitory poverty (May 2006). Equally important is the result for those households just above the poverty line in 1993: by 1998 about 50 per cent of these households had fallen back into poverty (May 2006). Indeed, while it is important to emphasise the significance of transitions into and out of poverty amongst South African households, the results also make it clear that the initial level of household income and wealth, which can in part be proxied by a variety of labour market indicators, is a significant predictor of movement out of poverty (May 2006; Cichello, Fields and Leibbrandt 2005).

Changes in the labour market remain possibly the key transmission mechanism for understanding the shifts in income poverty and inequality. Labour market developments, in turn, indicate a significant increase in the unemployment rate irrespective of the definition used. The broad unemployment rate increased from 31 to 42 per cent, while narrow unemployment rates rose from 18 to 31 per cent (Bhorat and Oosthuizen 2006). Hence the data for South Africa on employment and unemployment trends appear to strongly reinforce the income trends noted above. The data show that over the period 1995–2002, aggregate employment grew by some 1.5 million jobs, at an average rate of 2.3 per cent per annum. This remains slightly below the economic growth rate over the period. In turn, however, the labour force grew by some 5.2 million individuals, resulting in a massive rise in the national unemployment levels from 4.2 million in 1995 to close to 8 million in 2002 (Bhorat and Oosthuizen 2006). Thus, while the economy did not experience jobless growth in the post-apartheid period, employment absorption was sufficiently poor to result in rising unemployment rates for all races and both sexes. In turn, these labour market shifts reflect a continued trend of skills-biased labour demand needs as the share of skilled and semi-skilled workers continued to rise in the post-apartheid period. Other studies have also reported the worrying spectre of sharply rising graduate unemployment, driven by the qualities and types of tertiary qualification being accumulated by individuals (Bhorat 2004).

The above headline results dominate much of the policy discourse around the shifts in social and economic indicators since April 1994. The rise in income deprivation or income maldistribution – measured differentially by the Gini coefficient, the headcount index and the unemployment rate – is undoubted. This should not, however, mask some important movements in access to public services and in social indicators. These shifts are worthy of their own headlines. The post-1994 era is notable for the rapid reallocation of resources through the fiscus, from rich, white households to poor, African households. Broadly, while approximately 40 per cent of aggregate social spending was directed to whites and 43 per cent to Africans in the mid-1980s, by the late 1990s fully 80 per cent of total social spending was assigned to the African populace and less than 10 per cent to whites (Van der Berg 2006). The results of this fiscal switch are evident in the data on assets and services. Hence, the share of households with access to piped water increased from 80 to 85 per cent between 1996 and 2001 – with similar gains reported for related sanitation services (Bhorat, Poswell and Naidoo 2004). The share of households with access to electricity for lighting and cooking has shown particularly spectacular gains. For example, between 1996 and 2001, the share of African households with access to electricity for lighting increased from 44 to 62 per cent (Leibbrandt et al. 2006). While less significant, improvements in local government services (principally refuse removal) were also reported.

There has thus been a remarkable shift of fiscal resources toward poor households in post-apartheid South Africa. There are three key issues within this overall fiscal reallocation. Firstly, the magnitude of the shifts is important to understand, and is particularly interesting, given that over the same period government managed to reduce its deficit-to-GDP ratio. Secondly, the incidence of the shift is important, and the extent to which it was biased toward the poor must be analysed. Finally, aside from the magnitude of the shift in resources, we need to be sure that it has resulted in the intended outcomes.

In terms of aggregate shifts, social service expenditure (encompassing spending on education, health, housing and social security) increased from 12 to 17 per cent of GDP between 1993 and 2003. Proportionately, the largest increases were recorded for housing and social security, where expenditure (as a share of GDP) increased by 40 and 92 per cent respectively (National Treasury 2004). Government spending on water schemes and services also increased dramatically – from R847 million per annum in 1993 to R4 445 million in 2003 – a 76 per cent rise over the decade. Put differently, real per capita social expenditure (including water service provision) stood at R2 170 per person in 1983. By 2003, this figures was R3 451 per person, which represents close to a 60 per cent increase in total social spending. It should be clear, then, that a dramatic fiscal reallocation process took place in the post-apartheid era. Driven by a need to overcome severe backlogs in these different spheres, there was a sharp refocusing of expenditure towards potentially poverty-alleviating assets and services.

The second issue – the extent to which this redirection of expenditure did in fact reach its intended beneficiaries – is of course the domain of fiscal incidence analysis. Evidence indicates a consistent shift in expenditure toward poorer households. Between 1995 and 2000, per capita social spending increased by between 21 and 38 per cent for the 1st and 2nd deciles. In turn, social spending declined on a per capita basis by 9 per cent (6 per cent) for the 9th (10th) decile (Van der Berg 2005). By race, per capita social spending on Africans increased by 20 per cent between 1995 and 2000, while it declined for all other race groups (Van der Berg 2005). Allocation to rural areas increased by over 30 per cent, while that for urban areas declined. Summary measures of expenditure indicate that spending on education (particularly on schools, and less so for tertiary education), health, housing and water are equity-enhancing, while that on social security is strongly equity-enhancing (Van der Berg 2006). On the latter, for example, the introduction of a new state transfer, the child support grant (CSG), together with very high take-up rates in existing social grants – most notably the old-age pension – has made the state's social security provision the most effective anti-poverty intervention. Of total social security expenditure, in 2000, 61 per cent was allocated to individuals in the 1st and 2nd deciles (Van der Berg 2006).

Given this clear pro-poor orientation of fiscal expenditure, the outcomes that this has engendered are also important to capture. In the case of services – principally water, sanitation and electricity – the results point to a widening of access for vulnerable households. Relatively new work in the area has analysed the shift in entitlement deprivation over the 1993–2004 period (Naidoo and van der Westhuizen 2005). Applying the growth incidence curve methodology to these shifts, the results indicate absolute and relative pro-poor growth in access to services and assets, when measured against per capita household expenditure. For example, access to formal housing grew by 42 and 34 per cent for deciles 1 and 2 between 1993 and 2004, and by 21 and 16 per cent for deciles 3 and 4. Access to piped water increased by 187 per cent over this period, while the growth was 31 per cent in the 4th decile. Finally, a reflection of possibly the most successful of these interventions – access to electricity for lighting – expanded by 578 per cent for the poorest decile and 286 per cent for the 2nd-poorest decile.

In terms of state provision of education, panel data indicate that it remains the most important asset for extracting households out of poverty (May 2006) and the resource shift in this sense is extremely positive. However, more detailed evidence on the specific earmarking of this expanded budget indicates that much of the funds went toward increasing teacher salaries (Fiske and Ladd 2005). For example, expenditure per learner increased from R2 222 to R3 253 between 1995 and 2001, while over the same period, learner-educator ratios remained constant at 30 : 1 (Fiske and Ladd 2005).

Ultimately, though, the above analysis of welfare shifts in the post-apartheid period points to three important lessons. Firstly, that any exhaustive analysis of changes in household and individual well-being should also account for non-income measures of deprivation. As a consequence, a true appreciation of the shifts that have occurred in the post-apartheid period can be derived only through comparing and contrasting movements in income, assets and services available to the poor. Secondly, the importance of this comparative exercise is magnified in the context here, given that these non-income measures – measures of Sen's entitlement deprivation – have in fact moved counter to the standard income metrics of vulnerability. It is not possible to make an objective assessment of whether poverty, measured multi-dimensionally, has in fact increased in the post-apartheid period. New methods that have recently been designed to undertake such exercises (Duclos, Sahn and Younger 2005) would appear to be the next step in the country's domestic research programme. Finally, it should be kept in mind that increased expenditure allocations, independent of income poverty and inequality shifts, are a necessary but not sufficient condition for welfare improvements. In addition to the example of education outlays noted above, prices are an important predictor of welfare outcomes. Hence, recent evidence has indicated that the key drivers of aggregate inflation for poor urban households in the 1998–2002 period have been public services including water, electricity, transport and sanitation services (Bhorat and Oosthuizen 2004). The provision of the asset or service, therefore, remains only a first step in ensuring that vulnerable households are sufficiently empowered to extricate themselves from permanent or transitory poverty.

Policy: Growth and distribution

All of the trends in income and non-income measures of well-being have played out against the backdrop of poor overall economic growth performance by the South African economy. Economic growth rates since 1994 have been modest, with the highest recorded being 4.3 per cent in 1996. Furthermore, the trend over this short period has been downward until 1999, and then levelling-off to a range between 2 and 4 per cent since 2000. Importantly, though, the pre-1994 period was characterised by negative growth rates, and since the advent of democracy growth, while in absolute terms remaining insufficient, averaged about 3 per cent over the decade. The positive, yet tepid growth rates are manifest in the fact that over the 1994–2003 period, the mean population growth rate was over 2 per cent, resulting in a real per capita GDP growth rate of 0.9 per cent over the period. In addition, data available for middle-income and low-middle-income countries from the World Bank indicate that the mean growth rates for these composite countries for the period 1999 to 2003 were above that for South Africa over the same period[3] (World Bank 2005). There can be no doubt, therefore, that since 1994, the economy has remained in a low-level growth cycle.

It is widely accepted that consistent and high levels of economic growth will, holding income inequality constant, reduce levels of income poverty in a society (Dollar and Kraay 2002; Ravallion and Chen 2003; Kanbur 2005). This has, of course, been the implicit approach taken by policy authorities in post-apartheid South Africa: namely, that a multitude of policy interventions being pursued across all national government departments are simultaneously designed to place the economy on a significantly higher growth trajectory.

With this in mind, a burgeoning research agenda in South Africa is being focused on understanding the constraints on long-run growth. These can be categorised in terms of a number of broad determining factors which, thematically, include: the role of the labour market in growth; trade liberalisation; domestic market inefficiencies and the importance of social ills, specifically HIV/AIDS and crime. We turn now to a brief consideration of each of these elements, within the context of the extent to which they may act as a constraint on long-run growth.

The role of the labour market in constraining economic growth can be broadly cast in terms of three key concerns. The first is the role of labour legislation in hindering growth in domestic investment and hence employment creation. The second is South Africa's well-known skills mismatch – a high demand for skilled labour co-existing with an excess supply of unskilled labour – and its relationship to domestic economic growth. The third concern is the highly contentious wage–employment trade-off.

Firm survey evidence, based on the perceptions of employers, has indicated fairly consistently that they view employment constraints as partly operating through the labour regulatory environment. Secondly, within this regulatory framework, dismissal clauses in the amended Labour Relations Act of 2002 are viewed as particularly inimical to employment creation, production costs and productivity levels (Bhorat 2005; Chandra 2000; Rankin 2005). One objective measure of these costs indicates that the dismissal costs for labourers, as a ratio of own-mean wage, is three times that of managers (Bhorat 2005). Within the regulatory environment, there remain significant concerns about the extent to which South Africa's workplace grievance institution – the Commission for Conciliation, Mediation and Arbitration (CCMA) – has perhaps contributed to increased inefficiency within the labour market through a combination of having to adhere to specific regulatory provisions; its own internal procedural machinations; and, finally, general resource constraints, particularly relating to the shortage of skilled personnel (Benjamin and Gruen 2005; Cheadle 2005). Compounding this is the view that much of the legislation is biased against small businesses, purely by virtue of their inability to meet a myriad of requirements in the legislation – the so-called 'procedural burden' inherent in South Africa's regulatory environment (Small Business Project 2005).

In terms of South Africa's skills shortage, the rise in the demand for highly skilled workers has been well documented for South Africa (Bhorat and Hodge 1999; Edwards 2001), and the extent to which it acts as a constraint on the productivity levels of firms has also been shown (Chandra 2000). Also related to this, however, is the fact that this shortage of high-level human capital has hindered growth in fixed investment through constraining new investments in research and development (R&D) in higher educational institutions (Fedderke 2006; Fedderke, de Kadt and Luiz 2003). In addition, there continues to be skilled-immigration legislation that is not entirely suited to an economy such as South Africa's, with its chronic skills shortage.

Finally, the contentious issue of the wage–employment trade-off continues to be the subject of debate in South Africa. Estimates of South Africa's long-run wage elasticity of employment have been consistently negative and less than unity and at the aggregate level range from -0.5 to -0.7 (Bowles and Heintz 1996; Fallon and Lucas 1998; Fields, Leibbrandt and Wakeford 1999). With different specifications and according to skill classes, the elasticity can rise to as much as -2.23 (Fedderke 2006). There would seem to be two issues here. The first is that while the wage–employment trade-off cannot be doubted, the link between wages and household poverty still requires further analytical refinement. Hence, it is not clear whether wage increases will ultimately reduce levels of household poverty in the society. Although we now have an analytical framework to lean on (Fields and Kanbur 2005), this is a new line of enquiry critical to taking this debate forward. Secondly, independent of the veracity of the elasticity estimates, there remains a very powerful political economy fact: that wage repression of whatever scale and intensity in South Africa's highly unionised environment is a recipe for potentially severe social and political instability. This fact should never be discounted when considering the implications of pursuing a policy of mandated real wage reductions.

South Africa embarked on a process of trade liberalisation in the mid-1980s, intensifying this considerably in the post-apartheid period under World Trade Organisation commitments. There was, therefore, a significant reduction in average tariff rates, combined with a simplification of the tariff structure (Cassim et al. 2002; Edwards 2006). Evidence in turn indicates that this liberalisation process has resulted in a twin process of growth in exports and increased import penetration ratios. Furthermore, studies have shown that increased trade over time in South Africa is significantly associated with a growth in total factor productivity, with little evidence, if any, of de-industrialisation (Cassim et al. 2002; Tsikata,1999). The debate within South Africa on trade reform in the post-apartheid period has also, however, focused on the labour market effects of reducing these distortions. Tariff reduction seems to have been disproportionately applied to labour-intensive sectors, with the growth in net trade in the post-1994 period biased strongly in favour of skill-intensive sectors (Edwards 2006). A more detailed decomposition exercise designed to measure the sources of employment growth in the post-apartheid period, however, finds a small positive effect on employment from net trade, with many of the employment losses in the formal sector attributable to technological change (Edwards 2006). Perhaps one of the key determinants of trade performance in the first decade of democracy has been the exchange rate. There has been a significant increase in the volatility of the real effective exchange rate since 1994, which has resulted in considerable uncertainty amongst exporters (Cassim et al. 2002). Given that monetary policy is now guided by inflation targeting, the exchange rate has ceased to be a nominal anchor, and hence the search for a stable and competitive exchange rate becomes a key variable for export competitiveness in the future.

High levels of concentration in the South African economy have resulted in mark-ups that are significantly higher in South Africa than comparable international evidence suggests (Fedderke 2006). These mark-ups are as high as 80 per cent within the domestic manufacturing sector, with the USA manufacturing data indicating a mark-up of about 45 per cent (Fedderke 2006). In addition, evidence for the banking sector suggests that the margins here are high by international standards – and twice those for European banks (Okeahalam 2002). One consequence of these high margins in the banking sector is that they have acted as a constraint on the growth of small businesses in South Africa (Berry, von Blottnitz, Cassim and Kesper 2002). Within this context, then, the role of greater import competition and competition policy is enhanced. A combination of the two would ultimately result in reducing concentration levels in domestic industries, thereby inducing not only enhanced consumer welfare but also greater domestic and international competitiveness.

The role of institutions and governance in economic growth is clearly an important determinant of long-run growth. The literature on the subject in South Africa in the post-apartheid period is unfortunately relatively thin, with a few exceptions (Fedderke 2006). Hence, while we are aware that issues of corruption, contract enforcement, the perception of the legal system and political certainty are key, little formal empirical evidence currently exists to isolate their importance as constraints on growth. Two significant areas of uncertainty, though, are obvious, and deserve attention here, namely the extraordinarily high levels of crime in South Africa combined with the country's very high incidence of HIV/AIDS.

South Africa's incidence of both violent and non-violent criminal activity remains one of the highest in the world (Demombynes and Özler 2006). Firm survey evidence also indicates that employers view crime and theft as the most important constraints on firm growth (Rankin 2005). Apart from the uncertainty generated by these high levels of crime, thereby impeding long-run growth, it is also clear that they significantly increase the operating costs of firms. In addition, crime is a key contributor to skilled-labour emigration. The fortunes, though, of income inequality and criminal activity are also closely intertwined. Micro-evidence suggests that high levels of income inequality, particularly within-group inequality, are a significant and positive determinant of the incidence of burglary and vehicle theft, as well as of violent crime (Demombynes and Özler 2006). Ultimately, there exists a vicious triangle which links income inequality to crime, which in turn induces high levels of investment uncertainty. This acts as possibly one of the key constraints on long-run economic growth in South Africa.

South Africa's HIV/AIDS prevalence remains one of the highest in the world. Estimates suggest that the prevalence amongst adults aged 15–49 was 21.5 per cent in 2003. This compares with a global average of 1.1 per cent and a mean of 7.5 per cent for sub-Saharan Africa (UNAIDS 2004). In addition, the pandemic has disproportionately struck young, economically active adults as well as those categorised as semi-skilled or unskilled (Arndt and Lewis 2002). The pandemic's impact on long-run growth operates, of course, through a multitude of channels. These include, for example, declining productivity amongst the infected employed, increased pressure on health and other social services as the pandemic matures, reduced investment expenditure and savings in households treating infected individuals, and so on. Over a ten-year horizon, modelling exercises estimate that per capita GDP is likely to be on average 8 per cent lower given the impact of the pandemic (Arndt and Lewis 2002). Estimates of the impact on long-run growth indicate that the pandemic may result in a 0.5 to 1 per cent reduction in real GDP per annum (Arndt and Lewis 2002; Bureau for Economic Research 2001).

The above, then, has provided a quick, and by no means exhaustive, tour of some of the key constraints on long-run growth in South Africa. While steady progress is being made on some of these fronts, notably within the area of deregulating domestic markets and trade liberalisation, there has been a fair degree of policy inertia. The latter is particularly true in the case of crime and the HIV/AIDS pandemic, which, given their powerful impact on investment and uncertainty, suggests a need for some redirection of state commitment to focusing on these binding constraints on growth. Within the growth and distribution nexus, though, evidence for South Africa indicates that the nature of the economy's growth path is equally important. Evidence for the 1995–2000 period, for example, indicates that South Africa's growth trajectory has not been pro-poor in nature (Hoogeveen and Özler 2006). Complementary evidence indicates that South Africa's economic growth post-1994, while being positive, has induced a significant maldistribution of income. The latter has been large enough to erode any income benefits to the poor and has ultimately yielded an increase in national poverty levels. Hence, despite a growth in per capita expenditure between 1995 and 2000, this growth has not been sufficiently high to offset the accompanying rise in inequality. Put differently, most of the gains in income through economic growth in the post-apartheid period in the form of reduced poverty levels have been dissipated through increased income inequality.

What is interesting overall is the deep and organic connection between economic growth, which provides the resources for improving income and non-income dimensions of well-being, and distributional outcomes along these very dimensions, since research demonstrates that these distributional outcomes themselves influence the prospects for growth.

Conclusion

Five clear trends have emerged in the analysis of welfare shifts in the post-apartheid period. These are, firstly, an increase in both absolute and relative income poverty, when using the standard measures of poverty. Secondly, there has been an increase in income inequality, which is notably being catalysed by a rise in the share of within-group inequality. Thirdly, despite some employment growth, the rapid expansion of the labour force has resulted in increased unemployment rates irrespective of the definition used. Fourthly, a large and swift fiscal resource shift has engendered widened access to assets and basic services for poor households. These aggregate trends are fairly consistent across race and gender – with the shifts amongst the African population predictably influencing many of the results. One important, relatively new dimension to emerge from the above broad trends has been the declining share of rural poverty as a consequence of increased migration and urbanisation. Fifthly and finally, these changes in poverty and well-being in the post-1994 period have occurred within, and have influenced and been influenced by, an environment of tepid economic growth rates.

The constraints on growth identified above speak to the menu of policy options available to the government. While ensuring that a conducive environment to realise higher growth is critical, this should not marginalise the issue of income vulnerability. In this context, it is the nature of growth, together with growth itself, that is crucial, and the dissipating impact of inequality on economic growth is a key result. Given South Africa's severe income vulnerability, the growth-poverty-inequality nexus retains a particular relevance for the future.

The overview deliberately traverses a number of conceptual, research and policy challenges that still prevail some ten years after the advent of democracy. We hope that the rest of this volume expands appropriately on some of these ideas, in a bid to provide a more expansive assessment of welfare issues in the post-1994 period. We hope, finally, that this volume may also provide the seeds for fresh and new ideas on how this multitude of challenges can be dealt with in the country's second decade of democracy.

Acknowledgements

The authors are grateful to USAID for its support of this project through its collaborative agreement with Cornell University, Strategies and Analysis for Growth and Access (SAGA).

Notes

1   The state, through the Presidency of South Africa, did prepare its own ten-year review, which in fact drew directly or indirectly on many of the findings presented in this book (PCAS 2003).

2   The research unit that undertook the survey was the Southern Africa Labour and Development Research Unit (SALDRU) and the survey has in fact come to be known as the SALDRU 1993 data set.

3   Specifically the middle-income aggregate average growth rate was 3.7 per cent per annum while that for low-middle-income economies was 4.8 per cent per annum.

References

Arndt C & Lewis J (2002) *The HIV/AIDS pandemic in South Africa: Sectoral impacts and unemployment*. Discussion paper. World Bank: Washington, DC .

Benjamin P & Gruen C (2005) The regulatory efficency of the CCMA: A statistical analysis. Unpublished mimeo. University of the Witwatersrand: Johannesburg.

Berry A, von Blottnitz M, Cassim R & Kesper A (2002) *The Economics of SMMES in South Africa*. Working Paper: Trade and Industrial Policy Strategies (TIPS).

Bhorat H (2004) Labour market challenges in the post-apartheid South Africa, *South African Journal of Economics* 72(5): 940–977.

Bhorat H (2005) Labour supply and demand constraints on employment creation: A microeconomic analysis. Paper presented to the School of Development Studies 50th Anniversary Conference. University of KwaZulu-Natal: Durban.

Bhorat H & Hodge J (1999) Decomposing shifts in labour demand in South Africa, *South African Journal of Economics* 67(3): 348–380.

Bhorat H & Kanbur R (2006) *Poverty and policy in post-apartheid South Africa*. Cape Town: HSRC Press.

Bhorat H & Oosthuizen M (2004) The impact of inflation on the urban poor in South Africa: 1997–2002. Unpublished Research Report for the South African Reserve Bank: Pretoria.

Bhorat H & Oosthuizen M (2006) Evolution of the labour market: 1995-2002. In H Bhorat and R Kanbur (2006) *Poverty and policy in post-apartheid South Africa*. Cape Town: HSRC Press.

Bhorat H, Poswell L & Naidoo P (2004) *Dimensions of poverty in post-apartheid South Africa*. Development Policy Research Unit. University of Cape Town: Cape Town.

Bowles S & Heintz J (1996) Wages and jobs in the South African economy: An econometric investigation. Unpublished report prepared for the Presidential Labour Market Commission.

Bureau for Economic Research (2001) *The macroeconomic impact of HIV/AIDS in South Africa*. Economic Research Note 10. University of Stellenbosch: Cape Town.

Casale D, Muller C & Posel D (2004) Two million net new jobs? A reconsideration of the rise in employment in South Africa: 1995–2003, *South African Journal of Economics* 72(5): 978–1002.

Cassim R et al. (2002) *The state of trade policy in South Africa*. Trade and Industrial Policy Secretariat: Johannesburg.

Chandra V (2000) *Constraints to growth and employment in South Africa. Report 1: Statistics from the Large Manufacturing Survey*. World Bank Discussion Paper 14. World Bank: Washington, DC.

Cheadle H (2005) Regulated flexibility and small business: Revisiting the LRA and BCEA. Unpublished mimeo. University of Cape Town: Cape Town.

Cichello P, Fields G & Leibbrandt M (2005) Earnings and employment dynamics for Africans in post-apartheid KwaZulu-Natal: A panel study of KwaZulu-Natal, *Journal of African Economies* 14(2): 143–190.

Cronje M & Budlender D (2004) Comparing census 1996 and census 2001: An operational perspective, *Southern African Journal of Demography* 9(1): 67–89.

Demombynes G & Özler B (2006) Crime and local inequality in South Africa. In H Bhorat and R Kanbur (2006) *Poverty and policy in post-apartheid South Africa*. Cape Town: HSRC Press.

Dollar D and Kraay A (2002) Growth is good for the poor, *Journal of Economic Growth* 7(3): 195–225.

Duclos J-Y, Sahn D & Younger S (2005) Robust multidimensional poverty comparisons, *The Economic Journal*, forthcoming.

Edwards L (2001) Globalisation and the skill bias of occupational employment in South Africa, *South African Journal of Economics* 69(1): 40–71.

Edwards L (2006) Trade liberalization and labour demand in South Africa during the 1990s. In H Bhorat and R Kanbur (2006) *Poverty and policy in post-apartheid South Africa*. Cape Town: HSRC Press.

Fallon P & Lucas R (1998) *South African labor markets: Adjustment and inequalities*. Informal Discussion Paper No. 12. World Bank: Washington, DC.

Fedderke J (2006) From chimera to prospect: South African sources of and constraints on long-term growth, 1970–2000. In H Bhorat and R Kanbur (2006) *Poverty and policy in post-apartheid South Africa*. Cape Town: HSRC Press.

Fedderke JW, De Kadt RHJ & Luiz J (2003) A capstone tertiary educational system: Inefficiency, duplication and inequity in South Africa's tertiary education system, 1910–93, *Cambridge Journal of Economics* 27(3): 377–400.

Fields G & Kanbur R (2005) 'Minimum Wages and Poverty', May, 2005. Cornell University: Ithaca.

Fields G, Leibbrandt M & Wakeford J (1999) *Key labour market elasticities in South Africa*. Department of Finance: Pretoria.

Fiske EB & Ladd HF (2005) *Elusive equity: Education reform in post-apartheid South Africa*. Cape Town: HSRC Press.

Foster JE, Greer J & Thorbecke E (1984) A class of decomposable poverty indices, *Econometrica* 52: 761–766.

Hoogeveen J & Özler B (2006) Poverty and inequality in post-apartheid South Africa: 1995–2000. In H Bhorat and R Kanbur (2006) *Poverty and policy in post-apartheid South Africa*. Cape Town: HSRC Press.

Kanbur R (2005) Growth, inequality and poverty: Some hard questions, *Journal of International Affairs*, Spring.

Leibbrandt M, Levinsohn J & McCrary J (2005) *Incomes in South Africa since the fall of apartheid*. NBER Working Paper No. 11384. National Bureau for Economic Research: Cambridge.

Leibbrandt M, Poswell L, Naidoo P, Welch M & Woolard I (2006) Measuring recent changes in South African inequality and poverty. In H Bhorat and R Kanbur (2006) *Poverty and policy in post-apartheid South Africa*. Cape Town: HSRC Press.

May J (2006) Persistent poverty, asset accumulation and shocks in South Africa: Evidence from KwaZulu-Natal. In H Bhorat and R Kanbur (2006) *Poverty and policy in post-apartheid South Africa*. Cape Town: HSRC Press.

Meth C (2006) Half-measures revisited: The ANC's unemployment and poverty reduction goals. In H Bhorat and R Kanbur (2006) *Poverty and policy in post-apartheid South Africa*. Cape Town: HSRC Press.

Naidoo P & van der Westhuizen C (2005) Shifts in access to services and assets in South Africa: 1993–2004. Unpublished. Development Policy Research Unit: University of Cape Town.

National Treasury (2004) *Budget Review 2004*. National Treasury of South Africa. Government Printer: Pretoria.

Okeahalam C (2002) *Structure and conduct in the commercial banking sector of South Africa*. Working Paper No. 7. Johannesburg: TIPS.

Oosthuizen M & Naidoo P (2004) *Internal Migration to the Gauteng Province*. DPRU Working Paper 04/88. Development Policy Research Unit: University of Cape Town.

Posel D & Casale D (2006) Internal labour migration and household poverty in post-apartheid South Africa. In H Bhorat and R Kanbur (2006) *Poverty and policy in post-apartheid South Africa*. Cape Town: HSRC Press.

Rankin N (2005) The regulatory environment and SMMEs. Evidence from South African firm level data. Unpublished mimeo. University of the Witwatersrand: Johannesburg.

Ravallion M & Chen S (2003) Measuring pro-poor growth, *Economic Letters* 78(1): 93–99.

Rospabe S & Selod H (2006) Does city structure cause unemployment? The case of Cape Town. In H Bhorat and R Kanbur (2006) *Poverty and policy in post-apartheid South Africa*. Cape Town: HSRC Press.

Simkins C (2003) A critical assessment of the 1995 and 2000 income and expenditure surveys as sources of information on incomes. Unpublished. University of the Witwatersrand.

Small Business Project (2005) *Counting the costs of red tape to business in South Africa*. Small Business Project: Johannesburg.

Policy Co-ordination and Advisory Services (PCAS) The Presidency (2003) *Towards a ten year review: Synthesis report on implementation of government programmes*. Presidency of South Africa: Pretoria.

Tsikata Y (1999) *Liberalisation and trade performance in South Africa*. World Bank Informal Discussion Papers on Aspects of the South African Economy 13. World Bank: Washington, DC.

UNAIDS (2004) *2004 Report on the Global Aids Epidemic*. UNAIDS: Geneva.

Van der Berg S (2005) *Fiscal expenditure incidence in South Africa, 1995 and 2000*. A Report for the National Treasury. University of Stellenbosch: Cape Town.

Van der Berg S (2006) Public spending and the poor since the transition to democracy. In H Bhorat and R Kanbur (2006) *Poverty and policy in post-apartheid South Africa*. Cape Town: HSRC Press.

Whiteford AC & van Seventer DE (2000) South Africa's changing income distribution in the 1990s, *Journal of Studies in Economics and Econometrics* 24(3): 7–30.

World Bank (2005) *World Development Indicators Database*. World Bank: Washington, DC.

1 From chimera to prospect: South African sources of and constraints on long-term growth, 1970–2000

Johannes Fedderke

Introduction

South Africa's democratic transition now lies more than a decade in the past, a period long enough to allow us to take stock of the past growth performance of the country and recognise implications for its future pro-growth policies. The successful political transition raised hopes for an economic transition characterised by broadly shared growth and greater access of the majority of the population to economic opportunities, and hence to jobs. Economic policies have, indeed, been geared towards ensuring macroeconomic stability (with considerable success) and raising access to basic social services, especially education and health. A number of special initiatives have also aimed to promote a wider spread of economic benefits across the population. However, the outcomes in terms of growth of per capita income and employment have been below expectations. Two important questions, therefore, arise, one positive: what were the main determinants of and institutional constraints on long-term growth in South Africa? and the other normative: what are the implications of this positive analysis for future economic policies?

In this chapter we hope to shed light on both of these questions. Simply put, we are interested in identifying the main factors that have constrained output growth and, in particular, employment growth in South Africa, especially during the past ten years. Based on this analysis, we also offer some preliminary thoughts on what economic and social policies could do to engender more dynamic and broadly shared economic growth in the future.

We begin with a review and decomposition of the long-run performance in terms of real output and employment creation. Specifically, we decompose South Africa's growth into its primary sources, in order to identify any underlying structural changes. The evidence obtained in this way reveals that not only have growth and employment creation in South Africa been subject to a long-term, structural decline, but the sources of economic growth have also shifted from capital accumulation to growth in total factor productivity. Put differently, South Africa's growth pattern has simply *not* been labour-absorbing to the degree that was necessary to generate a sustained decline in the high unemployment rate. The question is: why is this so?

To answer this and related questions, we first focus on perhaps the most fundamental driver of long-term growth to date: investment in physical capital stock. The evidence suggests that rates of return on capital and the user cost of capital are fundamental to the determination of investment in fixed capital stock, but exercise their influence subject to the powerful impact of *uncertainty*. Moreover, uncertainty appears to be a crucial determinant not only of investment in physical capital stock, but also of international capital flows. Here, we also consider the impact of macroeconomic policy and financial markets on investment in physical capital and economic growth.

Given the importance of institutions for capital accumulation, we also discuss some institutional features of labour and output markets, as well as those governing international external trade flows. The core finding is that labour market distortions are present – and specifically that the strong negative wage elasticity associated with labour usage in South Africa has not been utilised as a vehicle of job creation. Equally, however, we report the existence of very significant price mark-ups over marginal cost of production in output markets, in part reflecting high industry concentration, as well as incomplete trade liberalisation. The net consequence of this combination of market distortions is a loss of competitiveness that limits the growth potential of South Africa's industry.

Furthermore, given the rising importance of total factor productivity for growth in South Africa, the chapter examines the long-run determinants of technological progress in this country. Specifically, we consider evidence on the importance of the factors identified by modern (endogenous) growth theory in determining South Africa's growth performance. While a number of different determinants are considered, emphasis is placed on the contribution of investment in human capital. The evidence suggests that what counts increasingly is the *quality*, not just the quantity, of human capital investment.

Finally, we consider the implications of these findings for economic and social policy geared towards more dynamic growth of output and employment, and a more rapid diffusion of economic benefits. We also suggest a few knowledge gaps and potential avenues of further policy research that, if addressed, could help to develop and implement more effective economic policies for broadly shared growth.

An important caveat is that the chapter focuses on and discusses mainly *macroeconomic*, *market-related*, and *institutional* determinants of and constraints on growth, largely ignoring the complex distribution and poverty issues dealt with elsewhere. The hypothesis supported by much of the literature is that growth is a *necessary condition* for economic progress and improvement in standards of living. This chapter focuses on growth and says little about how the benefits of growth have been shared among the South African population, although these are well-known facts. The chapter refers, however, to the numerous applied microeconomic studies that shed more light on the distribution/poverty pattern of South Africa's growth experience. A more comprehensive socio-economic accounting of the growth-cum-equity experience of South Africa would need to combine this analysis of factors of growth with the findings of these microeconomic studies.

Growth in South Africa, 1970–2000: Evidence and interpretation

Growth decomposition[1]

International evidence from *developed countries* has often pointed to the significant contribution of total factor productivity (TFP) growth to total growth, as compared with the contribution of factor inputs.[2] In effect, real output growth in developed countries is difficult to explain with reference to growth in factor inputs alone. Rather, most economic growth in this group of countries over the most recent decades of the twentieth century seems to be the result of technological progress.

Developing countries, including South Africa, are different.[3] Evidence from developing countries often shows a changing pattern of growth, beginning with a heavy reliance on capital growth and, more broadly, factor accumulation, then shifting to TFP-led growth with rising per capita real GDP. South Africa's aggregate growth experience largely mirrors that of many developing countries, although growth in South Africa has been markedly slower during the 1990s than in comparator countries (see Figure 1.1).

Figure 1.1 *Comparative growth performance of world, middle-income and East Asian countries*

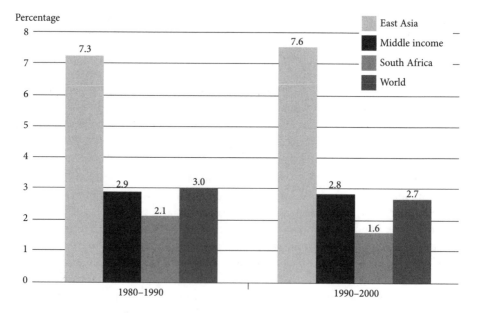

Source: World Bank Development Indicators Database

The empirical question, then, is whether factor accumulation or TFP gains led real output growth in South Africa during the period 1970–2000. With regard to the former, the policy imperative is to account for specific factors that determine investment in physical capital and employment. If, on the other hand, TFP growth is dominant, we must consider deeper determinants of technological progress in the South African context.

A standard decomposition of sources of growth indicates that during the period 1970–90, economic growth was driven largely by factor accumulation, and by gains in TFP in the 1990s (see Table 1.1; Figure 1.2 illustrates the same data). The 1970s and 1980s saw economic growth heavily led by capital and labour input accumulation, with very little contribution by technology. In the 1990s, however, the pattern of growth was reversed: growth in labour input contributed *negatively* and growth in capital input contributed relatively weakly to the overall growth. In contrast, the single strongest contributor to output growth during the course of the 1990s was a rapid augmentation in technology.

Table 1.1 *Contributions to growth by labour, capital and TFP*

Period	Real output growth	Labour	Capital	TFP
1970s	3.21	1.17	2.54	−0.49
1980s	2.20	0.62	1.24	0.34
1990s	0.94	−0.58	0.44	1.07

Part of the reason for the change in South Africa's pattern of growth in the 1990s towards the creation of a greater role for technology lies in a decline in formal-sector employment.[4] This change was associated with considerable restructuring and shedding of labour in major industries such as mining. As a result, with declining employment, growth in labour inputs alone could not have added to the growth in real output of the economy. At the same time, the declining contribution of capital to overall growth during this period is a result of the declining investment rate.[5] The contribution of technological progress has, therefore, been rising since the 1970s, although in the context of a declining overall growth rate in output.

This aggregate evidence conceals considerable variation across sectors.[6] The only consistent feature across the main sectors of the economy – agriculture, mining, manufacturing and services – is that the contribution of labour towards output growth has shown a downward trend from the 1970s to the 1990s. In terms of the contribution of growth in the capital stock, we find that in the agriculture, mining and services sectors capital has been of declining importance as a contributor towards output growth, while for manufacturing industry it has assumed increasing importance. Finally, in terms of the contribution of technological progress,

Figure 1.2 *Decomposition of growth in real GDP*

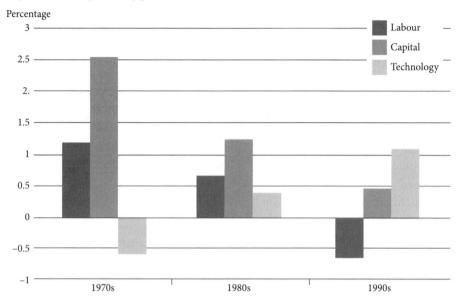

Source: Adapted from Fedderke 2002a

the strongest efficiency improvement is evident in agriculture, although this contribution by technology has declined during the 1990s. Mining, in contrast, while coming off a low rate of technological progress, has been on an upward trend, similar to that of services. These results confirm our initial finding: that technology as a contributor to economic growth in the South African economy has become increasingly important, though sectoral shifts have also affected the overall growth. The exception to this finding is the manufacturing sector, which has experienced a decline in the importance of technological innovation throughout the 1990s (see Table 1.2).

These basic findings lead to a number of further questions. Why, in particular, has the growth in capital stock contributed in declining measure to the growth in output? What is it about the labour market that has led to the decline in employment creation and, hence, a virtual absence of labour input as a positive contributor to output growth in South Africa? Further, what else specifically, besides growth in factor inputs, might be important in generating increases in real output? The rising contribution of TFP growth gives us one broad indication, but it also raises further questions related to the findings of new growth theory. How, in particular, are we to understand the role of human capital and the contribution of explicitly innovative activity (research and development) to TFP growth and, hence, output growth in the South African context?

Table 1.2 *Decomposition of growth in real output into contributions by factors of production and technological progress; evidence by principal economic sectors, 1970–2000*

	Percentage growth in real GDP	Of which:		
		Labour	*Capital*	*Technology*
Agriculture, forestry and fishing				
1970s	4.27	−0.10	2.00	2.37
1980s	4.30	−0.24	−0.56	5.10
1990s	2.40	−0.20	−0.92	3.52
Mining				
1970s	−1.08	0.51	3.81	−5.40
1980s	−0.55	0.18	3.90	−4.63
1990s	−0.60	−2.32	0.10	1.62
Manufacturing				
1970s	4.94	1.67	2.78	0.49
1980s	1.48	0.78	1.21	−0.52
1990s	0.43	−0.47	1.69	−0.79
Service industry				
1970s	3.41	1.49	2.80	−0.88
1980s	2.81	0.82	1.28	0.71
1990s	1.50	−0.59	0.44	1.65

Source: Fedderke 2002a

The foundation of long-run growth: Investment in physical capital stock

The investment rate in the physical capital stock has been documented in the literature as a core determinant of long-run economic growth. Whether we are referring to classical theories of economic growth (Solow 1956) or modern endogenous theories of economic growth (for example, Romer 1986, 1990; Grossman and Helpman 1991) and more recent contributions (Bosworth and Collins 2003; Kraay forthcoming), investment in physical capital is consistently considered a key source of economic growth. Empirical research confirms this centrality of the investment rate in physical capital. In a seminal paper, Levine and Renelt (1992), for example, have established investment in physical capital as the single most robust variable in empirical cross-sectional growth studies, and De Long and Summers (1991, 1993) have confirmed its importance as the key engine of long-run gains in per capita real output.

In the South African context, we have seen that the contribution of capital has been the dominant source of economic growth in the 1970–80 period, and the second most important source in the 1990s, after TFP. Moreover, the decline in the overall growth rate of real output is clearly associated with the observed decline in the importance of capital as a factor of growth. Hence a more in-depth look at investments in physical capital is needed for a fuller understanding of the growth puzzle of South Africa.

Determinants of investments in South Africa: Empirical evidence[7]

The modern theory of investment expenditure has focused on the impact of *irreversibility* and *uncertainty*. While the importance of irreversibility and uncertainty for changes in the capital stock has long been recognised (for example, Hartman 1972; Nickel 1978), recent debates (for example, Dixit and Pindyck 1994) have provided a more comprehensive understanding of the issues.

Irreversibility of investment decisions is associated with the possibility of waiting for better returns in the future. This means that the decision not to invest at a present point in time can be thought of as a purchase of an option that has value, since waiting to invest in an uncertain environment delivers additional information. The modern literature has been cast in terms of a stochastic, dynamic environment. One of the core – and straightforward – insights of the modern literature is that uncertainty generates a reward for waiting, and, hence, that increases in uncertainty will potentially *lower* investment.

The most important of these insights, however, has been the recognition that the impact of uncertainty on investment is ambiguous. A rise in uncertainty raises the threshold at which investment will be triggered, and this suggests a negative link between investment and uncertainty. However, uncertainty may at least in part be due to an increased *volatility* of profit flows, such that the higher threshold level of profitability is reached more frequently in an uncertain than in a certain environment, generating more rather than less frequent bursts of investment expenditure. In this case, increased uncertainty may be associated with *higher* investment expenditure on average, even though the net rate of return on investment required to justify the investment expenditure has increased due to the uncertainty. The net effect of uncertainty on investment is, therefore, ambiguous, and a matter of empirical analysis.[8]

We focus our analysis of determinants of investment expenditure on manufacturing – a key industry in South Africa – for which solid data are readily available. Our results are consistent with those of other studies based on the aggregate investment rates in South Africa.[9] A key issue in empirical implementation of irreversible investment models is that one must control for the impact of uncertainty.[10]

The results confirm the standard theoretical expectations about the impact of the rate of return on capital and the user cost of capital on investments (see Figure 1.3).[11] A rising expectation on the rate of return on capital, and rising user cost of capital, tend to increase and decrease the investment rate in physical capital stock respectively. In this regard, investment in physical capital stock in South Africa is, therefore, susceptible to the standard policy levers (such as tax policy, depreciation rules, measures that improve the efficiency of factor input markets, etc.) associated with stimulating investment expenditure.

A striking finding is that uncertainty exercises a statistically significant and strong *negative* impact on investment expenditure in the South African manufacturing industry (see again Figure 1.3). Importantly, both *systemic*[12] and *sectoral* uncertainty[13] appear to be significant for investment, with systemic uncertainty showing a stronger impact. Systemic uncertainty is defined here as political stability, measured as a weighted average of eleven indicators of repressive state responses to pressures for political reform, while sectoral uncertainty refers to the measured volatility of sector-specific output demand. The political instability index covers the 1970–2000 period of 24 years of apartheid and six years of the period of political liberalisation.[14] While the index tracks the rising political stability to 1994 and beyond, its close association with investments covers the whole period of analysis and captures the periods of peak instability in the mid-1970s and the 1980s. This result is a consistent and robust finding regardless of which other variables are controlled for in the estimation.[15] One explanation for the observed investment performance of the South African economy, therefore, is that uncertainty, including both systemic and sectoral uncertainty, continues to characterise the South African economic environment.[16]

On the surface, a major implication of these empirical findings is that the standard policy handles such as tax policy are important as a *potential* means of stimulating investment expenditure. Both the proxy for the rate of return on capital stock and the marginal cost of investment come to determine the long-run investment rate in South Africa. The implication of this is twofold. In the first instance, the policy factors that change the user cost of investment (or rate of return on capital) may deter or foster investment. Since changes in the real user cost of capital influence the investment rate of the manufacturing sector, public policy can influence long-run changes in investment rates by changing elements of real unit cost of capital (for example, tax rates on corporate incomes and dividends, depreciation rules). The basic point is that policy-makers could potentially play a role in creating the appropriate (or unfavourable) conditions for rising investment rates via changes in the real user cost of capital.

Figure 1.3 *Standardised coefficients in the investment relation*

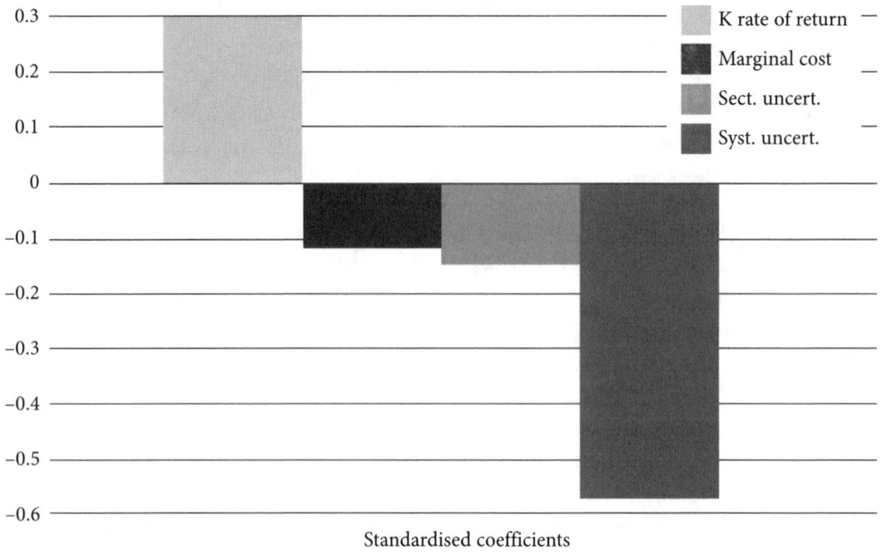

Standardised coefficients

Source: Adapted from Fedderke 2001a
Notes: 'K rate of return' denotes the proxy for the expected rate of return on capital.
'Marginal cost' denotes the user cost of capital.
'Sect. uncert.' denotes a measure of sectoral demand uncertainty.
'Syst. uncert.' denotes a measure of systemic uncertainty.[17]
Figures are standard deviations, denoting the standard deviation response in the investment rate to a one standard deviation change in the independent variable. All coefficients are statistically significant.

This finding, however, has to be qualified significantly because of both *direct* and *indirect* policy implications of the empirical results concerning the impact of uncertainty on investment. There are direct policy implications that arise from the direct (and large) negative impact of uncertainty on investment in South Africa: stability of the investment environment at a systemic level (i.e. the investment climate) appears crucial if investment rates in South African manufacturing industry are to rise. This implies the need for a stable and predictable macroeconomic policy stance resulting in price stability, but also signals the importance of a stable political environment conducive to credible policy adjustments over time.[18]

But the importance of uncertainty for investment arises in more than this direct sense. Uncertainty also raises the threshold rate of return below which investment is unlikely to occur. Firstly, this implies that any policy intervention designed to stimulate investment expenditure may face serious constraints where an industry is operating below the threshold rate of return on investment. Policy intervention may not trigger a physical investment response because the intervention has not been substantial enough to breach this threshold. Secondly, as a corollary, the creation of a macroeconomic as well as a microeconomic environment that is stable, predictable and devoid of sudden and arbitrary policy interventions is a policy goal that emerges not only because uncertainty has a direct negative impact on investment rates in manufacturing, but also because it serves to lower the threshold below which investment does not occur. In effect, lowering uncertainty directly stimulates investment, and indirectly it renders other policy levers more effective in achieving their objective. Moreover, further evidence presented below shows that the relevance of uncertainty is even deeper than its immediate significance in the context of investment in the physical capital stock.

Further evidence on the determinants of investment

Beyond uncertainty, there are also other factors, such as capital flows and the financial sector, that influence investment rates in South Africa. For example, the shortfall of private-sector savings relative to investment (see Figure 1.4) highlights the significance of the role of the financial sector in the South African economy in at least two distinct senses.

Firstly, it emphasises the need for inflows of foreign capital, as expected in developing countries. Therefore, understanding the determinants of capital flows into and out of the South African economy becomes a key to an understanding of constraints on the investment rate in the economy. Secondly, it raises the question of the efficiency of the South African financial sector as an intermediary between savers and investors in the economy. The crucial question here is what role the financial sector has played in effectively intermediating between economic agents with surplus funds (savers), and those with opportunities to utilise those funds productively (investors). The nature and role of the financial sector in the South African growth process becomes relevant.

THE IMPORTANCE OF CAPITAL FLOWS: THE RETURN OF UNCERTAINTY

The shortfall of savings relative to investments has been recognised as a longstanding structural constraint of the South African economy. Except for very brief periods in the 1960s and the early 1980s, South Africa's private sector has not produced sufficient savings to meet its demand for physical capital formation. The implication is that South Africa has been, and remains, reliant on capital inflows in order to finance its physical capital formation.

Figure 1.4 *Private savings[19] and investment rates[20]: South Africa, 1970–2000*

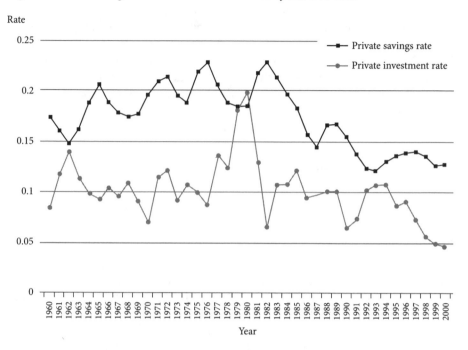

On the presumption that capital flows respond positively to higher domestic returns on assets, and negatively to risk and higher returns on foreign assets,[21] and employing a range of distinct measures of capital flow,[22] we report on estimates of the determinants of capital flows in Figure 1.5.

The results are, firstly, consistent with expectations of the underlying portfolio theory (Fedderke 2001b). Thus an improved rate of return on assets and reduced risk on assets will increase capital inflows into South Africa, although there are some differences between the various capital flow measures on the imputed magnitude of the impact of the various rates of return and risk dimensions.

Secondly, as expected, capital flows in South Africa prove to be positively associated with growth and negatively associated with political risk. More specifically, it turns out that both changes in the level of political rights and changes in the level of political instability affect capital flows. Higher instability and political liberalisation in South Africa were both initially associated with higher capital outflows. We note further that it is difficult to argue that the three capital 'flight' measures are more responsive to risk than the 'normal' capital flow measures of the balance of payments – with the one exception of the KFDRV measure. Capital inflows tend to respond to the already favourable growth performance; of course, any 'additional' capital inflow may further enhance the growth in output.

Figure 1.5 *Standardised long-run coefficients from ARDL estimation*

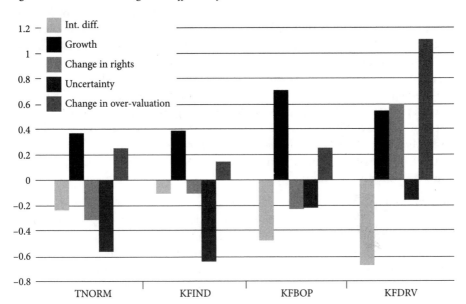

Source: Adapted from Fedderke and Liu 2002
Notes: 'Int. diff.' denotes the change in the exchange rate-adjusted interest differential, defined as the difference between the foreign and the domestic interest rates.[23]
'Growth' denotes the percentage change in gross domestic product.
'Change in rights' is defined as the change in an index of political rights.[24]
'Uncertainty' refers to the index of political instability employed in the investment estimations reported in Figure 1.3.
'Change in over-valuation' is defined as the change in the degree of over/undervaluation of the exchange rate in terms of PPP.
Figures are standard deviations, denoting the standard deviation response in the investment rate to a one standard deviation change in the independent variable. All coefficients are statistically significant.

The direct risk dimensions that were earlier shown to be crucial for investment in physical capital stock are also one of the key indirect enabling conditions for investment in South Africa. South Africa's reliance on capital inflows, therefore, strengthens the policy need to minimise any source of uncertainty that may detract from investment directly, or from capital inflows. A key policy implication is that the extent of transparency, predictability, and credibility of political processes will, therefore, determine how and to what extent the process of democratisation in South Africa brings about economic as well as political benefits for the majority of South Africans.

THE ROLE OF THE FINANCIAL SYSTEM

The financial system not only allocates scarce resources to the most efficient uses; it is also important for growth. Nowadays, most economists agree that the financial system is, in fact, essential for development.[25] They argue that a more efficient financial system leads to higher growth and reduces the likelihood and severity of crises. Kularatne (2002), for example, has recently investigated the role of financial deepening in South African growth in the post-war era. This study allows for both direct effects of the financial system on growth and indirect effects via a stimulus of the investment rate in the economy. In addition, Kularatne allows for the possibility that a rising level of per capita output (as an indicator of the level of development) may itself stimulate the development of the financial system, i.e. there may exist a feedback from output to financial deepening. Finally, the study controls for both the impact of credit extension by financial intermediaries in the South African economy and the liquidity of the stock market.[26] The central finding of this study is that *all* forms of financial deepening (both credit extension and stock market liquidity) stimulate economic growth.[27]

The two dimensions of financial deepening – credit expansion and stock market liquidity – are found to be complementary rather than substitutes for each other. Moreover, although the impact of financial deepening is indirect, by stimulating investment in physical capital, credit extension in the South African financial markets appears to serve as a means of improving the liquidity of the stock market rather than increasing investment in physical capital stock directly.

One possible explanation for the absence of a *direct* association between financial intermediation and the real sector may be attributed to the presence of credit rationing within the South African economy. Firms may find it difficult to source working capital from financial intermediaries for investment projects. Indeed, this is borne out by the evidence gathered by a recent World Bank Report on the constraints on growth in South Africa,[28] which supports the argument concerning the prevalence of credit rationing within the South African economy. This suggests that the full potential of the financial sector for growth stimulus in South Africa has not yet been realised.

THE ROLE AND LIMITS OF DEMAND-SIDE POLICY

Finally, macroeconomic stability is crucial in creating appropriate *levels* of the net return on physical capital to render investment attractive to the private sector, but, even more importantly, it is crucial in rendering the return *certain*. In effect, the conduct of monetary and fiscal policies represents another important channel by means of which uncertainty faced by investors can be minimised. Mariotti (2002) investigates the impact of two indicators of demand-side policy in the post-war South African growth experience: government consumption expenditure as a percentage of GDP as a proxy for fiscal policy stance,[29] and the CPI inflation rate as a proxy for monetary policy orientation. The study allows for both direct effects of policy on growth and indirect effects via a stimulus of the investment rate in the economy. This study takes into account the possibility that the impact of policy intervention on output may be non-linear.[30]

Government consumption expenditure and inflation are both found to have an unambiguously negative impact on long-run per capita GDP. But the results also indicate that there is an indirect impact of policy on output via its impact on investment. These results also suggest that the relationship between policy and long-run output growth and investment may be non-linear, implying the presence of an optimal level of government consumption expenditure and inflation. The estimated optimal level of government consumption expenditure turns out to be quite low (below 12 per cent of GDP), as is optimal inflation (below 3 per cent).

The significance of the findings regarding macroeconomic policy (i.e. demand-side policy interventions) in South Africa is that they do play a role in the growth process, but not as a means of providing positive demand-side stimulus to output growth. At best, the positive stimulus of an increase in government consumption expenditure tends to be short-lived, only to be succeeded by contractionary pressures. Instead, the role of government stabilisation policy is to provide a stable and predictable macroeconomic environment – lowering uncertainty in the economy, and improving predictability of the economic environment for investors, while providing public goods services. In short, there is no quick-and-easy demand-side policy panacea for the supply-side problem of economic growth. But the demand side has a role to play: to keep the economic environment as stable and predictable as possible, without distorting private sector incentives. In this area, arguably more than in any other, South Africa's policy performance has been exemplary for long-run growth purposes. At the same time, it is now recognised that markets and institutions also matter for economic growth, an issue we explore next.

The role of institutions and markets in economic growth

A more complete discussion of determinants of long-run growth requires a sense of the institutional factors that may exercise an influence on growth directly, as well as indirectly via capital formation and capital flows. In this section, we extend our understanding of institutions from specifically social and political institutions to what is perhaps the single most important set of institutions of all for long-run economic development: market institutions. Capital market distortions in the past allocation of capital in the South African economy have been identified as one constraint on capital accumulation[31] – and similar considerations may also be relevant to other markets.

Evidence is beginning to accumulate that the functioning of the market mechanisms in South Africa leaves considerable room for improvement. In particular, we consider the impact of *trade liberalisation* and the performance of *labour and output markets* in South Africa, as well as the evidence on the efficiency of output markets.

Institutional factors of output growth

The possible existence of a link between social and political institutions and long-run economic development has long been the subject of an extensive literature in its own right. From modernisation theory,[32] with its postulated positive association between economic and political development, the emphasis on property rights (hence markets) as critical to long-run development in the work of North (1981, 1990) and North and Thomas (1970, 1973), and the emphasis on the importance of the credibility of political institutions,[33] to the recent introduction of social capital,[34] explorations of the possibility of a link between institutions and economic development are a recurrent theme in the literature. Theoretical contributions have been accompanied by a growing body of empirical evidence.[35] Important questions can be raised on the link between institutions and growth in the South African context as well.

Which institutional dimensions are important to the growth process in South Africa, and are the channels of influence, direct or indirect? Fedderke, de Kadt and Luiz (2001b) explore the roles of political instability, political rights and property rights in South Africa's investment and growth performance. Figure 1.6 summarises their findings, which are consistent with the evidence presented on the investment function above, with some nuances. Firstly, the impact of the institutional dimensions on economic growth in South Africa appears to have been affecting investment, while political instability and property rights also appear to be important determining factors of capital accumulation. Secondly, where the agent (e.g. the state) responsible for setting the rules of the game is not seen to be fully and credibly committed to those rules which confer ownership, confidence, and hence investment, are inevitably going to be compromised. Thirdly, there is little evidence of a direct impact of institutional variables on growth, only of an indirect link via the investment rate. Instead, economic development drives institutional development both in terms of the rights structure within the political realm and in terms of the level of political instability. Hence, there is no evidence that political rights per se in the period of investigation supported either capital accumulation or per capita output. Instead, political institutions appear to be an outcome variable rather than a forcing variable in the estimations. All this has obvious implications for economic policy.

South Africa-specific and international analyses suggest that there is little doubt that sound macroeconomic stability is key to growth, but macroeconomic stability alone is not enough.[36] It is only part of the story, and, one might argue, the easy part. Far more demanding is the need to establish that the policy commitment to long-term growth is a credible one, and that the institutional framework within which it is achieved is one that will itself hold, and allow economic agents to realise fully the results of their work and entrepreneurial efforts. A major policy implication is that unless institutional stability requirements are met, the considerable achievements that South Africa has realised in the post-apartheid period, through its strict macroeconomic policy discipline, may be jeopardised.

Figure 1.6 *Patterns of association*

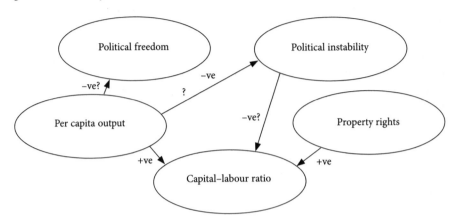

Source: Fedderke, de Kadt and Luiz 2001b

The impact of market distortions: Trade liberalisation

The 1990s have seen a laudable first attempt to initiate trade liberalisation in South Africa, but much remains to be done. The extent of the liberalisation of the economy constitutes one of the clear successes of the South African administration in the post-1994 period, and the country has continued its trade liberalisation, which has been a source of gains in total factor productivity. Within the context of the Doha negotiations, South Africa pushed for the removal of agricultural subsidies in industrial countries. While it is negotiating a number of bilateral agreements, it is also moving ahead with unilateral tariff reform. The average unweighted tariff rate was reduced from 22 per cent in 1998 to an estimated 11 per cent in 2003. Nevertheless, the tariff structure is unduly complex and there are a number of highly protected sectors (for example, textiles, footwear). On the customs and trade facilitation front, the Southern African Customs Union (SACU) has streamlined customs procedures based on the Automated System for Customs Data (ASYCUDA). Customs procedures are well defined and implemented. Despite these achievements, however, there remains a concern about whether trade liberalisation went far enough during the 1990s. Empirical evidence suggests that it did not.

An analysis of effective rates of protection across sectors shows that important sectors of the economy continue to enjoy very high levels of protection. Fedderke and Vaze (2001), for example, calculate effective protection rates (EPR) for 38 economic sectors, and the general changes are shown in Table 1.3 below.[37] When a rise in EPR of greater than 1 per cent has been recorded, the industry has been classified as more protected. Falls in EPR of greater than 1 per cent have been categorised as liberalised. The remaining sectors have been placed in the column indicating modest or no change. In each column, sectors have been ordered by the size of sectoral real GDP, averaged over the 1988–98 period.

Note that the three large sectors – finance and insurance; agriculture, forestry and fishing; and gold and uranium – have all come under increased protection. These three sectors make up on average 26 per cent of the total GDP of the 38 sectors during the period 1988 to 1998. When the other sectors of the economy in this column are added, the proportion of GDP where protection has increased rises to approximately 34 per cent of the GDP of the 38 sectors, on average, for the period from 1988 to 1998.

Table 1.3 *Classification of economic sectors according to changes in effective protection rates*

More protected	Modest or no change	Liberalised
Finance & insurance	Electricity, gas & steam	Basic iron & steel
Agriculture, forestry & fishing	Machinery & equipment	Motor vehicles, parts & access
Gold & uranium ore mining	Wholesale & retail trade	Paper & paper products
Other mining	Metal products excluding machinery	Basic chemicals
Food		Basic non-ferrous metals
Textiles	Other chemicals & man-made fibres	Electrical machinery
Tobacco	Coal mining	Wearing apparel
Leather & leather products	Transport & storage	Plastic products
	Beverages	Other industries
	Non-metallic minerals	TV, radio & communication equipment
	Coke & refined petroleum products	Furniture
	Printing, publishing & recorded media	Glass & glass products
	Medical, dental & other health & veterinary services	Footwear
	Wood & wood products	Professional & scientific equipment
	Rubber products	
	Building construction	
	Other transport equipment	

Source: Fedderke and Vaze 2001

While the number of sectors undergoing significant trade liberalisation appears impressive, large sectors (in terms of their contribution to GDP) experienced increased protection. The liberalised sectors constitute just over 15 per cent of total

GDP from the 38 sectors on average for the period 1988–98, whereas the sectors where there has been little or no change in the EPR constitute the remaining 51 per cent of total GDP. The overall impact of the change in the trade regime in South Africa is, therefore, likely to be complex, and at best incomplete. Evidence to suggest that the lowering of protection has led to increased import penetration is ambiguous at best, while there is far stronger evidence suggesting that those sectors subject to significant liberalisation have also been those realising the strongest successes in improved export performance in the economy.[38] In sum, the distortionary impacts of trade barriers matter, and there remains much to be done to remove these impediments to improved efficiency and productivity in the South African economy.

Labour market inefficiencies

South Africa's labour market has contributed in declining measure to long-term national growth in the period under investigation. The importance of inappropriate pricing (and its institutional underpinnings) and rigidities in South African labour markets is arguably one of the single most widely documented characteristics of the South African economy to have emerged during the course of the 1990s. The wage elasticity of employment has time and again been found to be negative, in empirical study after study. Supporting descriptive evidence points in the direction of continuing rigidities creating obstacles to employment creation (Lewis 2001, 2002; Arndt and Lewis 2000; Nattrass 2000; and Fields 2000). Here we note four additional pieces of evidence relevant to an understanding of the problem of labour mispricing and employment losses in the South African economy. Firstly, we examine evidence to emerge from the mining sector, in which employment losses were particularly severe during the 1990s. Secondly, we consider evidence on the linkage between labour productivity, real wage, and employment creation, considering both descriptive and econometric evidence. Thirdly, we consider some preliminary evidence concerning the impact of labour skills on the wage elasticity of labour demand. Finally, we examine the impact of trade liberalisation on the demand for labour in South Africa.

THE IMPACT OF THE MINING SECTOR ON EMPLOYMENT

During the 1990s, there were at least two salient features of the labour market in mining, traditionally one of the principal employers in the South African economy (Fedderke and Pirouz 2002). Two main conclusions are of interest.

Firstly, there was a substantial amount of labour-shedding during the 1990s, with the employment loss concentrated in unskilled occupational categories. This is illustrated in Figure 1.7, with reference to gold and uranium mining, but the pattern is found in other mining sectors (see Fedderke and Pirouz 2002 for additional detail). More generally, employment in three principal mining sectors fell from a high of 101 705 employees in coal mining in 1985 to 55 219 in 1997; for gold and uranium mining the decline was from 526 839 to 241 352 employees over the same period; while for diamond and other mining employment declined from 199 572 in 1990 to 136 543 in 1997. In short, employment losses in the mining sector during the 1990s were dramatic. Given the significant historical contribution of mining to employment in South Africa, such large-scale job losses raise immediate concerns about the reasons for this phenomenon.

Figure 1.7 *Gold mining: skills composition of labour force*

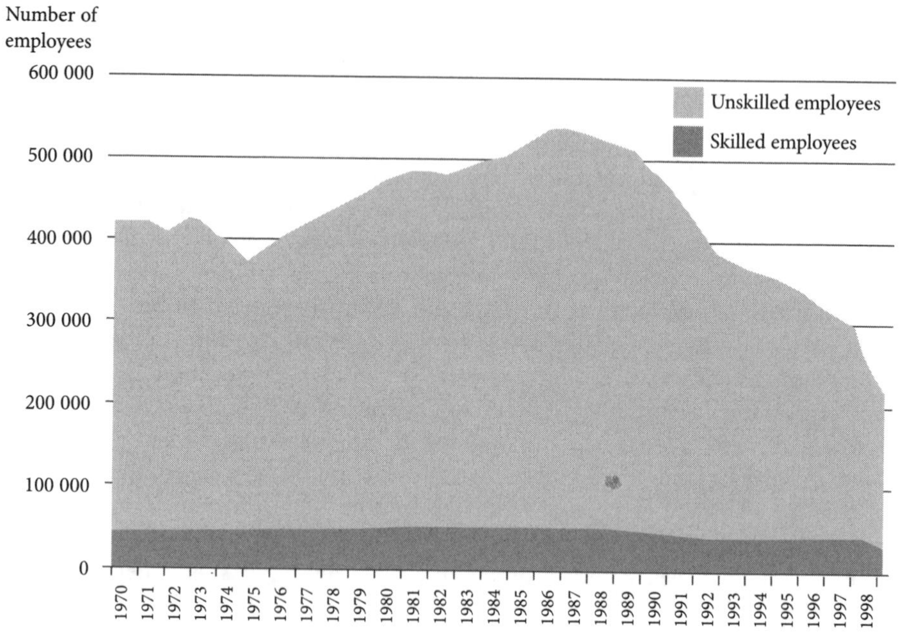

Source: Fedderke and Pirouz 2002

Secondly, a significant contributor, though not the only one, to the employment losses in mining has been the real cost of labour in production. This is illustrated by Figures 1.8 through 1.10, which show a substantial negative correlation between the real cost of labour and employment trends in all three principal mining sectors of the South African economy, over precisely the period in which substantial job losses were recorded in these sectors. The real wage elasticities for the coal, gold and uranium, and diamond and other mining sectors were –0.44, –0.69, and –1.45 respectively. The finding is further confirmed by a consideration of the relative rate of increase in labour productivity and the rate of increase in the real cost of labour in the mining sectors. Table 1.4 demonstrates that over the period in which significant job losses occurred, increases in real labour costs were consistently greater than improvements in labour productivity – with the inevitable consequence that the real unit cost of labour was increasing over the period.

Table 1.4 *Average percentage changes in labour productivity and real labour cost in the three aggregate mining sectors of South Africa, 1970–97*

Sector	Avg. % change in:	1970–75	1975–80	1980–85	1985–90	1990–95	1995–97
Coal	Labour productivity	3.19	7.95	11.27	−1.39	4.02	5.96
	Real cost of labour	3.98	−2.46	21.02	3.57	−0.94	10.91
Gold & uranium	Labour productivity	−4.47	−4.61	−4.31	−1.22	6.09	−1.28
	Real cost of labour	−8.55	−9.30	6.81	9.31	10.03	−0.59
Diamond & other	Labour productivity	2.40	0.58	5.64	1.19	5.11	8.58
	Real cost of labour	6.61	−4.88	14.70	3.98	2.17	15.58

Source: Fedderke and Pirouz 2002

Figure 1.8 *Coal mining: employment and real cost of labour*

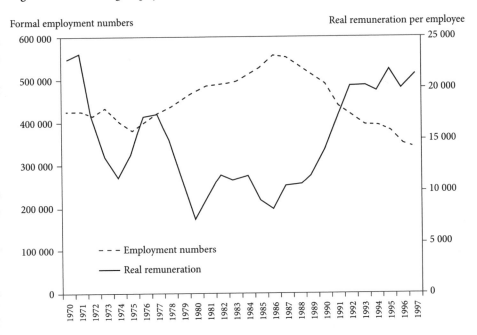

Source: Fedderke and Pirouz 2002

Figure 1.9 *Gold and uranium mining: employment and real cost of labour*

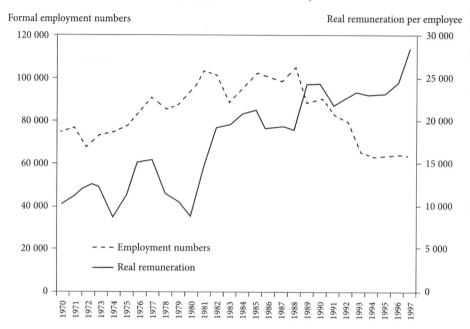

Source: Fedderke and Pirouz 2002

Figure 1.10 *Diamond and other mining: employment and real cost of labour*

Source: Fedderke and Pirouz 2002

THE IMPACT OF THE OTHER SECTORS OF THE ECONOMY ON EMPLOYMENT

The finding that labour mispricing constitutes a significant constraint on employment creation in South African mining, and hence acts as a brake on the economy's growth performance, generalises to other economic sectors. The impact of the link between the rate of increase in labour productivity and the rate of increase in the real wage on employment creation, considered for all 48 sectors of the South African economy over the 1970–97 period, shows that only where there is a strong positive correlation between growth in real labour remuneration and growth in labour productivity do economic sectors in South Africa create jobs on a sustainable basis (Fedderke and Mariotti 2002). Econometric evidence on real wage elasticities confirms the strong impact of the cost of labour on employment prospects in the economy. For the 28 manufacturing sectors of the South African economy, the aggregate real wage elasticity is in the region of –0.5 to –0.55. But in a fuller specification which controls for demand effects, skills composition of the labour force, openness of economic sectors, capacity utilisation in sectors, as well as industry concentration, the wage elasticity can be found to rise to –1.97 for manufacturing (see the extensive discussion of the estimation issues in labour markets in open economy contexts in Fedderke, Shin and Vaze 2003). The results hold across various skills levels for formal employment. The finding is consistently of negative wage elasticities for unskilled labour, with the wage elasticity for unskilled labour in the formal labour market ranging from –2.00 to –2.23, an elasticity considerably above that for skilled and highly skilled workers.

Given the substantial increases in the real cost of labour in the South African economy, labour mispricing continues to be an important factor in South Africa's poor track record of job creation, and constitutes the negative contribution of labour input to long-run real output growth in South Africa. The resulting employment losses hit hardest at the poorest segments of the population that have the fewest alternative skills for re-employment. Moreover, labour mispricing, and its institutional underpinnings governing wage determination for those who are already employed, result in limited opportunities for the unemployed to participate in the labour market, earn incomes and reduce poverty. A key policy implication is that realistic wage policies, guided more by improvements in labour productivity and not by maximisation of remuneration for those already employed, are needed to ensure more rapid absorption of unemployed labour into the formal economy and the wider spread of benefits of job opportunities across the population.

THE IMPACT OF GLOBALISATION ON THE SOUTH AFRICAN LABOUR MARKET

Has globalisation exercised a negative influence on the South African labour market? A study of the 28 three-digit manufacturing sectors in South Africa shows the opposite: that globalisation, or trade liberalisation, has resulted in positive earnings increases in sectors that are labour-intensive, as predicted by the Stolper-

Samuelson (SS) theorem (Fedderke, Shin and Vaze 2003). Trade liberalisation has been associated with increased demand for, and growth in, the earnings of labour. Technological change, however, has been substantially labour-saving. The net effect of these two countervailing forces maintains a net positive, mandated increase in real wages for labour for the 1970–2000 period. However, actual real wage increases have significantly outstripped the mandated rate of increase in wages (the actual growth rate has been twice the mandated growth rate). The implication, once again, is that factor mispricing may help to explain the poor employment creation record of the South African economy. The study further confirms the impact of limited output growth, high industry concentration, and slowly changing skills composition of the labour force as contributing factors to the slow employment growth in South Africa.

Mark-ups and inefficiencies in output markets

Inefficiencies are not restricted to labour markets in South Africa, as product markets also appear to be associated with considerable pricing power on the part of producers. In fact, Fedderke and Schaling (2005) suggest that the mark-up over unit labour cost in South Africa is several orders of magnitude greater than that found in similar studies for the USA, for example. This poses a challenge for the successful conduct of macroeconomic stabilisation policy, since cycles of price increases become self-reinforcing, rendering anti-inflationary policy more difficult. It also creates scope for the continued mispricing of labour through excessive wage settlement between big business and organised labour in the economy, with the attendant employment implications both for large firms and, especially, for small and medium-size firms to which such settlements tended to apply as well. But the presence of pricing power in South African output markets also suggests that the level of competitive pressure in output markets is not adequate, lowering the competitiveness of South African production internationally.

The average mark-up in South African manufacturing industry has been found to be in the region of 80 per cent,[39] twice the average mark-up in USA manufacturing industry, reported as 45 per cent in comparable international studies (Fedderke, Kularatne and Mariotti forthcoming). Furthermore, the openness of manufacturing sectors to international trade influences the magnitude of industry mark-up over marginal cost. Both increased import penetration and increased export penetration tend to decrease the mark-up of price over marginal cost, and this occurs regardless of whether the increase in openness of the sector occurs relative to the industry-specific mean or whether it occurs relative to the aggregate manufacturing mean.[40] The implication is thus that trade openness is one means by which excessive domestic market power in South African manufacturing can be curbed. This emphasises the importance of removing remaining forms of trade protection in South African industry.

High industrial concentration ratios further influence the magnitude of industry mark-ups. An important policy implication is that lowering industry concentration relative to the manufacturing sector mean does appear to lower the pricing power of industry. In addition to trade liberalisation, therefore, competition policy offers a means by which inefficiencies in output markets arising from the pricing power of industry can be curtailed.

Industry cost competitiveness, as measured by real unit labour costs relative to real unit labour costs in a basket of other countries, is also statistically significantly related to the observed mark-up.[41] This is the case for variation from both industry-specific and aggregate manufacturing mean relative real unit labour cost. The findings are divergent, however. An improvement in the cost competitiveness of an industry relative to its industry-specific mean reduces the price–marginal cost mark-up. An improvement in an industry's cost competitiveness relative to the manufacturing industry mean increases the price–marginal cost mark-up. Improvements in industry competitiveness are thus absorbed by firms as improved profitability, rather than by reducing prices. One explanation of this divergent finding is that in the presence of cost reductions within an industry, competition between rival firms does drive prices down. Between industries, such competition is absent, allowing industries to appropriate divergent profit rates.

Mark-ups over marginal cost, where marginal cost *includes* intermediate inputs, lie in the region of 7 per cent in South African manufacturing, which is below the corresponding figure reported for USA manufacturing (13 per cent).[42] Significantly, when industry mark-up over marginal cost, which includes intermediate inputs, is estimated while controlling for industry concentration ratios, significant increases in the mark-up due to increasing concentration ratios are found, again raising the mark-up to twice that found in USA manufacturing (or more). One explanation of this finding is that in South African industry concentration ratios are considerably higher than in the USA, and need to be controlled for in order to capture true mark-up of price over marginal cost.

The evidence, therefore, points to the presence of considerable pricing power in South African industry. A corollary is that the pricing power in South African industry may have generated inefficiencies in resource allocation over time – particularly since the incentive to invest in physical capital stock may be substantially affected. While rigidities in South Africa's labour markets have contributed to an underemployment of the labour input in production, inefficiencies in South African output markets may equally have contributed toward the poor investment performance over the past two decades. Whether or not this has been a relevant factor in the South African investment record is worthy of further research.

In combination, the evidence on the efficiency of market processes in South Africa, from both labour and output markets, suggests symptoms of what might be termed 'crony corporatism'. Crony corporatism is here defined as the explicit or tacit cooperation agreements between big business, big labour and, to some extent, government, to serve relatively narrow sectional interests, and curtails the efficient functioning of markets to a significant degree. The observed consequences of such corporatist behaviour are higher unemployment, greater industrial concentration, higher prices and lower competition, and therefore, likely lower long-term, labour-absorbing growth than would otherwise be the case.

Innovation, human capital and their relevance for South Africa

Endogenous technological change

Modern growth theory has come to place increased emphasis on innovation as a long-term driver of economic growth, with attention focusing on the source of technological innovation. As we have seen from the outset, in South Africa, total factor productivity growth has assumed increasing importance as a growth driver over time. Almost universally in new growth theory, innovation is seen as the outcome of investment of resources for technological advance, but debate continues on which resources precisely are required, and what the strength of their impact will be. For Romer-type models (1986), the source of innovation is spillovers attached to investment in the physical capital stock. For the Lucas-variant (1988), the spillovers can be argued to result from investment in human rather than physical capital stock. Finally, in variants of the Schumpeterian approach to long-run growth, innovation is the explicit outcome of the investment of resources in technical advances, rather than the production of final output.[43] The crucial questions for our purposes are, firstly, whether endogenous growth processes are present in South Africa and, secondly, what form such endogenous growth processes might take. The latter is especially important, given the divergent policy implications that the alternative conceptions carry.[44]

The impact of endogenous growth processes in South Africa

The key empirical question here is identifying determinants of growth in total factor productivity in South Africa. Since the results are symmetrical, we focus the discussion on the results for the spillover specification in Table 1.5, though the additional modifications emerge from the Schumpeterian considerations (Fedderke 2001c). While the results confirm the presence of spillover effects for South African manufacturing, it is important to note that the confirmation is not unconditional. To the extent that spillover effects are corroborated, they take the form suggested by Lucas (1988) rather than Romer (1986). The coefficient on the growth rate of the capital stock is consistently negative (even where we control for investment in human as well as physical capital) and statistically significant. Since the coefficient of the capital growth rate should control for the positive contribution of capital stock over and above that implied by its income share due to spillovers, this constitutes a rejection of Romer-type spillover effects in South African manufacturing industry (in favour of classical growth theory). On the other hand, Lucas-type spillover effects do find some support, in the sense that at least some of the human capital investment variables prove to have positive and significant coefficients. However, even here the support for Lucas spillovers is circumscribed. In particular, only very *specific* types of investment in human capital contribute positively to productivity growth. The proportion of matriculation students taking mathematics, and the proportion of degrees in the natural, engineering and mathematical sciences (NES) out of total degrees, are the only two human capital variables that provide a positive and significant contribution to productivity growth in South African manufacturing industry over the 1970–97 period.[45]

What counts, for purposes of the innovative activity associated with long-run output growth in South African manufacturing, is not so much the production of human capital per se as the production of *quality* human capital, as proxied by the mathematics and NES degree proportions. There are at least two good reasons why this finding is plausible. The first is that high quality human capital is simply more likely to have the positive spillover effects identified by Lucas (1988), while poor quality human capital is not. A second interpretation of the evidence might point to an improved quality of screening by an educational system (both primary and secondary, and tertiary) with rising mathematics and NES degree proportions. This, in turn, would reduce the risk faced by producers wishing to hire human capital for purposes of innovative activity.

The test of the Schumpeterian hypothesis confirms the presence of a positive impact of R&D expenditure on growth in total factor productivity. Thus the findings confirm the presence of the positive impact on output growth of innovative R&D activity undertaken by the private sector. Results from the range of human capital indicators again point to the possibility of a positive impact of human capital spillovers on productivity growth. However, just as for the spillover results, the particular dimension of human capital investment controlled for proves to be crucial. The positive impact on productivity growth emerges from the NES degree proportion variable (as it did for the spillover discussion), while a number of human capital variables prove to be negative and significant (WENROL, APPCAP) or insignificant. The interpretation of this evidence remains much the same as for the spillover results above. While the human capital dimension can legitimately be argued to have a positive impact on long-run productivity growth, it is above all the *quality* dimension of human capital that exercises this effect rather than the quantity of human capital.

Table 1.5 *Testing for spillover effects in TFP*

Dependent variable: Growth in Total Factor Productivity

Regressors	Spillover effects	Regressors	Schumpeterian effects
$\dfrac{\dot{K}}{K}$	−0.004* (0.000)	R&D	0.02* (0.01)
WENROL	−0.03 (0.34)	WENROL	−0.67* (0.30)
TOTENROL	−0.12* (0.04)	TOTENROL	−0.09 (0.05)
MATHPRP	0.11* (0.04)	MATHPRP	0.02 (0.04)
DEGREE	-0.1×10^{-4}* (0.1×10^{-5})	DEGREE	-0.1×10^{-5} (0.1×10^{-5})
NESDEG	0.00 (0.00)	NESDEG	-0.1×10^{-5} (0.1×10^{-5})
NESDEGPRP	0.79* (0.32)	NESDEGPRP	1.00* (0.39)
APPCAP	13.82 (15.13)	APPCAP	−50.75* (19.52)
LnPATENT	0.01* (0.004)	LnPATENT	0.02* (0.00)

Source: Fedderke 2001c
Notes: Figures in parentheses denote standard errors.
* denotes statistical significance at the 5% level.
WENROL denotes the primary and secondary school enrolment rate for 'whites', TOTENROL the primary and secondary school enrolment rate for all population groups, MATHPRP the proportion of matriculants sitting mathematics, DEGREE the total number of degrees issued by universities, NESDEG the number of degrees issued in the natural, engineering and mathematical sciences (NES), NESDEGPRP the proportion of NES degrees issued, APPCAP the per capita apprenticeship contracts issued, PATENT the number of patents registered, and R&D denotes an indicator of research and development expenditure.

South Africa's legacy of human capital creation

The empirical evidence from South African manufacturing industry appears to point to a positive impact of both explicit R&D activity and the quality of human capital. The implication is that we can isolate the core determinants of growth in total factor productivity for South Africa. Specifically, these are *investment in quality human capital*, as proxied by the proportion of school leavers and university graduates engaged in mathematical, scientific and engineering disciplines, and *R&D development activity*. In Figures 1.11 and 1.12 we report the proportion of white and African matriculants sitting mathematics (on any of the three grades available) and the proportion of university graduates by race in the NES degree categories. Table 1.6 reports the per-academic staff research output by university over the 1989–94 period.

In all three indicators of the capacity of the economy to undertake long-term innovation there is evidence of a substantial decline. Reflecting the legacy of the apartheid era, the proportion of matriculants in the historically 'best' parts of the schooling system has been in a steady decline, and in African schooling has been persistently low. As a result, the proportion of NES degrees has collapsed. R&D activity in the university system, in turn, has also shown a steady decline on a per capita basis. Even the best part of the university system in South Africa has at the very least manifested declining quality over time during the period under investigation. The white university research output has ceased to increase in absolute terms from the late 1980s, and in per-lecturer output terms the output declined through to the early 1990s, though it has since stabilised. In addition, most research in South Africa is done in a very small number of universities.

Figure 1.11 *Proportion of matric candidates with mathematics*

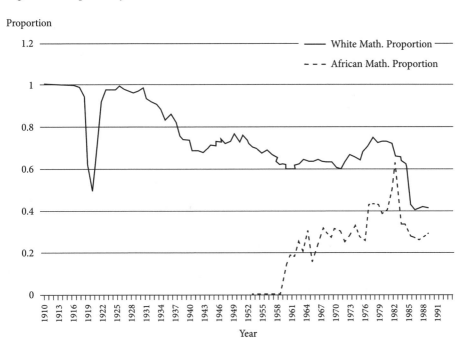

Source: Fedderke, de Kadt and Luiz 2000

Figure 1.12 *Proportion of degrees in natural and mathematical sciences*

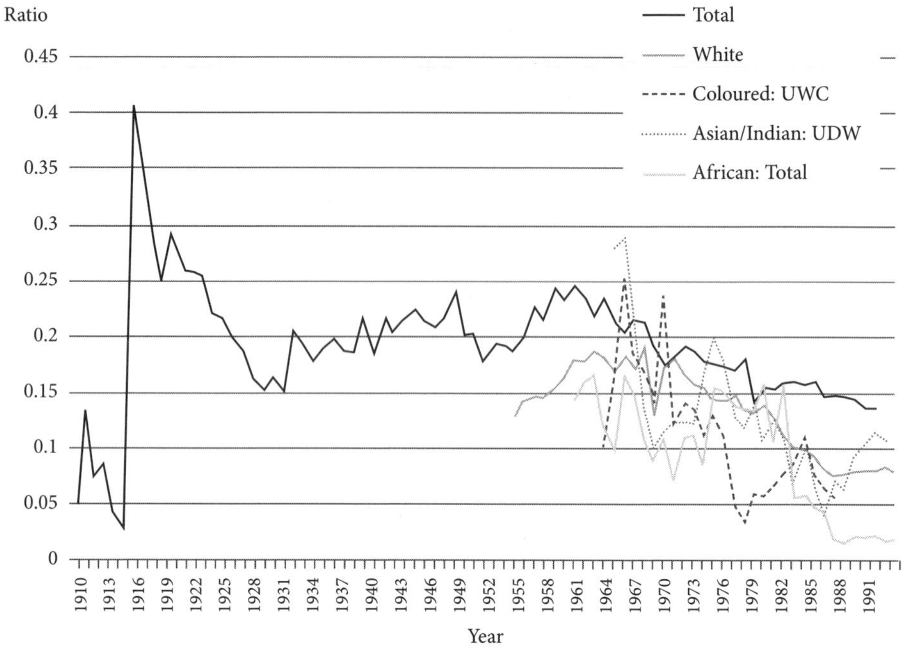

Source: Fedderke, de Kadt and Luiz 2003

In sum, the South African education system has achieved widening access in recent years,[46] but at the expense of quality; the key policy challenge in the future is how to safeguard and promote wide access while improving long-term quality. For example, gender equality in enrolment has been largely achieved. Public resources in education are increasingly being channelled towards the previously disadvantaged groups and communities. However, the system's capacity at all levels of education to deliver on what matters most for long-run economic development purposes – sound education in mathematics and science, and a deepening research capacity within the system – has been in decline. In sum, data on enrolments, matriculations and public expenditures suggest that much has been achieved to equalise access to education. Econometric evidence on South Africa also suggests a positive link between investment in human capital and growth. Also evident, however, is that the quality of human capital has been eroding. The challenge for public policy is, therefore, to continue efforts to equalise access while forcefully addressing the quality problem.

Table 1.6 *Per capita publication unit output by university, 1989–94*

	1989	1990	1991	1992	1993	1994	Rank 1989	Rank 1994
Wits	1.17	1.09	0.78	0.83	0.74	0.84	1	3
Cape Town	1.04	0.98	0.93	0.93	0.89	0.91	2	1
RAU	0.92	0.82	0.71	1.03	1.00	0.89	3	2
Natal	0.68	0.59	0.58	0.49	0.65	0.56	4	5
Rhodes	0.59	0.56	0.49	0.47	0.43	0.47	5	6
Stellenbosch	0.55	0.49	0.45	0.51	0.50	0.65	6	4
Pretoria	0.51	0.50	0.43	0.47	0.48	0.45	7	7
Free State	0.41	0.43	0.41	0.37	0.40	0.39	8	8
Potch	0.40	0.45	0.35	0.41	0.36	0.36	9	9
UPE	0.38	0.29	0.34	0.33	0.22	0.28	10	10
Medunsa	0.26	0.14	0.23	0.07	0.16	0.12	11	15
UNISA	0.24	0.25	0.24	0.25	0.23	0.25	12	11
UDW	0.20	0.19	0.21	0.22	0.18	0.24	13	12
Vista	0.15	0.10	0.11	0.11	0.09	0.09	14	17
UWC	0.14	0.09	0.11	0.13	0.20	0.22	15	13
Zululand	0.14	0.08	0.12	0.14	0.12	0.16	16	14
North	0.10	0.11	0.08	0.08	0.11	0.10	17	16

Source: Fedderke, de Kadt and Luiz 2003

Concluding remarks

The findings on the determinants of long-run growth in South Africa presented in this chapter cover three core sets of insights.

The first is that one of the central reasons for South Africa's structurally declining growth rate is its declining investment rate in fixed capital. The determinants of South Africa's investment rate are broadly consistent with those found in the wider literature. The South African investment function has the same structure as can be found elsewhere in the world, responding to the rate of return on and the real user cost of capital, thereby providing policy-makers with some immediate policy levers. But what proves to be key for investment expenditures is *uncertainty*, especially uncertainty that arises from institutional factors. In particular, uncertainty in South Africa has proved to be crucial not only to investment in the physical capital stock, but also to the capital flows that are required to meet the shortfall of private-sector savings relative to private-sector investment expenditure. Uncertainty affects investment both directly and indirectly, by lowering the effectiveness of the policy levers that the rate of return on capital and the user cost of capital provide.

Secondly, there remain significant market distortions in the South African economy in capital, labour and output markets, including external trade. This means that much remains to be done in improving microeconomic policy directions designed to increase the efficiency of resource allocation in the South African economy. The continued high level of protectionism in the economy, the size of the price mark-up over marginal cost of production, gives considerable cause for concern if South African production is to become globally competitive. But perhaps the most enduring concern relates to the now well-documented distortions in the labour markets. South Africa seems caught in an unfortunate pincer between inefficient labour and output markets which, unless addressed, will continue to constrain long-run growth prospects in the future.

Thirdly, the impact of human capital on growth reflects twin trends of declining contribution of human capital accumulation to growth and declining *quality* of education. The quality dimension of human capital investment with potentially significant impact on growth has been lacking. Even the best parts of the school and university systems do not produce the sorts of educational output required for long-term economic growth, and what they do produce comes at a relatively high cost.

These positive findings carry with them some normative policy implications that may be important for South African policy-makers as they contemplate policy posture in the second decade of the post-apartheid era:

(i) Improving the investment climate. With respect to stimulating investment expenditure, regardless of whether this is through the augmentation of physical capital or the attraction of capital inflows, two requirements are central – raising the net rate of return on capital, and providing a stable, predictable climate for private investment. In this regard South Africa has made some progress, but more needs to be done to create a favourable overall environment for private investment, entrepreneurship and growth.

(ii) Maintaining sound monetary and fiscal policies. The adoption of sound fiscal and monetary policy, through the Medium-Term Expenditure Framework and inflation-targeting, has provided macroeconomic conditions that are considerably more stable than has historically been the case. Such stability has provided the long-term platform for improved sustainable growth. The only remaining source of concern in the context of macroeconomic stability has been the behaviour of the currency. However, with further strengthening of the macroeconomic policy fundamentals in recent years (2003–04), the emphasis in the future is likely to be on the maintenance of the strong record to date.

(iii) Strengthening institutions and the functioning of labour and output markets. In contrast to the substantial achievements in the context of macroeconomic stabilisation policy, the institutional structure of the economy still leaves room for further improvement. This is true with respect to a number of distinct dimensions. The crucial objective here is to improve the functioning of markets – both labour and output markets.

a. Improving labour regulations for faster labour absorption. Labour market reform, geared towards creating a policy environment for faster labour absorption, remains one of the single most pressing needs in the economy. Excessive rigidity, inappropriate bargaining institutions for South African levels of development, excessive industry concentration, and associated mispricing of labour have led to poor employment growth in the economy. They have also disadvantaged the large pool of unemployed people who remain excluded from the benefits of the formal economy. It is time, therefore, to revisit labour market regulation and consider, for example, the possibility of introducing multi-tiered labour regulation that would allow more flexible and faster labour absorption for small and medium-size firms. The objective must be to allow the poor, who are often excluded from participation in the labour market through human capital endowments associated with past legacy and information asymmetries, access to employment under labour market regulation that is less onerous on the employer, and offers more chances of employment to jobseekers. Wage and non-wage costs in the labour entry market, for example, may need to be distinguished from those that govern the formal labour market – and they need to be considerably lower in order to create employment opportunities for the poor. International experience of multi-tiered labour market regulation exists – South Africa can learn much from this experience.

b. Making output markets more competitive. Output market reform is equally pressing. High industry concentration has led to mark-ups over marginal cost of production, which lowers incentives to expand production into international markets. Foregone employment opportunities and investment costs follow. Efficiency and competitiveness of output markets in South Africa require urgent attention, through continuation of the incomplete process of trade liberalisation, and the more aggressive pursuit of competition policy.

c. Deepening external trade and capital account liberalisation. Both further trade liberalisation and capital account liberalisation afford additional opportunity for further opening up of the economy to healthy competition that will result in longer-term gains in the productivity and competitiveness of South Africa's economy. Currently there remains scope for further trade reform, greater regional trade integration, and the reduction of excessive protection of some sectors of the economy. Also, restrictions on the movement of South African capital offshore continue to hamper both the opportunity for greater foreign direct investment and related technology transfers, and attempts to lower concentration levels in the South African economy. Given South Africa's level of development, greenfield investment is less likely than direct investment through equity acquisition. Yet the continued presence of constraints on South African firms wanting to move capital off-shore restricts the ability of foreign firms to acquire South African ventures into which technology transfer could take place. Increasing international entry into production in South Africa will require a further, systematic lifting of exchange controls.[47]

d. Fostering quality human capital accumulation. A significant achievement of the post-1994 government has been the large-scale expansion of access to education. This is a major policy achievement. But we have also seen that innovation is of increasing importance to South African growth, and that R&D and quality human capital formation are central to technological progress in South Africa. In neither dimension is policy yet sufficiently developed to reap potential gains in long-term growth. For example, incentives for R&D activity are poorly developed relative to international competitors. Human capital formation in South Africa, particularly in mathematics and the natural and applied sciences, remains poor – and lags behind competitor nations. Therefore, a more rigorous policy approach to innovation is required. R&D incentives can be brought into line with international competitors. More frequent standardised evaluation of school pupils can be implemented with computerised evaluation formats in order to test literacy and numerical ability. Incentives for school districts and pay incentives for teachers can be tied to the performance of pupils over time. Here, too, South Africa can learn from international experience (see, for instance, PROMESA in Mexico) about what does and does not work in such incentive schemes.

In conclusion, it is clear that South Africa has achieved much since 1994. But these achievements are best viewed as the platform for yet higher aspirations.

Notes

1   The discussion that follows draws substantially on Fedderke (2002a).

2   See, for instance, Abramovitz (1956, 1986, 1993); also Fagerberg (1994), Maddison (1987), Bosworth and Collins (2003).

3   See, for instance, Lim (1994).

4   See the more detailed discussion in Fedderke and Mariotti (2002); and Fedderke and Pirouz (2002).

5   See the more detailed discussion in Fedderke (2001a, 2004); and Fedderke, Henderson, Kayemba, Mariotti and Vaze (2001).

6   See Fedderke (2002a) for the full empirical evidence on sectors.

7   This section draws substantially on the more extensive analysis and discussion presented in Fedderke (2001a, 2004).

8   A comprehensive coverage of the modern debate can be found in Dixit and Pindyck (1994).

9   See Fielding (1997, 2000). Results are consistent with those presented here.

10 See, for example, Ferderer (1993); Guiso and Parigi (1999).

11 The reported results are panel estimation results for 28 manufacturing sectors. Aggregate results confirm the central findings – see Mariotti (2002); Kularatne (2002).

12 See Fedderke (2001a, 2004) and Fedderke, de Kadt and Luiz (2001a) for detail on this index.

13 Measured as a moving average of a variance of output demand measure by sector.

14 The index is available as far back as 1935.

15 In the regression, we also tested for the impact of credit rationing, openness of the manufacturing sectors to international trade, technological progress, the skills composition of the labour force, the real wage, and government crowd-in.

16 There is also new evidence to consider on the sources of systemic uncertainty in South Africa. This includes institutional factors as well as crime rates. See Fedderke and Luiz (2005).

17 For the systemic uncertainty measure we employ the data set contained in Fedderke, de Kadt and Luiz (2001a). For the precise definition of the other variables deployed, the reader is referred to the discussion in Fedderke (2001a, 2004).

18 New results suggest that lowering crime rates is also important – see Fedderke and Luiz (2005).

19 Defined as the sum of corporate saving (unit: R millions, current prices (Period)) [Source: SARB Quarterly Bulletin (S-129)] and saving by households (unit: R millions, current prices (Period)) [Source: SARB Quarterly Bulletin (S-131)], as a proportion of gross national product at factor cost (unit: R millions, current prices (Period)) [Source: SARB Quarterly Bulletin (S-127)].

20 Defined as the ratio of gross fixed capital formation at current prices by private business enterprises (unit: R millions, current prices (Period)) [Source: SARB Quarterly Bulletin (S-116)] to gross national product at factor cost (unit: R millions, current prices (Period)) [Source: SARB Quarterly Bulletin (S-127)].

21 For the detail, see Fedderke (2002b).

22 Estimations are for the standard short- and long-term capital flow measures reported in the balance of payments (TNORM), and three measures of capital flight constructed according to the indirect method (KFIND – see World Bank (1985) for its construction), the balance of payments method (KFBOP – see Cuddington (1987)) and the derived method (KFDRV – see Dooley (1988)).

23 Thus a positive Int. diff. should trigger capital outflows.

24 See Fedderke, de Kadt and Luiz (2001a) for a detailed description of the index underlying this variable.

25 For example see Levine (1997), Levine and Zervos (1998) and Levine, Loayza and Beck (2000).

26 This serves as the proxy for the ease of raising capital on equity markets in a wide range of international studies.

27 In particular, a percentage increase in the ratio of total value of shares traded increases the investment rate and per capita output by 0.28 per cent and 0.30 per cent, respectively. A percentage increase in credit extension and per capita GDP increases the ratio of value of shares traded by 0.26 per cent and 0.83 per cent, respectively. The effect of a percentage increase in credit extension on per capita GDP and the investment rate is relatively small, estimated to be an increase of 0.08 per cent and 0.07 per cent, respectively.

28   See World Bank (2000). The survey covers the 1998–99 period.

29   Government consumption expenditure consists of remunerations, depreciation of fixed capital and intermediate consumption less fees and charges. It does not include expenditure on education, given the potential importance of human capital formation for economic growth.

30   Linear estimation would imply one of two corner solutions as the optimal level of government consumption expenditure: 0 per cent or 100 per cent. Estimation proceeds in terms of both Johansen vector error correction techniques, as well as threshold autoregressive regression techniques in the presence of non-linearity.

31   See the discussion in Fedderke, Henderson, Kayemba, Mariotti and Vaze (2001).

32   See, for instance, the classic Lipset (1959); Diamond (1992) provides an overview of later developments.

33   See, for instance, Borner, Brunetti and Weder (1995).

34   See Coleman (1988, 1990); Putnam (1995); Fukuyama (1995a, 1995b).

35   Barro (1991) is the classic reference.

36   See the preceding discussion and Mariotti (2002) on evidence of the impact of macroeconomic policy on South African long-run economic growth.

37   For a recent dissenting view see Rangasamy and Harmse (2003), and the reply in Fedderke and Vaze (2004).

38   See the full discussion in Fedderke and Vaze (2001).

39   Ignoring intermediate inputs into production.

40   For a discussion of the economic as well as the statistical significance of these and other reported effects see Fedderke, Kularatne and Mariotti (forthcoming).

41   Data are obtained from Edwards and Golub (2002).

42   We report the results from Oliveira Martins and Scarpetta (1999).

43   For a non-technical discussion of the generic approaches to endogenous growth theory, and their implications for economic as well as institutional development, see Fedderke (2002c).

44   The methodology applies dynamic heterogeneous panel analysis to the South African manufacturing sectors. Estimation is of: $TFP = \frac{\dot{A}}{A} + \beta \frac{\dot{X}}{X} + \sum_{i=1}^{m} \gamma_i Z_i$ where $\frac{\dot{A}}{A}$ denotes exogenous technological change, $\frac{\dot{X}}{X}$ denotes either growth in physical capital stock (for the Romer (1986) type of approach), growth in human capital (for the Lucas (1988) type of approach), or growth in intermediate inputs or quality ladders (under Romer (1990), Grossman and Helpman (1991) or Aghion and Howitt (1992) type approaches), and Z_i denotes a range of additional regressors suggested by the literature. Here we skip the relatively complex range of estimation issues that arise, and proceed to salient estimation results directly. Full discussion of the estimation issues can be found in Fedderke (2001c).

45   In contrast, the total school enrolment rate, and the total number of degrees issued by South African universities, while significant, contributed negatively to TFP growth, while

the white school enrolment rate, the total number of NES degrees, and the number of apprenticeship contracts per capita proved to be insignificant.

46 We lack the space to develop evidence of the widening access here. But see Fedderke, de Kadt and Luiz (2000, 2003) for full details.

47 South Africa has Article VIII status with the International Monetary Fund (IMF) reflecting currency convertibility for current account transactions. Since 1994, it has also progressively eased exchange controls on capital transactions. For the latest status of the remaining exchange restrictions see, for example, the IMF Staff Report for the 2004 Article IV Consultation discussions on the IMF external website: www.imf.org under 'South Africa' keyword.

Appendix

The systemic uncertainty or political instability index

A measure of systemic uncertainty is provided by an index of political instability obtained from Fedderke, de Kadt and Luiz (2001a). It is illustrated in Figure 1A.1. Political instability was latent in South Africa throughout the twentieth century, and often became overt after 1948. The index is a weighted average of 11 indicators of repressive state responses to pressures for political reform. They are constructed from official and unofficial sources.

The indicators are:
* the number of prosecutions under the Defence Acts and Emergency regulations;
* the number of prosecutions for 'faction fighting';
* the number of people proscribed and/or banned under the Suppression of Communism Act of 1950;
* the number of people placed in detention;
* the number of political fatalities;
* the number of organisations officially banned;
* the number of actions against 'riots';
* declarations of official states of emergency;
* the number of publications subjected to censorship.

Weightings were determined by the Delphi technique on the basis of advice from leading political scientists in South Africa.[1]

Note

1 See the detailed discussion in Fedderke, de Kadt and Luiz (2001a).

Figure 1A.1 *Political instability in South Africa, 1935–95*

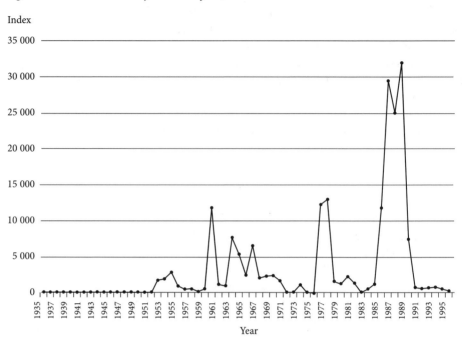

References

Abramovitz M (1956) Resource and output trends in the United States since 1870, *American Economic Review* 46(2): 5–23.

Abramovitz M (1986) Catching up, forging ahead, and falling behind, *Journal of Economic History* 46(2): 385–406.

Abramovitz M (1993) The search for the sources of growth: Areas of ignorance, old and new, *Journal of Economic History* 53(2): 217–243.

Aghion P & Howitt P (1992) A model of growth through creative destruction, *Econometrica* 60(2): 323–351.

Arndt C & Lewis JD (2000) The macro implications of the HIV/AIDS epidemic: A preliminary assessment, *South African Journal of Economics* 58(5): 856–887.

Barro RJ (1991) Economic growth in a cross-section of countries, *Quarterly Journal of Economics* 106: 407–443.

Borner S, Brunetti A & Weder B (1995) *Political credibility and economic development.* New York: St. Martin's Press.

Bosworth B & Collins S (2003) The empirics of growth: An update, *Brookings Panel on Economic Activity* September 4–5.

Coleman JS (1988) Social capital in the creation of human capital, *American Journal of Sociology* 94(Supplement): S95–S120.

Coleman JS (1990) *Foundations of social theory.* Cambridge, Mass.: The Belknap Press of Harvard University Press.

Cuddington JT (1987) Macroeconomic determinants of capital flight: An econometric investigation. In DR Lessard & J Williamson (eds) *Capital flight and third world debt.* Institute for International Economics: Washington, DC.

De Long JB & Summers LH (1991) Equipment investment and economic growth, *Quarterly Journal of Economics* 446–502.

De Long JB & Summers LH (1993) How strongly do developing countries benefit from equipment investment? *Journal of Monetary Economics* 32: 395–415.

Diamond L (1992) Economic development and democracy reconsidered, *American Behavioral Scientist* 35(4/5): 450–499.

Dixit AK & Pindyck RS (1994) *Investment under uncertainty.* Princeton: University Press.

Dooley MP (1988) Capital flight: A response to differences in financial risks, *IMF Staff Papers* 35: 422–436.

Edwards L & Golub SS (2002) South Africa's international cost competitiveness and productivity: A sectoral analysis. Report Prepared for South African National Treasury.

Fagerberg J (1994) Technology and international differences in growth rates, *Journal of Economic Literature* 32(3): 1147–1175.

Fedderke JW (2001a) Investment in fixed capital stock: Testing for the impact of sectoral and systemic uncertainty. Paper presented at the Royal Economic Society Conference, Durham, April. Econometric Research Southern Africa Working Paper No. 16. University of the Witwatersrand: Johannesburg.

Fedderke JW (2001b) Growth and institutions, *Journal of International Development* 13(6): 645–670.

Fedderke JW (2001c) *Technology, human capital and growth: Evidence from a middle income country case study applying dynamic heterogeneous panel analysis,* Econometric Research Southern Africa Working Paper No. 23.

Fedderke JW (2002a) The structure of growth in the South African economy: Factor accumulation and total factor productivity growth 1970–97, *South African Journal of Economics* 70(4): 611–646.

Fedderke JW (2002b) The virtuous imperative: Modelling capital flows in the presence of nonlinearity, *Economic Modelling* 19(3): 445–461.

Fedderke JW (2002c) Technology, human capital, growth and institutional development: Lessons from endogenous growth theory? *Theoria* 100: 1–26.

Fedderke JW (2004) Investment in fixed capital stock: Testing for the impact of sectoral and systemic uncertainty, *Oxford Bulletin of Economics and Statistics* 66(2): 165–187.

Fedderke JW, de Kadt RHJ & Luiz J (2000) Uneducating South Africa: The failure to address the need for human capital – a 1910–93 legacy, *International Review of Education* 46(3/4): 257–281.

Fedderke JW, de Kadt R & Luiz J (2001a) Indicators of political liberty, property rights and political instability in South Africa, *International Review of Law and Economics* 21(1): 103–134.

Fedderke JW, de Kadt RHJ & Luiz J (2001b) Growth and institutions: A study of the link between political institutions and economic growth in South Africa – a time series study, 1935–97, *Studies in Economics and Econometrics* 25(1): 1–26.

Fedderke JW, de Kadt RHJ & Luiz J (2003) A capstone tertiary educational system: Inefficiency, duplication and inequity in South Africa's tertiary education system, 1910–93, *Cambridge Journal of Economics* 27(3): 377–400.

Fedderke JW, Henderson S, Kayemba J, Mariotti M & Vaze P (2001) Changing factor market conditions in South Africa: The capital market – a sectoral description of the period 1970–1997, *Development Southern Africa* 18(4): 493–511.

Fedderke JW, Kularatne C & Mariotti M (forthcoming) Mark-up pricing in South African industry, *Journal of African Economies*.

Fedderke JW & Liu W (2002) Modelling the determinants of capital flows and capital flight: With an application to South African data from 1960–95, *Economic Modelling* 19(3): 419–444.

Fedderke JW & Luiz JM (2005) *The political economy of institutions, stability and investment: A simultaneous equation approach in an emerging economy – the case of South Africa*, Economic Research Southern Africa Working Paper No. 15.

Fedderke JW & Mariotti M (2002) Changing factor market conditions in South Africa: The labour market – A sectoral analysis of the period 1970–1997, *South African Journal of Economics* 70(5): 830–864.

Fedderke JW & Pirouz F (2002) The role of mining in the South African economy, *South African Journal of Economic and Management Sciences* 5(1): 1–34.

Fedderke JW & Schaling E (2005) Modeling inflation in South Africa: A multivariate cointegration analysis, *South African Journal of Economics* 73(1): 79–92.

Fedderke JW, Shin Y & Vaze P (2003) *Trade and labour usage: An examination of the South African manufacturing industry*, Econometric Research Southern Africa Working Paper No. 15, University of the Witwatersrand.

Fedderke JW & Vaze P (2001) The nature of South Africa's trade patterns by economic sector, and the extent of trade liberalisation during the course of the 1990's, *South African Journal of Economics* 69(3): 436–473.

Fedderke JW & Vaze P (2004) Response to Rangasamy and Harmse: Trade liberalisation in the 1990's, *South African Journal of Economics* 72(2): 408–413.

Ferderer JP (1993) The impact of uncertainty on aggregate investment spending: An empirical analysis, *Journal of Money, Credit and Banking* 25(1): 49–61.

Fielding D (1997) Aggregate investment in South Africa: A model with implications for political reform, *Oxford Bulletin of Economics and Statistics* 59(3): 349–369.

Fielding D (2000) Manufacturing investment in South Africa: A time series model, *Journal of Development Economics* 58: 405–427.

Fields GS (2000) The employment problem in South Africa. Keynote Paper, TIPS Annual Forum 2000.

Fukuyama F (1995a) The primacy of culture, *Journal of Democracy* 6(1): 7–14.

Fukuyama F (1995b) *Trust: The social virtues and the creation of prosperity*. London: Hamish Hamilton.

Grossman GM & Helpman E (1991) *Innovation and growth in the global economy*. Cambridge, Mass.: MIT Press.

Guiso L & Parigi G (1999) Investment and demand uncertainty, *Quarterly Journal of Economics* 185–127.

Hartman R (1972) The effects of price and cost uncertainty on investment, *Journal of Economic Theory* 5: 258–266.

Kraay AC (forthcoming) When is growth pro-poor? Cross-country evidence, *Journal of Development Economics*.

Kularatne C (2002) An examination of the impact of financial deepening on long-run economic growth: An application of a VECM structure to a middle-income country context, *South African Journal of Economics* 70(4): 647–687.

Levine R (1997) Financial development and economic growth, *Journal of Economic Literature* 35: 688–726.

Levine R, Loayza N & Beck T (2000) Financial intermediation and growth: Causality and causes, *Journal of Monetary Economics* 46(1): 31–77.

Levine R & Renelt D (1992) A sensitivity analysis of cross-country regressions, *The American Economic Review* 82: 942.

Levine R & Zervos S (1996) Stock market development and long-run growth, *World Bank Economic Review* 10(2): 323–340.

Levine R & Zervos S (1998) Stock markets, banks and growth, *American Economic Review* 88(3): 537–558.

Lewis JD (2001) *Policies to promote growth and employment in South Africa*. World Bank Discussion Papers on Aspects of the Economy of South Africa No. 16.

Lewis JD (2002) Promoting growth and employment in South Africa, *South African Journal of Economics* 70(4): 725–776.

Lim D (1994) Explaining the growth performances of Asian developing economies, *Economic Development and Cultural Change* 42(4): 829–844.

Lipset SM (1959) Some social requisites of democracy: Economic development and political legitimacy, *American Political Science Review* 53: 69–105.

Lucas RE (1988) On the mechanics of development planning, *Journal of Monetary Economics* 22(1): 3–42.

Maddison A (1987) Growth and slowdown in advanced capitalist economies: Techniques of quantitative assessment, *Journal of Economic Literature* 25: 649–698.

Mariotti M (2002) An examination of the impact of economic policy on long-run economic growth: An application of a VECM structure to a middle-income country context, *South African Journal of Economics* 70(4): 688–725.

Nattrass N (2000) Is South Africa's high productivity growth strategy appropriate in a labour surplus economy? Paper presented at the TIPS Annual Forum 2000.

Nickel SJ (1978) *The investment decisions of firms.* Cambridge: University Press.

North DC (1981) *Structure and change in economic history.* New York: Norton.

North DC (1990) *Institutions, institutional change and economic performance.* Cambridge: University Press.

North DC & Thomas RP (1970) An economic theory of the growth of the Western world, *The Economic History Review* 23(1): 1–17.

North DC & Thomas RP (1973) *The rise of the Western world.* Cambridge: University Press.

Oliveira Martins J & Scarpetta S (1999) *The levels and cyclical behaviour of mark-ups across countries and market structures,* OECD Economics Department Working Papers No. 213.

Putnam RD (1995) Bowling alone: America's declining social capital, *Journal of Democracy* 6(1): 65–78.

Rangasamy L & Harmse C (2003) Revisiting the extent of trade liberalisation in the 1990's, *South African Journal of Economics* 70(4): 705–728.

Romer PM (1986) Increasing returns and long-run growth, *Journal of Political Economy* 94(5): 1002–1037.

Romer PM (1990) Endogenous technological change, *Journal of Political Economy* 98(5): S71–S102.

Solow RM (1956) A contribution to the theory of economic growth, *Quarterly Journal of Economics* 65–96.

World Bank (1985) *World Bank Development Report.* World Bank: Washington, DC.

World Bank (2000) *Constraints to Growth and Employment in South Africa: Evidence from the large manufacturing firm survey.* World Bank: Washington, DC.

2 Poverty and inequality in post-apartheid South Africa: 1995–2000[1]

Johannes G. Hoogeveen and Berk Özler

Introduction

Apartheid in South Africa officially came to an end with the democratically held elections in 1994, and in its wake left a population with vast inequalities across racial groups.[2] Using a poverty line of R322 (in 2000 prices), at least 58 per cent of all South Africans, and 68 per cent of the African population, was living in poverty in 1995, while poverty was virtually non-existent for whites.[3] The Gini coefficient of expenditures was 0.56, making South Africa one of the most unequal countries in the world. The country also inherited vast inequalities in education, health, and basic infrastructure such as access to safe water, sanitation, and housing. For instance, while only a quarter of Africans had access to piped water in their houses, Asians and whites had universal access to this service.

Many other aspects of the South African economy are equally challenging. Crime is so prevalent that it leads to the emigration of South African professionals of all ethnic groups (Dodson 2002), and possibly also discourages investment and stifles growth. The broad unemployment rate is estimated to be between 30 per cent and 40 per cent and has been steadily increasing since 1995, making South Africa's unemployment rate one of the highest in the world. Many communities in the former homelands have little economic activity to speak of – mean unemployment rates in these communities approach 75 per cent.[4] The proportion of the workforce in the informal sector is no more than approximately 15 per cent in South Africa, a figure that is remarkably small when compared with, say, Latin American countries (Rama 2001; Kingdon and Knight 2004). According to UNAIDS, HIV prevalence increased from 10.5 per cent in 1995 to 22.8 per cent in 1998.[5] The Human Sciences Research Council (HSRC) projected that more than 375 000 South Africans would die from HIV/AIDS in 2003, a 30 per cent increase from the estimated number of deaths in 2000.[6]

Faced with these enormous challenges, the new government introduced the Reconstruction and Development Programme (RDP) in 1994, which described itself as an integrated, coherent socio-economic framework. The RDP set ambitious goals, such as job creation through public works programmes, redistribution via land reform, and major infrastructure projects in housing, services and social security. The Growth, Employment and Redistribution (GEAR) programme of

1996, which presented a formal macroeconomic framework for growth, followed the RDP and aimed to increase growth and stimulate job creation. It was an export-led macroeconomic strategy that included '...anti-inflationary policies, including fiscal restraint, continued tight monetary policies and wage restraint.'[7] Under this programme, the average annual GDP growth rate was to increase from a base projection of 2.8 per cent to 4.2 per cent between 1996 and 2000, and the deficit was to be reduced to a target rate of 3 per cent of GDP.[8] The main goals of the RDP were reiterated in GEAR, including reforms to make the labour markets more flexible, to improve productivity, and to increase training and employment of the unskilled.

During this period prices were stable, spending levels in education and pension programmes were adequate, and access to certain basic services and infrastructure improved significantly. However, GDP per capita grew at an annual rate of roughly 0.6 per cent that was more in line with baseline projections rather than with the Integrated Scenario projections of GEAR, and unemployment kept increasing steadily.[9,10] Final consumption expenditure by households also grew by less than 1 per cent per capita annually between 1995 and 2000.[11]

The failure of the economy to grow and to create enough jobs gave rise to an '...interrogation of the compatibility between GEAR and the labour legislation and a growing concern with rising unemployment and poverty' (Leibbrandt et al. 2001). The government reiterated its commitment to GEAR at the Presidential Jobs Summit in 1998, which brought together government, organised labour and the business sector. Despite consensus on the need for occupational training and job creation schemes, significant changes in labour market legislation did not follow. Nor did any significant land reform materialise, although this was identified as a source of improved prospects for long-term employment and rural income growth.

The narrow unemployment rate increased from 17 per cent to 24 per cent between 1995 and 1999, while the broad unemployment rate, which includes the so-called 'discouraged workers', increased from 29 per cent to 38 per cent during the same period (Klasen and Woolard 2000). During this period the demand for high-skilled labour increased, while it declined for low-skilled labour, a trend that Rama (2001) relates, to some extent, to trade liberalisation. Rama (2001) also reports a tendency towards outsourcing in the manufacturing sector, which led to an increase of workers in the informal sector between 1995 and 2000. Bhorat (2003) reports that the expansion of the informal sector accounted for 84 per cent of the 1.1 million jobs created between 1996 and 1999. However, the labour force expanded by 3.1 million over the same period, causing an overall increase in the rate of unemployment. Employers in manufacturing perceived labour market regulations as a major hindrance to the hiring of workers (Rama 2001; *The Economist* 2004).

The result is a segmented labour market, the high-skill tier of which is characterised by excess demand (Rama 2001), while the low-skill tier displays large excess supply.[12] Unemployment is very high in rural areas, highlighting not only the lack of economic activity in former homelands, but also the fact that unemployed individuals stay in or move back to rural areas to attach themselves to households with adequate public or private support (Klasen and Woolard 2000). Under these circumstances, one would expect an increase in inequality due to rising incomes for a small group of educated and skilled South Africans and stagnant or declining incomes for a much larger group of low-skilled individuals.[13]

Given this backdrop of very high levels of poverty and inequality in what is essentially an upper-middle-income country, knowledge of what has happened to the national distribution of household expenditures since the end of apartheid is important, but somewhat inadequate.[14] Various studies using the panel data generated by the KwaZulu-Natal Income Dynamics Study (KIDS) report on changes in welfare in KwaZulu-Natal, a large province of South Africa that is home to roughly one-fifth of its population. Carter and May (2001) find that poverty rates among the non-white population in KwaZulu-Natal increased from 27 per cent to 43 per cent between 1993 and 1998. Furthermore, they find that approximately 70 per cent of the poor may be dynamically so, unable to escape poverty. Using the same data source, but utilising income data instead of expenditures, Fields et al. (2003) do not present any figures on absolute poverty, but report that the Gini coefficient increased from 0.515 to 0.543 in KwaZulu-Natal. Also using income data from the same data sources used in this chapter (the Statistics South Africa (SSA) 1995 and 2000 Income and Expenditure Surveys (IES)), Lam and Leibbrandt (2003) find that incomes deteriorated for most South Africans. They also report that inequality within racial groups increased substantially, while between groups inequality declined only slightly, as a result of which total inequality increased in South Africa between 1995 and 2000.

In this chapter, we build on the existing literature and make three main contributions. Firstly, we utilise consumption aggregates in both the 1995 and 2000 IES that are carefully constructed so as to be as comparable to each other as possible. Secondly, using price data for each food item collected in the monthly Consumer Price Surveys conducted by SSA, we not only construct provincial and inter-temporal price indices, but also draw normative poverty lines to assess poverty in South Africa using the 'cost-of-basic-needs' approach. Finally, in addition to describing changes in real mean household expenditure, poverty and inequality across all of South Africa and for various sub-groups of the population for the 1995–2000 period, we also investigate whether the observed changes in welfare are due to changes in endowments, or changes in the returns to those endowments.

We find that the annual per capita growth rate of household expenditures between 1995 and 2000 is 0.5 per cent – very much in line with the GDP growth and the growth of final consumption expenditure by households.[15] Echoing Lam and Leibbrandt (2003), we find a deterioration of expenditures at the bottom end of the distribution, as a result of which poverty, especially extreme poverty, increased significantly. There were approximately 1.8 million more South Africans in 2000 living on less than $1/day, and 2.3 million more living on less than $2/day, than there were in 1995. However, these losses were not uniform: coloureds made significant gains against poverty over this period, as did several provinces, such as the Western Cape, Northern Cape and Free State. Overall inequality also increased, mainly due to a sharp increase of inequality within the African population. The fact that the growth rate was low and the reality that the materialised growth was not pro-poor were the main reasons for the lack of progress in the elimination of poverty in this period.

The next section of the chapter briefly discusses the data and methodology used, while the third section presents findings on the changes in poverty and inequality in South Africa, and provides breakdowns by ethnic group, province, and type of area. The fourth section discusses the sensitivity of our results with respect to the assumptions on sampling weights, the importance of home-grown food consumption, and urban/rural price differentials. The fifth section, using a multivariate regression framework, addresses the question of whether changes in endowments or returns to endowments are responsible for the results reported in this chapter. The final section discusses some remaining puzzles and concludes the chapter.

Data and methodology

In constructing household consumption aggregates to analyse changes in welfare in South Africa, we followed standard practice, in particular the guidelines put forth by Deaton and Zaidi (2002), Lanjouw et al. (1996), and Ravallion (2001).[16] Instead of discussing the construction and comparability of the consumption aggregates, the normative poverty lines, and the spatial and inter-temporal price adjustments in great detail, we refer the readers to Babita et al. (2003), which provides a very detailed account of these issues. Below, we briefly discuss the data and deviations we had to make from standard practice – mainly due to data constraints – that may affect our welfare estimates.

The data utilised in this chapter come from two surveys, each of which was conducted by SSA in both 1995 and 2000. The first is the October Household Survey (OHS) that is conducted annually. The second is the Income and Expenditure Survey (IES), which is held every five years among households surveyed by the OHS. Combined, these surveys provide information on household income and expenditure, along with information on other household characteristics such as demographics, work, access to services and housing characteristics for roughly 30 000 households in each of the survey years. Recently the annual OHS was transformed into a biannual Labour Force Survey (LFS) with a rotating panel. We utilise OHS 1995, IES 1995, LFS 2000 (2) and IES 2000 to build comparable welfare indicators for 1995 and 2000.

The income and expenditure modules in the IES hardly changed between 1995 and 2000, and hence it is possible to build comparable consumption aggregates based on a large set of common items that are included in both the 1995 and 2000 data.[17] The consumption aggregate includes the following expenditure categories: food, beverages and cigarettes (excluding home-grown foods); housing (imputed rental value of residence and utilities); compensation for domestic workers; personal care, household services and other household consumer goods; fuel (excluding firewood and dung); clothing and footwear; transport (excluding cost of purchased vehicles); communication; education; reading matter, cost of licences and other rental charges, and cost of insurance.[18] Rental values for housing were imputed in the same manner for each year using hedonic regressions.[19]

We used the 'cost-of-basic-needs' approach to draw normative poverty lines for our analysis (Ravallion 1994, 2001). According to these calculations, a reasonable poverty line for South Africa must lie between R322 (lower-bound poverty line) and R593 (upper-bound poverty line) per capita per month in 2000 prices. In this chapter, we report poverty using the lower-bound poverty line as well as the $2/day poverty line, which is equivalent to R174 per capita per month. The $2/day poverty line is close to the poverty line used by Deaton (1997), and also reasonably close to our food poverty line of R211.[20] While it is significantly lower than our preferred poverty line for South Africa, it is useful for international comparisons, and to describe what happens to the welfare of those at the bottom end of the distribution. Using these poverty lines, we report the Foster-Greer-Thorbecke (FGT) measures of headcount rate, poverty gap, and poverty gap squared. We also present three inequality measures for South Africa: the Gini index, the Theil index, and the Mean Log Deviation.

The data have three possible shortcomings that might bias the results presented in this chapter. Firstly, the issue of sampling weights for the 1995 and 2000 IES data has been a source of much controversy. Because of problems with the sampling frame for the 1995 OHS and IES, we report results using a set of sampling weights that was recalculated by SSA using information from the 1996 Census.[21] However, there is also reason to fear that the 2000 sampling weights might be inadequate (Simkins 2003). Secondly, the IES lacks the necessary information to impute a comparable value for consumption of home-grown products. In many countries, consumption of home-grown products is a significant component of the household consumption aggregate and hence its omission can lead to poverty being overestimated and the cross-sectional and inter-temporal poverty profiles being biased.[22] Thirdly, the IES neither collects information on quantities purchased to allow the construction of 'unit values', nor does it collect information on prices of various food items in the markets in the communities sampled. Hence, the price data we utilise to transform nominal household expenditures into real expenditures come from the price surveys that SSA conducts on a monthly basis. The Consumer Price Survey covers only metropolitan and urban areas throughout the nine provinces of South Africa. The lack of rural price data may cause an overestimation of poverty in rural areas, as well as biases in inter-temporal comparisons. For each of the potential problems discussed above, we perform sensitivity analysis and report the results in the fourth section of the chapter.

Results

Absolute poverty

Figure 2.1 shows the cumulative distribution functions (CDFs) for per capita expenditure in 1995 and 2000. The four vertical lines at R87, R174, R322, and R593 refer to the $1/day, $2/day, lower-bound and upper-bound poverty lines, respectively. The CDF for 1995 starts below that for 2000 and stays below it for most of the relevant range of poverty lines before crossing it, indicating a decline in real expenditures for those in the bottom half of the distribution.

Figure 2.1 *Cumulative distribution functions by year*

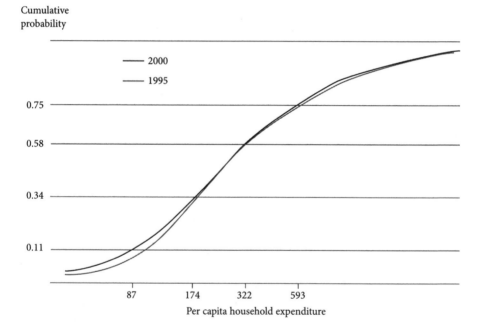

More than one in ten individuals lived on less than just $1/day in 2000, a large increase from 7.7 per cent in 1995 that translates into roughly 1.8 million additional individuals. These changes in poverty are presented in Table 2.1. Using the normative lower bound poverty line of R322 per month, we find that at least 58 per cent of the South African population were poor in both years. Roughly one-third of the population lived on less than $2/day (R174 per month) in 2000. For any poverty line below R322 per capita per month, the poverty gap and poverty severity (poverty gap squared) indices are significantly higher in 2000 than they were in 1995. These increases in poverty accompanied positive expenditure growth that was statistically insignificant.

Table 2.1 *Changes in poverty between 1995 and 2000*

Poverty line		$2/day poverty line (R174)		Lower-bound poverty line (R322)	
		1995	**2000**	**1995**	**2000**
South Africa	Headcount index*	0.32 (0.01)	0.34 (0.01)	0.58 (0.01)	0.58 (0.01)
	Poverty gap*ᵃ	0.11 (0.00)	0.13 (0.00)	0.27 (0.01)	0.29 (0.01)
	Poverty gap squared*ᵃ	0.05 (0.00)	0.07 (0.00)	0.16 (0.00)	0.17 (0.00)
	Mean expenditure	534 (10.5)	547 (11.0)	534 (10.5)	547 (11.0)
Africans	Headcount index*	0.38 (0.01)	0.40 (0.01)	0.68 (0.01)	0.67 (0.01)
	Poverty gap*ᵃ	0.13 (0.00)	0.15 (0.00)	0.32 (0.00)	0.34 (0.00)
	Poverty gap squared*ᵃ	0.06 (0.00)	0.08 (0.00)	0.19 (0.00)	0.21 (0.00)
	Mean expenditureᵇ	341 (6.8)	357 (5.9)	341 (6.8)	357 (5.9)
Coloureds	Headcount index*ᵃ	0.20 (0.01)	0.12 (0.01)	0.50 (0.02)	0.35 (0.02)
	Poverty gap*ᵃ	0.06 (0.00)	0.04 (0.00)	0.19 (0.01)	0.13 (0.01)
	Poverty gap squared*ᵃ	0.02 (0.00)	0.01 (0.00)	0.10 (0.01)	0.07 (0.00)
	Mean expenditureᵇ	474 (15.9)	659 (23.6)	474 (15.9)	659 (23.6)
Asians/ Indians	Headcount index	0.00 (0.00)	0.01 (0.01)	0.08 (0.01)	0.07 (0.02)
	Poverty gap	0.00 (0.00)	0.00 (0.00)	0.02 (0.00)	0.02 (0.01)
	Poverty gap squared	0.00 (0.00)	0.00 (0.00)	0.01 (0.00)	0.01 (0.00)
	Mean expenditure	1 108 (66.6)	1 146 (49.7)	1 108 (66.6)	1 146 (49.7)
Whites	Headcount index	0.00 (0.00)	0.00 (0.00)	0.01 (0.00)	0.01 (0.01)
	Poverty gap	0.00 (0.00)	0.00 (0.00)	0.00 (0.00)	0.00 (0.00)
	Poverty gap squared	0.00 (0.00)	0.00 (0.00)	0.00 (0.00)	0.00 (0.00)
	Mean expenditureᵇ	1 989 (39.0)	2 211 (51.7)	1 989 (39.0)	2 211 (51.7)
Urban	Headcount index*ᵃ	0.15 (0.01)	0.18 (0.01)	0.36 (0.01)	0.40 (0.01)
	Poverty gap*ᵃ	0.05 (0.00)	0.05 (0.00)	0.14 (0.00)	0.16 (0.00)
	Poverty gap squared*ᵃ	0.02 (0.00)	0.02 (0.00)	0.08 (0.00)	0.09 (0.00)
	Mean expenditureᵇ	811 (19.8)	764 (17.9)	811 (19.8)	764 (17.9)
Rural	Headcount index*ᵃ	0.45 (0.01)	0.55 (0.01)	0.75 (0.01)	0.80 (0.01)
	Poverty gap*ᵃ	0.16 (0.00)	0.22 (0.01)	0.37 (0.01)	0.44 (0.01)
	Poverty gap squared*ᵃ	0.07 (0.00)	0.12 (0.00)	0.22 (0.00)	0.29 (0.00)
	Mean expenditureᵇ	313 (8.3)	262 (6.1)	313 (8.3)	262 (6.1)

Notes: All figures have been weighted using person weights (household weight * household size).

Standard errors are given in parentheses and are corrected for complex survey design.

* indicates that the difference in the poverty figures between 1995 and 2000 is statistically significant at the 90 per cent level for z=174.

ᵃ indicates that the difference in the poverty figures between 1995 and 2000 is statistically significant at the 90 per cent level for z=322.

ᵇ indicates that the difference in mean expenditure levels between 1995 and 2000 is statistically significant at the 90 per cent level.

Figures 2.2 and 2.3 show the cumulative distribution functions for Africans and coloureds by year. Figure 2.2 demonstrates that the CDF for Africans looks very similar to the CDF for all South Africans, indicating that while some Africans made gains in their household expenditures over time, many others experienced losses. However, Africans are the only population group that exhibit this pattern. As can be seen in Figure 2.3, the CDF in 2000 for coloureds lies nowhere above that in 1995, meaning that poverty among this group is lower in 2000 for any poverty line. We find similar but more modest improvements for Asians/Indians and whites (figures not shown).

Figures 2.4 and 2.5 show the distribution of per capita expenditure by ethnic groups for 1995 and 2000, respectively. In both years, the CDF for coloureds first order dominates that for Africans, the CDF for Asians/Indians dominates that for coloureds, and the CDF for whites dominates that for Asians/Indians. However, somewhat surprisingly, the gap between coloureds and Africans increased over this period, while the gap between coloureds and the remaining population groups decreased. Nonetheless, poverty in 2000 was virtually zero among whites, and Africans were the poorest ethnic group followed by coloureds and Asians/Indians – closely mimicking the order established by the apartheid regime.

Figure 2.2 *Cumulative distribution functions by year for Africans*

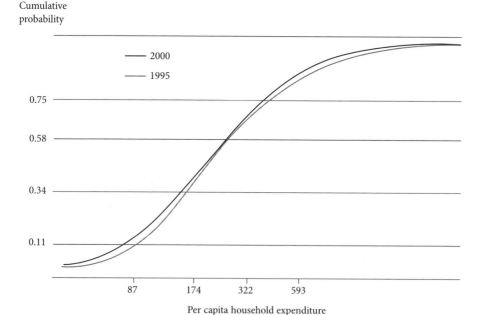

Per capita household expenditure

Figure 2.3 *Cumulative distribution functions by year for coloureds*

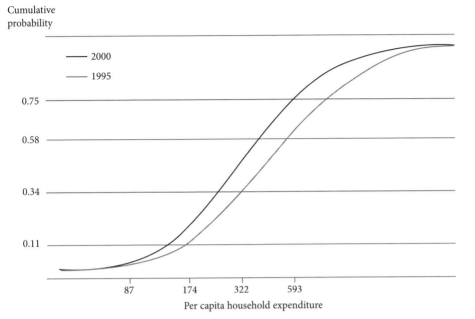

Figure 2.4 *Cumulative distribution functions by population group in 1995*

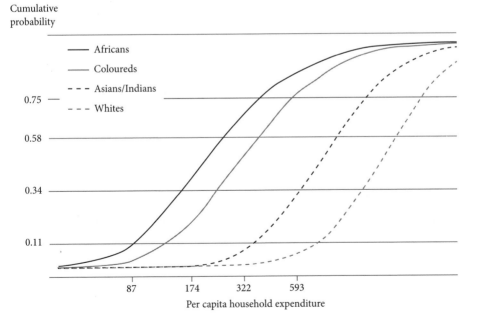

Figure 2.5 *Cumulative distribution functions by population group in 2000*

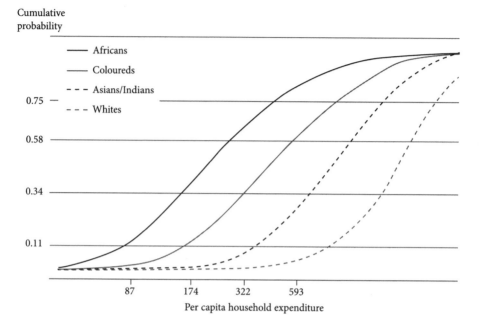

Changes in poverty by population group are also presented in Table 2.1. Among Africans, extreme poverty increased in terms of any of the three common Foster-Greer-Thorbecke (FGT) measures of poverty. In 2000, more than two-thirds of Africans in South Africa lived in poverty, while more than 40 per cent lived on less than $2/day. On the other hand, the substantial improvements in mean expenditure for coloureds resulted in a significant decrease in poverty. The poverty headcount among this group went down from 50 per cent in 1995 to 35 per cent in 2000, while extreme poverty declined from 20 per cent to 12 per cent. There was no change for Asians/Indians and whites, i.e. the headcount rate remained at a very low level for Asians/Indians and at virtually zero for whites.

Table 2.1 also presents changes in poverty for urban and rural areas. There is a large gap in poverty rates between urban and rural areas, both of which increased significantly over this period. No significant change in the overall headcount ratio (using the lower-bound poverty line of R322 per capita per month) in South Africa during this period is consistent with increases in that index in both urban and rural areas, as the share of the population living in urban areas increased significantly during this period.[23] More than three-quarters of the population in rural areas lived in poverty in both years, while the share living on less than $2/day increased from 45 per cent in 1995 to more than half of the rural population in 2000. Poverty in urban areas also increased – from 36 per cent to 40 per cent.

Table 2.2 *Changes in poverty by province*

		$2/day poverty line (R174)		Lower-bound poverty line (R322)	
		1995	**2000**	**1995**	**2000**
South Africa	Headcount index*	0.32 (0.01)	0.34 (0.01)	0.58 (0.01)	0.58 (0.01)
	Poverty gap*a	0.11 (0.00)	0.13 (0.00)	0.27 (0.01)	0.29 (0.01)
	Poverty gap squared*a	0.05 (0.00)	0.07 (0.00)	0.16 (0.00)	0.17 (0.00)
Western Cape	Headcount index*a	0.15 (0.02)	0.10 (0.01)	0.40 (0.02)	0.31 (0.02)
	Poverty gap*a	0.04 (0.01)	0.02 (0.00)	0.15 (0.01)	0.11 (0.01)
	Poverty gap squared*a	0.01 (0.00)	0.01 (0.00)	0.07 (0.01)	0.05 (0.00)
Eastern Cape	Headcount index*	0.49 (0.01)	0.56 (0.02)	0.76 (0.01)	0.76 (0.01)
	Poverty gap*a	0.18 (0.01)	0.23 (0.01)	0.39 (0.01)	0.44 (0.01)
	Poverty gap squared*a	0.08 (0.00)	0.13 (0.01)	0.24 (0.01)	0.29 (0.01)
Northern Cape	Headcount index*a	0.33 (0.03)	0.26 (0.02)	0.62 (0.03)	0.53 (0.03)
	Poverty gap*a	0.12 (0.04)	0.09 (0.01)	0.29 (0.02)	0.24 (0.02)
	Poverty gap squareda	0.05 (0.01)	0.04 (0.01)	0.17 (0.01)	0.13 (0.01)
Free State	Headcount index*a	0.48 (0.02)	0.38 (0.02)	0.70 (0.02)	0.61 (0.02)
	Poverty gap*a	0.19 (0.01)	0.14 (0.01)	0.38 (0.01)	0.32 (0.01)
	Poverty gap squared*a	0.10 (0.01)	0.07 (0.00)	0.24 (0.01)	0.19 (0.01)
KwaZulu-Natal	Headcount index*a	0.32 (0.02)	0.46 (0.02)	0.63 (0.02)	0.68 (0.02)
	Poverty gap*a	0.11 (0.01)	0.20 (0.01)	0.28 (0.01)	0.37 (0.01)
	Poverty gap squared*a	0.05 (0.01)	0.11 (0.01)	0.16 (0.01)	0.24 (0.01)
North West	Headcount indexa	0.39 (0.02)	0.35 (0.02)	0.66 (0.02)	0.61 (0.02)
	Poverty gap	0.14 (0.01)	0.13 (0.01)	0.33 (0.01)	0.30 (0.01)
	Poverty gap squared	0.07 (0.01)	0.06 (0.01)	0.20 (0.01)	0.18 (0.01)
Gauteng	Headcount index*a	0.08 (0.01)	0.14 (0.01)	0.23 (0.02)	0.37 (0.02)
	Poverty gap*a	0.02 (0.00)	0.04 (0.00)	0.08 (0.01)	0.14 (0.01)
	Poverty gap squared*a	0.01 (0.00)	0.02 (0.00)	0.04 (0.01)	0.07 (0.00)
Mpumalanga	Headcount index	0.31 (0.02)	0.29 (0.02)	0.62 (0.02)	0.59 (0.02)
	Poverty gap	0.09 (0.01)	0.09 (0.01)	0.28 (0.01)	0.26 (0.01)
	Poverty gap squared	0.04 (0.00)	0.04 (0.00)	0.15 (0.01)	0.14 (0.01)
Limpopo	Headcount index*a	0.36 (0.02)	0.47 (0.01)	0.65 (0.02)	0.76 (0.01)
	Poverty gap*a	0.12 (0.01)	0.16 (0.01)	0.31 (0.01)	0.38 (0.01)
	Poverty gap squared*a	0.06 (0.01)	0.07 (0.00)	0.18 (0.01)	0.23 (0.01)

Notes: All figures have been weighted using person weights (household weight * household size).

Standard errors are given in parentheses and are corrected for complex survey design.

* indicates that the difference in the poverty figures between 1995 and 2000 is statistically significant at the 90 per cent level for z=174.

a indicates that the difference in the poverty figures between 1995 and 2000 is statistically significant at the 90 per cent level for z=322.

Table 2.2 presents the changes in poverty for the nine provinces of South Africa. There is substantial variation in levels and changes in poverty across provinces. The only provinces that have experienced significant growth in their mean household expenditure levels – the Western Cape, Northern Cape and Free State – have experienced significant declines in poverty. In fact, by 2000, the Western Cape had the lowest poverty headcount rate in South Africa, replacing Gauteng. The declines in poverty in the Northern Cape and Free State were mainly driven by rural sector growth.[24] That the Western Cape and Northern Cape are also the two provinces in which coloureds form the majority of the population is consistent with the significant reduction in poverty experienced by coloureds. However, it wasn't only coloureds who benefited from poverty reduction in these provinces – the poverty headcount among Africans went down from 75 per cent to 62 per cent in the Northern Cape and from 62 per cent to 55 per cent in the Western Cape.

While a few provinces made progress, a number of provinces have seen dramatic increases in poverty. In the Eastern Cape, already the poorest province in South Africa in 1995, the extreme poverty rate increased from 49 per cent to 56 per cent, while the poverty gap and poverty severity have also worsened significantly. Limpopo, a mainly rural province, has seen the most dramatic increase in its poverty incidence, with approximately three-quarters of its population living in poverty by 2000 compared with 65 per cent in 1995. Poverty has also increased in KwaZulu-Natal, where close to half of the population was living on less than $2/day by 2000.[25] Finally, Gauteng, the wealthiest province in 1995, has experienced large increases in poverty, where more than one-third of the population was living in poverty by 2000, up from less than a quarter five years prior to that.[26]

Some of the dramatic increases in extreme poverty happened in provinces where mean expenditure levels stayed constant over time. In the Eastern Cape and KwaZulu-Natal, the increase in poverty is a result of a worsening of the distribution of expenditures. On the other hand, in North West and Mpumalanga, where growth rates were also zero, poverty stayed constant. Given this variation in outcomes regarding consumption growth and poverty, in the next two sub-sections of this discussion we examine whether South Africa's growth has been pro-poor for some, and describe the changes in inequality that have been experienced.

Pro-poor growth

Figures 2.6 and 2.7 present growth incidence curves (GIC) for South Africa and for the coloured population, respectively, for the period 1995–2000. The GIC is obtained by plotting the annual growth rate in each percentile p of the distribution of per capita expenditures while p is varied from 0 to 1.[27] The area under the GIC up to the headcount index in 1995 (normalised by the headcount rate in 1995) gives the mean growth rate for the poor. The vertical line in the graph indicates the headcount rate in 1995, while the horizontal line denotes the mean percentile growth rate. We define growth to be 'absolutely pro-poor' if the mean growth rate for the poor is positive, and 'relatively pro-poor' if, in addition, the mean growth rate for the poor is greater than or equal to the growth rate in mean expenditure. Hence, 'absolute pro-poor growth' only requires that the poor be better off on average in absolute terms, while 'relative pro-poor growth' requires the distributional shifts to be pro-poor as well.[28]

Figure 2.6 *Growth incidence curve for South Africa*

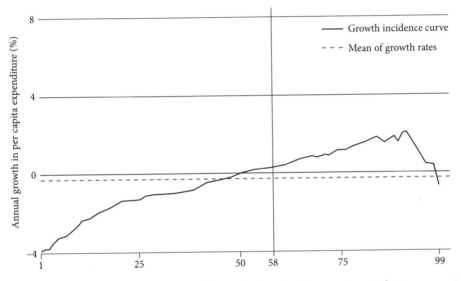

The poorest *p* percentage of the population ranked by per capita expenditure

A GIC that lies above zero for each percentile implies first order dominance of the expenditure distribution in 2000 over 1995, i.e. an unambiguous decline in poverty. A GIC that is downward-sloping implies that the poor benefit from growth more than the non-poor, leading to a decrease in inequality. Unfortunately, the GIC for South Africa during this period (Figure 2.6) satisfies neither condition: it is below zero everywhere for the poor and upward-sloping over most of the range. The annual growth rate in the mean is 0.5 per cent, while the rate of pro-poor growth is 1.4 per cent. Hence, the modest growth in South Africa has not been pro-poor between 1995 and 2000 – either absolutely or relatively.

As the poverty headcount has dropped sharply among coloureds, it is informative to contrast the GIC for coloureds with that for the whole country. Figure 2.7 shows that the GIC for coloureds lies entirely above the zero line and the rate of pro-poor growth is 4.8 per cent. However, the GIC is again upward-sloping, meaning that the non-poor benefited more from growth than the poor and that inequality among coloureds has risen. The growth in the mean for coloureds is 6.8 per cent. Hence, growth has been only 'absolutely pro-poor' for coloureds. The same pattern (not shown here) also holds for the three provinces with significant poverty reduction.

Figure 2.7 *Growth incidence curve for coloureds*

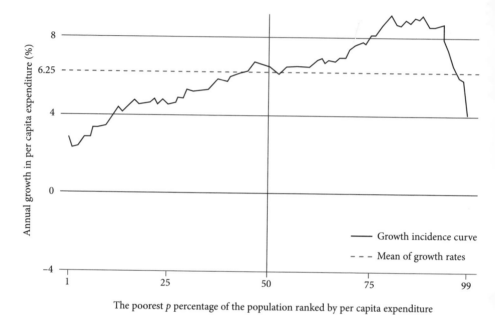

The poorest *p* percentage of the population ranked by per capita expenditure

Growth has not been pro-poor in South Africa as a whole, and in the instances where poverty declined for certain sub-groups, the distributional shifts were still not pro-poor. As a result, one expects inequality to have somewhat increased. We describe the changes in inequality below.

Inequality

Table 2.3 shows the changes in inequality in South Africa as a whole as well as the changes by population group and type of area, using three inequality measures: the Gini index, mean log deviation, and the Theil index. The Gini index went up only slightly from 0.56 in 1995 to 0.58 in 2000. This is not unexpected, as the Gini index is most sensitive to income differences in the middle of the distribution, while the observed changes in the South African expenditure distribution took place mostly at the tails. Mean log deviation, a general entropy class measure of inequality that is sensitive to changes at the bottom end of the distribution, went up from 0.56 to 0.61. Table 2.3 also shows that there was a significant increase in inequality among the African population. During this five-year period, the Gini index among Africans increased by more than three percentage points to 0.50 and the mean log deviation went up from 0.37 to 0.44. Inequality also increased slightly among coloureds and decreased somewhat among Asians/Indians and whites.

Table 2.3 *Changes in inequality between 1995 and 2000*

		1995	2000
South Africa	Gini index	0.565 (0.005)	0.577 (0.005)
	Mean log deviation	0.563 (0.011)	0.607 (0.012)
	Theil index	0.608 (0.014)	0.617 (0.012)
Africans	Gini index	0.467 (0.007)	0.501 (0.005)
	Mean log deviation	0.370 (0.011)	0.436 (0.010)
	Theil index	0.414 (0.015)	0.460 (0.012)
Coloureds	Gini index	0.439 (0.009)	0.453 (0.008)
	Mean log deviation	0.326 (0.014)	0.359 (0.012)
	Theil index	0.345 (0.016)	0.348 (0.013)
Asians/Indians	Gini index	0.398 (0.019)	0.374 (0.014)
	Mean log deviation	0.265 (0.025)	0.243 (0.021)
	Theil index	0.287 (0.034)	0.233 (0.018)
Whites	Gini index	0.344 (0.007)	0.319 (0.009)
	Mean log deviation	0.203 (0.008)	0.179 (0.011)
	Theil index	0.201 (0.007)	0.172 (0.011)
Urban	Gini index	0.527 (0.006)	0.533 (0.006)
	Mean log deviation	0.502 (0.013)	0.517 (0.013)
	Theil index	0.494 (0.013)	0.502 (0.013)
Rural	Gini index	0.493 (0.009)	0.502 (0.008)
	Mean log deviation	0.410 (0.016)	0.428 (0.014)
	Theil index	0.513 (0.022)	0.516 (0.022)

Notes: All figures have been weighted using person weights (household weight * household size).
Standard errors are given in parentheses and are corrected for complex survey design by utilising the ineqerr.ado file in STATA that provides bootstrap estimates of sampling the variances.
Mean log deviation and Theil index are General Entropy Class Inequality Measures with parameter values 'c' equal to 0 and 1, respectively.

General entropy class inequality measures are decomposable into components of inequality within and between groups, and the mean log deviation is decomposed as follows:

$$I_0 = [\sum_j g_j \log(\frac{\mu}{\mu_j})] + \sum_j I_j g_j, \qquad [1]$$

where j refers to sub-groups, g_j refers to the population share of group j and I_j refers to inequality in group j. The between-group component of inequality is captured by the first term to the right of the equality sign. It can be interpreted as measuring what would be the level of inequality in the population if everyone within the group had the same (the group-mean) consumption level, μ_j. The second term on the right reflects what would be the overall inequality level if there were no differences in mean consumption across groups but each group had its actual within-group inequality I_j.

Table 2.4 shows the results for such a decomposition exercise for South Africa, where the sub-groups are the four major population groups. We find that the share of inequality between ethnic groups went down from 38.3 per cent in 1995 to 33.2 per cent in 2000. However, this decrease in the share of between-group inequality can be attributed mostly to the increase in inequality within groups, as between-group inequality decreased slightly over the same period. The former can be explained mostly by the large increase in inequality among Africans, while the latter is mainly a result of the relative progress made by coloureds in their level of mean per capita household expenditure.

Table 2.4 *Inequality within and between population groups*

	1995	2000
Mean log deviation	0.563	0.606
Inequality within population groups	0.347	0.405
Inequality between population groups	0.216	0.201
Share of between-group inequality	38.3%	33.2%

Sensitivity analysis

Sampling weights

Throughout this chapter, we use a set of sampling weights for the 1995 data that were recalculated by SSA based on information from the 1996 Census. However, some have suggested (for example, Simkins 2003) that the sampling weights in the 2000 IES may also be problematic, in that they may lead to an overestimation (under-estimation) in the population share of Africans (whites). Following the end of apartheid, internal migration and emigration might have led to rapid shifts in demographic composition in South Africa, possibly making the 1996 Census – the sampling frame for the 2000 IES – somewhat outdated. A comparison of respective population shares of racial groups in the IES with those from the recent 2001 Census (Statistics South Africa 2003) confirms that this may be true to some extent. Table 2.5 shows that the share of whites is under-estimated significantly in the IES

(9.6 per cent versus 7.7 per cent), and this is particularly true in Gauteng (19.9 per cent versus 13.0 per cent). If the census figures of 2001 are a better representation of the 2000 population, this bias could lead to an under-estimation of the growth rate and an overestimation of the increase in poverty in South Africa.

Table 2.5 *Percentage population shares by race in 2000*

	South Africa		Gauteng	
	IES 2000	Census 2001	IES 2000	Census 2001
Africans	81.0	79.0	81.1	73.8
Coloureds	8.8	8.9	4.3	3.8
Asians/Indians	2.5	2.5	1.6	2.5
Whites	7.7	9.6	13.0	19.9

To test the robustness of our results, we employ a crude ex-post re-weighting scheme.[29] Using population shares from the 2001 Census at the province level for each racial group, we re-weight our 2000 IES sample so that the population share in each of the 36 province/race cells (9 provinces times 4 racial groups) is identical to that from the 2001 Census. The re-estimated welfare measures are presented in Table 2.6. Using the adjusted weights, mean expenditure grows from R534 to R587 over this period, a per capita growth rate of 1.9 per cent per year. This is more than double the GDP growth rate, and as such we can treat it as an upper limit on growth of per capita household expenditures over this period.

Despite this expenditure growth, the effect of re-weighting on poverty changes is minimal. The conclusion that poverty increased between 1995 and 2000 remains true for a wide range of poverty lines, especially for the poverty gap and poverty severity measures. On the other hand, inequality is higher using these adjusted sampling weights. These results are not completely surprising. As the population share of whites – who are clustered at the top end of the expenditure distribution – is significantly higher than originally estimated by the IES alone, the rate of growth and the level of inequality increase, but poverty levels are not significantly affected.

While our results with respect to changes in poverty and inequality generally hold regardless of the sampling weights used in the analysis, the magnitudes of some of these changes are different. For example, using the adjusted weights for 2000, the headcount index for Gauteng still increases significantly, but only to 33.8 per cent instead of 36.8 per cent. We conclude that adjustments to sampling weights alone cannot reverse the main conclusions reached in this chapter.

Table 2.6 *Sensitivity of poverty and inequality comparisons to sampling weights*

Poverty line		Revised 1995 sampling weights	Published 2000 sampling weights	Adjusted 2000 sampling weights
$2/day poverty line (R174)	Headcount index[a*]	0.317 (0.007)	0.339 (0.007)	0.334 (0.007)
	Poverty gap[a*]	0.109 (0.003)	0.128 (0.003)	0.126 (0.003)
	Poverty gap squared[a*]	0.050 (0.002)	0.065 (0.002)	0.064 (0.002)
Lower-bound poverty line (R322)	Headcount index	0.579 (0.007)	0.575 (0.007)	0.564 (0.007)
	Poverty gap[a]	0.272 (0.005)	0.286 (0.005)	0.281 (0.005)
	Poverty gap squared[a*]	0.157 (0.003)	0.174 (0.004)	0.171 (0.004)
	Mean expenditure*	534 (10.5)	547 (11.0)	587 (13.1)
	Gini index	0.565 (0.005)	0.578 (0.004)	0.588 (0.005)
	Mean log deviation	0.563 (0.011)	0.606 (0.010)	0.638 (0.012)
	Theil index	0.608 (0.014)	0.623 (0.011)	0.636 (0.012)

Notes: All figures have been weighted using person weights (household weight * household size).
Standard errors are given in parentheses and are corrected for complex survey design.
[a] indicates that the difference between the 1995 figures (column 3) and the published 2000 figures (column 4) for mean expenditure and poverty measures is statistically significant at the 90 per cent level.
* indicates that the difference between the 1995 figures (column 3) and the adjusted 2000 figures (column 5) for the same measures is statistically significant at the 90 per cent level.

Consumption from home-grown production

The importance of consumption from home-grown production seems to be small in South Africa compared with other countries. Deaton and Zaidi (2002) report that the budget share of this item was 2.2 per cent in South Africa in 1993, compared with 6.7 per cent in Brazil or 16.8 per cent in Vietnam. We have obtained the South Africa Integrated Household Survey, 1993 (SAIHS) – the same data set used by Deaton and Zaidi – and replicated this figure ourselves. Further examination of these data revealed no significant differences in the share of consumption from home-grown production across per capita expenditure deciles.

To examine whether this pattern has significantly changed over time, we calculated the share of maize consumption from home-grown production using our data sets for 1995 and 2000.[30] We use the market price of maize in each province to value home consumption. We find that while only 3 per cent of the population was consuming maize from own-production in 1995, this figure went up to approximately 11 per cent by 2000. The share of maize consumption from home production in the consumption aggregate also increased from approximately 0.5 per cent in 1995 to roughly 1.5 per cent by 2000. Furthermore by 2000, home-grown maize consumption constituted 3 per cent of the poorest quintile's consumption and virtually none of the richest quintile's, suggesting that home production of food may have become more important for the poor over this period.

However, these figures are still very small. Table 2.7 compares the poverty figures for 2000 using a consumption aggregate that includes home-grown maize (column 5) with those without this consumption item for 1995 (column 3) and 2000 (column 4). While poverty (and inequality) is slightly less in 2000 when this consumption of home grown maize is accounted for, the changes in the poverty gap and poverty gap squared measures over this period remain significant. We conclude that our general conclusions regarding inter-temporal comparisons of the mean growth rate, poverty and inequality are robust to the inclusion of home-grown food products. This conclusion remains the same regardless of whether we use the *published* sampling weights in the IES 2000 or the *adjusted* ones discussed above.

Table 2.7 *Sensitivity of poverty and inequality comparisons to consumption of home-grown food*

Poverty line		Consumption *excluding* home-grown maize (1995)	Consumption *excluding* home-grown maize (2000)	Consumption *including* home-grown maize (2000)
$2/day poverty line (R174)	Headcount index[a]	0.317 (0.007)	0.339 (0.007)	0.331 (0.006)
	Poverty gap[a]*	0.109 (0.003)	0.128 (0.003)	0.122 (0.003)
	Poverty gap squared[a]*	0.050 (0.002)	0.065 (0.002)	0.061 (0.002)
Lower-bound poverty line (R322)	Headcount index	0.579 (0.007)	0.575 (0.007)	0.573 (0.006)
	Poverty gap[a]	0.272 (0.005)	0.286 (0.005)	0.281 (0.004)
	Poverty gap squared[a]*	0.157 (0.003)	0.174 (0.004)	0.169 (0.003)
	Mean expenditure	534 (10.5)	547 (11.0)	549 (10.6)
	Gini index	0.565 (0.005)	0.578 (0.004)	0.574 (0.005)
	Mean log deviation	0.563 (0.011)	0.606 (0.010)	0.596 (0.012)
	Theil index	0.608 (0.014)	0.623 (0.011)	0.610 (0.012)

Notes: All figures have been weighted using person weights (household weight * household size).
Standard errors are given in parentheses and are corrected for complex survey design.
[a] indicates that the difference between figures excluding maize for 1995 (column 3) and for 2000 (column 4) for mean expenditure and poverty measures is statistically significant at the 90 per cent level.
* indicates that the difference between the 1995 figures (column 3) and the 2000 figures including maize (column 5) for the same measures is statistically significant at the 90 per cent level.

Rural/urban price differentials

Data on rural prices in South Africa are poor. As mentioned before, the IES data do not allow the calculation of unit values and there are no community price surveys. To get a basic idea of the rural/urban food price differentials, we again draw from the SAIHS of 1993. We fix a food bundle that makes up roughly 80 per cent of the food consumption in the 2000 IES and use the mean national urban and rural prices of these items from the SAIHS community questionnaire to construct crude rural and urban price indices for South Africa.[31] We find that the cost of this bundle in urban areas is approximately 4.5 per cent higher than it is in rural areas in 1993. This difference would lead to a slight overestimation of poverty in South Africa in general and the relative poverty of rural households in particular.

There is no data source available to us that can shed light on whether this small difference has changed between 1995 and 2000.[32] However, there is evidence from other countries on divergence of price indices between urban and rural areas. For instance, Friedman and Levinsohn (2002) report a co-movement of rural and urban prices in Indonesia over a 12-year period between 1984 and 1996.[33] Deaton and Tarozzi (2000) report that urban prices were 11.4 per cent higher than rural prices in India in 1987–88 and that this difference increased to 15.6 per cent by 1993–94. These numbers do not suggest a large divergence in rural/urban price differentials over time.

Table 2.8 *Sensitivity of poverty and inequality comparisons to changes in the urban/rural price differential*

Poverty line		If the base urban/rural price differential of 5% in 1995 doubled to 10%, tripled to 15%, or quadrupled to 20% by 2000:			
		1995 (5%)	2000 (10%)	2000 (15%)	2000 (20%)
$2/day poverty line (R174)	Headcount index	0.303 (0.007)	0.316 (0.007)	0.306 (0.006)	0.296 (0.006)
	Poverty gap	0.101 (0.003)	0.115* (0.003)	0.109* (0.003)	0.104 (0.003)
	Poverty gap squared	0.046 (0.002)	0.057* (0.002)	0.053* (0.002)	0.050* (0.002)
Lower-bound poverty line (R322)	Headcount index	0.570 (0.007)	0.561 (0.007)	0.555 (0.007)	0.549* (0.007)
	Poverty gap	0.262 (0.005)	0.271 (0.005)	0.264 (0.005)	0.257 (0.004)
	Poverty gap squared	0.149 (0.003)	0.161* (0.003)	0.155 (0.003)	0.150 (0.003)
	Mean expenditure	543 (10.6)	558 (11.0)	564 (11.0)	569* (11.0)
	Gini index	0.560 (0.005)	0.570 (0.005)	0.566 (0.005)	0.563 (0.004)
	Mean log deviation	0.552 (0.011)	0.586 (0.012)	0.577 (0.011)	0.569 (0.010)
	Theil index	0.598 (0.012)	0.601 (0.013)	0.593 (0.012)	0.586 (0.012)

Notes: The figures in parentheses in row 2 represent the percentage by which prices in urban areas exceed those in rural areas.
All figures have been weighted using person weights (household weight * household size).
Standard errors are given in parentheses and are corrected for complex survey design.
* indicates that the difference in mean expenditure and the poverty figures between 1995 and 2000 is statistically significant at the 90% level.

There are yet other factors to suggest that the small rural/urban price differentials are not likely to affect our results significantly. According to information collected on the area of purchase of goods and services in the 2000 IES, households in rural areas report buying a significant quantity of food items and most of their non-food items in nearby urban areas.[34] Nonetheless, we simulate the effect of changes in the rural/urban price differential over time and report the results in Table 2.8. We present revised poverty and inequality figures under three hypothetical scenarios: that the base rural/urban price differential increased from a reasonable 5 per cent in 1995 to 10 per cent, 15 per cent, or 20 per cent in 2000. We note that if we had assumed a 5 per cent price differential between urban and rural areas in 1995, the poverty figures would not be significantly lower than those reported in the third section (column 3). The table also shows that the increase in various FGT measures of poverty between 1995 and 2000 becomes insignificant only if the rural/urban price differential quadrupled in the five-year period between 1995 and 2000 (columns 4-6).

Correlates of household expenditure

In this section, we investigate the underlying reasons for the changes in household expenditures described in the previous section. We show that changes in the distribution of welfare between 1995 and 2000 are mostly attributable to changes in returns to endowments, such as education, and not to changes in the endowment levels themselves. In a manner that is analogous to wage regressions (for example, Lam 1999), we estimate a regression model to explain the variation in per capita household expenditures.[35]

Endogeneity – either as a result of reverse causality (for example, current household expenditure may affect decisions regarding the formation of new households) or due to omitted variables (for example, quality of education) – is a cause for concern. We try to minimise this concern through a careful selection of explanatory variables and the use of location fixed effects. Household size and composition, for instance, are responsive to the availability of resources, such as the receipt of old-age pensions, in South Africa (Klasen and Woolard 2000; Edmonds, Mammen and Miller 2001; Dieden 2003). The convention, however, is to include household size in regressions such as ours (see, for instance, Maluccio, Haddad and May 2000; Leibbrandt and Woolard 2001). We include household size and composition in our regressions for two reasons. Firstly, predicted poverty estimates (reported in Table 2.10) derived from the regression coefficients are closer to the 'true' poverty estimates for the regressions with household size included than without. Secondly, the remaining coefficients in the regression model are robust to the inclusion of household size and composition.

To estimate these regressions, we pool the data for 1995 and 2000 and regress the natural logarithm of per capita household consumption, $\ln y_{id}$, for the ith household in district d on its characteristics, X_{id}, and a set of district dummies, v_d. To capture changes over time, all household characteristics are interacted with a time dummy for year 2000. The model can be written as follows:

$$\ln y_{id} = X'_{id}\beta + tX'_{id}\gamma + v_d + \varepsilon_i, \tag{2}$$

where ε_i is an i.i.d. error term, and t a dummy taking the value one if the observation is from 2000 and zero otherwise. β is the vector of coefficients pertaining to 1995, and $(\beta + \gamma)$ is the vector of parameter estimates for the year 2000.

The explanatory variables can be divided into three categories: demographics, education and location effects. Demographic characteristics include household size, age and ethnic origin of the head of household, and whether the head of household is female or widowed. We also include variables reflecting the fraction of dependants in the household and distinguish between those aged 17 and below and those of pensionable age (65 for men, 60 for women).[36]

For heads of households who did not report obtaining a diploma or schooling certificate, we include dummies for each year of education between 2 and 10 years.[37] For those with high levels of education, i.e. those who obtained a diploma, dummy variables are included, and the years of education is set to zero.[38] All education variables are interacted with ethnic group dummies, because quality of education received conditional on attainment may differ for these groups (Case and Deaton 1999), and because there may be discrimination in the marketplace.

Finally, geographic effects, such as living in a former homeland, agro-ecological factors, access to markets, local institutions and infrastructure could be sources of variation in household consumption. We experimented with province, district, and primary sampling unit (PSU) level fixed effects, and settled for the inclusion of 362 district dummies.[39] We present two separate regression models for urban and rural areas.[40] There are very few Asians/Indians in rural areas and they are classified as whites in the rural regression model.[41]

Table 2.9 presents the regression results. The adjusted-R^2 is 0.68 for the urban regression and 0.67 for the rural one.[42]

Table 2.9 *Correlates of log per capita consumption*

	Urban		Rural	
	Coefficient	T-statistic	Coefficient	T-statistic
Household size	−0.24	−22.4	−0.23	−23.2
Household size, squared	0.01	9.9	0.01	12.9
Fraction of dependants aged 17 and less	−0.22	−10.6	−0.27	−13.6
Fraction of dependants of pensionable age	−0.15	−5.3	0.03	0.7
Age of head of household	0.02	10.5	0.02	9.9
Age of head of household, squared	0.00	−9.7	0.00	−8.6
D−household head is widow	0.02	1.3	−0.04	−2.1
D−household head is female	−0.14	−10.7	−0.03	−2.5
D-head is African	−1.09	−11.7	−0.80	−4.7
D-head is coloured	−1.00	−10.3	−0.77	−4.3

	Urban		Rural	
	Coefficient	T-statistic	Coefficient	T-statistic
D-head is Asian/Indian	−0.51	−3.5		
D-6 years of education, white	−0.10	−1.1	0.33	1.7
D-7 years of education, white	0.02	0.2	0.37	1.6
D-8 years of education, white	0.14	1.5	0.77	4.3
D-9 years of education, white	0.20	2.0	0.78	3.8
D-10 years of education, white	0.41	4.6	1.14	6.4
D-holder of certificate with less than Std 9, white	0.39	3.6	1.09	3.9
D-holder of certificate with Std 10, white	0.59	6.4	1.28	6.7
D-holder of degree, white	0.75	8.1	1.39	7.6
D-other diploma, white	0.10	0.8	1.24	4.0
D-2 years of education, Asian/Indian	0.09	0.5		
D-3 years of education, Asian/Indian	0.12	0.8		
D-4 years of education, Asian/Indian	−0.05	−0.4		
D-5 years of education, Asian/Indian	0.27	2.0		
D-6 years of education, Asian/Indian	0.26	2.2		
D-7 years of education, Asian/Indian	0.11	0.8		
D-8 years of education, Asian/Indian	0.38	3.1		
D-9 years of education, Asian/Indian	0.55	4.3		
D-10 years of education, Asian/Indian	0.65	5.4		
D-holder of certificate with less than Std 9, Asian/Indian	1.33	3.1		
D-holder of certificate with Std 10, Asian/Indian	1.04	7.6		
D-holder of degree, Asian/Indian	1.10	7.4		
D-other diploma, Asian/Indian	0.42	0.7		
D-2 years of education, coloured	0.08	1.3	0.05	0.8
D-3 years of education, coloured	0.14	2.8	0.10	1.7
D-4 years of education, coloured	0.18	3.8	0.26	5.0
D-5 years of education, coloured	0.20	4.6	0.26	4.3
D-6 years of education, coloured	0.28	7.0	0.27	4.4
D-7 years of education, coloured	0.43	9.2	0.26	2.2
D-8 years of education, coloured	0.60	11.4	0.53	4.6
D-9 years of education, coloured	0.63	9.4	0.61	2.4
D-10 years of education, coloured	0.93	18.6	1.14	6.7
D-holder of certificate with less than Std 9, coloured	1.26	7.0	0.65	1.5
D-holder of certificate with Std 10, coloured	1.18	18.7	1.30	6.0
D-holder of degree, coloured	1.51	14.0	1.46	4.3

→

	Urban		Rural	
	Coefficient	T-statistic	Coefficient	T-statistic
D-other diploma, coloured	0.92	4.0	−0.03	−0.2
D-2 years of education, African	−0.01	−0.4	0.12	6.1
D-3 years of education, African	0.04	1.0	0.08	4.1
D-4 years of education, African	0.13	4.0	0.14	6.9
D-5 years of education, African	0.12	4.2	0.22	10.9
D-6 years of education, African	0.24	8.9	0.30	14.2
D-7 years of education, African	0.27	8.2	0.39	13.2
D-8 years of education, African	0.40	12.0	0.42	14.0
D-9 years of education, African	0.42	11.2	0.54	13.6
D-10 years of education, African	0.69	21.4	0.74	19.0
D-holder of certificate with less than Std 9, African	0.78	9.3	0.78	10.3
D-holder of certificate with Std 10, African	1.06	24.5	1.24	22.3
D-holder of degree, African	1.18	19.7	1.41	11.6
D-other diploma, African	0.21	2.7	0.35	4.6
Interaction terms with D-2000				
Household size	0.01	1.1	−0.05	−3.5
Household size, squared	0.00	−0.7	0.00	2.1
Fraction of dependents aged 17 and less	−0.10	−3.3	−0.09	−3.0
Fraction of dependents of pensionable age	−0.02	−0.4	−0.09	−1.7
Age of head of household	0.00	−0.8	−0.01	−1.8
Age of head of household, squared	0.00	1.9	0.00	2.7
D-household head is widow	0.00	0.0	−0.02	−0.7
D-household head is female	−0.03	−1.4	−0.08	−4.3
D-head is African	−0.16	−1.0	−0.37	−1.1
D-head is coloured	0.02	0.1	−0.16	−0.5
D-head is Asian/Indian	0.07	0.3		
D-6 years of education, white	0.06	0.4	−0.30	−0.8
D-7 years of education, white	0.04	0.2	−0.23	−0.5
D-8 years of education, white	0.00	0.0	−0.11	−0.3
D-9 years of education, white	0.14	0.8	−0.70	−1.4
D-10 years of education, white	0.08	0.5	−0.27	−0.8
D-holder of certificate with less than Std 9, white	0.15	0.8	0.03	0.1
D-holder of certificate with Std 10, white	0.06	0.4	−0.43	−1.2
D-holder of degree, white	0.00	0.0	−0.20	−0.6
D-other diploma, white	0.73	3.9	−0.07	−0.2
D-2 years of education, Asian/Indian	0.24	1.1		
D-3 years of education, Asian/Indian	−0.20	−0.9		
D-4 years of education, Asian/Indian	0.03	0.2		

	Urban		Rural	
	Coefficient	T-statistic	Coefficient	T-statistic
D-5 years of education, Asian/Indian	−0.37	−1.9		
D-6 years of education, Asian/Indian	−0.10	−0.6		
D-7 years of education, Asian/Indian	−0.04	−0.2		
D-8 years of education, Asian/Indian	0.07	0.4		
D-9 years of education, Asian/Indian	−0.03	−0.2		
D-10 years of education, Asian/Indian	−0.07	−0.5		
D-holder of certificate with less than Std 9, Asian/Indian	−0.49	−1.1		
D-holder of certificate with Std 10, Asian/Indian	−0.13	−0.7		
D-holder of degree, Asian/Indian	0.00	0.0		
D-other diploma, Asian/Indian	0.41	0.6		
D-2 years of education, coloured	0.06	0.7	−0.11	−1.1
D-3 years of education, coloured	0.02	0.2	0.06	0.7
D-4 years of education, coloured	−0.08	−1.1	−0.13	−1.7
D-5 years of education, coloured	0.03	0.5	−0.12	−1.3
D-6 years of education, coloured	0.06	1.0	0.04	0.5
D-7 years of education, coloured	0.10	1.4	0.10	0.8
D-8 years of education, coloured	0.01	0.1	−0.02	−0.1
D-9 years of education, coloured	0.10	0.9	−0.22	−0.7
D-10 years of education, coloured	0.10	1.4	−0.60	−2.7
D-holder of certificate with less than Std 9, coloured	−0.09	−0.4	−0.01	0.0
D-holder of certificate with Std 10, coloured	0.13	1.4	0.08	0.3
D-holder of degree, coloured	0.15	1.1	0.17	0.5
D-other diploma, coloured	0.58	2.2		
D-2 years of education, African	0.11	2.4	0.03	1.0
D-3 years of education, African	0.09	2.0	0.05	1.7
D-4 years of education, African	0.00	0.0	0.07	2.2
D-5 years of education, African	0.07	1.8	0.04	1.2
D-6 years of education, African	0.02	0.6	0.01	0.3
D-7 years of education, African	0.06	1.4	−0.06	−1.5
D-8 years of education, African	0.06	1.3	0.00	0.1
D-9 years of education, African	0.06	1.4	−0.18	−3.6
D-10 years of education, African	0.08	2.0	−0.15	−2.7
D-holder of certificate with less than Std 9, African	0.26	2.5	0.07	0.5
D-holder of certificate with Std 10, African	0.26	4.7	0.07	0.9
D-holder of degree, African	0.38	4.8	0.06	0.4
D-other diploma, African	1.22	11.1	0.85	5.1

→

	Urban		Rural	
	Coefficient	T-statistic	Coefficient	T-statistic
D-year 2000	−0.04	−0.2	0.52	1.5
Constant	7.19	69.9	6.56	36.5
Number of observations	29 472		24 966	
R^2	0.68		0.67	

Note: District dummies are not reported.

Turning first to the results for 1995, we find that in both rural and urban areas, household size is negatively correlated with per capita expenditure.[43] The coefficient for the age of the household head reflects the expected life-cycle effects. Living in a household that is non-white, that includes young dependants or that is female-headed is negatively correlated with per capita expenditure. This comes over and above the negative correlations associated with household size. There is no correlation between households with a dependant of pensionable age and log per capita consumption for those living in rural areas, but a negative and significant correlation exists in urban areas. The fact that this coefficient is negative in urban areas, despite eligibility for a transfer, confirms a finding by Case and Deaton (1998), who report that median per capita income in pensioner households is lower than in households without a beneficiary of this transfer.

The parameter estimates for the education variables are consistently positive and significant, but vary significantly across ethnic groups and rural and urban areas. Note that the parameter estimates for education between whites and non-whites are not directly comparable as the omitted groups are different. Returns to education for Africans and whites seem to be higher in rural areas than in urban areas in 1995. We also observe sheepskin effects[44] in all population groups at ten years of education, as well as for degree holders and certificate holders with Standard 10.

Turning to the results for 2000, we find that in the rural and urban regression the sets of 2000 interactions are jointly significant, suggesting that a structural change took place.[45] The pattern of change, especially with respect to education, is strikingly different across rural and urban areas. In rural areas the year-interacted terms for demographic characteristics are all negative and mostly significant, implying an across-the-board worsening of these parameters. In urban areas, the results are similar but the declines in parameters are less significant statistically. More interesting are the changes in education coefficients. In urban areas, while the coefficients on education have not changed significantly for whites, Asians, or coloureds, they have increased for Africans. These gains are particularly large for Africans with high education, such as degree, certificate and other diploma holders. In rural areas, however, the picture is different. The year-interacted education parameters for whites and coloureds are mostly negative, although statistically insignificant, while those for Africans are mixed. As in urban areas, there were some small gains in returns to low levels of education (2–3 years), and there were declines in those for higher levels (9–10 years).

Since this is a household-level analysis and education reflects the level of education of the head of household, we cannot make definitive statements about the returns to education; however, one can interpret the education coefficients to capture the composite impact of differences in the quality of education and various trends in the labour market. Increasing unemployment since 1995, increased labour market opportunities for skilled labourers, deteriorating conditions for unskilled workers, and the decline of labour market discrimination are likely to have affected the education coefficients in various ways.

The results confirm a decline in the ethnic gap in education coefficients, a phenomenon some (for example, Mwabu and Schultz 1996; Moll 2000) attribute to the decline in labour market discrimination. The result that the returns to education accrued mostly to urban Africans with high levels of education – something also documented by Lam and Leibbrandt (2003) – is consistent with the high and rising demand for skilled workers, and an erosion of demand at the bottom end of the labour force. Note that the consequence of such a trend is a greater inequality within the African group, and a decline in inequality between ethnic groups, consistent with our earlier findings on changes in inequality.

In view of these results, it is natural to ask how many of the changes in poverty described earlier can be attributed to changes in the coefficients, as opposed to the changes in household endowments. To address this question, we construct counterfactual consumption distributions and examine the difference in the poverty headcount between the original and counterfactual distributions.[46] Table 2.10 presents the different counterfactuals, and the associated predicted poverty numbers.

Table 2.10 *Poverty headcounts for various counterfactuals in 1995 and 2000*

	Simulated log per capita consumption	Urban	Rural
1995 poverty incidence	$\ln \hat{y}_{95} = \beta_x X_{95} + \beta_e E_{95}$	37.0	75.2
2000 poverty incidence	$\ln \hat{y}_{00} = (\beta_x + \gamma_x) X_{00} + (\beta_e + \gamma_e) E_{00}$	41.5	80.1
Counterfactuals			
1. All parameters change	$\ln \hat{y}_{95} = (\beta_x + \gamma_x) X_{95} + (\beta_e + \gamma_e) E_{95}$	39.6	79.9
2. *Education* parameters change	$\ln \hat{y}_{95} = \beta_x X_{95} + (\beta_e + \gamma_e) E_{95}$	34.7	74.6
3. *Other* parameters change	$\ln \hat{y}_{95} = (\beta_x + \gamma_x) X_{95} + \beta_e E_{95}$	42.0	80.5
4. Old parameters	$\ln \hat{y}_{00} = \beta_x X_{00} + \beta_e E_{00}$	37.5	74.9
5. *Other* parameters unchanged	$\ln \hat{y}_{00} = \beta_x X_{00} + (\beta_e + \gamma_e) E_{00}$	35.5	74.8
6. *Education* parameters unchanged	$\ln \hat{y}_{00} = (\beta_x + \gamma_x) X_{00} + \beta_e E_{00}$	43.8	80.0

Note: Poverty is calculated as the expected probability of poverty, i.e. prob ($\ln \hat{y} < \ln z$), with z being the poverty line at R322.

Starting with rural areas, counterfactuals 1 and 4 demonstrate that the changes in poverty are entirely due to changes in the parameters and not in the endowments. Poverty headcount would have remained the same in rural South Africa if only the endowments had changed while the coefficients had remained the same between 1995 and 2000 (counterfactual 4). Similarly, the poverty headcount in 2000 would be the same if only the parameters had changed (counterfactual 1). Examining further which parameters are responsible for the increase in poverty in rural areas, we find that the decline in the parameters for demographic characteristics (counterfactual 3) and not in those for education (counterfactual 2) is responsible for this change.

In urban areas, the picture is slightly different. Again, counterfactual 4 shows that if only the endowments had changed, but the parameters had stayed the same, poverty in urban areas would be roughly the same in 2000 as in 1995. However, if only the parameters had changed (counterfactual 1), poverty would have increased (from 37.0 per cent to 39.6 per cent), but not as much as the realised poverty increase between 1995 and 2000 (from 37.0 per cent to 41.5 per cent). Interestingly, and consistent with the finding that there were increases in returns to education in urban areas, the direction of change in poverty as a result of a change in education parameters is different from that caused by a change in 'other' parameters. If only the education parameters had changed between 1995 and 2000 (counterfactual 2), poverty would have actually declined to 34.7 per cent in urban South Africa. However, these potential gains were cancelled by declines in other parameters: if only the 'other' parameters had changed between 1995 and 2000, then poverty would have increased to 42.0 per cent – very close to the realised poverty headcount of 41.5 per cent. Interestingly, poverty would have been highest in urban areas in 2000 if only education parameters had remained *unchanged* between 1995 and 2000.

Given the central importance of education, it may be useful to consider what happens to poverty if inequalities in education are reduced, as this is likely to translate into inequalities in per capita expenditure. This notion is intuitively appealing, although whether it holds depends on how education outcomes are mapped onto welfare outcomes (Lam 1999). A legacy of apartheid, the education gap between racial groups still exists in 2000 but is closing because of improvements in educational attainment, especially by Africans and coloureds (Lam and Leibbrandt 2003).

To explore how increases in educational attainment and returns to education might affect poverty reduction, we perform more simulations. For example, all else being equal, if every household head with less than seven years of education attained seven years of education, then poverty would decline by about eight percentage points in rural areas and five percentage points in urban areas.[47] If, in addition, the return to education for those with some education but without a diploma increased by 50 per cent, poverty would decline by 16 percentage points in rural areas and by about 14 percentage points in urban areas.

We conclude that most of the trends in poverty observed between 1995 and 2000 can be attributed not to the changes in household endowments, but rather to the returns to those endowments. Although there was some improvement in educational attainment over this period, these changes were not large for Africans.[48] In urban areas, where returns to education seem to be improving, these returns improved mostly for the highly educated – a very small percentage of the African population. The education parameters reflect the composite influence of education quality, labour market opportunities and (wage) returns to education. Disentangling these effects is beyond the scope of this chapter. However, we can say that microeconomic policies that focus on improving quality educational attainment for the poor, addressing labour market rigidities and providing safety nets are urgently needed if the trend of increasing poverty and inequality in South Africa is to be reversed in the short to medium run.[49]

Policy discussion and conclusions

This chapter has assessed the changes in poverty and inequality in South Africa between 1995 and 2000, the period that covers the first five years after the official end of apartheid in 1994. Consistent with GDP growth, we find that there was little growth in per capita household expenditures during this period. Roughly 60 per cent of all South Africans, and two-thirds of the African population, were poor in either year. The depth and severity of poverty increased as a result of declining expenditures at the bottom end of the expenditure distribution, and inequality among Africans rose sharply. By 2000, there were approximately 1.8 million more South Africans living on less than $1/day and 2.3 million more living on less than $2/day.

While substantial progress was made in other areas, such as access to safe water and sanitation, or coverage for social transfers like the old-age pension programme, the government's macroeconomic strategy failed to generate the projected growth and create enough jobs to bring down the high rate of unemployment. Even if the projected growth rates had been achieved, it should not be assumed that substantial reductions in poverty would have followed. Without a progressive shift in the expenditure distribution, even if South Africa grew at a remarkable annual rate of 8 per cent per capita – similar to China's growth rate in the 1990s – it would take approximately ten years for the average poor household to escape from poverty.[50] Hence, it is unlikely that growth alone – without explicit poverty reduction strategies – could have lifted many South Africans out of poverty. South Africa needs to grow in a way that also improves the distribution of incomes if it is to make significant progress against poverty in the short to medium run.

Some puzzles remain. Firstly, what explains the divergent paths taken by the African and coloured populations? The substantial decline in poverty experienced by coloureds is consistent with the finding that the Western Cape and Northern

Cape – the two provinces where coloureds form the majority of the population – also saw their poverty rates decline significantly during this period. The fact that African residents of these provinces also benefited from these reductions in poverty suggests a geographic rather than an ethnic explanation for this change, although we cannot provide any evidence as to whether there was a common underlying cause for poverty reduction in these areas for both population groups, or some positive spillover effects of the gains by coloureds for Africans.

Secondly, what explains the losses at the bottom end of the distribution? It is difficult to answer this question without further research, but it seems fair to say that the reasons behind these changes are complex. Gains in the levels and returns to education during this period seem to have been offset by demographic as well as labour market shifts. It is undisputed that the labour force growth was far higher than employment growth, causing the already high initial unemployment rates to swell. On the demographic side, there was a smaller number of adults per household in 2000 than in 1995, while the percentage of female-headed households was higher in 2000. It seems that there were more women without the necessary education or skills in the labour market in 2000 than there were in 1995. One possible explanation for this demographic shift could be the high prevalence of HIV/AIDS. HIV affects the African population in South Africa more than any other population group, and adult mortality (or morbidity) leads to the loss of assets and income-earners, causing other adults in the family, sometimes women who have never participated in the labour force before, to seek work outside the home. HIV could also partly explain the sluggish overall growth performance of South Africa during this period (Bell, Devarajan and Gersbach 2003).

Detailed answers to these questions are beyond the scope of this chapter. Future research that analyses the microeconomics of the complex distributional dynamics in South Africa is called for.

Acknowledgements

The authors would like to thank Miriam Babita, Harry Thema and Nozipho Shabalala for help with the construction of the data set used in the analysis. We are also grateful to Harold Alderman, Kathleen Beegle, Francois Bourguignon, David Dollar, Peter Lanjouw, Martin Ravallion and three anonymous referees for comments. These are the views of the authors, and do not necessarily reflect those of the World Bank or any affiliated organisation.

Notes

1   This chapter is a reprint of the *William Davidson Institute Working Paper* Number 739, Johannes G. Hoogeveen and Berk Özler, Not separate, not equal: Poverty and inequality in post-apartheid South Africa, January 2005. A revised version, Berk Özler, Not separate, not equal: Poverty and inequality in post-apartheid South Africa, is forthcoming in *Economic Development and Cultural Change*, University of Chicago Press, Journals Division.

2   In this chapter, we refer to four major population groups: Africans, coloureds, Asians/Indians, and whites. We use 'ethnic', 'racial', and 'population' groups interchangeably.

3   Authors' calculations using the SSA Income Expenditure Survey (1995).

4   Authors' own calculations using the 1996 Census.

5   <http://www.unaids.org/hivaidsinfo/statistics/fact_sheets/pdfs/Southafrica_en.pdf>. 1 October 2004.

6   *Mail and Guardian*, 7 February 2003. <http://www.mg.co.za/Content/l3.asp?ao=10925>.

7   Leibbrandt, van der Berg and Bhorat (2001: 16).

8   Government of South Africa (1996).

9   Authors' calculation using 'gross domestic product at constant 1995 prices (time series code KBP6006Y)' data from the South African Reserve Bank at http://www.reservebank.co.za/, accessed 1 October 2004.

10 Annual population growth in South Africa was approximately 2 per cent during this period.

11 Authors' calculation using 'final consumption expenditure by households (time series code KBP6007Y)' data from the South African Reserve Bank at http://www.reservebank.co.za/, accessed 1 October 2004.

12 According to *The Economist* (2004), blacks with sought-after skills are typically paid 15–20 per cent more than similarly qualified whites, as private companies compete for these workers in their effort to make their workplace more 'demographically representative'.

13 Old-age pensions, child support grants and unemployment insurance that provide social support to some families may counter these impacts.

14 The PPP-adjusted GDP per capita for South Africa (in current international $) was $8 642 in 1995 and $9 580 in 2000. Source: World Bank, International Comparison Programme database.

15 According to our household survey data, per capita household expenditures went from R534 in 1995 to R547 in 2000. However, this annual increase of 0.5 per cent is not statistically significant.

16 The literature on the choice of income versus expenditure to measure household welfare is well established and we abstract from that debate here. We believe, for empirical and theoretical reasons, that using data on household expenditures is preferable to using data on incomes.

17 However, there are two main shortcomings associated with the IES. Firstly, it is an expenditure survey as opposed to a consumption survey, making it difficult to deduce that the purchased amount was consumed during the period of recall. Secondly, the IES lacks the necessary information to impute reliable values of durable goods and as a result this item was excluded from the consumption aggregate.

18 Important categories of expenditures we have excluded from the consumption aggregate are: water; firewood and dung; health; imputed value of household durables; food consumption from home production; lobola/dowry, funerals, religious or traditional ceremonies, gambling; lumpy expenditures, such as furniture, appliances, vehicles, sound and video equipment, etc. See Babita et al. (2003) for details.

19 Again, see Babita et al. (2003) for details.

20 Deaton (1997) uses R105 per capita in 1993 prices as a poverty line. This is very close to R174 in 2000 prices.

21 The 1991 Census, which was the sampling frame for the 1995 OHS and IES (and for the widely used SALDRU survey), was carried out under the apartheid regime and had marked coverage problems.

22 For example, Deaton and Zaidi (2002) report that food consumption from home production accounts for 35 per cent of the consumption aggregate in Nepal in 1996 and 21 per cent in Ghana in 1988–89.

23 In our samples for the IES in 1995 and 2000, the share of population living in urban areas is 44.3 per cent and 56.7 per cent, respectively.

24 Rural poverty headcount declined from 87 per cent to 76 per cent in the Free State and from 70 per cent to 49 per cent in the Northern Cape between 1995 and 2000.

25 This increase is consistent with the results reported in Carter and May (2001) on changes in poverty in KwaZulu-Natal between 1993 and 1998.

26 There is reason to believe that the sampling problems that plagued the 1995 survey were most severe in Gauteng, leading to an undercount of the population there, especially of Africans. Hence, part of the increase in poverty in Gauteng during this period may be to the result of an underestimation of poverty in 1995. Another factor likely to be contributing to this increase is migration to Gauteng from poorer provinces after 1994. According to the 2001 Census, the population of Gauteng increased by 20 per cent between 1996 and 2001, a growth rate that is twice as large as that of South Africa as a whole. We discuss these issues further in the fourth section of the chapter.

27 It is important to remember that the households in the same percentile in two different periods need not be the same, i.e. these percentiles are 'anonymous'. See Ravallion and Chen (2003) for a detailed discussion of growth incidence curves and pro-poor growth.

28 For example, Ravallion and Chen (2003) report that the rate of pro-poor growth in China was 3.9 per cent between 1990 and 1999, while the growth rate in the mean was 6.2 per cent, an example of what we define as 'absolute pro-poor growth'. However, between 1993 and 1996, the same figures were 10 per cent and 8.2 per cent respectively, i.e. growth during this period was 'relatively pro-poor'.

29 Introducing ex-post inflation factors into surveys in this way is not uncommon. See, for example, Deaton (1997).

30 Among the home-grown products for which data are collected, maize is by far the most important item grown and consumed by households in our surveys.

31 This bundle includes mealie meal/maize flour, rice, bread, beef, mutton, pork, lamb, potatoes, tomatoes, cabbage, soft drinks, milk, milk powder, eggs, vegetable oil, margarine, butter, and sugar.

32 Carter and May (2001) use separate costs for rural and urban areas of KwaZulu-Natal that are borrowed from Potgieter (1993), but we were not able locate this study.

33 Specifically, they report that the rural prices increased by 182 per cent while urban prices increased by 187 per cent.

34 For example, approximately 60 per cent of rural households reported purchasing grain products in nearby urban areas.

35 Van de Walle and Gunewardena (2001) present a similar regression model to identify the determinants of living standards in Vietnam.

36 This old-age pension is arguably the most important social transfer in South Africa (Case and Deaton 1998). In 2000, the maximum pension benefit was R549 (or 1.7 times the lower-bound poverty line) per month per pensioner; the maximum disability grant was slightly larger: R685.

37 However, in our sample, the number of whites with low levels of education was very small. Hence, the omitted education group for whites is 5 years and below, rather than 0 or 1 year of education for other population groups.

38 We distinguish between four diploma types: (i) diploma obtained with Standard 9 or lower; (ii) diploma obtained with Standard 10; (iii) university degree; and (iv) other diplomas and certificates (including postgraduate diplomas).

39 The results are also robust to the inclusion of time-variant geographic fixed-effects.

40 We tested whether the correlates of poverty in rural areas are different from those in urban areas by including interaction terms for urban households for all variables. The null hypothesis that the interaction terms are jointly equal to zero was rejected.

41 Asians/Indians made up less than 0.3 per cent of the rural population in both years.

42 The high R^2 may be partly attributable to the endogeneity of household size. If household size is excluded from the regressions, the R^2 drops to around 0.5.

43 This result is robust to the choice of different parameters for adult equivalence and economies of scale.

44 This refers to the attainment of a diploma for primary, secondary, or higher schooling.

45 A potential concern is that changes in the estimated parameters pick up measurement error or changes in the omitted variables rather than structural changes (see for instance Malucio, Haddad and May (2000), who report large changes in the return to social capital between 1993 and 1998 in KwaZulu-Natal). As it is not clear how this could be addressed, we assume changes in measurement error are random and the observed parameter changes structural.

46 A detailed description of how we derive predicted poverty rates for each counterfactual is presented in Appendix 1.

47 This is the average level of education for the most recent cohort of household heads, defined as those aged 30 or below.

48 Average education levels for Africans remained roughly the same in urban areas between 1995 and 2000, possibly due to migration by low-skilled individuals from rural to urban areas. In contrast, the improvements in education were larger for coloureds in both urban and rural areas.

49 Kingdon and Knight (1999) find a negative relationship between wages and local unemployment rates in South Africa, concluding that wages are flexible with respect to unemployment, but not those of unionised workers.

50 Authors' own calculation. With a more reasonable growth rate of 5 per cent per year (3 per cent per capita), it would take more than 23 years for an average poor household to escape from poverty, assuming that the Lorenz curve stays unchanged.

Appendix

Poverty simulations

To calculate poverty incidence from the regressions we allow for the fact that even if predicted per capita consumption, $\hat{y}_i$, exceeds the poverty line, z, there is a non-zero probability that the household is in fact poor. Hence we derive a household's *probability* of being poor, and calculate the incidence of poverty as the mean of the household-specific probabilities (see Ravallion and Wodon (1999); Hentschel et al. (2000); Datt and Joliffe (2001)).

Using the model's parameters, the expected probability of being poor P_i for each household i, can be written as:

$$E(P_i \backslash X_i, \hat{\beta}, \hat{y}, \hat{v}_d, \hat{\sigma}) = prob\,(\ln \hat{y}_i < \ln z) \qquad \text{[A1]}$$

where $\hat{\sigma}$ indicates the predicted standard error of the regression. Assuming normally distributed errors, the expected probability P_i is non-zero for every household and given by:

$$E(P_i \backslash X_i, \hat{\beta}, \hat{y}, \hat{v}_d, \hat{\sigma}) = \qquad \text{[A2]}$$

$$prob\,(X_i\hat{\beta} + tX_i\hat{y} + \hat{v}_d < \ln z) = \Phi\left[\frac{\ln z - (X_i\hat{\beta} + X_i\hat{y} + \hat{v}_d)}{\hat{\sigma}}\right]$$

with Φ indicating the cumulative standard normal distribution. The predicted incidence of poverty P* for a group of households i with observable characteristics X_i and household weights w_i is then:

$$P* = \frac{\sum\limits_{i=1}^{N} w_i E(P_i \backslash X_i, \hat{\beta}, \hat{y}, \hat{\sigma})}{\sum\limits_{i=1}^{N} w_i} \qquad \text{[A3]}$$

References

Babita M, Özler B, Shabalala N & Thema H (2003) Changes in poverty and inequality in South Africa: 1995–2000. Unpublished manuscript.

Bell C, Devarajan S & Gersbach H (2003) *The long-run economic costs of AIDS: Theory and an application to South Africa*. Policy Research Working Paper No. 3152. World Bank: Washington, DC.

Bhorat H (2003) *The post-apartheid challenge: Labour demand trends in the South African labour market, 1995–1999*. DPRU Working Paper 03/82.

Carter MR & May J (2001) One kind of freedom: Poverty dynamics in post-apartheid South Africa, *World Development* 29(12): 1987–2006.

Case A & Deaton A (1998) Large cash transfers to the elderly in South Africa, *Economic Journal* 108(450): 1330–1362.

Case A & Deaton A (1999) School inputs and educational outcomes in South Africa, *Quarterly Journal of Economics* 114(3): 1047–1084.

Datt G & Joliffe D (2001) Poverty in Egypt: Modeling and poverty simulations. Unpublished manuscript.

Deaton A (1997) *The analysis of household surveys. A microeconometric approach to development policy*. Baltimore: Johns Hopkins University Press.

Deaton A & Tarozzi A (2000) Prices and poverty in India. Unpublished manuscript.

Deaton A & Zaidi S (2002) Guidelines for constructing consumption aggregates for welfare analysis. LSMS Working Paper No. 135. World Bank: Washington, DC.

Dieden S (2003) South African household's integration into the core economy: Micro level covariates. Unpublished manuscript.

Dodson B (2002) Gender and the brain drain from South Africa. The Southern African Migration Project. Migration Policy Series No. 23.

Edmonds E, Mammen K & Miller D (2001) Rearranging the family: Household composition changes to large pension receipts. Unpublished manuscript.

Fields GS, Cichello PL, Freije S, Menendez M & Newhouse D (2003) For richer or for poorer? Evidence from Indonesia, South Africa, Spain, and Venezuela, *Journal of Economic Inequality* 1(1): 67–99.

Friedman J & Levinsohn J (2002) The distributional impacts of Indonesia's financial crisis on household welfare: A 'rapid response' methodology, *The World Bank Economic Review* 16(3): 397–423.

Government of South Africa (1996) Growth, employment and redistribution: A macroeconomic strategy.

Hentschel J, Lanjouw JO, Lanjouw P & Poggi J (2000) Combining census and survey data to trace the spatial dimensions of poverty, *The World Bank Economic Review* 14(1): 147–165.

Kingdon G & Knight J (1999) *Unemployment and wages in South Africa: A spatial approach*. Working Paper WPS99-12. Centre for Study of African Economies, Department of Economics, University of Oxford.

Kingdon G & Knight J (2004) Unemployment in South Africa: The nature of the beast, *World Development* 32(3): 391–408.

Klasen S & Woolard I (2000) *Surviving unemployment without state support: Unemployment and household formation in South Africa*. IZA Discussion Paper No. 237.

Lam D (1999) Generating extreme inequality: Schooling, earnings and intergenerational transmission of human capital in South Africa and Brazil. University of Michigan, PSC Research Report No. 99–439.

Lam D & Leibbrandt M (2003) What's happened to inequality in South Africa since the end of apartheid? Unpublished manuscript.

Lanjouw P, Prennushi G & Zaidi S (1996) Building blocks for a consumption-based analysis of poverty in Nepal. World Bank. Unpublished manuscript.

Leibbrandt M & Woolard I (2001) The labour market and household income inequality in South Africa: Existing evidence and new panel data, *Journal of International Development* 13: 671–689.

Leibbrandt M, van der Berg S & Bhorat H (2001) Introduction. In Bhorat et al. (eds) *Fighting poverty*. Cape Town: UCT Press.

Maluccio J, Haddad L & May J (2000) Social capital and household welfare in South Africa, 1993–98, *Journal of Development Studies* 36(6): 54–81.

Moll PG (2000) Discrimination is declining in South Africa but inequality is not, *Studies in Economics and Econometrics* 24(3): 91–108.

Mwabu G & Schultz TP (1996) Education returns across quantiles of the wage function: Alternative explanations for the returns to education by race in South Africa, *American Economic Review* 86(2): 335–339.

Rama M (2001) Labor market issues in South Africa. World Bank. Unpublished manuscript.

Ravallion M (1994) *Poverty comparisons*. USA: Harwood Academic Publishers.

Ravallion M (2001) Poverty lines: Economic foundations of current practices. World Bank. Unpublished manuscript.

Ravallion M & Chen S (2003) Measuring pro-poor growth, *Economic Letters* 78: 93–99.

Ravallion M & Wodon Q (1999) Poor areas, or only poor people, *Journal of Regional Science* 39(4): 689–711.

Simkins C (2003) A critical assessment of the 1995 and 2000 income and expenditure surveys as sources of information on incomes. Unpublished manuscript.

Statistics South Africa (2003) *Census 2001: Census in Brief*. Second Edition.

The Economist (15 January 2004) Africa's Engine. Survey: Sub-Saharan Africa.

Van de Walle D & Gunewardena D (2001) Sources of ethnic inequality in Vietnam, *Journal of Development Economics* 65: 177–207.

3 Measuring recent changes in South African inequality and poverty using 1996 and 2001 census data

Murray Leibbrandt, Laura Poswell, Pranushka Naidoo and Matthew Welch

Introduction

Changes in inequality and poverty are key elements of the transformation of any economy. Two quantitative dimensions of this broad transformation process are changes in the distribution of income and changes in access to services. This chapter will discuss changes in the levels and composition of income, and access inequality and poverty, between 1996 and 2001, using the 10 per cent micro-samples from the 1996 and 2001 Censuses. The sizes of the data sets and their national reach make them well suited to such an assessment of changes in national well-being.

However, the usefulness of the comparison depends on the quality of the available data on incomes and access to services. We table a few major data issues in this introduction.[1] The second and third sections of the chapter, respectively, present the key results for changes in income inequality and in poverty. In the fourth section we present an analysis of access to goods and services; this section focuses on housing and access to clean water, electricity and sanitation. In the fifth section, we briefly compare the income-based measures of well-being and the access-based measures of well-being, before presenting our concluding discussion in the sixth section of the chapter.

The income data in the census are far from ideal (Cronje and Budlender 2004) and a great deal of work has been necessary to get the data sets into shape for analysis. In particular, a number of key data decisions had to be taken in order to ensure that the data were comparable over time and that our analysis was comparable with the work of others. Two major points are worth noting here.

Firstly, in both 1996 and 2001 data on personal income were collected in a set of income bands. These bands were not a consistent set of real income categories across the two years. This is especially true at the top end. The highest band for personal income in 1996 was R30 000 or more. This is lower than the real income equivalent of the top three bands in 2001. In order to compare the data across time, we compressed the top end of the 2001 distribution of personal incomes into the 2001 real income equivalent (R40 774) of the top band in 1996. As all of these bands are very far above any plausible poverty line, this has no impact on the analysis of poverty. However, it does have an impact on the inequality analysis.[2]

Secondly, on aggregating personal incomes into household incomes for both 1996 and 2001, a sizeable number of households are captured as having zero incomes or missing incomes. As shown in Table 3A1.1 in Appendix 1, these zero-income households and the missing-income households account for 23 per cent of households in 1996 and 28 per cent of households in 2001. This is a large percentage of each sample. It is highly unlikely that all of these zeros are genuinely households in which all adult members earned no income in 1996 or in 2001. For comparative purposes, we exclude these zeros from the poverty and inequality analysis presented in the body of the chapter.

As this decision effectively removes a group of households that currently make up the bottom of the distribution, it has a strong impact on measured poverty levels and also narrows inequality. Therefore, it is important to know as much as possible about these people and what sort of impact this decision has on the measure of poverty and inequality. Table 3A1.2 in Appendix 1 presents a profile of these missing and zero households. It shows that three of the poorest provinces, the Eastern Cape, KwaZulu-Natal and Limpopo, contributed the greatest proportion of total missing and zero values in 1996 and 2001. In all three cases, this was in excess of their total population share. It also shows that in both years Gauteng, the Western Cape, Limpopo and KwaZulu-Natal had the largest percentage of missing values. The proportion of missing values for these provinces was also in excess of their total population shares. Income shares and poverty shares also do not change significantly across provinces when the zeros are omitted and the magnitude of the narrowing of inequality is consistent across provinces, population groups and the rural/urban divide.[3] Thus, while this decision changes the levels of measured poverty, it should not skew the comparison of changes between 1996 and 2001.

One of the reasons for spelling out these two data adjustments in some detail is to illustrate the point that this chapter is directed at accurately assessing changes in inequality and poverty over time, rather than deriving the best estimates of poverty and inequality in any given year. Indeed, our emphasis on obtaining comparable data for the estimates of changes over time sometimes comes at the cost of deriving the best estimates of inequality or poverty within any given year. Figure 3.1 gives an aggregate snapshot of the change in per capita incomes in South Africa between 1996 and 2001, with 2001 incomes deflated to their 1996 equivalents for comparability purposes.[4] There are two plots for 2001. The 2001 distribution is plotted including all the top income brackets as they are found in the 2001 data (uncensored) as well as with the top brackets collapsed into a 1996 equivalent top band (censored). It is clear from the figure that this censoring of the 1996 distribution does indeed narrow 2001 inequality.

This figure gives us a foretaste of the key results of the income analysis in the chapter. Even with the censored data, the 2001 plot lies above the 1996 plot at the top end

Figure 3.1 *A distributional plot of South African incomes in 1996 and 2001*

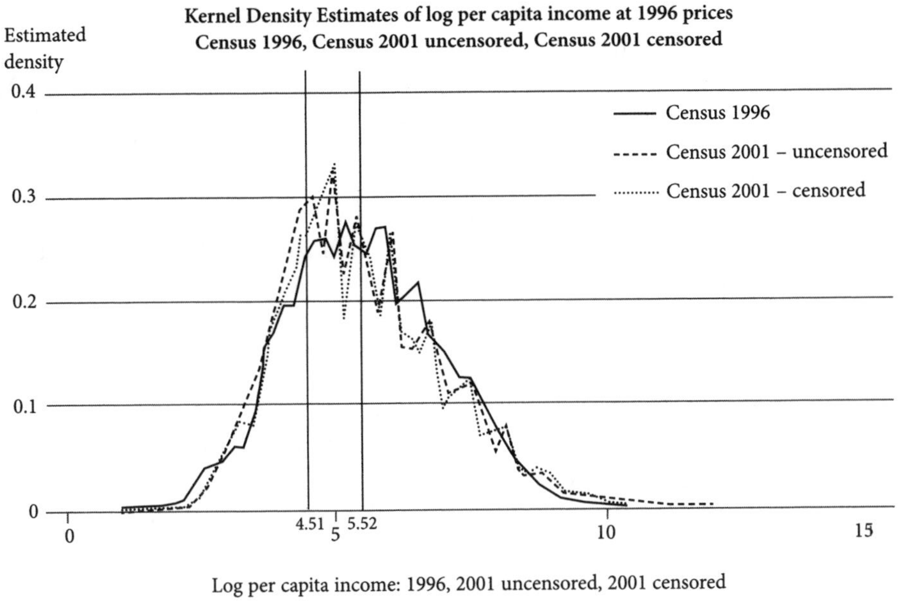

Log per capita income: 1996, 2001 uncensored, 2001 censored

Sources: Census 1996 and Census 2001, Statistics South Africa

of the income distribution. This suggests that the top end of the 2001 distribution contains a greater share of the population than it did in 1996. Thus, there is some evidence of improved real incomes at the top end. However, apart from this group at the top, the 2001 distribution evidences a leftward shift, implying decreased real incomes for the rest of the distribution. This is particularly pronounced in the middle and lower-middle sections of the distribution, with the situation at the bottom looking largely unchanged. In this chapter we show that the net effect of all of these changes is an unambiguous increase in inequality from 1996 to 2001.

The two vertical lines drawn on the figure represent the two poverty lines that we use for all of the poverty analysis in this chapter. Details of the calculation of these poverty lines are provided in Appendix 1. The lower line is a $2 per day poverty line, which is widely used for international poverty comparisons. The upper line is a R250-per person per month (in 1996 rands) poverty line, which was first suggested in the poverty-mapping work of Statistics South Africa (2000). The leftward shift of incomes in the middle and lower-middle areas of the 2001 distribution suggests a slight but unambiguous increase in measured poverty between 1996 and 2001. The poverty analysis presented in this chapter confirms this finding.

This income-based approach presents only one of many dimensions of the measurement of well-being in South Africa. The narrowness and limitations of this approach are revealed when we show that, over the same 1996–2001 period, there have been important improvements in access to basic goods and services for many households.

Changing patterns of income inequality

We begin our discussion of inequality at the national level. In Figure 3.2, we graph the Lorenz curves for the national distribution of per capita incomes for both 1996 and 2001. Such Lorenz curves are derived by ranking per capita incomes from the poorest to the richest, and then plotting the cumulative distribution of the population on the horizontal axis and the cumulative distribution of income on the vertical axis. Thus, for example, the figure on the vertical axis that corresponds to 0.2 on the horizontal axis is the proportion of per capita income accruing to the poorest 20 per cent of the population. The Lorenz curve labelled 'cumulative population proportion' represents a hypothetical line of income equality, because it shows a situation in which the poorest 20 per cent of the population accounts for 20 per cent of per capita income. The further an actual Lorenz curve falls below this line of equality, the higher the measured inequality. As the 2001 Lorenz curve lies below the 1996 curve, the figure shows a clear widening of inequality between 1996 and 2001. If Lorenz curves cross, then the changes in the income distribution are too complex to make definitive statements about inequality increasing or decreasing. In this case, the 2001 Lorenz curve is always below the 1996 curve, which implies that the finding of increased inequality between 1996 and 2001 is sound.

Figure 3.2 *National Lorenz curves at 1996 prices for Census 1996 and Census 2001*

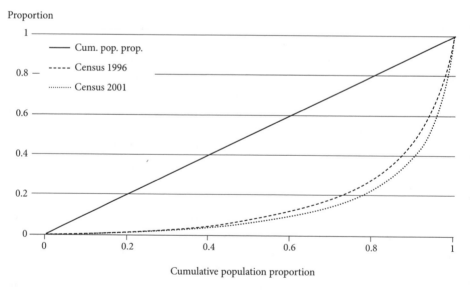

Sources: Census 1996 and Census 2001, Statistics South Africa

Next, in order to analyse inequality by population group, we present a set of Lorenz curves for each group. Figure 3.3 presents the 1996 situation and Figure 3.4 presents the 2001 situation. Both of these figures show the same clear ranking of inequality by group. Inequality for Africans is greater than for coloureds, which is greater than for Asians/Indians, which is greater than for whites.

Figure 3.3 *Lorenz curves by population group for Census 1996*

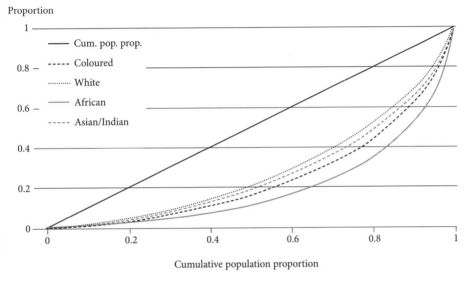

Source: Census 1996, Statistics South Africa

Figure 3.4 *Lorenz curves by population group for Census 2001*

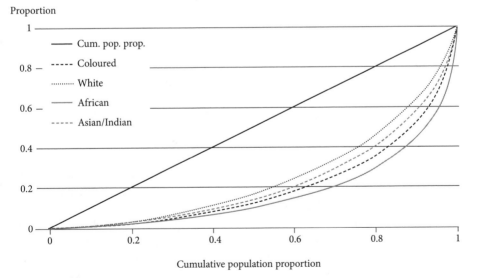

Source: Census 1996, Statistics South Africa

In order to use Lorenz curves to compare changes in inequality for different groups over the period 1996 to 2001, it is necessary to plot these Lorenz curves for both years on the same graph. This is done in Figure 3.5 for two groups – Africans and whites. The Lorenz curves confirm our earlier finding that African inequality is greater than white inequality. The curves go further to show that inequality increased for both groups between 1996 and 2001.

Figure 3.5 *Lorenz curves for the African and white groups, at 1996 prices, for Census 1996 and Census 2001*

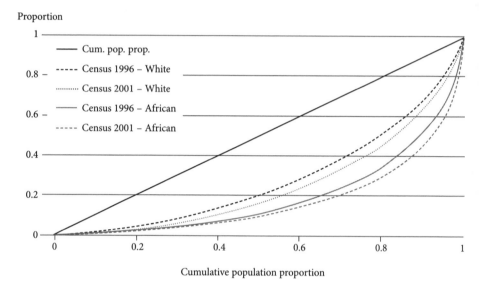

Cumulative population proportion

Sources: Census 1996 and Census 2001, Statistics South Africa

Given that the Lorenz curves do not cross in any of the above figures, all of these trends are unambiguous and are not dependent on the choice of a particular inequality measure. Any acceptable inequality measure will reveal the same pattern of increasing inequality over time and the same ranking of inequality by group.

Table 3.1 illustrates this through the presentation of a series of results using a well-known inequality measure, the Gini coefficient. This measure of inequality ranges from 0 to 1, with 0 being no inequality and 1 being extreme inequality. Thus, the fact that our measured coefficient at the national level rises from 0.68 in 1996 to 0.73 in 2001 reflects the increase in inequality that we observed above in the Lorenz curves of Figure 3.2. The fact that the Gini coefficients for each population group in both 1996 and 2001 are highest for the African group and lowest for the white group confirms the Lorenz curve analysis of Figures 3.3 and 3.4. Furthermore, the fact that the Gini coefficients rise for all groups between 1996 and 2001 confirms the analysis of Figure 3.5. Recent work by

Hoogeveen and Özler (2005)[5] comparing expenditure data from the 1995 and 2000 national Income and Expenditure Surveys supports these trends. Their reported Gini coefficients are notably lower than those derived by us using census data. However, in each case, between 1995 and 2000[6] their Gini coefficients increase.

Table 3.1 *Comparisons of inequality from 1975 to 2001, using the Gini coefficient*

	1975	1991	1996	1996	2001
	Whiteford & van Seventer estimates			Our estimates	
African	0.47	0.62	0.66	0.62	0.66
Coloured	0.51	0.52	0.56	0.53	0.60
Asian/Indian	0.45	0.49	0.52	0.48	0.56
White	0.36	0.46	0.50	0.44	0.51
National	0.68	0.68	0.69	0.68	0.73

Sources: Whiteford and van Seventer 2000 using 1975, 1991 and 1996 Census data; own calculations for 1996 and 2001, using Census 1996 and Census 2001, Statistics South Africa.

Table 3.1 also reports on comparable Gini estimates from Whiteford and van Seventer (2000). This study used 1975, 1991 and 1996 census data to undertake a longer-run comparison of South African inequality. We see from their Gini coefficients that the widening of inequality within each group between 1996 and 2001 is the continuation of a trend going back to 1975 and is particularly acute for Africans. However, it seems that the widening of inequality at the national level between 1996 and 2001 is a break with the trend from 1975 and 1996 – for Whiteford and van Seventer, measured inequality at the aggregate level remained high but stable over the 1975–96 period.

The Theil index is another well-known measure of inequality. It has the desirable property of allowing national inequality to be decomposed into a contribution due to inequality within groups and a contribution due to inequality between groups.[7] This is a particularly interesting exercise given that we are reporting an increase in inequality within each group as well as in aggregate inequality. As discussed by Bhorat, Leibbrandt and Woolard (2000), the strong between-group component of inequality has always been a stark marker of apartheid-driven inequality in South Africa. That said, Table 3.2 reproduces the findings of Whiteford and van Seventer (2000) based on the Theil decomposition to show a declining share of between-group inequality over the period 1975 to 1996. The table also records our own calculations of between- and within-group shares of inequality for 1996 and 2001. These shares show a continuation of the decline in the between-group component over this recent period. In addition, using expenditure data from the 1995 and 2000 Income and Expenditure Surveys, Hoogeveen and Özler (2005) do a similar decomposition and also find a decline in between-group inequality from 1995 to 2000. Thus, the finding of recent declines in between-group inequality seems to be sound.

Table 3.2 *Inequality comparisons within and between population groups, using the Theil index*

	1975	1991	1996	1996	2001
	Whiteford & van Seventer estimates (percentage)			Our estimates (percentage)	
Within-group inequality	38	58	67	57	60
Between-group inequality	62	42	33	43	40
Total inequality	100	100	100	100	100

Sources: Whiteford and van Seventer 2000 using 1975, 1991 and 1996 Census data; own calculations for 1996 and 2001, using Census 1996 and Census 2001, Statistics South Africa.

In the following three tables, we explore some additional dimensions of the racial composition of South African income distribution. In Table 3.3, we report on income and population shares for each group from 1970 to 2001. The results from 1970 to 1996 are from Whiteford and van Seventer (2000) and show that the share of income for the African group rises strongly from a very low base relative to population over the period 1970 to 1996. This corresponds to declining shares of income and population for the white group over the same period.

The table includes our estimates for 1996 and 2001. These show that the share of total income for Africans did not increase any further over this period. Rather, the white income share increased slightly. The lack of growth in the share of income attributed to Africans is striking when taking into account the growth of the total share of the African population. The slight growth in the share of white income is accompanied by a decrease in the population share of the white group. All in all, the 1996 and 2001 results suggest a break in the trend from 1970 to 1996.

Table 3.3 *Income and population shares, 1970–2001*

	Share of total income						Share of population					
	1970	1980	1991	1996	1996	2001	1970	1980	1991	1996	1996	2001
	Whiteford & van Seventer estimates (percentage)				Our estimates (percentage)		Whiteford & van Seventer estimates (percentage)				Our estimates (percentage)	
African	19.8	24.9	29.9	35.7	38	38	70.1	72.4	75.2	76.2	78	80
White	71.2	65.0	59.5	51.9	47	48	17.0	15.5	13.5	12.6	11	9
Coloured	6.7	7.2	6.8	7.9	9	9	9.4	9.3	8.7	8.6	9	9
Asian/ Indian	2.4	3.0	3.8	4.5	5	6	2.9	2.8	2.6	2.6	3	3
Total	100	100	100	100	100	100	100	100	100	100	100	100

Sources: Whiteford and van Seventer 2000 using 1970, 1975, 1980, 1991 and 1996 Census data; own calculations for 1996 and 2001, using Census 1996 and Census 2001, Statistics South Africa.
Note: Totals may not add up to 100% due to rounding.

We explore this further in Table 3.4, which reports on the ratios between mean white per capita income and the mean per capita income of other groups from 1970 to 2001. These ratios are known as disparity ratios. White per capita income increased from nine times higher than African per capita income in 1996 to 11 times higher in 2001. This is a break in the trend from 1970 to 1996, which showed the disparity decreasing over these years. The disparity between coloured and white incomes also increased between 1996 and 2001, while the disparity ratio with Asians/Indians remained constant. Thus, as with the movement of income shares by group, the movement of the disparity ratios between 1996 and 2001 contrasts with the decreasing inequality between 1970 and 1996.

Table 3.4 *Disparity ratios: whites to other population groups*

	1970	1980	1991	1996	1996	2001
	Whiteford & van Seventer estimates				Our estimates	
African	15.0	12.9	11.1	8.8	9.0	11.19
Coloured	6.0	5.3	5.7	4.5	4.3	5.26
Asian/Indian	5.1	3.9	3.0	2.3	2.3	2.39

Sources: Whiteford and van Seventer 2000 using 1970, 1980, 1991 and 1996 Census data; own calculations for 1996 and 2001, using Census 1996 and Census 2001, Statistics South Africa.

To probe these two findings a little further, Table 3.5 explores the racial composition of income deciles in 1996 and in 2001. It shows that the percentage of Africans in the upper six deciles has increased between 1996 and 2001, with a marked increase of 7 per cent in the second-highest decile since 1996. The share of African incomes in the lower deciles remains fairly constant over the period. Thus, this picture helps to explain some of the widening inequality within the African population, as shown earlier in our presentation of the changes in the Gini coefficients between 1996 and 2001.

The shares of whites in the bottom eight deciles remained constant between 1996 and 2001, with a decrease in the shares of the upper two deciles. The shares of coloureds and Asians/Indians in all deciles remained fairly constant over the period. These group shares help to make it clear that the increase in the white share of income over the 1996–2001 period and the increase in the white/African disparity ratio were being driven by a few very high-earning whites at the top of the distribution. The general trend is still one in which there is notable upward mobility of Africans into the top sections of the income distribution. At the same time, there is no real evidence of downward mobility of whites, especially not into the lowest few deciles.

Table 3.5 *Population-group composition of per capita income deciles, 1996–2001*

Decile	African (%)		White (%)		Coloured (%)		Asian/Indian (%)	
	1996	2001	1996	2001	1996	2001	1996	2001
1	97	96	0.4	0.3	3	4	0.2	0.2
2	95	95	1	0.3	4	5	0.4	0.4
3	93	92	1	1	6	7	0.4	1
4	89	90	1	1	10	9	1	1
5	84	85	2	1	13	12	2	1
6	79	81	3	2	15	14	3	2
7	72	74	5	6	18	16	5	4
8	63	63	12	12	17	17	7	8
9	43	50	35	30	14	13	8	8
10	21	23	67	63	6	7	5	7

Sources: Own calculations using Census 1996 and Census 2001, Statistics South Africa

This section has focused on changes in inequality at the national level and by population group. The increases in inequality that we have detailed are supported by increased inequality within each province and across the rural/urban divide. However, we do not dwell on these two dimensions of changing inequality. Rather, we give the provinces and the rural/urban situation more detailed attention in the poverty analysis that follows.

Changing patterns of poverty

In this section, we focus exclusively on 'money-metric' poverty – that is, we focus on the amount of money income available to households to purchase the goods and services they require. Clearly, the experience of poverty is not exclusively about a shortage or absence of income, but income poverty is a significant dimension of poverty. In the following section, we look at the advances that have been made in terms of other aspects of living standards such as access to clean water, decent housing and electrification.

Figure 3.6 presents the key picture of national poverty changes. In this figure, we make real income comparisons between 1996 and 2001 by deflating the 2001 distribution to 1996 equivalents. We then graph a series of cumulative distribution functions (CDFs) for these comparable 1996 and 2001 incomes. On the vertical axis, these functions show the proportion of the population with a per capita income that is less than or equal to each real income level on the horizontal axis. As the per capita income level rises, so the corresponding proportion of the population must rise. The pattern of the increase in the proportion tells us a lot about poverty. A CDF that reaches high proportions very quickly tells us that a high proportion of the population has a low per capita income. In addition, a CDF plot that lies above another plot implies that, at any per capita income level, a higher percentage of the population has that real per capita income or less. Therefore, they would be measured as being poorer at any chosen poverty line.

In Figure 3.6, the 2001 CDF graphs lie above the 1996 CDF graphs at all points and this tells us that measured poverty worsened between 1996 and 2001 at any poverty line. However, the magnitude of such worsening is very sensitive to a number of assumptions. Firstly, the fact that the 'with zero' graphs jump upwards shows how influential the distinction is between including and excluding the zero-income households from the analysis. As mentioned in the introduction, we generally exclude zero-income households from the analysis in this chapter, on the assumption that income in these households is mis-measured. However, the exclusion of zero-income households clearly has a large impact on the measurement of poverty, given that we are dropping the ostensibly poorest observations from the data set. Moreover, as we saw earlier, a higher percentage of the 2001 households report zero earnings. Thus, the inclusion of these households virtually guarantees that measured poverty will have worsened between 1996 and 2001.

Figure 3.6 *National cumulative distribution functions at 1996 prices*

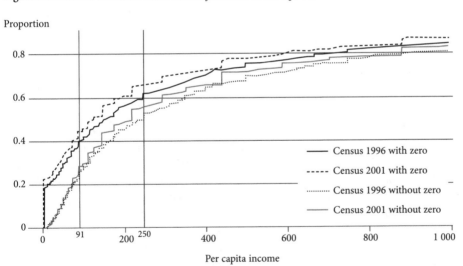

Sources: Census 1996 and Census 2001, Statistics South Africa

The graphs that exclude the zero-income households show that the percentage of households with less than or equal to the R91 per capita per month (a $2 per day poverty line) is very similar for 1996 and 2001. However, by the R250 (1996 rands) poverty line, there are more poor people in 2001 than in 1996. This evidence suggests that poverty worsened between 1996 and 2001 but that this worsening is not acute for the poorest of the poor.[8]

Table 3.6 shows this more precisely for the non-zero household case. Two poverty measures are used at the two poverty lines. The first is the headcount ratio – that is, the number of the poor as a percentage of the total population at each poverty line. This headcount ratio increases from 1996 to 2001 for both poverty lines. The actual value of the headcount ratio can be read off Figure 3.6 as it corresponds exactly to the value on the vertical axis where the poverty line cuts the CDF graph for each year. Thus, it can be seen that the low poverty line ($2 per day/R91 per month) cuts the 1996 graph at 26 per cent and cuts the 2001 graph (in 1996 real income terms) at 28 per cent.

The second measure, the poverty gap ratio, records the average household's proportionate shortfall from the poverty line. For example, using R250 per person per month, the 1996 census poverty gap ratio is 0.30. This means that the average household has an income that falls 30 per cent (0.30) short of this poverty line. This gap rises to 0.32 in 2001, reflecting the increase in measured poverty.

Table 3.6 *National poverty levels, 1996 and 2001*

Poverty line	Headcount	Poverty gap ratio	Headcount	Poverty gap ratio
	1996		2001	
$2 per day	0.26	0.11	0.28	0.11
R250 (1996) per month	0.50	0.30	0.55	0.32

Sources: Own calculations using Census 1996 and Census 2001, Statistics South Africa

The next CDF plot (Figure 3.7) allows us to examine poverty rankings by population group in both 1996 and 2001, as well as how poverty changed for each group from 1996 to 2001. Looking exclusively at either the 1996 CDF plots by group or the 2001 CDF plots by group, a robust poverty ranking emerges. At any poverty line, Africans are very much poorer than coloureds, who are very much poorer than Asians/Indians, who are poorer than whites. The gaps between these graphs show the yawning differences between the groups in terms of absolute income levels. For example, the graphs stop at R1 000 per capita per month. More than 90 per cent, 80 per cent and 60 per cent of Africans, coloureds and Asians/Indians, respectively, have this real monthly income or less. The equivalent proportion of whites is just over 20 per cent.

These same CDF graphs show that measured poverty increased for Africans, coloureds and Asians/Indians, especially in the range between the two poverty lines. The increase in coloured poverty is especially stark. White poverty appears to be unchanged.

Figure 3.7 *Cumulative distribution functions at 1996 prices by population group*

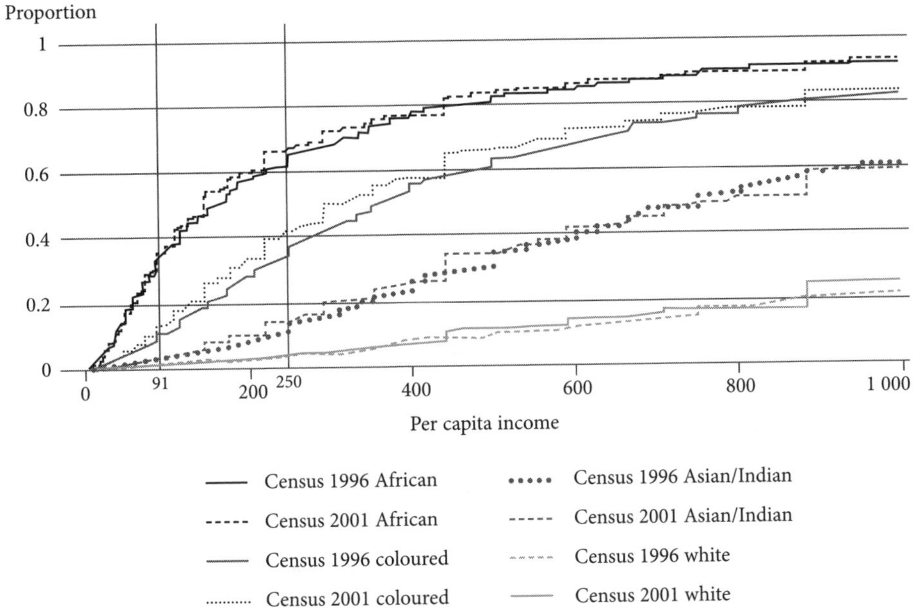

Sources: Census 1996 and Census 2001, Statistics South Africa

Given that these CDF plots do not cross at low income levels, the poverty rankings and changes over time are unambiguous and will be reflected in any acceptable poverty measure. Table 3.7 assesses this by measuring poverty for each population group in 1996 and 2001, using both the headcount poverty measure and the poverty gap ratio. These poverty measures confirm the group rankings of poverty and the large group differences in measured poverty at either poverty line. They also confirm that there were only small increases in poverty between 1996 and 2001 for Africans and coloureds when measured at the low poverty line ($2 per day) but fairly large increases in poverty for these two groups and the Asian/Indian group when the higher poverty line (R250) is used.[9]

One of the strengths of the headcount ratio and the poverty gap ratio as measures of poverty is that they can both be used to generate poverty shares to complement the poverty rates such as those reflected in Table 3.7. These poverty shares are derived by weighting the poverty rates of each subgroup (population groups in this case) by the share of the population that belongs to each sub-group. These poverty shares are shown in Table 3.8.

Table 3.7 *Poverty levels by population group*

	Headcount	Poverty gap ratio	Headcount	Poverty gap ratio
Poverty line	1996		2001	
$2 per day				
African	0.34	0.14	0.35	0.14
Coloured	0.10	0.03	0.13	0.04
Asian/Indian	0.03	0.01	0.03	0.01
White	0.01	0.00	0.01	0.00
R250 (1996)				
African	0.62	0.38	0.67	0.39
Coloured	0.34	0.16	0.41	0.19
Asian/Indian	0.11	0.05	0.14	0.06
White	0.03	0.02	0.04	0.02

Sources: Own calculations, using Census 1996 and Census 2001, Statistics South Africa

Table 3.8 *Poverty shares by population group*

	Headcount	Poverty gap ratio	Headcount	Poverty gap ratio
Poverty line	1996		2001	
$2 per day				
African	0.95	0.96	0.95	0.95
Coloured	0.04	0.03	0.05	0.04
Asian/Indian	0.00	0.00	0.00	0.00
White	0.01	0.00	0.00	0.00
R250 (1996)				
African	0.91	0.93	0.91	0.93
Coloured	0.07	0.06	0.08	0.06
Asian/Indian	0.01	0.00	0.01	0.01
White	0.01	0.01	0.01	0.01

Sources: Own calculations, using Census 1996 and Census 2001, Statistics South Africa

We have already seen that the African group has by far the highest poverty rates. When this is combined with their dominant population share, the result is the overwhelming African poverty shares that are reflected in Table 3.8. One subtlety reflected in the table is that this African share is higher for the poverty gap ratio than for the headcount ratio. This is a result of the fact that the poverty gap ratio accounts for how far a person's income is below the poverty line and not merely whether or not the person is poor. The African poor are over-represented in the poorest-of-the-poor group, and the poverty gap ratio reflects this as a higher percentage of poverty.

We introduce our discussion of provincial poverty through Figures 3.8, 3.9 and 3.10. Figures 3.8 and 3.9 allow us to examine provincial poverty rankings for each province for both 1996 and 2001.[10] The CDF graphs show that for the best-off and worst-off provinces, these rankings are unchanged over time. In both years, the Western Cape and Gauteng have the lowest poverty rates, while the Eastern Cape and Limpopo have the highest poverty rates, regardless of where we draw the poverty line.

Figure 3.10 focuses exclusively on the two richest provinces (the Western Cape and Gauteng) and the two poorest provinces (the Eastern Cape and Limpopo). This is useful in highlighting the magnitude of the differences in poverty between the richest and poorest provinces. In addition, as it presents comparable real income values for both 1996 and 2001 for each of these four provinces, it can show changes in poverty over time. There is evidence of an increase in poverty in all the provinces, including the two best-off provinces. This increase is particularly marked for real income levels between the low poverty line and the higher line, and less marked for incomes below the low poverty line.

Figure 3.8 *Cumulative distribution functions, without zero incomes, by province for Census 2001*

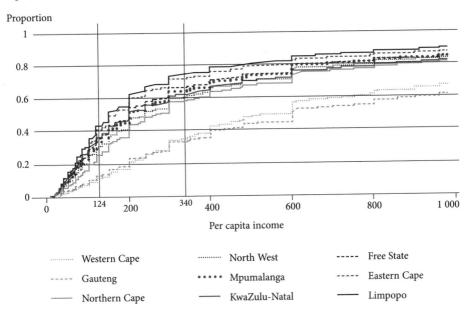

Source: Census 2001, Statistics South Africa

Figure 3.9 *Cumulative distribution functions, without zero incomes, by province for Census 1996*

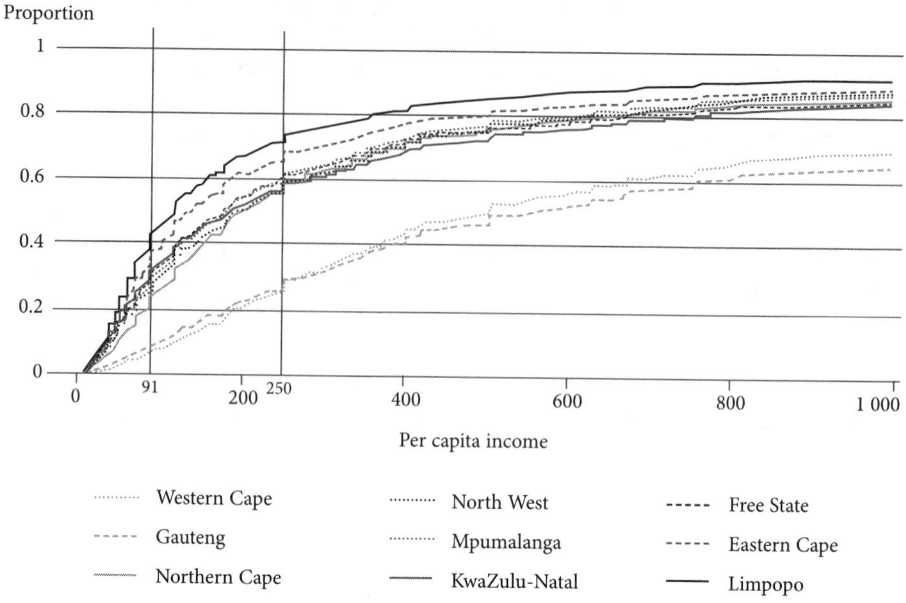

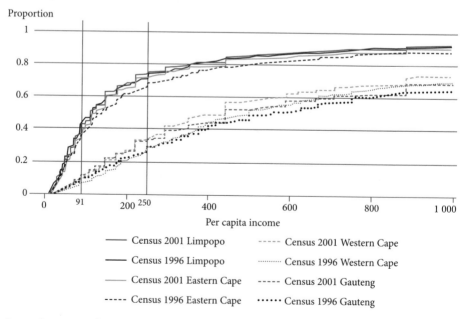

Source: Census 1996, Statistics South Africa

Figure 3.10 *Cumulative distribution functions, without zero incomes, for richest and poorest provinces for Census 1996 and Census 2001*

Sources: Census 1996 and Census 2001, Statistics South Africa

Table 3.9 confirms these provincial poverty profiles at the two selected poverty lines. In spite of excluding zero incomes (which, if included, would severely worsen the results), the poverty rates in the Eastern Cape, Free State, Limpopo, Mpumalanga and KwaZulu-Natal are all in excess of 30 per cent, even at the extremely low poverty line of $2 per day.

Table 3.9 *Poverty levels by province, excluding zero incomes*

	Headcount	Poverty gap ratio	Headcount	Poverty gap ratio
Poverty line	1996		2001	
$2 per day				
Western Cape	0.07	0.02	0.10	0.03
Eastern Cape	0.38	0.15	0.40	0.15
Northern Cape	0.24	0.09	0.24	0.09
Free State	0.32	0.13	0.35	0.15
KwaZulu-Natal	0.32	0.15	0.36	0.15
North West	0.28	0.12	0.30	0.12
Gauteng	0.09	0.04	0.12	0.04
Mpumalanga	0.30	0.13	0.33	0.14
Limpopo	0.44	0.19	0.43	0.18
R250 (1996)				
Western Cape	0.26	0.11	0.34	0.15
Eastern Cape	0.65	0.41	0.72	0.43
Northern Cape	0.57	0.31	0.58	0.31
Free State	0.59	0.35	0.66	0.39
KwaZulu-Natal	0.56	0.35	0.62	0.38
North West	0.56	0.33	0.60	0.34
Gauteng	0.26	0.13	0.33	0.16
Mpumalanga	0.59	0.35	0.64	0.38
Limpopo	0.71	0.46	0.74	0.46

Sources: Own calculations, using Census 1996 and Census 2001, Statistics South Africa

While it is clearly useful to know in which provinces the poverty rates are highest, in order to ascertain the provincial shares of national poverty these measures of provincial poverty incidence need to be weighted by the population share of each province. Table 3.10 presents the resultant provincial poverty shares. For example, using the lower poverty line, we find that 20 per cent of the poor live in the Eastern Cape and 25 per cent of the poor live in KwaZulu-Natal. Generally, the provincial poverty shares are quite stable across the two poverty lines, across the two poverty measures and across time. The most notable change is the fact that the two poorest provinces appear to have given up small shares of poverty to the two richest provinces between 1996 and 2001. Such a change in the shares would be consistent with a migration of poor South Africans from these very poor provinces to the better-off provinces.

Table 3.10 *Poverty shares by province, excluding zero incomes*

	Headcount	Poverty gap ratio	Headcount	Poverty gap ratio
Poverty line	1996		2001	
$2 per day				
Western Cape	0.03	0.02	0.04	0.03
Eastern Cape	0.20	0.19	0.18	0.17
Northern Cape	0.02	0.02	0.02	0.02
Free State	0.08	0.08	0.08	0.08
KwaZulu-Natal	0.25	0.26	0.26	0.27
North West	0.09	0.09	0.09	0.09
Gauteng	0.07	0.06	0.09	0.08
Mpumalanga	0.08	0.08	0.08	0.08
Limpopo	0.17	0.18	0.17	0.17
R250 (1996)				
Western Cape	0.06	0.04	0.07	0.05
Eastern Cape	0.18	0.19	0.17	0.18
Northern Cape	0.03	0.02	0.02	0.02
Free State	0.08	0.08	0.08	0.08
KwaZulu-Natal	0.23	0.24	0.23	0.24
North West	0.09	0.09	0.09	0.09
Gauteng	0.10	0.09	0.12	0.11
Mpumalanga	0.08	0.08	0.08	0.08
Limpopo	0.15	0.16	0.15	0.16

Sources: Own calculations, using Census 1996 and Census 2001, Statistics South Africa

We complete our discussion of income poverty by comparing rural and urban poverty. The rural/urban divide cuts across population groups and provinces. Figure 3.11 shows that rural poverty rates are substantially higher than urban poverty rates (regardless of the poverty line we choose). Nonetheless, the graph demonstrates that poverty rates unambiguously increased in urban areas over the inter-censal period, while this cannot be unequivocally concluded for rural areas.

Figure 3.11 *Urban and rural cumulative distribution functions at 1996 prices, Census 1996 and Census 2001*

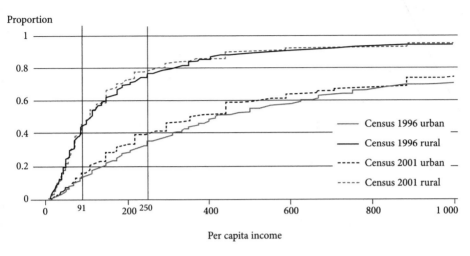

Sources: Census 1996 and Census 2001, Statistics South Africa

Table 3.11 confirms that at the two poverty lines that we use throughout this chapter, poverty in both rural and urban areas increased over the period 1996 to 2001. This increase is marked at the higher poverty line. The increase in urban poverty resonates with our earlier finding that poverty increased in Gauteng and in the Western Cape. In this context it is interesting to note that poverty also increased in KwaZulu-Natal.

Table 3.11 *Urban and rural poverty levels*

	Headcount	Poverty gap ratio	Headcount	Poverty gap ratio
Poverty line	**1996**		**2001**	
$2 per day				
Urban	0.13	0.05	0.16	0.06
Rural	0.45	0.19	0.46	0.19
R250 (1996)				
Urban	0.36	0.17	0.40	0.21
Rural	0.75	0.48	0.79	0.49

Sources: Own calculations, using Census 1996 and Census 2001, Statistics South Africa

Table 3.12 throws further light on this issue. While a much higher proportion of the rural population is poor, the proportion of the poor who are in rural areas is declining. Using the higher poverty line, 38 per cent of the poor were in urban areas in 1996, whereas 43 per cent of the poor were in urban areas in 2001. This is to be expected, given that a significant amount of rural to urban migration occurred over this period.

Table 3.12 *Urban and rural poverty shares*

Poverty line	Headcount	Poverty gap ratio	Headcount	Poverty gap ratio
	1996		2001	
$2 per day				
Urban	0.29	0.28	0.34	0.32
Rural	0.71	0.72	0.66	0.68
R250 (1996)				
Urban	0.38	0.34	0.43	0.39
Rural	0.62	0.66	0.57	0.61

Sources: Own calculations, using Census 1996 and Census 2001, Statistics South Africa

Changing patterns of access poverty and inequality

A comprehensive analysis of well-being stretches beyond the assessment of poverty and inequality based on income measures, to include other key indicators of living standards, which may not be fully accounted for using only the income approach. Access to basic services such as clean water, electricity, sanitation and telephones also has a major impact on quality of life, leading to improvements ranging from health to productivity. In this section we consider the types of dwelling that households occupy and access to basic services as further indicators of poverty and inequality. The shifts in measures are explored for the inter-censal period to see where gains have been made or setbacks experienced. The analysis is done at the national, population group, provincial and rural/urban levels.

Dwelling

Having adequate shelter is a basic necessity. From Census 1996 and Census 2001 we have identified four categories of dwelling: formal, informal in backyard, informal not in backyard (such as a squatter camp) and traditional. Formal dwellings are viewed as superior, more permanent fixtures with walls made of bricks or concrete, and tiled or corrugated iron roofs. Generally, informal dwellings have corrugated iron walls and roofs, whilst traditional dwellings are made of mud walls and an equal share of corrugated iron and thatch roofs. In terms of structural quality and overcrowding, informal dwellings appear to be most vulnerable to shocks such as adverse weather conditions or spreading fires within densely populated settlements. Informal dwellings are more vulnerable than traditional dwellings with regard to the condition of the dwellings' roofs and walls, thus rendering informal dwellings more susceptible to damage.

Figure 3.12 *Type of dwelling by population group, 1996 and 2001*

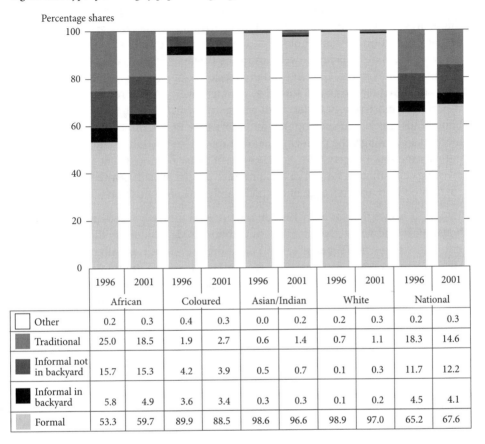

Percentage shares

	African 1996	African 2001	Coloured 1996	Coloured 2001	Asian/Indian 1996	Asian/Indian 2001	White 1996	White 2001	National 1996	National 2001
Other	0.2	0.3	0.4	0.3	0.0	0.2	0.2	0.3	0.2	0.3
Traditional	25.0	18.5	1.9	2.7	0.6	1.4	0.7	1.1	18.3	14.6
Informal not in backyard	15.7	15.3	4.2	3.9	0.5	0.7	0.1	0.3	11.7	12.2
Informal in backyard	5.8	4.9	3.6	3.4	0.3	0.3	0.1	0.2	4.5	4.1
Formal	53.3	59.7	89.9	88.5	98.6	96.6	98.9	97.0	65.2	67.6

Sources: Own calculations, using Census 1996 and Census 2001, Statistics South Africa
Note: Totals may not add up to 100 due to omission of 'unspecified' category.

Nationally, it is evident that in both 1996 and 2001 almost two-thirds of households occupied formal dwellings. During the inter-censal period, the proportion of households living in traditional dwellings decreased from approximately 18.3 per cent in 1996 to 14.6 per cent in 2001. Figure 3.12 shows that for both 1996 and 2001 more than 90 per cent of coloureds, Asians/Indians and whites lived in formal dwellings, whilst the proportion of Africans living in formal dwellings rose from 53 per cent in 1996 to 60 per cent in 2001. The increase in the proportion of Africans living in formal dwellings was offset by a decrease in the proportion of Africans living in traditional housing.

Furthermore, if we examine dwelling types on a provincial level, we see that during the inter-censal period, the proportion of households occupying formal dwellings increased in almost all provinces, especially in Limpopo where the proportion of households occupying formal dwellings increased by 10 per cent during this period. It is important to note that Limpopo, which is classified from census data as the poorest province in terms of income deprivation, has seen the largest increase in the proportion of households residing in formal dwellings, and the share of households residing in such dwellings in the province rivals those of the least poor provinces (for example, Gauteng and the Western Cape). The picture for the Eastern Cape, however, is consistent with the income poverty measures for this province. It performs most poorly in terms of access to formal dwellings, with only half of households residing in such homes, and more than one in three living in traditional dwellings. Although the performance of Limpopo seems quite extraordinary, given both its income poverty and rural nature, it must be noted that the majority of dwellings classified as formal in this province are simple shells with brick walls and corrugated iron or zinc roofs, and which rarely include a flush or chemical toilet.

Table 3.13 shows that for both 1996 and 2001, approximately three-quarters of urban households and more than half of rural households resided in formal dwellings. Informal settlements (squatter camps) are more prevalent in the urban areas of Free State, North West and Mpumalanga. As would be expected, traditional dwellings are more common in rural areas, especially in KwaZulu-Natal and the Eastern Cape, where more than 50 per cent and 60 per cent of households, respectively, reside in traditional dwellings. For rural areas, there has been a marked decrease in the proportion of households occupying traditional dwellings, from 43 per cent to 35 per cent. It is reassuring to note that this decrease was largely offset by an increase in formal dwellings as opposed to an increase in the more vulnerable informal dwellings.

Table 3.13 *Type of dwelling by province, 1996 and 2001*
(a) 1996

Province	Formal	Informal in backyard	Informal not in backyard	Traditional	Other	Total
Western Cape	82.2	3.4	13.3	0.9	0.2	100.0
Eastern Cape	47.4	2.3	8.6	41.4	0.3	100.0
Northern Cape	80.9	2.7	11.4	4.0	1.0	100.0
Free State	63.3	8.1	18.3	10.2	0.1	100.0
KwaZulu-Natal	56.1	2.7	8.6	32.4	0.2	100.0
North West	70.5	6.4	16.0	7.0	0.1	100.0
Gauteng	74.9	8.0	16.2	0.7	0.1	100.0
Mpumalanga	65.9	4.1	11.7	18.1	0.2	100.0
Limpopo	62.8	1.6	3.3	32.2	0.2	100.0
Rural	50.6	2.0	4.4	42.7	0.2	100.0
Urban	75.0	6.2	16.6	2.0	0.2	100.0
Total	65.2	4.5	11.7	18.3	0.2	100.0

(b) 2001

Province	Formal	Informal in backyard	Informal not in backyard	Trad- itional	Other	Un- specified	Total
Western Cape	80.4	4.0	12.1	2.1	0.3	1.2	100.0
Eastern Cape	50.2	2.1	8.9	37.8	0.2	0.9	100.0
Northern Cape	82.3	2.7	9.8	3.1	0.7	1.4	100.0
Free State	64.7	5.8	19.8	7.1	0.2	2.4	100.0
KwaZulu-Natal	60.1	2.3	8.4	27.5	0.3	1.4	100.0
North West	71.2	5.6	16.5	5.2	0.2	1.3	100.0
Gauteng	73.4	6.9	16.8	1.3	0.3	1.4	100.0
Mpumalanga	69.9	3.3	12.5	12.9	0.3	1.1	100.0
Limpopo	72.7	1.8	4.7	19.7	0.2	0.9	100.0
Rural	56.3	2.0	5.6	34.6	0.2	1.3	100.0
Urban	74.4	5.3	16.1	2.6	0.3	1.3	100.0
Total	**67.6**	**4.1**	**12.2**	**14.6**	**0.3**	**1.3**	**100.0**

Sources: Own calculations, using Census 1996 and Census 2001, Statistics South Africa

Water

Traditionally, people in poorer areas spend much time collecting water of varying quality from sources a great distance from their homes. A constant supply of clean water close to the home contributes positively to a household's well-being by promoting good health and freeing up time for alternative activities. The inter-censal period shows an increase in the proportion of households with access to piped water, and a subsequent reduction in the proportion of households using water from dams, rivers and springs.[11] In South Africa more than four out of every five households have access to piped water, be it in the home or outside the home.

The statistics for access to piped water shown in Figure 3.13 are encouraging; however, there remains a significant proportion of African households who in 2001 were still reliant on dams, rivers and springs as their main source of water for domestic use.

On a provincial level, as illustrated in Table 3.14, we see that yet again the income-poor Eastern Cape lags behind the other provinces in terms of access to piped water. Almost a third of households in the Eastern Cape obtain their water from dams, rivers and springs. The reliance of Eastern Cape households on water from dams, rivers and springs is particularly evident in the rural areas, where more than half of households obtain their water from these sources.

Figure 3.13 *Access to water by population group, 1996 and 2001*

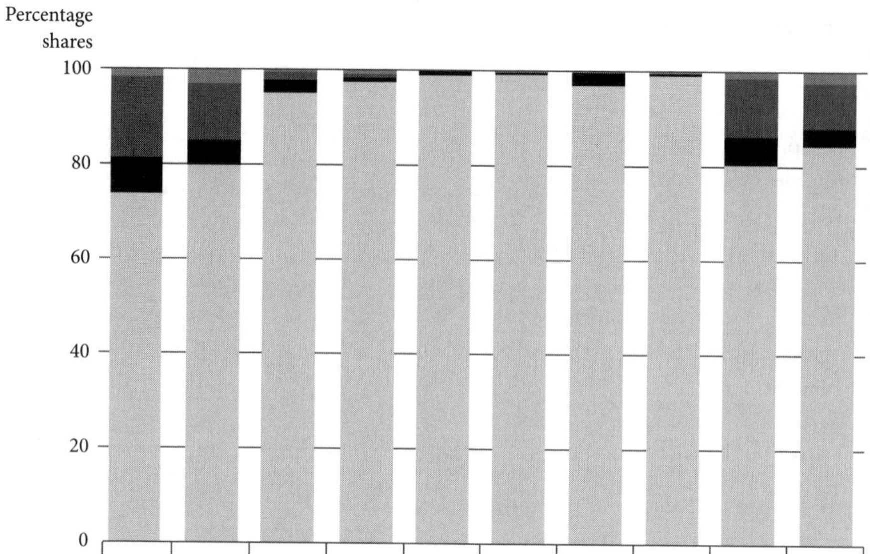

		African		Coloured		Asian/Indian		White		National	
		1996	2001	1996	2001	1996	2001	1996	2001	1996	2001
■	Other	1.6	2.9	0.4	0.7	0.1	0.2	0.0	0.2	1.2	2.3
■	Dam/river/ stream/ spring	16.9	11.9	1.6	0.8	0.2	0.1	0.2	0.1	12.4	9.2
■	Borehole/ rainwater tank/well/ water-carrier/ tanker	7.5	4.7	2.5	0.7	0.6	0.3	2.6	0.4	6.1	3.7
	Piped	73.6	78.3	95.4	94.7	98.9	95.7	96.9	95.8	80.0	82.2

Sources: Own calculations, using Census 1996 and Census 2001, Statistics South Africa
Note: Totals may not add up to 100 due to omission of 'unspecified' category.

Table 3.14 *Access to water by province, 1996 and 2001*

(a) 1996

Province	Piped	Borehole/ rainwater tank/well/ water-car- rier/tanker	Dam/river/ stream/ spring	Other	Un- specified	Total
Western Cape	97.0	1.2	0.6	1.0	0.2	100.0
Eastern Cape	53.6	4.7	40.7	0.6	0.5	100.0
Northern Cape	91.4	5.0	3.0	0.4	0.3	100.0
Free State	94.1	4.0	0.9	0.7	0.3	100.0
KwaZulu-Natal	66.4	7.8	24.4	0.9	0.4	100.0
North West	81.4	13.2	1.7	3.2	0.4	100.0
Gauteng	96.2	2.7	0.1	0.6	0.4	100.0
Mpumalanga	82.3	10.1	5.6	1.5	0.5	100.0
Northern Province	75.6	10.7	11.1	2.2	0.5	100.0
Rural	53.6	13.8	30.5	1.6	0.5	100.0
Urban	97.6	0.9	0.3	0.9	0.3	100.0
Total	**80.0**	**6.1**	**12.4**	**1.2**	**0.4**	**100.0**

(b) 2001

Province	Piped	Borehole/ rainwater tank/well/ water-car- rier/tanker	Dam/river/ stream/ spring	Other	Un- specified	Total
Western Cape	94.9	0.3	0.4	1.0	3.4	100.0
Eastern Cape	61.0	4.2	31.3	1.4	2.1	100.0
Northern Cape	94.8	0.8	1.4	1.2	1.9	100.0
Free State	93.6	1.0	0.5	2.8	2.1	100.0
KwaZulu-Natal	70.5	5.7	18.1	2.4	3.3	100.0
North West	84.9	9.0	1.1	3.4	1.5	100.0
Gauteng	94.4	0.7	0.2	1.6	3.1	100.0
Mpumalanga	84.9	4.4	4.9	3.8	2.0	100.0
Limpopo	76.9	7.4	10.4	4.0	1.2	100.0
Rural	62.0	9.0	24.0	3.4	1.6	100.0
Urban	94.4	0.5	0.3	1.6	3.1	100.0
Total	**82.2**	**3.7**	**9.2**	**2.3**	**2.5**	**100.0**

Sources: Own calculations, using Census 1996 and Census 2001, Statistics South Africa

It is interesting to note that although Limpopo is one of the poorest provinces in terms of income, it fares quite well with regard to access to piped water, with approximately three-quarters of households having access to piped water, even in the rural areas. More importantly, the proportion of households in KwaZulu-Natal with access to piped water is less than that in Limpopo. Although there has been an increase in the proportion of households with access to piped water during the inter-censal period, fewer than half of rural KwaZulu-Natal households obtain their water from this source. Thus the outbreak of waterborne diseases, such as cholera, in these rural regions is not surprising. Clearly, there is room for much improvement in terms of household access to piped water.

Energy for lighting

Electricity is viewed as the most desirable form of energy and is required for the functioning of various household assets, such as refrigerators and computers. However, poorer households often lack the means to access electricity (because of the lack of either infrastructure or income), and thus find themselves using other forms of energy such as wood, paraffin and candles. Nationally, from 1996 to 2001,

Figure 3.14 *Energy for lighting by population group, 1996 and 2001*

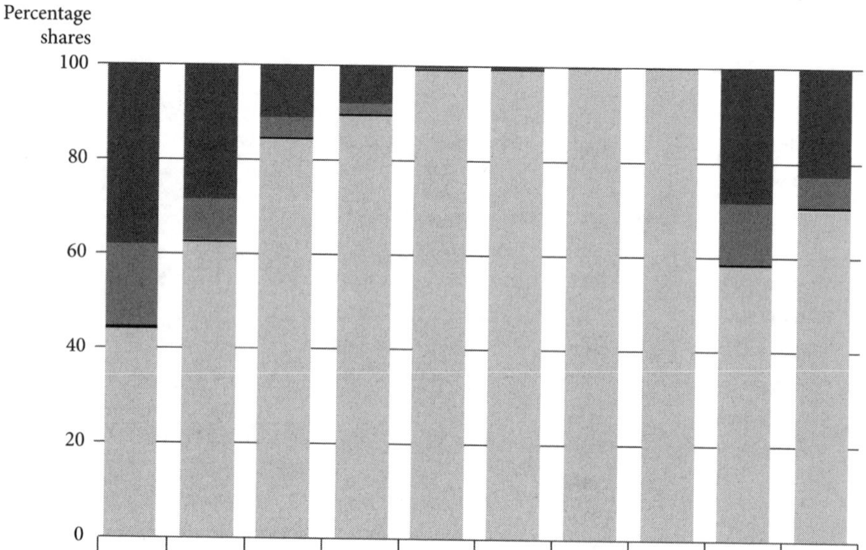

	African 1996	African 2001	Coloured 1996	Coloured 2001	Asian/Indian 1996	Asian/Indian 2001	White 1996	White 2001	National 1996	National 2001
Candles	38.1	28.5	11.2	8.2	0.5	0.6	0.2	0.3	28.5	22.6
Paraffin	17.0	8.5	4.4	2.2	0.3	0.2	0.1	0.1	12.7	6.7
Gas	0.5	0.3	0.3	0.2	0.1	0.1	0.1	0.2	0.4	0.3
Electricity	43.7	61.6	83.7	88.3	98.7	98.4	99.0	98.3	57.7	69.5

Sources: Own calculations, using Census 1996 and Census 2001, Statistics South Africa
Note: Totals may not add up to 100 due to omission of 'other' and 'unspecified' categories.

there has been a significant increase of more than ten percentage points in the proportion of households with access to electricity for lighting purposes. The success of the electrification programme has had specific ramifications for the African population of whom, in 1996, only two in five households used electricity for lighting. In 2001 this number had increased substantially to three in every five households, as illustrated in Figure 3.14. Notwithstanding the improvements, the racial discrepancies remain clear, with almost one-third of African households reliant on candles in 2001, compared with eight per cent of coloured and a negligible proportion of white and Asian/Indian households.

Stark provincial disparities in 1996 were somewhat smoothed by 2001, as is evident in Table 3.15. As in the case of formal housing and piped water, the income-poor Eastern Cape is the most deprived province, with only half of households there having access to electricity for lighting. It is interesting to note that the main alternative to electricity in most provinces is candles, but that in the Eastern Cape paraffin is also a major source of energy for lighting, and is used by just under a quarter of households. In Limpopo even greater successes in the electrification programme have been achieved: compared with five years earlier, an additional 25 per cent of households had access to electricity in 2001, with electricity largely replacing paraffin.

Table 3.15 *Energy for lighting by province, 1996 and 2001*

(a) 1996

Province	Electricity	Gas	Paraffin	Candles	Other	Un-specified	Total
Western Cape	85.4	0.3	8.2	5.8	0.0	0.4	100.0
Eastern Cape	31.7	0.6	38.8	28.4	0.0	0.6	100.0
Northern Cape	71.0	0.2	7.6	20.6	0.1	0.4	100.0
Free State	57.3	0.2	7.3	34.7	0.0	0.4	100.0
KwaZulu-Natal	53.7	0.5	5.2	40.0	0.0	0.7	100.0
North West	44.1	0.3	6.9	48.2	0.6	0.0	100.0
Gauteng	79.8	0.2	2.4	16.9	0.0	0.7	100.0
Mpumalanga	56.5	0.8	10.5	31.3	0.0	0.8	100.0
Limpopo	36.8	0.6	24.7	37.0	0.0	0.9	100.0
Rural	28.7	0.6	20.9	49.0	0.0	0.8	100.0
Urban	77.2	0.3	7.1	14.8	0.0	0.5	100.0
Total	**57.7**	**0.4**	**12.7**	**28.5**	**0.0**	**0.6**	**100.0**

→

(b) 2001

Province	Electricity	Gas	Paraffin	Candles	Other	Un-specified	Total
Western Cape	87.5	0.3	7.0	4.4	0.1	0.7	100.0
Eastern Cape	49.5	0.4	23.4	25.8	0.1	1.0	100.0
Northern Cape	76.4	0.2	3.9	18.4	0.4	0.8	100.0
Free State	74.4	0.2	4.7	20.2	0.1	0.5	100.0
KwaZulu-Natal	61.2	0.4	2.5	34.8	0.1	1.1	100.0
North West	70.2	0.1	3.1	26.1	0.1	0.5	100.0
Gauteng	80.4	0.2	2.9	15.8	0.0	0.8	100.0
Mpumalanga	67.9	0.3	4.2	26.7	0.1	0.8	100.0
Limpopo	63.7	0.2	7.6	27.4	0.1	1.0	100.0
Rural	50.3	0.3	8.7	39.2	0.5	1.1	100.0
Urban	80.8	0.2	5.6	12.6	0.2	0.7	100.0
Total	**69.5**	**0.3**	**6.7**	**22.6**	**0.1**	**0.9**	**100.0**

Sources: Own calculations, using Census 1996 and Census 2001, Statistics South Africa

In 1996, less than a third of rural households had access to electricity, but in 2001 approximately half of rural households used electricity for lighting, implying potential improvements in the standard of living in these more deprived areas.

Energy for cooking

The alternative sources of energy for cooking purposes are different to those for lighting purposes, and include electricity, gas, paraffin, wood, coal and animal dung. Furthermore, the choice between energy sources will be dependent largely on the cost, availability and effectiveness of the energy source to perform the given task, and on the asset available for cooking (for example, type of stove).

Even though there have been large increases in the reach of electricity used for lighting purposes, this has corresponded to only a three-percentage-point increase in the proportion of households using electricity for cooking purposes. In 2001, only half of South African households used electricity as the main source of energy for cooking purposes (see Figure 3.15). Furthermore, we see that only two in every five African households use electricity, while more than half of all African households are reliant on either paraffin or wood for cooking. Indeed, of our indicators examined thus far, it appears that fuel used for cooking is most closely linked to income status. The inequalities in access across provinces can be clearly seen in Table 3.16.

Figure 3.15 *Energy for cooking by population group, 1996 and 2001*

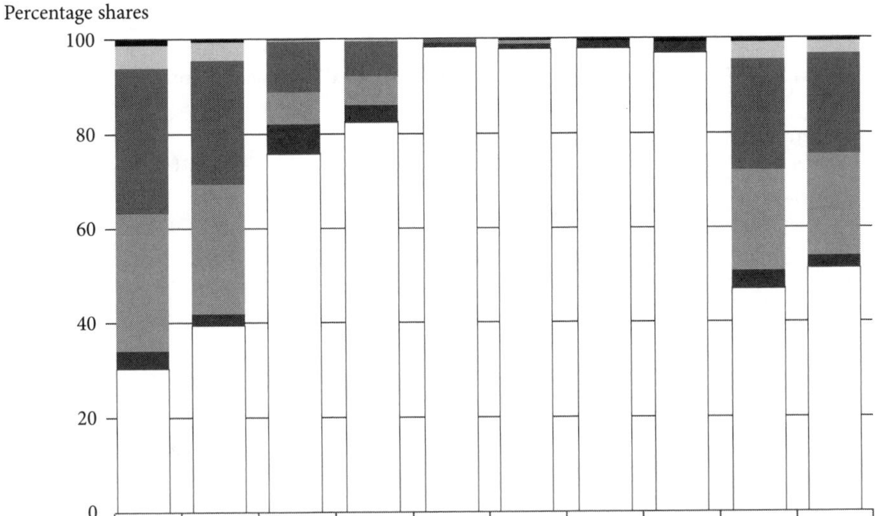

Percentage shares

	African		Coloured		Asian/Indian		White		National	
	1996	2001	1996	2001	1996	2001	1996	2001	1996	2001
Animal dung	1.6	1.2	0.1	0.1	0.0	0.1	0.0	0.1	1.2	1.0
Coal	4.8	3.5	0.5	0.4	0.0	0.1	0.1	0.1	3.6	2.7
Wood	30.4	25.6	10.8	7.5	0.2	0.2	0.2	0.3	22.9	20.3
Paraffin	28.9	27.0	6.7	5.9	0.5	0.6	0.1	0.2	21.5	21.3
Gas	3.3	2.5	5.8	3.3	1.1	1.3	1.8	2.4	3.2	2.5
Electricity	30.4	38.6	75.8	81.0	97.7	95.7	97.3	94.8	47.2	50.6

Sources: Own calculations, using Census 1996 and Census 2001, Statistics South Africa
Note: Totals may not add up to 100 due to omission of 'other' and 'unspecified' categories.

The financial constraints of households in Limpopo and the Eastern Cape are apparent in that they once again lag behind the other provinces with regard to access to electricity. In the rural areas of Limpopo, fewer than one in five households use electricity for cooking purposes, and more than two-thirds are reliant on often freely available wood. Rural households in the Eastern Cape appear to be worse off than their counterparts in Limpopo, with fewer than one in ten households using electricity for cooking. More than half of rural households use wood for cooking purposes. However, in urban areas where wood is not readily accessible, households are mainly reliant on electricity and paraffin. As such, poorer urban households are forced to use their little wealth to pay for this energy source. They become especially vulnerable to fluctuations in the price of paraffin, which varies greatly with changes in the oil price.

Table 3.16 *Energy for cooking by province, 1996 and 2001*

(a) 1996

Province	Electricity	Gas	Paraffin	Wood	Coal	Animal dung	Other	Un-specified	Total
Western Cape	76.8	4.9	13.3	4.5	0.1	0.0	0.0	0.4	100.0
Eastern Cape	23.3	3.3	29.4	37.9	0.3	5.4	0.0	0.5	100.0
Northern Cape	52.5	9.6	17.5	18.5	1.4	0.1	0.0	0.5	100.0
Free State	42.1	4.0	35.6	9.2	7.1	1.5	0.0	0.5	100.0
KwaZulu-Natal	46.0	3.2	17.9	29.5	2.3	0.6	0.0	0.5	100.0
North West	33.7	4.7	36.8	20.6	2.9	0.9	0.0	0.4	100.0
Gauteng	73.1	1.7	19.4	0.9	4.3	0.0	0.0	0.6	100.0
Mpuma-langa	35.5	2.4	17.3	25.9	17.8	0.5	0.0	0.6	100.0
Limpopo	19.5	1.7	12.2	63.3	2.2	0.5	0.0	0.5	100.0
Rural	15.3	3.1	19.8	54.6	3.7	2.9	0.0	0.5	100.0
Urban	68.5	3.2	22.6	1.7	3.5	0.0	0.0	0.5	100.0
Total	**47.2**	**3.2**	**21.5**	**22.9**	**3.6**	**1.2**	**0.0**	**0.5**	**100.0**

(b) 2001

Province	Electricity	Gas	Paraffin	Wood	Coal	Animal dung	Other	Un-specified	Total
Western Cape	77.6	3.4	13.9	2.9	0.2	0.3	0.2	1.6	100.0
Eastern Cape	27.6	2.9	29.3	35.6	0.3	3.3	0.3	0.7	100.0
Northern Cape	58.5	6.5	17.8	15.5	0.5	0.2	0.1	0.9	100.0
Free State	46.4	3.4	33.9	7.9	5.4	1.6	0.2	1.3	100.0
KwaZulu-Natal	47.3	3.0	17.9	26.7	2.0	1.0	0.4	1.8	100.0
North West	44.0	2.9	32.1	18.2	1.1	0.9	0.1	0.7	100.0
Gauteng	72.1	1.4	21.3	0.7	2.7	0.2	0.2	1.4	100.0
Mpuma-langa	39.4	1.9	17.3	23.2	16.0	0.8	0.3	1.1	100.0
Limpopo	24.7	1.7	11.0	59.3	1.6	0.4	0.3	0.9	100.0
Rural	21.8	2.8	17.8	51.3	2.7	2.1	0.6	0.9	100.0
Urban	67.7	2.4	23.3	1.7	2.8	0.3	0.4	1.5	100.0
Total	**50.7**	**2.5**	**21.3**	**20.3**	**2.7**	**1.0**	**0.2**	**1.3**	**100.0**

Sources: Own calculations, using Census 1996 and Census 2001, Statistics South Africa

Sanitation

During the inter-censal period, there was an increase in the proportion of households with access to a flush or chemical toilet. However, in 2001 a little more than half of the households in the country had access to toilets. Figure 3.16 shows that whilst the majority of coloureds, Asians/Indians and whites had access to a flush or chemical toilet, a mere 40 per cent of African households had this facility in 2001, which is nevertheless an improvement since only a third of African households had access to toilets in 1996.

Figure 3.16 *Access to sanitation by population group, 1996 and 2001*

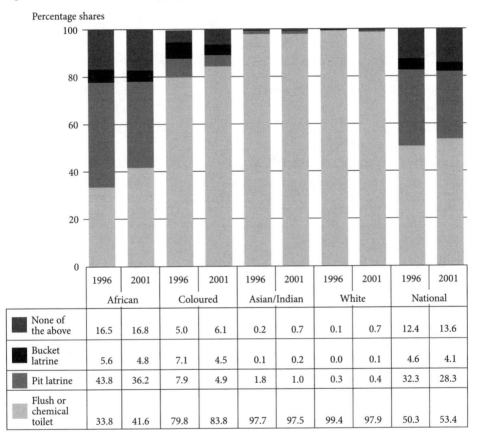

Percentage shares

	African 1996	African 2001	Coloured 1996	Coloured 2001	Asian/Indian 1996	Asian/Indian 2001	White 1996	White 2001	National 1996	National 2001
None of the above	16.5	16.8	5.0	6.1	0.2	0.7	0.1	0.7	12.4	13.6
Bucket latrine	5.6	4.8	7.1	4.5	0.1	0.2	0.0	0.1	4.6	4.1
Pit latrine	43.8	36.2	7.9	4.9	1.8	1.0	0.3	0.4	32.3	28.3
Flush or chemical toilet	33.8	41.6	79.8	83.8	97.7	97.5	99.4	97.9	50.3	53.4

Sources: Own calculations, using Census 1996 and Census 2001, Statistics South Africa
Note: Totals may not add up to 100 due to omission of 'unspecified' category.

Furthermore, as the analysis by province in Table 3.17 shows, in 2001 only a third of households in the Eastern Cape had access to toilets, whilst approximately 31 per cent had no access to either a toilet, or a pit or bucket latrine. A similar pattern holds for Limpopo, where fewer than one in five households had access to a toilet, and another one in five had no type of sanitation at all. Moreover, in 2001 fewer than 10 per cent of households in the rural areas of the Eastern Cape and Limpopo had access to a toilet.

Table 3.17 *Access to sanitation by province, 1996 and 2001*

(a) 1996

Province	Flush or chemical toilet	Pit latrine	Bucket latrine	None of the above	Unspecified	Total
Western Cape	85.8	4.8	3.8	5.4	0.2	100.0
Eastern Cape	30.7	33.7	6.2	28.9	0.5	100.0
Northern Cape	59.8	11.7	17.8	10.5	0.2	100.0
Free State	45.2	25.3	20.5	8.8	0.2	100.0
KwaZulu-Natal	41.9	41.7	0.9	15.1	0.4	100.0
North West	31.9	54.9	6.4	6.4	0.3	100.0
Gauteng	83.0	11.7	2.5	2.5	0.3	100.0
Mpumalanga	37.8	49.6	3.6	8.6	0.4	100.0
Limpopo	13.1	64.9	0.5	21.0	0.5	100.0
Rural	8.56	64.23	1.43	25.31	0.47	100.0
Urban	78.27	10.97	6.79	3.67	0.29	100.0
Total	**50.3**	**32.3**	**4.6**	**12.4**	**0.4**	**100.0**

(b) 2001

Province	Flush or chemical toilet	Pit latrine	Bucket latrine	None of the above	Unspecified	Total
Western Cape	85.8	2.1	3.7	7.7	0.7	100.0
Eastern Cape	34.6	28.5	5.6	30.7	0.7	100.0
Northern Cape	66.5	10.0	11.8	11.3	0.4	100.0
Free State	46.8	22.6	20.3	9.8	0.4	100.0
KwaZulu-Natal	46.5	35.5	1.1	16.0	0.9	100.0
North West	35.7	50.0	4.5	9.5	0.3	100.0
Gauteng	82.2	11.2	2.3	3.6	0.8	100.0
Mpumalanga	39.7	46.8	2.8	10.3	0.5	100.0
Limpopo	17.3	58.3	0.6	23.3	0.4	100.0
Rural	13.5	56.9	1.4	27.6	0.6	100.0
Urban	77.5	11.1	5.7	5.1	0.7	100.0
Total	**53.4**	**28.3**	**4.1**	**13.6**	**0.7**	**100.0**

Sources: Own calculations, using Census 1996 and Census 2001, Statistics South Africa

Thus it is evident that quality sanitation facilities are severely lacking in the income-poor provinces. In addition, rural households in North West and Mpumalanga also have relatively poor access to a toilet. Although there has been an increase in the proportion of rural households with access to a toilet, it is important to note that in both 1996 and 2001, more than a quarter of households in the rural areas of South Africa had no access to either a toilet, or a pit or bucket latrine.

Refuse removal

In terms of refuse removal by local authorities, there has been only a slight improvement over the inter-censal period, with a mere 56 per cent of households having access to this service in 2001, up from 53 per cent in 1996. Once again, this indicator of living standards is closely linked to income status. For the different population groups, a similar pattern holds to that found for sanitation, with the majority of coloureds, Asians/Indians and whites having their refuse removed on a regular basis (see Figure 3.17). Fewer than half of African households have their refuse removed on a regular basis, and a further two-fifths make use of their own refuse dumps.

On a provincial level, yet again the Eastern Cape and Limpopo perform quite poorly in terms of household access to regular refuse removal (see Table 3.18). In particular, only a third of households in the Eastern Cape and a discouraging 14 per cent of households in Limpopo have their refuse removed on a regular basis. More importantly, in 2001 fewer than 5 per cent of rural households had their refuse removed by a local authority on a regular basis. It appears that the majority of rural households are reliant on their own refuse dump, with almost three-quarters of households using their own dumps whilst a further 18 per cent of households have no outlets for rubbish disposal.

Figure 3.17 *Access to refuse removal by population group, 1996 and 2001*

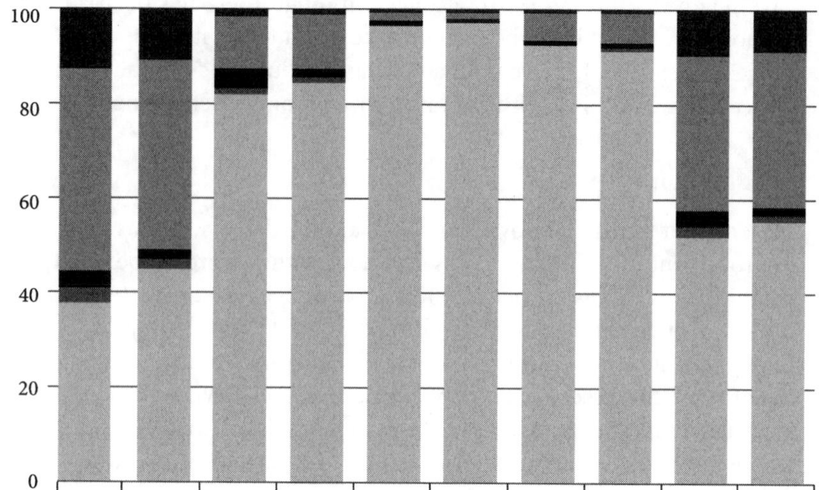

Percentage shares

	1996	2001	1996	2001	1996	2001	1996	2001	1996	2001
	African		Coloured		Asian/Indian		White		National	
No rubbish disposal	12.8	10.7	1.7	1.3	0.6	0.3	0.5	0.4	9.5	8.4
Own refuse dump	41.8	39.2	10.8	10.9	2.1	1.9	6.2	6.7	32.2	32.0
Communal refuse dump	3.7	1.9	4.2	1.9	0.3	0.3	0.9	0.7	3.2	1.7
Removed by local authority less often	2.8	1.7	1.2	1.2	0.4	0.5	0.5	0.7	2.2	1.5
Removed by local authority at least weekly	37.2	44.4	80.6	82.3	95.8	95.0	90.6	88.4	51.3	54.2

Sources: Own calculations, using Census 1996 and Census 2001, Statistics South Africa
Note: Totals may not add up to 100 due to omission of 'unspecified' category.

Table 3.18 *Access to refuse removal by province, 1996 and 2001*

(a) 1996

Province	Removed by local authority at least weekly	Removed by local authority less often	Comm-unal refuse dump	Own refuse dump	No rubbish disposal	Other	Un-specified	Total
Western Cape	82.4	2.5	3.7	7.7	2.0	0.1	1.6	100.0
Eastern Cape	33.9	1.7	1.7	39.6	21.6	0.1	1.4	100.0
Northern Cape	67.7	2.1	5.2	19.3	4.3	0.2	1.2	100.0
Free State	60.4	4.1	4.3	24.6	5.6	0.1	0.9	100.0
KwaZulu-Natal	42.1	1.2	2.9	40.6	11.3	0.5	1.5	100.0
North West	34.4	1.5	3.9	51.6	7.1	0.2	1.3	100.0
Gauteng	81.7	3.7	3.3	7.1	2.5	0.1	1.5	100.0
Mpumalanga	37.7	1.9	3.3	47.1	8.8	0.1	1.3	100.0
Limpopo	11.1	0.8	3.0	66.1	17.2	0.0	1.7	100.0
Rural	3.8	0.8	4.4	69.7	19.6	0.2	1.6	100.0
Urban	83.2	3.2	2.4	7.1	2.8	0.2	1.3	100.0
Total	51.3	2.2	3.2	32.2	9.5	0.2	1.4	100.0

(b) 2001

Province	Removed by local authority at least weekly	Removed by local authority less often	Comm-unal refuse dump	Own refuse dump	No rubbish disposal	Un-specified	Total
Western Cape	86.2	1.0	2.1	7.2	1.4	2.1	100.0
Eastern Cape	36.1	1.3	1.2	42.6	16.3	2.7	100.0
Northern Cape	67.7	3.0	2.5	21.5	3.6	1.7	100.0
Free State	57.6	3.1	3.4	24.8	9.3	1.7	100.0
KwaZulu-Natal	48.0	1.0	0.8	37.6	9.9	2.7	100.0
North West	35.9	1.0	1.9	51.6	8.3	1.4	100.0
Gauteng	82.1	2.1	2.3	8.4	2.5	2.6	100.0
Mpumalanga	38.0	1.6	1.7	47.0	9.9	1.9	100.0
Limpopo	13.8	0.7	1.0	67.2	15.5	1.8	100.0
Rural	4.9	0.7	1.8	72.4	17.9	2.3	100.0
Urban	83.9	1.9	1.6	7.6	2.7	2.2	100.0
Total	54.2	1.5	1.7	32.0	8.4	2.3	100.0

Sources: Own calculations, using Census 1996 and Census 2001, Statistics South Africa

The brief analysis of household access to services during the inter-censal period shows much improvement in terms of service delivery, but what is also evident is that households in provinces that contain former homeland areas (which were severely neglected during the apartheid regime) are particularly deprived of basic services.

Income and access

In this section, we bring together the analyses of income poverty and access to assets and services to create a more nuanced understanding of what it means to be the poorest members of society. We also identify who, across the income spectrum, has been most affected by changes in access to basic goods and services.

We begin by ordering households according to household income per capita. Households are then grouped into income quintiles. Specifically, the first income quintile reflects the poorest 20 per cent of households, the second income quintile the next poorest 20 per cent and the fifth income quintile, the 20 percent of highest 'income per person' households in the country. We will refer to the poorest 20 per cent as the ultra-poor and the next 20 per cent as the poor.

The derivation of these quintiles is described in detail in Appendix 2. Here we consider how the different income quintiles have fared with regard to changes in access to basic goods and services. Table 3.19 shows access rates by income quintile for 1996 and 2001.

Table 3.19 *Household services access by income quintile (excluding zeroes), 1996 and 2001*

	Quintiles 1996						Quintiles 2001					
	20%	40%	60%	80%	100%	Total	20%	40%	60%	80%	100%	Total
Dwelling types												
Formal	48.6	58.2	68.9	78.0	93.5	64.4	56.9	65.4	72.4	82.6	93.6	68.6
Informal	15.6	20.6	19.8	16.7	3.9	16.0	15.2	18.6	19.1	13.8	4.1	16.4
Traditional	34.7	20.0	9.9	3.9	1.5	18.1	27.7	15.7	8.2	3.3	1.9	14.8
Water access												
Piped	64.7	77.9	86.8	93.0	96.4	79.9	72.4	81.5	87.8	92.4	94.7	82.2
Borehole/tank/ vendor	10.0	7.3	5.5	3.4	2.1	6.1	5.9	4.4	3.1	1.7	0.9	3.7
Spring/river/dam/ pool	23.4	12.9	6.1	2.3	1.0	12.3	16.9	9.5	4.5	1.6	0.9	9.2
Energy source: Lighting												
Electricity	34.6	49.3	63.5	77.5	93.7	57.6	56.8	65.1	74.6	86.4	94.9	69.5
Paraffin	19.2	15.5	10.4	6.6	2.0	12.6	8.8	7.8	6.2	3.4	1.2	6.7
Candles	44.9	34.1	25.0	15.0	3.7	28.5	33.4	26.0	18.3	9.3	3.1	22.6
Energy source: Cooking												
Electricity	19.0	34.0	52.7	71.0	91.0	47.1	27.2	41.0	57.6	77.3	90.2	50.7
Paraffin	23.8	27.7	24.3	18.3	4.4	21.5	22.2	25.5	23.0	13.7	4.0	21.3
Wood	46.1	27.2	14.0	4.2	1.1	22.9	41.1	24.7	11.7	2.9	1.1	20.3

	Quintiles 1996						Quintiles 2001					
	20%	40%	60%	80%	100%	Total	20%	40%	60%	80%	100%	Total
Sanitation												
Flush/chemical toilet	20.7	37.5	57.1	76.2	93.0	50.2	29.0	43.5	60.2	78.5	91.6	53.4
Pit latrine	50.7	42.5	29.6	16.3	5.0	32.3	43.2	35.8	25.9	14.6	5.3	28.3
Bucket latrine	6.5	6.9	5.1	3.2	0.8	4.7	5.4	5.0	4.1	2.4	0.7	4.1
None	21.7	12.8	7.9	4.0	1.0	12.3	22.0	15.1	9.2	4.1	1.8	13.6
Refuse removal												
Removed by local authority	27.1	44.0	60.3	76.4	88.7	53.4	32.7	47.0	62.3	78.1	87.1	55.7
Own refuse dump	51.1	39.9	27.4	15.8	7.5	32.1	49.7	39.3	27.6	15.4	8.5	32.0
No rubbish disposal	16.3	10.1	6.1	3.5	1.3	9.5	14.0	9.6	5.9	2.9	1.2	8.4
Telephone												
In this dwelling/cellular phone	6.9	13.4	25.8	43.7	77.4	28.6	22.8	30.0	43.5	67.8	88.4	42.4
At a public telephone nearby	38.0	44.1	41.5	35.8	13.7	35.9	47.2	45.6	39.3	24.5	8.7	38.4
At another location	22.9	21.8	19.4	13.6	6.1	16.7	20.4	17.0	12.4	6.2	2.2	13.2
No access to a telephone	31.8	20.3	12.9	6.6	2.5	18.3	9.6	7.5	4.8	1.6	0.7	6.0

Sources: Census 1996 and Census 2001, 10 per cent samples
Note: This table including zero incomes shows a similar pattern and can be obtained from the authors.

The earlier discussion on access rates revealed that even though income poverty seems to have increased, access to basic services has improved, suggesting increases in well-being according to these measures. Table 3.19 shows that, unsurprisingly, in both 1996 and 2001, as household income rises so does access to better quality services. Indeed, the poor are the most severely deprived in terms of service delivery. It is apparent, nonetheless, that at the national level improvements have been made in all indicators over the five-year period. For most indicators the gains are less than five percentage points, or one percentage point per annum. In the cases of electricity used for lighting, and telephone access in the household, however, the increases in access have been impressive and in excess of ten percentage points.

When considering the extent of improvements in access by quintile, the evidence suggests that even though the poorest quintiles are most deprived, it is generally these households that are experiencing the greatest gains. The proportion of the ultra-poor living in formal dwellings increased from 49 per cent to 57 per cent in the period from 1996 to 2001. Access to piped water for this group rose from 65 per cent to 72 per cent, and even though electricity was used for cooking by a mere 27 per cent of households in 2001 (up from 19 per cent in 1996), electricity used for lighting rose from 35 per cent to 57 per cent of households, an increase of more than 20 percentage points over the period. Although sanitation improved, in that access to a flush or chemical toilet increased by eight percentage points to 29 per cent in 2001, this was mainly an upgrading from pit latrines to toilets. The proportion of households with no toilet, however, remained stable at a very high 22 per cent. While small gains have been made in refuse removal, only one in three of the poorest households had their refuse removed by a local authority in 2001. Finally, and most spectacular, is the marked increase in access to telephones over the inter-censal period. In 1996, 32 per cent of ultra-poor households had no access to a telephone at all. In 2001, this number fell to 10 per cent. Complementing this is the increase in households having a telephone or cellular phone in the home. This figure rose from a mere 7 per cent in 1996 to 23 per cent in 2001. Most of this improvement reflects the massive increase in uptake of cellular telephones.

The pattern of gains is similar for the second-poorest 20 per cent of households (quintile two), but generally the size of the improvements is slightly lower. The poorest 40 per cent of households outperform the remaining 60 per cent, in terms of advances in access to better quality services, on all measures except for telephones (while impressive gains have been achieved for the poor and ultra-poor, these have been even larger for the wealthier quintiles). Although income poverty has increased and access inequality is apparent, access has improved, and the gains have been greatest for the most deprived.

Conclusion

In this chapter, we have addressed changes in the well-being of South Africans between 1996 and 2001 across two dimensions – the distribution of income, and access to basic goods and services. The income-based analysis details increases in inequality and poverty at the national level. It also shows a persistent but changing population-group footprint in the structure of South African inequality and poverty. Inequality between population groups is still extremely high but continues to manifest a long-run decline in importance. The African group overwhelming dominates both the incidence and share of poverty. At the same time, the African group continues to increase its share in each of the top three income deciles. Inequality continues to widen within each group, evidencing something of the dynamism of post-apartheid South Africa. Within the African and coloured groups, and to a lesser extent the Asian/Indian group, this widening of inequality is a result of improvements at the top end of the intra-group distribution as well as increases in measured poverty at the bottom end. For white South Africans, the increase in inequality seems to be driven by increases in incomes for a few at the top of the distribution that are so large that they lead to a small increase in the aggregate income share of whites, and a widening of group disparity ratios. There is very little evidence of increasing white poverty.

Provincial poverty shares have remained fairly stable, with the important exceptions of an increase in the shares for the two best-off provinces (the Western Cape and Gauteng) as well as KwaZulu-Natal, and a decrease in the poverty share of the

Eastern Cape. These changes in the provincial poverty shares, together with a complementary increase in the urban share of poverty, give an indication of the importance of the migration of people from the poorest, predominantly rural provinces to major metropolitan centres.

The analysis of access poverty and inequality makes it clear that inequalities in access to basic services persist in South Africa on a population-group and regional level. Whites and Asians/Indians outperform coloureds, who, in turn, enjoy better access than Africans on nearly all measures. The wealthier provinces of Gauteng and the Western Cape have the greatest access rates to quality services, with the income-poor Limpopo and the Eastern Cape faring worst. Other provinces that perform quite poorly in terms of access to services include KwaZulu-Natal and Mpumalanga. Furthermore, we see that the urban/rural divide in terms of access to services is quite stark, with rural areas dramatically worse off than urban areas. Hence, we see that provinces that contain former homeland areas, which were severely neglected by the apartheid government, are particularly deprived of basic services.

Given these persistent inequalities in access, it is not surprising to find that households with poorer access tend to be found in the poorest income quintiles. However, it is important to note that between 1996 and 2001 access to basic goods and services improved for many households in South Africa, including those in the poorer quintiles. Thus, there is an optimistic lack of correspondence between the slight increase in poverty when measured in income terms and the decrease in poverty when measured in access terms.

Notes

1   Appendix 1 presents additional detail on the derivation of comparable 1996 and 2001 income variables as well as sensitivity analysis for many of these assumptions. On the whole, the access variables were measured in a consistent fashion across 1996 and 2001. Only the 'access to water' variable required detailed attention.

2   See Table 3A1.3 in Appendix 1 for a detailed set of results.

3   These results are presented in detail in Leibbrandt M et al. (2004: 43–55).

4   In order to keep the distribution within a narrower range without altering its shape, the graph plots the log of per capita income rather than per capita income itself. By logging we exclude all the zero-earning households. Figure 3.1, therefore, presents a picture of the income data as they are used in the rest of this chapter.

5   This paper forms the basis of Chapter 2 in the present volume.

6   Table 3A1.3 in Appendix 1 contains a more detailed set of these Gini coefficient results, including the standard errors and 95 per cent confidence intervals for all Gini coefficients.

7   See Bhorat et al. (2000) for a full explanation of such decompositions as well as a benchmarking against international results.

8   The rest of our graphical poverty analysis is conducted exclusively in terms of the non-zero income households.

9   Tables 3A1.4 and 3A1.5 in Appendix 1 reproduce racial headcount and poverty gap ratios presented in this section with standard errors and 95 per cent confidence intervals. In addition, these tables reproduce similar results if zero-income households are included.

10   As Figure 3.8 shows 2001 per capita incomes on the horizontal axis, the two poverty lines are merely the 2001 nominal equivalents of our R91 and R250 1996 poverty lines.

11   Questions on access to water differ for Census 1996 and Census 2001. However, Statistics South Africa provides a derived 'access to water' variable in the census data, which yields results that are comparable to those of the September editions of the Labour Force Survey for 2000, 2001 and 2002. In this chapter, the derived 'access to water' variable is used for analysis. A full discussion on the differences between the phrasing of questions in 1996 and 2001 can be found in Leibbrandt M et al. (2004: 56).

Appendix 1

Data decisions concerning the income variable

In addition to the two major data decisions that are described in the introduction to this chapter, a number of additional data decisions were made in order to prepare the income data for analysis. These are detailed in this appendix.

In both years, we find in the data that there are children below the age of 15 years with positive and often high incomes. We set these to zero. In 2001, a number of imputations were done on the income data to correct for missing data. We do not include the imputed data in our calculations for comparability with 1996.

To calculate the inequality and poverty indices, a continuous measure of income is required. Income is given in income bands in both censuses. To create a continuous measure of income, the midpoint of each band was assigned to each person in the band. The upper and lower (unbounded) bands were assigned the lower bound values. Furthermore, because we are interested in per capita income, we summed all positive individual income for each household and then divided by household size to obtain a monthly per capita measure of income.

For the poverty analysis, we chose two poverty lines to measure sensitivity. In 1996, we chose R250 per capita per month, and for comparability inflated this, using a CPI inflator, to R340 (the equivalent of R250 at 2001 prices). For the second line, we chose the $2 per day standard, which at Purchasing Power Parity, in 2001, equated to R4 per day per person or R124 per month.[1] This figure deflated, using a CPI deflator, equates to R91 in 1996.

For comparability between the two censuses and to avoid problems in calculating household size, we excluded all data on people living in institutions, and all results were weighted using the weights supplied by Statistics South Africa.

Table 3A1.1 shows that the exclusion of missing values and zero values reduces the household sample by close to 23 per cent in 1996 and close to 28 per cent in 2001.

These are large numbers. Table 3A1.2 then provides detailed information on these missing and zero values.

Table 3A1.1 *Descriptive statistics on zero and missing values in the 1996 and 2001 censuses*

	1996 households		2001 households	
Zero	1 750 790	18.62%	2 564 498	22.93%
Missing	412 173	4.38%	586 258	5.24%
Total	9 404 487		11 181 605	

Sources: Own calculations, using Census 1996 and Census 2001, Statistics South Africa

We provide a number of tables below to assess the impact of these data decisions.

Table 3A1.2 *Descriptive statistics on zero and missing percentage values in the 1996 and 2001 censuses, by province, population group and urban/rural area*

	1996				2001			
	Zero	Missing	Total zero + missing	Share of popu-lation	Zero	Missing	Total zero + missing	Share of popu-lation
Province								
Western Cape	3.28	7.66	3.99	9.69	4.32	14.17	6.14	9.86
Eastern Cape	24.70	11.55	22.56	15.85	19.11	18.94	19.08	14.56
Northern Cape	0.93	1.07	0.95	2.06	1.14	0.99	1.11	1.82
Free State	4.93	2.95	4.61	6.33	5.69	4.99	5.56	6.11
KwaZulu-Natal	23.11	22.99	23.09	20.69	24.51	23.53	24.33	21.24
North West	8.20	5.03	7.68	8.26	8.60	2.66	7.50	8.12
Gauteng	8.88	23.67	11.29	17.79	14.23	22.41	15.75	19.65
Mpumalanga	6.84	9.04	7.20	7.1	6.96	4.50	6.50	6.84
Limpopo	19.12	16.06	18.62	12.22	15.45	7.81	14.04	11.79
Total	100	100	100	100	100	100	100	100
Group								
African	94.29	72.36	90.77	76.74	94.02	72.06	89.96	79.18
Coloured	2.92	5.81	3.38	8.9	3.52	9.10	4.55	8.82
Asian/Indian	0.61	1.97	0.83	2.6	0.69	2.37	1	2.57
White	2.18	19.86	5.02	10.88	1.78	16.47	4.49	9.43
Total	100	100	100	100	100	100	100	100
Urban/rural								
Urban	29.23	54.80	33.40	53.33	41.51	59.16	44.77	55.97
Rural	70.77	45.20	66.60	46.67	58.49	40.84	55.23	44.03
Total	100	100	100	100	100	100	100	100

Sources: Own calculations, using Census 1996 and Census 2001, Statistics South Africa

Table 3A1.3 summarises the Gini coefficient at national, population group, provincial and urban/rural levels for 1996 and 2001 for various choices of income variable construction. The table is further broken down into whether people with zero incomes are included in the analysis or not.

The 'unconstrained' column in Table 3A1.3 refers to estimates obtained if we do not constrain the income bands in the 2001 census as described above. The 'constrained' results are for the variable used throughout the body of this chapter – that is, the upper category of 1996 (R30 001 per month) inflated to 2001 prices (R40 773.56). Not surprisingly, inequality estimates for the unconstrained income measure are much higher than for the constrained measure. For comparability with 1996, the constrained results are preferred in this chapter. The table also shows that measures of inequality are affected by whether we include the zero income estimates in the calculations or not. Including the zeros increases the Gini coefficient for both years. Standard errors for the estimates are very small. Importantly, though, ignoring the magnitude of the estimate and looking only at the trend, the reader will note that the observation of increased inequality between 1996 and 2001 is not affected by whether we include the zero incomes or not.

	1996				2001 Unconstrained				2001 Constrained			
	With zero		Without zero		With zero		Without zero		With zero		Without zero	
	Estimate	95% Conf. interval	Estimate	95% Conf. interval	Estimate	95% Conf. interval	Estimate	95% Conf. interval	Estimate	95% Conf. interval	Estimate	95% Conf. interval
National	0.7395 (0.0002)	0.7391 0.7399	0.6786 (0.0003)	0.6780 0.6791	0.8179 (0.0004)	0.8172 0.8187	0.7653 (0.0005)	0.7642 0.7664	0.7906 (0.0003)	0.7900 0.7912	0.7301 (0.0003)	0.7295 0.7307
Group												
African	0.7069 (0.0004)	0.7061 0.7076	0.6189 (0.0003)	0.6182 0.6196	0.7760 (0.0007)	0.7745 0.7776	0.6952 (0.0010)	0.6932 0.6972	0.7536 (0.0004)	0.7528 0.7543	0.6648 (0.0005)	0.6638 0.6657
Coloured	0.5550 (0.0009)	0.5531 0.5568	0.5261 (0.0007)	0.5245 0.5276	0.6584 (0.0013)	0.6557 0.6610	0.6248 (0.0025)	0.6195 0.6301	0.6345 (0.0006)	0.6331 0.6358	0.5985 (0.0012)	0.5961 0.6010
Asian/Indian	0.5016 (0.0017)	0.4980 0.5052	0.4787 (0.0016)	0.4754 0.4820	0.6234 (0.0032)	0.6167 0.6301	0.5994 (0.0024)	0.5945 0.6043	0.5830 (0.0016)	0.5795 0.5864	0.5563 (0.0015)	0.5531 0.5596
White	0.4645 (0.0006)	0.4633 0.4657	0.4428 (0.0007)	0.4413 0.4443	0.6044 (0.0012)	0.6020 0.6068	0.5862 (0.0012)	0.5837 0.5887	0.5276 (0.0007)	0.5262 0.5290	0.5059 (0.0006)	0.5047 0.5071
Province												
Western Cape	0.6190 (0.0006)	0.6177 0.6202	0.5931 (0.0007)	0.5916 0.5946	0.7358 (0.0015)	0.7328 0.7389	0.7063 (0.0015)	0.7032 0.7094	0.7011 (0.0007)	0.6997 0.7026	0.6678 (0.0008)	0.6661 0.6694
Eastern Cape	0.7807 (0.0005)	0.7797 0.7818	0.6901 (0.0006)	0.6887 0.6915	0.8322 (0.0010)	0.8302 0.8343	0.7606 (0.0016)	0.7572 0.7641	0.8091 (0.0007)	0.8077 0.8105	0.7278 (0.0007)	0.7263 0.7294
Northern Cape	0.6930 (0.0016)	0.6896 0.6965	0.6647 (0.0013)	0.6620 0.6673	0.7736 (0.0038)	0.7656 0.7815	0.7376 (0.0040)	0.7294 0.7459	0.7428 (0.0016)	0.7396 0.7461	0.7020 (0.0021)	0.6977 0.7063
Free State	0.7300 (0.0008)	0.7283 0.7317	0.6843 (0.0009)	0.6824 0.6862	0.8086 (0.0020)	0.8043 0.8128	0.7587 (0.0023)	0.7539 0.7636	0.7796 (0.0011)	0.7773 0.7819	0.7222 (0.0014)	0.7193 0.7251
KwaZulu-Natal	0.7547 (0.0005)	0.7536 0.7557	0.6884 (0.0006)	0.6872 0.6896	0.8245 (0.0009)	0.8228 0.8263	0.7627 (0.0011)	0.7604 0.7650	0.8011 (0.0005)	0.8000 0.8021	0.7311 (0.0006)	0.7298 0.7325
North West	0.7097 (0.0006)	0.7083 0.7110	0.6436 (0.0006)	0.6423 0.6448	0.7864 (0.0017)	0.7829 0.7900	0.7227 (0.0025)	0.7174 0.7280	0.7608 (0.0009)	0.7590 0.7626	0.6896 (0.0013)	0.6867 0.6924
Gauteng	0.6526 (0.0006)	0.6513 0.6539	0.6158 (0.0004)	0.6150 0.6166	0.7762 (0.0007)	0.7746 0.7777	0.7324 (0.0008)	0.7306 0.7341	0.7365 (0.0005)	0.7354 0.7376	0.6850 (0.0006)	0.6836 0.6863
Mpumalanga	0.7322 (0.0009)	0.7303 0.7341	0.6716 (0.0010)	0.6696 0.6736	0.8051 (0.0019)	0.8011 0.8091	0.7488 (0.0013)	0.7461 0.7514	0.7775 (0.0011)	0.7752 0.7798	0.7133 (0.0012)	0.7107 0.7159
Limpopo	0.7714 (0.0008)	0.7697 0.7732	0.6735 (0.0012)	0.6710 0.6760	0.8080 (0.0016)	0.8047 0.8114	0.7301 (0.0017)	0.7266 0.7335	0.7926 (0.0010)	0.7906 0.7947	0.7085 (0.0008)	0.7068 0.7102
Urban/rural												
Urban	0.6617 (0.0003)	0.6611 0.6623	0.6224 (0.0003)	0.6218 0.6231	0.7749 (0.0005)	0.7740 0.7759	0.7299 (0.0004)	0.7289 0.7308	0.7411 (0.0003)	0.7405 0.7417	0.6893 (0.0004)	0.6885 0.6901
Rural	0.7502 (0.0004)	0.7492 0.7511	0.6495 (0.0006)	0.6483 0.6507	0.8028 (0.0010)	0.8008 0.8048	0.7195 (0.0020)	0.7153 0.7237	0.7762 (0.0006)	0.7748 0.7775	0.6818 (0.0011)	0.6795 0.6841

Sources: Own calculations, using Census 1996 and Census 2001, Statistics South Africa

Note: Standard errors are given in parentheses.

Tables 3A1.4 and 3A1.5 summarise the poverty levels by race for the 'with zero income' and 'without zero income' estimates for 1996 and 2001.[2]

Table 3A1.4 Poverty levels by race, 1996

1996

Group	With zeros Headcount Estimate	With zeros Headcount 95% Conf. interval	With zeros Poverty gap ratio Estimate	With zeros Poverty gap ratio 95% Conf. interval	Without zeros Headcount Estimate	Without zeros Headcount 95% Conf. interval	Without zeros Poverty gap ratio Estimate	Without zeros Poverty gap ratio 95% Conf. interval
African								
$2 per day	0.4896 (0.0003)	0.4890 0.4902	0.3416 (0.0003)	0.3411 0.3421	0.3364 (0.0003)	0.3358 0.3371	0.1439 (0.0002)	0.1436 0.1443
R250 (1996)	0.7080 (0.0003)	0.7074 0.7085	0.5200 (0.0003)	0.5195 0.5205	0.6203 (0.0003)	0.6197 0.6210	0.3760 (0.0002)	0.3755 0.3765
Coloured								
$2 per day	0.1551 (0.0007)	0.1538 0.1564	0.0936 (0.0005)	0.0926 0.0945	0.1003 (0.0006)	0.0991 0.1014	0.0347 (0.0003)	0.0342 0.0352
R250 (1996)	0.3817 (0.0009)	0.3800 0.3835	0.2079 (0.0006)	0.2068 0.2091	0.3416 (0.0009)	0.3398 0.3433	0.1565 (0.0005)	0.1555 0.1575
Asian/Indian								
$2 per day	0.0695 (0.0008)	0.0679 0.0711	0.0530 (0.0007)	0.0516 0.0543	0.0267 (0.0005)	0.0257 0.0278	0.0094 (0.0002)	0.0090 0.0099
R250 (1996)	0.1471 (0.0012)	0.1449 0.1494	0.0878 (0.0008)	0.0862 0.0893	0.1080 (0.0010)	0.1059 0.1100	0.0458 (0.0005)	0.0448 0.0469
White								
$2 per day	0.0495 (0.0004)	0.0488 0.0502	0.0430 (0.0003)	0.0424 0.0437	0.0109 (0.0002)	0.0106 0.0113	0.0042 (0.0001)	0.0041 0.0044
R250 (1996)	0.0704 (0.0004)	0.0695 0.0712	0.0542 (0.0004)	0.0535 0.0549	0.0327 (0.0003)	0.0321 0.0333	0.0159 (0.0002)	0.0156 0.0162

Sources: Own calculations, using Census 1996, Statistics South Africa
Note: Standard errors are given in parentheses.

Table 3A1.5 *Poverty levels by race, 2001*

2001

	With zeros						Without zeros					
	Headcount			Poverty gap ratio			Headcount			Poverty gap ratio		
	Estimate	95% Conf. interval		Estimate	95% Conf. interval		Estimate	95% Conf. interval		Estimate	95% Conf. interval	
Group												
African												
$2 per day	0.5246 (0.0003)	0.5240	0.5252	0.3704 (0.0003)	0.3699	0.3709	0.3533 (0.0003)	0.3526	0.3540	0.1434 (0.0002)	0.1431	0.1438
R250 (1996)	0.7561 (0.0003)	0.7555	0.7566	0.5547 (0.0002)	0.5542	0.5552	0.6681 (0.0003)	0.6675	0.6688	0.3942 (0.0002)	0.3937	0.3947
Coloured												
$2 per day	0.2052 (0.0007)	0.2038	0.2066	0.1298 (0.0005)	0.1288	0.1309	0.1271 (0.0006)	0.1259	0.1284	0.0443 (0.0003)	0.0438	0.0449
R250 (1996)	0.4598 (0.0009)	0.4581	0.4616	0.2627 (0.0006)	0.2614	0.2639	0.4068 (0.0009)	0.4050	0.4086	0.1902 (0.0005)	0.1892	0.1913
Asian/Indian												
$2 per day	0.0921 (0.0010)	0.0902	0.0940	0.0699 (0.0009)	0.0683	0.0715	0.0342 (0.0006)	0.0329	0.0354	0.0106 (0.0003)	0.0101	0.0111
R250 (1996)	0.1940 (0.0013)	0.1914	0.1966	0.1142 (0.0010)	0.1124	0.1161	0.1426 (0.0012)	0.1402	0.1449	0.0577 (0.0006)	0.0565	0.0589
White												
$2 per day	0.0538 (0.0004)	0.0530	0.0546	0.0472 (0.0004)	0.0464	0.0480	0.0103 (0.0002)	0.0099	0.0107	0.0035 (0.0001)	0.0033	0.0036
R250 (1996)	0.0823 (0.0005)	0.0813	0.0834	0.0596 (0.0004)	0.0588	0.0604	0.0402 (0.0004)	0.0395	0.0410	0.0164 (0.0002)	0.0161	0.0168

Sources: Own calculations, using Census 2001, Statistics South Africa
Note: Standard errors are given in parentheses.

Appendix 2

The derivation of household income quintiles for a comparison of the distribution of household access with the distribution of household income

Tables 3A2.1 and 3A2.2 show the cut-off levels for the income quintile bands for 1996 and 2001 in real terms (1996 rands). It must be noted that these cut-offs reflect per capita income at the household level. We choose the household as the unit of analysis for this section, as service provision generally occurs at the household level. As poorer households have larger average household sizes, the share of the population relating to the bottom quintiles will be greater than the respective household share. For example, the poorest 20 per cent of households in 1996 account for 29 per cent of the population. In 2001, the poorest 20 per cent of households account for an even higher 34 per cent of individuals. In our income analysis in the chapter, we use individuals as the unit of analysis. Thus, those in the bottom quintile here make up close to the bottom two quintiles in the analysis of these sections. It is this re-division of households that accounts for the fact that per capita income appears to go up in most quintiles from 1996 to 2001 in this household-level analysis, whereas it falls in most quintiles in the analysis presented in the chapter.

Table 3A2.1 *Income quintiles (excluding zeroes), 1996*

Quintile	No. of households	Percentage	Cumulative percentage	Mean per capita household income	Min.	Max.	Share of population
1	1 396 336	20.0	20.0	62.7	3.0	110.3	29.1
2	1 414 445	20.3	40.3	180.8	110.9	275.3	24.1
3	1 383 028	19.8	60.1	396.8	275.3	600.1	18.2
4	1 392 766	20.0	80.0	923.0	600.1	1 400.1	15.2
5	1 393 693	20.0	100.0	3 501.6	1 400.2	30 001.0	13.4
Total	6 980 268	100.0	100.0	1 011.1	3.0	30 001.0	100.0

Sources: Own calculations, using Census 1996 and Census 2001, Statistics South Africa

Table 3A2.2 *Income quintiles (excluding zeroes), 2001*

Quintile	No. of households	Percentage	Cumulative percentage	Mean per capita household income	Min.	Max.	Share of population
1	1 822 208	22.7	22.7	91.4	7.4	150.1	34.2
2	1 655 735	20.6	43.3	237.8	150.2	300.3	20.6
3	1 598 556	19.9	63.1	522.9	300.3	600.5	16.9
4	1 369 577	17.0	80.2	1 138.2	616.8	1 800.3	14.7
5	1 595 643	19.8	100.0	5 751.1	1 800.3	40 773.6	13.6
Total	8 041 719	100.0	100.0	1 508.6	7.4	40 773.6	100.0

Sources: Own calculations, using Census 1996 and Census 2001, Statistics South Africa

Table 3A2.3 *Income quintiles (including zeroes), 1996*

Quintile	No. of households	Percentage	Cumulative percentage	Mean per capita household income	Min.	Max.	Share of population
1	1 734 612	20.03	20.0	0.40	0.0	14.4	20.4
2	1 729 214	19.97	40.0	77.9	14.6	145.2	28.5
3	1 847 902	21.34	61.4	265.6	145.4	375.3	21.0
4	1 616 027	18.66	80.0	694.6	375.3	1 166.8	17.3
5	1 730 851	19.99	100.0	3 067.3	1 166.8	30 001.0	12.9
Total	8 658 606	100.0	100.0	815.1	0.0	14.4	100.0

Table 3A2.4 *Income quintiles (including zeroes), 2001*

Quintile	No. of households	Percentage	Cumulative percentage	Mean per capita household income	Min.	Max.	Share of population
1	2 574 933	24.3	24.3	0.0	0.0	0.0	22.4
2	1 822 208	17.2	41.4	91.4	7.4	150.1	26.7
3	1 998 235	18.8	60.2	262.6	150.2	400.2	20.1
4	2 360 690	22.2	82.5	783.8	400.2	1 200.5	17.5
5	1 860 587	17.5	100.0	5 154.4	1 213.6	40 773.6	13.4
Total	10 616 653	100.0	100.0	1 142.7	0.0	40 773.6	100.0

Notes

1   World Bank (2003) *World Development Indicators*. World Bank: Washington, DC.

2   A complete set of poverty results at provincial and rural–urban levels for the income estimates, including and excluding zeros, is presented in Leibbrandt M et al. (2004).

References

Bhorat H, Leibbrandt M & Woolard I (2000) Understanding contemporary household inequality in South Africa, *Studies in Economics and Econometrics* 24(3): 31–52.

Central Statistical Service (1996) *Census 1996 10% sample*. Pretoria: Statistics South Africa.

Cronje M & Budlender D (2004) Comparing Census 1996 and Census 2001: An operational perspective, *Southern African Journal of Demography* 9(1): 67–89.

Hoogeveen JG & Özler B (2005) *Not separate, not equal: Poverty and inequality in post-apartheid South Africa*. William Davidson Institute Working Paper No. 739.

Leibbrandt M, Poswell L, Naidoo P, Welch M & Woolard I (2004) *Measuring recent changes in South African inequality and poverty using 1996 and 2001 Census data*. CSSR Working Paper No. 84. Centre for Social Science Research, University of Cape Town.

Statistics South Africa (2000) *Measuring poverty in South Africa*. Pretoria: Statistics South Africa.

Statistics South Africa (2001) *Census 2001 10% sample*. Pretoria: Statistics South Africa.

Whiteford AC and van Seventer DE (2000) South Africa's changing income distribution in the 1990s, *Journal of Studies in Economics and Econometrics* 24(3): 7–30.

World Bank (2003) *World Development Indicators*. World Bank: Washington, DC.

Evolution of the labour market: 1995–2002

Haroon Bhorat and Morné Oosthuizen

Introduction

Since 1994, the South African economy has undergone significant changes as the government has implemented various policies aimed at redressing the injustices of the past, fleshing out the welfare system, and improving the country's competitiveness as it becomes increasingly integrated into the global economy. These policies have, directly or indirectly, impacted on the labour market and, consequently, on the lives of millions of South Africans.

This chapter's chief objective is the analysis of some of the changes in the South African labour market in the post-apartheid era. The period between 1995 and 2002 began with much promise and many challenges, as the economy liberalised and normal trade relations were resumed with the rest of the world. In 1996, two years after the African National Congress (ANC) came to power, it unveiled the macro-economic strategy named 'Growth, Employment and Redistribution' (GEAR). This strategy predicted, amongst other things, employment growth averaging 270 000 jobs per annum from 1996 to 2000, with the number of new jobs created rising from 126 000 in 1996 to 409 000 in 2000 (Department of Finance 1996). Unfortunately, for a variety of reasons, these projections were not realised. In fact, in terms of the labour market, the experience of the second half of the 1990s appears to have fallen short of even the baseline scenario contained in the GEAR document, which projected a net increase in (non-agricultural formal) employment of slightly more than 100 000 jobs per annum (Department of Finance 1996: 7).

Consequently, the performance of the labour market and the various policies that impact on this critical factor market have come under increasing scrutiny. At the same time, there is a certain degree of confusion as to the actual performance of the labour market since 1994/5. This is largely a result of the flaws that exist in the period's early surveys, and the consequent refinement and improvement of the questionnaires. Furthermore, different groups of surveys estimate different employment numbers for the same period, because of differences in their design.

This chapter begins by looking at the labour force and how its two components, employment and unemployment, have changed since 1995. Attention is also paid to the composition of the labour force and to changes in the propensity of working-age individuals to enter the labour force. The next section then discusses in detail some of the key issues, in terms of employment and unemployment, that arise from the data, including the 'jobless growth' debate and the labour market issues surrounding three intertwined variables, namely race, education and age. A number of other issues are also dealt with, including formal- and informal-sector employment, the spatial distribution of employment and unemployment, and a brief consideration of so-called 'discouraged workseekers'.

The labour force

Aggregate employment and unemployment trends

The labour force is defined as comprising those individuals between the ages of 15 and 65 years who are economically active, and hence it is calculated as the sum of the employed and the unemployed. Figures for the labour force based on the official and expanded definitions of unemployment are presented in Table 4.1. This chapter uses two standard definitions of unemployment, namely the narrow definition of unemployment (used as the official definition in South Africa by the government) and the broad definition of unemployment. Individuals are narrowly unemployed if they '(a) did not work during the seven days prior to the interview, (b) want to work and are available to start work within a week of the interview, and (c) have taken active steps to look for work or to start some form of self-employment in the four weeks prior to the interview' (Statistics South Africa 2002c: xv). The expanded (or broad) definition of unemployment does not include criterion (c). Over 61 per cent of the national population, or 28.0 million people, were between the ages of 15 and 65 years in 2002, up from 24.2 million in 1995. Using the narrow (official) definition of unemployment, the labour force grew from 11.5 million in 1995 to 15.9 million in 2002, with almost two-thirds of the increase attributable to growing unemployment.. Similarly, growth in broad (expanded) unemployment accounted for over 70 per cent of the growth of the broad labour force of 5.2 million, to 19.0 million in 2002. Interestingly, employment growth managed to keep pace with the growth of the working-age population (those between 15 and 65 years of age), which expanded by around 2.1 per cent per annum on average. However, this rate of growth was far below that required to absorb the large number of individuals who entered the labour market over the period. Consequently, unemployment growth over the period was extremely rapid, with narrow unemployment more than doubling (equivalent to an average annual growth rate of 13.2 per cent) and broadly defined unemployment growing by an average of 9.4 per cent per annum.

Table 4.1 *The South African labour force, 1995 and 2002*

	1995	2002	Total change		
	thousands	thousands	thousands	percentage	average annual growth rate
15–65-year-olds	24 231	27 984	3 753	15.5	2.1
Employed	9 515	11 029	1 514	15.9	2.1
Narrow unemployed	2 032	4 837	2 806	138.1	13.2
Broad unemployed	4 239	7 925	3 686	87.0	9.4
Narrow labour force	11 547	15 866	4 320	37.4	4.6
Broad labour force	13 754	18 954	5 200	37.8	4.7

Sources: OHS 1995, LFS 2002 (2) (Statistics South Africa)

The combination of these two trends – relatively slow employment growth and rapid labour force growth – has resulted in significant increases in the unemployment rate, regardless of definition, between 1995 and 2002. Official unemployment stood at 31 per cent in 2002, up from 18 per cent seven years earlier, while the broadly unemployed comprised 42 per cent of the labour force in 2002, up from 31 per cent in 1995. It is therefore clear that the South African economy in the first decade of the twenty-first century faces an important challenge, one that it has been unable to meet successfully in the immediate post-apartheid era. By definition, labour force growth can be attributed to a combination of two trends, namely increased absolute employment and/or increased absolute unemployment. While employment has expanded, Table 4.1 shows that it has not been able to keep pace with labour force growth; hence, labour force growth has largely translated into increasing numbers of unemployed, with both broad and narrow unemployment rates having increased since 1995.

The broad labour force

The composition of the broadly defined labour force is presented in Table 4.2.[1] The labour force is dominated by African individuals (more than 70 per cent), with whites accounting for around 12 per cent in 2002, down from 14.4 per cent in 1995. Their dominance within and faster rate of entry into the labour force means that Africans account for about 85 per cent of the increase in the size of the labour force over the period. By 2002, the labour force was almost evenly split between males and females, marking a continuation of the trend of labour force feminisation identified by Casale and Posel (2002: 164), who estimated the 1999 female share of the broad labour force at 48.2 per cent based on the OHS 1999 (Statistics South Africa 2000). This rise in the female share is the result of a very rapid rise in the female labour force participation rate, and means that females account for more than 61 per cent of the net increase in the labour force. This pattern of increased female participation is evident within all race groups.

Approximately three in five labour force members are between the ages of 25 and 44, with the proportion in 2002 slightly lower than that in 1995. This change is due to increases in the proportions of worker in the 15–24-year and 45–54-year age groups. Most of the growth in the labour force (around 55 per cent) was located in the two youngest age groups, due at least in part to the country's bottom-heavy age-pyramid, which reveals that younger age groups are larger than older age groups. At the same time, it appears that the South African labour force is slowly becoming more educated, on average. The proportion of individuals with completed secondary education rose from 21 per cent in 1995 to 24 per cent in 2002, while completely uneducated individuals now account for only 6.0 per cent of the labour force, compared to 8.6 per cent in 1995. However, the increase in the number of tertiary-educated labour force members has barely kept pace with the rate of total labour force growth, while 19 per cent of the net increase in the labour force comprises individuals with complete or incomplete primary education. Those with incomplete and complete secondary education accounted for almost 70 per cent of the growth in the labour force.

Table 4.2 *Snapshot of the South African labour force (broadly defined), 1995 and 2002*

		1995		2002		Change	
		thousands	share	thousands	share	thousands	share
TOTAL		13 754	100.0	18 912	100.0	5 158	100.0
By race	African	9 875	71.8	14 271	75.5	4 396	85.2
	Coloured	1 485	10.8	1 837	9.7	352	6.8
	Asian/Indian	417	3.0	572	3.0	156	3.0
	White	1 976	14.4	2 231	11.8	254	4.9
By gender	Male	7 598	55.2	9 587	50.7	1 989	38.6
	Female	6 155	44.8	9 325	49.3	3 169	61.4
By age	15–24 years	2 403	17.5	3 704	19.6	1 301	25.2
	25–34 years	4 977	36.2	6 523	34.5	1 545	30.0
	35–44 years	3 670	26.7	4 900	25.9	1 231	23.9
	45–54 years	1 941	14.1	2 798	14.8	857	16.6
	55–65 years	762	5.5	991	5.2	229	4.4
By education level	No education	1 182	8.6	1 138	6.0	−43	−0.8
	Incomplete primary	2 441	17.8	3 070	16.2	628	12.2
	Complete primary	1 017	7.4	1 378	7.3	361	7.0
	Incomplete secondary	4 573	33.2	6 471	34.2	1 898	36.8
	Complete secondary	2 873	20.9	4 562	24.1	1 689	32.7
	Tertiary	1 430	10.4	1 962	10.4	532	10.3
	Other/unknown	237	1.7	335	1.8	98	1.9
By location	Urban	8 734	63.5	11 820	62.5	3 085	59.8
	Rural	5 020	36.5	7 134	37.7	2 115	41.0

Sources: OHS 1995, LFS 2002 (Statistics South Africa)

The bulk of the labour force is located in urban areas, with less than 38 per cent in rural areas in 2002. However, the proportion in rural areas increased slightly between the two surveys, with rural areas accounting for 41 per cent of the growth in the labour force. What makes this interesting is that the rural labour force grew more rapidly over the period, despite the continuing urbanisation of rural jobseekers. This phenomenon is likely to be linked to the increased labour force participation of females, as well as to improvements in the collection of data on informal-sector activity. In fact, rural African females account for almost one-quarter of the increase in the labour force between 1995 and 2002, although it is impossible to determine this group's full contribution because of migration to urban areas.

The trends presented above are not independent of race, and therefore sometimes very different patterns can be observed within race groups. Table 4.3 presents the age and education breakdowns for African and white individuals.[2] The gender breakdowns for the four race groups are very similar, with females accounting for around 61 per cent of the growth in the labour force, and are therefore not included here.

Population growth rate differences amongst the race groups have resulted in marked differences in the age structure of the labour force and in the contribution of different age groups to labour force growth. The bulk of the African and white labour force is between the ages of 25 and 44 years. The major difference between these two groups lies in the age groups responsible for labour force growth. Amongst Africans, nearly one-third of labour force growth occurred in the 25–34-year age group, with a further 28.9 per cent and 22.0 per cent occurring in the 15–24-year and 35–44-year age groups. The three youngest age groups therefore account for over 82 per cent of African labour force growth. In contrast, the bulk of net white labour force growth occurred in the three oldest age groups: 40.9 per cent were in the 45–54-year age group, 31.5 per cent in the 35–44-year age group and 27.0 per cent in the 55–65-year age group. Together, the increase in the size of these three age groups is almost exactly equal to the total growth in the white labour force, even though growth of the labour force amongst 25–34-year-olds was equivalent to 14.6 per cent of the net increase. However, this growth was negated by the fact that amongst 15–24-year-olds, the white labour force shrank. This could be partly a result of the declining birth rate amongst whites, and partly a result of young individuals continuing with their education for a longer period than in 1995.

Table 4.3 *Snapshot of the South African labour force (broadly defined) by race, 1995 and 2002*

		1995		2002		Change	
		thou-sands	share of race total	thou-sands	share of race total	thou-sands	share of race total
By race and age group							
African	15–24 years	1 628	16.5	2 898	20.3	1 270	28.9
	25–34 years	3 728	37.8	5 115	35.8	1 387	31.6
	35–44 years	2 678	27.1	3 647	25.6	969	22.0
	45–54 years	1 317	13.3	1 950	13.7	633	14.4
	55–65 years	524	5.3	664	4.6	140	3.2
White	15–24 years	312	15.8	276	12.4	−36	−14.1
	25–34 years	576	29.2	614	27.5	37	14.6
	35–44 years	541	27.4	621	27.8	80	31.5
	45–54 years	388	19.6	492	22.1	104	40.9
	55–65 years	159	8.0	227	10.2	69	27.0
By race and education							
African	No education	1 087	11.0	1 060	7.4	−27	−0.6
	Incomplete primary	2 133	21.6	2 778	19.5	645	14.7
	Complete primary	844	8.5	1 192	8.4	348	7.9
	Incomplete secondary	3 375	34.2	5 177	36.3	1 803	41.0
	Complete secondary	1 574	15.9	2 888	20.2	1 314	29.9
	Tertiary	682	6.9	973	6.8	291	6.6
	Other/unknown	179	1.8	206	1.4	27	0.6
White	No education	1	0.0	2	0.1	1	0.4
	Incomplete primary	7	0.3	6	0.3	−1	−0.3
	Complete primary	1	0.1	9	0.4	8	3.0
	Incomplete secondary	423	21.4	374	16.8	−50	−19.5
	Complete secondary	900	45.6	981	44.0	80	31.6
	Tertiary	599	30.3	792	35.5	193	75.8
	Other/unknown	45	2.3	67	3.0	23	8.9

Sources: OHS 1995, LFS 2002 (Statistics South Africa)

The validity of the latter possibility is confirmed by the fact that tertiary-educated individuals accounted for more than three-quarters of net white labour force growth over the period, with those with completed secondary education accounting for nearly one-third. This was balanced out by a decline in the number of white labour force participants with incomplete secondary education. This meant that by 2002, almost 80 per cent of the white labour force could boast either complete secondary (44.0 per cent) or tertiary (35.5 per cent) education. African labour force growth, in contrast, derived largely from the rapid increase in the number of African labour force participants with incomplete and complete secondary education (with growth rates of 41.0 per cent and 29.9 per cent respectively). Only about 27 per cent of African labour force participants had completed secondary or tertiary education, with the proportion of tertiary-educated individuals falling slightly to 6.8 per cent of the African labour force.

Labour force participation

The initial evidence presented suggests that an important root cause of unemployment is the fact that the labour force is growing at a rate far greater than both the population between the ages of 15 and 65 years and total employment. In particular, growth in the number of labour force members has occurred mainly amongst the younger sections of the population. This means that, on average, the probability of an individual being a member of the labour force is increasing over time. This overall probability is measured by the labour force participation rate (LFPR) and is defined as the proportion of labour force members within the total number of individuals between the ages of 15 and 65 years.

Table 4.4 presents broad labour force participation rates for the South African economy in 1995 and 2002 by various demographic and locational characteristics. Overall, the proportion of working-age individuals who are members of the broadly defined labour force rose from 57 per cent in 1995 to 68 per cent in 2002, with the narrow LFPR increasing by nine percentage points to 57 per cent. In general, labour force participation is highest amongst coloured and white adults,[3] at 71 per cent and 70 per cent respectively in 2002. Just less than two-thirds of females are labour force members, compared with 72 per cent of males. This gap may be artificially widened because of the fact that the female retirement age is 60 years, five years earlier than that of males. Labour force participation amongst urban dwellers, at 72 per cent in 2002, is more than ten percentage points higher than in rural areas, although this gap has narrowed substantially since 1995. This urban–rural pattern is clearly manifested in the provincial LFPR variations, with provinces with more urbanised adult populations such as Gauteng, the Western Cape, the Free State and the Northern Cape having higher LFPRs than those with more predominant rural adult populations. As expected, labour force participation is lowest amongst the youngest and oldest age groups (rates in the low forties in 2002), due respectively to relatively higher rates of attendance of educational institutions and retirement. In 2002, approximately 56 per cent of 15–24-year-olds were attending some type of educational institution, with around 95 per cent of these individuals being outside the labour force. Almost nine in ten 25–44-year-olds are economically active, up from around eight in ten in 1995.

Table 4.4 *Broad labour force participation rates in South Africa, 1995–2002*

Category	1995	2002	Change	Category	1995	2002	Change
African	54.3	67.1	12.8	15–24 years	29.4	41.2	11.8
Coloured	65.4	70.9	5.5	25–34 years	77.5	88.9	11.4
Asian/Indian	58.4	67.4	9.0	35–44 years	79.1	86.8	7.7
White	64.6	69.6	5.1	45–54 years	69.9	76.2	6.3
Male	65.8	72.0	6.2	55–65 years	34.6	43.5	8.9
Female	48.5	63.9	15.3	Western Cape	66.5	69.9	3.4
African male	62.5	70.1	7.6	Eastern Cape	47.3	59.6	12.4
African female	47.0	64.4	17.4	Northern Cape	59.7	68.3	8.6
Coloured male	73.9	77.9	4.0	Free State	62.6	69.1	6.5
Coloured female	57.6	64.7	7.2	KwaZulu-Natal	53.1	66.5	13.4
Asian/Indian male	77.9	79.2	1.3	North West	56.4	66.2	9.8
Asian/Indian female	40.2	56.3	16.2	Gauteng	68.7	77.3	8.6
White male	76.3	77.9	1.6	Mpumalanga	54.9	65.7	10.7
White female	53.2	61.3	8.2	Limpopo	39.9	61.8	21.9
Urban	63.8	72.2	8.4	**Total broad LFPR**	56.8	67.7	11.0
Rural	47.6	61.5	13.8	**Total narrow LFPR**	47.7	56.7	9.0

Sources: OHS 1995, LFS 2002 (2) (Statistics South Africa)

Several groups have seen substantial increases in labour force participation over the period. The key group here is probably African females, whose LFPR increased from 47 per cent to 64 per cent between 1995 and 2002. The reason why it is regarded as 'key' is that the impact of increased labour force participation amongst this group is evident in groups defined according to other characteristics. Adult females accounted for 54 per cent of all rural adults (African adult females alone are 51 per cent of the rural adult population) and consequently, the rural LFPR increased by almost fourteen percentage points, from 48 per cent to 62 per cent. At the same time, provinces with more rural adult populations, for example Limpopo, KwaZulu-Natal, the Eastern Cape and Mpumalanga, experienced the greatest increases in labour force participation. Large increases were also found to have occurred amongst the two youngest age groups, namely 15–24-year-olds and 25–34-year-olds. Relative to 1995 levels, labour force participation has increased most rapidly amongst Limpopo adults (equivalent to a 55 per cent increase on the 1995 LFPR), Asian/Indian females (40 per cent), 15–24-year-olds (40 per cent), African females (37 per cent), females in general (32 per cent), rural adults (29 per cent), Eastern Cape adults (26 per cent) and 55–65-year-olds (26 per cent).

The enormous task, in terms of job creation, is clearly evident. The economy, while still experiencing disappointingly low, though positive, rates of economic growth, has to deal with the original deficit in jobs from 1995 as well as the rapid increase in the number of labour force members. Thus, the target is not a stationary one, but continues to move seemingly beyond the reach of policy-makers. In order to address the rapidly increasing unemployment rate, it is vital for analysts to focus on understanding the reasons underlying the jump in labour force participation, particularly in the present context in which unemployment has been high and rising for an extended period of time. The inability of the economy to create jobs at the same pace at which the labour force has been growing is clearly illustrated in Table 4.5. The table compares employment, broad and narrow unemployment and the total labour force over the seven years between 1995 and 2002. Growth in unemployment over the period has been rapid, with the rates of broad and narrow unemployment growth exceeding that of employment growth by factors of 5.5 and 8.7 respectively, albeit from a relatively smaller base.

Table 4.5 *Employment and labour force growth, 1995–2002*

Category	1995 (Oct.) thousands	2002 (Sep.) thousands	Change absolute thousands	Change percentage	Target growth rate	Employ-ment absorp-tion rate
Broad definition estimates						
Employment	9 515	11 029	1 514	15.9		
Unemployment (broad)	4 239	7 925	3 686	87.0	54.6	29.1
Labour force	13 754	18 954	5 200	37.8		
Official definition estimates						
Employment	9 515	11 029	1 514	15.9		
Unemployment (narrow)	2 032	4 837	2 806	138.1	45.4	35.0
Labour force	11 547	15 866	4 320	37.4		

Sources: OHS 1995, LFS 2002 (2) (Statistics South Africa)

The final two columns provide a way of evaluating the actual performance in terms of job creation, namely the target growth rate of employment and the employment absorption rate for the period. The target growth rate (TGR) indicates how fast employment would have had to expand in order to provide jobs for all net entrants to the labour market over the period (say between time t and $t + 1$), and is defined as follows:

$$TGR_k = \frac{EAP_{k,t+1} - EAP_{k,t}}{L_{k,t}}$$

where EAP_k refers to the economically active population of group k, defined by any given covariate, and L_k is the number of employed group k individuals expressed as a percentage (Bhorat 2003a: 11). Note that because this target growth rate captures the growth required to provide employment only to the new entrants since 1995, it is essentially the rate of growth required to absorb all net entrants, independent of the unemployment numbers existent in the base year (1995). Employment growth at the target rate would serve to reduce the relevant group's overall unemployment rate. The employment absorption rate (EAR) is the ratio between actual employment growth and the desired or target rate, expressed as a percentage:

$$EAR_k = \frac{\dfrac{L_{k,t+1} - L_{k,t}}{L_{k,t}}}{\dfrac{EAP_{k,t+1} - EAP_{k,t}}{L_{k,t}}} = \frac{L_{k,t+1} - L_{k,t}}{EAP_{k,t+1} - EAP_{k,t}} \, .$$

The closer the employment absorption rate is to 100, the better the actual relative to the desired employment performance.

From the table, it can be seen that if all net entrants to the labour force between 1995 and 2002 were to have found work, employment would have had to increase by more than half, using the broad definition of unemployment. Using the official definition, employment would have had to grow by more than 45 per cent. In reality, however, actual employment grew at less than one-third of the rate required, based on the broad definition, and using the official definition of unemployment, the EAR was only 35 per cent. These figures call into question the notion of jobless growth since they indicate that the quantity of employment has increased and, by extension, more jobs were created over the period than lost. However, this aggregated view obscures the varied experiences of groups defined according to race, gender and other covariates. In Figure 4.1, the target and actual rates of employment growth, and the resultant employment absorption rates, for groups defined by race, gender and province are presented. Unsurprisingly, the target growth rates for non-white workers are relatively high, at 31 per cent for coloureds, 44 per cent for Asians/ Indians and a staggering 72 per cent for African individuals. This translates to an annual growth rate target of between 3.9 per cent and 8.0 per cent. The target growth rate for white workers is significantly lower at below 14 per cent. These differences may be traced to demographic differences, specifically the relatively low birth rate amongst whites compared to the rate among the other race groups during the 1980s, as well as changed labour force participation rates. Actual employment growth has been higher amongst Africans and Asians/Indians. However, the interaction between target and actual employment growth means that employment absorption has been significantly higher for white individuals at 66 per cent. The EARs for Africans, coloureds and Asians/Indians are 25 per cent, 43 per cent and 45 per cent respectively. Thus, for example, actual employment of Africans has grown at around one-quarter of the target rate, meaning that only one in four net labour force entrants found employment over the period. Simply stated, whites are reaping more of the benefits in the post-apartheid era in terms of employment growth than any other group, while African jobseekers seem to have drawn the short straw.

Figure 4.1 *Target and actual employment growth, 1995–2002*

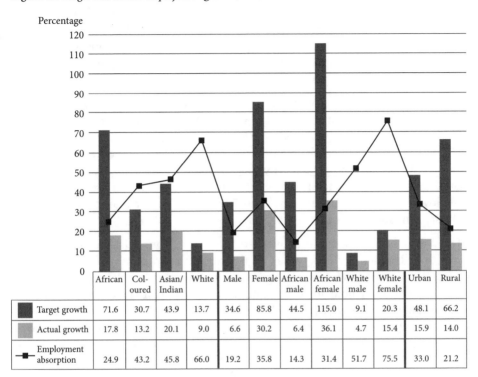

	African	Col- oured	Asian/ Indian	White	Male	Female	African male	African female	White male	White female	Urban	Rural
Target growth	71.6	30.7	43.9	13.7	34.6	85.8	44.5	115.0	9.1	20.3	48.1	66.2
Actual growth	17.8	13.2	20.1	9.0	6.6	30.2	6.4	36.1	4.7	15.4	15.9	14.0
Employment absorption	24.9	43.2	45.8	66.0	19.2	35.8	14.3	31.4	51.7	75.5	33.0	21.2

Sources: OHS 1995, LFS 2002 (2) (Statistics South Africa)
Note: The broad definition of unemployment is used here.

The seven years up to the end of 2002 have seen a large increase in the number of female labour-market participants in South Africa. As a result, the target growth rate for this period to ensure that all female net entrants are employed is more than 85 per cent, or more than 9 per cent annually. In contrast, the target growth rate for male workers is only 35 per cent. Despite this, female employment growth has been rapid, too, increasing by 30 per cent over the period, while the number of employed males rose by less than seven per cent. As a result, employment absorption has been almost twice as high amongst women, at 35 per cent, reflecting the increased feminisation of the South African workforce and related, in part, to the superior growth performance of the services sectors. However, the relatively high rate of employment absorption amongst females obscures marked racial differences. A comparison of employment absorption amongst African and white males and females reveals a substantial gap in the employment absorption rates between African females and white females (31 per cent and 76 per cent respectively) and between African males and white males (14 per cent and 52 per cent respectively).

This means that target and actual employment growth are most closely matched for white females and least closely matched for African males. The rapid growth in the number of female labour force participants is evidenced by the target employment growth rate for African females of 115 per cent, indicating that employment would have had to more than double to accommodate the net increase in the number of African females in the labour force.

Urban areas have proved more able to create the jobs required by the growing labour force. Target employment growth is, interestingly, lower in urban areas (48.1 per cent) than in rural areas (66.2 per cent), despite continued urbanisation. The actual increase in employment in these two types of areas occurred at similar rates, with urban employment expansion slightly outpacing rural expansion, although in both cases falling far short of the required rate. Consequently, urban employment absorption was more than 50 per cent higher than rural absorption (33 per cent and 21 per cent respectively).

The overarching message to be gleaned from these figures is, therefore, that the growth in the number of jobs has been far outstripped by the expanding labour force. While employment for some groups has grown rapidly relative to the increase in the size of the labour force, resulting in relatively high labour absorption rates (specifically, non-Africans, and white females in particular), none of the groups investigated experienced actual employment growth even in the region of the target growth rates. Thus, unemployment rates have continued to rise for these groups. The fact that the economy has been unable to provide sufficient employment opportunities for the South African population means that even greater demands for job-creating growth will be made on the future economy.

Key employment and unemployment issues

Jobless growth

Current perceptions of South African economic performance in the post-apartheid era hold that perhaps its greatest flaw is that it is characterised by so-called 'jobless growth'. Jobless growth is a term that can be interpreted in two ways, although generally the distinction is not explicitly made. Firstly, jobless growth may refer to a situation in which the general economy is growing but the absolute employment level is stagnant or falling. Alternatively, the term may be used to describe a situation in which the general economy is growing while the unemployment rate is rising, equating to employment growth lagging behind labour force growth (Altman 2003: 12). These two definitions respectively represent a very strict and a very broad interpretation of the term, with the latter not precluding an increase in the number of employed individuals, and with such assessments as 'given the national economy's level and trajectory of output expansion, the size of the increase in employment has been unsatisfactory' (Oosthuizen and Bhorat 2004) essentially representing a subjectively chosen point on the continuum. Given these definitions, can the economic growth of the past decade be accurately said to have been jobless?

Statistics South Africa and Reserve Bank data versus Household Survey data

The key piece of evidence upon which the assertion of jobless growth is based is presented in Figure 4.2, which illustrates the movement over the past three-and-a-half decades of indices of real Gross Domestic Product (GDP) and non-agricultural formal employment. From the beginning of the data series in 1967 until the early 1990s, employment tracked the movement of real GDP relatively closely. Output growth was associated with employment growth, while economic recessions saw stagnant or falling levels of employment. The economic recession of the early 1990s saw a sharp decline in non-agricultural formal employment. Whereas, prior to 1990, an upswing in the economy was accompanied by greater levels of employment, the economic recovery and expansion that occurred from 1993 and particularly after 1994 was not. Instead, employment continued to decline throughout the 1990s, falling by more than 12 per cent between 1994 and 2002. This left non-agricultural formal-sector employment almost 19 per cent lower in 2002 than it had been at its peak in 1989.

Figure 4.2 *Non-agricultural formal employment and real GDP, 1967–2002*

Index *(1994 = 100)*

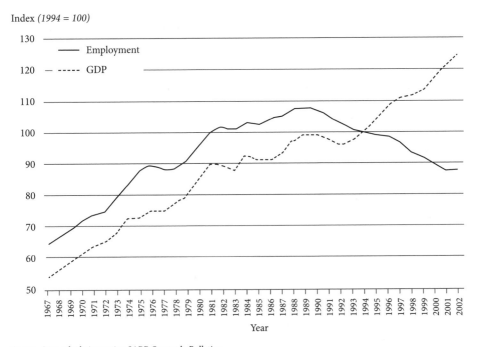

Source: Own calculations using SARB Quarterly Bulletins
Note: The employment indices published in the SARB *Quarterly Bulletins* are based on Statistics South Africa data from two sets of surveys: the Manpower Surveys and the Surveys of Employment and Earnings (from 1998 onwards).

Figure 4.2 is well known and certainly seems to indicate that recent economic growth has been jobless. The problem with it lies not in the deductions made on the basis of the data, but rather in the reliability of the underlying employment data (the Manpower Surveys (MPSs) and the Surveys of Employment and Earnings (SEEs)). The first problem is one of comparability. The real GDP data represent the total output of the South African economy, while the employment data exclude the agricultural sector as well as the informal sector, both of which are important sectors in terms of employment. In the former case, agriculture is the fourth-largest main-sector employer in the economy, while in terms of the informal sector there can be little doubt that this sector has been rapidly expanding its share of aggregate employment in the economy. The exclusion of these two sectors results in an underestimate of total employment, made more acute by their prominence in job generation in the domestic economy.

There is, however, a secondary and perhaps more fundamental flaw in the SEE data which form the basis of official employment series. This lies in the fact that core segments of economic activity, outside of agriculture and the informal sector, are explicitly not covered in the SEE. While ostensibly covering both private and public enterprises, a variety of sectors are omitted by the SEE. The complete list of omitted sectors within the SEE, as listed in the December 2002 Release, is as follows (Statistics South Africa 2002b: 7):[4]

- agriculture, hunting, forestry and fishing;
- restaurants and other eating and drinking places, boarding houses, caravan parks, guest farms;
- water and air transport;
- telecommunication services;
- financial institutions other than banking institutions, building societies and insurance companies;
- real estate and business services;
- educational services;
- medical, dental and other health services;
- welfare organisations;
- religious organisations;
- recreational and cultural services; and
- informal industries.

The SEE, therefore, is limited in its sectoral coverage and is likely to be biased towards firms in mining and manufacturing, and government. In addition, the bias against smaller enterprises in the sampling frame is evident in that the survey explicitly selects firms 'with a VAT turnover exceeding R300 000 per annum' (Statistics South Africa 2003b: 3). The SEE has also been found to be unable to pick up employment properly in newly established firms and is 'deficient in covering the SMMEs' (Stryker et al. 2001: v).

The SEE is, therefore, a problematic data series. In the first instance, there is the non-coverage of two key employment sectors of the domestic economy – agriculture and the informal sector. Secondly, and more importantly, a detailed examination of the coverage of the survey instrument makes it plain that the survey is omitting significant components of the economy. Thirdly, and rendering the use of the SEE data highly questionable, is the fact that omitted categories appear to vary across time periods, with certain sectors alternately included and excluded from the survey's coverage, making uniform time comparisons a treacherous, and ultimately error-ridden, exercise. Further, the affected sectors and sub-sectors predominantly form part of the tertiary sector, which previous labour market research has identified as the most significant job-generator in post-apartheid South Africa. For example, Bhorat (2003a: 2) estimates from October Household Survey (OHS) data that employment rose by 61 per cent in the finance sector, by 31 per cent in construction and by 22 per cent in domestic services between 1995 and 1999. Data from the March 2003 Labour Force Survey (LFS) indicate that the three most important sectors since 1995 are finance (an increase of 79 per cent), domestic services (52 per cent) and internal trade (46 per cent).

The earlier MPSs do not seem to be of much better quality. As with the SEE, the MPSs' coverage of the economy was incomplete, the major omissions being the agricultural sector (although not fishing), domestic workers and the entire informal sector (Roukens de Lange 1993: 53). Roukens de Lange (1993) points to a number of problems with the survey, including unstable occupational breakdowns of employment, particularly from the mid-1980s onwards, even when using very aggregated occupational or skill breakdowns. Furthermore, comparisons of population census data with MPS data have provided a poor match (Roukens de Lange 1993: 57).

Therefore, the often-used data presented graphically in Figure 4.2 can, in truth, not be considered conclusive proof of jobless growth. It is possible, though, to construct a picture of total employment in the South African economy between 1995 and 2002 using the October Household Surveys and the recent Labour Force Surveys conducted by Statistics South Africa. By sampling households, these surveys are able to provide a better picture of total employment than surveys, such as the SEE, that sample firms. These figures present a contrasting view of employment since 1995, revealing that aggregate employment has increased from 9.6 million in 1995 to 11.0 million in 2002 (based on the 1995 OHS and the September 2002 LFS). This translates into a growth in employment of 17.4 per cent over the period. This stands in stark contradiction to the SEE figures presented above and indeed begins to seriously question the notion of jobless growth.

TESTING THE JOBLESS GROWTH HYPOTHESES

Earlier, three interpretations of the term 'jobless growth' were presented, implying slightly different relationships between economic and employment change, namely:

- Economic growth is positive, but employment growth hovers around zero or is negative;
- Economic growth is positive, but employment growth is less than labour force growth and unemployment is therefore rising; or
- Economic growth is positive, but employment growth falls below a 'satisfactory' level.

We consider first the final definition, in which the specification of a 'satisfactory' level of employment growth will determine whether or not recent economic growth in South Africa can be deemed to have been jobless. As a fluid definition based on a normative decision, this definition bears no further investigation in this context.

It is, however, impossible to dispute the existence of jobless growth in South Africa in the sense of positive economic growth accompanied by rising unemployment, irrespective of whether one relies on the SEE/MPS data or the OHS/LFS data. Although the definition is relatively fluid, in that an absolute numerical value for employment growth is not specified, the core requirement is rising unemployment – a trend proven to be present by household survey data. The LFSs estimate the number of broadly unemployed individuals at 7.9 million people in September 2002, up from 4.2 million people in October 1995, an increase of 3.7 million. Recourse to the official definition of unemployment does not alter the picture, since official unemployment grew even more rapidly from 2.0 million to 4.8 million. Hence, if the second and broadest definition of jobless growth is applied in the South African context, then the post-apartheid South African economy has indeed been characterised by jobless growth.

The first definition of jobless growth is one that is used, consciously or sub-consciously, by South African politicians, the local media and, therefore, the general public. It is easy to see how the use of the official Statistics South Africa and Reserve Bank data 'confirms' the persistence of jobless growth throughout the post-apartheid era, satisfying the strictest criterion – zero or negative employment growth. However, as was shown above, the underlying data sets suffer important coverage and consistency problems, thus rendering such a conclusion invalid. This leads us to household survey data, the OHSs and LFSs, which, as discussed above, are likely to provide a more accurate picture of total employment.

Initial inspection of the OHS/LFS data reveals that, according to the strictest definition, the hypothesis of jobless growth is rejected outright, since total employment is estimated as having grown by 1.5 million jobs between 1995 and 2002, from 9.5 million to 11.0 million. However, while the SEE/MPS data have been argued to be inaccurate, some questions do exist about the OHS/LFS data. The main problem revolves around the quantification of employment in the nebulous informal sector. The 1995 OHS does not reliably distinguish between formal- and informal-sector employment, making only comparisons of total employment possible. Bhorat (1999) calculates from the OHS 1995 that of 1.2 million 'informal-sector' workers, only 569 000 are not domestic workers, a figure which, Bhorat concludes, 'is clearly a significant underestimate of the number of informally employed'. Part of the problem is the misspecification of informal workers as formal workers, implying that the survey's estimate of formal employment is inflated. However, another issue is that there may have been problems in accurately identifying informal-sector workers as being employed. In this regard, three inconsistencies or problem areas are addressed, namely:

- trend problems introduced by including the September 2000 LFS;
- sectoral patterns of employment growth; and
- provincial patterns of employment growth.

The inclusion of the September 2000 LFS (LFS (2)) in determining sub-period trends in employment creates some problems. Although total employment expansion between 1995 and 2002 is estimated at 1.5 million extra jobs, estimates from LFS (2) of 2000 indicate that total employment had declined by around 700 000 jobs between September 2000 and September 2002. This implies that all net employment growth previously attributed to the 1995–2002 period actually occurred prior to September 2000, representing employment growth between 1995 and 2000 of 2.2 million jobs at an average annual rate of 4.2 per cent, or more than twice the estimated employment growth rate for 1995–2002, but still only two-thirds of the average annual rate of growth of the broadly defined labour force. Further, informal-sector employment as a proportion of total employment has remained relatively stable, according to the LFSs, at around 15.5 per cent (if one excludes the anomalous estimates from LFS (3), February 2001). Thus, formal- and informal-sector employment between 2000 and 2002 were growing at roughly the same pace, which contradicts the general assertion that informal-sector employment is growing more rapidly than formal-sector employment. If we assume that employment in these two sectors grew at roughly the same pace from 1995 to 2002, an estimate of informal-sector employment (excluding domestic workers, amongst others) of 1.49 million people is reached – significantly higher than the approximately 631 000 non-domestic informal-sector workers recorded in the OHS 1995.

The sectoral pattern of employment growth, as set out in Table 4.6 – at a less aggregated level than main sector – is such that in some cases, most growth occurs in sub-sectors likely to include a large proportion of informal-sector employment. Three sectors account for more than four-fifths of net employment growth between 1995 and 2002, namely 'Wholesale and retail trade; repair of motor vehicles, motor cycles and personal and household goods; hotels and restaurants' (509 000 jobs, or 35 per cent of the net growth); 'Financial intermediation, insurance, real estate and business services' (440 000 jobs, or 30 per cent); and 'Private households' (241 000 jobs, or 16 per cent).

Beginning with domestic workers in the private households sector, it is estimated from the 1995 OHS that there were approximately 700 000 individuals employed as domestic workers. By 2000, slightly fewer than 1 million domestic workers were employed in South Africa, an increase of 43 per cent over the five-year period. However, the 2002 estimate is only 875 000, more than 12 per cent lower than the 2000 estimate.

Employment in the wholesale and retail trade sector has experienced the most rapid growth, from 1.7 million in 1995 to 2.2 million in 2002, which represents growth of 31 per cent over the period. But this is in fact down from the 2000 level of 2.4 million workers. Aside from this issue, the wholesale and retail trade sector is characterised by a large proportion of informal-sector activity. In 2002, 801 000 workers in this sector (37 per cent of the total) were employed in the informal sector. Superficially, therefore, it seems possible that much of the growth in this sector may in fact have been informal in nature. Within the divisions, 'Retail trade, except of motor vehicles and motor cycles; repair of personal and household goods' (division 2 in the table) accounted for 79 per cent of sectoral employment growth between 1995 and 2002 but only 63 per cent of the sector's employment in 1995. It is also the division where the informal sector is most dominant: 46 per cent of the division's employment is informal, and it accounts for 84 per cent of informal employment in the sector as a whole. Informal-sector employment is probably included in this division primarily through the 'Retail trade via stalls and markets' and 'Other retail trade not in stores' categories. Hence, it is possible that a substantial proportion of employment growth in this sector is attributable to the informal sector, and that this growth is biased upwards if the extent of informal-sector employment was underestimated in 1995.

The finance sector is different, though, in terms of its relatively small informal sector – less than 6 per cent of employment in the sector is informal. Almost three-quarters of sectoral employment growth – representing 326 000 jobs – is located in the 'Other business activities' division, but the division's informal sector consists of fewer than 40 000 jobs. This division is also the only division where the informal sector employs more than 10 000 individuals. Hence, unlike the wholesale and retail trade sector, the informal sector cannot be the main source of job growth in the finance sector since even if there was no (recorded) informal employment in the sector in 1995, the informal sector would account for only 13 per cent of total employment change.

Inconsistencies also appear when one looks at employment provincially (see Figure 4.3). Not totally surprisingly, 63 per cent of employment growth was concentrated in only three provinces. What does come as something of a surprise is that the three provinces are KwaZulu-Natal, the Eastern Cape and Limpopo. KwaZulu-Natal on its own accounts for one-quarter of the net increase in employment experienced nationally between 1995 and 2002. Further, these provinces' shares of employment growth far exceed their shares of total employment, by between 30 per cent and 127 per cent. Gauteng, the Western Cape, the Free State and North West have all seen declines in their total shares of employment.

Table 4.6 *Sectoral experiences of employment and informal sector employment growth, 1995–2002*

	1995	2002	Change		Informal sector 2002		
			thou-sands	percen-tage	thou-sands	rate	share
Wholesale and retail trade; repair of motor vehicles, motor cycles and personal and household goods; hotels and restaurants							
Wholesale and commission trades except of motor vehicles and motor cycles	141.0	109.0	−31.9	−6.3	3.1	2.8	0.4
Retail trade, except of motor vehicles and motor cycles; repair of personal and household goods	1 053.0	1 454.1	401.1	78.8	673.3	46.3	84.0
Sale, maintenance and repair of motor vehicles and motor cycles; retail trade in automotive fuel	303.9	313.2	9.3	1.8	53.0	16.9	6.6
Hotels and restaurants	170.3	301.0	130.7	25.7	71.7	23.8	8.9
Total	1 668.1	2 177.3	509.2	100.0	801.1	36.8	100.0
Financial intermediation, insurance, real estate and business services							
Financial intermediation, except insurance and pension funding	165.7	190.3	24.6	5.6	2.2	1.2	3.8
Insurance and pension funding, except compulsory social security	94.1	115.6	21.4	4.9	2.4	2.1	4.1
Activities auxiliary to financial intermediation	5.3	2.9	−2.5	−0.6	0.3	10.9	0.5
Real estate activities	29.1	53.9	24.7	5.6	9.0	16.8	15.6
Renting of machinery and equipment without operator and of personal and household goods	11.5	15.4	4.0	0.9	2.6	16.7	4.4
Computer and related activities	29.9	65.9	36.0	8.2	2.6	3.9	4.5
Research and development	10.9	16.6	5.6	1.3	0.2	1.2	0.4
Other business activities	234.1	560.2	326.1	74.1	38.6	6.9	66.7
Total	580.8	1 020.7	440.0	100.0	57.9	5.7	100.0

Sources: OHS 1995, LFS 2002 (2) (Statistics South Africa); SARB (2003)

Figure 4.3 *Provincial experiences of employment and informal sector employment growth, 1995–2002*

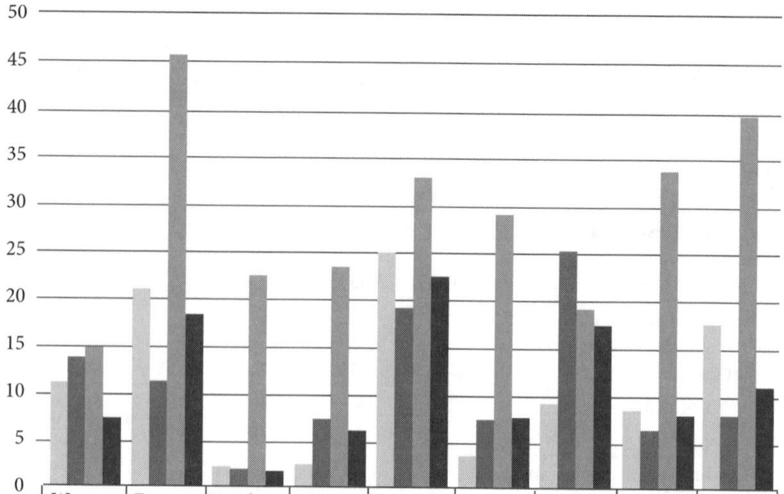

	Western Cape	Eastern Cape	Northern Cape	Free State	KwaZulu-Natal	North West	Gauteng	Mpuma-langa	Limpopo
Share of employment growth	11.1	20.9	2.3	2.6	24.8	3.4	9.1	8.3	17.5
Share of 2002 employment	13.8	11.2	2.2	7.2	19	7.3	25.2	6.5	7.7
Informal share of workforce	14.7	45.6	22.3	23.4	32.9	29.2	19.1	33.7	39.6
Informal share of total informal	7.3	18.4	1.8	6.1	22.5	7.7	17.4	7.9	11.0

Sources: OHS 1995, LFS 2002 (2) (Statistics South Africa); SARB (2003)

However, KwaZulu-Natal, the Eastern Cape and Limpopo were also the provinces, in 2002, with the largest proportions of people engaged in informal-sector activity (33 per cent, 46 per cent and 40 per cent respectively). Thus, if informal-sector activity is increasingly well captured, employment growth in these three provinces particularly is likely to be most overstated, as they have the largest proportions of workers in the informal sector. A further issue that may impact on the measurement of the informal sector relates to the quality of the fieldwork in various provinces; superior-quality fieldwork in Gauteng, for example, would mean that its informal sector was better recorded and not underestimated in 1995, and hence the provincial informal sector does not exhibit high growth.

In summary, in 1995 there were definitely problems in identifying formal-versus informal-sector employment, along with problems in the distribution of domestic workers versus non-domestic workers within the informal sector and possible undersampling of live-in domestic workers. This probably resulted in an underestimation of informal-sector employment and therefore also total employment, and this has a knock-on effect by inflating employment growth when 1995 is the base year. This seems to be confirmed by provincial breakdowns of employment growth: those provinces where most of the net national increase in employment is located are also the provinces with the largest proportions of the employed engaged in informal activities in 2002, and are home to the largest, second-largest and fourth-largest provincial informal sectors in absolute terms. Looked at in sectoral terms, in the wholesale and retail trade sector most of the employment growth stems from a division in which much informal-sector employment was recorded in 2002. At the same time, there is an ongoing process of improving questionnaires in order to better collect data on informal-sector employment in particular (see Devey, Skinner and Valodia 2002). This means that 'it is impossible to identify how much of the recorded increase in [informal] employment is as a result of real increases and how much is attributable to better data capture on this type of work' (Muller 2003: 14). Nevertheless, there is no evidence to suggest that the total employment in 1995 was underestimated to such an extent as to result in negative or near-zero employment growth over the period. The OHS 1995 data, therefore, although not perfect, are of sufficiently good quality to repudiate the strictest definition of jobless growth.

Ignoring the issue surrounding the actual magnitude of the rise in employment, and attributing the change to growing informal-sector employment, there is the all-important issue that formal- and informal-sector employment are not equivalent forms of employment. The former form is more stable, generally better paid and governed by national labour legislation. Briefly stated, recent evidence suggests a growing incidence of casualisation as a consequence of outsourcing and other cost-reducing strategies. According to Bhorat, Lundall and Rospabe (2002: 32), of 101 firms surveyed in the Outsourcing Survey 1994–98, 68 per cent had outsourced functions over the preceding five years, representing 5.7 per cent of the workforce (of whom more than 90 per cent were blue-collar workers). As a rule, outsourcing results in a decline in both employment and remuneration for affected workers. Outsourced operations generally employ 'two-thirds of the workers at two-thirds of the rate permanent workers were once paid' (Theron and Godfrey 2000). The poorer conditions of employment and lower wages received by retrenched workers who are re-employed by outsourcing firms are also pointed to by Bhorat et al. (2002: 32).

Evidence from the September 2002 LFS suggests that one in four employees is not employed on a permanent basis (see Table 4.7). This is not very different from the 22.6 per cent calculated by Bhorat et al. (2002: 32) on the basis of OHS 1999 data. Temporary and casual workers account for 12.5 per cent and 6.4 per cent of employees respectively (almost 19 per cent in total). Males are slightly more likely than females to be employed on a permanent basis. More than 90 per cent of whites are permanent employees, as opposed to 85 per cent, 77 per cent and 70 per cent of Asians/Indians, coloureds and Africans respectively. Conversely, female and African workers are most likely to be employed on a temporary or casual basis.

Table 4.7 *Type of contract of employed by gender and race, 2002*

	Permanent (%)	Fixed period contract (%)	Temporary (%)	Casual (%)	Seasonal (%)	Unspecified (%)
Total	75.7	4.1	12.5	6.4	0.7	0.7
Male	77.2	4.8	11.1	5.7	0.6	0.6
Female	73.6	3.2	14.3	7.2	0.8	0.8
African	70.2	4.3	16.9	7.0	0.9	0.7
Coloured	77.3	4.1	7.0	10.3	1.0	0.4
Asian/Indian	85.1	3.2	5.4	5.5	0.3	0.6
White	91.8	3.4	2.7	1.4	0.0	0.7

Source: Own calculations based on LFS (6) (Statistics South Africa 2002)

One manner of reconciling the above with the jobless growth tag is that the latter is perhaps a misleading description of a problem that may be more readily defined in terms of the notion of a general deterioration in employment *quality*, not quantity. This is because within total employment, a larger proportion is informal-sector employment and there is a greater proportion of more poorly remunerated outsourced employment. Informal-sector employment can be viewed as of inferior quality relative to formal-sector employment for a number of reasons. Kingdon and Knight (2001a: 6) offer evidence that formal sector employment income 'greatly exceeds income from self-employment [i.e. informal sector employment]... [suggesting that] wage employment is the preferred state'. At the same time, benefits such as annual and sick leave are 'sporadic or not granted' to informal-sector employees (South African Labour Bulletin 2002: 40). Casale and Posel (2002: 169) highlight the fact that informal-sector work is 'usually seen to have low returns and little security or protection for the worker', making informal-sector employment of inferior quality relative to formal-sector employment.

Racial inequalities in finding employment

The description of the labour force provides the framework within which employment and unemployment can be analysed. Unemployment remains one of the most pressing socio-economic problems facing South Africa and one that has a myriad of links to other issues and problems, such as poverty, inequality and crime. Unemployment has continued to increase steadily throughout the entire post-apartheid era. In 1995, the official unemployment rate was around 17 per cent of the labour force and expanded unemployment stood at 30 per cent. By 2000, these rates stood at 26 per cent and 36 per cent respectively, rising further to 31 per cent and 42 per cent respectively in 2002.

Unemployment problems are typically identified through investigations of unemployment rates, with higher rates indicating the most serious problems. However, unemployment rates, although important to our understanding of labour market conditions, tend to provide only part of the picture. Just as with poverty analyses, while it is important to know which group is most often afflicted by unemployment, policy must also be informed by the knowledge of which group constitutes the largest *share* of unemployment. Unemployment *rates* and *shares* represent a critical policy decision that must be made by governments concerned about the unemployed all over the world. In essence, the question is whether it is preferable to focus on helping the group most often afflicted by unemployment (the group with the highest unemployment rate) or whether the focus should be on helping the largest group of unemployed individuals (the group with the highest unemployment share). Probably one of the simplest ways to identify problems in terms of employment and unemployment is to compare the composition of these two groups. Thus, groups that constitute inordinately large proportions of the unemployed relative to the employed can easily be seen to be disadvantaged, for whatever reason. The further benefit of this approach is that one can get an idea of a group's unemployment share as well as its unemployment rate relative to the average. In situations where a group's unemployment share exceeds its employment share, that group's unemployment rate is above the average for the overall population, while the opposite is true where the unemployment share is lower than the employment share.

Employment and unemployment in the immediate post-apartheid era were quite different in racial structure (see Table 4.8). Of the 9.5 million employed individuals in the country, 65 per cent were African and 20 per cent were white, with coloureds and Asians/Indians constituting the remaining 16 per cent. In contrast, eight out of nine unemployed individuals were African and only three per cent were white. The differences between the employment and unemployment shares of the four race groups are quite stark. Whites and Asians/Indians account for a much smaller proportion of unemployment than employment, while the same is true, although to a lesser degree, for coloureds. In contrast, Africans account for a substantially larger unemployment share than their employment share. These differences indicate higher than average unemployment rates for Africans, and vice versa for other groups. This is indeed the case, with unemployment amongst Africans at 38 per cent in 1995, compared to the national average of 31 per cent. In 1995, fewer than six out of every hundred labour force members were unable to secure employment.

Table 4.8 *Employment and unemployment by race and gender, 1995 and 2002*

	1995			2002			Share of change	
	Employ-ment share	Un-employ-ment share	Un-employ-ment rate	Employ-ment share	Un-employ-ment share	Un-employ-ment rate	Employ-ment	Un-employ-ment
African	64.6	88.0	37.8	65.6	88.8	49.3	72.3	89.7
Coloured	12.1	8.0	22.8	11.8	6.8	29.3	10.0	5.4
Asian/Indian	3.8	1.4	13.8	3.9	1.8	24.9	4.8	2.3
White	19.6	2.7	5.8	18.4	2.5	9.0	11.1	2.3
Male	60.9	42.5	23.7	56.1	43.2	35.6	25.5	44.0
Female	39.1	57.5	39.6	43.9	56.8	48.2	74.3	56.0
African male	39.8	37.4	29.5	36.5	38.2	42.9	15.9	39.1
African female	24.8	50.6	47.6	29.1	50.5	55.5	56.2	50.5
Coloured male	6.9	3.4	17.9	6.5	3.0	24.8	3.6	2.5
Coloured female	5.1	4.6	28.4	5.3	3.8	34.1	6.5	2.9
Asian/Indian male	2.5	0.6	10.0	2.4	0.8	18.9	1.5	0.9
Asian/Indian female	1.2	0.7	20.6	1.5	1.0	32.7	3.2	1.4
White male	11.7	1.0	3.7	10.5	1.1	7.2	3.5	1.3
White female	7.9	1.7	8.7	7.9	1.4	11.2	7.6	1.0
Total	100.0	100.0	30.8	100.0	100.0	41.8	100.0	100.0

Sources: OHS 1995, LFS 2002 (2) (Statistics South Africa)

The post-apartheid era saw relatively little change, in that Africans still accounted for a disproportionately large share of unemployment at 89 per cent. The employment and unemployment shares for coloureds and whites declined marginally over the period, with relatively little change occurring for Asians/Indians. However, in line with the rapid rise in the overall unemployment rate to 42 per cent, the African unemployment rate stood at 49 per cent in 2002, equivalent to an increase of about 11 percentage points. Unemployment rates rose across the board, however, with the rise being particularly large for Asians/Indians (almost doubling from 14 per cent to 25 per cent). Whites still had the lowest unemployment rate in 2002 (9 per cent).

Education, employment and unemployment

The South African economy's increasing appetite for highly skilled labour, its continued mechanisation of manufacturing and industrial processes and its pursuit of international competitiveness mean that lower-skilled and poorly educated workers are likely to bear the brunt of unemployment (Bhorat 2003a; Oosthuizen

2003; Bhorat and Hodge 1999). The LFS data confirm that this trend is continuing, with employment growing fastest for those with higher levels of education (see Table 4.9). The bulk of the employed have not completed matric, although this proportion has declined from 62 per cent in 1995 to 58 per cent in 2002. The shares of employed individuals with completed secondary and tertiary education have both risen slightly over the period, confirming a continuation of the abovementioned trend. Fewer people with no education at all were employed in 2002 than in 1995. This is probably a result of a combination of the changing skills requirements of employers and the fact that individuals without any formal education tend to be significantly older than those with some education. In 2002, the average adult without education was aged 46 years, compared to just over 33 years for all adults. The largest proportion of employment growth accrued to individuals with completed secondary education (41 per cent), equivalent to an average annual growth rate of 3.8 per cent, which is also the fastest rate of growth of all the education categories. Tertiary-educated individuals filled 23 per cent of the net increase in total employment, their total employment having expanded at an average of 3.3 per cent per annum.

Table 4.9 *Employment and unemployment by highest level of education, 1995 and 2002*

	1995			2002			Share of change	
	Employ-ment share	Un-employ-ment share	Un-employ-ment rate	Employ-ment share	Un-employ-ment share	Un-employ-ment rate	Employ-ment	Un-employ-ment
None	8.1	9.7	34.7	6.7	5.0	35.0	–2.1	–0.3
Incomplete primary	16.2	21.2	36.9	15.3	17.4	45.0	9.6	13.1
Complete primary	6.7	9.0	37.3	6.8	7.9	45.6	7.4	6.8
Incomplete secondary	31.0	38.3	35.5	29.1	41.4	50.6	16.8	45.0
Complete secondary	22.0	18.3	27.0	24.6	23.5	40.7	40.9	29.4
Tertiary	14.0	2.2	6.6	15.2	3.6	14.6	22.8	5.2
Other/ unspecified	1.9	1.3	23.3	2.3	1.1	25.5	4.5	0.8
Total	100.0	100.0	30.8	100.0	100.0	41.8	100.0	100.0

Sources: OHS 1995, LFS 2002 (2) (Statistics South Africa)

The relatively disadvantaged position in the labour market in which less-educated individuals find themselves is evident from the comparison of their employment and unemployment shares. While those without matric accounted for 62 per cent of employment in 1995, over 78 per cent of the unemployed did not have matric certificates. A similar pattern was evident in 2002, with non-matriculants accounting for 58 per cent and 72 per cent of the employed and unemployed respectively. These higher unemployment shares are observed for all the sub-matric education groupings detailed in both years, except for those without education at all in 2002. Hence, these groups all have unemployment rates above the national average in each of the years. Unemployment rates range from 34 to 38 per cent compared to the national average of 31 per cent in 1995, and, ignoring those without any education, between 45 and 51 per cent compared to 42 per cent nationally in 2002. In contrast, holders of matric certificates, and particularly those with tertiary education, are more likely to find employment. The rise in the rates of unemployment amongst those with sub-matric levels of education has meant that 45 per cent of the growth of unemployment over the period occurred amongst those with incomplete secondary education. The South African economy's increasing appetite for highly skilled labour associated with its current growth path, its continued mechanisation of manufacturing and industrial processes, and its pursuit of international competitiveness underlie the fact that lower-skilled and poorly educated workers are bearing the brunt of rising unemployment.

A worrying development is the rapid rise in unemployment rates for those with completed secondary and tertiary education, up nearly 14 percentage points and more than doubling, respectively. Thus it appears that having completed matric does not vastly improve an individual's employment prospects. Increasingly, a tertiary qualification no longer seems sufficient to ward off unemployment, which appears contradictory to the belief that the South African economy is skills-constrained. However, the aggregate unemployment rates by level of education mask significant racial variation for those with completed secondary and those with completed tertiary education (see Table 4.10). Within both educational categories and in both years, Africans were significantly more often unemployed than any other race group. More than 55 per cent of Africans with completed secondary education were unemployed in 2002, significantly higher than in 1995 and 15 percentage points higher than the average for 2002. Similarly, one-quarter of African tertiary graduates were jobless in 2002, compared to the range of between 4 per cent and 8 per cent for other tertiary graduates. However, the African experience of rising unemployment rates over the period in these educational categories is not unique, as unemployment rose significantly for all secondary and tertiary graduates, with little difference for coloured and Asian/Indian tertiary graduates. The net effect of these changes is a narrowing of the differences in unemployment rates among coloureds, Asians/Indians and whites, and a widening of the gap between these groups on the one hand and Africans on the other.

Table 4.10 *Secondary and tertiary unemployment rates by race, 1995 and 2002*

		African	Coloured	Asian/Indian	White	Total
Completed secondary	1995	42.1	20.3	13.7	4.9	27.0
		(1.689)	(1.675)	(2.545)	(0.519)	(1.294)
	2002	55.7	23.8	24.1	8.6	40.7
		(1.241)	(1.950)	(2.252)	(0.741)	(1.749)
Completed tertiary	1995	10.1	8.3	5.6	2.5	6.6
		(1.128)	(1.814)	(1.361)	(0.448)	(0.566)
	2002	25.0	7.4	4.8	4.0	14.6
		(1.705)	(1.378)	(1.804)	(1.047)	(1.268)

Sources: OHS 1995, LFS 2002 (2) (Statistics South Africa)
Note: Standard errors are in parentheses, and are corrected according to frequency weights, the primary sampling unit and, in the case of 2002, sampling stratification.

The table therefore reveals that there are significant inter-racial differences in the likelihood of finding employment, irrespective of whether the individual has a secondary or a tertiary qualification. This is a critically important issue given that education is seen as one of the key mechanisms through which the apartheid legacy can be addressed and poverty levels be reduced. There are a number of possible reasons for this phenomenon. Firstly, inter-racial variation in unemployment rates may be the result of continued discrimination favouring whites in particular and, to a lesser extent, Asians/Indians and coloureds. Secondly, there may be issues surrounding perceptions of quality differences in the qualifications of individuals, which may not be linked to the individual's race but rather to the institution attended. Whether the differences in quality are real or only perceived, it is essential that the situation be addressed. A third possibility centres on possible mismatches between graduates' fields of study and the types of graduates required by employers. For example, Bhorat (2003b) finds that a large proportion of unemployed graduates have qualifications in the humanities and other fields where demand is relatively low.

The overall distribution of employment across educational categories once again obscures significant differences across race groups. The apartheid legacy is easily discernible from Figure 4.4, which depicts the distribution of employment across six educational categories for the four race groups. White workers are, in general, much better educated than average. Between 30 per cent and 40 per cent have a tertiary qualification and a further 45 per cent, approximately, have completed matric, with very few having lower levels of education. The profile of white employment also shifted markedly between 1995 and 2002, such that the proportion of the employed with tertiary education grew, while the proportion with incomplete secondary education declined. This may be part of a longer-term trend of increasing skill levels amongst the white population, but may also relate to the greater vulnerability, whether actual or perceived, of less-educated white workers forced to compete on more equal terms for employment. The aggregate pattern of

Asian/Indian employment most closely resembles that of whites, although there are some differences between the two. Specifically, amongst Asian/Indian workers there are, relative to white workers, fewer with tertiary education and significantly more with complete and incomplete secondary education. The 1995–2002 period has seen an increase of about ten percentage points in the share of employment of Asians/Indians with matric certificates, with a fall in the share of workers with less than matric education.

Figure 4.4 *Educational breakdown of employed by race (percentage), 1995 and 2002*

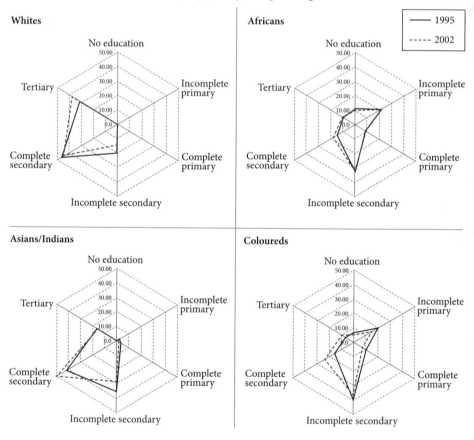

Source: OHS 1995, LFS 2002 (2) (Statistics South Africa)

The patterns of African and coloured employment are quite similar, and differ markedly from those of the other two population groups. Graphically, the weight of African and coloured employment is to the right and bottom of the diagrams, while that of Asian/Indian and white employment is almost exclusively to the left of the diagrams. African and coloured employment, in line with the skills profile, consists of large proportions of individuals with education levels ranging from no education to incomplete secondary education. A larger proportion of coloured workers has matric certificates, relative to Africans, while the proportions of tertiary-educated workers are similar, particularly in 2002. While coloured employment has shown a marked increase in the proportion of workers with completed secondary education, the change has been less substantial within African employment.

The various patterns highlighted above hold important implications for a number of government objectives, including poverty alleviation and reduction of inequality. Firstly, it is clear that a continuation of the trend in skills-biased employment expansion will slow progress towards attaining these objectives, particularly since whites have the greatest proportion of highly educated employed individuals. Secondly, and related to this, as far as it is possible to discern from the data, even where individuals have the same levels of education there does not seem to be equal access to employment opportunities. Whether this is because of continued deliberate discrimination, or because of actual or perceived differences in the quality of qualifications held by individuals from different institutions, or a result of differing patterns amongst races in terms of the fields in which the qualifications were obtained, is not clear and therefore requires further attention. Thirdly, the data show that increasing the output of matriculants in particular is not a sufficient condition for increasing employment levels, an issue that also requires investigation.

The discussion of education so far treats all individuals with the same level of education as being identical, or at least similar, apart from race. However, an important issue, particularly in an atmosphere of claims of falling educational standards, is the addition of an age dimension. Most important, particularly from a policy perspective, is whether the rise in unemployment amongst graduates of secondary and tertiary educational institutions represents the displacement of older workers by younger, newly qualified workers on the one hand, or the retention of their positions by older workers and the resultant 'exclusion' of new graduates from employment opportunities on the other. This can be determined by analysing the shares in the change in employment and unemployment by age groups (see Figure 4.5).

Between 1995 and 2002, the bulk of employment *and* unemployment expansion amongst those with secondary education occurred amongst 25- to 34-year-olds (46 per cent and 48 per cent respectively). However, the age distribution of the remainder of employment and unemployment growth is very different. Virtually all of the remaining 54 per cent of employment growth accrued to those aged 35 years and older: 35- to 44-year-olds accounted for one-third of employment expansion and 45- to 54-year-olds for 14 per cent. Barely 2 per cent of employment expansion amongst those with matric certificates accrued to 15- to 24-year-olds. This stands in stark contrast to the age distribution of unemployment growth. Almost 38 per cent of unemployment growth occurred amongst 15- to 24-year-olds, a proportion approximately 18 times higher than this age group's share of employment growth.

Consequently, older groups account for relatively low proportions of unemployment growth: 35- to 44-year-olds account for 10 per cent of unemployment growth while 45- to 65-year-olds represent less than 4 per cent. For secondary school graduates, therefore, it is clear that the bulk of employment growth has accrued to older individuals, while younger individuals have made up a large proportion of the growth in unemployment nationally.

Figure 4.5 *Employment and unemployment change by level of education and age group, 1995–2002*

Share of change (percentage)

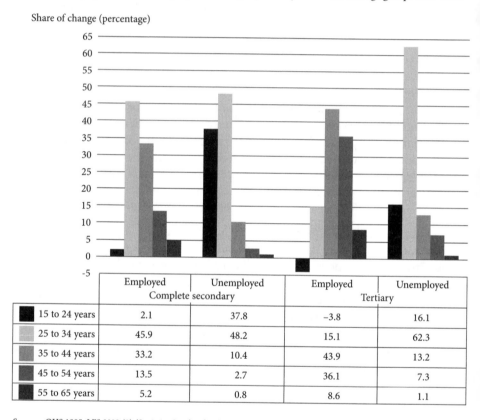

	Employed	Unemployed	Employed	Unemployed
	Complete secondary		Tertiary	
15 to 24 years	2.1	37.8	−3.8	16.1
25 to 34 years	45.9	48.2	15.1	62.3
35 to 44 years	33.2	10.4	43.9	13.2
45 to 54 years	13.5	2.7	36.1	7.3
55 to 65 years	5.2	0.8	8.6	1.1

Sources: OHS 1995, LFS 2002 (2) (Statistics South Africa)

The contrast is even starker for those with tertiary qualifications. Employment expansion amongst this group was concentrated amongst 35- to 54-year-olds. Individuals in this 20-year age group accounted for four-fifths of net employment expansion over the period, while 15 per cent of net new jobs accrued to 25- to 34-year-olds. The number of employed tertiary graduates under 24 years of age actually declined over the period. In terms of unemployment, close to four-fifths of unemployment growth occurred amongst 15- to 34-year-olds (16 per cent amongst

15- to 24-year-olds and 62 per cent amongst 25- to 34-year-olds). For 15- to 34-year-old tertiary graduates, therefore, the share of unemployment growth is nearly seven times their share of employment growth.

Overall, therefore, it appears that the increase in unemployment of those with secondary and tertiary qualifications during the post-apartheid era is indeed a case of job retention amongst older workers, with younger labour force members much less likely to find employment. This holds important implications for efforts to reduce poverty and inequality via the education system, and is an issue that needs to be addressed, given the huge amounts of money spent by the state and by households themselves on providing children with education. Without the opportunity to apply their recently acquired skills, young graduates run the risk of their skills and knowledge eroding, particularly in situations where they are unemployed for extended periods of time. Furthermore, the persistence of this bias of employment growth towards older individuals may hamper the transfer of skills within firms from older, more experienced workers to their younger and inexperienced counterparts, which may have a negative impact on the South African economy's longer-term competitiveness.

Over the period, employment gains have been biased towards higher-skilled and, therefore, generally better educated workers, while unemployment is highest amongst the less educated. At the same time, the evidence shows that a growing proportion of the unemployed are actually relatively well educated. An interesting question, therefore, is how the mean years of education vary by age for individuals according to their employment status, namely employed, broadly unemployed or outside the labour force. Generally speaking, within each age cohort, employed individuals have more years of education on average than those who are unemployed or not members of the labour force (see Figure 4.6). This is not surprising, given the evidence on education levels presented above. As one would expect, mean years of education decline as age increases, irrespective of labour market status, from a peak during the mid-twenties. The general pattern shows a rapid increase in the average years of education between the ages of 15 and 20 years as individuals pass through the education system, peaking amongst the 20- to 30-year-olds, and declining thereafter. The patterns for the unemployed and those outside the labour force are quite similar. Amongst the youngest, though, those outside the labour force have significantly more years of education on average than the unemployed (and employed), this difference being composed merely of individuals at educational institutions who will only enter the labour market later on.

Figure 4.6 *Mean years of education by broad labour force status, 1995 and 2002*

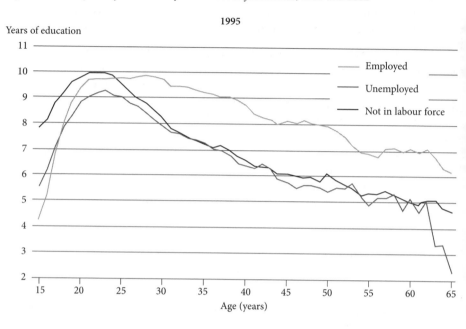

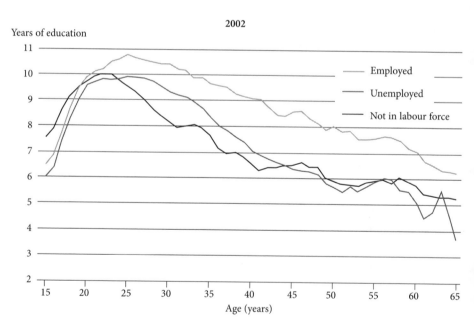

Sources: OHS 1995, LFS 2002 (2) (Statistics South Africa)
Note: Mean years of education is calculated as a three-year moving average for each age.

What is interesting is the fact that mean years of education have increased between 1995 and 2002 for virtually every age cohort whether employed or unemployed, particularly for the youngest labour force members. Education peaked around age 25 in 2002, compared to age 28 in 1995, amongst the employed. For the unemployed, the age at which mean years of education peaks rose from around 23 in 1995 to 25–27 in 2002. For those individuals who were not members of the labour force, mean years of education were basically unaltered. This means that while the employed were on average more educated in 2002 than they were in 1995, the same applies to the unemployed, indicating again that higher levels of education were less likely in 2002 than in 1995 to stave off unemployment. These changes were confirmed by investigation of the patterns derived from the September 2000 LFS.

Age group inequalities in finding employment

Not all age groups have benefited from employment expansion since 1995. Since 1995, 15- to 24-year-olds have flooded into the labour market at a rate that would require employment to have grown by more than 116 per cent in order for them to be absorbed into employment, which is more than twice the rate for the population as a whole (see Table 4.11). For other age groups, the target growth rate of employment is significantly lower, although still relatively high at between 35 per cent and 55 per cent. However, employment expansion has been highly biased towards older individuals: although 15- to 24-year olds represented almost 12 per cent of the employed in 1995, barely 2 per cent of employment expansion accrued to this group. This has meant that fewer than three in one hundred new labour force entrants in this age group were absorbed into employment between 1995 and 2002. Employment absorption has also been low for 25- to 34-year-olds (16 per cent), but has been relatively high amongst older groups, rising from 46 per cent for 35- to 44-year-olds to almost two-thirds amongst 55- to 65-year-olds.

Table 4.11 *Employment and unemployment performances by age group, 1995–2002*

		15–24 years	25–34 years	35–44 years	45–54 years	55–65 years	Total
Target growth rate		116.2	47.5	43.2	54.5	35.1	54.6
Employment absorption rate		2.6	15.9	46.1	59.0	66.0	29.1
1995	Employment share	11.8	34.5	30.1	16.7	6.9	100.0
	Unemployment share	30.1	40.0	19.0	8.3	2.5	100.0
	Unemployment rate	53.1	34.1	22.0	18.1	14.0	30.8
2002	Employment share	10.5	32.0	31.1	19.0	7.3	100.0
	Unemployment share	32.2	38.0	18.6	8.9	2.3	100.0
	Unemployment rate	68.8	46.0	30.0	25.2	18.6	41.8
Share of employment growth		2.2	16.3	37.6	33.8	10.0	100.0
Share of unemployment growth		34.6	35.6	18.1	9.6	2.1	100.0

Sources: OHS 1995, LFS 2002 (2) (Statistics South Africa)

Close to two-thirds (65 per cent) of the employed in 1995 were between the ages of 25 and 44 years, while only 12 per cent of jobs were filled by individuals under the age of 25 years. By 2002, though, these proportions had fallen to 63 per cent and 11 per cent respectively, meaning that older age groups expanded their proportion of employment over the period from under 24 per cent to over 26 per cent. In contrast, the bulk of the unemployed were young: in 1995, 30 per cent of the unemployed were under 25 years of age while a further 40 per cent were between 25 and 34 years old. Although the share of these two age groups in total unemployment remained at 70 per cent in 2002, the distribution had shifted slightly so that just over 32 per cent of the unemployed were under 25 years of age. This has been a result of the fact that these two age groups accounted for 70 per cent of unemployment growth over the period. The ratio of the share of unemployment growth to the share of employment growth amongst 15- to 24-year-olds is nearly 16:1, falling to 2:1 for 25- to 34-year-olds and a mere 0.2:1 for those over 45 years of age. These differences have resulted in a widening of the gap in unemployment rates between younger and older labour force members. Almost seven out of ten 15- to 24-year-olds were unemployed in 2002, compared to three in ten 35- to 44-year-olds and fewer than two in ten 55- to 65-year-olds, a spread of about 50 percentage points. In 1995, the spread was only around 39 percentage points.

The poor absorption of young labour market entrants into employment in South Africa has resulted in the age profiles of the employed and the unemployed differing substantially (see Figure 4.7). The major difference between the age profiles of employment and unemployment is that unemployment is concentrated largely amongst individuals between the ages of 20 and 28, while the employed are concentrated between the ages of 28 and 42 years. Here again, the economy's inability to absorb new jobseekers, specifically school-leavers, is evident. The surge in unemployment over the 1995–2002 period is particularly acute amongst labour force members in their twenties, with observed increases amongst older adults often a function of the seven-year gap between the two data sets. In other words, the number of unemployed 32-year-olds in 2002, for example, is closely related to the number of unemployed 25-year-olds in 1995, and in some cases the 1995 and 2002 figures are virtually identical. This is a rather important finding, in that it suggests that large proportions of individuals who have not found employment by their mid-twenties are unlikely to be employed seven years down the line. Although it is not possible to determine whether those employed in 2002 are the same individuals employed in 1995, it is likely that the two groups overlap to a large degree, particularly amongst older age groups. This issue has wide-ranging implications and requires further investigation.

Figure 4.7 *Broad employment status by age (thousands), 1995 and 2002*

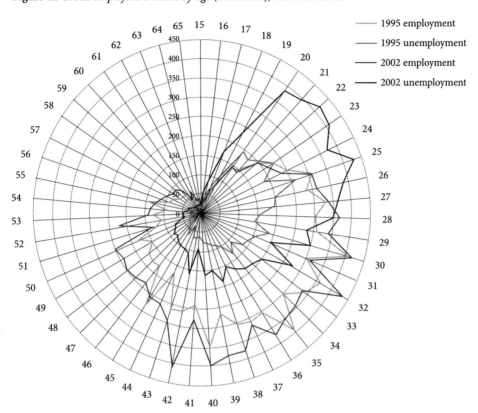

Sources: OHS 1995, LFS 2002 (2) (Statistics South Africa)

The length of time since an unemployed individual was last employed is a question posed in the LFSs, although this is not true of the 1995 OHS, and this provides a useful view of some of the dynamics underlying possible movements into and out of unemployment. The evidence seems to suggest that large proportions of the unemployed remain unemployed for extended periods of time. Granted, it is not possible to use the LFSs to determine the extent to which adults move in and out of the labour force over time, specifically the movements from being broadly unemployed to being out of the labour force and vice versa, as well as repeated movements from one state to the other and back again. If such movements are widespread, the assertion that a large proportion of the unemployed in 2002 were unemployed in 1995 is weakened. However, the existence of substantial proportions of the broadly unemployed who have never worked for pay, profit or family gain, even amongst the oldest groups, means that South Africa faces a serious problem in that large numbers of working-age individuals are chronically unemployed, a problem which has long-term ramifications as chronically unemployed individuals reach retirement age having been unable to provide for their old age.

A disturbingly large proportion (63 per cent) of the broadly unemployed has never been employed (see Figure 4.8). This amounts to approximately 5 million of the 7.9 million unemployed adults in 2002. The problem is, understandably, worst amongst the youngest of the unemployed, since they have had less time to find some form of employment relative to older adults. Thus, amongst 15- to 24-year-olds, nearly 85 per cent have never been employed, while the proportion is 66 per cent for 25- to 34-year-olds. The broad definition of work-utilised[5] means that these figures are likely to underestimate the proportion of individuals who have never had remunerative employment, formal-sector or stable employment.

Figure 4.8: *Broad unemployed according to time since last worked, 2002*

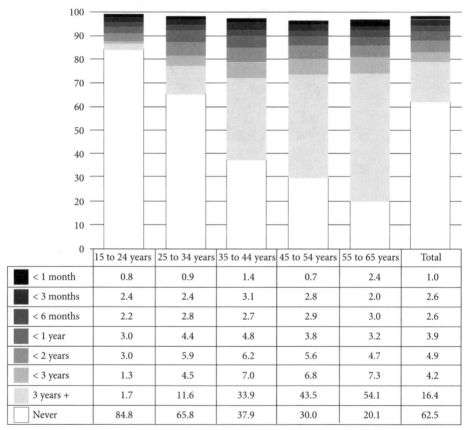

	15 to 24 years	25 to 34 years	35 to 44 years	45 to 54 years	55 to 65 years	Total
< 1 month	0.8	0.9	1.4	0.7	2.4	1.0
< 3 months	2.4	2.4	3.1	2.8	2.0	2.6
< 6 months	2.2	2.8	2.7	2.9	3.0	2.6
< 1 year	3.0	4.4	4.8	3.8	3.2	3.9
< 2 years	3.0	5.9	6.2	5.6	4.7	4.9
< 3 years	1.3	4.5	7.0	6.8	7.3	4.2
3 years +	1.7	11.6	33.9	43.5	54.1	16.4
Never	84.8	65.8	37.9	30.0	20.1	62.5

Source: LFS 2002 (2) (Statistics South Africa)
Note: Figures do not add up to 100 per cent since individuals who did not specify or did not remember when they last worked were omitted.

Interestingly, though, the gap between the age groups is substantially narrowed if one looks at the proportion of the broadly unemployed who have either never had a job or who have been unemployed for longer than three years. This group accounts for more than 86 per cent of unemployed 15- to 24-year-olds, 77 per cent of 25- to 34-year-olds, 72 per cent of 35- to 44-year-olds, 73 per cent of 45- to 54-year-olds and 74 per cent of 55- to 65-year-olds. This means that 79 per cent of the broadly unemployed in 2002 were broadly unemployed in 1999, indicating a large degree of stability within the unemployed as a group.

Other labour market issues

FORMAL- AND INFORMAL-SECTOR EMPLOYMENT

Differentiating between formal- and informal-sector employment remains a difficult task, both in South Africa and internationally. This is due to a number of reasons, and is complicated by the fact that individuals may not always view their informal-sector activities as work at all. Furthermore, surveys that aim to provide estimates of the size of the informal sector are almost certain to underestimate the importance of the sector, not least because of the overlap between the informal sector and illegal economic activities.

In South Africa, household survey estimates of the size of the informal sector are often incomparable because of the evolution of the questions that attempt to identify informal-sector employment. As a consequence, for example, the 1995 OHS is unable to provide a reasonable estimate of the size of the informal sector. Improved questions designed to pick up informal work have enabled the LFSs to better distinguish between formal- and informal-sector employment. Estimates of these sectors are provided in Table 4.12. According to the LFSs, between 20 per cent and 30 per cent of total employment in South Africa is to be found in the informal sector, representing 2.2 to 3.3 million workers.

Table 4.12 *Formal- and informal-sector employment, 2000–2002*

	Formal employment thousands	Informal employment thousands	Total employment* thousands	Informal employment as share of total employment
LFS 2000 (2)	7 509	2 899	11 713	24.7
LFS 2001 (1)	7 377	3 319	11 837	28.0
LFS 2001 (2)	7 539	2 232	10 829	20.6
LFS 2002 (1)	7 771	2 559	11 393	22.5
LFS 2002 (2)	7 845	2 223	11 029	20.2

Source: Own calculations, various LFSs (Statistics South Africa)
Note: * Total employment includes domestic workers and those in unknown/unspecified sectors.

In her study on the measurement of the informal sector, Muller (2003) investigates the ability of a number of recent South African national household surveys to identify informal sector employment. The surveys investigated were the 1993 Project for Statistics on Living Standards and Development survey, the October Household Surveys for 1995, 1997 and 1999, and Labour Force Surveys 2, 3 and 4 (September 2000, and February and September 2001). Muller (2003: 17) used the definition that 'employed persons with only one job, who are not classified as domestic workers or agricultural workers and who work in an unregistered (registered) enterprise are classified as informally (formally) employed', and her estimates for formal and informal employment from 1997 to 2001 are presented in Table 4.13.

Table 4.13 *Formal and informal employment, 1997–2002*

	Formal employment thousands	Informal employment thousands	Total employment* thousands	Informal employment as share of total employment
Estimates by Muller (2003), individuals 16 years and older				
OHS 1997	6 881	1 181	9 177	12.9
OHS 1999	7 083	1 635	10 562	15.5
LFS 2000 (2)	6 818	1 865	11 955	15.6
LFS 2001 (1)	6 627	2 679	12 134	22.0
LFS 2001 (2)	6 946	1 892	11 014	17.2
Own estimates, individuals between the ages of 15 and 65 years				
LFS 2000 (2)	6 768	1 820	11 713	15.5
LFS 2001 (1)	6 574	2 547	11 837	21.5
LFS 2001 (2)	6 883	1 841	10 829	17.0
LFS 2002 (1)	7 102	1 699	11 393	14.9
LFS 2002 (2)	7 156	1 690	11 029	15.3

Sources: Muller 2003: 12; own calculations, various LFSs (Statistics South Africa)
Notes: Own estimates are based on Muller's (2003) methodology, with slight changes.
* Total employment includes formal and informal employment, plus domestic workers, agricultural workers and individuals with multiple jobs.

Muller's figures seem to suggest that informal employment as a share of total employment may be rising slightly, particularly if one excludes the February 2001 LFS, whose reliability is questionable because of problems of interviewee fatigue during that survey (Muller 2003: 3). At the same time, it appears that the actual number of people employed in the informal sector rose between 1997 and 2000 and seems to have levelled out at just under 1.9 million workers. Updating the figures using the 2002 LFSs reveals the proportion of informal-sector employment in total employment to have returned to around 15 per cent, roughly the same level as in 1999/2000. Whatever the period one uses, it is evident that the number of informally employed workers identified at the end of the period is higher than the number identified in OHS 1997. The problem here is that it is impossible to discern the extent to which this increased number is a result of the surveys' improved ability to correctly identify informal-sector workers.

Sectoral distribution of employment change

The sectoral shift that characterised the South African economy from the 1970s through the mid-1990s, from primary and secondary activities to tertiary activities, continued after 1995. It is evident from Table 4.14 that employment growth since 1995 has been unevenly distributed among the various sectors, with most growth occurring in the tertiary sector. Tertiary-sector employment grew by 1.1 million, representing more than three-quarters of the total increase in employment over the period.

Table 4.14 *Sectoral composition of employment change, 1995–2002*

	1995		2002		Change		
	thousands	share	thousands	share	thousands	percentage	share
Primary sectors	*1 829*	*19.3*	*1 847*	*16.8*	*18*	*1.0*	*1.2*
Agric./Hunt./Forestry/ Fishing	1 236	13.0	1 347	12.3	111	9.0	7.6
Mining and quarrying	593	6.2	499	4.6	−94	−15.8	−6.4
Secondary sectors	*1 967*	*20.7*	*2 281*	*20.8*	*314*	*16.0*	*21.4*
Manufacturing	1 437	15.1	1 631	14.9	194	13.5	13.2
Electricity, gas & water supply	85	0.9	81	0.7	−4	−4.5	−0.3
Construction	446	4.7	570	5.2	124	27.8	8.5
Tertiary sectors	*5 700*	*60.0*	*6 836*	*62.3*	*1 135*	*19.9*	*77.4*
Wholesale & retail trade	1 668	17.6	2 177	19.9	509	30.5	34.7
Transport, storage & communication	477	5.0	550	5.0	74	15.5	5.0
Fin. int., insurance, real estate & bus. serv.	581	6.1	1 021	9.3	440	75.8	30.0
Community, social & personal services	2 175	22.9	2 046	18.7	−129	−5.9	−8.8
Private households	799	8.4	1 041	9.5	241	30.2	16.4
Other and unspecified	*171*	*1.8*	*65*	*0.6*	*−106*	*−61.9*	*−7.2*
Total	*9 496*	*100.0*	*10 964*	*100.0*	*1 468*	*15.5*	*100.0*

Sources: OHS 1995, LFS 2002 (2) (Statistics South Africa)
Notes: Mining figures for 1995 adjusted using official Chamber of Mines figures, given the exclusion of hostel dwellers in the 1995 OHS.
Individuals whose sectors were insufficiently defined or unspecified, or who are classified as working in the Exterior organisations and foreign government sector, were omitted.

Within the primary sectors, employment change was minimal with the total increase in agriculture, forestry and fishing employment balancing out the decrease in employment in mining and quarrying. This is a reflection of recent economic trends in these sectors, where growth has been relatively low or unstable and conditions difficult. Secondary-sector employment grew by 16.0 per cent over the period, equivalent to 2.1 per cent annually. Between them, manufacturing and construction added more than 300 000 jobs, while employment in the utilities sector, which is very small in terms of employment, barely changed. Overall, the rate of employment change was marginally higher than the rate for the entire economy.

The bulk of employment expansion between 1995 and 2002 occurred in the tertiary sectors, which added more than 1.1 million jobs, equivalent to an average annualised rate of 2.6 per cent per annum. Three sectors added jobs at a rate higher than the tertiary-sector average, namely finance, internal trade and so-called private households (the domestic worker sector). Employment in finance expanded by three-quarters over the period, representing an increase of 440 000 jobs, while growth in the internal trade sector of 500 000 jobs occurred at a rate of 30.5 per cent (or 3.9 per cent annually). The rapid growth of employment of domestic workers between 1995 and 2002 seems to contradict experience and is likely to be a reflection of an improvement of the ability of the surveys to correctly identify domestic workers, rather than of actual growth in this sector. This would be consistent with the decline in employment in community, social and personal services, of which private households would generally form a part. While employment expansion in finance and internal trade was most rapid, these sectors also accounted for a net increase of almost 950 000 jobs over the period.

Employment changes are closely related to the general and sector-specific economic conditions prevalent during a given period. Thus, one would expect that sectors that experience favourable economic conditions and increasing output would be more likely to create jobs than sectors that face a less favourable set of conditions. In Figure 4.9, growth in output and growth in employment are related sectorally in a manner that better identifies sectors that have performed best in terms of creating employment. Each of the nine major sectors is represented in the figure by a circle. For each sector, the rate of growth of real gross value added (GVA) and the rate of sectoral employment growth are used for the coordinates of the centre of the relevant circle. The size of each circle represents the relative size of employment in that sector in 1995. Thus a large circle represents a sector employing more people than a smaller circle.

Figure 4.9 *Gross value added and employment growth by sector, 1995–2002*

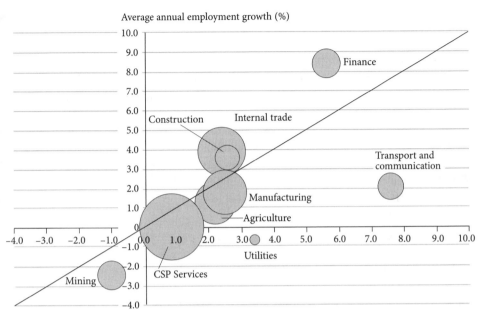

Sources: OHS 1995, LFS 2002 (2) (Statistics South Africa); SARB (2003)

Notes: 'Community, Social and Personal (CSP) services' include domestic workers in private households, and individuals whose sectors were insufficiently defined or unspecified, or who are classified as working in the 'Exterior organisations and foreign government' sector.

GVA data are calculated as a three-year moving average of the SARB's GVA estimates, where possible (for 2002, the value is an average for 2001–02).

While the location of sectors in specific quadrants is generally clear from the figure, that of CSP Services is not. CSP Services is located almost exactly on the line between the upper and lower right-hand sector, with GVA growth of 0.86 per cent and employment growth of 0.03 per cent.

The figure consists of four quadrants. The upper right quadrant is characterised by both GVA and employment expansion, while the lower left quadrant will contain sectors where both GVA and employment have been in decline. In the lower right quadrant, GVA is growing but employment is declining, while the reverse is true of the upper left quadrant. Further, the 45° line divides the figure into two sections. The upper section represents points where employment expansion is more rapid than GVA expansion, while the lower section represents points where employment expansion has been slower than GVA growth. Naturally, on this line employment growth and GVA growth are identical. The interpretation of these two areas can be extended further and conclusions may be reached regarding the labour intensity of gross value added. Thus, GVA in sectors above the 45° line has become more labour-intensive, since employment has grown (declined) more (less) rapidly than GVA. Stated differently, these sectors will have seen GVA per worker decline over the period. Industries below the 45° line have experienced falling labour intensity of GVA, or rising GVA per worker.

Most sectors in the national economy have experienced growth in both GVA and employment over the period. Only two sectors saw declining employment between 1995 and 2002, namely utilities, despite average GVA growth of 3.4 per cent per annum, and mining and quarrying, which also saw GVA fall be 1.0 per cent annually over the period. Employment in the aggregated community, social and personal (CSP) services sector was stable. At the same time, GVA per worker has risen in six of the nine sectors. In the finance, wholesale and retail trade and construction sectors, GVA per worker has fallen as employment has grown at a higher rate than has GVA over the period. Interestingly, transport and communications, utilities and mining and quarrying are revealed as the sectors where GVA per worker has grown fastest (34.9 per cent, 24.6 per cent and 11.9 per cent over the period respectively), despite the latter two sectors having shed jobs.

While output expansion or contraction at the sectoral level is an important correlate of sectoral employment change, what is also relevant in terms of labour demand patterns is the particular configuration of skills needs that can be identified within each sector. This provides another important layer in understanding the unevenness of economic growth at the sectoral level. The evidence shows that while different sectors have fared differently in respect of the relationship between output change and employment change, these responses mask significant differences within individual sectors when employment is divided into skilled, semi-skilled and unskilled employment.[6] Appendix 3 replicates Figure 4.9 for the three categories of employment for all the sectors except mining.

Of the eight sectors, the experience of four indicates a substitution process whereby lower-skilled workers are 'replaced' by more skilled workers. In the agriculture and manufacturing sectors, skilled and semi-skilled workers are replacing the unskilled workforce, while in CSP services and utilities skilled workers are replacing semi- and unskilled workers. Large losses of unskilled jobs occurred within agriculture, CSP services and manufacturing. In the wholesale and retail trade and construction sectors, interestingly, the reverse appears to have occurred, with the employment of less-skilled workers growing more rapidly than that of skilled workers. The two fastest-growing sectors in terms of GVA, finance and transport and communication, have seen employment growth in all three skills categories. Thus, growth in output over the seven years continued the trend of skills-biased employment growth.

Table 4.15 documents the changing nature of employment by three broad skills categories at the sectoral level. The national figure reflects the continuation of the long-run labour demand trend, namely that output growth continues to be skills-biased. Hence we see that, despite the evidence garnered above of aggregate employment growth, the share of unskilled workers in the workforce declined by three percentage points, from 31 per cent in 1995 to 28 per cent in 2002, while the shares of skilled and semi-skilled employment both increased by around two percentage points.

Table **4.15** *Skills breakdown of employment by sector, 1995 and 2002*

	Year	Skilled	Semi-skilled	Unskilled	Total
Agriculture, hunting, forestry & fishing	1995	0.02	0.46	0.52	1.00
	2002	0.28	0.61	0.11	1.00
Mining & quarrying	1995	0.07	0.74	0.18	0.99
	2002	0.38	0.56	0.06	1.00
Manufacturing	1995	0.07	0.81	0.11	1.00
	2002	0.43	0.48	0.09	1.00
Utilities (electricity, gas & water supply)	1995	0.12	0.68	0.19	1.00
	2002	0.45	0.39	0.15	0.99
Construction	1995	0.19	0.64	0.16	1.00
	2002	0.52	0.36	0.12	1.00
Internal trade	1995	0.18	0.67	0.13	0.98
	2002	0.00	0.02	0.97	1.00
Transport, storage & communication	1995	0.23	0.63	0.12	0.99
	2002	0.00	0.16	0.84	1.00
Financial intermediation, insurance, real estate & business services	1995	0.09	0.71	0.19	1.00
	2002	0.10	0.36	0.20	0.65
Community, social & personal services	1995	0.06	0.76	0.18	1.00
	2002	0.21	0.32	0.04	0.57
Private households	1995	0.17	0.64	0.20	1.00
	2002	0.20	0.48	0.31	0.99
Other & unspecified	1995	0.13	0.56	0.31	1.00
	2002	0.22	0.50	0.28	1.00
Total	1995	0.26	0.62	0.11	0.99
	2002	0.02	0.02	−0.03	0.00

Sources: OHS 1995, LFS 2002 (2) (Statistics South Africa)
Note: Unspecified occupations were omitted from the analysis.

In turn, at the sectoral level, these patterns of declining proportions of unskilled workers and higher shares of semi-skilled and skilled employees are reinforced. In agriculture, mining and quarrying, and private households, employment shifted significantly in favour of semi-skilled occupations and against unskilled occupations. In these sectors, the proportions of semi-skilled workers increased by 14, 7 and 14 percentage points respectively, while those of unskilled workers declined by 15, 7 and 13 percentage points. In manufacturing, utilities, finance and CSP services, the trend is one of skilled jobs displacing semi-skilled jobs and often unskilled jobs too. Only one sector bucked the trend with a significant rise in the proportion of unskilled workers relative to other workers, namely internal trade. Both skilled and semi-skilled workers gave way as the share of unskilled workers in total employment rose by eleven percentage points.

Pressures on the South African stock of skills are likely to continue to mount in the near future, as several of the sectors where employment expansion is most rapid (for example finance and construction) are also increasing their employment of skilled and semi-skilled workers relative to unskilled workers. Internal trade, while the fastest-growing sector in terms of employment, has seen a rise in the proportion of unskilled workers at the cost of employment of more highly skilled workers. This highlights the impact that informal-sector growth has on aggregate employment data, and may point to improvements in the capturing of informal-sector employment in the LFSs. Since informal vendors are classified as part of the internal (or wholesale and retail) trade sector, informal-sector growth has resulted in a downward change in the skills profile of this sector. Similarly, the two sectors where total employment has fallen over the period, namely mining and quarrying and utilities, are cutting unskilled jobs at a higher rate than skilled and semi-skilled jobs, as is evident from the shift in the skill composition of employment.

The above indicates a dual challenge for the domestic economy, in terms of producing an adequate economic growth strategy. Firstly, there is the challenge noted above of converting the current relatively low and erratic levels of economic growth to higher and more consistent rates of output expansion. Secondly, though, it remains likely that the nature of labour uptake as a result of economic growth will continue: namely, the disproportionate uptake of semi-skilled and skilled workers, relative to unskilled workers. This unevenness of growth requires the upgrading of the supply characteristics of those individuals entering the labour market each year in search of employment.

SPATIAL INEQUALITIES IN EMPLOYMENT AND UNEMPLOYMENT

Perhaps one of the most critical labour market issues is spatial. Economic activity in South Africa is not evenly distributed geographically, and neither is population. This, on its own, is not necessarily problematic, unless the distributions of economic activity and population differ. Where these distribution patterns differ markedly, the result is unemployment in certain areas and labour shortages in others. In South Africa, there are some considerable spatial mismatches between economic activity and population concentrations, due largely to the spatially based policies of the apartheid government.

Nationally, employment in 1995 was concentrated in three or four provinces, a situation that had not changed by 2002 (see Table 4.16). Almost seven in ten employed adults resided in Gauteng, KwaZulu-Natal, the Western Cape and the Eastern Cape in 2002, which is at best slightly lower than the 1995 proportion.

Gauteng, on its own, accounts for more than one-quarter of total employment, with KwaZulu-Natal accounting for a further 19 per cent. These four provinces saw a net increase in employment of around 950 000, or 63 per cent of the total. Employment increased at rates lower than the national average in the Western Cape, the Free State, North West and Gauteng, which means that these provinces have lost ground in terms of employment shares. While it is encouraging that much of the employment growth has occurred in some of the country's poorer provinces where, as will be discussed below, unemployment is such a pressing concern, as indicated earlier much of this occurred within the informal sector and may not represent a real increase in employment.

Table 4.16 *Spatial distribution of employment, 1995 and 2002*

	1995			2002			Employment change	
	Employment		Share of 15–65-year-olds (%)	Employment		Share of 15–65-year-olds (%)		
	thou-sands	share (%)		thou-sands	share (%)		thou-sands	share (%)
Western Cape	1 355.5	14.2	10.5	1 523.8	13.8	10.4	168.3	11.1
Eastern Cape	919.0	9.7	14.0	1 234.9	11.2	14.1	315.9	20.9
Northern Cape	213.7	2.2	2.1	247.8	2.2	2.0	34.1	2.3
Free State	753.6	7.9	6.8	793.4	7.2	6.6	39.7	2.6
KwaZulu-Natal	1 715.7	18.0	20.3	2 090.8	19.0	20.1	375.1	24.8
North West	750.6	7.9	8.3	801.6	7.3	8.1	51.0	3.4
Gauteng	2 639.4	27.7	20.9	2 777.5	25.2	20.7	138.0	9.1
Mpumalanga	585.4	6.2	6.7	711.7	6.5	6.8	126.3	8.3
Limpopo	582.0	6.1	10.4	847.3	7.7	11.3	265.2	17.5

Sources: OHS 1995, LFS 2002 (2) (Statistics South Africa)

However, employment and population are not identically distributed. A number of provinces, therefore, account for a larger proportion of employment than would be expected given their proportion of 15- to 65-year-olds (the working-age population, from whom the employed are drawn). In 2002, the employment shares of the Western Cape, the Free State and Gauteng were above their individual shares of the working-age population. In total, these three provinces were home to 38 per cent of the working-age population, but accounted for 46 per cent of employment, the difference being most marked in Gauteng (a difference of 4.5 percentage points) and the Western Cape (a 3.4 percentage point difference). On the other hand, however, there are provinces that have lower employment shares than would be expected, namely the Eastern Cape, KwaZulu-Natal, North West and Limpopo, the differences being most acute for the Eastern Cape (where the employment share is nearly 3 percentage points lower than the provincial share of the working-age population) and Limpopo (with a difference of 3.6 per cent). For the Northern Cape and Mpumalanga the shares are quite closely aligned. The differences in these shares translate into differences in unemployment rates (although indirectly, through differing labour force participation rates).

These differences (see Table 4.17) seem to have been influenced by the provinces' differing histories under apartheid. Specifically, provinces that include areas previously designated as 'homelands' or 'self-governing territories' and which experienced relative neglect under the apartheid system, have higher rates of unemployment than do other provinces, particularly in rural areas. The Western Cape, Northern Cape, Free State and Gauteng – provinces containing no or relatively small homeland areas – have higher unemployment in urban areas than in rural areas. This is because of the fact that in these areas there is virtually no subsistence agriculture, and individuals not employed in commercial agriculture had little option but to move elsewhere in search of work. The other provinces have significantly higher rates of unemployment in rural areas, especially Limpopo (a difference of 20 percentage points in 1995) and KwaZulu-Natal (19 percentage points). In 2002, the highest rates of unemployment were to be found in rural Limpopo (61 per cent), rural KwaZulu-Natal (52 per cent) and rural Eastern Cape (52 per cent). It is therefore clear that previous governments' neglect of homeland areas continues to manifest itself in high levels of unemployment in those areas, while economic decentralisation policies seem to have had limited employment effects.

Table 4.17 *Unemployment rates by province, 1995 and 2002*

| | Unemployment rates | | | | | | | |
| | 1995 | | | | 2002 | | | |
	Urban	Rural	Diff.	Total	Urban	Rural	Diff.	Total
Western Cape	22.7	4.4	–18.3	20.0	26.5	13.7	–12.9	25.1
Eastern Cape	34.7	50.4	15.7	42.6	42.3	51.5	9.2	47.4
Northern Cape	37.8	13.7	–24.1	29.5	41.7	25.0	–16.6	35.1
Free State	33.0	17.8	–15.2	26.8	41.1	31.7	–9.4	38.1
KwaZulu-Natal	25.0	44.4	19.3	34.3	37.8	52.1	14.3	44.1
North West	25.9	41.4	15.5	33.8	41.2	49.4	8.3	46.3
Gauteng	24.8	11.6	–13.2	24.1	38.4	27.3	–11.1	38.1
Mpumalanga	30.9	36.7	5.8	34.7	38.6	46.0	7.3	42.7
Limpopo	25.7	45.8	20.0	42.2	34.1	60.6	26.5	56.5
Total	26.6	38.2	11.6	30.8	37.1	49.6	12.4	41.8

Sources: OHS 1995, LFS 2002 (2) (Statistics South Africa)
Note: Differences are calculated by subtracting the urban unemployment rate from the rural rate.

DISCOURAGED WORKSEEKERS

The two definitions of unemployment, the broad and the narrow, while establishing the criteria for being defined as unemployed, also define two 'labour forces', with the broad labour force being, necessarily, larger than the narrow labour force. A person who is narrowly unemployed is by definition also broadly unemployed, although the opposite is not true. The group of individuals who are broadly unemployed but are regarded as outside the narrow labour force forms the focus of this section. These individuals are the discouraged workseekers, who no longer actively seek employment.

Table 4.18 presents a description of South Africa's discouraged workseekers according to various correlates. The rapid growth in the number of broadly and narrowly unemployed individuals since 1995 has meant that there has been substantial, although relatively slower, growth in the number of discouraged workseekers over the period, from 2.2 million in 1995 to 3.1 million in 2002. This represents an increase of about 40 per cent for the period, which equates to a growth rate of 4.9 per cent per annum.

Table 4.18 *Discouraged workseekers (percentage breakdowns), 1995 and 2002*

		1995			2002		
		Male	Female	Total	Male	Female	Total
TOTAL	*thousands*	875.0	1 332.2	2 207.2	1 163.1	1 924.4	3 087.5
	percentage	39.6	60.4	100.0	37.7	62.3	100.0
African		37.2	54.9	92.1	34.5	56.9	91.4
Coloured		1.9	3.5	5.5	2.0	3.5	5.5
Asian/Indian		0.2	0.5	0.7	0.4	0.5	0.9
White		0.3	1.4	1.7	0.8	1.3	2.2
15–24 years		12.5	16.1	28.6	14.2	19.6	33.8
25–34 years		15.2	24.5	39.6	12.2	22.3	34.5
35–44 years		6.9	13.1	20.0	6.0	12.5	18.5
45–54 years		3.6	5.4	9.0	3.8	6.4	10.2
55–65 years		1.5	1.4	2.9	1.5	1.5	3.0
Total		39.6	60.4	100.0	37.7	62.3	100.0
No education		10.6	13.2	12.2	6.2	7.7	7.2
Incomplete primary		26.1	22.2	23.8	24.5	19.3	21.2
Complete primary		8.6	9.8	9.3	8.7	9.5	9.2
Incomplete secondary		35.4	37.0	36.4	38.7	42.3	40.9
Complete secondary		16.0	14.8	15.3	18.9	18.3	18.6
Tertiary		1.4	1.5	1.5	2.1	2.3	2.2
Total		100.0	100.0	100.0	100.0	100.0	100.0

→

		1995			2002		
		Urban	Rural	Total	Urban	Rural	Total
TOTAL	thousands	1 011.6	1 195.6	2 207.2	1 202.8	1 884.7	3 087.5
	percentage	45.8	54.2	100.0	39.0	61.0	100.0
Western Cape		5.3	0.2	5.5	3.8	0.4	4.2
Eastern Cape		6.0	11.5	17.5	4.3	12.6	16.8
Northern Cape		1.3	0.2	1.6	1.0	0.8	1.8
Free State		5.6	2.1	7.7	3.6	1.6	5.2
KwaZulu-Natal		5.6	14.8	20.4	5.7	12.3	18.0
North West		3.2	7.1	10.3	2.3	7.8	10.1
Gauteng		15.1	0.5	15.6	14.9	0.3	15.2
Mpumalanga		2.5	6.3	8.9	2.0	5.4	7.3
Limpopo		1.2	11.5	12.7	1.4	19.7	21.2

Sources: OHS 1995, LFS 2002 (2) (Statistics South Africa)

More than three-fifths of discouraged workseekers are female, with the proportion rising slightly from 60.4 per cent in 1995 to 62.3 per cent in 2002. Unsurprisingly, more than 9 out of 10 discouraged workseekers are African, while a further 5.5 per cent are coloured. Whites and Asians/Indians form a very small proportion of the group. Consequently, the largest group of discouraged workseekers, defined by race and gender, are African females, constituting 56.9 per cent of the total in 2002, up 2 percentage points from 54.9 per cent in 1995.

In terms of age, there has been a slight shift in the distribution of discouraged workseekers across the age groups. At the start of the period, almost 40 per cent of the discouraged workseeker population was between the ages of 25 and 34 years, with just under 29 per cent being 15–24 years of age. This meant that slightly less than one-third were 35 years or older. The seven-year period that followed saw a significant increase in the proportion that were 15–24 years old, up to nearly 34 per cent, with a corresponding decline in the proportion aged 25–34 years (down to 34.5 per cent). The proportions of discouraged workseekers in the older age groups have remained relatively stable over the period. The predominance of females amongst the group means that females aged between 25 and 34 years accounted for between one-fifth and one-quarter of the group.

A rather disturbing trend is revealed when one examines the discouraged workseekers according to their highest level of education. Increasingly, discouraged workseekers are coming from the ranks of the relatively well-educated population. In 2002, nearly 60 per cent of discouraged workseekers had at least some kind of secondary education (specifically, 41 per cent had an incomplete secondary education with a further 19 per cent having completed their secondary education). This is a rise of around 8 percentage points from 1995, when 36.4 per cent had an incomplete secondary education and 15.3 per cent had matriculated. The rise in the number of unemployed individuals with these educational characteristics has been particularly stark amongst females. In 2002, 42.3 per cent of female discouraged workseekers had incomplete secondary education, 18.3 per cent had complete secondary education and 2.3 per cent had tertiary education, up from 37.0 per cent, 14.8 per cent and 1.5 per cent respectively in 1995. The proportion of female discouraged workseekers with at least some secondary education therefore rose from 53.3 per cent to 62.9 per cent over the period, a difference of nearly ten percentage points. Overall, this shift is in line with the trend observed in the composition of the labour force, which is shifting towards higher levels of education.

Although discouraged workseekers are predominantly poorly educated – around 80 per cent have not completed matric – there is also an increasing proportion that has completed secondary or tertiary education, a group which is often assumed to be more able to find employment than less educated individuals. This again points to the education system, which seems unable to produce the types of skills required by the labour market in the necessary quantities. While education is touted as the route to employment and a better life, the evidence suggests that for a growing number of people a matric certificate is no help in securing employment.

Most of the discouraged workseekers are resident in rural households (61.0 per cent in 2002, up from 54.2 per cent in 1995), and are concentrated in relatively few provinces. KwaZulu-Natal, the Eastern Cape, Gauteng and Limpopo provinces are home to the largest numbers of discouraged workseekers. Combined, they accounted for more than 71 per cent of the total in 2002, up from 66.2 per cent seven years earlier. Limpopo saw the biggest surge in its share, from 12.7 per cent in 1995 to 21.2 per cent in 2002, a rise of 8.5 percentage points. This has meant that Limpopo has taken over from KwaZulu-Natal as the province with the highest number of discouraged workseekers in the country. These two provinces accounted for almost 40 per cent of the national total in 2002.

The group of individuals who have given up actively seeking work – referred to in this section as discouraged workseekers – deserves further attention. This state is for many the final step before exiting the labour force. In fact, to a large degree, these individuals are already not active participants in the labour force. The problem of unemployment in South Africa can clearly not be properly addressed without improved understanding of this group and their reasons for terminating their search for employment.

Conclusion

The South African economy today, like that of 1995, faces some important challenges. Probably the most important, and one which characterised the economies of both 1995 and 2003, is the challenge of generating job opportunities in sufficient numbers so as to first halt the rise in unemployment and then reduce it. It has been shown that, while not jobless, economic growth has been unable to provide the necessary employment opportunities, resulting in a rapidly rising rate of unemployment, which now stands at 41.8 per cent of the labour force. The problem has been exacerbated by the high number of new entrants into the labour force, with labour force participation rates rising across the board. This has meant that actual labour absorption has been far lower than the rates required just to keep unemployment levels constant.

Equality in the labour force is still a long way off in terms of access to employment. Unemployment is concentrated in specific demographically and geographically defined groups. Thus, those worst affected by unemployment are African, female, poorly educated, and the young (15- to 24-year-olds specifically). Rural areas, specifically those of the former homeland territories, are the worst-hit regions. Even amongst groups who, in the past, would have found employment relatively easily, for example whites or highly educated people, jobs have become relatively scarcer. Unemployment in 2002 was also quite a permanent feature of life for many individuals, with almost nine in ten unemployed individuals having been unemployed for more than three years or having never had a job at all. This phenomenon has serious implications for the human capital of these individuals as extended periods of unemployment erode their skills or make their skills outdated, reducing their chances of re-employment even further.

Many of the trends discussed in this chapter have been previously identified. However, a number of new issues have also been highlighted. Firstly, evidence has been presented that questions the validity of the jobless growth argument. The argument rests on an incomplete data set of inconsistent coverage and, although October Household Survey and Labour Force Survey data are unable to refute the argument with total certainty, there are now serious doubts regarding the accuracy of this description of the post-apartheid South African economy.

Secondly, there was found to be a rapidly growing number of unemployed workers with relatively high levels of education (specifically matric and tertiary qualifications), despite the 1995–2002 period seeing a continuation of previous employment trends biased towards tertiary sectors and more highly skilled and better-educated workers. This problem is particularly acute amongst Africans, which seems to indicate perceived differences in the quality of graduates from different race groups, and may relate more to perceptions of an inferior quality of education provided at historically disadvantaged tertiary education institutions.

Thus, despite a skills shortage in South Africa, there are increasing numbers of highly educated people without employment. This represents one of the most important challenges facing government: ensuring that the education system produces the mix of skills required by the labour market, as well as ensuring quality education at all educational institutions. However, addressing these problems may still be insufficient as employers may still have misconceptions and stereotypes about certain institutions in terms of the quality of the education they provide.

Finally, it has emerged that the bulk of unemployment growth has occurred amongst the youngest labour-force members, to the extent that nearly four-fifths of the labour force between the ages of 15 and 24 years were unemployed in 2002. Furthermore, the vast majority of these individuals have never had a job before. This holds important implications for these individuals and for the wider economy, particularly in terms of the erosion of skills while they remain unemployed, as well as the loss of the opportunity for older workers to pass on skills and expertise to younger workers. Since these individuals have never before been employed, they are also not eligible for unemployment benefits, leaving them even more vulnerable than the average unemployed person. Even amongst older workers, substantial proportions have never been employed or have been unemployed for longer than three years.

It is clear that the South African economy's performance in terms of employment growth has been far from satisfactory and is a long way from making any real impression on unemployment and, by extension, poverty and inequality. The daunting task that faced the country's first democratically elected government in 1994 is no less daunting ten years later.

Notes

1   Although the narrow definition of unemployment is the official definition, there is a strong argument that in developing countries such as South Africa it is more appropriate to use the expanded definition of unemployment (see Kingdon and Knight (2001b: 84–87) for a detailed discussion). Thus, although some details of narrow unemployment are provided, most of the analysis that follows will use the expanded definition.

2   The full table for African, coloured, Asian/Indian and white individuals and including the gender breakdown can be found in Appendix 1.

3   For the sake of convenience, individuals between the ages of 15 and 65 years are referred to as 'adults', those below 15 years as 'children' and those over 65 years as 'elderly'.

4   What is interesting, and perhaps more vexing, is that the December 2000 issue of SEE includes, for example, telecommunication services and insurance companies, and *excludes* household services (meant to represent domestic workers). Comparing just these two time periods, with their contrasting coverage, therefore, is clearly impossible, rendering the notion of 'private non-agricultural employment' even more questionable.

5   The question in the LFS 2002 (2) defines work as '[f]ormal work for salary, wage, profit or unpaid in family business; informal work such as making things for sale, selling things or providing a service; work on a farm or land, whether for a wage or as part of the household's farming activities; casual/seasonal work' (LFS September 2002 Questionnaire, question 3.11).

6   'Skilled' refers to ISOC codes 1–3; 'semi-skilled' refers to ISOC codes 4–8; 'unskilled' refers to ISOC code 9.

Appendix 1

Table 4A1.1 *Snapshot of the South African labour force (broadly defined), by race, 1995 and 2002*

		1995		2002		Change	
		thou-sands	share of race total	thou-sands	share of race total	thou-sands	share of race total
African	Male	5 374	54.4	7 058	49.5	146	38.3
Coloured	Female	4 501	45.6	7 213	50.5	206	61.7
	Male	804	54.1	950	51.7	58	41.4
Asian/ Indian	Female	682	45.9	888	48.3	98	58.6
	Male	269	64.5	327	57.1	101	37.3
White	Female	148	35.5	246	42.9	153	62.7
	Male	1 152	58.3	1 253	56.1	1 989	39.7
African	Female	825	41.7	978	43.9	3 169	60.3
	15–24 years	1 628	16.5	2 898	20.3	1 270	28.9
	25–34 years	3 728	37.8	5 115	35.8	1 387	31.6
	35–44 years	2 678	27.1	3 647	25.6	969	22.0
	45–54 years	1 317	13.3	1 950	13.7	633	14.4
	55–65 years	524	5.3	664	4.6	140	3.2
Coloured	15–24 years	366	24.6	414	22.5	48	13.8
	25–34 years	538	36.2	598	32.5	59	16.9
	35–44 years	349	23.5	493	26.8	144	40.9
	45–54 years	172	11.6	258	14.1	86	24.5
	55–65 years	61	4.1	75	4.1	14	3.9
Asian/ Indian	15–24 years	98	23.5	116	20.2	18	11.5
	25–34 years	134	32.2	196	34.2	62	39.7
	35–44 years	103	24.6	140	24.5	38	24.2
	45–54 years	64	15.3	97	17.0	34	21.7
	55-65 years	19	4.4	25	4.4	7	4.3
White	15–24 years	312	15.8	276	12.4	–36	–14.1
	25–34 years	576	29.2	614	27.5	37	14.6
	35–44 years	541	27.4	621	27.8	80	31.5
	45–54 years	388	19.6	492	22.1	104	40.9
	55–65 years	159	8.0	227	10.2	69	27.0
African	No education	1 087	11.0	1 060	7.4	–27	–0.6
	Incomplete primary	2 133	21.6	2 778	19.5	645	14.7
	Complete primary	844	8.5	1 192	8.4	348	7.9
	Incomplete secondary	3 375	34.2	5 177	36.3	1 803	41.0
	Complete secondary	1 574	15.9	2 888	20.2	1 314	29.9
	Tertiary	682	6.9	973	6.8	291	6.6
	Other/unknown	179	1.8	206	1.4	27	0.6

→

		1995		2002		Change	
		thou-sands	share of race total	thou-sands	share of race total	thou-sands	share of race total
Coloured	No education	92	6.2	75	4.1	−17	−4.8
	Incomplete primary	289	19.5	275	15.0	−14	−4.0
	Complete primary	157	10.6	164	8.9	7	1.9
	Incomplete secondary	625	42.1	738	40.2	113	32.1
	Complete secondary	227	15.3	412	22.4	185	52.5
	Tertiary	86	5.8	126	6.8	40	11.4
	Other/unknown	10	0.7	48	2.6	38	10.9
Asian/Indian	No education	2	0.5	2	0.3	0	−0.2
	Incomplete primary	13	3.1	11	1.9	−2	−1.1
	Complete primary	14	3.4	13	2.3	−1	−0.8
	Incomplete secondary	150	36.0	182	31.8	32	20.7
	Complete secondary	172	41.2	282	49.2	110	70.9
	Tertiary	63	15.1	71	12.4	8	5.4
	Other/unknown	3	0.8	13	2.3	10	6.5
White	No education	1	0.0	2	0.1	1	0.4
	Incomplete primary	7	0.3	6	0.3	−1	−0.3
	Complete primary	1	0.1	9	0.4	8	3.0
	Incomplete secondary	423	21.4	374	16.8	−50	−19.5
	Complete secondary	900	45.6	981	44.0	80	31.6
	Tertiary	599	30.3	792	35.5	193	75.8
	Other/unknown	45	2.3	67	3.0	23	8.9

Sources: OHS 1995, LFS 2002 (2) (Statistics South Africa)

Appendix 2

Table 4A2.1 *Employment estimates, 1995–2002*

	Formal non-agricultural employment	Total employment					Real GDP
		P0317 (1999)	LFS	SSA (2002)	Combined series		
	Index	thousands	thousands	thousands	thousands	Index	Index
	SARB	SSA	SSA	SSA			SARB
1995	111.34			9 632	9 632	82.24	87.78
1996	110.59	9 287			9 287	79.29	91.56
1997	108.68	9 247			9 247	78.95	93.99
1998	104.90	9 390			9 390	80.17	94.70
1999	102.80	10 369		10 369	10 369	88.53	96.62
2000	100.00		11 712*		11 712	100.00	100.00
2001	98.39		11 335*		11 335	96.78	102.83
2002	98.54		11 211*		11 211	95.72	105.89

Sources: SARB *Quarterly Bulletins*, Statistics South Africa (2000, 2002), Bhorat (2003), and own calculations using LFSs (Statistics South Africa 2000–2002) and SARB *Quarterly Bulletins*.
Note: * Average of each year's February and September estimates.

Appendix 3

Figure 4A3.1 *Gross value added and employment growth by sector, 1995–2002: skilled workers*

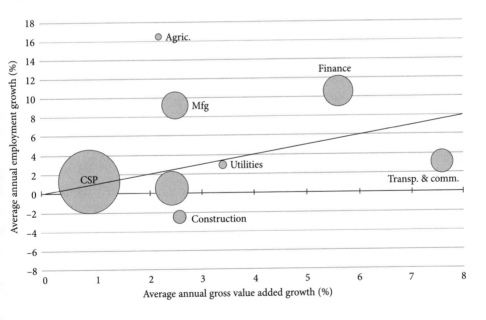

Figure 4A3.2 *Gross value added and employment growth by sector, 1995–2002: semi-skilled workers*

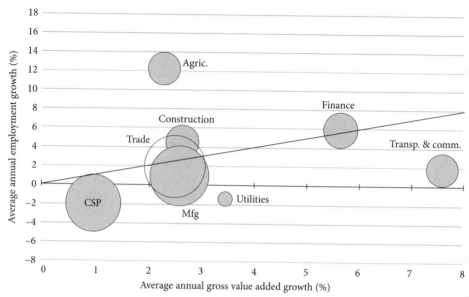

Figure 4A3.3 *Gross value added and employment growth by sector, 1995–2002: unskilled workers*

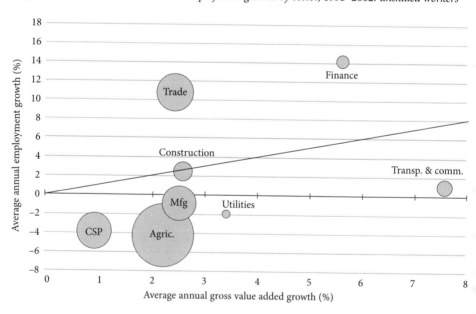

Sources: OHS 1995, LFS 2002 (2) (Statistics South Africa)

References

Altman M (2002) Jobless or job creating growth: Some preliminary thoughts. Paper presented at the TIPS/DPRU Annual Forum, 8–10 September, Johannesburg. Accessed online April 2004, http://www.hsrc.ac.za/research/output/outputDocuments/2294_AltmanEmploymentTrends Implications.pdf.

Bhorat H (1999) The October Household Survey: Unemployment and the informal sector: A note, *The South African Journal of Economics* 67(2): 320–326.

Bhorat H (2003a) *The post-apartheid challenge: Labour demand trends in the South African labour market, 1995–1999.* Development Policy Research Unit Working Paper No. 03/82. Accessed online March 2004, http://www.commerce.uct.ac.za/dpru/WorkingPapers/wpapers.asp.

Bhorat H (2003b) Employment and unemployment trends in post-apartheid South Africa. Paper prepared for the Presidency 10-Year Cabinet Review Process.

Bhorat H & Hodge J (1999) Decomposing shifts in labour demand in South Africa, *South African Journal of Economics* 67(3): 348–380.

Bhorat H, Lundall P & Rospabe S (2002) The South African labour market in a globalizing world: Economic and legislative considerations. ILO Employment Paper 2002/32. Geneva: ILO.

Casale D & Posel D (2002) The continued feminisation of the labour force in South Africa: An analysis of recent data and trends, *South African Journal of Economics* 70(1): 156–184.

Department of Finance (1996) *Growth, employment and redistribution: A macroeconomic strategy (GEAR).* Pretoria: Ministry of Finance.

Devey R, Skinner C & Valodia I (2002) The informal economy in South Africa: Who, where, what and how much? Paper presented at the Development Policy Research Unit Conference on Labour Markets and Poverty in South Africa, Glenburn Lodge, Johannesburg, 22–24 October. Accessed online March 2004, http://www.commerce.uct.ac.za/dpru/Conference2002/Conference2002.htm.

Kingdon G & Knight J (2001a) *Unemployment in South Africa: The nature of the beast.* CSAE Working Paper WPS 2001.15. Accessed online March 2004, http://www.econ.ox.ac.uk/Members/geeta.kingdon/homepage.htm.

Kingdon G & Knight J (2001b) What have we learnt about unemployment from microdatasets in South Africa? *Social Dynamics* 21(1): 79–95.

Muller C (2003) *Measuring South Africa's informal sector: An analysis of national household surveys.* Development Policy Research Unit Working Paper No. 03/71. Accessed online January 2004, http://www.commerce.uct.ac.za/dpru/WorkingPapers/wpapers.asp.

Oosthuizen MJ (2003) *Expected labour demand in South Africa 1998–2003.* Development Policy Research Unit Working Paper 03/81. University of Cape Town.

Oosthuizen MJ & Bhorat H (2004) The South African Labour Market 1995–2002. Paper presented at the DPRU/TIPS Forum 2004, 13–15 October, Cape Town, South Africa.

Roukens De Lange A (1993) Occupation and skill structure of manpower in South Africa: A critical analysis of manpower survey data, *Journal for Studies in Economics and Econometrics* 17(3): 53–64.

SALB (2002) How high is unemployment? *South African Labour Bulletin* 26(2): 39–41.

SARB (South African Reserve Bank) (2003) *Quarterly Bulletin* No. 228.

Statistics South Africa (2000) October Household Survey 1999. *Statistical Release P0317.* Pretoria: own publication.

Statistics South Africa (2002a) *The South African labour market: Selected time-based social and international comparisons.* Pretoria: own publication. Available online: http://www.statssa.gov.za. March 2004

Statistics South Africa (2002b) Survey of employment and earnings, December 2002. *Statistical Release P0271.* Pretoria: own publication.

Statistics South Africa (2002c) *Statistical Release P0210.* Pretoria: own publication.

Statistics South Africa (2003a) Labour Force Survey: September 2002. *Statistical Release P0210.* Pretoria: own publication.

Statistics South Africa (2003b) Survey of Employment and Earnings, March 2003. *Statistical Release P0275.* Pretoria: own publication.

Statistics South Africa (various years) *Labour Force Survey.* Pretoria: own publication.

Statistics South Africa (various years) *October Household Survey.* Pretoria: own publication.

Stryker JD, Cassim F, Rajaratnam B, Bhorat H, Leibbrandt M & Plunkett D (2001) *Increasing demand for labour in South Africa.* Accessed online April 2004, http://www.eagerproject.com/.

Theron J & Godfrey S (2000) *Protecting workers on the periphery.* Institute of Development & Labour Law, University of Cape Town.

5 Public spending and the poor since the transition to democracy[1]

Servaas van der Berg

Introduction

Fiscal incidence studies commonly investigate the net burdens and benefits of public expenditure and taxation in order to gauge a government's political and policy commitments to equity. Some such studies are concerned with equity in the post-fiscal distribution, i.e. with material outcomes of all economic processes, including the budget, as a household's command over goods and services depends both on its members' incomes and on government taxation and spending.

Just as the shifting of the tax burden leads to differences between the statutory incidence of taxation and its economic incidence, public expenditure, too, can affect economic behaviour and thereby have unintended consequences; for example, means-tested welfare grants may affect decisions on labour force participation, consumption, household formation (including marriage), and perhaps even fertility. To deal with this ideally requires a general equilibrium model incorporating assumptions of behavioural changes resulting from fiscal incentives, so as to be able to estimate the economic effects of such tax and expenditure shifts. Most incidence studies really only consider the static or statutory effects of the budget, and not the dynamic effects or the effects of previous rounds of taxation or spending. In an early overview of the incidence literature in developing countries, De Wulf (1975) was highly sceptical of attempts at full net fiscal incidence estimates, a view which still has relevance today:

> …it should be emphasized that the impression of preciseness left by the studies surveyed here is definitely questionable; the estimates obtained in these studies are at best approximations. In any study, the overall effective tax rate or the effective tax rates of those income classes that, from a political point of view, deserve more attention – the wealthy and the poor – can be changed considerably by altering the shifting assumptions or by using different consumption and income data (De Wulf 1975: 75).

Fiscal expenditure analysis, or benefit incidence analysis, as it is often called, deals with the distribution of the statutory incidence of public expenditure, usually by income group, although some studies incorporate geographic or even gender dimensions (see Demery n.d.). This is the topic dealt with in this chapter, although the South African situation requires that incidence analysis along racial grounds should also be considered. The chapter addresses a number of interrelated questions concerning targeting of, and shifts in, public social spending, but also relating to the capacity to transform social spending into social outcomes.

The chapter draws on the author's own previous and ongoing work, in particular Van der Berg (2000) and Van der Berg and Burger (2002), and on readily accessible sources of other researchers. It provides an overview of poverty and fiscal incidence in South Africa, before moving on to consider the link between fiscal incidence and social outcomes. This serves as a good illustration of more general social policy problems.

Figure 5.1 connects some of the issues relating to South African fiscal shifts. Inter-provincial and intra-provincial shifts in fiscal incidence, in combination, determine overall fiscal resource shifts which sometimes, but not always, translate into real resource shifts. Real resource shifts in turn can affect social outcomes, but again, this is by no means certain. The links between inter- and intra-provincial fiscal resource shifts and social outcomes lie in the budget (performance budgeting and the medium-term expenditure framework are of crucial importance) and in the social delivery process.

Figure 5.1 *A scheme for analysing the link between fiscal resource shifts and social outcomes*

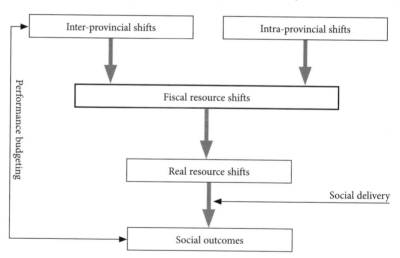

Research and publications on inter-provincial fiscal incidence in various fields include regular publications by the Financial and Fiscal Commission (FFC), the National Treasury's excellent Inter-Governmental Fiscal Reviews, more than one hundred budget information briefs by Idasa's Budget Information Service, and a paper on health inequalities between the provinces (Collins, Brijlal, Makan and

Cross 2000). These documents set out in some detail resource shifts aimed at achieving greater fiscal equity between provinces, which have also had consequences at the intra-provincial level. Intra-provincial shifts have not, however, received much separate attention, except for an unpublished paper by Fiske and Ladd (2002) on education in the Western Cape. The social policy dilemma is well analysed in some government documents (South Africa, Department of Finance 1998a and 1998b) and also discussed in a report by De Bruyn, McIntyre, Mthetwa, Naidoo, Ntenga, Pillay and Pintusewitz (1998).

This chapter first discusses trends in aggregate public expenditure, before dealing with an analysis of fiscal resource shifts both at the racial level and across income groups. Finally, the chapter moves on to a discussion of how these issues relate to social outcomes in health and in education. This provides some support for suggestions that the government's policy focus should shift to giving greater attention to *equity in outcomes* (requiring improved efficiency of social delivery and attention to quality) rather than *fiscal equity* only.

Public spending trends

When the new government came to power after the transition to democracy, investor confidence was constrained by fears that it might bow to populist pressure to rapidly expand public spending on its hitherto disenfranchised, fiscally neglected constituency. These fears were fed by the Reconstruction and Development Programme (RDP) that placed much emphasis on expenditures to address equity and poverty, but little emphasis on fiscal constraints. Yet it had been well recognised that fiscal constraints would prevent the raising of the per capita social expenditures of other groups to the levels of whites; this implied that fiscal equity would require a reduction in expenditures benefiting whites. Initially, the new government's pronouncements seemed to indicate that it would try to satisfy both white and black expectations by increasing expenditures for all to the levels historically associated with the privileged white group.

However, the macroeconomic strategy, Growth, Employment and Redistribution (GEAR), announced in 1996, committed the government to reducing its budget deficit to below 3 per cent of GDP whilst slightly reducing taxes as a share of GDP. Exceeding this deficit target improved the standing of the new government's macro-economic policies in the investor community, and also had the favourable longer-term consequence of reducing debt service payments, creating more space for the expansion of social expenditure in the longer term. Gross government loan debt reached a high of 49.5 per cent of GDP in 1995, but was brought down to 38.5 per cent in 2004 (South Africa, National Treasury Budget Review 2004: Annexure B, Table 7). Moreover, in the early years after the transition, capacity to utilise more resources productively in social programmes was limited – lifting spending constraints could well have encouraged wasteful expenditure. In fact, the budget deficit target might have been less restrictive, in terms of real government spending, than the unrealistically high wage demands acceded to in the public sector shortly after the transition, a lesson that the government has since taken to heart.

The longer-term success of the new government in shifting resources to social programmes can be seen in the continued expansion of social expenditures, which even accelerated from R2 092 per capita in 1982/83 to R2 545 in 1992/93 and R3 369 in 2002/03 (all figures in 2000 rand values) despite sluggish economic growth (see Table 5.1).[2] This was in part made possible by lower population growth. As these figures indicate, the last decade under apartheid did give rise to rapid increases in social expenditure and, as will be shown in a later section, this expenditure was indeed redistributive, reflecting attempts at social reform under apartheid. Such rapid expansion could not be sustained indefinitely by a new government. Social spending increased from 38.7 per cent to 44.4 per cent of consolidated general government expenditure in the decade 1982 to 1992, before the political transition, and rose further to 49.3 per cent in 2002.

Table 5.1 *Consolidated general government spending by function, 1982–83, 1992–93 and 2002–2003*

	R million			Percentage average annual real growth		Percentage of non-interest expenditure		
	1982/83	1992/93	2002/3	1982/83 –92/93	1992/93 –2002/3	1982/83	1992/93	2002/3
Protection services	4 819	22 451	58 132	1.90	1.90	19.6	17.5	15.8
Defence and intelligence	3 477	10 729	20 772	−2.20	−1.10	14.2	8.4	5.6
Police	897	8 576	24 928	9.50	3.10	3.7	6.7	6.8
Prisons	276	1 968	7 458	6.30	5.80	1.1	1.5	2.0
Justice	169	1 178	4 976	6.10	7.00	0.7	0.9	1.3
Social services	9 501	56 821	181 764	4.50	4.00	38.7	44.4	49.3
Education	4 349	27 154	68 686	4.90	1.60	17.7	21.2	18.6
Health	2 394	12 487	40 828	3.10	4.30	9.8	9.7	11.1
Welfare (incl. social security)	1 511	11 222	46 704	6.80	6.80	6.2	8.8	12.7
Housing	179	1 656	9 467	9.10	10.30	0.7	1.3	2.6
Community development	1 068	4 302	16 078	0.40	5.70	4.4	3.4	4.4
Economic Services	4 664	17 141	45 130	−0.50	2.00	19.0	13.4	12.2
Water schemes and related services	357	847	4 445	−4.80	9.30	1.5	0.7	1.2
Fuel and energy	37	653	2 588	16.40	6.30	0.2	0.5	0.7
Transport and communication	2 482	7 054	22 009	−3.00	3.80	10.1	5.5	6.0

	R million			Percentage average annual real growth		Percentage of non-interest expenditure		
	1982/83	1992/93	2002/3	1982/83 –92/93	1992/93 –2002/3	1982/83	1992/93	2002/3
Other economic services	1 788	8 587	16 088	2.20	-1.40	7.3	6.7	4.4
General government services and unallocatable expenditure	2 384	12 977	35 021	3.50	2.30	9.7	10.1	9.5
Interest	3 168	18 687	49 012	4.30	2.00	12.9	14.6	13.3
Consolidated expenditure	24 536	128 077	369 059	3.10	3.00	100	100	100
Non-interest expenditure	21 368	109 390	320 047	2.90	3.10	87.1	85.4	86.7
GDP at current basic prices*	78 951	351 854	1 048 840	16.12	11.54			
Social spending as % of GDP	12.0	16.1	17.3	2.98	0.71			
Population	30 759 200	39 173 150	46 070 995	2.45	1.64			
CPI (2000 = 100)*	14.77	57.00	117.12	14.46	7.47			
Real social spending: R'm (2000)	64 334	99 686	155 199	4.48	4.53			
Real social spending per capita: 2000 rand value	2 092	2 545	3 369	1.98	2.84			

Sources: Fiscal data: South Africa, National Treasury. 2004. Budget Review 2004. Table 1.10, p. 22. CPI and GDP figures from SARB series; population estimates based on Sadie 1993; Van Aardt and van Tonder 1999.
Note: * Fiscal years, calculated from SARB data.

Thus trends in the volume of social spending reflect the new government's commitment to addressing social equity and poverty, even though it was seriously constrained by the fiscal ceilings set by relatively weak economic growth, its own laudable commitment to fiscal discipline, and constraints on social delivery capacity. The following sections of this chapter will show that this commitment was reflected even more in the reallocation than in the expansion of social spending.

Fiscal inequality and fiscal incidence

The racial nature of inequality in South Africa is well known. Most of the poor are African, but not all Africans are poor. Inequality in income distribution is mainly a problem of inequality between white and African, but inequality is no longer only a racial issue: the top portion of the African population already exhibits relatively high levels of per capita household expenditure, although the largest portion of the African population remains poor.

The inequity of apartheid spending levels is summarised by the fact that social spending per capita on whites was approximately 8.5 times more than that on Africans in 1975, when spending inequality peaked. Although vast social spending inequalities along racial lines were some of the most visible features of apartheid, apartheid spending did, surprisingly, reach more deeply into rural areas than is often the case in developing countries, largely because of attempts to legitimise the homeland system, with attendant social reforms aimed at bringing schools, health services and particularly social grants to rural areas. Thus, despite discrimination in the fiscal expenditure, the distribution of *beneficiaries* (rather than *benefits*) was surprisingly equitable across the population, particularly under late apartheid. For instance, almost universal access to school education was achieved, despite severe quality issues, and Lam (1999) shows that mean educational attainment improved much more rapidly in South Africa than in Brazil, another middle-income country with high levels of inequality.

We now turn to an analysis of fiscal incidence, as the budget is crucial for meeting the aspirations and expectations of the newly enfranchised in a society where market redistribution is constrained by poor job creation. As a result of changes in economic behaviour in response to fiscal policies, the economic rather than the statutory incidence of taxes and public spending is extremely difficult to determine. Nevertheless, it is possible to draw some conclusions from statutory incidence. Earlier South African studies focused mainly on racial incidence of expenditure, the most comprehensive study being that by McGrath (1983) (see also Lachmann and Bercuson 1992). Until 1993, apartheid bookkeeping made it relatively easy to obtain such spending figures, because social expenditure was clearly demarcated by race. Since then, however, this has become more difficult, because of the deracialisation of expenditure. An earlier overview of such work (Van der Berg 2001a) concluded that rising social spending on Africans had ensured substantial budgetary redistribution since at least the 1930s, despite unequal spending patterns, as taxes were even more concentrated than expenditures. Figure 5.2 shows that expenditure redistribution accelerated in the mid-1970s, inter alia because of reduced white benefit levels. This shift in incidence towards Africans from the mid-seventies onwards is not as much of a historical anomaly as one would be tempted to think – repressive governments often respond to social pressures by introducing hesitant social reforms (including social spending shifts) to deflect pressure, before political reform comes onto the agenda. Thus, when the new government came to power, considerable shifts in fiscal incidence had already occurred and parity had even been reached in social grants (see Figure 5.3), although massive inequities remained in some fields, particularly school education.

Figure 5.2 *Social spending by race, 1949–97*

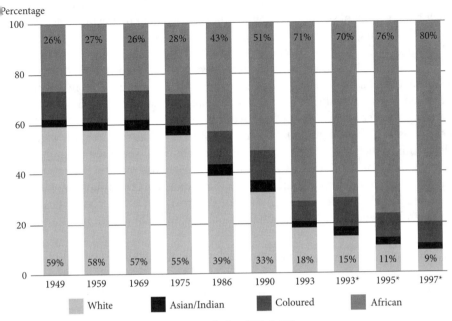

Source: Own calculations from various sources. See Van der Berg 2001a & 2001c.
Note: * Indicates that estimates were derived from surveys plus fiscal data rather than race-based fiscal data alone.

Note that while the data for the series until 1993 in Figure 5.2 were based on estimates obtained from racially allocated fiscal data, those observations marked with an asterisk (the second observation shown for 1993, and also those for 1995 and 1997) were obtained from survey data combined with fiscal data. Fortunately, the survey-based study gave results similar to those generated by the race-based data for 1993, thereby increasing confidence in the quality of this data source. As this study forms the core of the rest of this section, it will be described in some detail. The study was commissioned in 1999 by the Department of Finance; its purpose was to systematically investigate the incidence of social expenditure and of taxes. Van der Berg (2001a) provides more detail on the methodology used for the expenditure-side analysis. The aim was to arrive at reliable estimates of the benefit incidence of social spending by location (metropolitan/other urban/rural), race and income group, and to gain some understanding of shifts in incidence in the period immediately following the political transition, covering the years 1993 to 1997. The major data sources were government reports, budgets and budget reviews to derive expenditure figures for consolidated national and provincial spending; three household surveys, although because of considerable inconsistencies between them the 1995 OHS/IES survey was used as the standard; and 1997 school data sets for seven provinces (Van der Berg 2001b) for information on education costs.

Households were grouped into deciles *by level of pre-transfer income per capita*, to also assess the impact of social grants on distribution. (Social grants constitute a much higher share of social spending in South Africa than in any other developing country.) This required the calculation of income data from the survey, including subsistence agricultural production and imputed rent, and subtraction from that of social grants.[3] Note that although deciles were equal-sized in terms of number of households, larger household size in poorer deciles/quintiles implied that they contained more individuals, as the 1995 population estimates in Table 5.2 show. Spending was separately analysed for school education; tertiary education; health; social assistance (social grants); housing and related infrastructure; and water and related infrastructure,[4] as well as for the aggregate of all these spending items. A second study that replicates this work for 1995 to 2000 has recently been completed (van der Berg 2005). Other studies of a similar kind, apart from those by McGrath mentioned earlier, include Janisch (1996), Castro-Leal (1999), Castro-Leal et al. (1998) and, on education, Crouch (1996).

Figure 5.3 *Real maximum social pension by race per annum, 1975–2004*

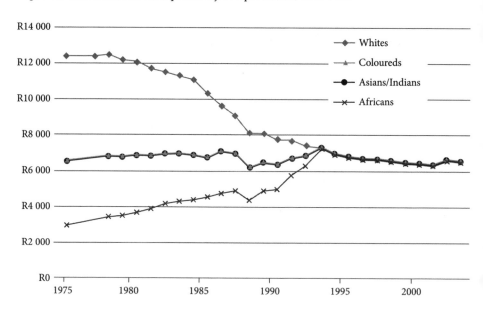

Source: Own calculations from official documents. Data not available for some years.
Note: Amounts are given using 2000 rand values.

Table 5.2 *Social spending by income group, 1993, 1995 and 1997*

	Year	Quintile 1	Quintile 2	Quintile 3	Quintile 4	Quintile 5	Total
Population	1995	10 493 223	10 350 669	8 483 660	6 677 025	5 195 422	41 214 778
Spending (R'm)							
School	1993	5 421	5 356	4 350	4 291	4 030	23 448
education	1995	7 253	6 954	5 187	4 308	3 398	27 100
	1997	9 197	8 662	6 127	4 470	2 941	31 397
Tertiary	1993	735	914	1 281	1 374	1 170	5 474
education	1995	849	1 056	1 479	1 558	1 234	6 176
	1997	974	1 213	1 697	1 762	1 304	6 950
Health	1993	3 911	3 775	3 580	2 619	1 011	14 896
	1995	4 369	4 152	3 788	2 583	1 015	15 907
	1997	5 425	5 131	4 645	3 172	1 378	19 751
Social	1993	8 727	2 599	1 961	1 161	338	14 785
assistance	1995	8 680	2 630	2 003	1 150	314	14 778
	1997	9 405	2 922	2 255	1 238	307	16 127
Housing	1993	155	216	350	511	578	1 810
	1995	289	405	111	163	184	1 151
	1997	1 508	2 114	218	319	361	4 520
Water	1993	226	244	249	225	215	1 160
	1995	641	674	603	371	281	2 570
	1997	893	895	796	560	470	3 614
Total	1993	19 176	13 103	11 770	10 182	7 342	61 574
	1995	22 081	15 871	13 172	10 133	6 425	67 682
	1997	27 041	20 937	15 739	11 521	6 761	82 359
Total	1993–95	2 905	2 768	1 402	–49	–917	6 108
spending	1995–97	5 321	5 066	2 567	1 388	335	14 677
increase	1993–97	8 226	7 833	3 969	1 339	–582	20 785
(R'm)							
Share of spending (%)							
School	1993	23.1	22.8	18.6	18.3	17.2	100.0
education	1995	26.8	25.7	19.1	15.9	12.5	100.0
	1997	29.3	27.6	19.5	14.2	9.4	100.0
Tertiary	1993	13.4	16.7	23.4	25.1	21.4	100.0
education	1995	13.7	17.1	23.9	25.2	20.0	100.0
	1997	14.0	17.5	24.4	25.4	18.8	100.0
Health	1993	26.3	25.3	24.0	17.6	6.8	100.0
	1995	27.5	26.1	23.8	16.2	6.4	100.0
	1997	27.5	26.0	23.5	16.1	7.0	100.0
Social	1993	59.0	17.6	13.3	7.9	2.3	100.0
assistance	1995	58.7	17.8	13.6	7.8	2.1	100.0
	1997	58.3	18.1	14.0	7.7	1.9	100.0
Housing	1993	8.6	11.9	19.3	28.3	31.9	100.0
	1995	25.1	35.2	9.7	14.1	16.0	100.0
	1997	33.4	46.8	4.8	7.1	8.0	100.0
Water	1993	19.5	21.1	21.5	19.4	18.5	100.0
	1995	24.9	26.2	23.5	14.4	10.9	100.0
	1997	24.7	24.8	22.0	15.5	13.0	100.0

→

	Year	Quintile 1	Quintile 2	Quintile 3	Quintile 4	Quintile 5	Total
Population	1995	10 493 223	10 350 669	8 483 660	6 677 025	5 195 422	41 214 778
Total	1993	31.1	21.3	19.1	16.5	11.9	100.0
	1995	32.6	23.4	19.5	15.0	9.5	100.0
	1997	33.3	25.4	19.1	14.0	8.2	100.0
Spending	1993	R1 969	R1 246	R1 364	R1 686	R1 569	R1 555
per capita	1995	R2 104	R1 533	R1 553	R1 518	R1 237	R1 643
	1997	R2 514	R1 947	R1 786	R1 661	R1 253	R1 924
Per capita	1993–95	6.9	23.1	13.8	–10.0	–21.2	5.7
increase	1995–97	19.5	27.0	15.0	9.5	1.3	17.1
(%)	1993–97	27.6	56.3	30.9	–1.5	–20.2	23.8

Table 5.3 *Social spending by race group, 1993, 1995 and 1997*

Population	Year	African	Coloured	Asian/Indian	White	Total
	1995	31 413 885	3 572 428	1 042 430	5 171 257	41 200 000
Spending (R'm)						
School	1993	13 634	3 360	1 387	5 068	23 449
education	1995	19 109	2 950	1 071	3 970	27 100
	1997	24 871	2 590	826	3 111	31 397
Tertiary	1993	4 246	200	190	838	5 474
education	1995	4 791	226	214	945	6 176
	1997	5 391	254	241	1 063	6 950
Health	1993	12 100	1 168	538	1 090	14 896
	1995	13 073	1 274	500	1 060	15 907
	1997	16 142	1 600	589	1 419	19 751
Social assistance	1993	11 420	1 843	366	1 156	14 785
	1995	11 644	1 716	341	1 076	14 778
	1997	13 071	1 674	333	1 049	16 127
Housing	1993	957	200	78	575	1 810
	1995	821	112	28	190	1 151
	1997	3 641	409	68	402	4 520
Water	1993	828	104	30	198	1 160
	1995	2 122	181	40	227	2 570
	1997	2 912	250	62	389	3 614
Total	1993	43 185	6 875	2 590	8 924	61 574
	1995	51 560	6 458	2 194	7 469	67 682
	1997	66 028	6 777	2 120	7 435	82 359
Total spending	1993–95	8 375	–417	–395	–1 455	6 108
increase (R'm)	1995–97	14 467	318	–74	–35	14 677
	1993–97	22 842	–99	–470	–1 490	20 785
Share of spending (%)						
School	1993	58.1	14.3	5.9	21.6	100.0
education	1995	70.5	10.9	4.0	14.7	100.0
	1997	79.2	8.2	2.6	9.9	100.0
Tertiary	1993	77.6	3.7	3.5	15.3	100.0
education	1995	77.6	3.7	3.5	15.3	100.0
	1997	77.6	3.7	3.5	15.3	100.0

Population	Year	African	Coloured	Asian/Indian	White	Total
	1995	31 413 885	3 572 428	1 042 430	5 171 257	41 200 000
Health	1993	81.2	7.8	3.6	7.3	100.0
	1995	82.2	8.0	3.1	6.7	100.0
	1997	81.7	8.1	3.0	7.2	100.0
Social assistance	1993	77.2	12.5	2.5	7.8	100.0
	1995	78.8	11.6	2.3	7.3	100.0
	1997	81.0	10.4	2.1	6.5	100.0
Housing	1993	52.9	11.1	4.3	31.7	100.0
	1995	71.3	9.7	2.4	16.5	100.0
	1997	80.6	9.0	1.5	8.9	100.0
Water	1993	71.3	8.9	2.6	17.1	100.0
	1995	82.6	7.0	1.6	8.8	100.0
	1997	80.6	6.9	1.7	10.8	100.0
Total	1993	70.1	11.2	4.2	14.5	100.0
	1995	76.2	9.5	3.2	11.0	100
	1997	80.2	8.2	2.6	9.0	100
Spending per capita	1993	R1 439	R2 014	R2 529	R1 732	R1 555
	1995	R1 641	R1 808	R2 105	R1 444	R1 643
	1997	R2 012	R1 812	R2 000	R1 435	R1 924
Per capita increase (%)	1993–95	14.1	–10.2	–16.8	–16.6	5.7
	1995–97	22.6	0.2	–5.0	–0.6	17.1
	1993–97	39.8	–10.0	–20.9	–17.1	23.8

Table 5.4 *Social spending by region-type, 1993, 1995 and 1997*

Population	Year	Metropolitan	Other urban	Rural	Total
	1995	11 173 440	12 121 040	17 905 520	41 200 000
Spending (R'm)					
School education	1993	8 168	8 429	6 851	23 449
	1995	8 777	9 238	9 086	27 100
	1997	9 642	10 286	11 469	31 397
Tertiary education	1993	1 935	1 561	1 978	5 474
	1995	2 140	1 755	2 281	6 176
	1997	2 367	1 969	2 614	6 950
Health	1993	3 899	3 822	7 175	14 896
	1995	3 949	3 941	8 017	15 907
	1997	4 895	4 878	9 978	19 751
Social assistance	1993	2 077	4 531	8 177	14 785
	1995	2 074	4 475	8 229	14 778
	1997	2 261	4 797	9 069	16 127
Housing	1993	914	896	0	1 810
	1995	463	688	0	1 151
	1997	1 584	2 936	0	4 520
Water	1993	344	418	398	1 160
	1995	707	1 034	830	2 570
	1997	876	1 183	1 555	3 614

→

Population	Year	Metropolitan	Other urban	Rural	Total
	1995	11 173 440	12 121 040	17 905 520	41 200 000
Total	1993	17 337	19 658	24 580	61 574
	1995	18 109	21 131	28 442	67 682
	1997	21 624	26 050	34 685	82 359
Total spending increase (R'm)	1993–95	773	1 473	3 862	6 108
	1995–97	3 515	4 919	6 244	14 677
	1993–97	4 287	6 392	10 106	20 785
Share of spending (%)					
School education	1993	34.8	35.9	29.2	100.0
	1995	32.4	34.1	33.5	100.0
	1997	30.7	32.8	36.5	100.0
Tertiary education	1993	35.3	28.5	36.1	100.0
	1995	34.7	28.4	36.9	100.0
	1997	34.1	28.3	37.6	100.0
Health	1993	26.2	25.7	48.2	100.0
	1995	24.8	24.8	50.4	100.0
	1997	24.8	24.7	50.5	100.0
Social assistance	1993	14.0	30.6	55.3	100.0
	1995	14.0	30.3	55.7	100.0
	1997	14.0	29.7	56.2	100.0
Housing	1993	50.5	49.5	0.0	100.0
	1995	40.2	59.8	0.0	100.0
	1997	35.0	65.0	0.0	100.0
Water	1993	29.6	36.0	34.4	100.0
	1995	27.5	40.2	32.3	100.0
	1997	24.2	32.7	43.0	100.0
Total	1993	28.2	31.9	39.9	100.0
	1995	26.8	31.2	42.0	100.0
	1997	26.3	31.6	42.1	100.0
Spending per capita	1993	R1 666	R1 741	R1 373	R1 555
	1995	R1 621	R1 743	R1 588	R1 643
	1997	R1 811	R2 011	R1 937	R1 924
Per capita increase (%)	1993–95	–2.7	0.1	15.7	5.7
	1995–97	11.7	15.4	22.0	17.1
	1993–97	8.7	15.5	41.1	23.8

The summary tables (Tables 5.2, 5.3 and 5.4) show that in 1997 most social programmes were progressive in their effect (i.e. the poor gained more than *proportionately to their pre-transfer income*) and most were also relatively well-targeted (i.e. the poor gained more than *proportionately to their population size*). This can be expressed graphically as in Figure 5.4, by means of a Lorenz curve (the cumulative proportion of *pre-transfer income* from the poorest to the richest quintiles) as well as concentration curves for different types of social expenditure (showing the cumulative proportion of spending for these groups). Concentration curves show the cumulative proportion of spending going to these same groups:

- Where concentration curves lie above the Lorenz curve, as is true in all instances reported here, spending is at least progressive or weakly equity-enhancing (Crouch 1996); i.e. it would redistribute aggregate resources even if funded by proportional taxes.
- Where the concentration curve in addition also lies above the diagonal, spending is targeted at the poor, i.e. it is strongly equity-enhancing or per capita progressive, and the poor benefit more than proportionately to their numbers.

Figure 5.4 *Lorenz curve and concentration curves for South Africa, 1997*

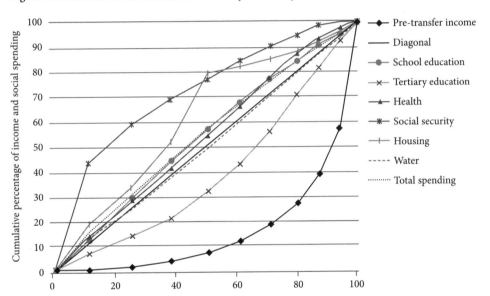

Source: Own calculations. See Van der Berg 2001a

Clearly, by 1997, social spending was relatively well targeted towards the poor, or not as skew as in many other developing countries. This applies to most social programmes investigated here, especially social grants, which lie well above the diagonal and are therefore extremely well targeted, illustrating this programme's redistributive role. Social grants are an important item of expenditure in the South African context, particularly for the poor, as their targeting and large size make them important for equity of overall spending. The notable exception is tertiary education, which is poorly targeted at the poor, mainly because of issues of access: high private costs of tertiary education and poor school results preclude most poor children from continuing to tertiary education. In contrast, the fiscal benefits of school education were in 1997 already almost equally distributed across the income range. Despite remnants of past discriminatory per pupil expenditure, the poor have more children, and almost all children are now at school until about age fifteen. Housing is targeted mainly at the middle income groups, as most of the poor are rural dwellers who cannot benefit from urban housing subsidies. Although water provision is not particularly well targeted, more recent initiatives aimed at improving rural water supply are likely to have improved its targeting. A similar situation applies to health spending.

Targeting accuracy can be summarised in the concentration index and the Kakwani progressivity index. The former is similar to the Gini coefficient, where a value of zero indicates complete equality of public expenditure. However, concentration curves, unlike Lorenz curves, can lie above the diagonal (the poorest quintile can receive more than one-fifth of benefits from public expenditure, but not of income); thus the area above the diagonal contributes to negative values, where

$$\text{Concentration index} = 1 - 2 \times (\text{Area under concentration curve})$$
$$\text{and}$$
$$\text{Kakwani progressivity index} = \text{Gini coefficient} - \text{Concentration index}$$

Where the Kakwani index is negative, expenditure is at least weakly equity-enhancing, while where the concentration index is negative, spending is per capita progressive or targeted, i.e. strongly equity-enhancing. Table 5.5 shows these two indices based on the study reported above.

Table 5.5 *Estimates of concentration index and Kakwani progressivity index for South African social spending programmes*

	Concentration index			Kakwani progressivity index
	1993	1995	1997	1995
School education	0.079	−0.016	−0.078	−0.697
Tertiary education	0.261	0.235	0.223	−0.445
All education: Total	0.113	0.030	−0.023	−0.650
Health	−0.038	−0.068	−0.064	−0.748
Social security	−0.437	−0.434	−0.433	−1.114
Housing	0.417	−0.020	−0.232	−0.700
Water	0.138	−0.019	0.008	−0.699
Total	−0.046	−0.097	−0.123	−0.777

Source: Own calculations, based on applying geometry (i.e. assuming straight lines between observations rather than fitting curves to the data). These calculations are based on decile data rather than on the quintile data reported in the table. The calculations were based on the distribution of individuals, not households. Deciles/quintiles are equal-sized in terms of households, not individuals.
Note: The Gini coefficient for pre-transfer income was 0.680 in 1995.

How does South African social spending equity compare with that in other countries? This is no easy question to answer, because of differences in the definitions used in many international studies; yet a fairly recent attempt at an overview of such studies for the *World Development Report 2000/1* (Yaqub 1999) gives some inkling of how South Africa compares. His results, as summarised in Table 5.6, relate to education and health in a number of countries, largely in the 1990s. South Africa's –0.023 in 1997 for all levels of education combined is somewhat below the mean of 0.01 for the 25 countries for which this information was available in his sample, indicating that South African education spending is better targeted than most, despite the poorly targeted university spending. But even for university spending, South Africa's concentration index is well below the mean of 0.39 for the 31 developing countries included in the sample, and South Africa's school education is also relatively well targeted, although direct comparisons are not possible here. (Because spending is higher per rich child than per poor child, South Africa's primary education concentration index is likely to be worse than average, but South Africa's surprisingly high secondary education participation rates may lead to somewhat better targeting than in most developing countries with poor access to secondary education.) In health, South Africa's negative concentration index points to a more equitable performance than that seen in any developing country covered by the table. This could probably be ascribed largely to the success of attempts to reach the poor through the public health system, whilst the more affluent have largely opted out of public health because of health insurance that allows them to access private health services.

Table **5.6** *Concentration indices for public spending on education and health in samples of developing countries, 1990s*

	Mean	Minimum	Maximum	Sample size	South Africa 1997
Education					
Lower (primary) levels	−0.14	−0.44	0.19	34	−0.078
Middle (secondary) level	0.12	−0.23	0.72	38	(all schools)
Tertiary	0.39	0.04	0.76	31	0.223
All education	0.01	−0.27	0.30	25	−0.023
Health					
Lower levels	21.3	7.5	67.0	23	
Hospitals	15.8	1.0	35.8	23	
All health	22.7	4.0	51.2	31	−0.064

Source: Yaqub 1999: Tables 2 and 5

In most political systems, budgetary redistribution occurs mainly on the expenditure side of the budget. Spending incidence in South Africa is indeed redistributive to poorer groups, and has become considerably more so since the political transition. Figure 5.5 shows a Lorenz curve for income from which all transfer incomes have been subtracted, in order to compare the distributional impact of government spending and taxes.[5] The Gini coefficient associated with this Lorenz curve is a very high 0.68,[6] which declines only slightly to 0.64 if taxes are also included.[7] If the impact of social spending is also included, however – in other words, if a wider concept of income is employed – the Gini declines to 0.44. (For comparison purposes it needs to be remembered, though, that this Gini of 0.44 cannot be compared to the pre-tax and pre-social spending Gini for other societies.)

Figure 5.5 *Lorenz curves for pre-transfer income, pre-transfer income after taxes and pre-transfer income after taxes and social spending, 1995*

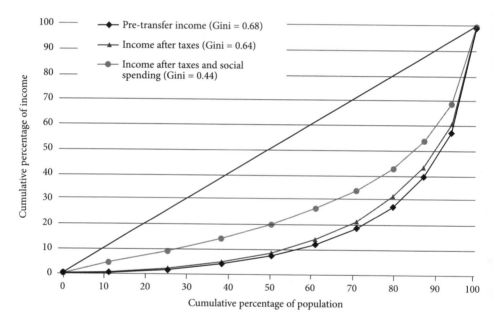

Source: Own calculations. See Van der Berg 2001a

This illustrates the fact that South Africa's moderately redistributive tax system has a limited redistributive impact, not uncommon for a developing country, whereas social expenditure incidence is strongly redistributive. As the poor receive a small share of income and therefore pay an even smaller share of taxes, social spending almost proportional to population considerably improves their relative situation.

As distribution of expenditure is already fairly equal, further shifts in expenditure incidence favouring the poor are likely to be constrained by fiscal resources and opposition to benefits cutbacks amongst the more affluent. Thus, from a redistributive perspective, the scope for further reducing inequality through more fiscal shifts is limited.

Figure 5.6 shows an alternative way of presenting the incidence of social spending, this time for 1995, the base year for most estimates. Across the different categories, spending incidence differs only moderately, but two aspects need explanation:

- In racial terms, lower than average spending on whites can be accounted for by less use by this group of public health services, and because the means test excludes many from benefiting from social assistance. The same factors account for the lower than average spending on the top income quintile, two-thirds of whom are white. Although spending per white child is still above average because of the lasting effects of previous discrimination, the impact of this is reduced as a result of whites having fewer children at school.
- The high spending incidence on the poorest quintile reflects the fact that quintiles were arranged by income *excluding social assistance*. Most grant-receiving households are often amongst the poorest in terms of pre-transfer income.

Figure 5.6 *Spending incidence per capita by subgroup and programme, 1995*

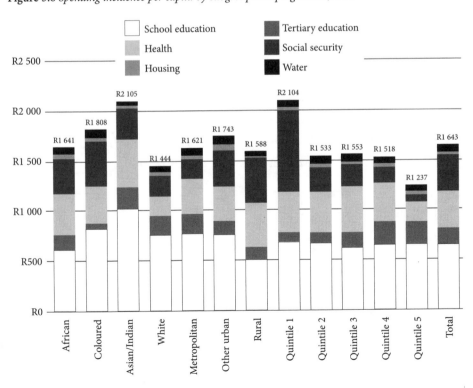

Figure 5.7 shows that aggregate social spending and spending on school education became more progressive after 1993. In 1993 aggregate social spending was close to proportional, after the worst inequities of the apartheid area, apart from those in schools, had diminished. School education still favoured the more affluent, particularly in *per pupil* terms. By 1997, however, school education had become substantially more targeted at the poor, despite some enduring spending bias towards richer schools (because of higher salaries for better-qualified teachers). The concentration index for all social spending improved from –0.046 in 1993 to –0.123 in 1997, and even more in school education, from 0.079 to –0.078 (see Table 5.5). Improved targeting here resulted from the major shifts in educational resources, given almost universal access and the fact that poor households had more children. Fiscal shifts towards poorer schools contributed much to improved aggregate spending incidence, but most of these shifts took the form of more money allocated for teachers in historically disadvantaged schools, often in the form of increased teacher salaries. Thus spending per African pupil increased by 63 per cent of spending in the six years to 1997, but teachers per 1 000 African pupils increased by only 17 per cent, the rest being largely accounted for by salary adjustments. Fiscal benefit incidence estimates therefore overestimate real resource shift to poorer groups, as spending was deflated by the consumer price index, whereas teacher costs rose much more rapidly (a trend also applicable to health spending). Nevertheless, real resources did also shift, although less so than the fiscal shifts.

Figure 5.7 *Lorenz curve and concentration curves for social spending, 1993 and 1997*

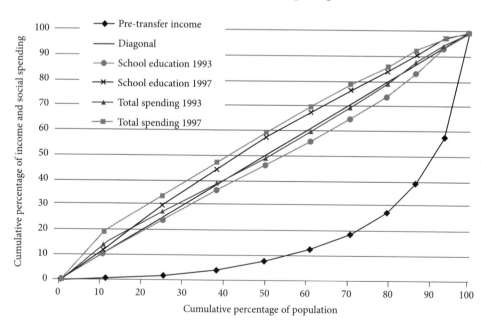

In the absence of much growth in the overall budget, fiscal resource shifts with implications for the poor took a number of forms:

- Budget shifts substantially increased resources allocated to social spending.
- The composition of social spending itself changed, with two relatively small programmes (housing and infrastructure, and water) growing strongly in relative size.
- There were shifts within social programmes, such as the large shifts of teachers between schools, or the greater emphasis on primary health care.

Table 5.2 shows a considerable increase in the resources going to the poorest 40 per cent of households, whilst the only income group to experience a marginal decline in benefits from public spending was the top quintile. In racial terms (Table 5.3), the net spending increment went fully to the African population, mainly through spending being redirected to formerly disadvantaged schools. Other racial groups experienced a small to moderate decline in benefits from public spending, again mainly because of the redirection of teaching resources. In geographic terms (Table 5.4), all region-types gained in net terms from greater educational spending, but the rural population gained by far the most.

The column second from the right in Figure 5.8 shows the geographic distribution of the population across metropolitan areas, other urban areas and rural areas – a graphical representation of the data in Table 5.4. Total social spending (the final column on the right) closely follows this geographic distribution of the population. This is exceptional for developing countries, which usually experience considerable urban bias in public spending because of strong urban pressure groups, difficulties of rural social service delivery and lower rural participation in education. But close to universal access to education, fairly good targeting of social old-age pensions and disability grants, and opting out of public health services by the affluent have contributed to surprisingly good targeting of rural areas.

Individual social spending items do show some quite stark deviations from the overall pattern. So, for instance, housing spending is disproportionately targeted at metropolitan and even other urban areas, and does not reach rural areas. In contrast, social grants are extremely well targeted at the rural areas, which receive 56 per cent of such spending, as against their 42 per cent population share.

Figure 5.8 *Geographic distribution of social spending and population, 1997*

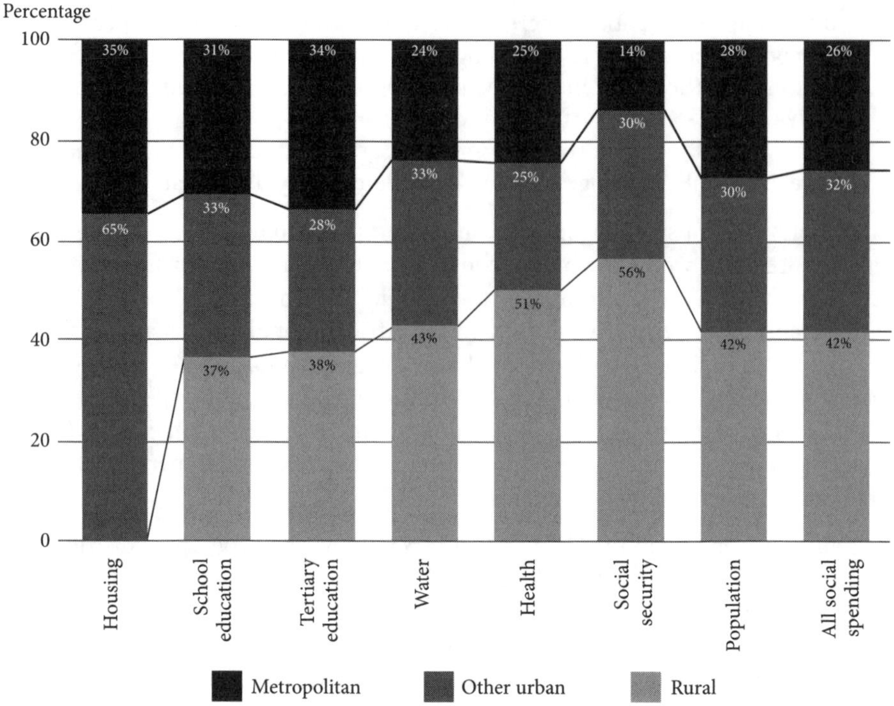

Percentage

Source: Own calculations. See Van der Berg 2001a

The good targeting of South African social spending partly results from the fact that a large section of the affluent population does not use public social services to the same extent as their share of the population. For instance, not many of the rich use public health services, particularly clinics, nor do many receive social grants, and the affluent usually have fewer children who can benefit from public school spending. This trend towards improved targeting has probably continued since 1997, given:

- the completion of the shift to equity in allocation of teacher resources between schools, along with almost universal access to school education for most of the primary and secondary age groups;
- increased opting out of poor-quality public health services by the affluent; and
- the expansion and targeting (through the means test) of the social grant system, mainly through the introduction and rapid expansion of the Child Support Grant.

The problem of dealing with *efficiency in the delivery of services* is one that the government is still grappling with, and one which is crucial for the future, so as to ensure that fiscal equity translates into greater equity of social outcomes. We now turn to this topic.

Linking outputs to inputs: Health and education

Even if social spending is relatively well targeted, does it make a difference, i.e. does it improve social outcomes? International inter-country evidence indicates that government health spending has a limited impact on health outcomes (see for example Filmer, Hammer and Pritchett 1997; Gupta, Verhoefen and Tiongson 1999; Inter-American Development Bank 1998). Figure 5.9 illustrates the very indirect way in which public spending impacts on health outcomes. The effect of public spending on health is mediated by how it affects the composition of spending, which in turn may have an impact on public provision of effective health services, which is not necessarily the same as total consumption of effective health services because of possible shifts between private and public health services. But even consumption of effective health services is only weakly linked to health outcomes, because many other factors also influence health, for example nutrition, sanitation, clean water, etc. The strength of these different links determines whether public spending translates into health outcomes. A similar situation holds in other social services, i.e. there is often a long chain between public spending and social outcomes.

Figure 5.9 *Linking public health spending to health outcomes*

Strength of links determine whether inputs translate into outputs

Source: Based on Filmer, Hammer and Pritchett 1997

Government attempts at improving health services have largely focused on attempts to improve access. Shifts of health spending to historically poorly endowed provinces (see for example Collins et al. 2000), and within provinces to primary health care, particularly clinics, were accompanied by the provision of free health care to pregnant women and young children. Data are not yet available to assess fully how successful this strategy has been in affecting utilisation rates and improving access of the poor to health facilities.

However, consumers still seem to prefer private health facilities, or more centralised health facilities where access is possible. Thus, although primary health facilities are supposed to be the first point of service before referral to secondary or tertiary facilities, the health authorities have problems implementing this because of the aversion of health users to visiting clinics when they are ill. Palmer (1999) identified four themes from the responses she received in ten focus group discussions in five rural towns in the Western Cape and Eastern Cape as to why people choose private services over public services:

- *Quality and choice come from paying for a service:* Respondents felt that paying for a service meant there was an incentive for good service delivery;
- *Public sector care is not effective:* Respondents felt that the public sector did not provide effective care – a number claimed that nurses 'merely prescribe pills';
- *Public sector care is not appropriate:* The perception was that public sector care (particularly clinics) is primarily for pregnant mothers, babies and tuberculosis sufferers;
- *Poor attitudes from public sector staff:* Many felt that public sector health workers (particularly nurses) treat patients badly, in marked contrast to the friendly attitude of private doctors.

The demand for health care reflects an overwhelming preference for private health care where this is available and affordable (see for example Palmer, Mills, Wadee, Gilson and Schneider 2002); public health care is an inferior good in economic terms, the demand for which declines as people's incomes increase. Figure 5.10, based on research by Booysen (2002) utilising the 1998 Demographic and Health Survey, clearly illustrates this. Even amongst the poorest wealth quintile, where only 1.1 per cent of the population are covered by medical aid, 8 per cent visited private health facilities in the month preceding the survey, indicating that many of the poor are prepared to pay from own funds to visit private health care providers. Public health facilities are utilised less by people in the top quintile, where own income as well as access to medical aid make private health care more affordable. Even amongst the second-richest wealth quintile, where only one-fifth of people are covered by medical insurance, utilisation of private health care exceeds that of public care.

Thus it would be surprising if public resource shifts were to have a large impact on the utilisation of public health resources. Except for some of the rural poor, who are constrained in their access to private facilities, utilisation of private facilities is surprisingly large throughout the population, as is also illustrated by the conditional probability plot shown in Figure 5.11 for 1993. This preference for private health services among all income groups probably still holds. From a policy perspective, this could imply that government should place greater emphasis on improving access to private health care, for example through subsidising such care or through measures to encourage private practitioners to move to rural areas. The quality of public health care, at least in the perception of potential users, requires attention, otherwise the expanded provision of public health resources would be a costly but largely useless exercise from the perspective of the intended beneficiaries.

Figure 5.10 *Medical aid coverage and utilisation of public and private health care facilities in the month preceding the 1998 Demographic and Health Survey, by wealth quintile*

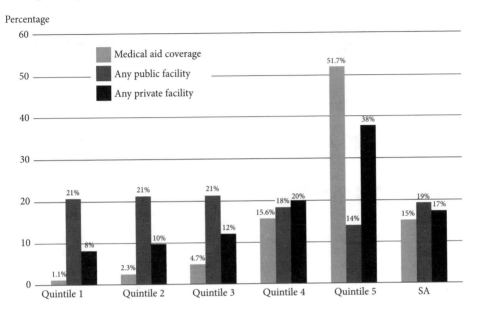

Source: Own calculations from Booysen 2002

In education there is also no clear link between resource shifts to the poor and social outcomes. South Africa allocates almost 7 per cent of GDP to public education spending, which is amongst the highest ratios in the world. As Figure 5.12 shows, overall real spending on school education increased substantially after 1994, with a dramatic shift towards spending benefiting African pupils. But as discussed earlier, such fiscal resource shifts were overshadowed by wage increases for teachers (some aimed at eliminating apartheid-era discrimination in teacher salaries), implying slower real resource shifts. In contrast to international experience, the relative burden of teacher salaries (relative to per capita GDP) increased.[8]

Much of this shift was driven by inter-provincial fiscal redistribution through the equitable share process, but equally important shifts in real teacher resources also took place within provinces. A Western Cape study shows that the remaining fiscal inequalities between schools largely reflect differences in qualifications and experience of teachers (Fiske and Ladd 2002) (ignoring school fees, a type of user fee or tax imposed on parents and used to supplement public teaching resources). By 2002 there was complete equalisation of the pupil:teacher ratio across former departments and by poverty ranking of schools.

Figure 5.11 *Conditional probability plot of health demand by income group, 1993*

Income quintile

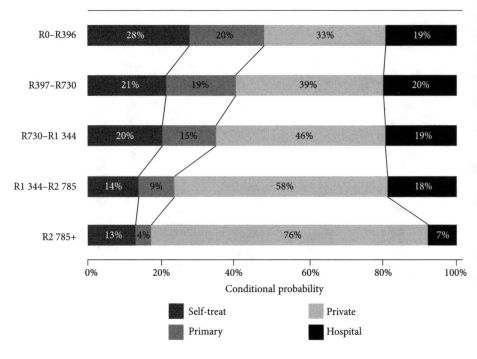

Source: Haveman and van der Berg 2002
Interpretation: A conditional probability plot graphically presents the results of a discrete choice model. This plot analyses the effect of changing the *income* variable while keeping other variables constant at their means. This separates the effect of *income* on health care demand from other factors.

Nationally, state-paid teachers per 1 000 students increased from 24 to 31 in formerly African schools, and decreased from 59 to 31 in formerly white schools (see Table 5.7). Another 12 teachers per 1 000 students, on average, are paid for by parents in formerly white schools. Even considering these privately funded teachers, teachers per 1 000 students declined from 59 to 43 in formerly white schools and increased from 24 to 31 in African schools. However, despite these real resource shifts, between 1991 and 2000[9] results deteriorated somewhat in formerly African schools (perhaps because some better-off African students moved to historically white schools, which maintained their results over the period). Lags in outcomes may also explain some of the perseverance of performance differentials despite resource shifts, but there is strong evidence that resource efficiency is a severe problem.

Figure 5.12 *Public spending on school education by race, 1991–97*

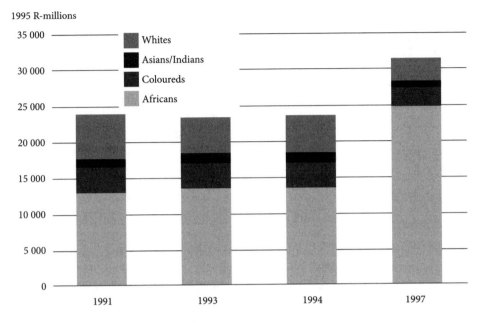

1995 R-millions

Source: Own calculations. See Van der Berg 2001b

Table 5.7 *Teacher resources and matric pass rates over a decade, by former school race category*

Year	Former school type	Teachers per 1 000 students			Pass rates (percentage)
		Public	Private	Total	
1991	White schools	59	0	59	97
1999 & 2000	White schools				97
2002	White schools	31	12	43	
1991	African schools	24	0	24	49
1999 & 2000	African schools				43
2002	African schools	31	0	31	
1991	All schools	30	0	30	
2002	All schools	31	2	33	

Despite the fiscal resource shifts, there are still stark differences in teacher qualifications between more and less privileged schools. Poorer schools struggle to attract better-qualified teachers. Good teachers are scarce and it is difficult to entice them to work in deep rural areas and townships, where they are most needed. Equally, a factor that appears to be particularly crucial for well-functioning schools, management, is in scarce supply in many poor schools and is little influenced by fiscal shifts.

Matriculation pass rates still differ substantially by race and by the socio-economic background of the school community. Table 5.8 shows that Western Cape average pass rates and school matriculation aggregates (out of 2 100) differ systematically and greatly by former racial department and poverty level. In the poorest quintile of schools, pass rates are 71 per cent and the average aggregate matric mark 844; in the richest quintile, the pass rate is 97 per cent and the aggregate 1 264.[10] Yet differences in school performance are striking, particularly when the focus is on some measure of quality, such as the matric aggregate. Former white schools in the Western Cape deliver 34 per cent of matriculants, 41 per cent of matric passes, 72 per cent of endorsements (those qualifying to go on to university studies), and 87 per cent of higher grade mathematics passes. Clearly, outcomes still differ very greatly across the education system, particularly when quality of outputs is considered.

Table 5.8 *Pass rate and matric aggregate in the Western Cape by former department and poverty quintile, 2002*

Former department or poverty quintile	Pass rate (percentage)	Matric aggregate (2 100 = 100%)
DET (former African department)	68	823
HOR (former coloured department)	83	919
CED (former white department)	99	1 289
Quintile 1	71	844
Quintile 2	81	891
Quintile 3	88	997
Quintile 4	94	1 192
Quintile 5	97	1 264

The above analysis illustrates that inequalities in access to education and in *educational resources* have increasingly become less important than inequalities in outcomes. In particular, quality is what matters, particularly *quality of outcomes* rather than of inputs. (See for example Archer 1995; Fuller, Pillay and Sirur 1995; Crouch and Mabogoane 1998; Case and Deaton 1999; Case and Yogo 1999; Lam 1999; Chamberlain 2001; Simkins 2002; Taylor and Vinjevold 2003; Van der Berg, Wood and le Roux 2002; Van der Berg 2002; Van der Berg and Burger 2003).

Concluding comments

In the light of inherited inequalities and poverty, the emphasis on shifting fiscal resources to benefit the poor was understandable, and the evidence assessed here shows that the government has been amazingly effective in accomplishing fiscal and even real transfers of resources to social services for the poor. But fiscal resource shifts, although necessary, have been insufficient to reduce the inequality of social outcomes – and if they do not translate into improved social outcomes, they are rather meaningless. Indeed, the available evidence indicates that this was often the case: in education resources were shifted to the poor, but outcomes remained largely unchanged, particularly when measured in terms of higher-quality outcomes; and in health, the services provided by the public health sector are not highly rated by the population, with even the poor often opting for higher-quality and higher-cost private health care. Only in the case of social grants (where resources are shifted directly to the intended beneficiaries) and perhaps in the case of housing, physical infrastructure and water provision (where provision of services often brings direct benefits) was there an unequivocal improvement in the position of the poor, but these are areas not dealt with in this chapter.

It would appear that the government has performed commendably in shifting fiscal resources to overcome inherited inequalities. However, the next step is far more difficult. At the time of the transition, Donaldson (1993: 147) noted perceptively that the binding constraint was 'not (only) finance, but the limited real resources available to the economy. Competent teachers, nurses, doctors and community workers are scarce, as is the capacity to produce books, medical supplies, and building materials. So the growth and improved distribution of social services must be viewed as the growth and improved distribution of the inputs required for delivering these services.'

But even more constrained than real resources is management capacity. Applying the necessary management to those areas most in need of attention requires information on which parts of the social delivery system's performance are deficient, in order to ameliorate the situation. This is crucially dependent on data and other information on system performance. The budgetary process and social delivery processes are crucial. The performance budgeting system acknowledges the imperative of performance measurement for social services, but measurement is difficult and scarce – and to a large extent only available for matriculation results.

An overall assessment therefore has to be that government has been quite effective in the past ten years in reaching its objectives in terms of resource shifts. In terms of its ultimate goals, however, namely improvement in the living standards of the poor, social policy objectives should be reformulated in terms of measurable improvement in social outcomes for the poor, which would require that much more attention be given to the quality of social delivery. This is the central social policy challenge for the next ten years.

Notes

1   This chapter is in part based on input papers to the World Bank's World Development Report 2004, focusing on social delivery (Van der Berg and Burger 2002) and to the Presidency's Ten Year Review of Government Policy (Van der Berg 2002), funded by the German Agency for Technical Cooperation (gtz).

2   But even though economic growth was low, it was sustained even during the 1998 Asian crisis that negatively impacted on other emerging market economies. Thus, in the ten years since the transition, South Africa has yet to experience a recession – the longest uninterrupted economic upswing in South African history.

3   The term *social transfers* is used here synonymously with *social assistance*. Social security incorporates both social assistance and *occupational insurance*, but as we deal here only with public financial resources, the latter is not included. Here, social transfers, social assistance and social security are thus synonyms.

4   Capital spending is not usually included in benefit incidence studies, as the proper methodology requires summing the stream of benefits in a particular year by beneficiary from capital expenditures that have occurred over a long period. It is thus not directly linked to a particular budget. However, water provision was specifically included in this study at the request of the government, and dealt with as if it reflected recurrent expenditure. It is a small component, however, and does not greatly affect overall incidence. Housing expenditure, taking the form of once-off subsidies, was correctly dealt with as for current expenditure.

5   These Lorenz curves were drawn for grouped (decile) data, and thus do not allow for differential impacts of social spending or taxes *within* a group that change the ranking of individuals or households.

6   To separate out the effects of social spending from personal income obtained in the market, *social grants were not included with incomes for this purpose, thus increasing the Gini* above its already high level, as social assistance substantially reduces income inequality. See for example Leibbrandt, Woolard and Bhorat (2001).

7   Using personal income tax, value added tax and customs and excise duties, as estimated in the tax incidence study that accompanied the study on expenditure incidence (Simkins and Woolard 2000).

8   Lee and Barro (1997: 17–18) provide some international evidence of the relative decline of teachers' wages.

9   Figures for 2002 are not available on the same basis.

10   The Western Cape has far less poverty and experiences far better matric results than many poorer provinces, and poor former African schools are least present in this province. Some poorer provinces have pass rates lower than the 71 per cent experienced by the poorest Western Cape quintile.

References

Archer S (1995) *Quality and efficiency indicators in education: A survey*. EDUPOL research report. Johannesburg: EDUPOL.

Booysen F le R (2002) *Urban–rural inequalities in health: Evidence from the South African Demographic and Health Survey (DHS)*. Paper 9 of country background report for FASID (Foundation of Advanced Studies on International Development) on 'Poverty and the role of rural institutions in a globalising South African economy'. Stellenbosch: March 2002.

Case A & Deaton A (1999) School inputs and educational outcomes in South Africa, *Quarterly Journal of Economics* 114(3): 1047–1084.

Case A & Yogo M (1999) *Does school quality matter? Returns to education and the characteristics of schools in South Africa.* NBER Working Paper W7399. Cambridge, Mass.: National Bureau of Economic Research.

Castro-Leal F (1999) *The impact of public health spending on poverty and inequality in South Africa.* South Africa: Poverty and Inequality Informal Discussion Paper Series. Washington, D.C.: World Bank.

Castro-Leal F, Dayton J, Demery L & Mehra K (1998) *Public social spending in Africa: Do the poor benefit?* Processed. Washington, DC: World Bank.

Chamberlain D (2001) Earnings functions, labour market discrimination and quality of education in South Africa. Unpublished Master's dissertation. Stellenbosch: Department of Economics, University of Stellenbosch.

Collins D, Brijlal V, Makan B, & Cross P (2000) *Why do some South African provincial governments spend more on health care than others?* Discussion paper, Equity project. Mimeo. Pretoria: Department of Education. March.

Crouch L (1996) Public education equity and efficiency in South Africa: Lessons for other countries, *Economics of Education Review* 15(2): 125–137.

Crouch L & Mabogoane T (1998) When the residuals matter more than the coefficients: An educational perspective, *Studies in Economics and Econometrics* 22(2): 1–14.

De Bruyn J, McIntyre D, Mthetwa N, Naidoo K, Ntenga L, Pillay P & Pintusewitz C (1998) *Public expenditure on basic social services in South Africa.* An FFC report for UNICEF and UNDP. Midrand: Financial and Fiscal Commission.

De Wulf L (1975) Fiscal incidence studies in developing countries: Survey and critique. *IMF Staff Working Papers* 22(1).

Demery L (n.d.) *Benefit incidence analysis.* Washington, DC: Poverty Anchor, PREM, World Bank.

Donaldson AR (1993) Basic needs and social policy: The role of the state in education, health and welfare. In: M Lipton & C Simkins (eds) *State and market in post-apartheid South Africa.* Johannesburg: University of the Witwatersrand Press: 271–320.

Filmer D, Hammer J & Pritchett L (1997) *Health policy in poor countries: Weak links in the chain,* Policy Research Working Paper No. 1874. Washington, D.C.: World Bank.

Fiske EB & Ladd HF (2002) *Financing schools in post-apartheid South Africa: Initial steps towards fiscal equity.* Mimeo. Stanford Institute of Public Policy.

Fuller B, Pillay P & Sirur N (1995) *Literacy trends in South Africa: Expanding education while reinforcing unequal achievement?* Mimeo. Cape Town: SALDRU.

Gupta S, Verhoeven M & Tiongson E (1999) *Does higher government spending buy better results in education and health care?* IMF Working Paper. Washington, DC: International Monetary Fund.

Havemann R & Van der Berg S (2002) *The demand for health care in South Africa.* Mimeo. Department of Economics, University of Stellenbosch.

Inter-American Development Bank (1998) *Facing up to inequality in Latin America.* Economic and Social Progress in Latin America 1998–1999 Report. Washington, DC: Johns Hopkins University Press.

Janisch CA (1996) An analysis of the burdens and benefits of taxes and government expenditure in the South African economy for the year 1993/94. Unpublished Master's dissertation. Pietermaritzburg: University of Natal.

Lachman D & Bercuson K (eds) (1992) *Economic policies for a new South Africa.* IMF Occasional Paper (91). Washington, DC: International Monetary Fund.

Lam D (1999) *Generating extreme inequality: Schooling, earnings, and intergenerational transmission of human capital in South Africa and Brazil.* Research Report 99–439. Ann Arbor: Population Studies Center, University of Michigan.

Lee J-W & Barro RJ (1997) *Schooling quality in a cross section of countries.* NBER Working Paper 6198. Cambridge, MA: National Bureau of Economic Research.

Leibbrandt M, Woolard I & Bhorat H (2001) Understanding contemporary household inequality in South Africa. In: H Bhorat, M Leibbrandt, M Maziya, S van der Berg & I Woolard *Fighting poverty: Labour markets and inequality in South Africa.* Cape Town: UCT Press.

McGrath MD (1983) The distribution of personal income in South Africa in selected years over the period from 1945 to 1980. Ph.D. dissertation. Durban: University of Natal.

Palmer N (1999) Patient choice of primary health care provider. *South African Health Review 1999.* Durban: Health Systems Trust. Accessed online, November 2004, http://www.hst.org/sahr.

Palmer N, Mills A, Wadee H, Gilson L & Schneider H (2002) *A new face for private providers in developing countries: What implications for public health?* Mimeo. London: London School of Hygiene and Tropical Medicine.

Sadie JL (1993) *A projection of the South African population, 1991–2011.* Bureau of Market Research, Research Report No. 195. Pretoria: University of South Africa.

Simkins C (2002) *The jagged tear: Human capital, education, and Aids in South Africa, 2002–2010.* CDE Focus. Johannesburg: Centre for Development and Enterprise.

Simkins C & Woolard I (2000) *An analysis of the burden of taxes in the South African economy for the years 1995 and 1997.* Report to the Department of Finance, Pretoria, funded by Deutsche Gesellschaft für Technische Zusammenarbeit (German Agency for Technical Cooperation, gtz). Mimeo. Stellenbosch.

South Africa, Department of Finance (1998a) *1998 medium term expenditure review: Education.* Pretoria: Department of Finance.

South Africa, Department of Finance (1998b) *1998 medium term expenditure review: Health.* Pretoria: Department of Finance.

South Africa, National Treasury. (Various years) *Budget Review.* Pretoria: National Treasury.

South Africa, National Treasury. (Various years) *Intergovernmental Fiscal Review.* Pretoria: Government Printer.

South African Health Review (various years) Durban: Health Systems Trust.

Taylor N, Muller J & Vinjevold P (2003) *Getting schools working*. Cape Town: Pearson Education.

Van Aardt CJ & Van Tonder JL (1999) *A projection of the South African population, 1996–2021*. Bureau of Market Research, Research Report No. 270. Pretoria: University of South Africa.

Van der Berg S (2001a) Redistribution through the budget: Public expenditure incidence in South Africa, *Social Dynamics* 27(1): 140–164.

Van der Berg S (2001b) Resource shifts in South African schools after the political transition, *Development Southern Africa* 18(4): 309–325.

Van der Berg S (2001c) Trends in racial fiscal incidence in South Africa, *South African Journal of Economics* 69(2): 243–268.

Van der Berg S (2002) Education, poverty and inequality in South Africa. Paper presented to the Conference of the Centre for the Study of African Economies, Oxford. March.

Van der Berg S (2005) Fiscal expenditure incidence in South Africa, 1995 and 2000. Report to National Treasury. University of Stellenbosch. Accessed online May 2005, http://www.finance.gov.za/documents/budget/2005/review/Fiscal%20Incidence%20Report.pdf Appendices by various authors accessed online May 2005, http://www.finance.gov.za/documents/budget/2005/review/Fiscal%20Incidence%20Report%20%20-%20Appendices.pdf

Van der Berg S & Burger R (2002) The stories behind the numbers: An investigation of efforts to deliver services to the South African poor. Background study to *World Development Report 2004*. Stellenbosch. November 2002. Accessed online November 2004, http://econ.worldbank.org/files/28003_van_der_berg.pdf

Van der Berg S & Burger R (2003) Education and socio-economic differentials: A study of school performance in the Western Cape, *South African Journal of Economics* 71(3): 496–522.

Van der Berg S, Wood L & Le Roux N (2002) Differentiation in black education, *Development Southern Africa* 19(2): 289–306.

Yaqub S (1999) *How equitable is public spending on health and education? Background paper to World Development Report 2000/1*. Poverty Research Unit, Sussex University. September. Accessed online November 2004, http://www.worldbank.org/poverty/wdrpoverty/background/yaqub.pdf.

6 Trade liberalisation and labour demand in South Africa during the 1990s

Lawrence Edwards

Introduction

The 1990s heralded a period of increased globalisation of the South African economy. The new democratically elected government of 1994 initiated a range of policy reforms that were designed to encourage economic growth as well as to uplift the standard of living of the previously disenfranchised majority. These reforms included significant tariff reductions in accordance with the government's 1995 Offer to the World Trade Organisation (WTO). A new macroeconomic policy, Growth, Employment and Redistribution (GEAR), was also implemented with the aim of transforming South Africa into a 'competitive, outward orientated economy' (Republic of South Africa 1996).

In response to these initiatives, trade flows increased rapidly during the 1990s, particularly within the manufacturing sector. Merchandise exports as a share of Gross Domestic Product (GDP) rose from 8 per cent in 1990 to 15 per cent in 2001. The ratio of imports to GDP rose from 13 per cent to 20 per cent over the same period. Output growth also recovered from the recession during the early 1990s, but only moderately.

In contrast, growth in formal employment, particularly of semi-skilled and unskilled labour, has been poor, despite the modest improvement in output growth.[1] Estimates based on the South African Standardised Industrial Database (Quantech 2004) suggest that manufacturing employment declined by 1.5 per cent per annum between 1994 and 2003. The decline amongst semi- and unskilled labour was particularly strong (–2.1 per cent per annum).

The coincidence of 'jobless growth', rising skill- and capital-intensity of production and increased integration of South Africa into the international economy has resulted in a growing literature exploring the links between trade liberalisation, structural change and employment growth (Bell and Cattaneo 1997; Nattrass 1998; Bhorat 1999; Birdi, Dunne and Watson 2001; Edwards 2001a, 2001b, 2003; Fedderke, Shin and Vaze 2003). Yet there is still no consensus on the impact of trade liberalisation on employment and factor returns relative to other influences such as technological change, factor market rigidities and fiscal restraint.

For example, Bell and Cattaneo (1997), Nattrass (1998), Bhorat (1999) and Birdi et al. (2001) argue that trade liberalisation negatively affected employment during the 1990s. In contrast, Fedderke et al. (2003) and Edwards (2001a) argue that trade benefited labour and that technological change accounts for most of the decline in employment. Evidence of skill-biased technological change is also found by Bhorat and Hodge (1999) and Edwards (2002), who find that *within-sector* shifts (i.e. technology), as opposed to *between-sector* shifts, are the primary cause of the rising skill intensity of production in South Africa.

The lack of consensus on the impact of trade liberalisation on labour in South Africa arises from a number of methodological and theoretical limitations in existing research. Firstly, there is considerable debate concerning whether South Africa significantly liberalised its trade regime during the 1990s (Holden 1992; Bell 1997; Belli, Finger and Ballivian 1993; Fedderke and Vaze 2001, 2004; Van Seventer 2001; Rangasamy and Harmse 2003).

Secondly, South Africa, as a middle-income country, does not fit in well with the one-cone two-product two-country Heckscher-Ohlin-Samuelson (HOS) model generally used to analyse the impact of trade liberalisation between developed and developing countries. According to the Stolper-Samuelson (SS) theorem, trade liberalisation is predicted to raise wage inequality in developed economies, but reduce wage inequality in developing economies. However, middle-income countries like South Africa compete with both developed and developing countries, leading to potentially ambiguous outcomes arising from trade liberalisation. This relationship has not been sufficiently explored in the South African literature.

Thirdly, empirical applications draw upon different empirical methodologies that are not directly comparable with each other. For example, the Stolper-Samuelson (SS) theorem relates product price changes to factor returns and not to changes in employment. Yet only Fedderke et al. (2003) directly analyse the relationship between product prices and factor returns in South Africa, using Leamer's (1996) SS-consistent 'mandated wage' regressions. Most South African studies analyse changes in the structure of trade or the factor content of trade and then infer an impact on employment or wages (Bell and Cattaneo 1997; Bhorat 1999; Hayter, Reinecke and Torres 1999; Edwards 2001a). In these 'factor-content' studies, labour embedded in imports is assumed to reduce the demand for domestic labour while labour embedded in exports increases the demand for domestic labour. Few studies have attempted to merge the 'price-effect' and 'factor-content' approaches into a consistent analysis of the impact of trade on labour in South Africa.

The fourth reason for a lack of consensus in this debate is that none of the existing studies adequately links trade liberalisation using tariff or non-tariff data to changes in product prices, trade flows and employment or labour remuneration.[2] As a consequence, the relationship between trade liberalisation, production, trade flows and labour is mostly *inferred* from changing trends during the 1990s. Such inferences are doubtful as the 1990s are characterised by, amongst other things, structural breaks such as the election of a democratic government, the ending of sanctions, a new macroeconomic programme and new labour legislation.

Finally, few South African studies (see Jenkins 2002 and Edwards 2003) have incorporated the effect of trade-induced technological change on labour. In order to compete against cheaper foreign imports, firms may be forced to raise productivity through 'unskilled labour saving technical progress' or 'defensive innovation' as Wood (1994) refers to it. Trade also increases skill-biased technological transfers (through imitating foreign technology or through the transfer of goods) from developed countries (Pissarides 1997).[3] The failure to account for trade-induced technological change implies that the impact on labour ascribed to trade in many South African studies may be underestimated.

Drawing on these shortcomings, this chapter makes a number of contributions to research on the impact of trade on labour demand in South Africa.

The next section of the chapter clarifies the debate on the extent to which South Africa has liberalised its trade during the 1990s by using appropriate tariff schedule data constructed from government gazettes. The chapter then estimates the impact of trade on labour demand, by analysing the changing structure and factor content of South African trade during the 1990s. Although similar factor content approaches have been used by Edwards (2001a) and Jenkins (2002), this chapter presents a more regional focus on trade flows as well as investigating the role of trade-induced technological change in driving the estimated impact of trade flows on employment. Finally, the 'mandated factor return' methodology developed by Leamer (1996) and modified by Feenstra and Hanson (1999) is used to estimate the impact of tariff liberalisation on factor demand. This extends similar work on South Africa done by Fedderke et al. (2003), by explicitly capturing the impact of tariff liberalisation rather than product price movements on the returns to capital and skilled and unskilled labour. The chapter closes with various conclusions derived from the analysis presented.

Trade liberalisation during the 1990s

The impact of trade liberalisation on labour in South Africa is strongly dependent on the degree to which protection barriers have fallen. On this matter, there is substantial disagreement within the South African research environment (Holden 1992; Bell 1997; Belli et al. 1993; Fedderke and Vaze 2001, 2004; Van Seventer 2001; Rangasamy and Harmse 2003). Although nominal tariffs have fallen since 1994, Fedderke and Vaze (2001) argue that effective protection rates have risen or are still high for many sectors. Rangasamy and Harmse (2003), in contrast, argue that protection fell significantly during the 1990s. However, these studies are based on collection rates (Fedderke and Vaze 2001) and the WTO bound rates (Rangasamy and Harmse 2003), rather than on applied tariff rates. Hence neither of these studies presents an adequate representation of liberalisation during the 1990s.

To investigate tariff reform during the 1990s, this chapter draws on scheduled tariff rates and surcharge revenue at the 8-digit Harmonised System (HS) level for the years 1990 to 2004. These data are obtained from the Trade Analysis and Information System (TRAINS) database, the Economic Research Division of the Industrial Development Corporation (IDC), the Trade and Industry Policy Strategies (TIPS) and South African government gazettes.

South Africa's early industrial development was driven by a policy of import-substitution industrialisation that began in the 1920s with the substitution of imports of consumer goods by domestic manufactures, but then shifted in the 1970s and 1980s towards import replacement in downstream industries, particularly the chemical and basic metals sub-sectors. As a consequence, the democratically elected government in 1994 inherited a protectionist trade regime characterised by high levels of protection, a wide dispersion of tariffs, and a complicated array of tariff types (Belli et al. 1993).

Although some initiatives had been undertaken to open the economy from the 1970s (the Export Development Assistance scheme in 1970s, the General Export Incentive Scheme (GEIS) in 1990 and the relaxation of quantitative restrictions), reform of the trade regime gathered momentum with South Africa's formal Offer in 1995 to the WTO. In this Offer South Africa agreed to bind 98 per cent of all tariff lines, reduce the number of tariff rates to six, rationalise the more than 12 000 tariff lines and replace quantitative restrictions on agricultural products with tariffs.

Substantial progress has been made in simplifying the tariff structure of the early 1990s (see Table 6.1). The total number of 8-digit HS tariff lines fell from more than 12 000 in 1990 to 7 914 in 2003.[4] The tariff structure has also been simplified with the share of 8-digit HS lines bearing formula, mixed or specific duties declining from 31.4 per cent in 1994 to between 0.7 per cent (SADC) and 25.3 per cent (most favoured nation (MFN)) in 2003. Finally, the number of *ad valorem* tariff rates facing the European Union (EU) (27) and SADC (27) countries fell, but still exceeds the six tariff rates proposed in South Africa's GATT/WTO Uruguay Round Offer. Further progress in simplifying the tariff structure is thus possible.

Table 6.1 *Summary tariff statistics (including* ad valorem *equivalents)*

	1990	1994	1998	2003 average*	2003 MFN	2003 EU	2003 SADC
Number of tariff lines	12 466	11 231	7 773		7 914	7 914	7 914
Number of *ad valorem* tariff rates	38	37	45		38	27	27
Number of non-*ad valorem* rates	694	686	230		178	77	24
Ad valorem tariffs as % all tariffs	69.6	68.6	74.5		74.7	96.2	99.3
Non-*ad valorem* tariffs as % all tariffs	30.4	31.4	25.5		25.3	3.8	0.7
Max	445.7	639.3	353.7		102.2	102.2	102.2
Min	0.0	0.0	0.0		0.0	0.0	0.0
% lines zero rated	25.6	27.3	42.7		44.0	45.5	64.6
% lines with tariff rate > 30%	19.7	29.1	29.2		26.7	10.3	5.0
Coeff. of variation	1.0	1.2	1.3		1.1	1.1	1.6
Mean collection rate excl. surcharges	8.3	7.9	7.1	6.1			
Unweighted mean							
Total	13.2	17.5	14.1	10.6	11.3	9.7	5.1
Agriculture	4.5	5.1	5.2	5.0	5.4	4.6	1.5
Mining	3.7	2.8	1.2	0.6	0.9	0.2	0.0
Manufacturing	13.6	18.0	14.7	11.0	11.8	10.1	5.3
Unweighted mean incl. surcharges							
Total	20.5	21.9	14.1	10.6	11.3	9.7	5.1
Agriculture	10.4	8.9	5.2	5.0	5.4	4.6	1.5
Mining	3.7	2.8	1.2	0.6	0.9	0.2	0.0
Manufacturing	21.1	22.5	14.7	11.0	11.8	10.1	5.3

Notes: These rates include surcharges and *ad valorem* equivalents (AVE) of formula, specific, compound and mixed duties and are based on HS8-digit tariff lines.
Duty collection rates are used to calculate the AVE.
For formula duty and mixed duties the AVE are equal to the collection rates if these exceed the *ad valorem* component of the tariff. See Edwards (2005) for further details.
* Calculated using import values in 2003 as weights.

Average nominal and effective protection rates have also fallen. The simple average MFN tariff rate, inclusive of surcharges, fell from 22 per cent in 1994 to 11.3 per cent in 2003 (Table 6.1), with most of this decline occurring prior to 2000. From 2000, tariff barriers facing EU and SADC countries fell more rapidly than MFN tariffs in accordance with the SA–EU Free Trade Agreement and the SADC Free Trade Protocol.

By 2003 average tariffs facing EU and SADC countries had fallen to 9.7 per cent and 5.1 per cent respectively. Further simplifications of the tariff structure initiated in early 2004 have led to additional reductions in average tariff rates facing MFN (8.3 per cent), EU (7.1 per cent) and SADC (2.4 per cent) countries. Average effective rates of protection (ERP) have also fallen, but remain high, particularly in manufacturing where they averaged 24.3 per cent in 2003 (see Table 6.1 and Table 6.2).[5]

All aggregate sectors experienced a decline in nominal and effective protection between 1994 and 2003, but protection remains high in some sectors (see Table 6.2). Nominal tariff reductions were biased against labour-intensive and semi- and unskilled labour-intensive sectors, with relatively strong declines experienced in textiles, footwear, wearing apparel and communication equipment.[6] Despite these declines, nominal protection remains high in many of the labour-intensive sectors such as textiles, clothing and footwear, where average tariffs exceed 20 per cent. Other highly protected sectors are tobacco (33 per cent), furniture (17 per cent), beverages (15 per cent) and motor vehicles (15 per cent). The structure of effective protection rates is similar to nominal protection rates and high ERP are also found in the tobacco (257 per cent), textiles (76 per cent), clothing (94 per cent), footwear (51 per cent) and furniture (46 per cent) sectors.[7] The levels of protection in these sectors are, however, substantially lower than in 1994, when ERP often exceeded 100 per cent.

Table 6.2 *Measures of sectoral protection*

| | | Scheduled tariffs including surcharges (percentage) | | | | | ERP[2] (percentage) | |
	1994	2003 MFN	2003 EU	2003 SADC	2003 Average	Percentage change[1]	1994	2003
Total	21.9	11.3	9.7	5.1	10.6	−9.3	38.6	18.9
Agriculture	8.9	5.4	4.6	1.4	4.4	−4.1	7.3	3.8
Coal mining	0.0	0.0	0.0	0.0	0.0	0.0	−5.5	−2.3
Gold mining	10.0	0.0	0.0	0.0	0.0	−9.1	11.4	−2.1
Other mining	2.9	1.0	0.3	0.0	0.9	−1.9	1.7	0.2
Manufacturing	22.5	11.8	9.9	5.2	10.9	−9.5	48.4	24.3
Food	18.8	11.8	11.3	5.2	11.5	−6.2	55.3	38.3
Beverages	29.3	14.3	16.0	5.4	15.4	−10.8	51.9	28.4
Tobacco	41.7	36.0	35.3	17.0	32.9	−6.2	340.5	257.2
Textiles	41.3	22.6	18.1	10.8	20.3	−14.8	149.7	76.2
Wearing apparel	75.1	35.0	27.1	19.7	33.4	−23.8	218.4	94.1
Leather products	25.9	11.6	11.3	6.8	11.3	−11.5	59.7	18.8
Footwear	48.0	22.7	22.4	18.8	22.7	−17.1	106.0	51.1
Wood products	14.5	9.1	9.1	2.6	8.5	−5.3	21.7	14.0
Paper products	11.3	6.2	6.2	0.1	6.2	−4.7	15.8	10.3

→

	1994	2003 MFN	2003 EU	2003 SADC	2003 Average	Percentage change[1]	1994	2003
		Scheduled tariffs including surcharges (percentage)					ERP[2] (percentage)	
Printing & publishing	16.1	4.8	4.5	0.0	4.6	−9.9	22.2	4.5
Coke & petroleum	5.1	3.3	3.4	0.8	3.3	−1.8	10.0	8.2
Basic chemicals	8.1	1.7	1.6	0.1	1.6	−5.9	14.4	1.4
Other chemicals	16.2	4.5	4.4	1.1	4.4	−10.2	32.3	7.4
Rubber products	18.6	11.4	10.1	2.4	10.8	−6.5	46.6	31.7
Plastic products	19.8	9.8	9.7	1.8	9.8	−8.4	36.2	20.3
Glass products	17.2	7.7	6.5	1.8	7.2	−8.5	32.1	13.3
Non-metallic minerals	15.0	5.6	5.6	1.9	5.6	−8.2	29.9	10.8
Basic iron & steel	8.8	4.3	4.3	0.0	4.3	−4.2	20.1	11.0
Non-ferrous metals	10.8	2.2	2.2	0.1	2.1	−7.9	17.9	2.9
Metal products	18.3	8.1	7.8	3.4	7.9	−8.8	36.7	16.1
Machinery & equipment	10.4	3.7	3.4	1.1	3.6	−6.2	11.9	2.9
Electrical machinery	18.3	7.7	6.5	1.9	7.1	−9.4	33.0	13.8
Communication equipment	24.2	3.1	2.7	1.5	2.9	−17.1	35.5	1.2
Professional & scientific	12.2	0.3	0.3	0.1	0.3	−10.6	9.5	−5.9
Motor vehicles	25.9	15.7	14.9	10.8	15.2	−8.5	45.1	32.3
Other transport	12.3	0.9	0.8	0.3	0.8	−10.2	14.9	−3.2
Furniture	32.1	17.7	17.7	11.8	17.4	−11.2	82.6	46.4
Other manufacturing	26.5	6.0	5.9	3.3	5.9	−16.2	96.5	17.5

Notes: Nominal protection rates are the simple unweighted average calculated using HS8-digit data.
Tariffs include surcharges and AVE for formula duties, specific duties and mixed duties.
1   Calculated as $((t_1 - t_0)/(1 + t_0) - 1)$.
2   The averages are calculated using ERP at the 2- and 3-digit SIC level. Total output values between 1988 and 2002 are used as weights.

In conclusion, South Africa has experienced a considerable reduction in tariff protection since the beginning of the 1990s. The tariff structure has been simplified and tariff levels have fallen by roughly half, which is similar to the pace of liberalisation in other developing economies. Tariff reductions are also found to be biased against sectors that use labour, particularly semi- and unskilled labour, relatively intensively. This suggests that tariff liberalisation may have contributed towards the decline in employment, particularly of less-skilled labour. This relationship is explored in more detail in the following sections.

The structure and factor content of South African manufacturing trade

Tariff liberalisation alters the relative incentive to produce for the domestic and export markets. Import-competing sectors contract, while export-orientated sectors expand. According to traditional trade theory, the changing pattern of trade will also reflect the economy's relative factor endowments. This section of the chapter investigates South Africa's comparative advantage vis-à-vis various regions and briefly analyses the changing factor intensity of South African manufacturing trade. Further, decomposition techniques are used to decompose growth in factor usage (employment and capital) into changes arising from domestic demand, exports, imports and technological change.

The factor bias of South African regional trade flows

Traditional trade theory predicts that the composition of an economy's regional trade will reflect its factor endowment relative to its partners. To test this hypothesis in the case of South Africa, Table 6.3 presents the coefficients from regressions of regional net trade in 28 manufacturing sectors against (i) the ratio of highly skilled labour (managerial and professional occupations) to less-skilled labour (other occupations) and (ii) the capital intensity of production (machinery and equipment capital stock per worker). Following Baldwin (1971), the sign of these coefficients 'reveals' a country's relative factor endowments.[8]

Net trade for total manufacturing is shown to be negatively related to the skill intensity of production within manufacturing. This suggests that South Africa is relatively abundant in less-skilled labour and hence has a comparative advantage in products that use less-skilled labour relatively intensively. However, this relationship is driven by the large share of total South African trade accounted for by developed economies. Relative to Africa, China and India, and South America, South African net trade is biased towards skilled-labour-intensive sectors. This result is consistent with a study by Alleyne and Subramanian (2001), who find that South African net trade during the 1990s 'reveals' the country to be unskilled-labour-abundant relative to high- and middle-income economies, but skilled-labour-abundant relative to low-income economies.

However, South African net trade paradoxically 'reveals' the country to be capital-abundant relative to all the regions in the sample, a result also found by Alleyne and Subramanian (2001). This is a paradox as South Africa is generally considered to be capital-abundant vis-à-vis high-income and many middle-income economies.[9]

Table 6.3 *Factor bias of net trade in manufacturing, 1990–2002*

	Highly skilled/ less-skilled	Capital/Labour	Adj. R^2	F-stat	Share total trade (%)
Total	−14.2***	6.5***	0.53	16.0***	
Africa	8.1*	2.3	0.16	3.7**	10
Rest of Asia	−12.7*	9.0**	0.18	3.9**	14
China & India	6.7	4.2	0.02	1.3	4
S. America	1.4	6.7**	0.14	3.3*	2
Developed	−20.6***	6.6***	0.61	22.4***	66

Notes: Highly skilled/Less-skilled is measured as the ratio of professional, managerial and skilled technical to the remaining occupations.
Capital/Labour measures the value of machinery and equipment capital stock (R million, 1995 prices) per worker.
Net trade is measured as the average natural logarithm of exports/imports over the period 1990–2002. Estimations are weighted using average output between 1990 and 2002.
Share total trade is calculated as regional imports plus exports over total South African imports plus exports.
Trade data are sourced from Customs and Excise in current values and are deflated to 1995 prices using an import price deflator obtained from Quantech (2004).
Developed economies include the EU, USA, Canada, Japan, Australia and New Zealand. Rest of Asia excludes China and India.
*, ** and *** reflect significance at the 10, 5 and 1 per cent significance levels respectively.

However, the 'revealed' abundance in capital is not necessarily a paradox. Capital is internationally mobile and links between domestic and international capital markets result in similar costs of capital (Wood and Mayer 2001). As a result, capital cannot be regarded as a resource of which a large fixed 'endowment' gives some countries a comparative advantage in the production and export of capital-intensive goods. The sectors driving the positive relationship between capital intensity and net trade are the basic metals (iron and steel, and non-ferrous metals) and chemicals sectors, which are highly capital-intensive. Exports of basic metals, for example, reflect South Africa's rich endowments of natural resources rather than an abundance of capital.[10]

Significant state support for the beneficiation of natural resources, particularly during the 1970s and early 1980s, also exacerbated the capital intensity of exports. Even during the 1990s, capital-intensive sectors received state support. Between 1993 and 1997 the bulk of IDC funds were utilised in the basic metals sector and covered projects such as the Alusaf expansion, Columbus Stainless Steel and Saldanha Steel (Department of Trade and Industry 1997). Export incentives, provided under the GEIS, were also biased towards capital- and intermediate-capital-intensive sectors. This support has contributed to the failure of South Africa to diversify into more labour-intensive manufacturing exports, particularly to developed economies where it is revealed to have a comparative advantage in products that use less-skilled labour relatively intensively.

Deeper investigations show that the sectoral composition of imports drives the difference in the composition of net trade across regions. High-technology products from the machinery and equipment, motor vehicles, communication equipment and basic chemicals sectors dominate imports from developed countries. Imports from Africa are largely concentrated in natural resource and labour-intensive products such as food, non-ferrous metals and clothing. Imports from China and India are concentrated in labour-intensive industries such as wearing apparel, textiles and footwear, as well as in relatively skilled-labour-intensive sectors such as machinery and equipment and communication equipment. In contrast to imports, the sector composition of South Africa's manufactured exports is remarkably similar across regions, with basic chemicals, basic iron and steel, machinery and equipment, and motor vehicles dominating exports to most regions.

Two main implications emerge from the analysis in this section. Firstly, South Africa's net trade in manufacturing is characterised by substantial heterogeneity across regions. The relative factor endowments 'revealed' by South African trade appear consistent with data on factor endowments, suggesting that the Heckscher-Ohlin model performs well in predicting South African trade flows, at least when measuring labour according to skills. However, this conclusion requires an extended version of the standard two-country Heckscher-Ohlin model, namely one where middle-income countries such as South Africa compete against more developed and less developed economies.

Secondly, the heterogeneity in trade flows suggests that the various bilateral trade negotiations the government is currently engaged in are likely to result in non-uniform impacts on factors of production. Open trade with developed economies is likely to benefit less-skilled labour, whereas trade with developing economies will place downward pressure on the wages and employment of less-skilled labour.

Changing factor intensity of trade

Despite a 'revealed' comparative advantage in unskilled-labour-intensive exports, and a macroeconomic framework explicitly aimed at encouraging export-led employment growth, little progress has been made in raising the relative share of unskilled-labour-intensive products in total exports. This is clearly shown in Figure 6.1, which plots the relationship between the skill intensity of production within 28 manufacturing sectors and the average annual growth in net trade. Diagrams using exports, as opposed to net trade, show the equivalent relationship and are therefore not presented. The skill intensity of production is calculated as the ratio of skilled labour (managers, professionals, technicians, clerks, skilled service workers, skilled agricultural workers, artisans) to less-skilled labour (operators, elementary workers).[11]

The results show that during the 1970s, growth in net trade was strongly biased in favour of sectors that use less-skilled labour relatively intensively, a result also found by Bhorat (1999). During the 1980s a weak positive relationship emerged, but this relationship disappeared during the early 1990s. From 1994, however, growth in net trade was again biased strongly in favour of skilled-labour-intensive sectors, with high export growth experienced in relatively skill-intensive sectors such as coke and refined petroleum products, other chemicals, motor vehicles, parts and accessories, and other transport equipment. Poor export growth, combined with strong import growth, occurred in less-skilled-labour-intensive sectors such as textiles, wearing apparel, leather and footwear.

Constructing similar diagrams using the capital intensity (machinery and equipment capital per worker) of production within manufacturing sectors reveals no consistent pattern in any period. Overall, there has been no noticeable shift in the structure of net trade towards labour-intensive sectors. These trends suggest a diminished capacity of trade to generate employment, particularly of less-skilled labour. Estimates of the impact of trade on employment from the 1970s are explored in more detail in the next section of this chapter.

Figure 6.1 *Skill bias of manufactured net export growth*

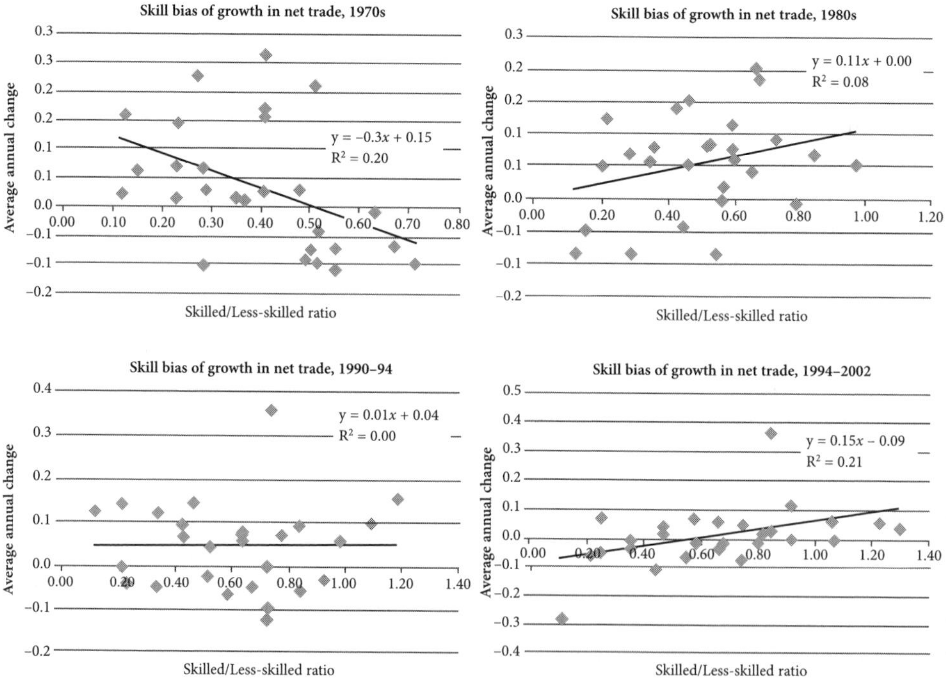

Notes: Printing and publishing has been excluded as it is an outlier. The exclusion of this sector does not affect the trends. Net trade is measured as the natural logarithm of exports/imports.

Sources of employment and output growth in manufacturing

To assess the contribution of trade to employment growth, the gross value of manufacturing production is disaggregated into demand effects arising from changes in final demand, exports, import penetration and technology using a Chenery-style decomposition technique (Chenery 1979). Using the simple accounting relationship, gross output can be expressed as:

$$X = D + E - M, \quad\quad\quad [1]$$

where X is gross output, E is exports and D is demand (final plus intermediate demand). Imposing the assumption that exports do not include re-exports, this can be re-formulated as:

$$X = dD + E, \quad\quad\quad [2]$$

where d is the ratio of domestically produced goods to total demand. Through manipulations, changes in gross output can therefore be decomposed into changes in demand (ΔD), export expansion (ΔE) and import penetration (ΔdD) as follows:

$$\Delta X = d\Delta D + \Delta dD + \Delta E. \quad\quad\quad [3]$$

Total factor usage (N) is given by nX where n is the row vector of factor requirements (capital, high-skilled labour, skilled labour and low-skilled labour) per unit output. The change in total factor usage can therefore be expressed as:

$$\Delta N = n\Delta X + \Delta nX = nd\Delta D + n\Delta dD + n\Delta E + \Delta nX, \quad\quad\quad [4]$$

where factor usage is affected by improvements in productivity (ΔnX) in addition to changes in demand, export expansion and import penetration. Similar methodologies have been used by Edwards (2001a, b) and Jenkins (2002), although these do not calculate the sources of growth in capital usage.

The analysis in this chapter is conducted for the periods 1970–79, 1980–89, 1990–94 and 1994–2002. The last period coincides with increased trade liberalisation, although other changes in the global and domestic environment will also have affected trade flows. The results of this decomposition for total labour, skilled labour, less-skilled labour and capital stock (machinery and equipment) are presented in Table 6.4 and Figure 6.2. Values represent the average annual growth in factor demand during the periods.

Table 6.4 *Sources of factor growth in manufacturing, average annual change*

	Final demand %	Exports %	Imports %	Net trade %	Tech-nology %	Total %	Δ factor
1970s							
Total employment	2.7	0.1	1.7	1.8	−2.1	**2.8**	353 653
Skilled	2.9	0.1	1.8	1.9	−0.2	**4.2**	146 573
Less-skilled	2.6	0.2	1.6	1.8	−2.8	**2.2**	207 080
Capital	3.1	−0.9	4.4	3.9	3.1	**7.8**	63 692
1980s							
Total employment	0.9	0.8	−0.1	0.7	−1.0	**0.7**	103 302
Skilled	1.1	0.9	−0.1	0.8	1.1	**2.7**	132 983
Less-skilled	0.8	0.7	−0.1	0.6	−2.0	**−0.3**	−29 681
Capital	1.6	1.2	0.0	1.2	−0.6	**2.2**	28 445
1990–94							
Total employment	0.6	1.7	−2.3	−0.5	−2.3	**−2.2**	−131 165
Skilled	0.8	1.7	−2.4	−0.6	−1.2	**−1.0**	−20 868
Less-skilled	0.5	1.7	−2.2	−0.4	−3.0	**−2.9**	−110 296
Capital	−0.4	2.4	−0.9	1.6	1.6	**2.7**	16 690
1994–2002							
Total employment	1.4	1.1	−0.6	0.6	−4.0	**−1.5**	−156 399
Skilled	1.4	1.3	−0.6	0.8	−3.2	**−0.5**	−21 724
Less-skilled	1.4	1.0	−0.6	0.4	−4.4	**−2.1**	−134 675
Capital	1.8	2.5	−0.8	1.8	−1.4	**2.3**	33 473

Note: Skilled labour consists of managers, professionals, technicians, clerks, skilled service workers, skilled agricultural workers and artisans. Less-skilled labour consists of all remaining occupations.

The decline in manufacturing employment growth and rising capital intensity of production from the 1970s is clearly shown in Table 6.4 and Figure 6.2. Formal-sector employment grew at 2.8 per cent per annum during the 1970s, but fell to 0.7 per cent per annum in the 1980s before becoming negative in the 1990s. The decline in employment was particularly severe during the period 1990–94, and continued to fall during 1994–2002, despite the recovery in output growth. In contrast, growth in capital stock was positive in all periods, although the rate of capital accumulation declined from the highs reached in the 1970s. The growth in the capital–labour ratio, however, has not declined from the 4–5 per cent range per annum, and was driven in the 1990s by a combination of capital growth and falling employment. Employment growth was also strongly biased towards high-skilled labour, which was positive in all periods, even during the 1990s (Table 6.4).

A number of observations can be made with regard to the various sources of employment growth. Firstly, changes in domestic demand are more important than trade in explaining changes in manufacturing employment in most periods. For example, domestic demand expansion accounted for over 100 per cent of manufacturing employment growth in many of the periods analysed.

Secondly, the contribution of import substitution towards manufacturing output, employment and capital growth closely follows changes in South Africa's industrial policy. During the 1970s the positive contribution of import substitution towards employment growth (0.8 per cent per annum) exceeded that of export expansion (0.4 per cent per annum). The contribution of import substitution declined absolutely and relative to export expansion during the 1980s, in response to the partial liberalisation of the economy and the expansion of manufacturing exports from the mid-1980s. During the recessionary period 1990–94 and the period of accelerated trade liberalisation, domestic firms were unable to retain domestic market share and import penetration reduced employment. The contribution of exports to employment growth, however, rose in response to trade liberalisation and the export subsidies provided by GEIS.

Figure 6.2 *Sources of factor growth in manufacturing, 1994–2002*

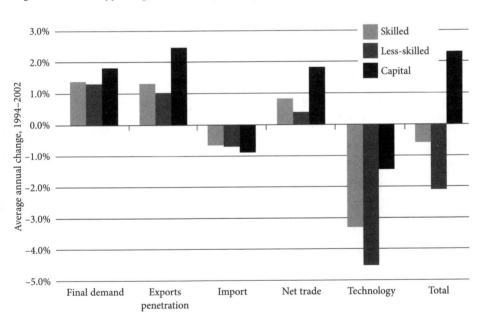

Thirdly, trade has had a net positive impact on employment since 1994 (0.6 per cent per annum), but the net impact is small compared to that of the 1970s and the 1980s and has also lagged population growth. Employment generated through trade has thus been insufficient to offset unemployment arising from technological change and new entrants into the labour force. South Africa's poor manufacturing export growth during the 1990s, relative to other middle-income economies and natural resource-based economies, has contributed to this problem (Alves and Edwards 2005). The economy has thus not realised its pursuit of 'employment creating international competitiveness' (Republic of South Africa 1996: 11).

Fourthly, the positive impact of net trade was also biased in favour of skilled labour during the 1980s and 1994–2002. During the latter period, net trade raised employment of skilled labour by 0.8 per cent per annum, compared to 0.4 per cent per annum for less-skilled labour. This bias arises from the relatively high export growth within skilled-labour-intensive sectors, as shown earlier in Figure 6.1. Sectoral losses in employment as a result of import penetration show no relationship to the skill intensity of production.[12] These results suggest that trade-induced changes in the sectoral composition of employment and production since 1994 are not being driven by imports, but rather by exports.

The decomposition analysis suggests that the dominant source of the decline in employment and the skill bias of employment growth is technological change. Technological change raised the employment of highly skilled labour during the 1970s, 1980s and early 1990s, but reduced employment of less-skilled labour during these periods. From 1994 onwards, technological change reduced employment of both skill categories, but the bias against less-skilled labour remained. The effect of technological change was also pervasive across sectors, with all but three of the 28 sectors experiencing a decline in employment because of technology.

The pervasiveness of technological change across sectors and the skill bias associated with it are consistent with the studies by Bowles (1995), Bhorat and Hodge (1999) and Edwards (2002), who decompose changes in the economy-wide average skill or capital intensity of production into *between-* and *within-sector* employment shifts. Edwards (2002), for example, finds that *within-sector* shifts account for over 80 per cent of the rise in skill intensity of aggregate manufacturing during the 1970s, 1980s and 1990s. Bhorat and Hodge (1999) report similar results. The results are also consistent with those of other developed and developing economies, suggesting that these changes are partly driven by global skill-biased technological change (Berman, Bound and Griliches 1994; Berman and Machin 2000).

A serious limitation of these decomposition studies is that they fail to account for the interaction between the various sources of demand and the impact of supply-side factors, including the labour market.[13] When taking into account labour market factors, the negative impact of technology on employment may reflect labour shedding in response to labour market rigidities and strong real wage growth. Lewis (2001) estimates that the real wages of semi- and unskilled workers increased by 150 per cent between 1970 and 1999. Real wages of highly skilled workers declined while those of skilled workers rose by approximately 10 per cent over the same period. The 1990s also saw the enactment of legislation and regulations aimed at redressing some of the inequalities inherited from the apartheid era. These included the Labour Relations Act (LRA) of 1996, the Basic Conditions of Employment Act (BCEA) of 1997 and the Employment Equity Act of 1998. Lewis (2001) argues that, although it is difficult to quantify the collective impact of this legislation, overall it appears to have contributed to the impression of *inflexibility*. Citing the World Economic Forum's Global Competitiveness Report (1999), he notes that South Africa came last in most matters concerning flexibility, labour relations and the work ethic of the labour force.

The very strong growth in capital, combined with improvements in labour productivity driven largely through labour shedding, also suggests that much of the productivity improvement is caused by capital/labour substitution (Edwards and Golub 2003). The relatively poor total factor productivity growth during the 1990s (Edwards and Golub 2003; Fedderke 2002) that accompanied the growth in capital stock is also consistent with this interpretation.

A second limitation of the decomposition technique is that trade liberalisation and import penetration indirectly affect employment and factor remuneration via technological change (Wood 1994; Pissarides 1997). There is some evidence that trade induces technological change in South Africa (Belli et al. 1993; Fallon and Pereira de Silva 1994; Hayter et al. 1999; Jonsson and Subramanian 2000), but the magnitude of the effect on the level and composition of employment has not been fully ascertained. Jenkins (2002), for example, estimates that rising import penetration led firms to rationalise their use of labour, leading to an estimated reduction in total employment in manufacturing of 100 000 between 1990 and 2001. Edwards (2003) uses firm-level data and finds some evidence that trade-induced technological change reduced employment, but the effect was small.

The data used in the decomposition analysis provide some evidence of a relationship between trade and technological change, but mainly on the export side. Improvements in labour productivity appear to be concentrated in sectors experiencing relatively high export growth. Consistent relationships between labour productivity and export performance have been found by Golub and Ceglowski (2001), Edwards (2003) and Edwards and Golub (2004). However, it is difficult to infer the direction of causality from these relationships. Productivity improvements may have led to improved export performance, or may be a consequence of export-induced transfers of technology. Nevertheless, the relationship between exports and productivity suggests that estimates of employment growth due to export expansion shown in Figure 6.2 are biased upwards.

On the import side, there is no significant correlation between tariff reductions and employment lost as a result of technological change. Further, the correlation coefficients are of the incorrect sign (−0.31 for highly skilled labour and −0.33 for less-skilled labour), which suggests that the sectors experiencing the largest reductions in labour because of technology are also those experiencing the smallest declines in tariffs. This is inconsistent with Wood's (1994) defensive innovation hypothesis.

Overall, the decomposition analysis indicates that employment lost as a result of import penetration is counteracted by employment gained through export expansion. The dominant source of the decline in employment appears to be skill-biased technological change. No evidence of defensive innovation is found, suggesting that the loss of employment as a result of imports is not significantly underestimated. However, a positive correlation between export growth and improvements in labour productivity suggests that the gains in employment due to exports may be biased upwards.

Tariff liberalisation and factor remuneration

A more serious limitation of the factor content approach used above is that its theoretical foundations are weak. Most importantly, the methodology uses trade flows, which are an endogenous outcome, to proxy price changes arising from liberalisation (Leamer 2000). Such a relationship is valid only under restrictive assumptions regarding the nature of the production and consumption functions (Deardorff and Staiger 1988; Deardorff 2000).

An alternative approach is one based on the SS theorem, which draws theoretically consistent relationships between product price movements and factor returns.[14] According to the SS theorem, a decline in the output price of the unskilled-labour-intensive sector relative to the skilled-labour-intensive sector lowers the relative wage of unskilled labour relative to skilled labour. This arises because the price shock induces a shift in resources out of the unskilled-labour-intensive sectors towards the skilled-labour-intensive sectors, which in turn reduces the relative demand for unskilled labour. Thus, the model predicts that trade liberalisation raises wage inequality in developed economies as the relative price of skilled-labour-intensive products rises, but reduces wage inequality in developing economies as the relative price of unskilled-labour-intensive products rises.

Few studies in South Africa have used the price-effect approach to estimating the impact of trade liberalisation on factor demand. The most extensive research following the SS approach is that of Fedderke et al. (2003), who use a panel of 28 manufacturing industries over the period 1970–97 to estimate the impact of product price changes on the returns to capital and labour. They find that product price movements were biased against capital, leading them to conclude that 'demand factors, and trade liberalisation related factors in particular, did not prove to carry a negative impact on labour in South African manufacturing' (Fedderke et al. 2003: 35).

A limitation of the Fedderke et al. (2003) study, however, is that it does not directly estimate the impact of tariff liberalisation on factor returns. The study also does not capture the impact of trade on skilled and unskilled labour. As noted earlier, capital may be a poor determinant of comparative advantage relative to labour endowments as it is internationally mobile. This section therefore uses the tariff data presented earlier to estimate the returns to capital, highly skilled, skilled and semi- and unskilled labour mandated by trade liberalisation.

Empirical methodology

The key equation that drives the SS relationship is the zero profit condition:

$$P = AW \qquad\qquad [5]$$

where P is a vector of N industry-level domestic value-added prices,[15] W is a vector of M domestic factor prices and A is an (N × M) matrix of input intensities in which element A_{ij} is the share of factor i per unit of output j. Differentiating these zero-profit conditions and rearranging produces:[16]

$$\hat{P} + \hat{TFP} = \theta\hat{W}. \qquad\qquad [6]$$

$\hat{P}$, $\hat{W}$ and $\hat{TFP}$ represent the percentage change in value-added prices, wages and total factor productivity, respectively. θ is an (N × M) initial cost-share matrix in which element θ_{ij} is the share of factor i in the average cost of producing one unit of product j. Equation [6] represents a system of equations in which changes in product prices and technology are equal to economy-wide changes in factor prices (factors are perfectly mobile within the country), weighted by initial factor shares.

Given data on exogenously determined changes in value-added prices ($\hat{P}^{Exog}_{va,\,jt}$), TFP growth ($\hat{TFP}^{Exog}_{jt}$) and factor cost shares (θ), the zero-profit condition [6] can be estimated directly as:

$$\hat{P}^{Exog}_{va,\,jt} = \Sigma\,\theta_{ijt}\,\beta_i + \varepsilon_{jt} \qquad\qquad [7]$$

and:

$$\hat{TFP}^{Exog}_{jt} = \Sigma\,\theta_{ijt}\,\delta_i + v_{jt}. \qquad\qquad [8]$$

Leamer (1996: 23) refers to these as 'mandated wage' regressions, where the estimated δ_i's and β_i's are changes in factor payments 'that are needed to keep the zero profits condition operative in the face of changes in technology and product prices', respectively. The approach therefore estimates the economy-wide factor payments that are consistent with changes in product prices and technology. These can then be compared with actual wage changes to identify the contribution of product price changes and technological change towards the overall change in factor prices.

A key feature of the zero profit relationship [4] is that relative factor returns are influenced by the sector bias of changes in product prices and technological change. Thus price increases or technological improvements in sectors that use less-skilled labour relatively intensively cause resources to shift towards these sectors, which in turn raises the relative demand for less-skilled labour. The wage of less-skilled labour relative to skilled labour rises as a result.

Equation [7] forms the base specification used to estimate the impact of trade liberalisation on factor returns in this section. To calculate the exogenous change in value added ($\hat{P}_{va,\,jt}^{Exog}$) arising from trade liberalisation, the simplifying assumption is made that domestic firms price up to the import parity price.[17] The tariff-induced change in output price can then be calculated as $\hat{P}_j = \dfrac{(t_{j,\,fin} - t_{j,\,ini})}{1 + t_{j,\,ini}}$, where $t_{j,fin}$ and $t_{j,ini}$ represent the final and initial tariff rates for product j, respectively. A 43-sector Social Accounting Matrix (SAM) for 1997, obtained from the World Bank, is then used to calculate tariff-related changes in value added, $\hat{P}_{VA,j} = \hat{P}_j - \sum_{i=1}^{N} a_{ij}\hat{P}_j$, where a_{ij} represents the intermediate input coefficient. Factor cost shares for capital, skilled and less-skilled (semi- and unskilled) labour are also calculated from the SAM.

Results

Figure 6.3 presents scatter-plot diagrams that capture the factor bias of tariff reductions within manufacturing between 1994 and 2003. The weighted (using import values) average EU, SADC and MFN tariff is used for 2003. As is clearly shown in the first diagram, tariff liberalisation between 1994 and 2003 led to relatively large declines in value added within semi- and unskilled-labour-intensive sectors. According to the SS theorem, this bias will have led to a decline in wages of semi- and unskilled labour relative to skilled labour, i.e. a rise in wage inequality.

A positive bias emerges between tariff-related changes in value added and the capital intensity of production within manufacturing sectors. However, substantial variation around this trend exists, suggesting that the relationship, if any, is weak. Hence it is not possible to derive any priors on the expected impact of trade liberalisation on the returns to capital relative to labour.

Figure 6.3 *Factor bias of tariff changes in manufacturing*

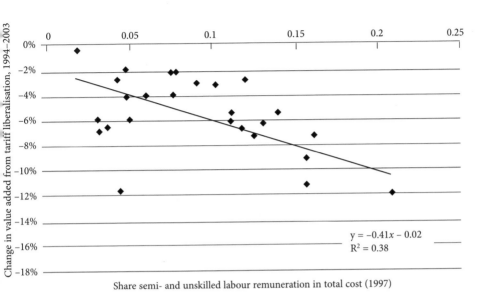

Share semi- and unskilled labour remuneration in total cost (1997)

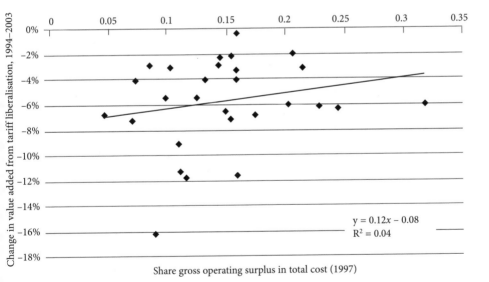

Share gross operating surplus in total cost (1997)

Note: Change in value added calculated using the weighted (using import values) average EU, SADC and MFN tariffs for each sector in 2003.

Table 6.5 presents the estimated mandated factor returns from two different liberalisation scenarios: liberalisation from 1994 to 2003 and a reduction of 2003 tariffs to zero. The second scenario therefore simulates the impact of a comprehensive programme of liberalisation from 2003. What is not captured is the positive impact that bilateral and multilateral trade agreements have had on the prices of South African exports. The analysis is thus at best partial.

Results for the manufacturing sector and all sectors (agriculture, mining, manufacturing and services) are presented separately. In each case the weighted average tariff for EU, SADC and MFN countries is used for 2003. The appendix to this chapter presents the results of separate mandated wage regressions for each region.

The estimated coefficients reflect the percentage change in factor returns that are consistent with changes in value added, induced by trade liberalisation between 1994 and 2003. These changes in factor returns do not necessarily reflect actual changes experienced, as numerous other changes to the factor and product markets between 1994 and 2003 will also have affected factor returns. The coefficients, however, provide some insight into the general equilibrium contribution of bilateral and multilateral tariff reductions to changes in factor returns.

Looking at the results for capital and labour, tariff liberalisation between 1994 and 2003 mandated a sharp decline in the return to labour relative to capital. The mandated decline in wages is estimated to range between 26 per cent and 29 per cent. In contrast, the mandated return to capital ranges between –5 per cent and 11 per cent. Although the estimates for capital are only weakly significant, the difference in return between capital and labour is significant at the 5 per cent level. The mandated decline in wages also exceeds the decline in product prices arising from tariff liberalisation (9–10 per cent), pointing to a mandated decline in real wages of between 17 per cent and 19 per cent. The mandated real return to capital ranges between 5 per cent and 20 per cent.

Further investigation reveals substantial heterogeneity in the impact of tariff liberalisation on labour. Tariff liberalisation negatively affected the demand for semi- and unskilled workers the most, leading to a mandated decline in semi- and unskilled wages of 47 per cent when only including manufacturing sectors and 40 per cent in the complete sample. The mandated decline in wages is significantly (at the 5 per cent level) lower than the mandated return to capital and skilled labour. Thus trade liberalisation between 1994 and 2003 appears to have raised the return to capital and skilled workers relative to semi- and unskilled workers.

Table 6.5 *Mandated factor returns from trade liberalisation, 1994–2003, and full liberalisation from 2003*

	Liberalisation, 1994–2003		Full liberalisation from 2003	
	Manufacturing	All sectors	Manufacturing	All sectors
	Coef.	Coef.	Coef.	Coef.
Capital and labour				
Capital	–0.05	0.11*	–0.13	0.03
Labour	–0.29***	–0.26***	–0.19*	–0.15**
Difference in mandated factor returns				
Capital – labour	0.24**	0.36***	0.05	0.18
Capital and labour according to skill				
Capital	–0.08	0.07	–0.20*	–0.01
Skilled	–0.02	–0.05	0.37*	0.05
Less-skilled	–0.47***	–0.40***	–0.58***	–0.30***
Difference in mandated factor returns				
Capital – skilled	–0.06	0.12	–0.57**	–0.06
Capital – less-skilled	0.39***	0.47***	0.38*	0.29**
Skilled – less-skilled	0.45**	0.35***	0.94***	0.36**
Obs.	28	43	28	43
% change in product price	–0.10	–0.09	–0.08	–0.05

Notes: The weighted average tariff for EU, SADC and MFN is used for 2003. Consistent results are obtained when using 94-sector Supply-Use tables for 1993 and 2000 to calculate changes in value added.
*, ** and *** reflect significance at the 10, 5 and 1 per cent significance levels respectively.

To investigate the potential impact of further liberalisation on factor demand, Table 6.5 presents the results from estimations where full liberalisation from 2003 is assumed. The results suggest further real reductions in the return to aggregate labour (5 per cent to 11 per cent), although these declines are not significantly different from the mandated return to capital. When analysing the returns to labour according to skill, the results show that further liberalisation will continue to raise the demand for skilled labour relative to less-skilled labour. This result reflects the relatively high tariffs that remain on sectors that use semi- and unskilled labour relatively intensively.

These results strongly suggest that tariff liberalisation from 1994 to 2003 placed substantial downward pressure on the demand for semi- and unskilled labour relative to capital and skilled labour. The results therefore contrast starkly with the results of Fedderke et al. (2003), although, as mentioned earlier, their study does not capture the impact of trade liberalisation directly. The tariff-induced decline in demand for semi- and unskilled labour is therefore consistent with the decline in employment and rising skill and capital bias experienced in the manufacturing sector during the 1990s. However, real wage rigidity may have exacerbated the impact of trade on employment. Real wages of semi- and unskilled labour are estimated to have grown by approximately 4 per cent per annum over this period.[18] The lack of wage moderation in the face of increased international competition will have encouraged firms to shed labour. The substantial decline in the employment of semi- and unskilled labour may therefore reflect real wage rigidity in the face of trade and technology-induced declines in labour demand.

Conclusion

This chapter draws on a variety of empirical methodologies to analyse the impact of trade flows and trade liberalisation on employment and factor remuneration in South Africa during the 1990s. During this period, the economy made significant progress in reducing tariff protection, although tariff levels and ERP remained high in certain sectors and the tariff schedule remained complex. The economy also experienced substantial changes in the level and composition of manufacturing exports and imports during this period. The objective of this chapter has been to analyse the impact of these changes on the demand for labour.

Various conclusions are derived from the analysis.

Firstly, the factor content of trade flows differs across regions, reflecting the middle-income status of the South African economy. South Africa is revealed to be abundant in skilled labour relative to Africa, but abundant in unskilled labour relative to developed and many Asian economies. The bilateral trade agreements currently being negotiated by the government will therefore have non-uniform impacts on the demand for labour. Open trade with developed economies is likely to benefit less-skilled labour, while trade with low-income countries should benefit skilled labour. The impact of regional trade on labour in South Africa is yet to be fully explored.

Secondly, using a decomposition analysis, the chapter shows that employment created through export growth has been matched by employment lost through import penetration. The net effect of trade on employment between 1994 and 2003 is slightly positive. However, there is a rising skill bias associated with net trade, a trend driven predominantly by export growth. The capacity to generate employment of unskilled labour through export growth has thus diminished.

Thirdly, the mandated wage regression shows that tariff liberalisation has reduced the demand for less-skilled labour relative to skilled labour. Tariff liberalisation between 1994 and 2003 is estimated to have mandated a wage decline of 40 per cent for semi- and unskilled workers. Further liberalisation is expected to mandate additional declines in wages for labour, particularly semi- and unskilled labour, as tariffs remain high in sectors that use this labour relatively intensively.

There are some important caveats to this conclusion. In estimating the mandated wages, the impact of greater access to foreign markets (and prices) for South African exports is not taken into account. The analysis is therefore biased towards presenting a negative representation of the impact of tariff liberalisation on labour. For example, improved access to the EU market under the Free Trade Agreement is expected to raise the return to less-skilled labour relative to skilled labour. This is an area that requires further research.

In addition, no correlation is found between the change in tariffs and employment growth, suggesting that non-trade-related factors have dominated the employment decision within firms. These factors may include labour market rigidities, real wage growth and skill-biased technological change. The effect of these factors is not sector-specific, which may explain why within-sector shifts in employment have dominated between-sector shifts.

Notes

1. Much controversy surrounds the reliability of South African statistical series. Statistics South Africa's *Survey of total employment and earnings* shows a decline in formal-sector (excluding agriculture) employment during the late 1990s. In contrast, the October Household Surveys show a small rise in employment once agriculture and the informal sector are included. However, in all cases employment growth has been insufficient to reduce unemployment significantly during the 1990s.

2. Edwards (2003) uses two firm-level surveys to estimate the impact of tariff reductions on labour demand. No consistent relationship is found for various categories of labour.

3. A further problem is that many of these studies are conducted using a partial equilibrium framework where skill-biased technological change reduces relative employment and wages of less-skilled labour. In a general equilibrium framework, skill-biased technological change does not necessarily raise wage inequality, as the impact depends on the sector bias and not the factor bias of technological change (Leamer 1996; Haskel and Slaughter 2001).

4. Further reforms were introduced in 2004. The number of tariff lines fell to 6 707 and the percentage of non-*ad valorem* tariffs to 3 per cent.

5. ERP are calculated as $ERP_j = (t_j - \sum_i a_{ij}t_i)/(1 - \sum_i a_{ij})$ where t_j is the tariff on outputs, t_i is the tariff on inputs and a_{ij} is the quantity of intermediate input i used in the production of one unit of j. The Balassa (1965) approach is followed and services are given a zero output tariff. See Holden and Holden (1975), Greenaway and Milner (1993) and Holden (2001) for a critical evaluation of ERP.

6. Pairwise correlation coefficients indicate a significant negative relationship between the decline in tariffs from 1994–2003 and the share of low-skilled labour in total employment and the ratio of labour to machinery and equipment capital stock. No significant correlation is found between the decline in tariff protection and changes in employment, irrespective of the skill classification used (highly skilled, skilled and low-skilled).

7. The correlation between ERP and nominal protection rates exceeds 0.79 in all cases.

8   Drawing on the Heckscher-Ohlin-Vanek relationship, a comparison of the factor content of net trade with the factor content of consumption or production can also 'reveal' a country's relative factor endowment (Leamer 1980).

9   Edwards and Golub (2002) find that South African capital-labour ratios in aggregate manufacturing are lower than those of France, Canada, Italy, Japan, the USA, the UK, Korea and Singapore, but higher than those of Zimbabwe and India.

10   The revealed capital abundance, however, is still remarkably robust to the exclusion of natural resource-based products. This may also reflect internationally low electricity costs which have encouraged investments in capital-intensive sectors. The capital-intensive structure of production has also been encouraged by rising real wages (Fallon 1992) and under-investment in labour-intensive sectors in response to political uncertainty (Kaplinsky 1995).

11   The trends shown in the diagrams are robust to the inclusion of agriculture and mining.

12   A significant positive correlation (0.44) is found between the skill intensity of production and employment changes caused by export expansion. The correlation coefficient between skill intensity of production and employment changes as a result of import penetration is negative (–0.26), but not significant.

13   Wood (1994) also argues that the use of domestic labour coefficients rather than foreign coefficients may understate the impact of trade on labour, as many of the imported goods are 'non-competing' since they are no longer produced in the home country.

14   See Slaughter (1998) for a review of many of the international studies. This model also suffers from some severe limitations. For example, the impact of product price changes on factor returns breaks down once more products are introduced. Technology is also assumed to be exogenous, which has been critiqued by Wood (1994). Further, the two-country model is less adept at analysing the impact of trade liberalisation on factor returns within middle-income economies (Davis 1996; Wood 1997).

15   Value-added price is calculated as $P^G - ZP^G$, where P^G is a vector of gross-output prices and Z is the $(N \times N)$ intermediate input requirement matrix.

16   See Leamer (1996) for details or Feenstra and Hanson (1999) for an alternative derivation of this relationship using the dual measure of total factor productivity growth.

17   See Feenstra and Hanson (1999) and Haskel and Slaughter (2001), who use a two-step approach to dealing with the identification of exogenously induced changes in prices and technology. Leamer (1996) deals with the endogeneity problem by assuming that all sectors have the same rate of technological pass-through to value-added prices, namely $\hat{P} = -\lambda T\hat{F}P$, where λ is the pass-through rate. This enables the identification of exogenous price changes $(\hat{P}_{jt} + \lambda T\hat{F}P)$ and technological change $((1 - \lambda)T\hat{F}P)$ from observed data.

18   Calculated using Quantech (2004) data.

Appendix

Table 6A.1 *Mandated factor returns from trade liberalisation by region, 1994–2003*

	EU		SADC		MFN	
	Manufacturing	All sectors	Manufacturing	All sectors	Manufacturing	All sectors
	Coef.	Coef.	Coef.	Coef.	Coef.	Coef.
Capital and labour						
Capital	−0.02	0.12**	−0.18**	0.09	−0.04	0.11**
Labour	−0.31***	−0.27***	−0.30***	−0.29***	−0.28***	−0.25***
Difference in mandated factor returns						
Capital – labour	0.29**	0.39***	0.12	0.37**	0.24**	0.36**
Capital and labour according to skill						
Capital	−0.06	0.08	−0.23***	0.03	−0.07	0.07
Skilled	0.00	−0.06	0.03	−0.03	−0.03	−0.06
Less-skilled	−0.53***	−0.43***	−0.55***	−0.48***	−0.46***	−0.39***
Difference in mandated factor returns						
Capital – skilled	−0.06	0.13	−0.26	0.06	−0.05	0.13
Capital – less-skilled	0.47***	0.50***	0.32**	0.51***	0.38***	0.46***
Skilled – less-skilled	0.53**	0.37***	0.58**	0.45**	0.43**	0.33**
Obs.	28	43	28	43	28	43
% change in value added	−0.06	−0.04	−0.08	−0.05	−0.06	−0.04

Note: *, ** and *** reflect significance at the 10, 5 and 1 per cent significance levels, respectively.

Table 6A.2 *Mandated wages under full liberalisation by region from 2003*

	EU		SADC		MFN	
	Manufacturing	All sectors	Manufacturing	All sectors	Manufacturing	All sectors
	Coef.	Coef.	Coef.	Coef.	Coef.	Coef.
Capital and labour						
Capital	−0.16	0.02	0.01	0.05	−0.13	0.03
Labour	−0.16	−0.14*	−0.16**	−0.12**	−0.19*	−0.16**
Difference in mandated factor returns						
Capital – labour	0.00	0.16	0.17	0.17*	0.06	0.19
Capital and labour according to skill						
Capital	−0.22**	−0.02	−0.05	0.02	−0.21*	−0.01
Skilled	0.35	0.06	0.31**	0.03	0.37*	0.06
Less-skilled	−0.52***	−0.28***	−0.50***	−0.22***	−0.59***	−0.31***
Difference in mandated factor returns						
Capital – skilled	−0.56*	−0.07	−0.37*	−0.01	−0.58*	−0.07
Capital – less-skilled	0.30	0.26*	0.44***	0.25**	0.39*	0.30*
Skilled – less-skilled	0.86**	0.33*	0.81***	0.25**	0.97***	0.37**
Obs.	28	43	28	43	28	43
% change in value added	−0.06	−0.03	−0.03	−0.02	−0.06	−0.03

Note: *, ** and *** reflect significance at the 10, 5 and 1 per cent significance levels, respectively.

References

Alleyne TS & Subramanian A (2001) *What does South Africa's pattern of trade say about its labor markets?* International Monetary Fund Working Paper 01/148.

Alves P & Edwards L (2005) South Africa's export performance: Determinants of export supply. Mimeo.

Balassa B 91965) Tariff protection in industrial countries: An evaluation, *Journal of Political Economy* 73: 573–594.

Baldwin RE (1971) Determinants of the commodity structure of U.S. trade, *American Economic Review* 61: 126–146.

Bell T (1997) Trade policy. In J Michie and V Padayachee (eds) *The political economy of South Africa's transition*. London: Dryden Press.

Bell T & Cattaneo N (1997) Foreign trade and employment in South African manufacturing industry. Occasional Report No. 4, Employment and Training Department, International Labour Office, Geneva.

Belli PM, Finger MJ & Ballivian A (1993) South Africa: A review of trade policies. World Bank Informal Discussion Papers on Aspects of the South African Economy No. 4, The Southern Africa department, The World Bank.

Berman E, Bound J & Griliches Z (1994) Changes in the demand for skilled labor within US manufacturing: Evidence from the annual survey of manufacturers, *Quarterly Journal of Economics* 109(2): 367–397.

Berman E & Machin S (2000) Skill-biased technology transfer around the world, *Oxford Review of Economic Policy* 16(3): 12–22.

Bhorat H (1999) Decomposing sectoral employment trends in South Africa. Paper presented at the Trade and Industrial Policy Secretariat Annual Forum, Muldersdrift, September 1999.

Bhorat H & Hodge J (1999) Decomposing shifts in labour demand in South Africa, *South African Journal of Economics* 67(3): 348–380.

Birdi A, Dunne P & Watson D (2001) Labour demand and trade in South Africa: A dynamic panel analysis. Paper presented at the Annual Conference on Econometric Modelling for Africa, July 2001.

Bowles S (1995) Choice of technology, sectoral priorities and employment: The challenge of job creation in the South African economy. Report to the Labour Market Commission, Cape Town.

Chenery H (1979) *Structural change and development policy.* New York: Oxford University Press.

Davis DR (1996) *Trade liberalisation and income distribution.* Harvard Institute of International Development Discussion Paper No. 551.

Deardorff AV (2000) Factor prices and the factor content of trade revisited: What's the use? *Journal of International Economics* 50: 73–90.

Deardorff AV & Staiger RW (1988) An interpretation of the factor content of trade, *Journal of International Economics* 24: 93–107.

DTI (Department of Trade and Industry) (1997) *Annual Report 1996–97.* Pretoria: Department of Trade and Industry.

Edwards L (2001a) Globalisation and the skill bias of occupational employment in South Africa, *South African Journal of Economics* 69(1): 40–71.

Edwards L (2001b) Trade and the structure of South African production, 1984–97, *Development Southern Africa* 18(4): 471–491.

Edwards L (2002) Trade, technology and employment in South Africa, *Trade & Industry Monitor* 23: 11–15.

Edwards L (2003) A firm level analysis of trade, technology and employment in South Africa, *Journal of International Development* 17: 1–17.

Edwards L (2005) Has South Africa liberalised its trade? Paper prepared for the Trade and Poverty Project, Southern Africa Labour and Development Research Unit, University of Cape Town. Accessed online 1 December 2005, http://www.cssr.uct.ac.za/saldru_trade&poverty.html

Edwards L & Golub SS (2002) *South Africa's international cost competitiveness and productivity: A sectoral analysis.* Report prepared for the South African National Treasury under a USAID/Nathan Associates SEGA Project.

Edwards L & Golub SS (2003) South African productivity and capital accumulation in manufacturing: An international comparative analysis, *South African Journal of Economics* 71(4): 659–678.

Edwards L & Golub SS (2004) South Africa's international cost competitiveness and productivity in manufacturing, *World Development* 32(8): 1323–1339.

Fallon P (1992) An analysis of employment and wage behaviour in South Africa. World Bank Informal Discussion Papers on Aspects of the South African Economy, The Southern Africa department, The World Bank.

Fallon P & Pereira de Silva LA (1994) South Africa: Economic performance and policies. World Bank Informal Discussion Papers on Aspects of the South African Economy No. 7, The Southern Africa department, The World Bank.

Fedderke J (2002) The structure of growth in the South African Economy: Factor accumulation and total factor productivity growth 1970–97, *South African Journal of Economics* 70(4): 611–646.

Fedderke J & Vaze P (2001) The nature of South Africa's trade patterns by economic sector, and the extent of trade liberalisation during the course of the 1990's, *South African Journal of Economics* 69(3): 436–473.

Fedderke J & Vaze P (2004) Response to Rangasamy and Harmse: Trade liberalisation in the 1990s, *South African Journal of Economics* 72(2): 407–412.

Fedderke J, Shin Y & Vaze P (2003) *Trade and labour usage: An examination of the South African manufacturing industry.* Econometric Research Southern Africa Working Paper, No. 15.

Feenstra RC & Hanson GH (1999) The impact of outsourcing and high-technology capital on labor: Estimates for the United States, 1979–90, *Quarterly Journal of Economics* August: 907–940.

Golub SS & Ceglowski J (2001) South African real exchange rates and manufacturing competitiveness, *South African Journal of Economics* 70(6): 1047–1075.

Greenaway D & Milner C (1993) *Trade and industrial policy in developing countries.* Basingstoke, Hampshire: Macmillan Press.

Haskel JE & Slaughter MJ (2001) Trade, technology and U.K. wage inequality, *Economic Journal* 111(468): 163–187.

Hayter S, Reinecke G & Torres R (1999) South Africa: Studies on the social dimensions of globalisation. Task force on country studies on globalisation, International Labour Office, Geneva.

Holden M (1992) The structure and incidence of protection in South Africa. In P Black and B Dollery (eds) *Leading Issues in South African Microeconomics*, Johannesburg: Southern Book Publishers.

Holden M (2001) Effective protection revisited: How useful a policy tool for South Africa? *South African Journal of Economics* 69(4): 659–673.

Holden M & Holden P (1975) An intertemporal calculation of effective rates of protection for South Africa, *South African Journal of Economics* 43(3): 370–379.

Jenkins R (2002) The labour market effects of globalisation in South Africa. Paper presented at the seminar on Globalisation, Production and Poverty in South Africa, Cape Town, 27 June 2002.

Jonsson G & Subramanian A (2000) *Dynamic gains from trade: Evidence from South Africa.* International Monetary Fund Working Paper No. 00/45.

Kaplinsky R (1995) Capital intensity in South African manufacturing and unemployment, 1972–90. *World Development,* 23(2): 179–192.

Leamer EE (1980) The Leontief paradox reconsidered, *Journal of Political Economy* 88(3): 495–503.

Leamer EE (1996) *In search of the Stolper Samuelson effects on US wages.* National Bureau of Economic Research Working Paper No. 5427, Cambridge, MA.

Leamer EE (2000) What's the use of factor contents? *Journal of International Economics* 51(1): 17–49.

Lewis J (2001) *Reform and opportunity: The changing role and patterns of trade in SA and SADC.* Africa Region Working Paper Series, No. 14. World Bank.

Nattrass N (1998) *Globalisation, employment and labour market institutions in South Africa.* South African Network for Economic Research Working Paper No. 14.

Pissarides CA (1997) Learning by trading and the returns to human capital in developing countries, *The World Bank Economic Review* 11(1): 17–32.

Quantech (2004) South African Standardised Industry Database, Sources and Descriptions. Accessed online 1 December 2005, http://www.tips.org.za/data/

Rangasamy L & Harmse C (2003) Revisiting the extent of trade liberalisation in the 1990s, *South African Journal of Economics* 70(4): 705–728.

Republic of South Africa 1(996) *Growth, employment and redistribution: A macroeconomic strategy.* Pretoria: South African government printers.

Slaughter MJ (1998) *What are the results of product-price studies and can we learn from their differences?* National Bureau of Economic Research Working Paper No. 6591, Cambridge, MA.

Van Seventer DE (2001) The level and variation of tariffs rates: An analysis of nominal and effective tariff rates in South Africa for the years 2000 and 2001. Paper presented at the Trade and Industrial Policy Strategies Annual Forum, Muldersdrift, September 2001.

Wood A (1994) *North South trade, employment and inequality.* Oxford: Oxford University Press.

Wood A (1997) Openness and wage inequality in developing countries: The Latin American challenge to East Asian conventional wisdom, *The World Bank Economic Review* 11(1): 17–32.

Wood A & Mayer J (2001) Africa's export structure in a comparative perspective, *Cambridge Journal of Economics* 5(3): 369–394.

7 Does city structure cause unemployment? The case of Cape Town

Sandrine Rospabe and Harris Selod

Introduction

In June 1998, the South African newspaper *The Star* told the story of a 46-year-old single mother who lives in the suburbs of Cape Town and commutes every day to a job located in a central part of the city. Up before dawn, she has a one-kilometre walk to a taxi rank and often waits an hour before being able to board her only transport to work, at about 6 a.m. If she could afford it, she would buy a car, but half her wages are spent on transport already and the rest goes towards school fees for her daughters, who attend an inner-city school.[1] Such stories of long and costly commuting trips are not uncommon for South African township dwellers, and illustrate two of the major problems faced by today's South African cities: *urban sprawl* and *a high level of segregation of population groups*. This situation has been inherited in part from the former apartheid policy which allowed only whites to live in the city centre where most of the jobs were located. Hence, urban non-whites were forced to reside in peripheral areas, far away from jobs and organised in racially segregated townships separated from each other by unoccupied buffer zones.[2] Today, even though land-use restrictions have been abolished, urban fragmentation remains the norm (see Brueckner 1996 and Selod and Zenou 2001a for urban models comparing apartheid and post-apartheid uses of urban land).

In this context, it is not difficult to imagine that a stratified city structure may strongly affect local labour-market outcomes, and particularly exacerbate unemployment and poverty. Indeed, an abundant literature in both sociology and urban economics suggests that the spatial organisation of cities can drive unemployment because of (i) *the harmful effect of residential segregation* along ethnic or socio-economic lines, or (ii) *the negative impact of the disconnection between places of work and places of residence* (the so-called *spatial mismatch hypothesis* initiated by Kain 1968; see Gobillon, Selod and Zenou 2005 for a theoretical survey of the literature, and Ihlanfeldt and Sjoquist 1998 for an empirical review). These theories linking labour-market outcomes to the spatial organisation of cities have been tested in metropolitan areas (see O'Regan and Quigley 1996; Immergluck 1998) in the USA, but the issue has seldom been investigated in cities in the developing world, although city fragmentation is a major issue in many developing countries. The objective of the present work is to investigate how city structure can affect employment prospects in the particular case of Cape Town. The first section of the chapter presents a brief synthesis of the economic literature that links the formation of unemployment to city structure. The next section presents some relevant descriptive statistics on Cape Town, related to its population and its economic structure. The third section presents our methodological approach and carries out the empirical analysis.

Urban unemployment and city structure: A brief review of the literature

An abundant literature in sociology and urban economics suggests that the spatial organisation of cities can exacerbate unemployment and deteriorate the income of disadvantaged communities. In this perspective, labour market outcomes should depend on individual characteristics (age, education, ethnicity...) but also on location within the city. The present section surveys the two major explanations put forward by economists that underpin this theory. The first explanation stresses the role played by the physical distance from job opportunities, whereas the second one underlines the harmful effects of residential segregation.

The physical disconnection between jobs and residential locations

The first reason why city structure might influence labour market outcomes is that the physical disconnection between places of work and places of residence (i.e. *spatial mismatch*) can be a source of long journeys and expensive commuting costs, which in turn hinder the mobility of workers. Moreover, the costs associated with the physical disconnection from jobs may be further accentuated by congestion and, for those who do not own a car, by the poor quality of public transport systems (as a result of incomplete network coverage, long waits at connection nodes, or the lack of coordination between transportation modes). Some workers – notably unskilled workers who are likely to hold part-time jobs or start working very early in the morning or late at night – may be confronted with low public transport frequencies, if not with the closing of the network at the times when they need it. In this context, unemployed workers residing in neighbourhoods disconnected from job opportunities face temporal and monetary commuting costs that are often very high in comparison with the wages they are offered. This can lead to very low net wages, and deter workers from accepting any job at all. In this respect, Brueckner and Martin (1997) and Brueckner and Zenou (2003) propose urban models in which commuting costs are indeed the main source of both low wages and urban unemployment.

Distance from job opportunities may also discourage job search (when it is too costly) or even deteriorate its efficiency. In this respect, it has been shown that the quantity and quality of information that workers have about job opportunities within a specific metropolitan area decrease with distance from jobs, which in turn reduces the efficiency of job search (see Rogers 1997; Ihlanfeldt and Sjoquist 1990; Ihlanfeldt 1997). There are several reasons for the fact that information about jobs decreases with distance. For instance, many employers resort to spatially-limited search modes such as posting 'wanted' signs in shops, or having advertisements published in local newspapers (Turner 1997). Another explanation is that job candidates usually experience difficulties in identifying potential recruiters in distant zones with which they are unfamiliar. In this respect, Davis and Huff (1972) have shown that jobseekers search efficiently only in a restricted perimeter around their place of residence, even if this zone hosts only poor-quality jobs that pay little. These mechanisms are at the core of theoretical models that aim to explain the formation of urban unemployment (see Wasmer and Zenou 2002, who argue that job search efficiency decreases with distance to jobs, or, in a different context, Ortega 2000 who postulates that search costs are higher outside a worker's zone of residence).

Residential segregation

Physical disconnection between jobs and residential locations is not the only way in which space can deteriorate the socio-economic opportunities of workers. Researchers also stress the role of socio-economic and often ethnic segregation (see, for example, Cutler and Glaeser 1997; Selod and Zenou 2001b), which may have four main consequences.

Firstly, residential segregation can be a hindrance to human capital acquisition, which may in turn deteriorate the employability of segregated workers, and especially that of young individuals. The links between residential segregation and poor school results are indeed well documented: residential segregation often concentrates low-skill learners in certain schools, and this concentration exerts a negative pressure on the learning process (Benabou 1993). This is because, as shown by the literature on education production functions, the success of a given student largely depends on the socio-economic characteristics of all the other students in the class (Summers and Wolfe 1977; Arnott and Rowse 1987). In other words, in neighbourhoods where low-ability students are concentrated, human capital externalities can further deteriorate school achievements.

A second consequence of residential segregation is that it fuels the emergence of social problems that also deteriorate the employability of workers. In this respect, Crane (1991) develops an *epidemic theory of ghettos* in which the propensity of youngsters to adopt socially deviant behaviour (for instance, dropping out of schools or yielding to criminality) depends on the proportion of same-behavior individuals in the neighbourhood. This contagion is all the more prevalent when the adults in the neighbourhood are themselves unemployed and do not provide role models of social success with which youngsters could identify.

A third consequence of residential segregation is that it can deteriorate social networks in disadvantaged communities. This is a crucial point, since a significant proportion of jobs are usually found through personal contacts (Mortensen and Vishwanath 1994) and since low-skilled workers, young adults, and ethnic minorities often resort to such informal search methods (Holzer 1987, 1988). In other words, social network quality is a key factor in the job-acquisition process of unskilled workers and ethnic minorities, but since many such individuals reside in disadvantaged neighbourhoods, they usually benefit from social networks of poor quality. In particular, the local unemployment rate in these neighbourhoods is usually higher than average, so that local residents know fewer employed workers who could refer them to their own employer or provide them with professional contacts. In this respect, Reingold (1999) concludes that the poor quality of social networks explains a significant portion of unemployment problems in disadvantaged urban areas in the USA. These issues have recently been the focus of several formalisations: Calvo-Armengól and Zenou (2005) present a non-spatial theoretical model of social network and unemployment formation, while Selod and Zenou (forthcoming) provide an urban model in which residential segregation can exacerbate unemployment through low-quality social networks.

Finally, a fourth mechanism that links bad labour market outcomes to segregation involves the reluctance of employers to hire workers residing in disadvantaged communities. The stigmatisation of these neighbourhoods is at the root of *redlining*, a practice in which employers draw an imaginary red line around a stigmatised neighbourhood and beyond which they discriminate against residents (see Zenou and Boccard 2000 for a formalisation in an urban model).

To sum up, several theoretical mechanisms have been proposed to explain how city structure can have harmful effects on the labour market. The remainder of this chapter tries to relate these elements of theory to the particular case of Cape Town.

The city of Cape Town: Racial segregation, the disconnection between places of work and places of residence, and labour market outcomes

In the present section, we provide descriptive statistics for Cape Town, an urban area that covers more than 25 km and encompasses almost 2.7 million inhabitants.[3]

Figure 7.1 *The Cape Town urban area*

Figure 7.2 *Residential locations in Cape Town*

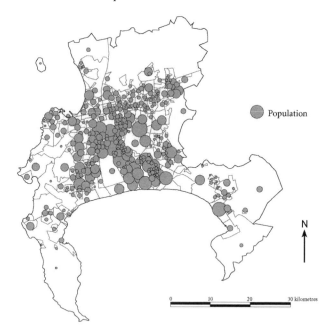

Source: Census 1996 (Statistics South Africa)

Figure 7.2 represents the spatial distribution of people within the Cape Town Urban Area (CTUA), each circle being proportional to the local population in the corresponding suburb.

According to the old apartheid classification, the population can be broken down into four population groups (see Table 7.1). Coloureds broadly represent half of the population of Cape Town, whereas whites and Africans each amount to about one-quarter of the population. Asians/Indians form a small minority of 1.4 per cent.

Table 7.1 *The population of the Cape Metropolitan Area, 1996*

	Population (in thousands)	Percentage
Africans	702	26.2
Coloureds	1 313	48.9
Asians/Indians	37	1.4
Whites	631	23.5
Total	2 683	100

Source: Dorrington 2000

Residential segregation

In this multiracial context, the rule is nevertheless residential segregation. Indeed, under apartheid, only whites were authorised to live close to the city centre. The non-white labour force (i.e. Asians/Indians, coloureds and Africans) were forced to live on the peripheries of cities, sometimes very far away from the city centre. Even though a certain amount of residential desegregation started to occur at the end of the 1980s, these spatial patterns of segregation continued to prevail throughout the 1990s. In other words, a high level of what is now market-driven segregation remains. In Cape Town, for instance, the African–white index of dissimilarity was still above 97 per cent in 1991 (Christopher 1993).[4] We have calculated that in 1996 the African–white index of dissimilarity still exceeded 92 per cent. Table 7.2 presents the dissimilarity indices for the four population groups in Cape Town in 1996. It is striking that the level of residential segregation between any two population groups in 1996 is correlated with the 'racial distance' between these two groups in the old apartheid classification. In particular, whites were less segregated from Indians than from coloureds or Africans. Africans were almost completely segregated from all other groups.

Table 7.2 *Dissimilarity indices (Cape Town Urban Area, 1996)*

Africans/ whites	Africans/ Asians (Indians)	Africans/ coloureds	Whites/Asians (Indians)	Whites/ coloureds	Coloureds/ Asians (Indians)
92.8%	94.5%	93.5%	76.3%	86.1%	63.3%

Source: Calculated by the authors, using data from Census 1996 (Statistics South Africa).

The disconnection between places of work and places of residence

In Cape Town, jobs occupy central locations and most jobs are located around one edge of the city: the central business district and its close surroundings (*Mail & Guardian* 1999). The central areas comprise centres of employment laid out along corridors extending outward from the port and city centre (see Figure 7.3).[5]

Figure 7.3 *Job locations in Cape Town*

Source: RSC Levy 2000 database

When one compares residential and job locations, it is clear that there exists a major disconnection between places of work and places of residence (see Figure 7.4). This problem has long been identified by Cape Town's urban planners (see, for instance, the Cape Metropolitan Council's *Metropolitan spatial development framework* 1996).

Figure 7.4 *Population and jobs in Cape Town*

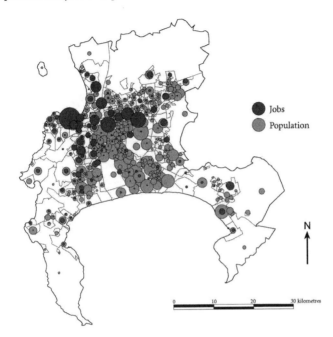

Sources: RSC Levy 2000 database and Census 1996 (Statistics South Africa)

This physical disconnection or *spatial mismatch* does not affect the four population groups equally. In fact whites and Asians/Indians reside relatively close to jobs, whereas coloureds and especially Africans are located at a much greater distance from job locations (see Figures 7.5 to 7.8).

Figure 7.5 *The location of whites in Cape Town*

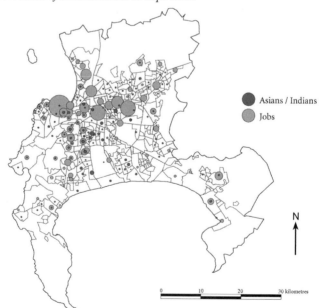

Sources: RSC Levy 2000 database and Census 1996 (Statistics South Africa)

Figure 7.6 *The location of Asians/Indians in Cape Town*

Sources: RSC Levy 2000 database and Census 1996 (Statistics South Africa)

Figure 7.7 *The location of coloureds in Cape Town*

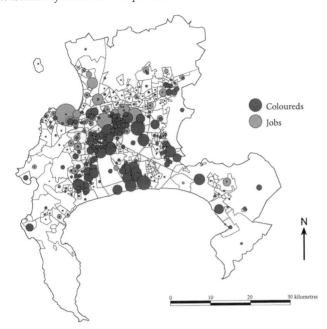

Sources: RSC Levy 2000 database and Census 1996 (Statistics South Africa)

Figure 7.8 *The location of Africans in Cape Town*

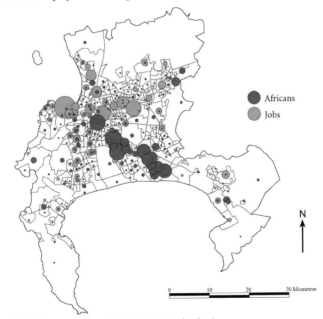

Sources: RSC Levy 2000 database and Census 1996 (Statistics South Africa)

This situation results in very different degrees of job access across population groups – all the more so since mode choices also differ across population groups. The 1998 study on *Migration and Settlement in the Cape Metropolitan Area* (discussed in detail in the next section of this chapter) provides interesting statistics with respect to commuting that we summarise in Table 7.3. It is striking that whites and Asians/Indians mainly use their cars to go to work, whereas coloureds and Africans mainly resort to public transport.

Table 7.3 *Transport modes by population group (percentage use) Cape Town, 1998*

	Walk/ bicycle	Public transport (minibus, train)	Private (car)	Provided by employer	Other	Total
Africans	12	58	6	13	11	100
Coloureds	23	39	25	11	2	100
Asians/Indians	19	14	53	12	2	100
Whites	16	4	58	16	6	100

Source: Calculated by the authors on a sample of 1 394 workers in the 1998 *Migration and Settlement in the Cape Metropolitan Area* data set.

In this context of different access to jobs and different modes of transport, population groups in Cape Town face very different commuting times and commuting costs (see Table 7.4 below, where it can be seen that Africans have the longest commuting trips and incur the highest costs).

Table 7.4 *Commuting times and commuting costs by population group (Cape Town, 1998)*

	Mean commuting time (one-way journey, in minutes)	Median commuting time (one-way journey, in minutes)	Mean commuting cost (return trip, in rands)	Median commuting cost (return trip, in rands)
Africans	39	30	3.57	3
Coloureds	25	20	3.89	3
Asians/Indians	19	15	3.06	3
Whites	23	15	6.31	4
All groups	30	25	4.03	3

Source: Calculated by the authors on a sample of 1 394 workers in the 1998 *Migration and Settlement in the Cape Metropolitan Area* data set.

Differences in labour market outcomes

Labour market outcomes vary considerably across population groups in Cape Town. Table 7.5 presents the disparities in terms of unemployment rates and median income. The unemployment rate for Africans in Cape Town is close to 38 per cent, whereas it is only slightly above 4 per cent for whites. The median income of an African worker is less than one-tenth of that of a white worker.

Table 7.5 *Unemployment and income by population group (Cape Town, 1996)*

	Africans	Coloureds	Asians/Indians	Whites	Total
Employed	182 633	427 689	13 408	245 481	869 211
Unemployed, looking for work	110 791	91 483	1 590	10 522	214 386
Unemployment rate	37.8%	17.6%	10.6%	4.1%	19.8%
Median income (rands per annum)	4 200	15 000	24 000	48 000	15 000

Sources: Space-Time Research, and *A Socio-Economic Profile of the Cape Metropolitan Area* by the Cape Metropolitan Council, based on data from Census 1996 (Statistics South Africa).

Of course, these differences in labour market outcomes stem largely from very different levels of education inherited historically (see Selod and Zenou 2001a, 2003 for figures on education imbalances). We will now investigate the extent to which these differences can also be attributed to differences in location, taking into account the role of job accessibility and residential segregation, as the theory suggests.

Econometric analysis

Methodological issues

The objective of our work is to investigate the possible causes of unemployment, with a particular focus on spatial factors. In order to do so, we want to estimate unemployment probabilities at the individual level by taking into account both personal and household characteristics as well as the role played by location characteristics, such as neighbourhood composition or job accessibility.

The endogeneity of location choice

The search for neighbourhood effect is complicated by the fact that individuals choose their locations. Selective migration introduces the possibility that any correlation between locations and employment outcome might not truly represent a 'treatment effect'. The existing literature offers three ways to circumvent the problem of endogenous location choices:

- The first solution is to focus on residential relocation experiments which attempt to randomly assign individuals to locations with different characteristics (Katz, Kling and Liebman 2001).
- The second approach to the problem is to concentrate on the outcomes of children or young adults who presumably do not directly choose their places of residence (O'Regan and Quigley 1998; Case and Katz 1991). However, Vigdor (2002) stresses an important limitation of this line of analysis by showing that selective migration to a city in the parent generation has a significant impact in the child generation.
- Finally, to obtain unbiased estimates of neighbourhood effects, some researchers control for non-random sorting into neighbourhoods by modeling the location choice (Ioannides and Zabel 2002). As Brock and Durlauf (2001) show, identification of neighbourhood effect is enabled by selection bias correction.

These analyses are all very demanding in terms of data set availability, requiring for instance a sample large enough either to select only young labour force participants who live with their parents or to model neighbourhood choice. The 1998 study, *Migration and Settlement in the Cape Metropolitan Area*, that we will use provides information on each person's relationship with the head of the household. However, restricting our sample to children (aged from 15 to 25) who are members of the labour force would reduce the sample to just 255 individuals, which would not allow for any robust econometric estimates. On the other hand, modelling the location choices in the 25 randomly selected areas that were surveyed would raise the same issue of sample size: there are not enough observations in each area to run a multinomial logit. Thus, the econometric analysis presented below does not correct for this endogeneity since, so far, we have not come across a good way of dealing with this issue.[6]

The logit model

We estimate the unemployment probability P_i of an individual i using the following logistic model:

$$Log \left[\frac{P_i}{1 - P_i} \right] = \alpha + \beta I_i + \gamma H_i + \delta N_i, \qquad [1]$$

where I_i is a vector of personal characteristics (race group, gender, age, level of education, marital status, head of the household status, birth type of area (rural or urban), date of arrival in the dwelling), H_i is a vector of household characteristics (house ownership, access to electricity), and N_i is a vector of neighbourhood characteristics (median earnings, local employment density, average commuting distance of workers living in the area).[7]

From [1], the individual probability of unemployment P_i is given by:

$$P_i = \frac{e(\alpha + \beta I_i + \gamma H_i + \delta N_i)}{1 + e(\alpha + \beta I_i + \gamma H_i + \delta N_i)} \qquad [2]$$

The determinants of unemployment

THE DATA AND SAMPLE

The data we use are derived from three sources. The 1998 study, *Migration and Settlement in the Cape Metropolitan Area* (also referred to as the 'migration study'), carried out jointly by the University of Stellenbosch and the Cape Metropolitan Council (see Cross and Bekker 1999), provides a great deal of information on 990 households (4 299 individuals) living in 25 randomly selected areas (*Enumerator Areas* or EAs[8]) in Cape Town (see Figure 7A2.1 in Appendix 2, which maps the locations of these EAs).[9] Excluding one of the investigated EAs which was not located in our definition of the CTUA, and excluding any household with missing values, we are left with 4 066 individuals belonging to 950 different households residing in 24 different neighbourhoods. The sample we use for the econometric analysis is limited to economically active individuals, between the ages of 15 and 65, for whom all attributes are available, restricting the final sample size to 1 870 individual observations.

The data on the social and economic composition of these EAs come from the 1996 Census. The Regional Service Council (RSC) Levy database provides detailed information on job locations for the year 2000 which enable us to compute the local job density within a defined geographical perimeter.[10]

THE RESULTS

Table 7.6 displays the results of our logistic regressions, taking into account the different groups of variables. We present four models explaining the probability of unemployment in the CTUA. We first consider individual characteristics as in a standard labour market analysis (model I). Model II introduces some cross-term effects. Then the household's characteristics are added among the independent variables (model III), as well as the neighbourhood features (model IV). Considering household and neighbourhood variables significantly increases the fit of the regression (see the likelihood ratios). Variations in our results are small from one model to the other, so we focus on the model that incorporates the three groups of variables (model IV).

Table 7.6. *The influence of individual, household and neighbourhood characteristics on unemployment probabilities*

	Model I		Model II		Model III		Model IV	
Individual variables								
Race group								
White	<Ref.>		<Ref.>		<Ref.>		<Ref.>	
African	0.931***	(2.537)	0.966***	(2.628)	0.930***	(2.536)	0.629**	(1.875)
Coloured	−0.276[NS]	(0.759)	−0.290[NS]	(0.748)	−0.215[NS]	(0.806)	−0.455[NS]	(0.634)
Asian/Indian	−0.052[NS]	(0.949)	−0.037[NS]	(0.964)	−0.046[NS]	(0.955)	−0.251[NS]	(0.778)
Male	−0.340***	(0.712)	0.030[NS]	(1.031)	−0.347***	(0.707)	−0.352***	(0.703)
Age	−0.179***	(0.836)	−0.182***	(0.834)	−0.186***	(0.830)	−0.192***	(0.825)
Age square	0.002***	(1.002)	0.002***	(1.002)	0.002***	(1.002)	0.002***	(1.002)
Schooling splines								
Primary	−0.027[NS]	(0.974)	−0.031[NS]	(0.970)	−0.021[NS]	(0.979)	−0.027[NS]	(0.973)
Secondary	−0.092***	(0.912)	−0.095***	(0.910)	−0.075**	(0.928)	−0.068*	(0.934)
Tertiary	−0.262**	(0.769)	−0.251**	(0.778)	−0.232**	(0.793)	−0.212*	(0.809)
Couple	−0.244*	(0.784)	−0.240*	(0.787)	−0.233*	(0.792)	−0.205[NS]	(0.814)
Head of the household	−0.947***	(0.388)	−0.935***	(0.393)	−0.999***	(0.368)	−0.996***	(0.369)
Time spent in the present dwelling	0.017**	(1.017)	0.017**	(1.017)	0.021***	(1.021)	0.021***	(1.021)
Rural birth area	0.434***	(1.543)	0.811***	(2.250)	0.394**	(1.482)	0.394**	(1.483)
Cross term effect								
Rural birth area*male			−0.792***	(0.453)				
Household variables								
Ownership of the dwelling					−0.397***	(0.672)	−0.393***	(0.675)
Access to electricity					−0.509***	(0.601)	−0.366**	(0.693)
Neighbourhood variables								
Median income of the EA							−0.175**	(0.840)
Average commuting distance of workers living in the EA							0.035*	(1.036)
Job density							0.267[NS]	(1.306)
Intercept	2.915***		2.805***		3.583***		4.012***	
Likelihood ratio	363.4		375.2		376.7		385.1	
Correctly predicted obs.	77.0%		76.5%		76.6%		76.6%	
Number of obs.	1 877		1 877		1 870		1 870	

Notes: Figures in brackets give the odds ratios.
* significant at a 10 per cent level; **significant at a 5 per cent level; ***significant at a 1 per cent level; [NS] not significant at a 10 per cent level

Model I presents the influence of individual variables on unemployment probability. Firstly, given South African history, the results confirm some expectations: Africans have a higher probability of being unemployed than whites. Indeed, Rospabé (2002) and Kingdon and Knight (2001) estimate the incidence of African-white discrimination in access to employment in the whole country. The greater economic integration of coloureds and Asians/Indians is reflected in the insignificance of the coefficient for these two population groups. Being a female increases the risk of being unemployed. To test how the employer's hiring choice and the worker's decision to enter the labour market are affected by the individual's endowment of human capital, three splines of education are introduced.[11] The incidence of unemployment decreases dramatically with education. However, primary education does not make individuals less likely to be unemployed. But an additional year of secondary education decreases the probability of being unemployed and this effect is reinforced with regard to tertiary education. One should note that these variables only reflect quantity of education, and thus can be poor indicators of the real level of education especially for African people, who suffered from low-quality schooling under apartheid. Indeed, Case and Yogo (1999) find that poor school quality significantly reduces the probability of employment for Africans. However, Kingdon and Knight (2001) estimate, on 'available weak evidence', that racial differences in unemployment probability do not seem to be, even partially, a result of differences in educational quality. The influence of age on the probability of unemployment is significantly negative, with diminishing returns. As Kingdon and Knight (2001) observe, younger people have a smaller chance of getting a job because employers might recoil at their high degree of job mobility. According to them, there is also evidence that younger people are more likely to enter unemployment voluntarily.

Being born in a rural area increases the probability of being unemployed. This result is difficult to interpret as we do not know when the individual leaves her birthplace to come to an urban area. One might think that recent migrants are more hampered in their job search than those who have been in urban areas for longer, as their labour market network is probably very limited. The only variable available to approximate roughly the time that migrants have spent in the CTUA is the date of arrival in the dwelling. But crossing this date of arrival with the rural origin does not provide any significant result. In a somewhat related perspective, two econometric studies (Van der Berg, Burger, Leibbrandt and Mlatsheni 2002; Posel and Casale 2003) underline the importance of taking gender into account in the study of internal labour migration in South Africa. To test whether gender matters in the influence of rural origin on unemployment, we introduce a cross term male/rural origin (model II). Results show that rural origin disadvantages more females than males in finding a job. We also include among the independent variables the time spent in the present dwelling, so as to capture the social integration of the individual into her area of residence. The longer time individuals have spent in the dwelling, the more likely they are to be unemployed. We do not have any straightforward interpretation for this finding. We might think that these individuals have a low housing mobility, which impedes them in their search for a job. However, one should also highlight the endogenous nature of this variable, as being unemployed prevents one from moving. Finally, it is found that being married or the head of the family limits the probability of unemployment. On the supply side, this partly reflects the fact that greater family responsibilities induce entry into the labour market and lower the reservation wages. On the demand side, it may also indicate employers' preferences for workers with higher probabilities of staying with their current employers. Kingdon and Knight (2001) choose to exclude these two variables from their probit specification on account of their endogenous nature.

Turning to household variables (model III), we see that housing tenure decreases the probability of unemployment. This finding is in contradiction with the general literature which shows that home ownership impedes labour mobility and migration (and thus employment), because of higher associated transaction costs compared to renting (Cameron and Muellbauer 1998; McCormick 1997). Previous results on South Africa presented by Rospabé (2002) and Kingdon and Knight (2001) are consistent with this literature when considering Africans only, whereas for whites, home ownership is associated with a lower probability of unemployment. In this context, the negative effect can be explained if home ownership is a proxy for household wealth and is endogenous to unemployment (i.e. unemployment determines the chances of owning one's home). In order to test for these racial differences, we introduce a variable crossing the race group and ownership, but it does not appear to be significant.[12] Access to electricity has the same effect as home ownership, and decreases the risk of being unemployed.[13] Thus our findings mean either that it is easier for an individual in a wealthier household to find a job or that this variable might be endogenous.

Introducing neighbourhood variables in the regression, model IV shows that median income in the EA decreases the probability of unemployment. This result is consistent with some elements of the theory mentioned in the first section of the chapter: a socio-economic environment of higher quality facilitates human capital acquisition, and provides a better social network which may in turn improve the employability of individuals. We complement model IV by also taking into account spatial mismatch variables. The effect of local employment density[14] is not significant, whereas the average commuting distance of workers surveyed in the 'migration study' and living in the EA plays a positive and significant role in the unemployment probability. This means that controlling for all other variables, individuals who reside in EAs where employed workers occupy jobs far away are more likely to be unemployed. This result is in accordance with the theory on physical disconnection from jobs.[15]

Conclusion

The explanation of unemployment usually revolves around well-known determinants (notably the lack of formal education or the skill mismatch between labour supply and labour demand). Alternative theories suggest that unemployment may also be determined by the spatial organisation of cities which concentrate disadvantaged families in poverty zones and/or distance them from job opportunities. This chapter has examined the particular case of Cape Town, and investigated the extent to which its spatial organisation could affect the labour market, an important issue for a country such as South Africa which is characterised by spatially stratified cities. We have studied the link between residential location and labour market outcomes by estimating the unemployment probability of individuals surveyed in different neighbourhoods of Cape Town. Although there remain some technical issues to resolve, our preliminary results suggest that, controlling for individual and household characteristics, there are important spatial factors that exacerbate unemployment: distance from jobs, rural origin (especially for women), and the length of time spent in the present dwelling. The next step required will be to deepen the econometric analysis and try to propose adapted policy measures to counter the identified spatial mechanisms of urban exclusion.

Acknowledgements

Harris Selod is grateful to the South African Data Archive and the City of Cape Town for providing the data used in this study. His warmest thanks go to Simon Bekker, Jens Kuhn, Saleem Mowzer, Phillip Romanovski, Amanda van Heerden and Rae Wolpe for their much-appreciated help. The authors are also grateful to researchers at DPRU, University of Cape Town, and especially Haroon Bhorat and Eckart Naumann for their kind help and advice. All opinions expressed in the present paper are the authors' own.

Notes

1   This example was provided in Selod and Zenou (2001a).

2   See Selod (2001) for a detailed presentation of South African city structures.

3   Official data are usually given for the Cape Metropolitan Area (CMA), an aggregation of several hundred suburbs which, in the recent past, were grouped into six local municipalities. In the econometric analysis that we present in the following section, however, we use a somewhat different definition of the metropolitan area which in our view better corresponds to a functional definition of Cape Town in terms of economic integration. In our definition, we have excluded from the CMA the suburbs that belong to the northern part of the Blaauwberg municipality such as Atlantis which, in our opinion, should be viewed as a town in itself. We have labelled our working definition of Cape Town the 'Cape Town Urban Area' (CTUA). Like the CMA, the CTUA does not include distant places to the east and north-east such as Stellenbosch or Paarl. It extends south-east as far as Strand or Gordons Bay (see Figure 7.1). The CTUA hosts almost 2.4 million inhabitants, who reside in 401 different suburbs.

4   The dissimilarity index for Africans and whites for instance is given by:

$$\frac{1}{2} \sum_i \left[\frac{Africans_i}{Africans} - \frac{Whites_i}{Whites} \right]$$

where $Africans_i$ and $whites_i$ are the respective numbers of Africans and whites in suburb i and $Africans$ and $whites$ are the respective numbers of Africans and whites in the whole urban area (Duncan and Duncan, 1955). This index represents the percentage population of one of these two groups which would have to be relocated in order to obtain a uniform mix of both groups in each suburb of the urban area. In the USA, a city with an index above 60 per cent is usually considered highly segregated.

5   The location of salaried jobs has been obtained by our treatment of the RSC Levy database, which we will explain in the third section of the present chapter.

6   However in South Africa, more than anywhere else, the endogenous risk of residential localisation is alleviated by the effect of apartheid policy, which did not leave much freedom to individuals in selecting their residential area.

7   Descriptive statistics on variables can be read in Table 7A1.1 in Appendix 1. Table 7A1.2 in Appendix 1 presents the correlation matrix.

8   An Enumerator Area (EA) is the smallest statistical area in South Africa and is the direct subdivision of a suburb. The Cape Town Urban Area, as we define it, is divided into 401 suburbs and 4 622 enumerator areas. The average size of an EA is 518 inhabitants (for a standard deviation of 277). This means that an EA corresponds to a small neighbourhood where individuals are likely to interact with one another. The largest EA in the CTUA has 2 006 residents.

9   In this stratified survey, 40 dwellings were randomly investigated in a random sample of 25 EAs. Africans are over-represented, since they account for 46.6 per cent of the sample (coloureds, whites, and Asians/Indians respectively account for 38.4 per cent, 12.3 per cent and 2.7 per cent of the sample).

10   The RSC Levy database contains information on all companies operating in Cape Town and paying a municipal tax to fund the provision of basic municipal services. In particular, companies are asked to declare their number of workers. In most cases, the registered address is the same as the address where the economic activity actually takes place. We were able to identify the locations of 407 348 salaried jobs within the CTUA as we define it.

11   These three splines cover primary, secondary and tertiary schooling respectively. The splines allow the effect on unemployment of each of the three schooling levels to vary, while implicitly assuming that the annual effects within each of the three schooling levels are identical. (See Moll 2000 and Rospabé 2002 for the use of similar variables.)

12   In our sample, 84 per cent of Africans are owners of their dwelling. As a result, taking into account the large number of shacks in the African informal areas surveyed in the 'migration study', home ownership does not seem to be a relevant measure of wealth for Africans.

13   This variable is more likely to be an indirect measure of wealth for Africans in the 'migration study' since only 62 per cent of them live in a household that has access to electricity.

14 We constructed several job density variables depending on the choice of the geographical perimeter: 5, 10 or 15 km. None of these variables were significant. We retain, in model IV, the job density within a 10 km perimeter.

15 In order to test whether this effect could be different for different race groups, we ran separate regressions for each race group. In all cases, distance to job is not significant. The most obvious interpretation is that racial residential segregation makes distance to job very homogenous within each race group, and thus erases any physical disconnection effect.

Appendix 1

The determinants of unemployment

Table 7A1.1 *Variables used to estimate unemployment probabilities*

Variable	Description	Database	Mean and standard deviation
Dependent variable			
Unemployed	= 1 if unemployed according to the official definition (excludes discouraged jobseekers)	Migration study (1998)	0.276 (0.447)
Individual variables			
Race group			
African	= 1 if African	Migration study (1998)	0.483 (0.500)
Coloured	= 1 if coloured	Migration study (1998)	0.390 (0.488)
Asian/Indian	= 1 if Asian/Indian	Migration study (1998)	0.028 (0.164)
White	= 1 if white	Migration study (1998)	0.100 (0.300)
Male	= 1 if male	Migration study (1998)	0.542 (0.498)
Age	= age in years	Migration study (1998)	34.49 (11.17)
Age square	= age square	Migration study (1998)	1 314 (857.1)
Schooling splines			
Primary	$\begin{cases} x, 0 \leq x \leq 7 \\ 7, x > 7 \end{cases}$ where x = years of schooling	Migration study (1998)	6.479 (1.467)
Secondary	$\begin{cases} 0, x \leq 7 \\ x - 7, 7 < x \leq 12 \\ 5, x > 12 \end{cases}$	Migration study (1998)	2.618 (2.031)
Tertiary	$\begin{cases} 0, x \leq 12 \\ x - 12, x > 12 \end{cases}$	Migration study (1998)	0.306 (0.758)
Couple	= 1 if married or living together	Migration study (1998)	0.479 (0.500)
Head of the household	= 1 if is the head of the household	Migration study (1998)	0.345 (0.476)
Time spent in the present dwelling	= number of years spent in the present dwelling	Migration study (1998)	12.02 (10.86)
Rural birth area	= 1 if was born in a rural area	Migration study (1998)	0.398 (0.490)

Variable	Description	Database	Mean and standard deviation
Household variables			
Ownership of the dwelling	= 1 if the household owns the dwelling	Migration study (1998)	0.750 (0.433)
Access to electricity	= 1 if the household has access to electricity	Migration study (1998)	0.804 (0.397)
Neighbourhood variables			
Median income of the EA	= income class (1 to 13) of the median worker	Census 1996	3.789 (1.189)
Average commuting distance of workers living in the EA	= average distance (in km) between the EA where the individual is living and the suburb where she is working	Migration study (1998)	8.852 (4.068)
Job density	= number of jobs/active population (in a 10 km radius around the EA of residence)	Cape Town RSC Levy 2000	0.484 (0.374)

Table 7A1.2 *The correlation matrix*

Variable	Unem.	White	African	Asian/Indian	Coloured	Male	Age	Age sq.	Prim.	Sec.	Tert.	Couple	Hhead	Dwell.	Rural	Own.	Elect.	Incom.	Dist. jobs	Job density
Unemployed	1.00																			
White	-0.12*	1.00																		
African	0.22*	-0.32*	1.00																	
Asian/Indian	-0.05*	-0.06*	-0.16*	1.00																
Coloured	-0.13*	-0.27*	-0.77*	-0.13*	1.00															
Male	-0.09*	0.06*	-0.02	0.03	-0.03	1.00														
Age	-0.25*	0.14*	-0.05*	0.04	-0.05*	0.05*	1.00													
Age square	-0.23*	0.15*	-0.07*	0.05*	-0.04	0.05*	0.99*	1.00												
Primary	-0.06*	0.12*	-0.16*	0.05*	0.07*	-0.01	-0.17*	-0.18*	1.00											
Secondary	-0.13*	0.29*	-0.29*	0.10*	0.08*	-0.01	-0.17*	-0.17*	0.46*	1.00										
Tertiary	-0.15*	0.27*	-0.22*	0.08*	0.03	0.00	0.03	0.02	0.14*	0.47*	1.00									
Couple	-0.17*	0.09*	0.01	0.01	-0.07*	0.08*	0.43*	0.39*	-0.04	-0.06*	0.00	1.00								
Household head	-0.23*	0.07*	0.11*	-0.01	-0.16*	0.20*	0.45*	0.43*	-0.06*	-0.08*	0.07*	0.29*	1.00							
Time in dwelling	-0.04	-0.11*	-0.34*	0.14*	0.37*	0.01	0.16*	0.17*	0.05*	0.01	-0.02	-0.15*	-0.09*	1.00						
Rural origin	0.17*	-0.15*	0.61*	-0.14*	-0.48*	-0.01	0.03	0.02	-0.22*	-0.32*	-0.20*	0.10*	0.11*	-0.34*	1.00					
Ownership	0.00	-0.08*	0.19*	0.05*	-0.17*	-0.02	0.04	0.04	-0.03	-0.01	0.04	0.00	-0.02	0.02*	0.14*	1.00				
Electricity	-0.17*	0.17*	-0.44*	0.08*	0.32*	-0.01	0.07*	0.08*	0.19*	0.27*	0.17*	-0.01	-0.07	0.28*	-0.39*	-0.24*	1.00			
Area income	-0.20*	0.47*	-0.38*	0.12*	0.06*	0.02	0.17*	0.17*	0.16*	0.41*	0.36*	0.14*	0.05*	0.07*	-0.26*	-0.13*	0.42*	1.00		
Distance to jobs	0.13*	-0.21*	0.50*	-0.13*	-0.34*	-0.03	0.02	0.00	-0.03	-0.11*	-0.11*	0.02	0.06*	-0.19*	0.37*	0.12*	-0.29*	-0.24*	1.00	
Job density	-0.11*	0.13*	-0.43*	0.33*	0.25*	0.04	0.01	0.02	0.11*	0.27*	0.18*	0.02	-0.06*	0.23*	-0.35*	-0.24*	0.29*	0.42*	-0.59*	1.00

Note: * significant at 5 per cent level.

Appendix 2

Migration and settlement in the Cape Metropolitan Area (1998)

Figure 7A2.1 *The surveyed neighbourhoods*

References

Arnott R & Rowse J (1987) Peer group effect and the educational attainment, *Journal of Public Economics* 32: 287–305.

Benabou R (1993) Workings of a city: Location, education, and production, *Quarterly Journal of Economics* 108: 619–652.

Brock W & Durlauf S (2001) Interactions-based models, 3297–3380. In Heckman JJ and Leamer EE (eds) *Handbook of Econometrics*, Vol. 5, Amsterdam: North Holland.

Brueckner J (1996) Welfare gains from removing land-use distortions: An analysis of urban change in post-apartheid South Africa, *Journal of Regional Science* 36: 91–109.

Brueckner J & Martin R (1997) Spatial mismatch: An equilibrium analysis, *Regional Science and Urban Economics* 27: 693–714.

Brueckner J & Zenou Y (2003) Space and unemployment: The labor-market effects of spatial mismatch, *Journal of Labor Economics* 21: 242–266.

Calvo-Armengól A & Zenou Y (2005) Job matching, social network and word-of-mouth communication, *Journal of Urban Economics* 75: 500–522.

Cameron G & Muellbauer J (1998) The housing market and regional commuting and migration choices, *Scottish Journal of Political Economy* 45: 420–446.

Cape Metropolitan Council (1996) Metropolitan spatial development framework: A guide for development in the Cape metropolitan functional region. Technical report, April.

Cape Metropolitan Council, Department of Housing and University of Stellenbosch, Department of Sociology (2000) *Migration and settlement in the Cape Metropolitan Area (CMA)*. South Africa: Cape Metropolitan Council and South African Data Archive (distributor).

Cape Metropolitan Council (2000) RSC Levy database 2000.

Case A & Katz L (1991) *The company you keep: The effect of family and neighbourhood on disadvantaged youth*. NBER Working Paper 3705.

Case A & Yogo M (1999) *Does school quality matter? Return to education and the characteristics of schools in South Africa*. NBER Working Paper 7399.

Christopher A (1993) Urban segregation levels in South Africa, 1985–1991, *South African Journal of Sociology* 24: 121–127.

Crane J (1991) The epidemic theory of ghettos and neighborhood effects on dropping out and teenage childbearing, *American Journal of Sociology* 96: 1226–1259.

Cross C & Bekker S (1999) En waarheen nou? Migration and settlement in the Cape Metropolitan Area. Occasional Paper 6, Department of Sociology, University of Stellenbosch.

Cutler D & Glaeser EL (1997) Are ghettos good or bad? *Quarterly Journal of Economics* 112: 827–872.

Davis S & Huff D (1972) Impact of ghettoization on black employment, *Economic Geography* 48: 421–427.

Dorrington R (2000) Projection of the population of the Cape Metropolitan area 1996–203. Accessed online, www.capetown.gov.za.

Duncan O & Duncan B (1955) A methodological analysis of segregation indexes, *American Sociological Review* 41: 210–217.

Gobillon L, Selod H & Zenou Y (2005) *The mechanisms of spatial mismatch*. CEPR Discussion Paper 5346.

Holzer H (1987) Informal job search and black youth unemployment, *American Economic Review* 77: 446–452.

Holzer H (1988) Search method used by unemployed youth, *Journal of Labor Economics* 6: 1–20.

Ihlanfeldt K (1997) Information on the spatial distribution of job opportunities within metropolitan areas, *Journal of Urban Economics* 41: 218–242.

Ihlanfeldt K & Sjoquist D (1990) Job accessibility and racial differences in youth employment rates, *American Economic Review* 80: 267–275.

Ihlanfeldt K & Sjoquist D (1998) The spatial mismatch hypothesis: A review of recent studies and their implications for welfare reform, *Housing Policy Debate* 9: 849–892.

Immergluck D (1998) Job proximity and the urban employment problem: Do suitable nearby jobs improve neighbourhood employment rates? *Urban Studies* 35: 7–23.

Ioannides Y & Zabel J (2002) Interactions, neighborhood selection and housing demand. Mimeo.

Kain J (1968) Housing segregation, negro employment and metropolitan decentralization, *The Quarterly Journal of Economics* 82: 175–183.

Katz L, Kling J & Liebman J (2001) Moving to opportunity in Boston: Early impacts of a housing mobility program, *Quarterly Journal of Economics* 116: 607–654.

Kingdon G & Knight J (2001) Race and the incidence of unemployment in South Africa. Mimeo.

Mail & Guardian (1999) New plans to revitalize the Mother City, 1–7 October.

McCormick B (1997) Regional unemployment and labour mobility in the UK, *European Economic Review* 41: 581–589.

Moll P (2000) Discrimination is declining in South Africa but inequality is not, *Studies in Economics and Econometrics* 24: 91–108.

Mortensen D & Vishwanath T (1994) Personal contacts and earnings: It is who you know! *Labour Economics* 1: 187–201.

O'Regan K & Quigley J (1996) Spatial effects upon employment outcomes: The case of New Jersey teenagers, *New England Economic Review* May/June: 41–58.

O'Regan K & Quigley JM (1998) Where youth live: Economic effects of urban space on employment prospects, *Urban Studies* 35(7): 1187–1205.

Ortega J (2000) Pareto-improving immigration in an economy with equilibrium unemployment, *Economic Journal* 110: 92–112.

Posel D & Casale D (2003) What has been happening to internal labour migration in South Africa, 1993–1999? *South African Journal of Economics* 71: 455–479.

Reingold D (1999) Social networks and the employment problem of the urban poor, *Urban Studies* 36: 1907–1932.

Rogers C (1997) Job search and unemployment duration: Implications for the spatial mismatch hypothesis, *Journal of Urban Economics* 42: 109–132.

Rospabe S (2002) How did labour market racial discrimination evolve after the end of apartheid? An analysis of the evolution of employment, occupational and wage discrimination in South Africa between 1993 and 1999, *The South African Economic Journal* 70: 156–189.

Selod H (2001) *Structure des villes et ghettos urbains: le cas des Etats-Unis et de l'Afrique du Sud.* Ph.D. dissertation, University of Paris 1 Panthéon-Sorbonne.

Selod H and Zenou Y (2001a) Location and education in South African cities under and after Apartheid, *Journal of Urban Economics* 49: 168–198.

Selod H and Zenou Y (2001b) Social interactions, ethnic minorities and urban unemployment, *Annales d'Economie et de Statistique* 63–64: 183–214.

Selod H and Zenou Y (2003) Private versus public schools in post-Apartheid South African cities: Theory and policy implications, *Journal of Development Economics* 71: 351–394.

Selod H and Zenou Y (forthcoming) City structure, job search, and labor discrimination, *Economic Journal* 116.

Statistics South Africa (2006) *Census 1996.* Pretoria: Statistics South Africa.

Summers A & Wolfe B (1977) Do schools make a difference? *American Economic Review* 67: 639–652.

Turner S (1997) Barriers to a better break: Employer discrimination and spatial mismatch in metropolitan Detroit, *Journal of Urban Affairs* 19: 123–141.

Van der Berg S, Burger R, Leibbrandt M & Mlatsheni C (2002) Migration and the changing rural-urban interface in South Africa. What can we learn from census and survey data? DPRU/FES conference paper.

Vigdor J (2002) Locations, outcomes and selective migration, *The Review of Economics and Statistics* 84: 751–755.

Wasmer E & Zenou Y (2002) Does city structure affect search and welfare? *Journal of Urban Economics* 51: 515–541.

Zenou Y & Boccard N (2000) Labor discrimination and redlining in cities, *Journal of Urban Economics* 48: 260–285.

8 *Crime and local inequality in South Africa*[1]

Gabriel Demombynes and Berk Özler

Introduction

Crime is among the most difficult of the many challenges facing South Africa in the post-apartheid era. The country's crime rates are among the highest in the world and no South African is insulated from its effects. Beyond the pain and loss suffered by crime victims, crime also has less direct costs. The threat of crime diverts resources to protection efforts, exacts health costs through increased stress, and generally creates an environment unconducive to productive activity. Additionally, the widespread emigration of South African professionals in recent years is attributable in part to their desire to escape a high-crime environment.[2] All of these effects are likely to discourage investment and stifle long-term growth in South Africa. Consequently, it is important to understand the factors that contribute to crime.

Both economic and sociological theory have linked the distribution of welfare to criminal activity. Economists have suggested that inequality may capture the differential returns from criminal activity and thereby have an association with crime rates. If criminals travel, not only the welfare distribution in the local area, but that in neighbouring areas as well may be linked to local crime levels. Sociologists have hypothesised that inequality and social welfare in general may have effects on crime through other channels. Inequality may be associated with a lack of social capital, a lack of upward mobility, or social disorganisation, all of which may cause higher levels of crime. Furthermore, economic inequalities between groups may engender conflict in a society by consolidating and reinforcing ethnic and class differences (Blau and Blau 1982).

In this chapter, using data on crime and estimates of welfare measures by police station jurisdiction[3] in South Africa, we consider three questions. Firstly, we examine the extent to which economic versus sociological theories explain the variation in crime rates, by comparing the implications of various theories for violent crime and property crime separately. Next, we consider how the relative economic position of a community among neighbouring areas may be associated with crime. Finally, we examine whether crime is particularly prevalent in areas with high inequality between racial groups.

The next section of the chapter discusses the reasons why there might be an association between economic welfare and crime at the community level. The third section summarises the empirical literature on inequality and crime and explains the contribution of this chapter. This is followed by a section that outlines the empirical approach and describes our data sources. The fifth section presents the regression results for various types of crime, and the concluding section summarises our findings and discusses possible implications for policy implementation.

Crime and economic welfare

There are a number of reasons why the local distribution of economic welfare might be associated with the prevalence of crime. Various arguments on this issue have been advanced by economists, sociologists and public health specialists.

Firstly, community welfare measures may be associated with crime levels via a relationship with the returns from criminal and non-criminal activities. In his seminal work, Becker (1968) proposes an occupational choice model in which the incentives for individuals to commit crime are determined by the differential returns from legitimate and illegitimate pursuits. At an aggregate level, researchers have suggested various approaches to approximating these returns. For example, Machin and Meghir (2000) argue that criminals are more likely to come from the bottom end of the wage distribution, and they measure the returns to legitimate activities with the 25th percentile wage. Ehrlich (1973) postulates that the payoffs to activities such as robbery, burglary and theft depend on the level of transferable assets and can be proxied by median income in the community.

Under certain conditions, a Becker-type economic model can generate a relationship between property crime and local inequality. Suppose, for example, that the expected returns from illegitimate activities are determined by the mean income of households in the community. Also suppose that the returns from crime for potential criminals are equal to the incomes of those at the lower end of the local income distribution. Then the relative benefits of crime will be determined by the spread between the community mean and the incomes of the relatively poor. This implies that the expected level of crime will be greater in a community with higher inequality. Using variations on this argument, Ehrlich (1973), Chiu and Madden (1998) and Bourguignon (2001) all suggest that economic incentives for crimes are higher in areas with greater inequality in the community. A Beckerian model does not imply that inequality per se causes crime, but rather that empirically, inequality may capture the incentives for criminal activity. This leaves no reason to suspect that crime should be correlated with inequality if the costs and benefits of crime are controlled for.

Secondly, local economic welfare may also be associated with the level of protection from crime. Private crime protection measures may include guard dogs, bars on windows, electric fences, and alarm systems with armed security response. Chiu and Madden (1998) provide a model that allows for richer neighbourhoods to have lower crime rates, partly because they may employ effective defence strategies against crime. Wealthier people may also have better access to legal protection (Black 1983). Inequality may also be positively correlated with crime if, as Pradhan and Ravallion (2003) suggest, concern for public safety at the household level is a concave function of income, thereby creating a negative correlation between public concern for safety and inequality at the aggregate level. The provision of protection against crime through collective action such as neighbourhood watch programmes may also be low in communities with low social capital. Lederman, Loayza and Menéndez (2001) suggest that social capital may decrease crime rates by lowering the cost of social transactions and attenuating free-rider problems of collective action. If inequality is correlated with lack of social capital in a community, then one expects to observe a positive correlation between inequality and crime.

Thirdly, lack of upward mobility in the society may be linked to the prevalence of crime. Coser (1968, cited in Blau and Blau 1982: 119) argues that people who perceive their poverty as permanent may be driven by hostile impulses rather than rational pursuit of their interests. Wilson and Daly (1997) hypothesise that sensitivity to inequality, especially by those at the bottom, leads to higher risk tactics like crime, when the expected payoffs from low-risk tactics are poor. If income inequality, a static measure, is correlated with social mobility, a dynamic concept, then these theories imply a higher prevalence of criminal behaviour in more unequal areas.

Fourthly, closely related to theories involving social mobility are those related to social disorganisation and crime. In an influential paper, Merton (1938) proposes that '...when a system of cultural values emphasises, virtually above all else, certain *common* symbols of success *for the population at large* while its social structure rigorously restricts or completely eliminates access to approved modes of acquiring these symbols *for a considerable part of the same population*, ...antisocial behavior ensues on a considerable scale'. Hence, the lack of upward mobility in a society, combined with a high premium on economic affluence, results in anomie, a breakdown of standards and values. According to Merton, poverty or even 'poverty in the midst of plenty' alone is not sufficient to induce high levels of crime. Only when their interaction with other interdependent social and cultural variables is considered can one explain the association between crime and poverty.

Finally, people may be particularly sensitive to inequalities across ethnic, racial or religious groups, or across geographical areas.[4] Blau and Blau (1982) argue that three concepts are central to theories on social relations in a population: heterogeneity, inequality, and the extent to which two or more dimensions of social difference are correlated and consolidate status distinctions. For example, racial heterogeneity and income inequality, both correlated with status in the community, could inhibit marriage between persons in different positions or spell potential for violence. They suggest that '...great economic inequalities generally foster conflict and violence, but ascriptive inequalities do so particularly' (Blau and Blau 1982: 119). Their theory suggests that inequality between racial groups is an especially strong force behind high crime rates.

A departure from the literature in this chapter is the incorporation of the effects of characteristics of neighbouring communities on crime. With respect to the sociological theories of crime, such as Merton (1938), Coser (1968, as cited in Blau and Blau 1982: 119) and Wilson and Daly (1997), it is not clear whether it is inequality within the community or within a larger geographical unit that should matter in relation to crime. The relevance of neighbouring communities can also be considered in the context of the Beckerian economic theory of crime. For ease of exposition, we use 'own neighbourhood' to refer only to the neighbourhood itself, while we define the 'criminal catchment area' for a neighbourhood to include that neighbourhood itself and all bordering neighbourhoods. One can think of 'own neighbourhood' as the police precinct in which a reported crime has taken place. 'Criminal catchment area' is then defined as the larger area containing that precinct and the bordering precincts, where the perpetrator(s) of said crime may reside. Because individuals may travel from surrounding communities to commit crimes, or to neighbouring areas to work, the relevant returns for potential criminals to legitimate activities are the returns available in the criminal catchment area. The relevant returns to crime, however, are those in the own neighbourhood alone.

Suppose two adjoining neighbourhoods are identical and have identical income distributions, except that in one neighbourhood households have incomes and transferable assets worth twice those of households in the other neighbourhood. Consequently, inequality is equal within each of the two neighbourhoods. Further suppose that individuals can observe the mean income (or assets) of households in a neighbourhood, but not the welfare levels of individual households. In economic theories of crime, such as Ehrlich (1973), where crime rates are a positive function of the absolute differential returns from crime and a negative function of punishment, it is not clear why crime levels should be higher in the richer neighbourhood. When travel between neighbourhoods is not considered and punishment is by imprisonment only, then the effect of the difference in mean incomes between the two neighbourhoods could be zero, as the returns from legitimate and illegitimate activities and, hence, the opportunity cost of crime, are all higher by the same proportion in the richer neighbourhood.[5] On the other hand, if individuals can travel freely between the two neighbourhoods at negligible cost, every individual who allocates some time to property crime will prefer to conduct their activity in the richer neighbourhood, where the expected returns are twice as high. Thus, if criminals can travel, economic theory predicts that crime will be higher in wealthier neighbourhoods, even controlling for inequality.

Crime rates may also be partially determined by the wealth of the own neighbourhood relative to other neighbourhoods in the catchment area. As above, consider a criminal catchment area that consists of multiple neighbourhoods instead of just two, where the neighbourhoods differ only in their mean level of income and assets. In such a case, criminals will conduct all their illegitimate activity in the richest neighbourhood. Property crimes may still take place in the poorer areas if travel is costly, if the amount of protection from crime varies across neighbourhoods, or if criminals have better information on returns from crime in their immediate neighbourhood.

The relationship between community welfare and property crime may vary with the specific type of crime. The travel scenario seems best suited to explain residential burglary, because the benefits – the value of transferable assets – are most clearly linked to local household wealth. This scenario is less applicable to other property crime, such as vehicle theft or robbery, because the crime may take place while the victim is away from his or her neighbourhood. Consequently, wealth in the area in which the theft is reported may not be linked to the return from crime.

In summary, a variety of theories suggest that higher inequality may be associated with crime. Standard economic theories, which seem most applicable to property crime, imply that inequality may be positively correlated with crime through its effect on the differential returns from criminal activity versus legitimate pursuits. This would suggest that there is no relationship between crime and inequality, controlling for the benefits and costs of crime participation. However, sociological theories of crime imply that inequality also has a direct effect on crime. These theories suggest that inequality leads to higher levels of both property crime and violent crime, independently of the net returns to such crimes. Higher inequality may also lead to more crime through lower levels of protection from crime, if inequality suppresses collective action or concern for public safety at the aggregate level.

The theoretical literature on crime does not generally address the relationship between aggregate income levels and crime. We have argued above that if mean level of income adequately captures the level of transferable assets in the community and if individuals travel to commit crimes, then, all else being equal, *property* crime should be positively correlated with mean income. At the same time, higher incomes may lead to lower property crime levels through more effective protection. *Ex ante*, there is no obvious reason to expect *violent* crime levels to be associated with mean income levels.

Evidence from the literature

The empirical evidence on the crime–inequality relationship, based mainly on comparisons across states and cities in the USA, or across countries, generally shows a positive correlation between inequality and crime. A meta-analysis of 34 aggregate data studies (Hsieh and Pugh 1993) shows that 97 per cent of bivariate correlation coefficients for violent crime with either poverty or inequality were positive, with 80 per cent of the coefficients above 0.25. Ehrlich (1973) finds a positive relationship between relative poverty (percentage of the population under half the median income in the state) and crime, with higher elasticities for property crime than for violent crime. Ehrlich also finds median income in a state to be positively associated with property crime. Machin and Meghir (2000) argue that higher wages at the bottom end of the wage distribution reduce crime, while criminal activity is positively correlated with returns from crime in the UK. Gould, Weinberg and Mustard (2002) also find mean wages of non-college-educated men and unemployment rate to be significantly related to crime, but find no consistent relationship between mean income and crime rates across counties in the USA. Kelly (2000) finds a strong relationship between income inequality and violent crime across USA counties, but finds no such relationship for property crime. Kelly does not control for mean or median income. Blau and Blau (1982) find that both between-race and within-race economic inequality are associated with criminal violence across states in the USA. Lederman et al. (2002) argue that increases in income inequality and lower growth rates lead to increases in violent crime across countries. Using panel data for approximately 39 countries, Fajnzylber, Lederman and Loayza (2002a) report similar findings for homicide and robbery rates across countries. Lederman et al. (2001) also argue that higher social capital, measured using levels of trust in each country, leads to lower rates of homicides. Kennedy, Kawachi, Prothrow-Stith, Lochner and Gupta (1998), using data on 39 states of the USA, find that inequality affects violent crime mostly through its effect on social capital.

There are several important limitations of this literature that are worth mentioning. The first is that the unit of observation for which crime is examined is relatively large. The works cited above refer mostly to cross-country studies and to analyses of states and large metropolitan areas in the USA. It is unlikely that the underlying process that produces crime is the same across countries. Various authors (Kelly 2000; Chiu and Madden 1998; Wilson and Daly 1997) suggest that the appropriate geographical unit to study might well be much smaller, such as a neighbourhood, rather than a state, county or large metropolitan area. Recent papers by Fafchamps and Moser (2002), Di Tella and Schargrodsky (2001) and Glaeser, Sacerdote and Scheinkman (1996) examine crime at the commune, city block and police precinct level, respectively, but none of these papers addresses the issue of local inequality and crime.

The second limitation is that comparability of definitions of crime categories and welfare indicators poses serious problems for most cross-country studies, as does aligning data for various countries for the same time period. For example, Fajnzylber et al. (2002b) use the Deininger-Squire inequality data (Deininger and Squire 1996), the problems with which are well documented (Atkinson and Brandolini 2000).

A third limitation is that most studies treat crime markets as closed, meaning that only the characteristics of the own area, and not those of neighbouring areas, are allowed to influence the crime rates. This may be a justifiable assumption when the unit of observation is a country or a state, but it quickly loses its appeal when geographical units are such that travel between them for legitimate or illegitimate activities is plausible. Even the theoretical work on the determinants of crime has not addressed this issue, despite the fact that it is not constrained by the availability of data for small geographical units.[6]

Finally, very few studies address the relative importance of economic inequality between groups (for example, racial or geographical groups), rather than within groups, as a determinant of crime. One study that attempts to address this issue (Blau and Blau 1982) does not utilise a direct measure of within-group inequality.

In this chapter, we address the limitations summarised above. The geographical unit used in the analysis is the police precinct, which is smaller than the units employed in most empirical work that we have encountered in the literature.[7] Using geographical information for each of the police precincts, we are able to allow explicitly for spatial effects in the analysis. The data further provide us with a detailed breakdown of different types of crimes, defined in the same manner for the whole of South Africa.[8] Finally, utilising well-known inequality decomposition techniques, we analyse the relationship between crime and inequality within and between racial groups in South Africa.

Empirical strategy

We first establish the bivariate relationships between two welfare indicators (inequality and mean expenditure) and various types of crime in South Africa across police precincts. Next, we consider whether the observed relationships are more consistent with the economic or the sociological theories of crime, by controlling for costs and benefits of crime and by comparing the results for violent and property crimes. We also examine the effect on crime of the relative position of a community among neighbouring communities in terms of its wealth. Finally, we analyse whether inequalities between racial groups are more relevant in explaining crime levels than inequalities within racial groups.

The dependent variable for the analysis is the number of crimes reported, by police precinct. We regress crime counts by police precinct on inequality and a set of regressors, always including precinct population as a control, along with dummy variables for each of the nine provinces in South Africa. In the data, there is a non-negligible number of police precincts with crime counts equal to zero or very small values. Hence the distribution for each crime is skewed to the left, but has a long tail as there are also police precincts with a high prevalence of crime. These features of the data motivate the application of special models for count regression, which can improve on least squares.[9] In preliminary analysis with the Poisson regression model, goodness of fit tests (as implemented in STATA) indicated overdispersion. Consequently, throughout the chapter we employ the negative binomial regression model, which is more appropriate in the case of overdispersion. To test the sensitivity of all of our results to the choice of functional form, we perform the main analysis using ordinary least squares (OLS) as well, with the per capita crime rate as the dependent variable. This analysis yields results similar to those from negative binomial regressions.

Data

The data employed for the analysis come from three main sources. Firstly, each household in the 1996 Census of South Africa was matched to its local police precinct to generate information on household composition, race and employment status for each precinct. Secondly, crime data for 1996 were obtained from the South African Police Service (SAPS). The crime information is a comprehensive database of crimes reported for the entire country by police precinct. Thirdly, mean per capita expenditure and per capita expenditure inequality were estimated for each police precinct by applying a recently developed small area estimation technique to the 1996 Census, along with the 1995 October Household Survey (OHS) and Income and Expenditure Survey (IES). The estimation method is described in Appendix 2.

Dependent variables

We analyse six categories of crime: residential burglary, vehicle theft, serious assault, rape, armed robbery with aggravating circumstances, and murder. Summary statistics for these crimes are presented in Table 8A1.1 in Appendix 1. Because there are different theoretical implications for property crime and violent crime, we select crimes that fall, as much as possible, exclusively into one category or the other. Burglary and vehicle theft are property crimes that are generally non-violent, while serious assaults and rapes are violent crimes with no apparent direct pecuniary benefit to perpetrators.[10] We also examine two additional crimes that do not fall cleanly into one category but are often studied in the literature: armed robbery and murder. Although both crimes are violent in nature, robberies – and sometimes murders – are primarily motivated by a desire for material gain.

Welfare indicators

The measure of inequality employed in the analysis is the mean log deviation (Generalised Entropy inequality measure with c = 0).[11] Mean log deviation takes the following form:

$$I_0 = -\sum_i f_i \log \left(\frac{y_i}{\mu}\right)$$

where f_i refers to the population share of household i, y_i is the household's per capita expenditure, and μ is mean per capita expenditure for the area in question.

To control for the returns from crime, we use mean expenditure in own precinct, as this will likely be highly correlated with transferable assets. One would also like to control for the legitimate earnings opportunities for individuals who are likely to commit crimes. We use unemployment rate in the catchment area as a proxy for the opportunity cost of crime.[12] We also introduce a dummy variable that indicates whether the police precinct is the richest in the criminal catchment area.

We decompose our inequality measure to examine inequalities within and between racial groups in relation to crime.[13] Generalised Entropy inequality measures can be additively decomposed into a between- and within-group component along the following lines:

$$I_0 = [\sum_j g_j \log (\frac{\mu}{\mu_j})] + \sum_j I_j g_j$$

where j refers to sub-groups, g_j refers to the population share of group j and I_j refers to inequality in group j. The between-group component of inequality is captured by the first term to the right of the equality sign. It can be interpreted as measuring what would be the level of inequality in the population if everyone within the group had the same (the group-average) consumption level μ_j. The second term on the right reflects what would be the overall inequality level if there were no differences in mean consumption across groups but each group had its actual within-group inequality I_j.

Other explanatory variables

In addition to the welfare indicators above, we include additional control variables that may be associated with crime levels in our models. Population density may be an important determinant of crime, either by increasing the supply of potential victims who do not know the criminal or by reducing the chances of apprehension (Kelly 2000). Population density is defined as the number of persons per square kilometre. We also employ the percentage of households headed by a female, which has been used as an indicator of instability, disorientation and conflict in personal relations in the sociological literature (for example, Blau and Blau 1982). It has been suggested that youth may be more prone to crime (Cohen and Land 1987). We have created a variable that is equal to the percentage of the population aged 21–40 for use in the empirical models.[14]

Finally, we include race and racial homogeneity as control variables.[15] Kelly (2000) argues that race is a predictor of crime through social isolation and feelings of hopelessness in black communities in the USA. Race may also be associated with other factors linked to crime. For example, our analysis of the South African 1998 Victims of Crime Survey (VCS) (Statistics South Africa 2001) shows race to be a strong correlate of private protection. Africans are less likely than those in other racial groups to have private forms of protection, such as alarms, high walls, fences, armed security or guns.[16] Like inequality, racial heterogeneity in the police precinct may also hinder private provision of protection from crime by inhibiting collective action. It may also be negatively correlated with institutional quality in general (Mauro 1995; Easterly 2002), leading to the ineffective provision of public safety by the police.

Results

Main results

Figures 8.1–8.4 show log-log scatter plots of per capita crime levels versus inequality. There is a positive correlation for all four crimes shown, although this correlation is the least pronounced for vehicle thefts. The bivariate correlations between mean per capita expenditure and crime rates are shown in Figures 8.5–8.8. Figures 8.5 and 8.6 show that, absent any additional controls, property crimes are strongly and positively associated with average estimated expenditure in the police precinct. The correlation between violent crimes and mean expenditure has an inverted U-shape in Figures 8.7 and 8.8, showing violent crime rates increasing with mean expenditure levels for the bottom half of the police precincts, then decreasing for richer districts.

Figure 8.1 *Inequality and residential burglaries per capita*

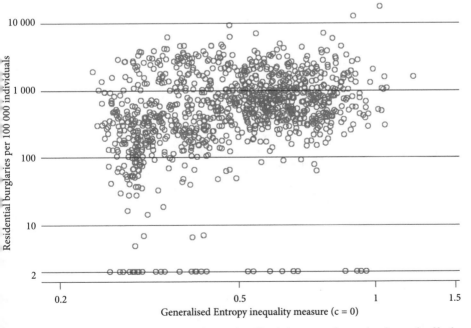

Note: Both variables are in logarithms. Observations where residential burglaries were equal to zero have been replaced by the smallest values in the sample.

Figure 8.2 *Inequality and vehicle thefts per capita*

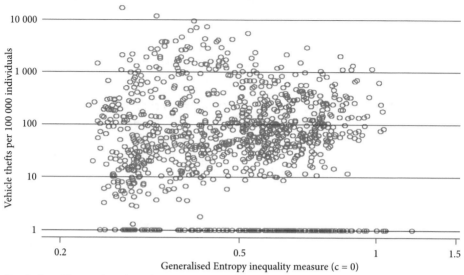

Note: Both variables are in logarithms. Observations where vehicle thefts were equal to zero have been replaced by the smallest values in the sample.

Figure 8.3 *Inequality and serious assaults per capita*

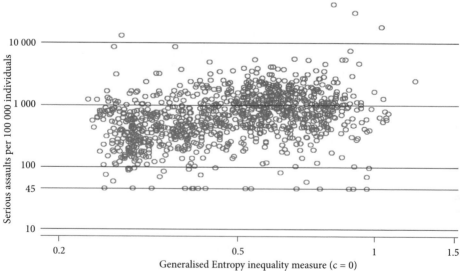

Note: Both variables are in logarithms. Observations where serious assaults were equal to zero have been replaced by the smallest values in the sample.

Figure 8.4 *Inequality and rapes per capita*

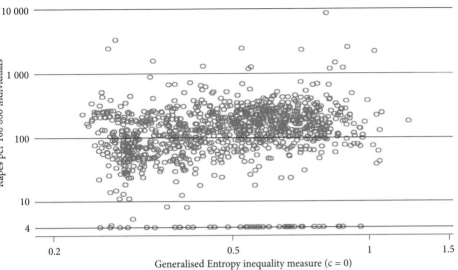

Note: Both variables are in logarithms. Observations where rapes were equal to zero have been replaced by the smallest values in the sample.

Figure 8.5 *Average expenditure and residential burglaries per capita*

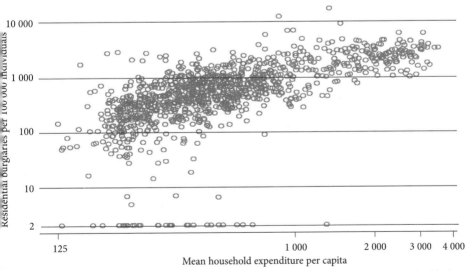

Note: Both variables are in logarithms. Observations where residential burglaries were equal to zero have been replaced by the smallest values in the sample.

Figure 8.6 *Average expenditure and vehicle thefts per capita*

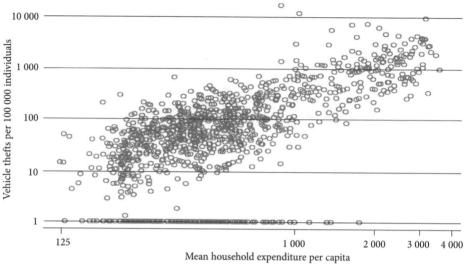

Note: Both variables are in logarithms. Observations where vehicle thefts were equal to zero have been replaced by the smallest values in the sample.

Figure 8.7 *Average expenditure and serious assaults per capita*

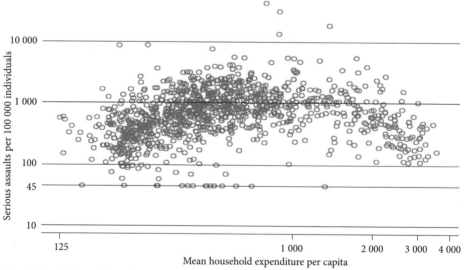

Note: Both variables are in logarithms. Observations where serious assaults were equal to zero have been replaced by the smallest values in the sample.

Figure 8.8 *Average expenditure and rapes per capita*

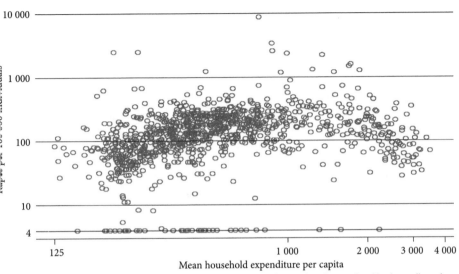

Note: Both variables are in logarithms. Observations where rapes were equal to zero have been replaced by the smallest values in the sample.

Table 8.1 presents the results of the negative binomial regression models, which include the welfare indicators and the additional explanatory variables discussed above. These regressions have crime counts as the dependent variable and always include population and province dummies on the right-hand side. Because all non-dummy variables are in log form, the coefficients can be interpreted as elasticities. Inequality in the police precinct has a positive and significant correlation with property crimes, but no correlation with violent crimes. The elasticity of burglary with respect to inequality is larger and more significant than that for vehicle theft.

The coefficients on mean expenditure indicate a strong relationship with property crime. The elasticities on mean expenditure for burglary and vehicle theft are high, 0.64 and 1.27 respectively, consistent with our assertion that mean expenditure per capita may proxy the returns to property crime.[17] For violent crime, the correlation with mean expenditure is strongly positive and the correlation with squared mean expenditure is strongly negative, consistent with the inverted U-shape that was evident in Figures 8.7 and 8.8.[18]

Table 8.1 *Negative binomial regressions*

	Property crimes		Violent crimes	
	Residential burglary	Vehicle theft	Aggravated assault	Rape
Inequality in police precinct	0.63 (0.11)**	0.30 (0.14)*	−0.21 (0.12)	−0.11 (0.11)
Mean expenditure in police precinct	0.64 (0.06)**	1.27 (0.08)**	5.48 (0.62)**	3.51 (0.58)**
(Mean expenditure)² in police precinct			−0.44 (0.05)**	−0.27 (0.04)**
Unemployment in criminal catchment area	−0.00 (0.06)	0.01 (0.09)	0.07 (0.06)	0.10 (0.06)
Richest precinct in criminal catchment area	0.25 (0.07)**	0.21 (0.09)*	0.19 (0.07)**	0.14 (0.06)*
Population density	0.09 (0.02)**	0.15 (0.03)**	0.03 (0.02)	0.06 (0.02)**
Female-headed households	0.24 (0.09)**	0.56 (0.12)**	0.36 (0.09)**	0.20 (0.08)*
Percentage aged 21–40	0.88 (0.18)**	1.67 (0.22)**	1.45 (0.18)**	1.58 (0.18)**
Percentage African	−0.01 (0.03)	0.01 (0.05)	−0.09 (0.03)**	0.00 (0.03)
Index of racial homogeneity	−0.47 (0.13)**	−0.59 (0.17)**	−1.05 (0.12)**	−0.68 (0.11)**
Population	0.71 (0.03)**	0.81 (0.04)**	0.71 (0.03)**	0.74 (0.03)**
Constant	−5.06 (0.54)**	−11.71 (0.71)**	−17.53 (2.23)**	−13.42 (2.09)**
Province dummies	Yes	Yes	Yes	Yes
Pseudo R²	0.125	0.187	0.101	0.157
Observations	1 064	1 064	1 064	1 064

Notes: Standard errors are given in parentheses.
* significant at 5 per cent; ** significant at 1 per cent

We find no significant association between unemployment in the criminal catchment area and crime, although the coefficients are positive for violent crime. In the absence of earnings data for potential criminals, we have suggested that the employment rate may capture the opportunity cost of crime. However, unemployment may have a more complicated relationship with crime rates. For example, unemployment may capture not only opportunity costs for potential criminals, but also part of the value of transferable assets, and thus the benefits of crime. It may also be the case that the criminal catchment area for a precinct does not adequately capture the relevant job market. Nonetheless, an insignificant or weak negative relationship between unemployment and crime is not an uncommon finding in the literature (Kelly 2000; Ehrlich 1973) and we revisit the issue later in the chapter.

To measure the impact of the rank of a precinct's wealth among its neighbours, we include a dummy variable equal to one if the precinct has the highest per capita expenditure among other precincts in its criminal catchment area. We find a positive association between this variable and all types of crime, with the correlation more significant for burglary and assault, and the elasticity highest for burglary. Controlling for the benefits and costs from crime participation, burglary rates are 25 per cent higher in precincts that are the wealthiest among their neighbours. This is consistent with the hypothesis that burglars travel to neighbouring areas where the expected returns are highest. The OLS results in Table 8.2 discussed below indicate that the positive relationship is not robust for vehicle theft and rape.

Finally, Table 8.1 shows that the coefficients for the other explanatory variables have the expected signs and are in most cases statistically significant. Racial heterogeneity in the precinct is strongly correlated with all types of crime, with the correlation stronger for violent crime, especially assaults. Population density is also significantly correlated with property crime levels, although the elasticity is small. The percentage of female-headed households in the police precinct and the percentage of individuals aged 21–40 are positively and significantly correlated with all four crime types, while race (measured by the percentage of African households in the precinct) has no consistent correlation with crime levels.

We have used a count model for the regression analysis of crime *levels*, with a control for population. However, some researchers have utilised OLS regressions for similar analysis of crime *rates* (typically, crimes per 100 000 individuals).[19] To test the sensitivity of the results to the regression specification, we re-estimate the models using an OLS specification, regressing log crime rates on logs of the same explanatory variables.

Table 8.2 presents the same models as Table 8.1, using OLS instead of negative binomial regressions. The results are qualitatively the same. The correlation coefficient for richest precinct is significant only for burglary and assault in the OLS regressions. That we find a consistent and significant link between a precinct's relative rank and burglary, but not vehicle theft, is not surprising, as vehicle thefts are much less clearly linked to the characteristics of the area in which the crime is reported.

Table 8.2 *OLS regressions*

	Property crimes		Violent crimes	
	Residential burglary	Vehicle theft	Aggravated assault	Rape
Inequality in police precinct	0.84 (0.17)**	0.92 (0.23)**	−0.12 (0.13)	0.22 (0.16)
Mean expenditure in police precinct	0.76 (0.10)**	1.37 (0.13)**	5.21 (0.68)**	3.54 (0.84)**
(Mean expenditure)^2 in police precinct			−0.42 (0.05)**	−0.28 (0.06)**
Unemployment in criminal catchment area	−0.06 (0.09)	−0.07 (0.13)	0.02 (0.07)	−0.00 (0.08)
Richest precinct in criminal catchment area	0.31 (0.11)**	0.26 (0.15)	0.21 (0.08)**	0.08 (0.10)
Population density	−0.02 (0.03)	0.30 (0.04)**	−0.07 (0.02)**	0.04 (0.02)
Female-headed households	0.23 (0.12)	0.62 (0.17)**	0.34 (0.09)**	0.38 (0.11)**
Percentage aged 21–40	1.33 (0.27)**	0.40 (0.37)	1.59 (0.20)**	1.61 (0.25)**
Percentage African	−0.01 (0.05)	0.06 (0.07)	−0.12 (0.04)**	0.00 (0.04)
Index of racial homogeneity	−0.32 (0.19)	−0.99 (0.26)**	−0.95 (0.13)**	−0.83 (0.16)**
Constant	−7.69 (0.73)**	−16.51 (1.00)**	−19.14 (2.44)**	−15.60 (3.02)**
Province dummies	Yes	Yes	Yes	Yes
Adjusted-R^2	0.47	0.56	0.37	0.23
Observations	1 064	1 064	1 064	1 064

Notes: Standard errors are given in parentheses.
* significant at 5 per cent; ** significant at 1 per cent

Next we examine the relationship between crime and inequality within and between racial groups. Table 8.3 presents the results of the decomposition of overall inequality in each police precinct into its within- and between-racial group components. It shows that, on average, 37 per cent of inequality in a police precinct can be attributed to differences in mean levels of expenditure between racial groups. Table 8.4 repeats the analysis shown in Table 8.1, but reports parameter estimates for within- and between-group inequality instead of overall inequality. The motivation here is to shed some light on the hypothesis that economic inequalities between racial groups are particularly important in the generation of crime, especially violent crime. The results are surprising. While the elasticities of property crime with respect to *between*-group inequality are positive and significant, they are very small.

In fact, most of the correlation between burglary and inequality can be attributed to inequality *within* racial groups. Furthermore, there is no correlation between violent crime and inequality *between* racial groups. Both violent crimes are positively correlated with *within*-group inequality, but this relationship is significant only for aggravated assault. Decomposing inequality into within- and between-group components does not substantially affect the other parameter estimates.

Table 8.3 *Inequality within and between racial groups*

	Mean	Minimum	Maximum
Overall inequality	0.514	0.234	1.228
Within-group inequality	0.324	0.198	0.839
Between-group inequality	0.189	0	0.785
Share of between-group inequality in overall inequality	36.8%	0%	63.9%
Percentage of communities where one racial group accounts for more than 95% of precinct population	32.2	0	1
Index of racial homogeneity	0.735	0.334	1

Note: In South Africa, the population census allows for four specific population groups (African, white, coloured, Asian/Indian) and a fifth category, 'other'. For reasons related to the availability of data, the inequality and racial heterogeneity measures presented here refer to three population groups: African, white, and other. Index of racial homogeneity is equal to the sum of squared shares of each racial group. It can be interpreted as the probability of two households selected at random belonging to the same racial group.

Table 8.4 *Crime and inequality between racial groups*

	Property crimes		Violent crimes	
	Residential burglary	Vehicle theft	Aggravated assault	Rape
Within-racial group inequality in police precinct	0.67 (0.17)**	−0.06 (0.21)	0.35 (0.18)*	0.11 (0.17)
Between-racial group inequality in police precinct	0.09 (0.01)**	0.11 (0.02)**	−0.01 (0.01)	−0.01 (0.01)
Mean expenditure in police precinct	0.59 (0.06)**	1.24 (0.08)**	4.89 (0.58)**	3.32 (0.55)**
(Mean expenditure)² in police precinct			−0.40 (0.04)**	−0.26 (0.04)**
Unemployment in criminal catchment area	0.01 (0.06)	0.06 (0.08)	0.04 (0.06)	0.08 (0.06)
Richest precinct in criminal catchment area	0.23 (0.07)**	0.22 (0.09)*	0.18 (0.07)*	0.13 (0.06)*
Population density	0.11 (0.02)**	0.20 (0.03)**	0.04 (0.02)*	0.06 (0.02)**
Female-headed households	0.14 (0.09)	0.57 (0.11)**	0.33 (0.08)**	0.18 (0.08)*

	Property crimes		Violent crimes	
	Residential burglary	Vehicle theft	Aggravated assault	Rape
Percentage aged 21–40	0.69	1.56	1.42	1.58
	(0.18)**	(0.22)**	(0.19)**	(0.18)**
Percentage African	0.00	0.03	−0.10	−0.01
	(0.03)	(0.05)	(0.03)**	(0.03)
Index of racial homogeneity	−0.43	−0.42	−1.03	−0.68
	(0.12)**	(0.16)**	(0.12)**	(0.11)**
Population	0.71	0.81	0.72	0.77
	(0.03)**	(0.04)**	(0.03)**	(0.03)**
Constant	−4.40	−11.71	−15.15	−12.87
	(0.59)**	(0.78)**	(2.15)**	(2.02)**
Province dummies	Yes	Yes	Yes	Yes
Pseudo R^2	0.129	0.191	0.103	0.162
Observations	1 062	1 062	1 062	1 062

Notes: Negative binomial regressions. Standard errors are given in parentheses.
* significant at 5 per cent; ** significant at 1 per cent

Misreporting in crime

Under-reporting is a potentially serious but frequently neglected problem in the crime literature. There is often the danger that the observed relationships between crime and other variables reflect correlations with crime misreporting. It is generally difficult to deal with this problem, because of the absence of independent data on crime reporting.[20] In South Africa, however, the nationally representative VCS was conducted in 1998; in the survey households were asked whether crimes they experienced were reported to the police. Summary statistics for selected crimes are presented in Table 8.5. As the definitions of the crime categories in the VCS differ from those in the SAPS data, the figures in this table are meant only to be suggestive of possible under-reporting. According to the VCS data, under-reporting is a particularly serious problem for robbery and is least serious for vehicle theft.

Measurement error in the dependent variable is a problem in regression analysis to the extent that it is correlated with some of the regressors in the model. In the case of crime misreporting, if, for example, only wealthy people reported crime or the police filed official reports only for complaints by the rich, then one would find a correlation between wealth and *reported* crime regardless of the true relationship between wealth and crimes committed.

Table 8.5 *Reporting in selected crime categories*

Crime category	Percentage reported to the police
Theft of cars, vans, trucks or bakkies	95.0 (2.0)
Housebreaking and burglary	59.1 (2.2)
Deliberate killing or murder	84.2 (3.7)
Robbery involving force against the person	41.8 (4.8)

Source: All the numbers are authors' own calculations using the VCS 1998 (Statistics South Africa 2001).
Note: There are 3 899 observations in the VCS. The percentages and the standard errors (in parentheses) reflect the complex sample design of the survey, including household weights, stratification, and clustering. The definitions of the crime categories in the VCS are somewhat different than those in the data from SAPS, and hence the figures in this table are meant only to be suggestive of possible under-reporting in the SAPS data.

To examine the extent to which misreporting affects the results presented in Table 8.1, we repeat the analysis using adjusted crime statistics. We conduct the analysis exclusively for residential burglary, which, unlike other crimes, both appears frequently in the victims survey and has nearly identical definitions in the VCS and SAPS data. For respondents in the VCS who said they had been victims of burglary in the five years prior to the survey, we estimate a probit regression for whether the crime was reported to the police. We use the same explanatory variables, at the police precinct level, as in our earlier analysis. The results of this regression are shown in the first column of Table 8.6. Mean per capita expenditure is positively correlated with the probability of a residential burglary being reported by a household, while unemployment in the criminal catchment area and richest precinct have negative parameter estimates, none of which is significant. We use the coefficient estimates from this regression to predict for each police precinct the probability p that a burglary was reported to the police. We then calculate an adjusted count of burglaries for each police precinct by multiplying the reported number of crimes by $1/p$.

Table 8.6 *Correcting for misreporting in residential burglary*

	Probit results using	Negative binomial regression results using	
	Household reporting of burglaries	*Unadjusted burglaries*	*Adjusted burglaries*
Inequality in police precinct	0.02 (0.36)	0.63 (0.11)**	0.58 (0.12)**
Mean expenditure in police precinct	0.31 (0.21)	0.64 (0.06)**	0.41 (0.06)**
Unemployment in criminal catchment area	−0.25 (0.22)	−0.00 (0.06)	0.09 (0.06)
Richest precinct in criminal catchment area	−0.27 (0.24)	0.25 (0.07)**	0.43 (0.07)**

→

	Probit results using	Negative binomial regression results using	
	Household reporting of burglaries	*Unadjusted* burglaries	*Adjusted* burglaries
Population density	−0.17	0.09	0.20
	(0.05)**	(0.02)**	(0.02)**
Female-headed households	0.67	0.24	−0.10
	(0.35)	(0.09)**	(0.09)
Percentage aged 21–40	1.01	0.88	0.32
	(0.56)	(0.18)**	(0.18)
Percentage African	−0.16	−0.01	0.03
	(0.13)	(0.03)	(0.03)
Index of racial homogeneity	0.12	−0.47	−0.52
	(0.45)	(0.13)**	(0.13)**
Population		0.71	0.69
		(0.03)**	(0.03)**
Constant	0.89	−5.06	−4.39
	(1.66)	(0.54)**	(0.57)**
Province dummies	Yes	Yes	Yes
Pseudo R²	0.112	0.110	0.125
Observations	627	1 064	1 064

Notes: Negative binomial regressions. Standard errors are given in parentheses.
* significant at 5 per cent; ** significant at 1 per cent.
Probit regressions are at the household level using data on reporting of residential burglary to the police from the VCS.
Adjust number of burglaries in a police precinct is the number of actual burglaries reported divided by the probability of a burglary being reported in that precinct.

Column 2 in Table 8.6 redisplays the earlier results (the same as Table 8.1, column 1), using the unadjusted count as the dependent variable, and column 3 presents the results using the adjusted burglary count as the dependent variable for the same model. Compared with the earlier results, the elasticities of inequality and per capita expenditure are still positive and significant but somewhat attenuated. Conversely, as under-reporting is more likely in areas with higher unemployment, the adjustment causes the elasticity of unemployment to also become positive, but still not statistically significant. The elasticity of burglary with respect to the richest precinct is also stronger in the regression adjusted for misreporting. Overall, the results we derive for residential burglary remain broadly the same: burglaries are more likely to take place in wealthier areas which are unequal, and in particular in those that have the highest mean expenditure among their neighbours.

Local inequality or inequality in the criminal catchment area?

Earlier, we argued that it is not clear whether it is inequality within the community or inequality within a larger geographical unit that should matter in relation to crime. This chapter focuses on the relationship between local inequality and crime. However, there may be reasons to consider inequality in the criminal catchment area as well. For example, it may be inequality in the larger area, and not local inequality, that is highly correlated with low social mobility in certain precincts. It could also be that crime prevention is more effective when neighbouring precincts coordinate their efforts, and inequality in the catchment area is the more pertinent factor for collective action than inequality levels in each precinct. In this subsection, we repeat the regressions performed in Table 8.1, replacing inequality in police precinct with inequality in criminal catchment area.[21]

Table 8.7 presents the results. The elasticity of burglary with respect to inequality in the criminal catchment area is positive and significant, but substantially smaller, while inequality is not correlated with vehicle thefts. Interestingly, inequality in the catchment area is significantly correlated with violent crime. Other parameter estimates are not significantly altered. It seems that while inequality at the precinct level is more salient with respect to *property* crime, it is inequality in the larger area that is associated with *violent* crime.

Table 8.7 *Inequality in catchment area*

	Property crimes		Violent crimes	
	Residential burglary	Vehicle theft	Aggravated assault	Rape
Inequality in catchment area	0.38 (0.11)**	−0.25 (0.14)	0.27 (0.11)*	0.44 (0.10)**
Mean expenditure in police precinct	0.70 (0.06)**	1.30 (0.08)**	4.67 (0.58)**	2.67 (0.54)**
(Mean expenditure)^2 in police precinct			−0.38 (0.04)**	−0.21 (0.04)**
Unemployment in criminal catchment area	0.06 (0.06)	−0.00 (0.09)	0.12 (0.06)	0.18 (0.06)**
Richest precinct in criminal catchment area	0.29 (0.07)**	0.19 (0.09)*	0.20 (0.07)**	0.16 (0.06)*
Population density	0.04 (0.02)*	0.12 (0.02)**	0.06 (0.02)**	0.08 (0.02)**
Female-headed households	0.27 (0.09)**	0.48 (0.12)**	0.42 (0.09)**	0.28 (0.08)**
Percentage aged 21–40	1.11 (0.17)**	1.77 (0.21)**	1.44 (0.18)**	1.59 (0.17)**
Percentage African	0.01 (0.03)	0.03 (0.05)	−0.10 (0.03)**	−0.01 (0.03)

$\longrightarrow$

	Property crimes		Violent crimes	
	Residential burglary	Vehicle theft	Aggravated assault	Rape
Index of racial homogeneity	−0.64	−0.77	−0.96	−0.61
	(0.12)**	(0.16)**	(0.12)**	(0.11)**
Population	0.72	0.83	0.70	0.73
	(0.03)**	(0.04)**	(0.03)**	(0.02)**
Constant	−5.16	−12.50	−14.24	−9.92
	(0.56)**	(0.73)**	(2.11)**	(1.96)**
Province dummies	Yes	Yes	Yes	Yes
Pseudo R^2	0.124	0.187	0.101	0.159
Observations	1 064	1 064	1 064	1 064

Notes: Negative binomial regressions. Standard errors are given in parentheses.
* significant at 5 per cent; ** significant at 1 per cent.

Murder and robbery

Many studies on crime examine murders and robberies. Murder is often studied because it is thought to suffer least from reporting problems and is one of the most violent crimes. Armed robberies are also usually categorised as violent crimes in the literature, despite the fact that the primary motivation of a robbery is economic. Table 8.8 shows the results of negative binomial and OLS regressions for murder and armed robbery. Inequality is not correlated with either armed robbery or murder. Like other property crimes, robbery is highly correlated with mean expenditure in the precinct. Murder, on the other hand, exhibits the same inverted U-shaped relationship with mean expenditure as assault and rape. Unemployment in the catchment area is positively associated with both crimes, with the relationship being especially strong for armed robbery. Racial heterogeneity is unrelated to robbery, but strongly associated with murder. Not surprisingly, murders fit well within the general picture of violent crimes, while robberies fit much better with property crimes.

Table 8.8 *Armed robbery and murder*

	Armed robbery		Murder	
	Negative binomial	OLS	Negative binomial	OLS
Inequality in police precinct	−0.10	0.21	−0.19	0.34
	(0.16)	(0.20)	(0.13)	(0.18)
Mean expenditure in police precinct	0.74	0.86	2.48	2.87
	(0.09)**	(0.11)**	(0.69)**	(0.92)**
(Mean expenditure)² in police precinct			−0.19	−0.23
			(0.05)**	(0.07)**

	Armed robbery		Murder	
	Negative binomial	OLS	Negative binomial	OLS
Unemployment in criminal catchment area	0.57 (0.09)**	0.54 (0.11)**	0.22 (0.07)**	0.11 (0.09)
Richest precinct in criminal catchment area	0.03 (0.10)	0.03 (0.12)	0.12 (0.07)	0.08 (0.10)
Population density	0.20 (0.03)**	0.18 (0.03)**	0.02 (0.02)	0.07 (0.03)**
Female-headed households	0.33 (0.13)**	0.29 (0.14)*	0.10 (0.10)	0.33 (0.12)**
Percentage aged 21–40	1.79 (0.24)**	1.47 (0.31)**	1.27 (0.20)**	1.13 (0.28)**
Percentage African	0.07 (0.05)	0.09 (0.06)	−0.02 (0.04)	−0.07 (0.05)
Index of racial homogeneity	−0.14 (0.18)	0.09 (0.21)	−0.64 (0.13)**	−0.70 (0.18)**
Population	0.66 (0.04)**		0.85 (0.03)**	
Constant	−7.22 (0.76)**	−11.94 (0.84)**	−12.20 (2.49)**	−14.78 (3.31)**
Province dummies	Yes	Yes	Yes	Yes
Pseudo R^2 (Adjusted–R^2 for OLS)	0.175	0.55	0.166	0.21
Observations	1 064	1 064	1 064	1 064

Notes: Standard errors are given in parentheses.
* significant at 5 per cent; ** significant at 1 per cent.

Conclusion

Both theoretical and empirical papers in the crime literature have called for an analysis of crime at a smaller level of geographical disaggregation than countries, states or large metropolitan areas. When the unit of analysis is large, not only is there a loss of information regarding relative welfare levels across neighbourhoods, but in addition the fact that individuals may travel to conduct criminal activities is ignored. In this chapter, utilising data on crime and welfare in all police precincts in South Africa, we have analysed the effect of local inequality on crime. Although the contribution of this chapter is mainly empirical, we have also suggested a pathway for the generation of property crimes in a precinct that takes into account the distribution of welfare in the surrounding area, and not just within its own borders.

Starting with property crimes, the empirical results indicate that inequality in the precinct is highly correlated with both burglary and vehicle theft. Property crime is strongly correlated with mean expenditure in the precinct, indicating that returns from crime are major determinants of property crimes. If wealthier communities have more effective protection from crime, the elasticity of residential burglaries with respect to mean expenditure, controlling for protection, may be even higher. Considering the welfare levels in neighbouring precincts, we show that precincts that are the wealthiest in their criminal catchment areas have higher levels of burglary. That the locally wealthiest neighbourhoods are hotspots for residential burglary is consistent with the story that burglars travel based on information on welfare levels of different neighbourhoods. At the same time, that burglaries do not occur exclusively in such areas suggests that there are travel costs, that burglars have more idiosyncratic information regarding houses in their own neighbourhood, or that the level of protection varies between precincts.

Violent crimes, our results indicate, are more likely to occur in areas with high inequality at the criminal catchment area level. Inequality in the precinct is not associated with violent crime. The relationship between violent crime and mean expenditure levels has an inverted U-shape. With respect to unemployment in the criminal catchment area, we find no consistent correlation for rape and assault, but a positive and significant correlation for armed robbery and murder.

Inequality between racial groups within a precinct has a very small correlation with property crime and no correlation with violent crime. Within-group inequality explains most of the correlation between burglary and inequality. This finding is at odds with the suggestion that '...economic inequalities matter, but ascribed inequalities do so particularly' (Blau and Blau 1982: 125). However, while inequality between groups does not appear to be too important with respect to crime, racial heterogeneity in the precinct is highly correlated with all types of crime.

The results support the sociological theories of crime. Beckerian economic theory of crime does not predict any correlation between inequality and crime other than via a correlation with the differential returns from such crimes. While we acknowledge the possibility that our results may reflect aspects of the costs and benefits of criminal activity not captured by the regressors, the fact that we find a conditional correlation between inequality and crime lends support to theories that suggest that inequality may lead to higher crime levels through other, non-economic, channels.

Some economic and sociological theories of crime suggest that there may be a positive relationship between poverty and crime levels. We have not explored this in our empirical analysis, mainly because mean expenditure and poverty are very highly and negatively correlated in our data set – the correlation coefficient is –0.87.

We hesitate to draw policy implications from an analysis using cross-sectional data without a strong identification strategy, especially given that a direct indicator of the most visible policy tool, public expenditures on crime prevention, is missing from the empirical analysis. Nonetheless, we note the following. Firstly, regarding prevention efforts for various property and violent crimes, policy-makers may want to focus on different elements, as it is likely that different mechanisms are responsible for the generation of each type of crime. Secondly, increasing the public supply of resources for prevention in high-property-crime areas would be regressive, because these crimes are most likely to occur in richer neighbourhoods. Governments may care as much about the equitable distribution of public resources as about the marginal benefit of the extra resources spent (Behrman and Craig 1987). Thirdly, policies that help reduce economic inequalities between neighbourhoods within a local administration may also help to reduce property-crime levels, particularly residential burglaries. Finally, policy-makers would do well to worry about the distribution of income – both within and between racial groups – when devising strategies for economic growth, as the welfare benefits from growth may be attenuated by decreased safety if such growth is accompanied by increased inequality.[22]

Acknowledgements

The authors would like to thank Statistics South Africa for help with the generation of our data set. We are grateful to Harold Alderman, Jere Behrman, Eliana La Ferrara, Peter Lanjouw, Misha Lokshin, Martin Ravallion and two anonymous referees for comments on previous drafts of this chapter. These are the views of the authors, and do not necessarily reflect those of the World Bank or any affiliated organisation.

Notes

1   Reprinted from the *Journal of Development Economics* 76(2), Gabriel Demombynes and Berk Özler, Crime and local inequality in South Africa, pp. 265–292, 2005, with permission from Elsevier.

2   According to a survey conducted by the South African Migration Project, Africans and whites both '...rated security and safety as the most significant push factor, reinforcing the national importance of addressing the crime problem as a deterrent to the brain drain' (Dodson 2002).

3   For simplicity, we refer to police station jurisdictions as police precincts or simply precincts throughout the rest of this chapter.

4   Kanbur (2003: 6) argues that '...spatial units may develop special identities even without the basis of ethnicity, race or religion.'

5   Ehrlich (1973) argues that the changes in optimal time allocation between legitimate and criminal activities due to such a 'pure wealth effect' depend on the offender's relative risk aversion.

6   Chiu and Madden (1998) model residential burglaries with an implicit focus on small neighbourhoods, but ignore the issue of possible spatial effects by citing empirical work that suggests burglars do not travel too far to commit crime.

7   The median population for a police precinct is 18 297, while the median area is approximately 588 km^2. These figures are much smaller in urban areas.

8   There may be differences in interpretation and reporting across police precincts.

9   See Cameron and Trivedi (2001) and Greene (1997) for detailed discussions of models for count regression.

10   Vehicle thefts exclude carjackings.

11   We have also used the Theil index (General Entropy measure with $c = 1$) for the same analysis and the results are similar to those reported here.

12   Gould et al. (2002) suggest that wages may be a better measure for labour-market prospects of potential criminals, because, they argue, unemployment is often short-lived and cyclical. However, the duration of unemployment in South Africa is significantly higher. According to Rama (2001), 38 per cent of the unemployed had stayed out of a job for more than three years in 1999. In any event, data on wages are not available for police precincts in South Africa.

13   In South Africa, the census allows for five 'population groups': African, white, coloured, Asian/Indian, and 'other'. Because of data availability limitations, we collapse these into three separate categories – African, white, and other – which we refer to throughout the chapter as 'racial groups'.

14   Analysis with alternative definitions of this variable, using different age groups or only males, produced results similar to those presented in this chapter.

15   Index of racial homogeneity is equal to the sum of squared shares of each racial group. It can be interpreted as the probability of two households selected at random belonging to the same racial group. We use an index of racial *homogeneity* instead of racial *heterogeneity* in our regressions to avoid zero values, as all our explanatory variables are in natural logarithms.

16   Detailed information available from the authors.

17   A model including a squared mean expenditure term showed no evidence of a U-shaped (or inverted U-shaped) relationship for either property crime, so the regression model for property crime includes mean expenditure only, while that for violent crime includes the squared term as well.

18   The predicted values for communities at the 5th, 50th, and the 95th percentiles of the mean expenditure distribution are 187, 262, and 92 for assaults, and 39, 51, and 30 for rapes, respectively.

19   It should be noted that other studies typically have units of analysis that are relatively large, such as metropolitan areas or countries. The motivation for count models is obviously weaker in such settings.

20   Glaeser and Sacerdote (1999) adjust reported crime rates in the Uniform Crime Reports using independent data on reporting from the National Crime Victimisation Survey in the USA.

21   It is possible that inequality at both levels is important with respect to crime levels. However, the two inequality measures are highly correlated with each other, so we include only inequality in the catchment area in the analysis here.

22 Hoogeveen and Özler (2003) show that the significant increase in inequality in South Africa between 1995 and 2000 (mean log deviation significantly increased from 0.56 to 0.61) is largely a result of increases in inequality within the African population (from 0.37 to 0.44).

Appendix 1

Table 8A1.1 *Summary statistics by type of crime*

Variable	Mean	Minimum	Maximum
Residential burglary	963	0	17 834
Vehicle theft	319	0	16 553
Serious assault	1 002	0	41 848
Rape	185	0	8 696
Murder	89	0	3 804
Robbery with aggravating circumstances	155	0	7 781

Notes: Crime variables are reported per 100 000 inhabitants for the year 1996.
The figures are for 1 066 police precincts.
The means reported here are simple means, i.e. not weighted by population size.

Table 8A1.2 *Correlations between welfare indicators*

		1	2	3	4	5	6	7
1	Inequality in police precinct	1.0000						
2	Mean expenditure in police precinct	0.102	1.0000					
3	Unemployment in catchment area	−0.114	−0.622	1.0000				
4	Richest precinct in neighbouring area	0.113	0.297	−0.077	1.0000			
5	Inequality within racial groups	0.359	0.019	0.332	0.139	1.0000		
6	Inequality between racial groups	0.725	0.314	−0.392	0.116	−0.075	1.0000	
7	Racial homogeneity	−0.559	−0.540	0.480	−0.200	0.057	−0.665	1.0000

Note: All variables are in logarithms except the richest precinct in neighbouring area, which is a dummy variable.

Table 8A1.3 *Correlations between selected variables*

		1	2	3	4	5	6	7
1	Population	1.0000						
2	Mean expenditure in precinct	0.0094	1.0000					
3	Inequality in precinct	−0.5053	0.1024	1.0000				
4	Population density	0.7448	0.3034	−0.6285	1.0000			
5	Female-headed households	0.4910	−0.4349	−0.4753	0.2956	1.0000		
6	Percentage aged 21–40	−0.0713	0.6340	0.2225	0.2159	−0.6479	1.0000	
7	Percentage African	0.2305	−0.4549	−0.0188	0.1000	0.3785	−0.2554	1.0000

Note: All variables are in logarithms.

Appendix 2

Brief methodological description of small-area estimation of welfare indicators

What follows is an overview of the methodology we employ to construct welfare indicators for small geographical areas, such as the police precincts in South Africa. We provide this section so that the reader is clear about the source of the welfare measures utilised as explanatory variables in the crime regressions throughout the chapter. Please see Elbers, Lanjouw and Lanjouw (2003) for a fuller discussion, and Babita, Demombynes, Makhatha and Özler (2002) for details regarding the specific application to the South African data.

The basic methodology applied in linking surveys and census-type data sets is very similar to that of synthetic estimation used in small-area geography. Prediction models are derived for consumption or income as the endogenous variable, on the basis of the survey. The selection of right-hand-side variables is restricted to those variables that can also be found in the census (or some other large data set). The parameter estimates are then applied to the census data and poverty and inequality statistics derived. Simple performance tests can be conducted which compare basic poverty or inequality statistics across the two data sets (at representative levels for the household survey). For Ecuador, Madagascar and South Africa, Demombynes, Elbers, Lanjouw, Lanjouw, Mistiaen and Özler (2004) show that stratum-level poverty estimates derived from consumption measured directly in the household survey are very similar to those calculated on the basis of imputed household consumption in the census.

The calculation of poverty and inequality statistics using predicted income or consumption has to take into account that each individual household income or consumption value has been predicted and has standard errors associated with it. Elbers et al. (2003) show that the approach yields estimates of the incidence of poverty and of inequality that are consistent, and that the standard errors are reasonably precise for small geographic units, such as parroquias in Ecuador. Furthermore, a recent case study[1] demonstrates that these estimates are precise enough to permit meaningful pair-wise comparisons across second and third levels of administration.

As described above, the concept of imputing expenditures for each household in the census is simple to grasp, yet it requires great attention to detail, especially regarding the computation of standard errors. This also makes the exercise computationally quite intensive. It involves constructing an association model between per capita household expenditure and household characteristics that are common to both the census and the household survey. After carefully constructing the variables in exactly the same manner in each data set, we estimate a regression model of logarithmic per capita household expenditure on the other constructed variables that consist of household composition, education, primary occupation, quality of housing and access to services.

The basis of the approach is that per capita household expenditure for a household h in cluster c can be explained using a set of observable characteristics. These observable characteristics must be found as variables in both the survey and the census:[2]

$$\ln y_{ch} = E[\ln y_{ch}|\mathbf{x}_{ch}] + u_{ch}. \qquad [1]$$

Using a linear approximation to the conditional expectation, the household's logarithmic per capita expenditure is modelled as

$$\ln y_{ch} = \mathbf{x}_{ch}'\beta + u_{ch}. \qquad [2]$$

More explicitly, we model the disturbance term as

$$u_{ch} = \eta_c + \varepsilon_{ch}$$

where η_c is the cluster component and ε_{ch} is the household component. This complex error structure will allow not only for spatial autocorrelation, i.e. a 'location effect' for households in the same area, but also for heteroskedasticity in the household component of the error. The two error components are independent of one another and uncorrelated with observable characteristics.

The model in [2] is estimated by Generalised Least Squares (GLS) using the household survey data. The results from this first stage of the analysis are a set of estimated model parameters, including the beta vector, an associated variance–covariance matrix, and parameters describing the distribution of the disturbances.

To avoid forcing the parameter estimates to be the same for all areas in South Africa, we run the first-stage regressions separately for each of the nine provinces. The explanatory power of the nine regressions ranges from an adjusted-R^2 of 0.47 (Eastern Cape) to 0.72 (Free State), with the median adjusted-R^2 equal to 0.64.[3]

In the second-stage analysis we combine these parameter estimates based on the *survey data* with household characteristics from the *census data* to estimate welfare measures for sub-groups of the census population. It is possible to produce these estimates for any sub-groups that can be identified in the census. For the purposes of this chapter, we perform the calculations at the police precinct levels.

Specifically, we combine the estimated first-stage parameters with the observable characteristics of each household in the census to generate predicted log expenditures and relevant disturbances. We simulate a value of expenditure for each household, $\hat{y}_{ch}$, based on both predicted log expenditure, $\mathbf{x}_{ch}'\beta$, and the disturbance terms, $\tilde{\eta}_c$ and ε_{ch}, using bootstrap methods:

$$\hat{y}_{ch} = \exp\left(\mathbf{x}_{ch}'\tilde{\beta} + \tilde{\eta}_c + \tilde{\varepsilon}_{ch}\right). \qquad [3]$$

For each household, the two disturbance terms are drawn from distributions described by parameters estimated in the first stage.[4] The beta coefficients, $\tilde{\beta}$, are drawn from the multivariate normal distribution described by the first-stage beta estimates and their associated variance–covariance matrix. We then use the full set of simulated $\hat{y}_{ch}$ values to calculate expected values of the average expenditure, poverty, and inequality measures for the two spatial sub-groups described above.

We repeat this procedure 100 times, drawing a new set of beta coefficients and disturbances for each set of simulations. For each sub-group, we take the mean and standard deviation of the welfare indicators over all 100 simulations. For any given location, these means constitute the point estimates of the welfare indicators, while the standard deviations are the standard errors of these estimates.

There are two principal sources of error in the welfare measure estimates produced by this method.[5] The first component, referred to as *model error* in Elbers et al. (2003), is a result of the fact that the parameters from the first-stage model in equation [2] are estimated. The second component, described as *idiosyncratic error*, is associated with the disturbance term in the same model, which implies that households' actual expenditures deviate from their expected values. While population size in a location does not affect the *model error*, the *idiosyncratic error* increases as the number of households in a target population decreases.

Notes

1 See Mistiaen et al. (2002).

2 The explanatory variables are observed values and thus need to have the same definitions and the same degree of accuracy across data sources. In Babita et al. (2002), the criteria and approach used to select these explanatory variables are explained in detail. Finally, note that from a methodological standpoint it does not matter whether these variables are exogenous.

3 The R-squared values that we report are from OLS models. We do this to give our readers a sense of the explanatory power of our regression models, as there is no precise counterpart to R-squared in a GLS model. See Greene (1997: 508) for details.

4 Please note that these errors are not necessarily drawn from a normal distribution. For details, please refer to Babita et al. (2002).

5 A third potential source of error is associated with computation methods. Elbers et al. (2003) found this component to be negligible with a sufficiently high number of simulation draws.

References

Atkinson AB & Brandolini A (2000) *Promise and pitfalls in the use of 'secondary' data sets: Income inequality in OECD countries.* Banca d'Italia. Temi di Discussione. No. 379: 1–57.

Babita M, Demombynes G, Makhatha N & Özler B (2002) Estimated poverty and inequality measures in South Africa: A disaggregated map for 1996. Unpublished manuscript.

Becker GS (1968) Crime and punishment: An economic approach, *Journal of Political Economy* 66(2): 169–217.

Behrman JR & Craig SG (1987) The distribution of public services: An exploration of local governmental preferences, *The American Economic Review* 77(1): 37–49.

Black D (1983) Crime as social control, *American Sociological Review* 48(1): 34–45.

Blau JR & Blau PM (1982) The cost of inequality: Metropolitan structure and violent crime, *American Sociological Review* 47(1): 114–129.

Bourguignon F (2001) Crime as a social cost of poverty and inequality: A review focusing on developing countries. In S Yusuf, S Evenett & W Wu (eds) *Facets of globalization.* Washington, DC: World Bank.

Cameron AC & Trivedi PK (2001) Essentials of count data regression. In BH Baltagi (ed.) *A companion to theoretical econometrics.* Oxford: Blackwell.

Chiu WH & Madden P (1998) Burglary and income inequality, *Journal of Public Economics* 69: 123–141.

Cohen LE & Land KC (1987) Age structure and crime: Symmetry versus asymmetry and the projection of crime rates through the 1990s, *American Sociological Review* 52(2): 170–183.

Deininger KW & Squire L (1996) A new data set measuring income inequality, *World Bank Economic Review* 10: 565–591.

Demombynes G, Elbers C, Lanjouw JO, Lanjouw P, Mistiaen J & Özler B (2004) Producing an improved geographic profile of poverty: Methodology and evidence from three developing countries In R van der Hoeven & A Shorrocks (eds) *Growth, inequality, and poverty: Prospects for pro-poor economic development.* Oxford: Oxford University Press.

Di Tella R & Schargrodsky E (2001) *Using a terrorist attack to estimate the effect of police on crime.* Center for Research on Economic Development and Policy Reform. Working Paper No. 90.

Dodson B (2002) *Gender and the brain drain from South Africa.* The Southern African Migration Project. Migration Policy Series No. 23.

Easterly W (2002) *Inequality does cause underdevelopment: New evidence.* Center For Global Development. Working Paper No. 1.

Ehrlich I (1973) Participation in illegitimate activities: A theoretical and empirical investigation, *The Journal of Political Economy* 81(3): 521–565.

Elbers C, Lanjouw J & Lanjouw P (2003) Micro-level estimation of poverty and inequality, *Econometrica* 71(1): 355–364.

Fafchamps M & Moser C (2003) Crime, isolation, and law enforcement, *Journal of African Economies* 12(4): 625–671.

Fajnzylber P, Lederman D & Loayza N (2002a) What causes violent crime? *The European Economic Review* 46(7): 1323–1357.

Fajnzylber P, Lederman D & Loayza N (2002b) Inequality and violent crime, *The Journal of Law and Economics* 45: 1–39.

Glaeser EL & Sacerdote B (1999) Why is there more crime in cities? *The Journal of Political Economy* 107(6, Part 2): S225–S258.

Glaeser EL, Sacerdote B & Scheinkman JA (1996) Crime and social interactions, *The Quarterly Journal of Economics* 111(2): 507–548.

Gould ED, Weinberg BA & Mustard DB (2002) Crime rates and local labor market opportunities in the United States, *The Review of Economics and Statistics* 84(1): 45–61.

Greene WH (1997) *Econometric analysis*. New Jersey: Prentice-Hall, Inc.

Hoogeveen J & Özler B (2003) Not separate, not equal: Poverty and inequality in post-apartheid South Africa. The World Bank. Unpublished manuscript.

Hsieh C & Pugh MD (1993) Poverty, inequality, and violent crime: A meta-analysis of recent aggregate data studies, *Criminal Justice Review* 18(2): 182–202.

Kanbur R (2003) The policy significance of inequality decompositions. Unpublished manuscript.

Kelly M (2000) Inequality and crime, *The Review of Economics and Statistics* 82(4): 530–539.

Kennedy BP, Kawachi I, Prothrow-Stith D, Lochner K & Gupta V (1998) Social capital, income inequality, and firearm violent crime, *Social Science and Medicine* 47(1): 7–17.

Lederman D, Loayza N & Menéndez AM (2002) Violent crime: Does social capital matter? *Economic Development and Cultural Change* 50: 509–539.

Machin S & Meghir C (2000) *Crime and economic incentives*. The Institute for Fiscal Studies Working Paper 00/17.

Mauro P (1995) Corruption and growth, *The Quarterly Journal of Economics* 110(3): 681–712.

Merton RK (1938) Social structure and anomie, *American Sociological Review* 3(5): 672–682.

Mistiaen J, Özler B, Razafimanantena T & Razafindravonona J (2002) *Putting welfare on the map in Madagascar*. Africa Region Technical Working Paper Series No. 34. The World Bank.

Pradhan M & Ravallion M (2003) Who wants safer streets? Explaining concern for public safety in Brazil, *Journal of Economic Psychology* 24(1): 17–33.

Rama M (2001) Labor market issues in South Africa. Processed. The World Bank.

Statistics South Africa (2001) Victims of crime survey, 1998. Pretoria: South African Data Archive (distributor).

Wilson M & Daly M (1997) Life expectancy, economic inequality, homicide, and reproductive timing in Chicago neighborhoods, *British Medical Journal* 314: 1271.

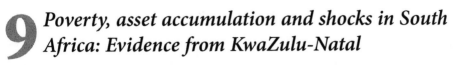

9 Poverty, asset accumulation and shocks in South Africa: Evidence from KwaZulu-Natal

Julian May

Introduction

Although their use has become widespread, approaches to poverty measurement such as the Foster, Greer and Thorbecke (FGT) class of measures discussed by Leibbrandt and Woolard (1999) for South Africa are necessarily static in nature. Such measurements regard poverty as a deficiency, measured in terms of the proportion of the population who are categorised as poor or, perhaps more usefully, in terms of the distance that separates those who are poor from the least well-off of the non-poor: the individual or household whose income is exactly equal to the poverty line. From the perspective of policy, poverty becomes a circumstance to be resolved by appropriately targeted transfers rather than the outcome of social and economic structures: a poverty that is 'produced' or, in the language of some analysts, a poverty that is 'perpetrated' (Øyen 2002). Beyond the identification of possible target groups and some of the ways in which poverty is experienced, those factors which lead to the production, reproduction and persistence of poverty are concealed. As a result, little can be offered in the way of concrete issues for poverty reduction strategies in a country such as South Africa, where the legacy of past policies continues to burden efforts to reduce poverty.

While a comparatively new literature on poverty transitions offers some ways to address this shortcoming, through its focus on chronic versus transitory poverty, such analysis still does not identify those who are structurally mobile from those who may be in a poverty trap. However, merging elements of Sen's entitlement approach with the economic theory of the household in imperfect market environments, Carter and May (2001) present non-parametric estimates of the mapping between household assets and poverty. This chapter builds on their analysis, to identify an alternative categorisation of poverty using panel data collected in 1993 and again in 1998 in KwaZulu-Natal.[1] The chapter goes further to describe the shocks that result in persistent poverty and the characteristics of those in different dynamic poverty categories in terms of the assets that might eventually lead to their mobility. This discussion draws out some important themes for poverty reduction, including redistributive strategies and microeconomic reform.

Conceptualising and measuring persistent poverty

The causes of persistent poverty

From a dynamic perspective, a change in a household's well-being over a period of time can be thought of as having three components:

- changes in the quantity or quality of assets available to the household;
- changes in the output derived from the assets through productivity changes, diversification or changes to the terms of exchange;
- changes in a diverse set of factors that include unobservable characteristics of household members such as entrepreneurship, good or bad luck, and the shocks that have affected the household's asset base or livelihood activities.

In addition to these, as several analysts have argued, there are structural causes of persistent poverty that result in the inability to make the minimum level of investment required to maintain or enhance different assets. Such adverse 'initial conditions' have been termed 'investment poverty' by Reardon and Vosti (1995: 1498) or 'economically persistence poverty' by Zimmerman and Carter (1995). These structural causes produce unfavourable outcomes for some people, and result in persistent vulnerability and poverty, maintaining existing economic and social inequalities. Several categories of such structural conditions can be identified, of which asymmetric markets that discriminate against the less well-off are perhaps the best known. This refers to situations in which the allocation of costs and benefits of exchange occurs in a manner that consistently prejudices the least well-off. The lumpiness of finance markets is a frequently cited example, whereby small sums of money cannot be easily or cheaply obtained from the formal financial sector, forcing poor households to make use of informal money-lenders at high interest rates. Information markets have more recently been included as another example of asymmetric markets, while transaction costs have also been identified as another important cost that falls asymmetrically on the poor (Bardhan 1989; Hoff, Braverman and Stiglitz 1993).

In addition to asymmetric markets, poor producers frequently confront thin markets when attempting to sell their goods and are unable to transport their goods elsewhere. These are conditions in which there are few buyers, and those that exist are poorly resourced. As a result, prices are low and sellers have difficulty trading. Missing markets are more frequently encountered by the poor, many of whom may rely upon non-market sources to meet essential needs, or for whom opportunities for exchange are limited. Access to common property resources such as grazing land, water and other natural resources are examples of the first; access to commodity markets for cash crops are an example of the second.

All of these factors are argued to produce asset accumulation failures, whereby the forces mentioned above combine to reduce the ability of the less well-off to accumulate, use and protect their assets over time, despite their effort and saving. An emerging economics literature provides some support for this conceptualisation of dynamic poverty (see Dasgupta 1997a, 1997b; Carter and Zimmerman 2001). In all these analyses, vulnerability and imperfect financial markets play key roles in preventing initially poor agents from using time as a means to build up asset stocks and achieve a high level of well-being.

Davies (1996) offers complementary insights from an anthropological perspective that show how a poverty trap situation can emerge for asset-poor households when negative events or shocks occur. Davies notes that three forces interact when households experience an economic shock: sensitivity, resilience and susceptibility. While the first refers to the depth or the severity of a shock on a household's well-being, resilience refers to the ability of the household to recover from the shock. Susceptibility refers to the frequency with which shocks take place, and all three factors determine the vulnerability of the household. Those that are highly sensitive to shocks, with a low resilience, are in an extremely hazardous state and may be forced to sell off or neglect productive assets in order to survive. Over time, the third dimension becomes important: the susceptibility of the household to multiple shocks. Households that are highly susceptible face multiple shocks over time, and may ratchet down over time to the point at which they eventually become trapped in a situation of structural poverty.

As in the economic analyses, accumulation failure rests at the heart of Davies' understanding of persistent, structural poverty. Although asset-rich households may spend spells below the consumption poverty line, they are affected less, recover more quickly, are better able to return to their initial position, and are able to avoid certain shocks altogether. As a result, they remain on a successful accumulation trajectory over time. In contrast, asset-poor households eventually ratchet below the consumption poverty line to become enmeshed in a poverty trap, are unable to maintain or build assets and, indeed, may have to shed assets as a coping mechanism. In this way, these households experience asset accumulation failure.

Both the economic and the anthropological work support the view that initially poor agents may be caught in a poverty trap from which neither time nor the opportunity to save and accumulate assets will deliver them. Their economic vulnerability precludes those who are in this position from ever realising their full potential as economic or social agents. A parallel implication is that it should be feasible to distinguish some minimum level of assets below which it becomes impossible to overcome structural constraints, and thus to accumulate assets or improve productivity. If this is so, the starting point for a dynamic analysis of poverty is the development of a method for identifying and measuring this asset threshold.

Developing an asset-based poverty line

In their attempt to measure persistent poverty, Carter and May (2001) develop a model of accumulation failure that provides a useful categorisation of households in the KwaZulu-Natal Income Dynamics Study (KIDS) sample based on their mobility between 1993 and 1998. The first step in this analysis is the construction of an asset-based poverty threshold, which replaces the standard consumption-based money-metric poverty line discussed earlier. To do this, the standard poverty line is rephrased so that the threshold is denoted as $\underline{c}$, whereby a person, i, is said to be poor in period t if:

$$c_{it} \leq \underline{c}. \tag{1}$$

This single-period poverty analysis can be cast in terms of realised levels of well-being, c_{it}, and the various measures discussed earlier can then be applied to produce a poverty profile that can show the incidence, depth and severity of poverty in terms of distance from the threshold. This is the conventional and static approach to poverty measurement that is widely used in most of the poverty profiles prepared for poverty reduction strategies.

An alternative approach is suggested by Carter and May (1999), who directly estimated $\hat{c}(A)$, that is to say, the expected consumption level, $\hat{c}$, for a household given its assets, A. These would consist of the human, social, natural, productive and financial capitals to which household members have access. This estimation is used to explore the structural or asset basis of poverty by developing 'asset poverty lines', $(\underline{A})$, defined as:

$$\underline{A} = \{A | \hat{c}(A) = \underline{c}\}. \tag{2}$$

Thus $\underline{A}$ is the combination of assets that yield an expected level of well-being exactly equal to the single-period poverty line.

Carter and May (2001) then go on to define a dynamic poverty line $(\underline{J})$ as:

$$\underline{J}(\underline{u}, \delta_p) = \left(\sum_{t=0}^{\infty} \delta_p^t \underline{c} \right), \tag{3}$$

where t indexes years and δ_p is a discount factor. $\underline{J}$ is then the present value of a sequence of poverty level living standards.

From this, the standard definition of poverty is extended to a multi-period context in which a household is defined as being dynamically poor if:

$$J^*(A_{0i}) < \underline{J}. \tag{4}$$

A household is thus dynamically poor if its members' expected long-term stream of well-being, $J^*(A_{0i})$, is less than the certain equivalence value of a stream of single-period poverty living standards. This is conditional on optimal accumulation behaviour, in which the household must balance current needs with anticipated future needs, and the anticipated ability to meet these.

The notion that there are initial asset positions from which successful accumulation and upward mobility are not possible suggests a dynamic analogue to the single-period asset poverty line defined in [2] above. Carter and May (2001) define this dynamic asset poverty line, $\underline{A}$, as:

$$\underline{A} = \{A \mid J^*(A_0) = \underline{J}\}. \qquad [5]$$

This dynamic asset poverty line divides those asset combinations from which it is possible to achieve successful accumulation and escape from poverty, from those combinations from which it is not.

Chronic poverty or structural poverty?

Studies using multiple observations on the well-being of a sample of households often distinguish between chronic and transitory poverty. A household that is observed to be poor using a criterion such as the consumption poverty line shown in [1] above in each wave of observation is said to be chronically poor. Households that move between poor and non-poor categories are labelled 'transitorily poor'.

In terms of Carter and May's (2001) analysis, an alternative conceptualisation is possible in which households can be divided between those that are structurally poor (with asset holdings below $\underline{A}$) and those that are structurally non-poor (with asset holdings above $\underline{A}$), irrespective of the consumption level at which the household is observed at a particular point in time. The structurally poor can, in turn, be subdivided between those that are caught in a poverty trap below $\underline{A}$, unable to accumulate, and those that are not. Finally, at any point in time, households may be stochastically poor (such as a household with asset holding $A''' > \underline{A}$ that has received a shock, $\varepsilon''' < 0$ and is likely to return to its expected livelihood level in time, $\hat{c}(A''') > \underline{c}$); or, stochastically non-poor (such as a household with asset level A'' that receives a windfall, $\varepsilon'' > 0$, but that is also likely to return to its expected livelihood level of $\hat{c}(A'') < \underline{c}$).

If this conceptualisation applies, very different kinds of household could be inappropriately grouped together if conventional chronic and transitory poverty concepts are used, especially in short panels with observations at only two or three points in time. Included in the conventional transitory category will be households that were initially structurally poor, but have escaped structural poverty through effective asset accumulation. Also in this category will be households that were never structurally poor, but which in one period were stochastically poor, as well as households that were structurally poor in all periods but were once stochastically non-poor. Similarly, the conventional chronically poor category could include households bound by a poverty trap as well as those twice observed to be stochastically (but not structurally) poor.

Measuring poverty: KIDS 1993–98

The KIDS study can be used to operationalise this approach in the context of South Africa. Firstly, the extent and depth of poverty measured by the KIDS study can be calculated using conventional static money-metric instruments. In other words, this analysis treats the data as if they represented two cross-sectional surveys such as the October Household Survey (OHS) and Income and Expenditure Survey (IES) data collected by Statistics South Africa (SSA). The data can then be described using cumulative distribution functions (CDF) that allow inspection of changes in the entire distribution of well-being between 1993 and 1998, and by means of the transition matrix approach favoured by most analyses of panel data. Finally, the data are examined through a joint distribution frequency and by testing for mobility trends.

A static approach to poverty measurement

Using the poverty line approach, based on a scaled Household Subsistence Level (HSL) consumption-based poverty line described by May et al. (2000), poverty thresholds have been estimated where average monthly expenditure per urban female adult equivalent was less than R172.36 in 1998 prices, and R118.89 per urban female adult equivalent in 1993 prices. In addition, a fixed cost comprising housing and transport expenditure has been added to each household. On average, this equalled R55.13 per urban female adult equivalent in 1993 and R79.83 per urban female adult equivalent in 1998. Table 9.1 shows the FGT class of poverty measures for households and individuals in the KIDS sample in 1993 and 1998.[2] Two poverty lines are used for each measure: the HSL and ½HSL representing an indigence line.

Table 9.1 *FGT poverty measures (total)*

	Households		Individuals	
	1993	1998	1993	1998
Headcount ratio ($P\alpha = 0$)				
c = HSL	25.9	41.5	29.6	48.9
c = ½HSL	3.7	11.0	4.0	13.1
Poverty gap ratio ($P\alpha = 1$)				
c = HSL	0.073	0.143	0.082	0.170
c = ½HSL	0.011	0.022	0.013	0.026
Squared poverty gap ($P\alpha = 2$)				
c = HSL	0.031	0.065	0.035	0.078
c = ½HSL	0.005	0.007	0.006	0.006
Number of cases	1 246	1 031	11 125	9 956

Comparing the 1998 measures with the same cohort of African and Asian/Indian households interviewed in 1993, it is evident that poverty, defined in terms of the consumption-based measures, has increased. The headcount ratio or incidence of poverty between 1993 and 1998 for the sample increased from approximately 26 per cent to 42 per cent of households, while the headcount using the lower poverty line, equal to half of the HSL, rose from 4 per cent to 11 per cent. For individuals, the headcount ratio increased from 29.6 per cent in 1993 to 48.9 per cent in 1998. As with other surveys in South Africa, the higher headcount for individuals shows the larger household sizes of poor families. In addition, Table 9.1 reveals that the depth of poverty has undergone a marked increase. The same holds true for the lower poverty line and for individuals, though the increase in depth is proportionally smaller for ultra-poor households than for poor households as a whole. This finding also holds true for the severity measure, although there is no change when the lower poverty line is used for individuals.

Despite the relative sophistication of the FGT measures, the conclusions that are reached may still be affected by the choice of poverty line. A CDF resolves this problem by testing whether differing poverty lines are robust, in that the poor are consistently identified and ranked whatever poverty line is used. If the CDFs of the indicators for different groups do not intersect, then one group can be definitively considered to be poorer than the other(s). Figure 9.1 provides this information for the two waves of KIDS after correcting to 1993 prices.

Figure 9.1 *Cumulative distribution frequency (1993–98)*

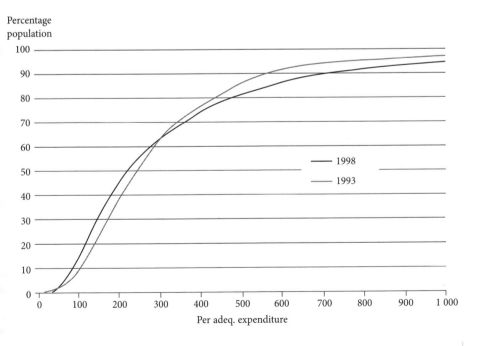

First-order dominance cannot be concluded since it is apparent that the CDFs for the two years cross over. However, as noted by Jenkins and Lambert (1997), second-order dominance can be shown since the data for 1998 lie to the left of those for 1993 until approximately R300 per urban adult female equivalent in 1993 prices. It is possible to conclude that households in 1998 are poorer than households in 1993 for all poverty lines up to twice the threshold used.

Turning to the characteristics of those who are poor, the FGT class of poverty measures has been disaggregated by location into non-urban and urban (towns and metropolitan) households in Table 9.2. This table shows the persistent geographical concentration of poverty that exists within KwaZulu-Natal, and which is similar to that of South Africa as whole.[3]

Table 9.2 *FGT poverty measures (by location)*[4]

| | Urban | | Non-urban | |
	1993	1998	1993	1998
Headcount ratio ($P\alpha = 0$)				
c = HSL	13.0	18.7	33.0	53.9
c = ½HSL	1.4	5.0	2.5	15.6
Poverty gap ratio ($P\alpha = 1$)				
c = HSL	0.033	0.053	0.095	0.191
c = ½HSL	0.012	0.021	0.042	0.090
Squared poverty gap ($P\alpha = 2$)				
c = HSL	0.002	0.004	0.016	0.031
c = ½HSL	0.001	0.001	0.008	0.010
Number of cases	440	363	806	668

In both 1993 and 1998 the risk of being a consumption-poor household in a non-urban area was more than double that experienced by urban households. The headcount ratio shows that households in non-urban locations in the province experienced a considerable increase in the incidence of poverty in the intervening five years between the waves, whereas urban households showed a more moderate increase. However, the depth of poverty for both locational groupings rose. This implies that poverty was not only becoming more pervasive in non-urban areas, but that the severity of the poverty was deepening. Even where, in the urban areas, there had been little change in the level of poverty, those that were poor had become progressively more impoverished since 1993, with the average shortfall increasing from 0.3 per cent of the poverty line to 0.5 per cent.

Finally, Table 9.3 provides the same set of FGT measures broken down by the sex of the household head.

Table 9.3 *FGT poverty measures (by sex of household head)[5]*

	De facto male head		De facto female head		De jure female head	
	1993	1998	1993	1998	1993	1998
Headcount ratio (Pα = 0)						
c = HSL	22.7	36.2	20.3	46.6	34.3	47.2
c = ½HSL	3.8	9.3	1.6	11.7	4.7	13.0
Poverty gap ratio (Pα = 1)						
c = HSL	0.065	0.121	0.050	0.156	0.100	0.167
c = ½HSL	0.012	0.017	0.002	0.033	0.014	0.024
Squared poverty gap (Pα = 2)						
c = HSL	0.029	0.055	0.017	0.074	0.043	0.077
c = ½HSL	0.006	0.005	0.000	0.014	0.007	0.008
Number of cases	662	516	192	103	382	409

Almost all of the Pα values for both poverty lines are higher for *de jure* female-headed households than for *de facto* male- and female-headed households in both years, in line with Klasen's (1997) finding for South Africa, as well as with the majority of research in sub-Saharan Africa (see Lachaud, 1994). While all types of household have experienced a decrease in their well-being as reflected by any of these consumption-based measures, the decline in the fortunes of *de facto* female-headed households is particularly striking for all the poverty measures.

A transition matrix approach

The conventional transition matrix approach is the next step necessary to complete this analysis. Transition matrices, depicting the position of households interviewed in both rounds in the income distribution over time, are a widely used and simple way to represent movement in and out of poverty. A transition matrix for KwaZulu-Natal is depicted in Table 9.4, once again using HSL-based poverty. Households that had split between 1993 and 1998 have been excluded for the purposes of this table, while those that refused to be re-interviewed have been excluded from the 1993 data.

Table 9.4 *Poverty transition matrix 1993–98 (percentage of row)*

		HSL codes 98					
		0–0.49 HSL	0.5–0.99 HSL	1–1.49 HSL	1.5–1.99 HSL	2+ HSL	Total in 1993
HSL codes 93	0–0.49 HSL	21.2	54.5	21.2		3.0	3.4
	0.5–0.99 HSL	18.9	47.9	16.1	8.8	8.3	22.0
	1–1.49 HSL	11.5	42.5	22.2	14.3	9.5	25.6
	1.5–1.99 HSL	7.3	26.4	22.3	17.6	26.4	19.8
	2+ HSL	2.0	10.2	13.9	13.9	60.0	29.1
	Total in 1998	9.8	31.3	18.4	13.1	27.4	n = 995

Based on their scaled per capita expenditure, households are placed in different expenditure groups according to their position relative to the money-metric poverty line used in the earlier tables. The mobility information is presented in the form of a percentage of each 1993 *expenditure* class (given by rows in the table) that was observed in each 1998 expenditure class (the columns of the table). The main diagonal elements of the matrix are printed in bold, and show the percentage of households in each row that did not change their position over the 1993–98 period. Households to the left of the bold diagonal line of figures experienced a decline in their well-being as measured by the poverty line that has been used. Each cell of the table thus shows the percentage of households that were in a specific poverty category in 1993 (the categories on the left side) that were subsequently in a poverty category in 1998 (the categories above).

As an example, 21.2 per cent of the households who received an income of less than half the HSL poverty line in 1993 were still in this position in 1998, while 54.5 per cent of this group had improved their position and were now earning between half the poverty line and the poverty line. With the exception of the best-off group in 1993, none of the main diagonal elements exceeds 50 per cent, signalling substantial mobility among expenditure classes.[6]

Focusing on those households that were below the scaled HSL poverty line in 1993, just over two-thirds (67.9 per cent) remained below the poverty line in 1998; in other words, two-thirds of the poor households were persistently or chronically poor. The other third of households below the poverty line in 1993 had exited poverty in 1998: these formed part of that category of households that can be considered to be transitorily poor. Looking at the next two expenditure classes (those that had 1993 expenditures between one and one-and-a-half times the HSL poverty line), while about one-third of them had moved up to higher categories in 1998, just over one-half had fallen below the scaled HSL poverty line. These households entering poverty make up another portion of the transitorily poor. It appears that not only were those in poverty in 1993 at high risk of remaining there (about two-thirds did so), but also those just above the poverty line were at substantial risk of falling into poverty (about half did so). As is seen elsewhere in the world, in addition to those who are chronically poor, the poor includes a large group of households who cycle in and out of poverty (Bane and Ellwood 1986; Ruggles and Williams 1989).

Table 9.4 can be simplified to depict those who are chronically poor (below the HSL in both periods), transitorily poor (below the HSL in either 1993 or 1998) and never poor (above the HSL in both periods). This is shown in Table 9.5, which once again excludes the split households.

Table 9.5 *Chronic and transitory poverty classes*

		98: Poverty category		Total 1993
		Not poor	Poor	
93: Poverty category	Not Poor	50.8% (never poor)	24.0% (transitory poor)	74.8
	Poor	8.0% (transitory poor)	17.2% (chronic poor)	25.2
Total 1998		58.5%	41.5%	n = 995

Using the language of conventional studies of chronic poverty, the table shows that 17.2 per cent of the KIDS sample can be described as being chronically poor between 1993 and 1998, and below the poverty line in both periods; 32.0 per cent can be termed transitory poor, with over 70 per cent of this group being those who were non-poor in 1993 but poor in 1998; and finally 50.8 per cent can be described as never poor.

Taken together, Tables 9.4 and 9.5 present a picture of money-metric mobility for the majority of the KIDS sample, with some instances of those furthest below the poverty line able to improve their situation, if not to escape to a position above the line; but generally there is a deterioration in well-being between 1993 and 1998 as expressed by consumption, especially for those near to the poverty line. Of course, because this is longitudinal data and the 1998 round is not representative, statements about overall poverty rates in KwaZulu-Natal cannot be made, however seductive this possibility may seem. Nonetheless, this worrying result requires further investigation to ascertain whether these changes are simply the result of measurement errors in one or either of the surveys, or a product of the money-metric approach that has been adopted, or whether they are both robust and can be explained.

Mobility and mobility tests

While provocative in its portrayal of an unequalising post-apartheid income distribution process within, at least, the African and Asian/Indian populations, the analysis in the prior section is uninformative about whether initially poor households have become systematically worse off over time, or whether the matrix has been generated by significant upward and downward mobility in which initially poor and non-poor households have swapped places in the income distribution.

As a first insight into this question of mobility, Carter and May (2001) graphically portray the estimated joint distribution of well-being (expenditures divided by subsistence needs) using the KIDS data. They find that a large clump of initially poor households has either held steady or fallen behind. To return to the language of conventional poverty dynamics analysis, these households are chronically poor. Upward mobility appears concentrated among households that were initially better off. Together, these two observations suggest that a pattern of class-based mobility underlies the shift in the cumulative distribution of income shown in Figure 9.1, as the probability of getting ahead is correlated positively to initial income level.

While the estimated joint distribution of well-being permits the full pattern of mobility to be seen, it is not amenable to any simple tests of the degree to which the visually distinct patterns of mobility across initial income classes are in fact significantly different from each other in statistical terms. However, to return to the transition matrix given in Table 9.4, mobility information is provided in the form of the percentage of households in each 1993 well-being class (given by the rows of the table) that was observed in the 1998 well-being classes (the columns of the table). Following Hout (1983), Carter and May (2001) ask whether these observed transition frequencies in Table 9.4 are sufficiently different from what would be expected under various models of homogenous or class-independent mobility, that the models can be rejected. The simplest such model is one of perfect mobility, in which a household's destination in the 1998 income distribution is independent of its 1993 starting position. Perfect or class-independent mobility is decisively rejected, as the p-value for the L^2 statistic is less than 0.0001.

Rejection of this perfect mobility model is not, however, especially surprising. Inertial forces might at least make it more likely that households will tend to maintain their initial position, rather than exhibiting upward or downward mobility. Carter and May (2001) go on to use the class of log-linear models to test a range of hypotheses, and conclude that the data reject the restrictions implied by the full series of increasingly less-restricted log-linear models that ask whether there are any common mobility patterns that cut across classes. Even the most general model tested (the 'Quasi-Diagonals' model in Hout's nomenclature) is rejected at the 5 per cent level, giving a clear indication that the mobility patterns are heterogeneous across income classes. Not only is 1993 livelihood position significantly related to 1998 income position, but the upward and downward mobility patterns are highly different across initial income classes. Statistically unable to accept any of the restrictions implied by commonly used mobility models, the observed transition matrix frequencies may be used as the best estimates of the mobility pattern.

The observed shift in the CDF seen in Figure 9.1 is thus the product of a relatively large group of chronically poor and a process of bifurcation among those just above the poverty line in 1993, with just over half that group falling behind, and the others holding steady or moving ahead. As a final test, Carter and May (2001) examine the longer-run implications of this class-based mobility pattern on the assumption that income distribution follows a stationary Markov process. Once again the data give clear evidence of a pattern of downward mobility.

Applying the asset-based poverty line to South Africa

Entitlement failure and endowment loss

While the analysis above provides further information on the incidence of chronic versus transitory poverty, and on mobility patterns across a well-being distribution, it is still not possible to determine whether the mobility of the transitorily poor is the result of successful accumulation, or whether this is simply driven by stochastic factors.

Two types of shock can be related to mobility and poverty transitions. Firstly, there are those that impact on the income stream that is derived from household assets: ε_{it}. Examples of such income shocks may be an unexpected bad harvest because of drought, or additional income from a business as a result of higher sales. To emphasise that these shocks refer to occasions when the use of available assets does not lead to the anticipated outcome, the language of Sen's entitlement literature is evoked, and these income shocks are thus termed 'entitlement failures' when they are negative and 'entitlement windfalls' when they are positive. The second type of shock occurs when the household experiences an unexpected, permanent reduction in its asset base, which may be defined as Θ_{it}. Examples here are when a wage earner suddenly dies; a fire destroys a business; or a friend, family member or government abandons or reneges on a longstanding remittance or other financial transfer. These asset shocks will be called 'endowment losses' to draw attention to their permanent and structural impact.

By estimating the livelihood function, or expected well-being, $\hat{c}_{it}(A_{it})$, Equation 2' can be recast to obtain an estimate of entitlement shocks, ε_{it}:

$$\varepsilon_{it} = c_{it} - \hat{c}(A_{it}).$$

However, these estimated shocks will contain measurement and other random errors, as well as genuine shocks experienced by the household. In general, the less precise the estimate of $c_{it}(A_{it})$, the larger will be the estimate of ε_{it} irrespective of the magnitude of shocks experienced by the household. To control for the precision of the underlying estimation of $\hat{c}_{it}(A_{it})$, Carter and May (2001) check each household to see whether the following hypotheses for each year of the data can be rejected:

Household is expected to be poor if reject H_1: $\hat{c}_{it} > HSL_{it}$.

Household is expected to be non-poor if reject H_2: $\hat{c}_{it} < HSL_{it}$.

A household that is observed to be poor, but for whom the hypothesis that they are expected to be poor can be *rejected*, is said have suffered an entitlement shock or to be *stochastically poor*. Similarly, a household that is observed to be non-poor, but for whom the hypothesis that they are expected to be non-poor can be *rejected*, is said to have enjoyed an entitlement windfall and to be *stochastically non-poor*.

By using stringent criteria requiring that the confidence band around the estimate of $\hat{c}_{it}$ lies completely above the HSL, it becomes possible to say that an observed poor household is stochastically poor, and if not, to deduce that the household is instead structurally poor and lacking the assets necessary to generate $\hat{c}_{it} > HSL_{it}$.

For reasons detailed in Carter and May (1999), there are a number of reasons why $\hat{c}_{it}(A_{it})$ should depart from strict linearity or asset additivity. Following on the methodological suggestion of that paper, flexible local regression methods were employed to derive an 80 per cent confidence interval estimate $\hat{c}_{it}(A_{it})$ for each time period.[7] The 80 per cent interval estimate allows the above (one-sided) hypotheses to be tested at the 10 per cent significance level. Hence, there will be a 10 per cent (Type I error) probability that any household that is deemed to be stochastically poor is not.

To measure endowment losses, in other words, a permanent reduction in available assets, Θ_{it}, the KIDS survey questioned all respondents about the economic shocks experienced over the 1993–98 period. For each shock, information was solicited to measure its economic costs. In the case of the theft or destruction of a physical asset, respondents were asked to supply the (asset) value of the item lost. When a wage earner was permanently disabled, a social welfare payment eliminated, or a source of remittance cut off, respondents were asked to report the resulting decrease in monthly income.[8] A present value calculation over a 20-year time horizon, using a 5 per cent real discount rate, was then utilised to approximate the asset value of the lost endowment. In principle, this present value formulation makes the loss of human capital or of a remittance comparable to the loss of non-human income-earning assets.

Valuing assets

To test this approach to measuring stochastic and structural poverty empirically, the incidence of ownership, and values of assets identified, must first be attempted. In many instances, actually measuring the assets listed is complex. The measurement of social capital, for example, remains an imprecise and disputed 'science', while the value of common property is also difficult to allocate among households who may enjoy access to such property.[9] Following Moser (1995) and others, a five-fold categorisation of assets is invoked: human capital and capabilities, social, legal and political capital, natural resources, productive capital and financial capital. The KIDS database contains information on the distribution and extent of some of these assets, and Table 9.6 shows the percentage that can be identified of the households surveyed in both 1993 and 1998 which had access to those assets. Using the approach just described to estimate the present value endowments lost through shocks, present values have been calculated for the combinations of assets used for the main income-generating activities for which data were gathered in the two waves of KIDS.

Table 9.6 *Access to assets: 1993 and 1998*

Assets	KIDS 1993 (%)	KIDS 1998 (%)
Human capital and capabilities		
Educated labour (Std 8 and above)[10]	60.7	82.1
Literate labour (Std 4 and above)	86.3	95.6
Social, legal and political capital		
Membership of a group[11]	57.3	70.9
Person of pensionable age	32.9	46.8
Migrant family member	40.8	40.3
Natural resources		
Land for farming	35.4	47.6
Access to private grazing land	3.3	2.2
Access to communal grazing land	24.9	20.3
Access to irrigation on farm land	5.5	4.4
Productive capital		
Livestock (MLU)	20.9	24.2
Agricultural equipment	27.6	53.0
Other productive equipment	15.4	12.6
Brick or block walls	47.3	50.6
Piped water connection	37.9	42.1
Electricity connection	44.8	55.2
Financial capital		
Savings in a bank or elsewhere	24.2	61.1
Durable household goods	95.2	98.8

Note: n = 1 031
MLU: Mature livestock units

In 1993 over 20 per cent of households had no fungible assets, meaning any assets which the household could convert to cash in some way. That is to say, households in this group had no safety net of their own, and were extremely vulnerable to any loss of income. They were unable to liquidate an asset to cover unexpected expenses or invest in new opportunities and, finally, lacked any possible resource that could be used as security against credit.

Forty-three per cent did not have land in either wave; 9 per cent had land in 1993 but not in 1998; 19 per cent had acquired land by 1998 and 29 per cent had land in both periods. Fifty-seven per cent of the 'never poor' did not have land in either wave, while 42 per cent of the structurally downward had land in both waves.

Just over a quarter of the households surveyed in 1993 (26.1 per cent) had access to a plot of land for the cultivation of crops. Average land size for these households was 2.2 ha. A similar pattern was repeated with respect to the ownership of livestock, with some 24 per cent of households in KwaZulu-Natal owning livestock with an average holding of 5.4 Mature Livestock Units (MLU) valued at approximately R4 300. The incidence of ownership was lower than that reported by studies undertaken in the early to mid-1980s, suggesting that there had been a decline in access to this particular endowment (May and Peters 1985; Muller, May and Krone 1987; Ardington 1988). This trend may be a result both of drought conditions and of the population expansion in dense rural settlements that do not have access to grazing land.

Ownership of agricultural and other productive equipment was limited to 18 and 8 per cent of the surveyed households, respectively. As this refers to important agricultural tools such as ploughs and harvesters, as well as tools which could be used in small and medium enterprise (SMME) manufacturing activities such as welding and sewing, rural non-farm income generation activities are likely to be severely constrained as a result of the lack of such equipment. Finally, 30 per cent of households included a person of pensionable age and 35 per cent had a member of the household who was a migrant in another area.

Although the ownership of assets is unevenly split according to the composition of the household, measuring the distribution of assets within the household is problematic. As with many studies, in Table 9.7 households have again been divided into three categories of headship as a way of reflecting gender inequalities. As before, the categories used are: households headed *de facto* by men, households headed *de jure* by absent men and thus *de facto* by women; and households headed *de jure* by women. Once again, only households surveyed in both 1993 and 1998 have been included, and split households have not been combined but have been included in the table.

Table 9.7 *Access to assets (by sex of head of household)*[12]

	De facto male head		De facto female head		De jure female head	
	1993	1998	1993	1998	1993	1998
Human capital and capabilities						
Educated labour (Std 8 and above)	66.0	82.8	50.6	75.7	63.5	82.6
Literate labour (Std 4 and above)	88.8	96.1	83.5	96.1	87.0	94.9
Social, legal and political capital						
Membership of a group	55.1	68.2	53.5	73.2	61.6	73.4
Person of pensionable age	24.7	39.1	23.2	39.8	51.7[1]	57.9[1]
Migrant family member	25.4	25.4	99.4	86.4	47.2[1]	47.4[1]
Natural resources						
Land for farming	30.3	38.8	60.4	70.9	38.4[1]	53.9[1]
Access to private grazing land	3.2	2.1	4.9	3.9	4.6	2.1
Access to communal grazing land	20.9	16.7	46.3	43.7	24.5[1]	19.1[1]
Access to irrigation	5.8	3.5	7.3	3.9	4.3	5.6
Productive capital						
Livestock (MLU)	20.2	22.3	44.5	50.5	15.2[1]	20.0[1]
Agricultural equipment	22.4	48.8	57.9	66.0	27.2[1]	54.8[1]
Other productive equipment	16.3	15.3	17.1	11.7	13.6	9.3[1]
Brick or block walls	57.0	59.3	24.4	28.2	43.7	45.2[1]
Piped water connection	48.2	51.7	9.2	12.6	35.3[1]	37.2[1]
Electricity connection	55.3	59.3	17.1	28.2	41.5[1]	45.2[1]
Financial capital						
Savings in a bank or elsewhere	28.8	65.5	19.5	69.9	18.3[1]	53.1[1]
Durable household goods	96.1	98.8	95.1	98.1	93.8	99.0
n =	535	516	164	103	323	409

Note: 1 refers to cases where the Chi square test shows a significant difference between the headship groups (0.05 level of confidence).

The table highlights several important differences in the ownership of assets between male- and female-headed households. Perhaps most significant is that a greater proportion of these female-headed households have some household members who are educated, and this proportion is considerably higher in households where the female head is absent. Some 64 per cent of all households headed by an absent female head have access to 'educated labour' in the household, compared to only approximately 34 per cent of households headed by a resident male head. It would seem therefore that higher poverty risks among female-headed households, and particularly among those where the head is absent, cannot be explained simply with reference to levels of education.

More than half (51 per cent) of all households headed by a resident female have access to pensions, compared to only 23.8 per cent of equivalent male-headed households. This finding suggests that a large proportion of these households are headed by women who are pensioners, which might in turn offer a partial explanation for the higher incidence of poverty among this household type.

There are also important differences between households where the head is resident and where the head is absent. An overwhelming majority of both male- and female-headed households with absent heads have household members who are migrant workers. For example, 93.3 per cent of all households headed by an absent male have migrant family members, compared to only 16 per cent of households where the male head is resident in the household. Several studies have argued that remittances from migrant household members in South Africa are often not received on a regular basis and are too low to meet the household's basic needs. A greater reliance of households with an absent head on remittances might therefore be significant in accounting for higher poverty risks in these household groupings.

Finally, in terms of spatial location, Table 9.8 shows the access to assets of households surveyed in both waves of KIDS, according to their spatial classification.

Table 9.8 *Access to assets (by spatial location)[13]*

	Urban		Non-urban	
	1993	1998	1993	1998
Human capital and capabilities				
Educated labour (Std 8 and above)	84.6	92.0	51.2[1]	76.6[1]
Literate labour (Std 4 and above)	97.2	98.3	82.2[1]	94.2[1]
Social, legal and political capital				
Membership of a group	51.5	62.3	60.5[1]	75.6[1]
Person of pensionable age	22.9	37.7	38.3[1]	51.6[1]
Migrant family member	19.3	14.3	56.3[1]	54.3[1]
Natural resources				
Land for farming	1.1	8.8	57.6[1]	68.7[1]
Access to private grazing land	0.3	1.1	5.8	2.8
Access to communal grazing land	0.3	0.0	40.1[1]	31.3[1]
Access to irrigation	0.6	3.0	8.2[1]	5.1
Productive capital				
Livestock (MLU)	0.6	0.6	34.4[1]	37.1[1]
Agricultural equipment	1.7	36.1	44.8[1]	62.1[1]
Other productive equipment	12.9	11.0	16.7	13.5
Brick or block walls	92.3	93.7	22.9	27.3[1]
Piped water connection	95.6	96.5	6.5[1]	12.5[1]
Electricity connection	82.1	94.2	24.6[1]	49.4[1]
Financial capital				
Savings in a bank or elsewhere	29.8	69.1	21.1[1]	56.7[1]
Durable household goods	98.6	99.4	93.4[1]	98.5
n =	363	363	668	668

Note: 1 refers to cases where the Chi square test shows a significant difference between the spatial location groups (0.05 level of confidence).

Substantial and statistically significant differences emerge between households in urban and non-urban areas in terms of their access to most assets.

Financial cost of positive and negative shocks

In 1998, in order to ascertain the incidence and cost of economic shocks, respondents were asked whether the surveyed household had experienced any bad or good surprises that had hurt or benefited the family financially during the past five years. A list of possible negative and positive shocks was then read out to the respondent, and an opportunity was allowed for any unprompted responses as well. If a shock was identified, the respondent was then probed as to the timing of the shock, its duration, the resultant loss or gain in income and the economic value of the positive or negative shock. In the case of negative shocks, the respondent was also asked to estimate the expenses that might have been incurred. Table 9.9 shows the percentage of households in each of the conventional transition matrix classes that experienced positive and negative shocks, and the mean number of shocks that were experienced by those who reported such events.

Table 9.9 *Incidence of negative and positive shocks*

	Chronic poor	Becoming poor	Becoming non-poor	Never poor	Total
Negative shock	70.2	70.4	79.0	68.6	70.1
Positive shock	26.0	23.6	37.0	31.4	29.0
Mean no. of shocks	1.7	1.6	1.9	1.7	1.7

Note: n = 1 031

On average, the majority (70 per cent) of households reported negative shocks, with just fewer than 30 per cent reporting positive shocks. Although those who were non-poor in 1993 and poor in 1998 reported a higher incidence of negative and positive shocks, as well as a higher average number of shocks, unlike Hunter and May's (2002) finding for the Durban region, there was no statistical difference between the groups, and poor households were not more likely to report a greater occurrence or number of shocks than wealthier households.

Information was collected on three options for the financial impact of the shock: firstly, the loss of gain in terms of income over the past five years, next the expenses that were incurred as a result of a negative shock, and finally the value of the item that was lost or gained. This information is shown in current prices for the entire sample in Table 9.10, which reports the mean value over the five-year time period for each category as well as the standard error of the mean in italics.

Table 9.10 *Financial impact of shocks: mean value, 1993–98 (in rands)*

	Chronic poor	Becoming poor	Becoming non-poor	Never poor	Total
Total income loss	2 320.66	3 392.89	4 123.33	4 581.62	3 191.75
	509.89	*688.35*	*1 353.30*	*819.86*	*388.0*
Total expenses	1 010.81	1 418.26	2 655.35	3 034.25	1 866.38
	131.31	*176.60*	*420.49*	*313.62*	*143.0*
Total value	632.65	977.87	1 229.81	2 311.03	1 329.60
	142.01	*250.22*	*392.81*	*544.15*	*235.5*
Total income gained	847.65	1 120.44	5 325.68	3 219.82	2 033.68
	283.41	*512.26*	*1 579.22*	*645.16*	*310.7*
Total value gained	13.76	907.60	444.44	1 299.60	753.71
	8.24	*524.03*	*444.44*	*484.45*	*229.5*

Notes: n = 1 031. Standard error of the mean shown in italics.

For those who experienced both positive and negative shocks, the 'becoming non-poor and the 'never poor' experienced the highest financial loss or gain, as might be anticipated given their greater initial wealth, while the chronic poor experienced the least loss or gain. Moreover, the total of expenses and the value of the loss is somewhat correlated with total household expenditure for 1993 and for 1998.[14] However, when expressed as a percentage of consumption, the income loss amounted to 17.2 per cent of total expenditure estimated for all shocked households over the five-year reporting period, but 31 per cent for the 'becoming poor' category compared to 12 per cent for the 'never poor'. Expenses amounted to 4 per cent of the expenditure of all shocked households over five years, but 6 per cent for the 'becoming poor' and 3.8 per cent for the 'never poor', while the value of the lost items amounted to 5 per cent of expenditure of all shocked households and 8 per cent for the 'becoming poor'. Income gains equalled 12 per cent for the total sample, but 16 per cent for the 'becoming non-poor' compared to 9 per cent for the 'becoming poor'.[15] For the 30 households that reported a gain in assets through the value of the positive shock, this amounted to 25 per cent of total expenditure over five years.

Turning to the type of shock that was received, Table 9.11 shows the negative and positive events that were reported most frequently by the transition matrix classes, in order of their frequency of being reported. The table also shows the mean value of the loss or gain in current prices, as well as the standard error of the mean for this value.

Table 9.11 *Type of shock received*[16]

	Chronic poor	Becoming poor	Becoming non-poor	Never poor	Total	Mean value of (loss)/gain (rands)	SE mean
Death	34.3	34.0	54.3	35.6	36.5	(4 249.92)	233.6
Illness	21.5	27.6	24.7	18.9	21.9	(1 544.31)	377.0
Loss of job	24.3	19.2	24.7	18.3	20.1	(14 296.15)	1 219.9
New job	17.1	12.8	27.2	19.3	17.9	19 582.61	2 920.5
Theft	13.3	12.8	16.0	16.0	14.7	(4 792.62)	969.2
Death of livestock	10.5	10.0	14.8	6.9	8.9	(4 277.83)	754.6
Crop failure	8.3	5.2	4.9	5.4	5.8	(694.91)	145.2
Higher grant	6.1	7.2	7.4	3.1	4.9	2 733.32	689.1
Abandonment	3.3	1.6	2.5	2.9	2.6	(2 095.24)	95.2

Note: n = 1 031

Death of a family member was the most frequently reported shock, with 37 per cent of households reporting this event. There is little difference between the transition classes, although the much higher incidence of death in the 'becoming non-poor' group does stand out. This suggests that for this group mobility out of poverty is the result of a smaller household, and thus higher per capita incomes, rather than a structural improvement in well-being. Illness and job loss are the next most frequently reported shocks, with households in the 'chronically poor' and 'becoming poor' categories experiencing a higher incidence of these shocks, although once again these differences are not statistically significant. Acquiring a new job was both the most frequently reported positive shock and the largest mean value of the shocks reported, and was especially frequent among the 'becoming non-poor' class.

Mobility and assets

Structural poverty classes

Using these data on assets and shocks, the model of persistent poverty can be used to generate a dynamic poverty typology. This breaks the KIDS sample into the seven groups shown in Table 9.12. For purposes of comparison, the data are presented by first eliminating the split-off households and then recombining these households. As can be seen, the difference is marginal.

Table 9.12 *Structural poverty classes*

Structural poverty classes	Split hhs excluded	Split hhs combined
Dual failures	1.4	1.5
Structurally poor	16.5	16.2
Stochastically upward	4.4	5.3
Structurally upward	3.7	3.9
Stochastically downward	2.6	3.8
Structurally downward	21.6	21.1
Never poor	49.7	48.2
n =	995	1 031

The categories can be explained as follows:

- Dual failures refer to households whose assets are such that they are expected to be above the poverty line in both periods, but which have experienced entitlement failures in periods during which data were collected and, subject to measurement error, would be observed as being chronically poor.
- Structurally poor households are those which are both observed to be poor in both periods, and which do not have sufficient assets with which incomes can be generated that can ensure that they will not be poor. They, too, would be observed to be chronically poor.
- Stochastically upward households are those that are observed to be poor in the first period, and then non-poor in the second period as a result of entitlement windfalls, but which still lack the assets to generate sufficient income to be non-poor. These households would be observed to be transitory poor.
- Structurally upward households are those that are observed to be poor in the first period, and then non-poor in the second period, and which have accumulated the assets required to generate sufficient income to be non-poor.
- Stochastically downward households are those that are observed to be non-poor in the first period, and then poor in the second period because of entitlement failure, but which have the assets to generate sufficient income to be non-poor in both periods. These households would also be observed to be transitory poor.
- Structurally downward households are those that are observed to be non-poor in the first period, and then poor in the second period, and which have experienced endowment shocks, thereby losing assets, and as a result can no longer generate sufficient income to be non-poor. Once again, these households would be observed to be transitory poor.
- And finally, the never poor are both structurally non-poor and are observed to be non-poor in both periods.

Decomposing mobility

The structure of Table 9.13 is the simplified version of the earlier poverty transition matrix (Table 9.4) in which the various well-being categories have been compressed into the poor and the non-poor. However, this table breaks these groups into the new structural poverty classes.

Table 9.13 *Recasting the transition matrix*

		Transition matrix classes			Total
		Chronic poor	Becoming poor	Becoming non-poor	Never poor	
Mobility classes	Dual failures	8.0	0.0	0.0	0.0	1.4
	Structurally poor	91.4	1.7	1.3	0.0	16.5
	Stochastically upward	0.0	0.0	55.8	0.2	4.4
	Structurally upward	0.0	0.0	42.9	0.8	3.7
	Stochastically downward	0.0	10.9	0.0	0.0	2.6
	Structurally downward	0.6	87.4	0.0	1.0	21.6
	Never poor	0.0	0.0	0.0	98.0	49.7
	Total	17.5	24.0	7.7	50.8	n = 995

As already shown in Table 9.5, some 18 per cent of all households are chronically poor and are observed to be poor in both periods of the KIDS data, 24 per cent are transitory poor and are observed to have become poor between 1993 and 1998, 8 per cent are transitory poor and are observed to have become non-poor between 1993 and 1998, and, finally, 51 per cent are never poor. However, as mentioned earlier, not all the chronically poor households are necessarily structurally poor (and candidates for being stuck in a poverty trap). Some of these households may have experienced entitlement failures in both periods of the KIDS study. Similarly, not all the transitory households in the off-diagonal cells can be said to be structurally non-poor (and therefore outside a poverty trap) as some of them may have experienced entitlement windfalls in the period in which they were non-poor, while others may be structurally non-poor but experienced entitlement failures in the period in which they were poor.

Using the shock data, bounds on the degree of structural and stochastic poverty in each of these groups can now be estimated. For 8 per cent of the chronically poor, the hypothesis that they were structurally poor in both periods can be rejected, meaning that they are likely to have suffered dual entitlement shocks. This defines an upper bound estimate of 92 per cent of the chronically poor who are actually structurally poor. It may of course be that some of these 92 per cent also suffered dual entitlement shocks, but the hypothesis that they are structurally poor cannot be rejected, and, for at least the five-year period covered by KIDS, it can be accepted that these households are enmeshed in the circumstances of a poverty trap.

We look next at the households that were described as transitory poor, and moved from non-poor to poor status between 1993 and 1998: for 11 per cent, the hypothesis that they were stochastically poor in both periods cannot be rejected, meaning that they are likely to have suffered entitlement failures in 1998 and are expected to return to their 'true' position as non-poor in time. They are thus classified as stochastically downward. For 87 per cent, the hypothesis that they were stochastically poor in the second period cannot be rejected, meaning that they are likely to have suffered endowment losses in the second period and are thus classified as structurally downward, and unlikely to recover to a non-poor position.

We turn now to the households that were described as transitory poor, and that moved from poor to non-poor status between 1993 and 1998: for 56 per cent, the hypothesis that they were stochastically poor in both periods cannot be rejected, meaning that they are likely to have suffered entitlement windfalls in 1993, and had returned to their 'true' position as poor in 1998. This group had received entitlement shocks in 1993 and the hypothesis that they were expected to be poor in 1993 can be rejected. The upward mobility of this group can thus be inferred to be a regression to their expected level of livelihood, rather than a story of successful accumulation or escape from structural poverty. For 43 per cent, the hypothesis that they were stochastically non-poor in the second period cannot be rejected, meaning that they have been able to accumulate assets successfully, placing an upper bound of 43 per cent on the number of the upwardly mobile who escaped poverty though accumulation. It was impossible to identify unambiguously any of the upwardly mobile as beneficiaries of a 1998 entitlement windfall, so this upper bound estimate cannot be further reduced.[17]

Finally, 15 per cent of the downwardly mobile households suffered a 1998 entitlement failure, in the sense that the hypothesis that their expected level of well-being was below their HSL could be rejected. The other 85 per cent of these households are potentially structurally poor, although it was impossible to identify any of them as a 1993 entitlement windfall beneficiary that had regressed to an expected level of well-being below the poverty line.

However, a large number of these households that fell behind (and that did not appear to have received an entitlement shock in 1998) were struck by asset shocks between 1993 and 1998. As many as 51 per cent of the households that fell below the poverty line in 1998, but were not stochastically poor, were victims of asset shocks. (This figure contrasts with the sample average of 30 per cent of households as victims of asset shocks.) While this group cannot be precisely decomposed into stochastically and new structurally poor, it seems likely that a significant portion of the households that fell behind are in a structural, as opposed to a stochastic, poverty situation – perhaps as many as 85 per cent of them.

Assets, shocks and structural poverty classes

To return to the assets that underpin these classes, Table 9.14 shows the groups identified as structurally poor or mobile and compares their access to assets in 1993 and 1998.

Table 9.14 *Assets and structural poverty classes[18]*

Assets	Structurally poor 1993 (1998)	Structurally upward 1993 (1998)	Structurally downward 1993 (1998)	Never poor 1993 (1998)
Human capital and capabilities				
Educated labour (Std 8 and above)	40.8 (66.9)	41.5 (73.2)	48.2 (73.2)	79.4[1] (92.2)[1]
Literate labour (Std 4 and above)	77.5 (90.5)	70.7 (92.7)	79.0 (93.8)	95.5[1] (98.4)[1]
Social and political capital				
Person of pensionable age	32.5 (55.0)	43.9 (58.5)	40.2 (52.2)	26.7[1] (38.6)[1]
Migrant family member	41.4 (52.1)	43.9 (46.3)	57.1 (54.0)	39.6[1] (30.6)[1]
Natural resources				
Land for farming	40.8 (57.4)	43.9 (61.0)	56.3 (66.5)	30.8[1] (37.5)[1]
Access to grazing land (private)	4.7 (2.4)	7.3 (0.0)	1.3 (1.3)	4.5 (2.7)
Access to communal grazing land	26.0 (26.0)	24.4 (30.0)	46.0 (29.5)	19.8[1] (13.9)[1]
Access to irrigation	4.1 (10.3)	0.0 (0.0)	6.7 (8.7)	6.7 (8.9)
Productive capital				
Livestock (MLU)	29.0 (33.1)	24.4 (34.1)	34.8 (34.8)	15.7[1] (17.1)[1]
Agricultural equipment	34.3 (57.4)	36.6 (61.0)	50.0 (58.9)	21.0[1] (50.2)[1]
Other productive equipment	(8.3)	(7.3)	(13.8)	(15.1)[1]
Permanent house (Brick or block)	22.5[1] (24.3)[1]	14.6[1] (39.0)[1]	23.2[1] (22.3)[1]	67.3[1] (71.6)[1]
Financial capital				
Savings	9.5[1] (34.9)[1]	2.4[1] (56.1)[1]	21.4[1] (42.0)[1]	34.1[1] (66.7)[1]
Durable household goods	85.2 (96.4)	90.2 (97.6)	96.0 (98.7)	98.4 (99.6)
n =	169	41	224	510

Note: 1 refers to cases where the Chi square test shows a significant difference between poverty groups (0.05 level of confidence).

Several trends emerge from this table. Firstly, the 'never poor' were substantially better endowed with educated labour than any other group. All groups did see an increase in the percentage of households with educated labour between 1993 and 1998. However, other groups still lag behind the 'never poor'; 92 per cent of the households in this group had at least one person with more than a Standard 8 education by 1998. In terms of literate labour, the four groups are similar, and all experienced a similar improvement.

Turning to the presence of a person of pensionable age in the household, the 'structurally poor' and the 'never poor' were less well endowed with this type of asset in 1993, which could reflect no more than the demographic structure of households in this group. Interestingly, though, by 1998 the 'structurally poor' appear similar to the other groups, while the 'never poor' remain less well endowed. Access to a pensioner does not therefore appear to improve the chances for a household to move permanently out of poverty, a finding consistent with other studies that have reported the extensive sharing of pensions in poor families.

All groups experienced an improvement in terms of access to farmland, livestock and agricultural equipment, although the 'structurally upward' appear to have done somewhat better than the other groups. All groups also experienced an improvement in terms of the building materials of their houses, although the 'structurally upward' appear to have done much better than the other groups and the 'never poor' were always far better endowed than the other groups. Finally, in terms of financial assets, while all groups have improved their position, the 'never poor' were far better endowed with access to savings accounts in 1993 and continued to have this advantage in 1998. Noteworthy, though, is the dramatic improvement in access to savings that has been achieved by the 'structurally upward' group. In sum, the asset profile of the 'never poor' confirms that they were relatively well resourced in 1993, while the improvements seen in housing, educated labour and access to savings confirms the positive mobility of the 'structurally upward'.

Conclusion

This chapter has further developed the concept of asset-based dynamic measurement of poverty proposed by Carter and May (2001), and has put forward a new typology of poverty. Assessing the components of this approach, namely, entitlement failure, entitlement windfalls and endowment loss, it is argued that the dynamic approach provides a better fit for the events encountered by the surveyed households over time than does the conventional transition matrix approach used by most analysts of chronic poverty. Instead, seven groups of households have been identified according to their structural position, as determined by the changes in assets and consumption-based well-being that the household has experienced between 1993 and 1998. Four of these groups represent structural positions: the structurally poor; the structurally upward; the structurally downward; and the never poor. Three are transitory positions dependent upon bad or good fortune between 1993 and 1998. These are the dual failures (unlucky in both years); the stochastically upward (fortunate in 1998); and the stochastically downward (fortunate in 1993). Comparing the data reported by the KIDS respondents with information from the South African Participatory Poverty Assessment (SA-PPA), which was undertaken during the same period as KIDS, provides useful corroborating evidence. Participants in the SA-PPA provide commentary on job losses, the death and illness of household members, the theft and destruction of property and, in each case, link these shocks to permanent declines in income. Education is perceived as an important route out of poverty, while access to land provides a buffer against misfortune, unreliable remittances from migrants and job loss. Limited access to finance is also identified as an important constraint.

As Carter and May (2001) note, distinguishing between these different types of chronic and transitory poverty is important for a variety of reasons. A society in which even structural poverty is transitory is clearly very different from a society in which large numbers of the poor are caught in a structural circumstance of accumulation failure. The policy implications, clearly, also differ for the two sets of circumstances. In one case, time is an ally that eliminates chronic poverty and interventions can be confined to reducing the time required to achieve this mobility, and implementing social protection policies that alleviate the ill effects of transitory poverty. In the other case, time merely oversees the reproduction of a chronically poor class, and structural changes, such as asset redistribution or market reforms, may be required if poverty is ever to be eliminated.

Notes

1   Known as the KwaZulu-Natal Income Dynamics Study (KIDS), this survey of 1 171 households is described in May et al. (2000). Alderman et al. (2000) discuss the impact of attrition on the data that were collected, while Roberts (2001) uses these data to distinguish the chronic from the transitory poor.

2   The results in this chapter will differ from previously published work because of a number of refinements made to the construction of the consumption-based poverty threshold that is used. These include adjustments to the community-specific price index, equivalence scales and household economies-of-scale. These adjustments have changed the magnitudes reported previously, but not the trends.

3   Because of the sample frame of the original sample, KIDS has followed the official classification of areas used in the 1985, 1991 and 1996 censuses, in which non-urban refers to areas that were historically not in the demarcated municipal authorities. By and large this corresponds with rural settlements, although there are important exceptions. In 2001, Statistics South Africa abandoned this definition in favour of a population-density classification.

4   Chi square tests show that the headcounts for urban and non-urban areas are statistically different.

5   *De facto* female headship refers to households in which a non-resident male head was identified. Chi square tests show that the headcounts for c = HSL are statistically different.

6   The stability of the best-off group is in part an artefact of it being an open-ended category.

7   Explanatory variables used in the local regression analysis are educated labour, uneducated labour, rural/urban dummy variable, productive capital, transfer income, and number of adult equivalent consumers. Social capital was not explicitly included because of the difficulty of measuring this asset in an already complex task. See Cleveland et al. (1988) for details on local regression methods.

8   Only when there was evidence of a permanent loss of the income stream was a shock considered an endowment loss.

9   Much has been written on social capital, and it is not the purpose of this chapter to enter into these debates. Following previous work on social capital using the KIDS data, it is assumed that group membership can be included as a potential resource to households (Maluccio et al. 2000).

10 Educated and literate labour refer to a person in the economically active age group (16–63) listed as a household member, although not necessarily resident for at least 15 days out of the previous 30 days.

11 Information on group membership was gathered only in 1998, and the data for 1993 were recorded through a retrospective question. Obviously the memory and identity of the respondent is a potentially important source of error and it is likely that the 1993 figures have been understated.

12 A Chi square test shows a significant difference between the headship groups at the 0.05 level of confidence.

13 A Chi square test shows a significant difference between the headship groups at the 0.05 level of confidence.

14 For those that experienced shocks only, the Pearsons correlation statistics are 0.274 and 0.382 for the expense of the shock correlated with expenditure in 1993 and 1998 respectively, and 0.307 and 0.421 when the value of the lost item is correlated with expenditure. In both cases the correlation is significant at the 0.01 level.

15 While indicative, the comparatively small sample results in the means being statistically different only in the first of these results.

16 Shocks that were reported by less than 2 per cent of the sample have been excluded.

17 It also proved impossible to identify unambiguously any of the upward movers as households that were structurally poor in 1993 (by rejecting the hypothesis that they were non-poor) and structurally non-poor in 1998.

18 The Chi square test shows a significant difference between groups at the 0.05 level of confidence.

References

Alderman H, Watkins S, Kohler H, Maluccio J & Behrman J (2000) Attrition in longitudinal household survey data. *FCND briefs from International Food Policy Research Institute* (IFPRI) No. 96. Washington.

Ardington EM (1988) *Nkandla revisited: A longitudinal study of the strategies adopted to alleviate poverty in a rural community*. Rural Urban Studies Unit Working Paper No. 16. University of Natal: Durban.

Bane MJ & Ellwood DT (1986) Slipping into and out of poverty, the dynamics of spells, *Journal of Human Resources* 21(1): 1–23.

Bardhan P (1989) *The Economic Theory of Agrarian Institutions* Oxford: Clarendon Press.

Carter MR & May J (1999) Poverty, livelihood and class in rural South Africa, *World Development* 27(1): 1–20.

Carter MR & May J (2001) One kind of freedom: Poverty dynamics in post-apartheid South Africa, *World Development* 29(12): 198–2006.

Carter MR & Zimmerman F (2001) The dynamic costs and persistence of asset inequality in an agrarian society, *Journal of Development Economics* 63(2): 265–302.

Cleveland W, Devlin S & Grosse E (1988) Regression by local fitting: Methods, properties and computation algorithims, *Journal of Econometrics* 37: 87–114.

Dasgupta P (1997a) Nutritional status, the capacity for work, and poverty traps, *Journal of Econometrics* 22: 5–37.

Dasgupta P (1997b) Poverty traps. In D Kreps & K Wallis (eds) *Advances in Economics and Econometrics: Theory and Applications* Vol. 2: 114–159. Cambridge: Econometric Society Monograph, Cambridge University Press.

Davies S (1996) *Adaptable Livelihoods: Coping with Food Insecurity in the Malian Sahel*. London: Macmillan Press.

Hoff K, Braverman A & Stiglitz J (1993) *The Economics of Rural Organization*. Oxford: Oxford University Press.

Hout M (1983) *Mobility tables*. Beverley Hills: Sage.

Hunter N & May J (2002) *Poverty, shocks and school disruption episodes among adolescents in South Africa*. Centre for Social and Development Studies Working Paper No. 35. School of Development Studies, University of Natal: Durban.

Jenkins SP & Lambert PJ (1997) Three 'I's of poverty curves, with an analysis of UK poverty trends, *Oxford Economic Papers* 49(3): 317–328.

Klasen S (1997) Poverty and inequality in South Africa: An analysis of the 1993 SALDRU survey, *Social Indicators Research* 41: 51–94.

Lachaud JP (1994) *Pauvreté et marché du travail urbain en Afrique subsaharienne: Analyse comparative*. Geneva: International Institute for Labour Studies.

Leibbrandt M & Woolard I (1999) A comparison of poverty in South Africa's nine provinces, *Development Southern Africa* 16(1): 37–54.

Maluccio JA, Haddad L & May J (2000) Social capital and development in South Africa: 1993–1998, *Journal of Development Studies* 36(6): 54–81.

May J, Carter MR, Haddad L & Maluccio J (2000) KwaZulu-Natal Income Dynamics Study (KIDS) 1993–1998: A longitudinal household data set for South African policy analysis, *Development Southern Africa* 17(4): 567–581.

May J & Peters A (1985) A study of income and expenditure and other socio-economic structures in rural KwaZulu – Nqutu. KwaZulu Finance Corporation occasional publication, *Studies in Development* No. 5/85.

Moser C (1995) Urban social policy and poverty reduction, *Environment and Urbanization* 7(1): 159–171.

Muller N, May J & Krone A (1987) *Upper Tugela Base Line Data Study*. Development Studies Unit Report, University of Natal: Durban.

Øyen E (2002) Poverty production: a different approach to poverty understanding. Downloaded from http://www.crop.org/publications/files/report/Poverty_production.pdf on 13 October 2005.

Reardon T & Vosti SA (1995) Links between rural poverty and the environment in developing countries: Asset categories and investment poverty, *World Development* 23(9): 1495–1506.

Roberts B (2001) Chronic and transitory poverty in post-apartheid South Africa: Evidence from KwaZulu-Natal, *Journal of Poverty* 5(4): 1–28.

Ruggles P & Williams R (1989) Longitudinal measures of poverty: Accounting for income and assets over time, *Review of Income and Wealth* 35(3): 225–243.

Zimmerman F & Carter MR (1995) The microeconomics of induced institutional change: Asset markets as a displaced innovation. Mimeo.

10 Internal labour migration and household poverty in post-apartheid South Africa

Dorrit Posel and Daniela Casale

Introduction

The migrant labour system has been a key feature of the economic development of South Africa. Throughout the twentieth century, until the lifting of influx control legislation in the late 1980s, labour migration within the country was closely regulated (Murray 1981; Spiegel 1980; Nattrass 1976). Restrictions were placed on Africans concerning where they could migrate, for how long and with whom. African labour migrants were mostly not permitted to settle permanently at places of employment, nor could they migrate with spouses and family members. These restrictions, together with the contractual nature of urban employment, gave rise to patterns of circular or oscillating migration: many labour migrants would retain a base in the household from which they had migrated, to which they would return each year and which was their 'permanent' home.

Even though restrictions on African urbanisation were lifted by the late 1980s, nationally representative household survey data suggest that these migration patterns may be continuing in post-apartheid South Africa (Posel and Casale 2003). The first objective of this chapter is briefly to describe and discuss trends in labour migration over the period 1993 to 2002, using these household survey data. We show that a growing number of rural African households report labour migrants as (non-resident) household members and we discuss possible reasons why individuals may continue to migrate temporarily to places of employment.

Our second objective is to explore the economic status of those who remain behind in the household of origin. We find that total household income, on average, is significantly and consistently lower in migrant households than in non-migrant households. Remittance transfers are a more important source of income than the earnings of employed resident members in migrant households. Since 1993, however, both the receipt and the average real value of remittance income have fallen. We conclude our study with a discussion of factors that may account for this trend, and the possible development implications of migration for rural African households.

The analysis in this chapter is descriptive only, and using cross-sectional data it is difficult to disentangle causality between migration and access to resources: are households poorer because of migration, or are poorer households more likely to have or to need labour migrants? At the aggregate level, however, there is little to suggest that labour migration is associated with upward mobility among rural African households.

Internal labour migration patterns, 1993–2002

Since 1993, nationally representative household surveys have been conducted annually, and more recently bi-annually, in South Africa. Some of these surveys have asked questions specifically about 'migrant workers', defined as individuals who remain members of the household of origin but who are away for a period of time each year to work or to look for work. These individuals therefore represent, at least by definition, the 'traditional' temporary or circular labour migrants associated with apartheid South Africa. In Table 10.1 we summarise the extent of this migration, using information available in four cross-sectional household surveys: the 1993 Project for Statistics on Living Standards and Development (PSLSD), the 1997 and 1999 October Household Surveys (OHS) and the 2002 (September) Labour Force Survey (LFS).[1]

Between 1993 and 2002, labour migration within South Africa increased significantly in absolute terms. Most labour migration, and most of the increase in this migration, originated from rural areas where there are limited employment and income-generating opportunities (Aliber 2003; Bhorat and Leibbrandt 2001; May and Rogerson 2000). The analysis that follows in this chapter focuses, therefore, on rural African households. In 1993, approximately 33 per cent of all rural African households were migrant households; by 2002, this had increased to more than 38 per cent, representing an increase of over 300 000 households that reported at least one migrant worker as a household member.[2]

During the late 1980s, formal restrictions on internal African migration were lifted, making it possible for labour migrants to move with their families and to settle permanently at places of employment. A number of factors, however, may continue to discourage permanent (family) migration in the post-apartheid period. The risks attached to labour migration increase with high and rising levels of unemployment in the country (Bhorat 2004; Bhorat, Lundall and Rospabé 2002; Casale, Muller and Posel 2004), and the rural household may provide insurance in the context of growing labour market insecurity. Higher costs of living in urban settlements, and a preference to retire and be buried in a rural area (James 2001; Todes 1998) may further help explain why individuals continue to migrate 'temporarily'. The rural household may also play an important role in taking over care of young children, making it possible for working-age women in particular to move in search of work.

Table 10.1 *The extent of temporary labour migration across households, 1993–2002*

Households with migrant worker(s)	1993 PSLSD	1997 OHS	1999 OHS	2002 LFS
Number				
All households	1 469 279 (33 136)	1 610 084 (19 630)	1 779 818 (27 644)	1 875 986 (27 645)
African households	1 313 312 (30 195)	1 556 965 (19 371)	1 722 400 (27 344)	1 802 799 (27 220)
African rural households	1 170 210 (26 651)	1 287 481* (17 182)	1 418 364 (25 030)	1 497 504 (25 072)
Percentage				
All households	17.8 (0.41)	17.4 (0.22)	16.5 (0.25)	17.3 (0.26)
African households	22.5 (0.52)	23.1 (0.28)	21.6 (0.33)	22.1 (0.32)
African rural households	32.6 (0.72)	37.6* (0.45)	35.8 (0.54)	38.3 (0.55)

Notes: All data in the table are weighted. Migrants are aged 15 years and older.
Standard errors are given in parentheses.
* The coding of rural areas in the 1997 OHS is different from that in the other survey years, in which the data are coded so that 'rural' includes also semi-urban areas. In the 1997 OHS, Statistics South Africa coded the sample so that 'urban' included semi-urban areas, and there is insufficient information in the data to recode the sample for comparability. Because labour migration is likely to be greater from rural areas than from semi-urban areas, measures of labour migration from rural African households in 1997 are probably overestimated.

Historically, most labour migrants in South Africa have been men, but the increase in labour migration over the past decade has been driven specifically by the rise in female labour migration (Posel and Casale 2003). Data reported in Table 10.2 show that in 1993, just under 30 per cent of all African labour migrants were female, but by 2002, this had increased to approximately 37 per cent. The shift in the gender composition of labour migrants reflects a more general feminisation of the labour force in South Africa, where labour force participation rates have risen across all female age cohorts (Casale and Posel 2002). Women may continue to retain ties with and membership in their household of origin, particularly if children remain behind in the care of other household members.

Table 10.2 *African migrant workers by gender (15 years and older)*

Percentage of all migrant workers	1993	1997	1999	2002
Female	29.6	32.4	33.7	37.2
Male	70.4	67.6	66.3	62.8
Total	100.0	100.0	100.0	100.0

Note: The data are not weighted.[3]

However, it may be that what is identified in household surveys as temporary migration in fact signals the permanent out-migration of individuals. In a case study of migration between the Eastern Cape and Western Cape areas in 1997–98, for example, Bekker (2001) found that few migrants were reported to have returned permanently to rural sending areas: while many new migrants expressed their intention to return, this desire weakened with length of stay in the destination area (see also Van der Berg, Burger, Leibbrandt and Mlatsheni (2004) on Eastern Cape – Western Cape migration patterns).

Table 10.3 *Remittances received in rural African migrant households*

	1993	1997	1999	2002
Percentage of migrant households receiving remittances	78.5 (1.15)	84.2 (0.56)	85.4 (0.69)	76.4 (0.77)
Average yearly nominal value of total remittances received by the household (rands)	3 246.13 (91.051)	3 990.72 (54.119)	—	4 069.80 (100.43)
Average yearly real value of total remittances received by the household (rands, 2000 prices)	5 598.25 (148.776)	4 728.341 (64.121)	—	3 526.69 (87.03)

Notes: Remittance values are conditional on remittances being received in migrant households.
The data are weighted.
Standard errors are given in parentheses.

Certainly, more research is needed to investigate questions of return migration. Nonetheless it is significant that the majority of migrant households also report receiving remittance transfers (Table 10.3), suggesting that most individuals who are identified as migrant household members retain ties and specifically economic ties with their household of origin.

Between 1993 and 1999, the proportion of rural African migrant households that received remittance transfers increased; by 2002, however, this proportion had fallen considerably. Furthermore, although the average value of remittances (conditional on a positive transfer) increased in nominal terms over the period, in real terms[4] it fell consistently from 1993.[5] There is therefore some suggestion that economic ties between migrants and households of origin may be weakening over time. We consider this trend further in the next section, where we explore the economic characteristics of migrant households.

The economic characteristics of migrant households

The literature on migration broadly identifies two different scenaria associated with the effects of migration on the economic development of 'sending' or migrant households. On the one hand, many studies provide examples of migration promoting investment and development in sending communities (see, for example, Taylor and Wyatt 1996; Adams 1991; Stark 1980, 1991), largely through the contribution of remittance transfers. Remittance income may make it possible for households to overcome credit or risk constraints on income-generating activities, allowing households to adopt new technologies and increase productivity (Taylor and Wyatt 1996; Stark 1980).

On the other hand, some studies suggest that although remittances support consumption, they do not provide a firm basis for sustaining this consumption in the future. Rather than migration facilitating investment and development, it is associated with an increasing dependence of rural households on remittance income (see Irfan 1986; Lipton 1980; Rempel and Lobdell 1978).

The dominant view of labour migration in South Africa is that it has contributed to agricultural decline in sending areas. At the same time as migration deprived households of labour needed for agricultural production, migrant workers were paid below-subsistence wages and the costs of reproducing labour had to be subsidised by the rural household (Beinart 1980; Wolpe 1972).

A few studies, however, have identified that a more positive role can be played by migrant remittances in rural economies of the southern African region (Morapedi 1999; Sharp and Spiegel 1990). In his study of migration in Botswana, for example, Morapedi (1999: 198) argues that

> [d]espite low pay and its exploitative nature, migrancy contributed to the acquisition of production inputs on the part of poor peasants, with the result that it raised their economic and social positions above those of their contemporaries who did not migrate.

In this section, we begin to explore the economic 'consequences' of labour migration in South Africa over the past decade, given the constraints imposed by the availability and comparability of national household survey data. We are not able to investigate the economic outcomes of migration for the migrants themselves. Labour-market conditions deteriorated in the first decade after apartheid, with both average real earnings and the probability of finding employment declining (Bhorat 2004; Casale et al. 2004). However, there are no data available on the earnings and employment of labour migrants specifically.[6]

Our study therefore investigates the economic status of those who 'remain behind' in the migrant household, and we compare the economic resources of households with migrants to those without. Because national household data are cross-sectional, we cannot identify the impact of migration more directly by examining the household's access to resources before and after migration. Furthermore, given differences in the quantity and quality of information collected on economic status across the years, we are limited even in the comparison of consecutive cross-sections. Of the four household surveys where data on migration are captured in the migrant household (or household of origin), only two (the 1993 PSLSD and the 1997 OHS) also provide information on total income in the household (both earned and non-earned).[7] We would also expect within-survey comparisons of reported income to be more reliable than those across the two surveys.

As Table 10.4 illustrates, in both years for which there are data, reported aggregate income in migrant households is on average significantly lower than in non-migrant households. In 1997, the gap in reported economic status between these household types is also considerably larger than in 1993. In 1993, the ratio of average income in migrant and non-migrant households was above 0.8; in 1997 it was approximately 0.6.

Table 10.4 *The economic status of migrant and non-migrant rural African households*

	1993	1997
Total real income **(earned + non-earned income, rands per month, 2000 prices*)**		
Migrant households	1 010.00 (30.8)	951.44 (21.55)
Non-migrant households	1 139.27 (26.26)	1 573.15 (29.88)
Household size (number of resident adult equivalents)		
Migrant households	4.736 (0.073)	4.630 (0.035)
Non-migrant households	3.997 (0.049)	4.299 (0.028)
Adult equivalent real monthly income (rands, 2000 Prices)		
Migrant households	265.60 (9.45)	232.62 (5.58)
Non-migrant households	395.03 (9.94)	482.75 (10.79)
Poverty (R410 per adult equivalent per month, 2000 prices)		
Migrant households (%)	84.17 (1.03)	85.6 (0.52)
Non-migrant households (%)	71.06 (0.89)	55.9 (0.58)
Ultra-poverty (R172 per adult equivalent per month, 2000 prices)		
Migrant households (%)	54.22 (1.39)	54.6 (0.74)
Non-migrant households (%)	40.21 (0.96)	28.6 (0.53)

Notes: The data are weighted.
Standard errors are given in parentheses.
Non-earned income includes remittances as well as income from state transfers, private insurance and pensions.
* Income values are converted into real values using the Consumer Price Index (CPI) published by Statistics South Africa. In 1993, 1997 and 2002, the CPI was equal to 61.2, 84.4 and 115.4 respectively, with 2000 as the base year.

In migrant households, a smaller income is also 'shared' among a larger number of resident household members. Differences in the economic well-being of migrant and non-migrant rural African households are therefore more pronounced when expressed in per capita or adult equivalent terms. In 1997, average adult equivalent income in non-migrant households was more than double that in migrant households.

Rural African households in post-apartheid South Africa continue to be disproportionately represented amongst the poor (Woolard and Leibbrandt 2001: 60; Carter and May 1999). Table 10.4 shows that rural African households with labour migrants are even more likely to be income-poor than those without. Furthermore, although it is difficult to identify a trend using only these data, there is the suggestion that this gap has widened over time.

There is no commonly used or agreed-upon poverty line in South Africa. We describe poverty using two absolute lines – the first is the per adult equivalent Household Subsistence Level (HSL) line, set by the Institute for Development Planning Research at the University of Port Elizabeth, of R251.10 per month at 1993 prices (Woolard and Leibbrandt 2001: 49) and R410 at 2000 prices. The second line, used by some agencies to make international comparisons, is a 'dollar a day' line, equivalent to a monthly R172 per adult equivalent at 2000 prices,[8] and could be thought of as identifying the 'ultra-poor'.

In both 1993 and 1997, the majority of all rural African households, whether they contained labour migrants or not, reported an average adult equivalent income below the HSL. However, the incidence of income poverty is clearly larger in migrant households – in 1997, for example, more than 80 per cent of these households could be defined as poor, compared to slightly over half of non-migrant households.

The extent of income poverty is also more severe in migrant households – poor migrant households are more likely to be ultra-poor than poor non-migrant households. In 1997, 65 per cent of those rural African migrant households with income below a 'household subsistence level' were in fact subsisting on the equivalent of less than a dollar a day, compared to approximately 52 per cent of poor non-migrant households.

The lower economic status of migrant households corresponds to clear differences in household composition and sources of income across the two broad household types. Although migrant households are larger than non-migrant households, they contain a comparable number of working-age resident adults on average, but a significantly smaller number of these adults report employment. As shown in Table 10.5, therefore, the lower aggregate income in migrant households is associated particularly with smaller earned income.

Table 10.5 *Employment and earned income in migrant and non-migrant rural African households, 1993–2002*

	1993	1997	2002
Number of resident working-age adults in:			
Migrant households	2.787	2.589	2.414
	(0.049)	(0.025)	(0.029)
Non-migrant households	2.581	2.719	2.319
	(0.033)	(0.019)	(0.023)
Number of resident *employed* working-age adults in:			
Migrant households	0.404	0.279	0.427
	(0.020)	(0.009)	(0.014)
Non-migrant households	0.998	0.734	0.858
	(0.017)	(0.010)	(0.016)
Total earned real income (rands per month, 2000 prices) in:			
Migrant households	421.40	328.58	329.21
	(27.79)	(19.82)	(21.74)
Non-migrant households	877.53	1028.50	889.48
	(26.17)	(25.93)	(24.74)

Notes: The data are weighted.
Standard errors are given in parentheses.
Working-age adults are women aged 16–59 years and men aged 16–64 years.

An obvious explanation for fewer resident employed adults in migrant households is that at least one (absent) member of the household is employed, or looking for employment, elsewhere. Income from the migrant's employment is received (and recorded) in the household not as earnings but as remittances, and as Table 10.6 illustrates, rural African migrant households are more likely to report remittances than earnings as their main source of income support.[9]

Table 10.6 *Main source of income support in rural African households (2002)*

Percentage of households for which the main source of income support is:	Migrant households	Non-migrant households
Remittances	36.3	9.1
Earned income	22.5	53.9
Pension	34.3	25.7
Other	6.9	11.3
Total	100.0	100.0

Note: The data are weighted.

Remittances sent by migrants are only a share, or a fraction, of what migrants earn, at the least because migrants incur living costs at places of employment. But individual remittances received in rural households are also significantly smaller than what rural (resident) Africans with employment earn. In both 1997 and 2002, average individual remittances were less than a quarter of average earnings in rural areas (Table 10.7).

Migrants tend to be older and better educated than non-migrants.[10] Because rural earnings increase positively and strongly with education and age, we would expect migrants' predicted earnings, *ceteris paribus* and conditional on their finding employment, to be even larger than actual earnings reported by rural African adults. These arguments would suggest, therefore, that had individuals not migrated, but remained in the rural area and found employment, all else being equal, average adult equivalent income in migrant households would have been considerably greater.[11]

To assume that all migrants would find rural employment, and further that there would be no general equilibrium implications of this employment, however, is particularly inappropriate given the nature of rural labour markets in South Africa. In fact, very high unemployment in rural areas is likely to be a key factor necessitating or encouraging labour migration in the first place (see Table 10.7). But the descriptive comparison suggests the potential contribution to the rural household's resources of expanded rural employment relative to labour migration.

Table 10.7 *Individual remittances and earnings among rural Africans*

	1997	2002
Monthly average individual remittances (rands)		
Nominal	269.91	264.97
	(3.28)	(5.48)
Real (2000 prices)	319.79	229.60
	(3.88)	(4.75)
Monthly average earnings in rural areas (rands)		
Nominal	1 243.48	1 272.21
	(21.78)	(26.73)
Real (2000 prices)	1 473.32	1 102.43
	(25.81)	(23.16)
Unemployment rates in rural areas (16 years and over)[12]		
Searching	30.22	34.08
	(0.464)	(0.506)
Non-searching	52.38	52.69
	(0.417)	(0.449)

Notes: Individual remittance data are not weighted.
Standard errors are given in parentheses.
Average remittances and earnings are calculated conditioned on positive remittances and earnings.

The exercise also highlights a key difficulty in evaluating the development implications of migration – we do not know how households would have fared had labour migration not occurred. Households with migrants are clearly poorer than households without, but migrant households may have been even poorer had there not been migration. Because nationally representative data are cross-sectional, we also cannot track changes over time in the economic well-being of migrant households. Nonetheless, for each cross-section of the rural population there is little suggestion that labour migration is associated with economic prosperity.

The key mechanism through which labour migration would be expected to promote rural development is through the contribution of remittance income. Although most migrant households receive remittances, this income is not sufficient to pull households out of poverty. Furthermore, between 1993 and 2002 both the receipt and the real value of remittance transfers fell.

A number of changes in the institutional environment may be relevant in accounting for a decline in remittance transfers. More insecure employment and a greater probability of becoming unemployed may increase the incentives for migrants to retain a rural alternative. But growing labour market insecurity and falling average real wages could mean that migrant workers are less able to afford remittances. In this case, and as Sharp (2001: 156) identifies in a study of migrants in Cape Town, it will be those migrants who have achieved 'some form of modest security in the city' who can sustain rural relationships (see also Sporton, Thomas and Morrison's 1999 study of migration in the Kalahari).

The increase in the coverage and the value of the social pension, paid to all age- and means-qualified individuals, may also have reduced the (perceived) need for migrants to remit income (Jensen 2003; Posel 2001).

Case-study research suggests further that falling remittances may reflect different investment choices made by migrants. In his study of two migrant communities in the Northern Province (now Limpopo), for example, Baber (1996: 293) writes that investment in livestock has been reduced as 'alternative savings instruments, such as pension and other savings policies with the major financial institutions have become more familiar to migrants'. Bank's (2001: 144) research on migrants in Duncan Village in the Eastern Cape identifies women migrants preferring 'to invest their income in clubs and commodities rather than directly in the rural economy', in part because the former are seen to be better investments.

An earlier study by Sharp and Spiegel (1990) of two migrant communities located in the old Bantustan regions along the rural periphery in South Africa illustrates how the investment environment may influence the development implications of labour migration.

In the one community, Matatiele, Sharp and Spiegel found that many village residents still had access to a wide variety of resources, including arable land. In contrast, the residents in the other community, Qwaqwa, had 'no agricultural resources; nor ... despite the density of habitation, [did] they have access to any of the facilities normally associated with urban townships' (Sharp and Spiegel 1990: 529).

In Qwaqwa, remittances received were lower than those received in Matatiele: 'Since none of them had access to land they did not remit lump sums to fund cultivation' (Sharp and Spiegel 1990: 545). In Matatiele, migration was associated with more positive development outcomes. The existence of arable resources, to which many households had direct access, 'meant that there was a whole sphere of income-generating activity for women to which men lent positive support (through remittances)' (Sharp and Spiegel 1990: 531).

Where there are few options for investment, migrants therefore may send remittances for consumption but they may make alternative investment decisions. In this case, poor migrant households could remain caught in a poverty trap, where remittance transfers are simply consumed.

Conclusion

The pattern of 'temporary' migration from rural areas in search of work that characterised the apartheid era appears to have remained an important feature of the post-apartheid decade. Using household survey data from 1993 to 2002, we find that an increasing proportion of African rural households reports non-resident members who are labour migrants.

It is possible that what is captured as 'temporary' migration in the household surveys is in fact permanent out-migration from rural areas, and more research on questions of return migration is needed. Nonetheless, labour migrants continue to be identified by the household of origin as household members, and the survey data indicate that most migrants do retain economic ties with these households through remittance transfers.

Notwithstanding the income support received from absent members, the majority of African migrant households in rural areas are found to be poor. They are also significantly more likely to be poor than non-migrant rural households. Although there are across-survey comparability concerns, there is some further suggestion that the income gap between migrant and non-migrant households may be widening over time.

While it is not known how migrant households would have fared if a member had not left to search for work elsewhere, there is little descriptive evidence that migration has been effective in lifting rural African households out of poverty.

The evidence summarised in the last section of this chapter suggests the importance of institutional interventions that would increase opportunities in rural areas – as a means of both expanding resident employment opportunities and increasing incentives for migrants to invest part of their earnings in rural development.

Notes

1   See Posel (2003) for a detailed discussion of how data on migrant workers are captured in these surveys.

2   The average number of labour migrants per rural African household also increased from a mean of 0.489 (0.014) in 1993 to a mean of 0.592 (0.011) in 2002 (standard errors in parentheses).

3   These data could not be weighted because there are no *individual* weights for migrant workers in either the 1997 and 1999 OHSs or the September LFS 2002. In these surveys, weights at the individual level are available only for the total resident population, and migrants are captured 'outside' the resident household roster. Where the data are reported at a *household* level, however, the weighted figures are presented, as weights for households that report migrant workers exist for all the years under review (Posel and Casale 2003).

4   The estimated real value of income in rural areas may be underestimated here. Incomes have been converted into real values using the Consumer Price Index (CPI) published by Statistics South Africa, and the CPI covers only metropolitan and urban areas in South Africa (Hoogeveen and Özler 2004). However, it seems highly improbable that nominal remittances kept pace with even more modest rural price increases over the period.

5   Unlike the 1993 and 2002 surveys, the 1997 and 1999 OHSs collected information only on income remitted and not also on remittances sent in kind. The value of total remittances in 1997, and remittance receipt in both 1997 and 1999, therefore will be underestimated. However, in-kind remittances form a significantly smaller part of the total value of remittances (approximately 13 per cent and 7 per cent in 1993 and 2002 respectively); moreover, their inclusion in the intervening years would only serve to reinforce the fall in 2002.

6   Most of the available household surveys in South Africa do not collect detailed information on the labour migrant at the household of origin. This is not surprising, given that labour migrants are non-resident members of the household and respondents are unlikely to provide reliable information, particularly about their earnings. The surveys also do not identify labour migrants in the destination household so that it is not possible to distinguish migrant workers from other labour force participants. The one exception is the 1995 OHS, but here labour migrants cannot be matched to the household of origin. Furthermore, a much lower number of migrant workers was found using the 1995 data, which suggests that when identified in the destination household, a different sample of migrant workers is being captured (Posel and Casale 2003).

7   The information on total household expenditure in these surveys also could not be used here because of concerns about the reliability and comparability of the data. Whereas the 1993 PSLSD collects detailed expenditure information, total expenditure in the other surveys is based on a single question which contains only a very brief prompt on what should be included in the estimate by the respondent. Detailed expenditure information is collected in the 1995 and 2000 Income and Expenditure Surveys, which can be linked to the 1995 OHS and the 2000 LFS, but neither of the latter household surveys collects migrant information. See Casale and Desmond (2004) for further discussion of problems involved in measuring economic status using nationally representative household survey data in South Africa.

8   Woolard and Leibbrandt (2001: 49) give this line as R105 per capita per month at 1993 prices. We used this figure flexibly as an adult equivalent measure and scaled the amount up to 2000 prices.

9   Pension income is a key source of support in migrant households, corresponding to there being significantly more adults of pensionable age in migrant households. One explanation consistent with these characteristics is that the social pension facilitates migration, by helping individuals overcome constraints (both income and time) to this migration (Posel, Fairburn and Lund 2004).

10   In 2002, for example, the average age of working-age Africans employed in rural areas and of migrants was approximately 39 years and 43 years respectively. Fewer than 10 per cent of labour migrants were reported as having no schooling, compared to almost 20 per cent of employed rural Africans; the percentages for completed Grade 12 are the exact reverse.

11   It is not possible to estimate this using the data available. Information on the value of individual remittances from each migrant is collected only in the 1997 OHS and the 2002 (2) LFS. However, the 1997 survey does not include a question on the age of the migrant, which is a key variable that would predict the migrant's wage. Although this information is available in the 2002 survey, it is not possible to measure total household income in this survey.

12   While the data indicate that there was not much change in rural unemployment rates between 1997 and 2002, urban unemployment rates did increase significantly over the same period: from 28.24 (0.41) to 39.26 (0.45) according to the strict definition and from 40.63 (0.40) to 47.17 (0.43) using the broad/non-searching definition (standard errors in parentheses). That there has been a rise in urban unemployment, and searching unemployment in particular, is consistent with increased migration from rural areas in search of work in urban areas.

References

Adams RH (1991) The economic uses and impact of international remittances in rural Egypt, *Economic Development and Cultural Change* 39(4): 695–722.

Aliber M (2003) Chronic poverty in South Africa: Incidence, causes and policies, *World Development* 31(3): 473–490.

Baber R (1996) Current livelihoods in semi-arid rural areas of South Africa. In M Lipton, M de Klerk & M Lipton (eds) *Land, labour and rural livelihoods in rural South Africa*, Vol. 2. University of Natal: Indicator Press.

Bank L (2001) Living together, moving apart: Home-made agendas, identity politics and urban-rural linkages in the Eastern Cape, South Africa, *Journal of Contemporary African Studies* 19(1): 129–147.

Beinart W (1980) Labour migrancy and rural production: Pondoland c.1900–1950. In P Mayer (ed.) *Black villagers in an industrial society*. Cape Town: Oxford University Press.

Bekker S (2001) Diminishing returns: Circulatory migration linking Cape Town to the Eastern Cape, *SA Journal of Demography* 8(1) 2001–2002: 1–8.

Bhorat H (2004) The labour market in post-apartheid South Africa: A brief overview. Development Policy Research Unit, Policy Brief No. 04/P2, University of Cape Town.

Bhorat H & Leibbrandt M (2001) Correlates of vulnerability in the South African labour market. In H Bhorat, M Leibbrandt, M Maziya, S van der Berg & I Woolard (eds) *Fighting poverty: Labour markets and inequality in South Africa*. Cape Town: UCT Press.

Bhorat H, Lundall P & Rospabé S (2002) The South African labour market in a globalising world: Economic and legislative considerations. Employment paper 2002/32, International Labour Organisation, Geneva.

Carter MR & May J (1999) Poverty, livelihood and class in rural South Africa, *World Development* 27(1): 1–20.

Casale D & Desmond C (2004) The economic well-being of the family: Households' access to resources in post-apartheid South Africa. Forthcoming in A Amoateng & L Richter (eds) *Families and Households in Post-Apartheid South Africa*. Cape Town: HSRC Press.

Casale D, Muller C & Posel D (2004) 'Two million net new jobs': A reconsideration of the rise in employment in South Africa, 1995–2003, *South African Journal of Economics* 72(5): 978–1002.

Casale D & Posel D (2002) The feminisation of the labour force in South Africa: An analysis of recent data and trends, *The South African Journal of Economics* 70(1): 156–184.

Hoogeveen JG & Özler B (2004) Not separate, not equal: Poverty and inequality in post-apartheid South Africa. Unpublished manuscript, World Bank.

Irfan M (1986) Migration and development in Pakistan: Some selected issues, *The Pakistan Development Review* 24(4): 743–755.

James D (2001) Land for the landless: Conflicting images of rural and urban in South Africa's Land Reform Programme, *Journal of Contemporary African Studies* 19(1): 93–109.

Jensen R (2003) Do private transfers 'displace' the benefits of public transfers? Evidence from South Africa, *Journal of Public Economics* (88): 89–112.

Lipton M (1980) Migration from rural areas of poor countries: The impact on rural productivity and income distribution, *World Development* 8(1): 1–24.

May J & Rogerson C (2000) The spatial context. In J May (ed.) *Poverty and inequality in South Africa: Meeting the challenge*. Cape Town: David Philip.

Morapedi WG (1999) Migrant labour and the peasantry in the Bechuanaland Protectorate, 1930–1965, *Journal of Southern African Studies* 25(2): 197–214.

Murray C (1981) *Families divided. The impact of migrant labour in Lesotho*. Cambridge: Cambridge University Press.

Nattrass J (1976) The migrant labor system and South Africa's economic development, *South African Journal of Economics* 44(1): 65–83.

Posel D (2001) How do households work? Migration, the household and remittance behaviour in South Africa, *Social Dynamics* 27(1): 165–189.

Posel D (2003) Moving out of the household and out of the household questionnaire: The coverage of labour migration in national surveys in South Africa (1993-2001), *Development Southern Africa* 20(3): 361–368.

Posel D & Casale D (2003) What has been happening to internal labour migration in South Africa, 1993–1999? *The South African Journal of Economics* 71(3): 455–479.

Posel D, Fairburn J & Lund F (2004) Labour migration and households: A reconsideration of the effects of the social pension on labour supply in South Africa. Unpublished manuscript, University of KwaZulu-Natal.

Rempel H & Lobdell RA (1978) The role of urban-to-rural remittances in rural development, *Journal of Development Studies* 14(3): 324–341.

Sharp J (2001) Review Article. Copperbelt and Cape Town: Styles and rural connections in comparative perspective, *Journal of Contemporary African Studies* 19(1): 149–158.

Sharp J & Spiegel A (1990) Women and wages: Gender and the control of income in farm and Bantustan households, *Journal of Southern African Studies* 16(3): 527–549.

Spiegel A (1980) Rural differentiation and the diffusion of migrant labour remittances in Lesotho. In P Mayer (ed.) *Black Villagers in an industrial society.* Cape Town: Oxford University Press.

Sporton D, Thomas D & Morrison J (1999) Outcomes of social and environmental change in the Kalahari of Botswana: The role of migration, *Journal of Southern African Studies* 25(3): 441–459.

Stark O (1980) On the role of urban-to-rural remittances in rural development, *Journal of Development Studies* 16(3): 369–374.

Stark O (1991) *The migration of labour.* Massachusetts: Basil Blackwell.

Statistics South Africa (2001) *South Africa in transition: Selected findings from the October Household Survey of 1999 and changes that have occurred between 1995 and 1999.* Pretoria: Statistics South Africa.

Taylor JE & Wyatt TJ (1996) The shadow value of migrant remittances, income and inequality in a household-farm economy, *The Journal of Development Studies* 32(6): 899–912.

Todes A (1998) Gender, place, migration and regional policy in South Africa. In A Larsson, M Mapetla & A Schlyter (eds) *Changing gender relations in Southern Africa: Issues of urban life.* Lesotho: The Institute of Southern African Studies and the National University of Lesotho.

Van der Berg S, Burger R, Leibbrandt M & Mlatsheni C (2004) Migration and the rural-urban interface in South Africa: What can we learn from census and survey data? Paper presented at workshop on Migration and Poverty, Stellenbosch, 4 March 2004.

Wolpe H (1972) Capitalism and cheap labour power in South Africa: From segregation to apartheid, *Economy and Society* 1(4): 425–456.

Woolard I & Leibbrandt M (2001) Measuring poverty in South Africa. In H Bhorat, M Leibbrandt, M Maziya, S van der Berg & I Woolard (eds) *Fighting poverty: Labour markets and inequality in South Africa.* Cape Town: UCT Press.

11 Half-measures revisited: The ANC's unemployment and poverty reduction goals[1]

Charles Meth

Introduction

A recently published paper by Ravi Kanbur posed 'some hard questions about growth, inequality and poverty'. Prominent among them is that of

> ...what exactly it is that we are buying into when we accept the number one Millennium Development Goal of the United Nations – halving the incidence of income poverty by the year 2015 (Kanbur 2004: 1).

The question is of more than passing interest in South Africa, committed as the country is to meeting the Millennium Development Goals (MDGs).[2] In addition, the social partners in South Africa (government, business and labour) have committed themselves to halving unemployment. The target year for meeting these goals is the year 2014, the 20th anniversary of the advent of democracy in South Africa. These laudable aims featured prominently in the most recent general election; at the head of a list of 'Some of the most important targets and objectives making up Vision 2014' in the 2004 election manifesto of the African National Congress (ANC) we find:

- Reduce unemployment by half through new jobs, skills development, assistance to small businesses, opportunities for self-employment and sustainable community livelihoods.
- Reduce poverty by half through economic development, comprehensive social security, land reform and improved household and community assets (African National Congress 2004: 8).

It is unreasonable to expect an election manifesto to spell out precisely what all of its aspirations entail. For purposes of the monitoring and evaluation of performance that must take place, however, greater precision is necessary. This chapter looks behind the manifesto, at policy and other documents, in an attempt to discover what is understood by these commitments. Finding little evidence of a considered view, the chapter delves into unemployment and poverty statistics in South Africa in an attempt to see whether or not greater precision than that displayed so far in specifying each of these targets is possible. In each case, the search opens a window overlooking an impressively wide plain of ignorance. In view of this, the chapter ends with some recommendations about what to do about the two commitments made in the election manifesto.

The chapter's limitations must be stated at the very outset. It does not concern itself unduly with the question of whether proclaiming commitment to the 'halving' targets is a good or a bad thing. The attempt it makes to evaluate progress towards the achievement of these goals is perfunctory. In the case of the poverty target, the chapter focuses primarily on income poverty, doing so in full awareness of the fact that approaches that have the reduction of income poverty as their sole end have long since slipped into disfavour.[3] There is, however, virtue in looking at income poverty – as long as one does not lose sight of the fact that it is one aspect of what is a complex multi-dimensional problem.

Government's position on 'halving': Unemployment

From pronouncements made by senior politicians, it is possible to infer that when it comes to halving unemployment, government has in mind the official rate of unemployment.[4] It is not easy, though, to find an explicit statement to this effect. First port of call in the search for greater specificity was the 'programme of action' on the government website. Informative though it undoubtedly is, the programme of action is devoted, however, to medium- and short-term targets. There is nothing on the unemployment goal under the Economic, Investment and Employment cluster, and nothing on poverty reduction under the Social cluster.[5] That avenue being closed, the next set of documents consulted were those prepared for, and emerging from, the ANC's 51st National Conference in December 2002. For our purposes, the most important among these were two papers prepared for the National Policy Conference held in September 2002 to formulate views to be taken forward to the National Conference. These papers (African National Congress 2002a and 2002b) outlined economic and social policy in a way that shaped the resolutions adopted at the National Conference. References to poverty and unemployment abound in each paper. Neither of them, however, quantifies the problem in such a way as to facilitate the drafting of resolutions that set clear and comprehensible targets. Of course, information on poverty and unemployment (particularly the latter) was widely available elsewhere. Even so, the omission of any discussion of feasible targets in the background papers could have hampered delegates whose access to, and understanding of, the nature of both problems was limited.

Given the silence of the background papers on the matter, it comes as little surprise to find no specific poverty reduction target in the place where one would expect to find it, namely, the resolutions adopted by the 51st National Conference of the ANC on Social Transformation, in the section headed 'On Attacking Poverty and Comprehensive Social Security' (African National Congress 2002c). None of the 13 resolutions adopted refers to any poverty reduction target. Likewise, the place to find an unemployment target, one would have thought, would have been among the 12 resolutions in the section 'Unemployment & Under-employment' in the resolutions on Economic Transformation. It is not there; instead it is to be found in the 'Appendix to Economic Resolutions: Comments on Key Performance Indicators for Outcomes: Employment'. In the Appendix, 'The unemployment rate' (which rate is not specified) is one of the key performance indicators identified. Below the list of indicators is a paragraph of comments, the first sentence of which reads, 'We want to halve the current level of unemployment by 2014.'

Since '[t]he unemployment rate' (which one is not stated) is to serve as a key performance indicator, it seems safe to assume that 'level' means 'rate of unemployment'. Attempts to find a more specific commitment have not proved successful. The unemployment reduction target agreed upon at the Growth and Development Summit of 2003 (GDS) is very similar to the ANC conference resolution. Paragraph 2.2.1 of the GDS Agreement states simply that '[t]he constituents aim to halve unemployment by 2014' (Nedlac 2003). This succeeds, by virtue of its failure to indicate whether the goal is the rate of unemployment, or the number of unemployed, in being even less communicative than the ANC conference resolution. There is no indication of which of the two measures of unemployment – the official or the expanded – the constituents had in mind. Establishing that outcomes will differ when one, rather than the other, of these possible goals is chosen, is the work of but a few moments. That being so, it may seem a little surprising that greater effort was not devoted to achieving clarity. It may have been feared or suspected that an attempt to do so at the Summit, a step that would, inevitably, have exposed the large differences between different targets, would lead to serious disagreement. Difficult as it may be to believe, it is also possible that people simply took it for granted that if one form of unemployment is halved, the other(s) would follow suit. For the framers of the resolution to halve unemployment, the most attractive candidate would have been the 'official' rate, a target that is appealing both because of its official (i.e. internationally accepted) status and because the official rate, being so much lower than the expanded rate, would appear to be easier to halve. Further speculation on this matter is pointless – interviews with participants in the discussions would be necessary to settle the question.

Someone, somewhere, however, is or has been working on the question. The website of the Expanded Public Works Programme (EPWP), a relative newcomer on the scene, informs us that

> [t]o reach government's target of halving unemployment by 2014 (i.e. reducing the unemployment rate from 30% to 15%) 546,000 new jobs would have to be created each year – 276,000 more than has hitherto been the case.[6]

From this, one may infer that it is the official rate of unemployment which is to be halved. The statement is repeated in a paper by the person in charge of the EPWP, Dr Sean Phillips, Chief Operations Officer in the National Department of Public Works. The paper in question was delivered at a recent conference called 'Overcoming underdevelopment in South Africa's second economy'.[7] As his source for these figures, Phillips cites Statistics South Africa's September 2003 Labour Force

Survey (LFS) (Phillips 2004: 1). An examination of that document discloses it to be entirely innocent (as one would expect) of such information. At the time of writing, the source remains unknown.[8]

So much for the likely target; discovering which year is to constitute the base against which to measure progress in the attempt to halve unemployment is also not straightforward. The statement taken from the Appendix to the Resolutions of the 51st National Conference of the ANC suggests that it could be the year 2002. The official rate of unemployment was 25.8 per cent in September 2000, and 30.2 per cent in September 2002. By September 2003, it had dropped back to 28.2 per cent.[9] Given the volatility of the numbers, it is not unduly pedantic to request some clarity on this matter.

Government's position on 'halving': Poverty

Poverty eradication rather than mere reduction, an ambitious goal,[10] exercised the minds of those who attended the Copenhagen World Summit on Social Development in 1995. Paragraph 25 of the Programme of Action published after the Copenhagen gathering said that there was an urgent need for

> [n]ational strategies to reduce overall poverty substantially, including measures to remove the structural barriers that prevent people from escaping poverty, with specific time-bound commitments to eradicate absolute poverty by a target date to be specified by each country in its national context…

In Paragraph 26, governments were urged to give

> greater focus to public efforts to eradicate absolute poverty and to reduce overall poverty substantially by (inter alia): …elaborating, at the national level, the measurements, criteria and indicators for determining the extent and distribution of absolute poverty. Each country should develop a precise definition and assessment of absolute poverty, preferably by 1996, the International Year for the Eradication of Poverty.

In the Programme of Action there is a guideline for developing a precise definition of poverty. Absolute poverty, it says, is

> a condition characterized by severe deprivation of basic human needs, including food, safe drinking water, sanitation facilities, health, shelter, education and information. It depends not only on income but also on access to social services. (Paragraph 19, Chapter 2)

In the year 2000, the UN Millennium Declaration added dates and specific targets to the Copenhagen exhortation.[11] Participating governments committed themselves

> [t]o halve, by the year 2015, the proportion of the world's people whose income is less than one dollar a day[12] and the proportion of people who

suffer from hunger and, by the same date, to halve the proportion of people who are unable to reach or to afford safe drinking water. (United Nations 2000a)

South Africa was committed to the Copenhagen Programme of Action – the Minister of Social Development reaffirmed this in the year 2000.[13] Numerous statements affirming South Africa's commitment to the MDGs, made at the World Summit on Sustainable Development in Johannesburg in 2002, can be found. Once again, however, it is not clear what base year the state has in mind for setting its poverty reduction goal. If poverty has been increasing, the year 2000 may be a more attractive base year than 2002, or 2004.[14]

Although the MDGs are quite specific, confusion has still managed to arise within the South African government. In its *Strategic Plan for the years 2002/03–2004/05* the Department of Social Development states that

> [t]he challenge for the Department is to ensure that its short term and medium term poverty relief and poverty alleviation measures contribute towards the Millennium Goal of *halving the number of people* who live in extreme poverty by 2015. (Department of Social Development 2002. Emphasis added)

Misunderstandings of this sort are likely to give rise in the future to the sort of acrimonious debate that took place in the run-up to the 2004 election over the extent of job creation between 1995 and 2002.[15] If goals are not agreed upon with greater precision than is evident above, disparities between actual outcomes and people's understanding of them (loosely worded as they are) could be the cause of considerable strife. In the absence of a clear statement of what, precisely, the goals are, commentators on the economy have already begun to insert their own interpretations into the discourse. Professor Sampie Terreblanche, for example, having done this, is adamant that the poverty and unemployment reduction targets, as he understands them, will not be met. It is interesting to note, in the passage cited below, that Professor Terreblanche assumes it is the expanded rate of unemployment that is to be halved. In any event, here he is in full cry, after having berated the ANC for being unwilling to acknowledge during its election campaign that '…the poverty problem has become more severe over the past decade', and after claiming that 'more than 48 per cent of the population – or 22 million – live under the poverty line'.[16]

> 'The ANC election manifesto,' he says, 'promises that poverty and unemployment will be cut by half over the next 10 years. This implies that by 2014 only 24 per cent of the population will live below the poverty line and that unemployment will be cut from 42 per cent to 21 per cent of the labour force. These goals are completely unattainable, especially if the government is to stick to its economic approach of neo-liberalism and free marketeerism.

'Owing to the sharp increase in the population over the past 20 years, the potential labour force will have 3 million more people in 2014 than at present. To cut unemployment to 21 per cent will necessitate the creation of almost 7 million new jobs. That is impossible.'[17]

The date when these chickens come home to roost lies quite far in the future – the fact that the article contains estimates of conditions at that distant point implies that the figures must have been cranked out by a model of some sort. Some critical assumptions have to be made in order to convert unemployment reduction targets into 'numbers of jobs'. There are two major determinants of the level of unemployment that operate independently of the number of jobs created or destroyed. One of these is mentioned in the article cited above: the growth of the working-age population (roughly, those between the ages of 15 and 64 years). The other is the growth of the participation rates – the proportion of the working-age population that is either working or is unemployed (according to either of the two definitions of unemployment, the official or the expanded). Participation rates can, and do, grow at different rates, depending upon the numbers of former workseekers who become 'discouraged'.

Without access to Professor Terreblanche's calculations, it is not easy to see how he arrived at his results. If he had used the same data as those used in the simulations reported on below (for the period 2003–14), then a growth rate of 1.5 per cent per annum for the working-age population, coupled with a static participation rate, would have been associated with a target of seven million jobs to meet the unemployment reduction target. The problem is that the working-age population grows in this scenario by 5.3 million.[18] There is an important lesson to be learned from this experience, one that flows from the fact that making assumption about the values these variables take is unavoidable. The lesson is the following: if rational debate is going to take place, the assumptions used to arrive at any conclusion have to be spelled out in detail so that (a) their plausibility may be considered, and (b) the results may be replicated. This is of particular importance in dealing with 'difficult to predict' numbers such as these. We consider below the sorts of assumption that have to be made to deal with problems of this nature, and then present a possible set of outcomes based upon these assumptions.

Halving unemployment

Either of the two forms of unemployment measured by the official statistics – that according to the 'official' definition, which counts as unemployed only those actually seeking work, or that according to the expanded definition (the officially unemployed plus the 'discouraged' or 'non-searching unemployed'), could have been specified as the goal. Although the evidence suggests that it is a rate that is targeted, it would also be possible to target the numbers of unemployed. Discovering what 'halving' implies, if it is taken to mean reducing the number of unemployed to half their total at some date, is simplicity itself – simply divide the relevant total by two. The arithmetic involved in trying to determine the numbers by which unemployment totals have to be reduced if it is the rate of unemployment that is to be halved, is not much more difficult. The presence, however, of two unknowns – the rate of growth of the population of working age (the potentially economically active population) and the participation rates – about which recent history is not very forthcoming, makes the always difficult job of guessing what the future holds, more difficult still. The only way to guess at this future is to build a model capable of generating scenarios under a wide variety of assumptions about the values that these unknowns might take. In order to discover the feasible ranges these variables might occupy, it is necessary to consider their past behaviour.

Unemployment: The basic data

Table 11.1 summarises the position as portrayed in the official statistics. The lines across the table below the 1999, September 2002, September 2003 and March 2004 results signify discontinuities of varying degrees of significance. In the case of the 1999 figures, the break was caused by the changeover from the October Household Survey (OHS) to the LFS as the main instrument for collecting data on labour market activity. The break after September 2002 arises because the March 2003 and September 2003 LFS results have been weighted to the 2001 population census results, whereas the earlier LFS and the OHS figures are weighted to the 1996 Census. The March 2004 LFS contains a series of minor adjustments to the September 2003 results. Although the size of the working-age population remained the same, the numbers of unemployed, and hence the numbers of economically active, according to both definitions, rose.

Revised mid-year population estimates, necessitated by the production of new mortality figures, saw the September 2004 LFS revise the March 2004 figures, thus introducing another break in the series. As the penultimate column in the table shows, this last revision was substantial, cutting the working-age population by almost 1.3 million. Re-benchmarking of earlier surveys is currently under way at Statistics South Africa (SSA). Until such time as the revised series becomes available, researchers are advised to proceed with caution.

The most remarkable features of the table are (a) the almost five-percentage point increase in participation rates between 1995 – and 1999, (b) the break in the series at 1999/2000 which sees the official and expanded participation rates increase by ten and eight percentage points respectively, and (c) the steady decline in the official participation rate between February 2000 and September 2004.

Table 11.1 *Participation rates and the working-age population*

	Participation rates (percentage)		Working-age population		Official non-participation rate (percentage)	Discouraged as percentage of official economically active population
	official	expanded	(thousands)	percentage change		
Oct. 96	46.7	56.2	24 657	–	53.3	20.3
Oct. 97	46.6	57.5	25 112	1.85	53.4	23.5
Oct. 98	48.8	58.4	25 710	2.38	51.2	19.7
Oct. 99	51.5	61.8	26 280	2.22	48.5	20.1
Feb. 00	61.3	69.7	26 455	–	38.7	13.7
Sept. 00	58.7	67.9	26 894	1.66	41.3	15.7
Feb. 01	59.3	69.3	27 121	0.84	40.7	16.9
Sept. 01	56.1	67.7	27 364	0.90	43.9	20.7
Feb. 02	58.3	69.6	27 673	1.13	41.7	19.5
Sept. 02	56.7	67.7	27 984	1.12	43.3	19.5
Mar. 03	56.9	67.6	29 555	–	43.1	18.9
Sept. 03	54.1	66.7	29 917	1.22	45.9	23.2
Sept. 03	54.4	67.2	29 917	–	45.6	23.5
Mar. 04	54.5	67.0	30 429	1.71	45.5	22.9
Mar. 04	54.3	67.2	29 131	–	45.7	23.8
Sept. 04	53.8	67.3	29 305	0.60	46.2	25.0

Source: LFSs and OHSs for the relevant periods
Note: See file 'Unempl_(1996–2001).xls', available from the author on request.

If the 1995–99 increase in the participation rate is not a statistical artefact caused by under-measurement of informal and subsistence agricultural employment, then a possible explanation for the bulge in participation rates in the late 1990s could lie in rapid population growth and pent-up demand for additional years of schooling in the early 1990s (along with other aspects of the social transition described in the *Ten Year Review* (PCAS 2003)). Those effects, however, must long since have worked their way through the system.

It is clearly better collection of statistics, rather than any major structural change, that accounts for the jump in activity rates at the 1999/2000 break (the working-age population, it will be observed, increases by a little less than the 'appropriate' amount). There was an unprecedented increase of 2.7 million in the number of economically active individuals, according to the official (strict) definition. The average for all other years (October to October for the OHSs, or September to September for the LFSs) is about 420 000.[19] The 2.7 million consist of 1.2 million additional officially unemployed, 1.2 million subsistence agricultural workers and about 200 000 domestic workers. Most other employment changes are trivial. To suggest, as the first LFS does, that there could have been an increase in the number of subsistence agricultural workers from an improbably low 300 000 in October 1999 to a plausible 1.5 million in February 2000 (only to fall back to an unbelievable 360 000 by September 2001) is to stretch the imagination beyond breaking point. Both low figures simply have to be incorrect.

On average, the number of officially unemployed grew by about 340 000 or so annually over the period 1996–2002. The changeover from the OHS to the LFS yields a figure almost four times greater than that average.[20] When the first LFS results were published, SSA included in the publication an appendix in which a number of ways of reconciling the OHS and LFS unemployment totals were considered (Statistics South Africa 2001: 12–13). The unemployment total that finally makes its way into the official statistics for the month of February 2000, 4 333 000, is one of several that could have been used. After adjustment, it can be reduced to 3 545 000. Instead of continuing the series with the relevant adjustments built into it, SSA chose to use the definition that produces the higher figure. Some large part of the increase between October 1999 and February 2000 is therefore accounted for by this change. In other words, there is a radical discontinuity in the unemployment series at this point – the number of officially unemployed did not actually increase from 3 158 000 in October 1999 to 4 333 000 in February 2000, nor did the official rate of unemployment suddenly jump from 23.3 to 26.7 per cent. The break in the series makes it impossible to compare the numbers.

For all practical purposes, the apparent increase in participation rates from 1996 to 2000 can be ignored – it is extremely unlikely to have happened. This means that the explanation trumpeted by the government in its *Ten Year Review* for the increase in unemployment rates, the 'fact' that 'the economically active labour force grew by about 4% although the population growth was only 2% per year' (PCAS 2003: 96) is almost certainly wrong.[21]

Prior to the publication of the September 2004 LFS, it seemed possible that the LFSs were picking up about two million more economically active individuals than the OHSs. The most recent revisions to the figures allow us to make a guess at growth rates of the economically active population that is possibly more reliable than previous estimates. The revisions push the March 2004 economically active population, according to both the official and the expanded definitions, down by approximately 800 000 (the 'new' March 2004 official figure is lower than the 1996 population-weighted figure for September 2002). Although it might be possible to re-estimate population sizes for the years immediately preceding the 2001 population census (there is an unavoidable element of arbitrariness in the choice of year prior to 2001 in which to stop using 2001 weights and to use 1996 Census weights instead), it is going to be very difficult to navigate around the discontinuity at 1999/2000. Although the 'true' story of the behaviour of the estimates of the economically active population in this critical period of South Africa's history can never be told, it is not unreasonable to assume that the 1996 OHS under-counted informal economy workers and subsistence producers, possibly by as many as 1.5 million (a modest estimate). If that were the case, then the implied growth rate of the economically active population over the period 1995–2004 would have been somewhere in the region of about 2.7 per cent per annum. This may have been greater than the rate of job creation (and the rate of population growth), but not by so much as to be responsible for any significant proportion of the tremendous surge in the numbers of unemployed.

The third feature in Table 11.1 that attracted our attention was the fall in the official participation rate after the LFS was introduced in February 2000. Can the figures be trusted? It is clear that estimates of the absolute size of the workforce in the period with which we are concerned cannot. Must the same be said about ratios such as the participation rate estimated from the now discredited absolute numbers? One assumes that since it is only the weights that will be changing, the answer to this question is that the ratios will not be too badly affected.[22] If this assumption is reasonable, then the LFSs will have uncovered a disturbing social phenomenon that is all the more remarkable for having gone unremarked thus far. The fall in the official participation rate between February 2000 and September 2004 is an astonishing 7.5 percentage points. If it is not appropriate to compare the 1996-weighted results with the 2001-weighted figures, the decline between February 2000 and September 2002 is a still not inconsiderable 4.6 percentage points. The problem in South Africa is thus apparently not one of participation rates outstripping both population growth rates and job creation growth rates, but, at least as far as the official participation rate is concerned, a rising official non-participation rate (100 minus the official participation rate) after the year 2000. This is accompanied by, and partly caused by, an increase in the ratio of the discouraged (non-seeking) unemployed to the officially economically active. In short, although the proportion of the working-age population wanting to work has fallen slightly since the year 2000, the proportion of people actively involved, either working or seeking work, has apparently fallen precipitously.[23]

One of the determinants of future participation rates might be the rate of growth of the working-age population (the potential workforce). To see how the latter is likely to behave, an examination of its history, and of the literature on its future, is necessary (even though history is often a poor guide to the future). There are two ways (at least) to gain access to its history. The first of these uses the results published in the LFSs. Inter-censal figures pop out of a demographic model, ready for insertion into the LFSs. Scanning the figures in Table 11.1, it would seem that the number of people of working age grows by about 600 000 to 700 000 per annum. The breaks in the table remind us, however, that estimating the size of the working-age population by this method is not plain sailing. In part, this is because the availability of revised population census figures means that existing estimates have to be revised as well. The 2001 Census figures have twice inflicted grievous bodily harm on existing series. The first instance may be seen by comparing the September 2002 and September 2003 figures. Instead of the half-million or so new people of working age one would have expected in the absence of a revision, the first attempt at revising the estimates to take account of the 2001 Census results in a jump of almost two million in the working-age population. The second instance may be seen by comparing the September 2004 and September 2003 estimates of the size of the working-age population. As has been noted above, the re-benchmarking process will almost certainly drive the existing September 2003 estimate, and all previous estimates, downwards.[24] If we believe the 1996 estimate of the size of the working-age population, then the growth rate of the potential workforce in the period 1996–2004 was about 2.4 per cent per annum.[25]

The other way to discover the history of the growth of the working-age population is to consult the AIDS model built by ASSA, the Actuarial Society of South Africa. This device also allows the researcher to peep into the likely future of the variable. It is not a happy story. Two sets of projections are made by the model, one labelled 'change' and the other 'no-change'. Changes in individual behaviour and institutional practice can lower mortality. One set of projections thus refers to possible outcomes if nothing changes, while the other predicts outcomes if a specified set of changes does take place. Their publication 'Actuarial Projection of the Epidemic: Summary Statistics' states quite clearly that there is no presumption that the necessary changes will, in fact, take place. The estimate of the growth rate of the working-age population over the period 1996–2003 from the ASSA model (2.3 per cent per annum) is very close to that estimated above from the LFS data (2.4 per cent per annum). For the period 2003–14, the AIDS epidemic bites deeply into population growth. In the 'change' scenario, the growth rate for working-age males is 0.05 per cent per annum, while that for females is –0.1 per cent per annum. This yields an overall growth rate of –0.04 per cent per annum. For the 'no change' scenario, the figures are –0.03 for men, –0.2 for women, to give an overall rate of –0.12 per cent per annum.[26]

To guesstimate the numbers that may be involved if unemployment is to be 'halved', one has to engage in a little simulation. To do that, it is necessary to assume boundary values for the growth rates of the variables discussed above. In the face of the confusion spelt out above, it is clear that the estimates of the values that the variables at issue might take over the period ending in 2014 must be, at best, one part science and nine parts guesswork. What might happen to participation rates and to the size of the potential workforce (the working-age population) in the future is anybody's guess. The best that one can do is to ensure that the guesswork is as well informed as possible.

To accommodate the many possible outcomes, the results of two runs made on a simple simulation model are presented below. The two runs span what could be regarded as a pair of extremes, one optimistic, the other pessimistic. In the optimistic runs, the impact of AIDS on the size of the workforce is either ignored (Run 1, Scenario 1), or muted (Run 1, Scenario 2). In the pessimistic runs, Run 2, Scenario 1 differs from Run 2, Scenario 2 in being more pessimistic about the growth rates of participation and of the working-age population. Because of the criticism that the ASSA model has attracted (a charge that its results are unduly pessimistic), the working-age population growth rates assumed in Run 2, although small, are both positive. This stands in strong contrast to the ASSA figures reported above, which are negative for both the 'change' and the 'no-change' model variants. If anything, therefore, the Run 2 assumptions may err on the side of generosity.

In Run 1, Scenario 1, it is assumed that the trend of the participation rate to decline continues. Although unlikely, such an outcome is not impossible. Run 1, Scenario 2, the story of what might have been in the absence of the AIDS epidemic (a useful counterfactual for highlighting the human cost of this tragedy), assumes that the working-age population carries on growing as it did in the period 1996–2003. It also assumes that desperation drives people back into the labour market, thereby reversing somewhat the fall in participation rates observed over the period 1996–2004. This applies to both the official and the expanded participation rates. In all other scenarios, the expanded participation rate is assumed to be stationary, or close to stationary.

Run 2, Scenario 1 assumes a weak response in the official participation rate to the rapid fall in the growth rate of the working-age population. Run 2, Scenario 2, by contrast, assumes that people bestir themselves more energetically (recall here the speculation above that the growth rate of the working-age population might be a determinant of the participation rate). It could well be that as death carries off an increasing number of the potentially economically active, those who survive might be driven (if not AIDS-sick) to a more active job search because perceived probabilities of finding employment have improved.

The boundary values selected for Run 2 serve to demarcate the area within which it is thought that the true values of these variables might lie. Although they 'feel' feasible, they are not cast in stone – anyone who disagrees can easily substitute figures that are believed to be more appropriate.[27]

To judge whether or not the 'halving unemployment' goal has been met, some base period figures are required. If unemployment rates are changing rapidly, the outcome will be sensitive to the choice of base period. The GDS at which the 'halving unemployment' goal was formally adopted took place in June 2003. One possible candidate is thus the latest set of figures available at the time that the commitment was made. The relevant base period figures would be those for September 2002. Another possibility is the latest set of figures available at the time that the ANC resolved to 'halve the current level of unemployment by 2014'. Those would be the February 2002 figures, published in September 2002.[28]

Between March and September 2003 the numbers of unemployed, according to the official definition, fell. By how much they fell depends on which set of September figures one uses. It was either 680 000 or 623 000 (from 5.25 million in March 2003 to 4.57 million or 4.63 million in September 2003).[29] Since there was not a similar fall in the number of expanded unemployed (by the first set of results the number fell from 8.4 to 8.3 million; by the second it was roughly the same at 8.4 million in March and September), the fall in the official unemployment rate from 31.2 to 28.2 (or 28.4) per cent is accounted for mainly by an increase in the number of discouraged unemployed.[30]

Regardless of what the 'correct' unemployment totals might be, being required to halve a rate of 28.2 (or 28.4) per cent is easier than being required to halve one in excess of 30 per cent. From the policy-maker's point of view, the September 2003 figures are thus the more attractive. To give the benefit of the doubt to those prone to boasting about the great strides made towards the achievement of the 'halving' goal, the September 2003 figures are used in the simulations whose results are presented in Table 11.2. The September figures are used in the simulations, because unlike the February figures, they are less susceptible to the effects of the flood of new entrants to the labour market at the beginning of the year.[31]

Unemployment halving simulation results

In order of appearance, Table 11.2 presents the baseline statistics (Rows 1–4) first. The assumed values of the two variables that generate Scenarios 1 and 2 are given next (Rows 5–10). Then come the increases in the size of the working-age population and the number of economically active, implied by the assumed rates of growth of these variables (Rows 11–16). Following these are the results of attempts to halve either the official or the expanded rates of unemployment (Rows 17–32). There are figures for the reductions in the numbers of unemployed required to yield the various 'halvings' (Rows 17–20).

Then we have the changes that government policy has found most difficult to facilitate, the increases in employment required to deliver the various 'halvings' (Rows 21–24). After that come the estimates of the numbers of people still unemployed after 'halving' has been achieved (Rows 25–28).

Finally, in the rate-halving section of the table, we give the expanded unemployment rates that would obtain in 2014 (under the given assumptions) if the goal of halving the official rate were prosecuted successfully (Rows 29–30), and the official rate of unemployment if the expanded rate were halved. Below this, in Rows 33–42, is a set of estimates of what might happen if, instead of aiming at halving the rate of unemployment, policy were directed (if such a thing were possible) to halving the numbers of unemployed (either official or expanded), a much more ambitious goal.

Table 11.2 *'Halving' unemployment by 2014 – some possibilities*

Base year results – unemployment in September 2003		Run 1	Run 2
1	Official unemployment rate (%)		28.4	
2	Expanded unemployed rate (%)		42.0	
3	No. of officially unemployed (millions)		4.6	
4	No. of expanded unemployed (millions)		8.4	
Assumptions				
5	Growth rate of working-age pop. (%/annum)	Scenario 1	1.0	0.3
6		Scenario 2	2.4	0.5
7	Growth of official participation rate (%/annum)	Scenario 1	–0.1	0.1
8		Scenario 2	0.3	0.3
9	Growth of exp. participation rate (%/annum)	Scenario 1	0.0	0.0
10		Scenario 2	0.2	0.1
Increase in working-age population, 2003–2014 (millions)				
11		Scenario 1	3.5	1.0
12		Scenario 2	8.9	1.7
Increase in number of economically active, 2003–2014 (millions)				
13	Official definition	Scenario 1	1.5	0.9
14		Scenario 2	6.1	2.0
15	Expanded definition	Scenario 1	2.3	0.7
16		Scenario 2	6.8	1.5
Reduction in no. of unemployed to halve unemployment rate by 2014 (millions)				
17	Scenario 1	Official	2.1	2.2
18		Expanded	3.7	4.1
19	Scenario 2	Official	1.4	2.0
20		Expanded	2.8	3.9
Required increase in no. employed to halve unemployment rate by 2014 (millions)				
21	Scenario 1	Official	3.6	3.1
22		Expanded	6.1	4.8
23	Scenario 2	Official	7.6	4.0
24		Expanded	9.6	5.4
Number of unemployed in 2014 (millions)				
25	Halving the rate of unemployment: Scenario 1	Official	2.5	2.4
26		Expanded	4.7	4.4
27	Halving the rate of unemployment: Scenario 2	Official	3.2	2.6
28		Expanded	5.7	4.5
Expanded rate of unemployment after official rate has been halved (2014)				
29	Scenario 1		31.9	29.1
30	Scenario 2		28.6	27.5

→

Official rate of unemployment after expanded rate has been halved (2014)			Run 1	Run 2
31	Scenario 1		0.5	4.4
32	Scenario 2		5.0	6.6
Rate of unemployment after number of unemployed has been halved by 2014 (%)				
33	Scenario 1	Official	13.0	13.5
34		Expanded	18.8	20.3
35	Scenario 2	Official	10.3	12.7
36		Expanded	15.7	19.6
Required increase in no. employed to halve no. unemployed by 2014 (millions)				
37	Scenario 1	Official	3.8	3.2
38		Expanded	6.5	4.9
39	Scenario 2	Official	8.4	4.3
40		Expanded	11.1	5.7
Number of unemployed in 2014 (millions)				
41	Halving the number of unemp.: Both scenarios	Official	2.3	
42		Expanded	4.2	

The job is tackled by working through the Run 1 figures (the might-have-beens) in some detail. Having done that, it becomes a relatively simple matter to contrast the optimistic population growth outcomes (with their huge job creation challenges) with the pessimistic population growth outcomes and their more modest challenges. Surprisingly, as we shall see, AIDS does not, as has sometimes callously been argued, 'solve' the unemployment problem.

By inspection we may see that halving the unemployment rates requires that the official rate fall to 14.2 per cent (Row 1), and the expanded rate to 21 per cent (Row 2). Halving the number of officially unemployed would require a fall of 2.3 million in their number (Row 3). To halve the number of expanded unemployed, their number would need to fall by 4.2 million (Row 4).

Rows 11 and 12 give the first hint of obstacles that would have had to be faced. It has been argued above that over the period 1996–2004, the growth rate of the working-age population was probably about 2.4 per cent annum. On average, the size of the working-age population increased by about 580 000 per annum. If growth in the period 2003–14 had continued at the previously observed rate (Scenario 2), about 811 000 people on average each year would have joined the potential workforce. This is shown in Row 12, where we observe that the working-age population would have grown by 8.9 million. Slow growth in the working-age population (Scenario 1) sees its size increase by a modest 300 000 or so per annum on average (Row 11).

With the modest Scenario 2 increase in the official participation rate (the three percentage point recovery this would produce over a decade is much smaller than the drop over the period 2000–04), the increase in the number of economically active would have been a hefty 6.1 million (Row 14).[32] In the face of this possibly harsh reality, any comfort that might have been drawn from the small numbers by which (official) unemployment has to fall in order to achieve the halving goal would have evaporated. Under Scenario 2 conditions (the fast labour force growth option), the total number of officially unemployed would have needed to fall by only 1.4 million (Row 19) over the period to halve the rate, apparently the easiest of targets. The Scenario 1 assumptions push this up a little, to 2.1 million (Row 17). Behind such seemingly easily attainable targets, however, would have lain some quite formidable employment creation tasks. Possible sizes of this burden, obviously a function of the rate of growth of the workforce and the participation rate, are shown in Rows 21–24. These figures give the numbers of jobs that would have to be created in order to get unemployment rates down to the desired levels.

The Scenario 1 conditions (slow growth of the potential workforce and a slight decline in participation rates) would have set the easiest employment targets. Creating 330 000 jobs per annum (the Row 21 figure divided by 11) may be possible. On average, halving the expanded unemployment rate would have required 550 000 jobs to be created each year (Row 22), a task that is probably beyond the capacity of the economy. Had the Scenario 2 conditions obtained, almost 8 million jobs (Row 23) would have had to be created in a decade to halve the official rate of unemployment.

Numbers of unemployed in the year 2014 for each of the halvings discussed above are given in Rows 25–28. At best, there would still have been 2.5 million officially unemployed (Row 25) and, at worst, some 5.7 million unemployed according to the expanded definition (Row 28). Corresponding to the latter numbers is a set of unemployment rates in 2014, in Rows 29–30. These show what the expanded rate would have been if the goal were a halving of the official rate. Hovering near the 30 per cent mark, such a blight would surely be intolerable some 20 years after the advent of democracy in South Africa.

More acceptable official rates of unemployment would result if the goal were to be a halving of the expanded rate of unemployment. Rows 31–32 have official unemployment all but disappearing. Unfortunately, the job-creation miracle that would have been required to produce an outcome of that sort (the 6.1 or 9.6 million jobs listed in Rows 22 and 24) is highly unlikely to have been forthcoming. Halving the official rate of unemployment is seen to leave behind it an unacceptably high residue of misery. Halving the number of unemployed (Rows 33–42) would have more than halved unemployment rates in both scenarios (Rows 33–36), and would have reduced the numbers of unemployed (Rows 41–42) below the numbers achieved by a rate-halving (Rows 25–28). The number of jobs that would have been required to achieve this would have climbed to 11.1 million (about 1 million jobs per annum) in the worst case (Row 40).[33]

So much for Run 1. The Run 2 results are a mixed bag. Growth in the numbers of economically active is small, because of the minuscule growth in the size of the working-age population (Rows 11–16). Reductions in the numbers of unemployed required to halve the unemployment rates (Rows 17–20) are slightly larger than those obtained in Run 1.[34] At 3.1 million and 4.0 million respectively in Scenarios 1 and 2 (Rows 21 and 23), the job-creation efforts required to halve the official unemployment rate are moving into the feasible range. Creating somewhere between 280 000 and 360 000 jobs per annum, even if not all are quality jobs, should be possible. After the necessary jobs have been created, however, the numbers of people unemployed remain high (Rows 25–28). What is more, the expanded rate of unemployment after the official rate has been halved is still close to 30 per cent (Rows 29–30).

It seems likely that the government's concern is primarily with the officially unemployed. In the body of the text of the *Ten Year Review*, for example, when unemployment totals are discussed, it is only the officially unemployed to whom reference is made, and then only once (PCAS 2003: 36). The composite index of economic participation specifically excludes the discouraged (the non-searching) unemployed, stating that '... this group is no longer considered economically active ...' (PCAS 2003: 126). Yet shortly before this, in the list of performance indicators, one finds under the heading 'Employment', 'Number employed, broad definition, (alternate) Percentage unemployed, broad definition.' (PCAS 2003: 119). What 'broad definition' has to do with employment is not clear, nor indeed is the reason for the sudden appearance of the 'broad' definition of unemployment.[35]

Clearly, if a goal has to be specified, then from the point of view of feasibility of attainment a halving of the official rate of unemployment is the most sensible, if not the most humane, candidate. Its achievement would require somewhere between 3.1 and 4.0 million jobs to be created (Rows 21 and 23), the number of officially unemployed would fall by between 2.2 and 2.0 million (Rows 17 and 19) between 2003 and 2014, and there would be between 2.4 and 2.6 million people officially unemployed in 2014 (Rows 25 and 27). The political problem, as pointed out above, would be the fact that after the target had been met, there would still be between 4.4 and 4.5 million unemployed according to the expanded definition (Rows 26 and 28), with rates of unemployment in the region of 28–29 per cent (Rows 29 and 30). Although somewhat lower than the figures obtained under the 'optimistic' Run 1 conditions, these outcomes are still unacceptable.

Which of the indicators of unemployment causes the most alarm and despondency (or bears witness to the worst suffering) is not known. One could hazard the guess that it is the absolute number that is most distressing.[36] The matter is, however, more complex than is suggested by the figures in the table. This is because the incidence of unemployment is probably as important as its magnitude. A simple example illustrates this. Consider two households with comparable dependency rates and comparable access to social grants. Let one of them be a multiple-adult household, two of whose members are employed and one of whom is unemployed, and the other, a single-adult household where the adult is unemployed. The former will almost certainly be better off than the latter. Although the distribution of the unemployed among households of different types is known, it is not possible (or, at least, not easy) to build a model that will predict which households will be favoured by spurts of job creation. The looming presence of all the unknowns discussed above, overshadowed by an AIDS epidemic whose incidence (in occupational terms) cannot be predicted with sufficient accuracy, makes an already difficult job that much harder. It is likely that much of the burden will fall on households least able to cope: workerless households, households whose members are poorly educated, households without access to the social networks so necessary to the functioning of the labour market, households far from centres of growing economic activity, and so on. In other words, much of the burden of such unemployment as remains after the official rate has been halved is likely to fall upon society's weakest households.

Whatever the government's intentions, the analysis above suggests strongly that making a political commitment to a goal, the achievement of which is at the mercy of three variables whose magnitude cannot be predicted with any accuracy, may not be such a clever thing to do. As has been shown, the magnitude of the undertaking depends on the rate of growth of the working-age population (the potential workforce) and the growth of the two participation rates, with the outcome in the target year determined by the performance of these over time, and by that of the third variable, the actual rate of job creation. If the detractors of the ASSA model are proved to be right, then the number of jobs that would have to be created to achieve the unemployment-halving goal would probably be beyond the capacity of the economy, at any plausible growth rate, to deliver. If, as seems likely, something like the ASSA predictions comes to pass, then the goal may be achieved, but only because millions of people have died an early death. Even after this decimation, the absolute number of unemployed would remain unacceptably high. It is time for the social partners to reconsider their commitment. With that in mind, we turn to the 'halving' poverty goal.

Halving poverty

In this section of the chapter, we commence with a glance at the state of existing academic studies. Hampered by paradoxical shortages of appropriate data (paradoxical because there are now more household survey data available than ever before), these studies languish in a state of relative impotence to help address the nation's most pressing problem. Having glanced at the literature, we take a brief look at the contradictions (the antinomies) of definition and measurement. The assumption that a shared commitment to poverty eradication will somehow produce agreement on even the most basic of the steps that has to be taken is shown to be naïve. This is followed by an overview of the steps that the government has taken to gauge the extent of the poverty problem in South Africa, and of its attempts to monitor progress in the fight against this social evil. Widespread criticism of the government's failure to stem an alleged increase in poverty and inequality, its numerous policies and programmes notwithstanding, has provoked a defensive response, visible in official publications and in speeches by senior politicians. This polarisation bodes ill for the fight against poverty. It is almost with relief that we turn from this to a discussion on some of the technical hazards of estimating income poverty. The difficulties, however, as will be seen below, are formidable. Having mapped out the minefield through which the estimator must travel, some estimates of the numbers of poor in South Africa, based on research I have recently undertaken (Meth 2004b), are presented. These form the basis of an attempt to gauge the size of the problem of halving, by the year 2014,[37] the proportion of South Africa's people that is absolutely poor.

In the academic world, the MDGs (with their dollar-a-day definition of the income part of absolute poverty) are beginning to attract increasing attention. The goal itself has come under scrutiny by Kanbur (2004), Maxwell (2004a; 2004b), and Clemens, Kenny and Moss (2004), as has the likelihood of countries achieving it (Hanmer and Naschold 2003). Accepting the MDG of halving 'by the year 2015, the proportion of the world's people' that is absolutely poor, Deaton (2003a) has offered a comprehensive analysis of ways in which MDGs could (should) be monitored. In the present chapter we climb no further up Deaton's proposed list of steps than the questioning of the appropriateness, in South Africa's case, of starting '... from the $1993 PPP poverty lines in Chen and Ravallion (2001)...' (Deaton 2003a: 362). Instead, it is proposed that in the absence of an official poverty line to identify the absolutely poor in South Africa,[38] a poverty line proposed by Deaton himself (1997) and applied to the 1993 SALDRU/World Bank data set, be used. The reasons for this will become clear as we proceed. As noted above, we also restrict ourselves mainly to income poverty, in full awareness of the artificiality of doing so – as everybody knows, poverty is multi-dimensional. Limiting ourselves in this way means that the estimates of the numbers of poor presented may well understate the real extent of poverty, something that ought be borne in mind before indulgence in premature congratulation at the extent of poverty reduction is contemplated.

Poverty: Definition, measurement, monitoring and politics

As will have been gathered from the summary above of the concerns of this section of the chapter, the measurement of poverty and the monitoring of anti-poverty programmes and policies are beset by more than mere technical and managerial problems. Behind these problems is a struggle over the extent of redistribution required to eradicate poverty. To put the matter crudely, those on the 'left' argue that significant redistribution is necessary – on the 'right', the preferred option is to limit redistribution to some minimum, and to rely for the rest on the workings of the market to lift the poor out of their poverty. Sandwiched awkwardly between the demands of the have-nots and their champions, and the defenders of (as much as possible of) the status quo as far as the distribution of income and wealth is concerned, is the government (which, of course, is not without strong views of its own on the matter).

Since the ANC's major constituency is supposed to be the poor, the government goes to great lengths to reel off statistics on the magnanimity of redistributive policies introduced, or reinforced and deracialised, since its accession to power. This trumpet-blowing has, however, to be done in such a way as not to antagonise the well-off too much. It must be reassuring for this jittery audience to hear the stand taken by government against such proposals as the Basic Income Grant (BIG). The President's repeated (and unfounded) assertion of the 'dependency' that would inevitably result from extensions of the social grant system to adults must be music to the ears of conservatives. The struggle over the form of anti-poverty policy is the context within which the problems of definition, measurement and monitoring must be understood.

POVERTY STUDIES IN SOUTH AFRICA: THE CURRENT STATE OF AFFAIRS

In the discussion on halving unemployment, it was argued that, without a clear specification of the target, confusion must reign. The same applies to the goal of 'halving' poverty, although, as has been argued above, it is possible, at least for a while, for the government to take refuge from its critics in the confusion. The poverty studies in South Africa that should be able to inform us of the progress (or lack thereof) in the fight against poverty are not in good shape. They are beset by two separate but related problems. It is not easy to say which is the more serious of them. The first is concerned with the absence of a rigorous distinction between the conceptualisation, definition and measurement of poverty. These terms feature in the title of a recent paper by Noble, Ratcliffe and Wright (2004), one that argues for a consensual approach to the problem. Critically examining some of the more prominent poverty studies in South Africa (most of which are referred to in the present chapter), the Noble et al. piece (pp.15ff) discloses slippage between the three necessary stages of conducting a poverty study. Giving examples of cases where 'measurement...does not follow from a concept and definition employed', they argue that

> [c]urrent South African poverty studies tend predominantly to be based around subsistence income or expenditure measures which do not neces- sarily have any firm definitional or conceptual underpinnings.... . (Noble et al. 2004: 18)

The second problem is that the studies themselves have to work with data which, in some respects (for example, sample frames) have improved over time, but in others (weighting, non-response rates) have deteriorated. Within the limitations described by Noble et al. (2004) there exists a reasonably reliable[39] set of poverty estimates for 1995, a year or so after the advent of democracy in South Africa. Based, as Noble et al. point out, on subsistence expenditure measures, these estimates use the information in the 1995 IES, the 1995 OHS and the 1996 Census (Woolard and Leibbrandt 2001). Much had been hoped for from the results of the long-awaited IES for the year 2000. The 2000 IES should have made it possible to gauge the extent of poverty (and inequality) in that year. This would have provided a report card on progress (or the lack of it) during the first five years of democratic rule. The SSA publication based on the IES, *Earning and spending in South Africa*, suggested substantial increases in income and expenditure poverty (Statistics South Africa 2002b: 29). The income share of the bottom quintile of households was also found to have fallen (Statistics South Africa 2002b: 46). Unfortunately, this analysis, which should have been authoritative, was so bedevilled by problems that its findings have been widely criticised, not least by the government. In the wake of the failure of the 2000 IES to deliver definitive answers on poverty and inequality, the public debate has sometimes floundered in a morass of poorly supported assertions. These emanate both from those who claim poverty and inequality have worsened and from those who deny that this is so.[40]

Extensive work has been done by SSA on the 2000 IES to repair (to the extent that it is possible to do so) its major deficiencies: faulty weighting of the survey results, and non-response – the latter occurring especially among better-off households. The debate will take another lurch forward when the revised figures are published. Out of this work of reconstructing the 2000 IES results has flowed a much-discussed paper, which although widely circulated, was hitherto non-quotable and non-citable (Hoogeveen and Özler 2004).[41] The paper, which was the subject of heated controversy, and recently received the public imprimatur of no less a luminary than Angus Deaton,[42] will probably become part of the received wisdom on this question in South Africa. The authors find that both poverty, especially extreme poverty, and inequality increased over the period 1995–2000. They report that

> [f]or any poverty line below 322 Rand per capita per month, the poverty gap and poverty severity (poverty gap squared) indices are significantly higher in 2000 than they were in 1995. These increases in poverty accompanied positive expenditure growth that was statistically insignificant. (Hoogeveen and Özler 2004: 10–11)

Inequality among the population as a whole fell slightly, but it rose among the African population (2004: 16). Hoogeveen and Özler refer to a paper by Lam and Leibbrandt (2003) which, using income data from the same data sources as they do, concludes 'that incomes deteriorated for most South Africans'. Lam and Leibbrandt also

> report that inequality within racial groups increased substantially while between group inequality declined only slightly, as a result of which total inequality increased in South Africa between 1995 and 2000. (cited in Hoogeveen and Özler 2004: 6)

Few other studies have appeared since the *Earning and spending* débâcle. One of them (Van der Berg and Louw 2003) tries, *inter alia*, to reconcile survey income data with national accounting statistics. The authors estimate the poverty headcount at 16 033 948 in 1995, and either 16 261 294 (their 'Optimistic' estimate) or 17 239 710 (their 'Pessimistic' figure) in the year 2000. Corresponding poverty headcount ratios would have been 38.8 per cent in 1995, and either 36.4 per cent (Optimistic) or 38.6 per cent (pessimistic) in 2000. According to them, the sustained fall in the headcount ratio of poverty (it fell from 49.8 per cent in 1970 to 35.3 per cent in 1990) went into reverse at some point thereafter. The number of poor increased by about 3 or 4 million between 1990 and 2000, depending on whether their 'Optimistic' or 'Pessimistic' figures are used (Van der Berg and Louw 2003: 18).

Focusing more on inequality, a paper by Fedderke, Manga and Pirouz (2004) is agnostic in its findings, the results being sensitive to choice of data set. A paper by Leibbrandt, Poswell, Naidoo, Welch and Woolard (2004) that made use of the 1996 and 2001 census figures, concluded that both the poverty and the inequality dimensions of well-being, as measured by income, worsened.[43] Access measures, however, 'show that well-being in South Africa…improved in a number of important dimensions' (Leibbrandt et al. 2004: 1). A more recent paper by Leibbrandt, this time with a different set of co-authors, took advantage of the fact that when Statistics South Africa conducted its five-yearly IESs in 1995 and 2000, it also carried out, in the same years, another large household survey that used the same sample (Leibbrandt, Levinsohn and McCrary 2005).[44] It is thus possible to merge and match the 1995 IES data with those from the OHS for 1995. Similarly, the data collected from the 2000 IES may be merged and matched with the LFS figures for September 2000. Using these data sets, they arrived at the conclusion that

> [i]n broad strokes, our analysis supports the view that an individual sampled at random in South Africa was (economically) better off in 1995 than in 2000. We interpret that contrast to be the relevant one for evaluating social welfare, abstracting, of course, from improvements in political freedoms and 'psychic income' generally. (Leibbrandt et al. 2005: 4)

The brief trawl above through the literature (there may be other studies that have been overlooked) gives a flavour of academic endeavours on the topic. It discloses a community divided in its assessment of the conditions of the poor ten years after the advent of democratic rule. The difficulties of measuring well-being in a more rounded manner, i.e. taking account of both income and access (and asset and time) poverty, appear to be insurmountable – the question of whether negative movement on one axis (for example, income poverty) can be, or has been, offset by positive movement in another (for example, asset poverty) is not readily answerable.[45]

Addressing the problems that plague South African poverty studies – (i) the absence of 'firm definitional or conceptual underpinnings' and (ii) the weaknesses of the available data sets – is no simple matter. The work by Noble and his collaborators in the Centre for the Analysis of South African Social Policy (CASASP) at Oxford University (Noble et al. 2004), which should help to tighten the 'concept–definition–measurement' nexus, is still in its preliminary stages. For the second category of problems, there are some defects in data sets which, once created, cannot be removed.

The difficulty of measuring well-being overall, when change is taking place in different directions along different axes in South Africa, has had attention drawn to it by the state's response to claims of increasing poverty and inequality. Going on the offensive, state spokespersons have demanded (legitimately) that the impact of the 'social wage' on the welfare of the poor be taken into account. We return to this issue below.

THE CONTRADICTIONS OF DEFINITION AND MEASUREMENT

For purposes of measuring income poverty, a poverty line (or preferably, a 'poverty critical range' between two poverty lines [Woolard and Leibbrandt 2001: 49]) must be identified. South Africa does not have an official poverty line (or pair of lines identifying a poverty critical range). This is not a desirable state of affairs. As Everatt points out,

> [t]he failure to define poverty is not an academic matter: it directly impacts on delivery. If poverty is undefined, programmes lack focus: it is not clear why this or that service is being provided, or to whom, or where and measuring progress and impact becomes near-impossible. (Everatt 2003: 89)[46]

The conclusions of a paper by Ravallion and Sen capture, with admirable brevity, the central problems involved in choosing between poverty lines. They observe that

> [p]overty measurement requires value judgements and behavioural assumptions to help interpret the available – and invariably imperfect – data. That will always be true. The more interesting question is how much bearing the choices made by analysts have on the key conclusions drawn. (Ravallion and Sen 1996: 785)

If a poverty line (or range) is to be acceptable, it must satisfy two conditions:

> ...[first], that the methods on which it is based reflect 'best practice' scientific research methodology and data; and second, that the judgments on which it is based are broadly in line with community opinion on the meaning and measurement of poverty. The poverty line should be regularly exposed to these two criteria of *scientific integrity* and *community credibility* if it is to be a valuable tool for monitoring trends and policy impacts. (Saunders 2004: 3)[47]

As far as scientific integrity is concerned, the criticisms made by Noble et al. (2004) about the absence of 'firm definitional or conceptual underpinnings' to current poverty studies in South Africa cast something of a pall over proceedings which, at least for the foreseeable future, must consist of more of the same. It is not necessary, however, for paralysis to set in – Noble et al. acknowledge that

> there is a need for a measurement of poverty (or poverty line) for South Africa based on an absolute concept and defined, perhaps, by reference to the Copenhagen Declaration (1995).... (Noble et al. 2004: 4)

Measurement of poverty using such a line, and variants of it, is what we attempt below. Community credibility, the second of the two criteria that have to be met to make a poverty line acceptable, is precisely what Noble et al. seek in their quest for a poverty line based on a consensual approach. They draw attention to the 'pressing need for a carefully thought out relative measure of poverty', and they argue that 'a "consensual" or "democratic" definition of poverty in South Africa is the most appropriate approach to help the country overcome the deep social divisions that are apartheid's legacy and become a more equal and unified society ...' (Noble et al. 2004: 4).

There is an interesting tension between this passage and the reference above in the citation from the Ravallion and Sen paper to 'the choices made by analysts'. In one instance, technocrats 'choose' the poverty measure; in the other, what constitutes poverty is discovered by consultation. Although it does not follow from this that Ravallion and Sen are insensitive to the need for consensus on poverty, the contrast between the two positions highlights the differences between technicians, politicians and the polity. Even if the poverty lines that are established meet with general acceptance, there can be no guarantee that they will be deployed by government in a manner that satisfies all concerned. This is because of the conflicting demands of politicians and programme managers, not to mention the public at large, a body whose heterogeneity is often the source of strong disagreements. The tensions between the needs of politicians and programme managers, and their relevance for the debate on poverty definition and measurement in South Africa, are captured by Everatt in an excellent piece of work called 'The politics of poverty' (Everatt 2003). It offers a guide through the complex terrain within which the debate about definitions, and their use (or non-use) in the design of policies, and the more nebulous business of articulating goals, takes place. Everatt offers an analysis of the conflicting needs of the two constituencies, and then shows how the struggle for ownership of the concept of poverty has marginalised the poor. Having just insisted that the failure to define poverty is not merely academic, he goes on to qualify the claim by stressing as well that[48]

> we should be realistic: politicians and programme managers have opposing needs. The latter require specificity, while the former prioritise political above technical considerations and prefer opacity to a definition of poverty eradication that 'implies...[that] someone else will have to forego

those resources'. Most poverty experts argue strongly that a detailed defi-nition of poverty is a prerequisite for appropriate policy selection, but ignore the political realm and the balancing act it requires…

Where poverty specialists are insufficiently sensitive to political consid-erations, political analysts pay inadequate attention to the programmatic needs of anti-poverty interventions. Balancing political and technical considerations is clearly needed.

Whether that would be sufficient (assuming it can be done) to return poverty eradication to its status as a national priority is questionable. While poverty has been repeatedly redefined and an unceasing string of indicators and targets provided, in South Africa its meaning has suf-fered a further hollowing out through endless repetition. Poverty and 'the poorest of the poor' have been both undefined since the days of the RDP and ubiquitous in political discourse. 'The poorest of the poor' are invoked by politicians, civil society activists, the private sector and oth-ers as the intended beneficiaries of (and thus justification for) their every action, from the privatisation of state assets to black economic empower-ment to enhanced social security provision. The unceasing mantra-like invocation of poverty has drained it of urgency.

It is not that poverty is meaningless: it has too many meanings, in the ANC-led alliance and the public service… .(Everatt 2003: 89–90)

If an explanation is sought for the absence of clarity on what is required to achieve the MDGs, it could do worse than to take the argument above as its starting point. Promises to achieve this or that goal can be attractive. The very act of making such promises, however, carries with it the risk of having to explain why, in the event of the goal not being achieved, the government has 'failed'. The unedifying debate on the extent of job creation in the run-up to the 2004 general election is an example of how unpleasant the recriminations can become, whether or not there are any specific promises over which to quarrel.[49] A promise to halve poverty is a double-edged sword.

GOVERNMENT MONITORING AND MEASUREMENT INITIATIVES

A significant, albeit piecemeal, role in monitoring government progress towards the achievement of the MDGs is being played by the Human Sciences Research Council (HSRC). In the second issue by that organisation of a major publication called *State of the nation: South Africa 2004–2005* (Daniel, Southall and Lutchman 2005), there is an overview of the state of poverty and inequality in the country, written by Benjamin Roberts. Although he acknowledges that 'there exists incontrovertible evidence of improvements in the lives of many South Africans over the last decade…' (Daniel et al. 2005: 504), the account he gives of the government's capacity to formulate anti-poverty policy and to measure its effects in a rational manner is not flattering. The following lengthy passage, culled from the conclusion to his piece, tells it all:

> [A]n adequately conceived programme of reforms to address poverty requires the development of detailed, empirically informed and well-reasoned policy packages, and cannot rest on a disparate set of … epigrams and axiomatic musings. The outcomes of government interventions on the poor [are] effectively determined by reasoned assessment of the nature of economy, society and indeed poverty. In South Africa, policy formulation has yet to be firmly based on such a nuanced understanding of social dynamics. Government departments have experimented with, and continue to initiate, monitoring systems that provide information on the impact of policies and programmes. Nonetheless, there is not yet a deeply-rooted culture of evidence-based policy-making whereby decisions about policy and programmatic reforms are based on empirical evidence of the outcomes on intended beneficiaries. This is particularly true of poverty monitoring at the aggregate level. The Poverty and Inequality Report (1997) lamented the absence of an effective form of monitoring and evaluating programmes in the country and recommended that 'a system and procedures for monitoring the impact of government policy on poverty and inequality be established as a matter of priority'. It is disheartening that, more than half a decade later, a co-ordinated poverty monitoring system has not been effectively instituted, though discussions have occurred on the possibility of establishing a poverty monitoring unit in the National Treasury. Unless this situation is addressed, the ability for policy to remain adaptive to the needs of the poor, and make a sustained impact on poverty, will continue to remain elusive objectives. (Roberts 2005: 503–504)

On at least three occasions since taking office, the democratic government has commissioned research directly or indirectly concerned to measure the extent of poverty (and inequality) in the country. The final report of the first of these research undertakings, Poverty and inequality in South Africa, was completed in 1998 (May 1998a). Next came the Report of the Committee of Inquiry into a Comprehensive System of Social Security for South Africa, commonly referred to as the Taylor Committee Report (2002). More recently, and not yet in the public domain,[50] is a report on The Social and Economic Impact of South Africa's Social Security System, a document prepared by the Economic Policy Research Institute (EPRI) (Samson 2003).

Recognising the urgency of the poverty problem, President Mbeki, while still Deputy President, commissioned the preparation of the Poverty and Inequality Report. The final document (May 1998a), a monumental work, told the government much of what it needed to know about poverty in the early days of democracy in South Africa. The report offered, as well, a comprehensive set of recommendations which, if carried out in the manner suggested, might have taken some of the sting out of the often acrimonious debates about poverty in South Africa. Aware of the critical importance of monitoring, the report devoted considerable energy to suggesting ways in which this could be carried out.[51] These recommendations were accepted by the then Minister of Welfare and Population Development (the department now called the Department of Social Development (DSD)), Geraldine Fraser-Moleketi.[52] Like many other government departments, the DSD has been a little slow in implementing the recommendations on monitoring and evaluation that would make thorough analysis of the impact of its anti-poverty programmes (chiefly, but not exclusively social security grants) possible. This, however, is changing.

Having examined South Africa's conditions through the prisms of most of the standard poverty measures, and having commented on the essentially arbitrary nature, in varying degrees, of all poverty lines, May, following the RDP, described the bottom 40 per cent of households as 'poor' (with monthly adult equivalent expenditure of less than R352.23 in 1995). The bottom 20 per cent of households (where expenditure was less than R193.77 per adult equivalent) was described as 'ultra-poor'. A little under 50 per cent of the population (about 19 million people) fell into the 'poor' category', while the ultra-poor (about 27 per cent of the population) numbered about ten million (May 1998a: 27).

Chapter 5 of the Taylor Committee Report is devoted to an examination of the impact of existing and proposed social policies (especially the BIG) on poverty. Figure 10 in this chapter provides a graphic illustration of the numbers still in poverty (below a poverty line of about R400 per person in 1999 prices), assuming full take-up of existing social security benefits. Figure 11 superimposes on the Figure 10 results the impact of a BIG of R100 per month, while Table 3 gives figures for the headcount and poverty gap reductions of moving from actual to full take-up of existing policies, and of the adoption of a BIG.

Much of the work for the poverty chapter in the Taylor Committee Report was done by EPRI. The fruits of this are to be seen in EPRI's latest work for the DSD, the draft report referred to above (Samson 2003). The report should by now have been released, but I can find no record of this having happened. Its findings will, therefore, not be cited. Suffice it to say, however, that it delves deeply into the question of the construction of subsistence-type poverty lines, performing simulations on the basis of a wide range of such lines. These examine the impact of existing and planned social grants on poverty (both headcounts and poverty gaps, the latter measured in three separate ways). With this report in hand, government will have some of the information required to make informed judgements about the extent to which its policies make possible the meeting of the MDGs.

Perhaps because it lacked the sort of information provided by Samson (2003), and possibly because the target date is so far in the future, the South African government, until recently, showed little sign of having applied its collective mind to the question of whether existing and proposed anti-poverty policies will enable it to meet the goal of halving poverty by 2014. That has started to change. Statistics South Africa has taken the first of the steps necessary for the performance of such an evaluation, the construction of poverty lines that define the levels of consumption that separate the poor from the rest of the population. In the discussion above on poverty lines, reference was made to what, in due course, will probably become South Africa's official poverty lines. Although Hoogeveen and Özler (2004), to whom we owe our knowledge of the existence of the poverty lines, do not describe it as such in so many words, it appears that a poverty line set at about R174 per person in 2000 is to be the line marking off the absolutely poor. The document in which the derivations of this poverty line, and its slightly more generous counterparts for identifying the 'merely' poor[53] as opposed to the destitute, are described (Babita, Özler, Shabalala and Thema 2003) has not yet been made available for public scrutiny. The government will not have complied with the Copenhagen injunction until such time as the paper is released and its contents have been found not wanting (i.e. it must be shown to have both scientific integrity and community credibility).[54]

Establishing what absolute poverty means is, however, merely the start. Rigorous research into the social wage is also long overdue. The DSD has made a start with the commissioning of the report by Samson et al. (2003) into the social and economic impact of the country's social security system. That investigation is, however, limited to social grants. Much more work is required before the effects on the poor of the very wide range of anti-poverty interventions initiated by the state can be ascertained. In his Budget Speech to Parliament on 3 June 2004, the Minister of Social Development said that

> [a]s part of the provision of basic social assistance services we will do further work to improve the understanding of the composition, value, distribution and targeting of the social wage. We will report to Cabinet on this matter by November 2004. (Skweyiya 2004)

The study commissioned by the DSD was, according Dr Yasmin Dada-Jones of the Presidency, supposed to cover all components of the social wage.[55] The outcome, a paper by the HSRC (Human Sciences Research Council 2004), on which we will have a little more to say below, advances the debate. It falls foul, however (as must all such enterprises, my own efforts not excepted), of the internationally recognised problems of valuing publicly provided goods and services. No satisfactory methodology for doing so exists. The benefit incidence (supply side) approach can lead to the kind of nonsense published in the *Ten Year Review* about dramatic falls in inequality (see below), while the 'behavioural' (demand side) approach starves in a 'dataless void' (Cornes 1995: 88). Valuing the social wage is a major challenge.

Some progress on monitoring and evaluation appears to have been made, although just how much remains to be seen. In his 2004 Budget Speech, the Minister of Social Development also said that

> the Department of Social Development, Stats SA and The Presidency have commissioned research to audit poverty measures used by different departments. The final report and recommendations on poverty measures will be ready by September 2004. (Skweyiya 2004)

It is not entirely clear what this means. The research could be a follow-up to that done for the report on monitoring and evaluation of anti-poverty programmes in 15 government departments, commissioned by the Department of Provincial and Local Government (Department of Provincial and Local Government (DPLG) 2001). Attention was drawn in that report to the non-uniformity and, in the case of seven of the departments concerned, the absence of definitions of poverty (DPLG 2001: 13–14; Everatt 2003: 86).[56] The authors of the DPLG report use the 'cart-before-horse' metaphor to describe the (then existing) practice of defining poverty in relation to anti-poverty programmes (para. 23).[57] Although one would hope that matters have improved since the DPLG report was published, the poor quality of the information on the social wage in the *Ten Year Review* does not encourage the belief that such improvements are widespread.

Scanning the government's Programme of Action website, under the heading 'Evidence-based decision making' (Action 6) in the programme of the Governance and Administration Cluster for 2004, one sees Action 6.01 described thus: 'Create strong information base for good governance and service the developmental state.' Progress towards achieving this is reported as follows:

> The National Statistical System has been established to develop a strong culture of information collection, collation and management to support good governance and developmental initiatives. (South African Government 2004)

If this reference to the National Statistical System, still far from complete, is all the government has to say about its intentions as far as evidence-based policy formation is concerned, then the strictures by Roberts (2005) with which this section commenced are richly merited.

Turning to monitoring and evaluation (M&E), we observe that Action 6.02 commits the government to

> [c]reate government-wide M&E framework to track impact of government programmes against goals and effectiveness and efficiency of service delivery outputs.

The progress report said that '[a] proposal on the architecture and implementation is under development' (South African Government 2004).

By 2005, the monitoring and evaluation programmes (still under the Governance and Administration [G&A] Cluster) Action 3.4.1 required the government to

> [f]inalise research, proposal and design of the government-wide M&E framework to track impact of government programmes against goals and effectiveness and efficiency of service delivery outputs. (South African Government 2004)

The report of steps taken and work still to be done said:

> The conceptualisation framework was accepted by the M&E task team. The project was presented to the G&A cluster of FOSAD [Forum of South African Directors-General] and is in progress. Expected completion – November 2005. (South African Government 2004)

Action 3.4.2 meanwhile, requires the government to '[f]inalise a plan to improve monitoring and evaluation across government, including the electronic information management system for phased implementation', with progress reported as:

> A proposal on the design of a government-wide monitoring and evaluation system has been developed. An audit of reporting requirements and departmental monitoring and evaluation systems in the public service is underway. (South African Government 2004)

The proposed design of the 'electronic' system is being piloted (Action 3.4.3), with roll-out to all provinces and departments promised by April 2007.[58] The Presidency is the lead department for much of the work spelt out above.

As a way of informing citizens about the government's plans and progress, the Programme of Action website is a commendable and brave departure. One predictable effect it has is to whet the appetite for more information. In the President's State of the Nation address on 11 February 2005, monitoring and evaluation, like capacity-building, was important enough to rate a mention. By June 2005, the President informed us,

> the plan to improve monitoring and evaluation across government, including the electronic information management system will have been completed for phased implementation. (Mbeki 2005)

Could this be a reference to the actions described above? If so, it would appear to contradict the Programme of Action report. Updated on 27 June 2005, the programme pencilled in a target date of November 2005. Whatever the answer, one must again lament the fact that so many years have elapsed since May and his colleagues called for the urgent creation of tools for monitoring and evaluating policy. It is a matter of more than a little concern that, apart from silly estimates of the Gini coefficient that we glance at below, there is no official estimate of what the impact has been of the expenditure of billions upon billions of rands on anti-poverty measures. We have already looked at the few academic estimates of the numbers in poverty; to the best of my knowledge, apart from the rough (and outdated) figures cited below, there is no official estimate.

GOVERNMENT'S RESPONSE TO CLAIMS OF RISING POVERTY AND INEQUALITY

Alarmed at persistent claims in the media that poverty was on the increase, the government has gone on the offensive against poverty studies that do not take into account the 'social wage'.[59] The government's attempt to deal with the social wage problem is, however, far from satisfactory. The basis of the challenge made by the government to the 'rising poverty and inequality story' is a set of studies undertaken for the report on the decade of democracy, the *Ten Year Review* (PCAS 2003). Although the government's criticism of existing poverty studies in South Africa is useful insofar as it has stimulated research into the impact of the social wage on the welfare of the poor, the published figures in the *Ten Year Review* have given rise to confusion. If the *Ten Year Review* does represent the most recent thinking of the South African government on the extent of the poverty problem, then the consideration of what the poverty reduction goal might be begins with the statement that in 1995

> [a]ccording [to] Statistics South Africa, it is estimated that approximately 28% of households and 48% of the population were living below the estimated poverty line – calculated on the basis of expenditure, *thus excluding access to services and assets.* In 1999, there were 3.7 million such households out of 11.4 million (just under 33%) living below the poverty line. Of these, most were Africans. Part of this increase in income poverty would be due to large-sized poor households unbundling into smaller households. The unbundling has the effect of removing additional income earners from the household and would therefore reflect an increasing number of households being classified as poor... .[60] (PCAS 2003: 17. Emphasis added)

Elsewhere in the *Ten Year Review*, the indicator for income poverty is said to be the '[p]ercentage below minimum living level (defined in terms of expenditure)' (PCAS 2003: 119). It is not clear what this is supposed to mean. A poverty measure with the name of the 'minimum living level' used to be estimated by the Bureau for Market Research of the University of South Africa (UNISA). Available only to subscribers (mainly businesses, presumably interested to know how far their wages are from starvation level), this surely cannot be the measure chosen by the state to disclose the extent of income poverty.

The phrase in italics in the passage cited immediately above signals the likelihood of what promises to be a major debate about the extent to which the 'social wage' has reduced poverty (Meth 2004b). If the outrageous claims in the *Ten Year Review* about the reduction in inequality brought about by the social wage were to be believed, all existing estimates of income poverty would have to be called into question.

The impact of social spending in 1997 was an alleged reduction in inequality as measured by the Gini coefficient, from a 'pre-social transfer value' of 0.68 to 0.44. By the year 2000, pre-social transfer inequality is asserted to have fallen to 0.59. Social spending, it is claimed, reduces this to 0.35 (PCAS 2003: 90ff).[61]

What this means for income poverty is not explained. I have argued that these results are fundamentally flawed, resulting as they do from the careless application of the benefit incidence measurement technique to social spending (Meth 2004b). It should be a relatively simple matter, given adequate administrative records, to determine the (first round) distributional impact of social grants (tax incidence studies are a lot harder to perform). Valuing the services that constitute a large proportion of social spending, (for example, health and education) is another matter altogether. An important part of the cause of the huge drops in inequality reported above is the imputation of shares of the total costs of production of government services to the different deciles of the income distribution. By doing so, the analyst responsible for them has fallen into the trap of conflating these results with the values that would be placed upon them by those 'consuming' the services. As Demery (2000) points out, although the benefit incidence technique allows

> benefit flows to *recipients* of government services [to be] distinguished from the income flows government spending generates to the providers of those services and other government administrators...,

this cannot be taken to imply that

> benefit incidence analysis is an accurate tool for measuring benefits to service recipients. Perhaps a better term to describe the technique is beneficiary incidence since this avoids the suggestion that true benefits are measured, but simply conveys the message that spending is imputed to the beneficiaries. (Demery 2000: 50)

In place of the meaningless estimates of the impact of the social wage presented in the *Ten Year Review*, the present chapter offers a set of estimates of the possible impact of the social wage on the ability of households to consume. These, admittedly rough and ready, estimates suggest that between 1997 and 2003, the poverty headcount rose, the social wage notwithstanding (Meth 2004b). The results are sensitive, amongst other things, to the assumptions underlying them, as are all poverty estimates. They do start, however, from a reasonably good base – the pre-social wage poverty headcounts are not wildly out of line with other estimates of the numbers of poor.[62]

As we have seen above, the 1995 Copenhagen Programme of Action required each country to 'develop a precise definition and assessment of absolute poverty', preferably by 1996. South Africa has been tardy in complying with this. Although, as noted above, Statistics South Africa has worked on this problem, the poverty lines they have estimated have not as yet been declared official. In the absence of an official poverty line with which to estimate the number of 'absolute poor', one on which it is possible to begin assessing the magnitude of the task of halving the proportion of absolute poor, some results from the work referred to above (Meth 2004b) are reproduced below. This makes use of poverty lines similar to those in the as yet unpublished SSA paper (Babita et al. 2003). Before digging into those results, a small digression concerning the set of obstacles facing the would-be estimator of income (or expenditure) poverty levels is necessary.

Some hazards of poverty measurement

Several well-known obstacles exist to the production of reliable poverty estimates. They are dealt with in a substantial literature. The brief survey above on the state of poverty studies in South Africa referred to some of the major problems. The point of this section of the chapter is not to delve more deeply into the literature, but rather to discuss the way in which some of these problems affect the South African poverty estimates. These are sensitive to a wide range of factors. The particular sensitivities dealt with below are the following:

- poverty lines, in particular, the dollar-a-day rate converted by purchasing power parity (PPP), and the differences between per capita and per adult equivalent poverty lines;
- the factors required to yield adult equivalents: the child cost ratio, and the household economies of scale parameter;
- the treatment of means and distributions in surveys that collect expenditure (or income) data in classes or categories;
- the extent of under-reporting of expenditure (or income) in social surveys;
- the reliability (consistency) of the surveys from which the basic data are drawn.

POVERTY LINES

It is scarcely original to point out that when estimating poverty levels, the choice of a poverty line (itself an arbitrary construct) can have a significant effect on the level of poverty disclosed by whatever study it is that is being carried out. In the present case, the range of options open should be relatively small – we are concerned, after all, with the reduction of absolute poverty, and that has been defined in the Copenhagen Programme of Action. Absolute poverty, it may be recalled, is said to be

> a condition characterized by severe deprivation of basic human needs, including food, safe drinking water, sanitation facilities, health, shelter, education and information. It depends not only on income but also on access to social services. (United Nations 2000b: Paragraph 19, Chapter 2)

Focusing, as is our intention, mainly but not solely on the income dimension of poverty, an interest in the absolute poor sends us initially to the MDG, where they are identified as those living below the dollar-a-day poverty line. Although there are numerous well-documented problems associated with this poverty line, not least of them the need to convert it into local currencies using estimates of PPP,[63] it is not without its defenders.[64] Chen and Ravallion (2001), re-evaluating the line in the light of a re-estimation of PPPs by the World Bank, argue that poverty rates estimated on the basis of the dollar-a-day (actually, $1.08) must be 'conservative' ('...a close approximation to the poverty line one would expect to find in the poorest country...') (Chen and Ravaillon 2001: 288).

Having outlined both the general problems with PPP exchange rates, and the specific problems of 'PPP indexes used in world poverty counts', Deaton (2003a: 357–361) nevertheless proposes the use of the Chen and Ravallion (2001) PPP poverty lines as a starting point for monitoring poverty. This suggestion, he argues, 'recognizes the rhetorical value of the $1-a-day concept, retaining the trademark'. Noting the arbitrariness of poverty lines, he goes on to say that

> [t]he hope is that within that range of arbitrariness, we can find a poverty line for each country that is: (a) close to $1-a-day at 1993 PPP, and (b) meaningful and that makes sense to people in the country for the purpose of the international (not domestic) counts. (Deaton 2003a: 362)

Countries not included in the 'benchmark' sample have PPP exchange rates imputed them by

> a regression procedure that effectively adjusts their official exchange rate by an amount that is similar to the adjustment for countries at a similar level of development for which benchmark data exist. This procedure, while clearly sensible, can also be subject to substantial error, and in some extreme cases in the past, the Bank has published PPPs and associated poverty rates that were clearly incorrect. (Deaton 2003a: 360)

South Africa is not one of the benchmark countries – its PPPs are produced by the regression method. Adjustments to the PPP rate have had some strange effects on the dollar-a-day rate when expressed in rand terms. Woolard (2002: 1) notes that the pre-1993 PPPs yielded a poverty line of R92 per month in 1993. The newly benchmarked figures reduced this to R55 (both in 1993 prices). According to Ahmad (2003: Annex B: 25), South Africa's 1993 PPP exchange rate (units of local currency per US$) was 1.672. This gives a dollar-a-day poverty line of R50.86 in 1993. Inflating this to the prices of the year 2002, using the very low-income CPI as inflator, yields an amount of R103.88, or R3.42 per day.[65] Deaton (1997: 157) used as poverty line, an amount of R105 per person per month in 1993, noting as he did that it was 'much lower than poverty lines commonly discussed in South Africa, but ...approximately equal to $1 (US) per person per day...'.[66] Inflating this poverty line to 2002 prices produces a figure of R214.48, or about R7.05 per day.[67] Because the consumption level it yields is so far below any poverty line in use in South Africa (and because it does not have its origins in a benchmark study), there would seem to be little further use that can be made of the PPP-adjusted dollar-a-day line. It is, however, used below to illustrate the argument about the sensitivity of poverty estimates to the choice of poverty line.

A characteristic of the dollar-a-day poverty line (both the PPP version and the Deaton 1997 version above) is that they are per capita lines (as opposed to per adult equivalent lines). In one of the early papers on the dollar-a-day line (Ravallion, Datt and van de Walle 1991), the poverty lines measure consumption per person (based on 'average families').[68] Apart from the problems inherent in working with such a nebulous concept as the 'average family', it is clear that poverty lines measured in this way (per capita) embody implicit values of the child cost ratio and the household economies of scale parameter. If these could be estimated, it should be possible to estimate the corresponding per adult equivalent poverty line. For a given per capita poverty line, the existence of reduced child costs, and the presence of household economies of scale, have the effect of raising the level of the per adult equivalent poverty line.[69] First prize in the poverty measurement stakes would be an accurate per adult equivalent poverty line. Such a measure is invariant to changes in household (and demographic) structures. Coping with the social transitions experienced in South Africa in recent times (increasing proportions of single- and two-adult households, falling household sizes generally) would present no problems. The errors involved in using per capita poverty measures are not easy to estimate. The problem with per adult equivalent poverty lines, of course, is precisely that child cost ratios and household economies of scale parameters are extremely difficult to determine.[70]

For the purposes of the present chapter, the income (and expenditure) dimension of absolute poverty in South Africa follows Deaton (1997) – the absolutely poor are assumed to be all of those whose expenditure was less than R214.48 per month per person in 2002. In line with Woolard and Leibbrandt's suggested use of two poverty lines to create a '..."poverty critical range"' (Woolard and Leibbrandt 2001: 49), we turn to a measure suggested by Chen and Ravallion to capture relative poverty. They argue that

> to be deemed 'not poor' a person must meet *both* the '$1 per day' abso-
> lute consumption standard and consume more than some constant pro-
> portion of the mean consumption in the country of residence. We set the
> constant of proportionality to avoid social exclusion[71] at one third... .
> (Chen and Ravaillon 2001: 294. Emphasis in original)

In South Africa in 2002, mean monthly per capita consumption was about R1 267;[72] one-third of this is about R422. It follows that if that level of consumption is regarded as modest, leaving, as it will do, most of those below it, and many above, far from being able to participate fully in society, then the MDG goal itself, although laudable, is itself extremely modest. The poverty critical range in 2002 used in this study requires that people consume between R214 and R422[73] per month. The lower figure separates the absolutely poor from the poor, while the higher figure separates the poor from the non-poor.

To place these figures in perspective, one of the more 'commonly discussed'[74] poverty lines in South Africa, Potgieter's Household Subsistence Level (HSL), in its adult equivalent form, would have had a value of about R557 per month in 2002 if what Woolard and Leibbrandt (2001: 54) describe as the 'widely accepted' (May, Carter and Posel 1995) scales, i.e. a child cost ratio of 0.5, and an economies of scale parameter of 0.9,[75] were used to obtain the numbers of adult equivalents. Converting this to a per capita measure (by setting the child cost ratio and household economies of scale parameter to unity) would yield a poverty line of R344 per month. This is more modest than both the Hoogeveen and Özler line (R387) and the Chen and Ravallion line (R422).

Each of the three Poverty Line Sets contains six poverty lines. Presenting the results for all of them has the advantage of showing how the numbers in poverty change as the level of the poverty line changes. The interest of the chapter is, however, focused on a limited number from each set. Most important, in Poverty Line Set No. 1, given the extent of deprivation it represents (and given the MDG commitment), is the line measuring absolute poverty, taken here as R214 per capita per month in 2002. Next is the line derived from Chen and Ravallion's work, of R422 per capita per month. Falling between these are the scaled HSL 1 and 'Official' poverty lines. We look in passing at the poor unfortunates located below the R104 per month line, being careful not to suggest that this line has any validity as a poverty line. Poverty Line Sets Nos 2 and 3 contain a series of scaled variants on the dollar-a-day line (the 'Deaton' version), the Chen line and the 'Official' line, in which household composition is allowed to vary between two adults and two children, or two adults and three children. The primary focus, however, is on the two per adult equivalent variants of the HSL, HSL 1 and HSL 2.

CHILD COST RATIOS AND HOUSEHOLD ECONOMIES OF SCALE PARAMETERS

In the model from which the results presented in this chapter are extracted, children are 'converted' to adult equivalents[76] by the application of a child cost ratio of whatever level is deemed appropriate. Similarly, the household economies of scale parameters may assume any value between unity and zero. Setting the child cost ratio at 1.0 implies that the cost of living for a child is the same as that of an adult, while a household economies of scale parameter of 1.0 implies that there are no economies of scale. These, obviously, are the values for per capita poverty lines such as the dollar-a-day poverty line. A rough indication of the effect of the presence of 'non-average families' may be obtained by allowing child cost ratios to vary between 0.5 to 1.0, while household economies of scale parameters float between 0.8 and 1.0.

Changing either or both of the coefficients α (the child cost ratio), and θ (the household economies of scale factor) is tantamount to changing the level of the corresponding per capita poverty line. When that happens, poverty estimates are affected. Woolard and Leibbrandt (2001: 53ff) have demonstrated that poverty headcounts are relatively insensitive to changes in α and θ when poverty lines themselves are relatively high. As the value of a poverty line declines, say, towards bare subsistence, the sensitivity of the poverty estimates to changes in the level of the poverty line increases.[77] Whatever their shortcomings, the most common per adult equivalent poverty lines in South Africa, the HSLs, are based on surveys conducted over a number of years. Since data on child costs, and implicitly, on household economies of scale, are available, the effects of varying household composition can be simulated. The same cannot be said of the most important of the per capita poverty lines mooted above.[78] The sensitivity of the Deaton (1997) R105 line (which converts to R214 per capita in 2002 prices) to changes in the composition of whatever 'average family' (or household) it is based on cannot be established (i.e. the implicit values of α and θ cannot be determined). There have been significant changes in household composition over the period in which we are interested (1997–2002).[79] The use of the same value for the poverty line in each year could thus lead to significant error. Until such time as an official poverty line that meets the 'scientific integrity and community credibility' criteria is created, the range within which the 'true' headcount of poverty might lie must remain unknown. History will continue to be difficult to write because such a line (or lines) did not exist in the past.

MEANS AND DISTRIBUTIONS WITHIN EXPENDITURE CATEGORIES

The study from which the poverty estimates are drawn (Meth 2004b) restricts its gaze to those in the two bottom expenditure categories (R0–399 and R400–799 per household per month). In 2002, the bottom expenditure category contained about 10.4 million people, and the category second from the bottom, a further 11.6 million. Together they accounted for almost half of the total population of somewhat more than 45 million. There will be more poor people in the expenditure categories above these. Comparison of the numbers of poor revealed by the present study and those in studies referred to above suggest that the 'missing poor' should be relatively few in number. The decision to limit the study to just those in the two bottom categories was taken because of the difficulties of distributing the social wage in the model. Although this misses some poor people, it is not fatal to the aims of the study, namely, to examine the impact of the social wage on people in poverty.

Possibly of equal or greater potential ability to cause the study to undercount the poor are the ways in which the means and distributions of expenditure within the expenditure categories have been determined. With the exception of the year 1997, the OHS and LFS data on which the results in the chapter are based do not allow these to be estimated with any ease. The 1997 OHS collected point estimates of consumption. For 1999 and 2002,[80] all that is available are the expenditure estimates by category. For those years, means and distributions have to be guessed at – a tricky process. To address this problem, distributions of adults and children in the various households were extracted from the survey data. Households containing only adults have been sorted (categorised) into those containing one adult, those containing two adults, and those containing between three and ten adults. Households containing adults and children are sorted into those containing up to 12 children and six adults (households of the latter composition or type may exist, but the surveys did not discover any). There are thus 80 possible 'types' (household compositions) into which a household could be classified. Dividing the boundary values of the expenditure categories (R0–399 and R400–799 per month) by the numbers of people (or adult equivalents) in each household 'type' yields maximum and minimum potential per capita expenditure.

Within each of the household types where expenditure lies in the R400–799 range, maximum and minimum potential expenditure are fixed by the boundaries (for example, in a two-adult household, per capita expenditure must be between R200 and R399.50). What is not known is the distribution of individuals within each category. For people in the expenditure range R0–399 per month, in addition to the distribution of individuals within each category being unknown, it is unreasonable to have R0 as the bottom bound, even though there will have been people with close to zero expenditure during the survey month. Within each household 'type', expenditure is assumed to be distributed in a linear fashion. For the bottom expenditure category, the lower bound is assumed to be set at 50 per cent of the upper bound, i.e. approximately R200. With a linear distribution, mean expenditure within this category (for a household containing a single individual) would be about R300 per month, or 75 per cent of the upper bound of R399.[81] In the expenditure category R400–799, a linear distribution obviously yields a mean that lies at the midpoint of the range, i.e. about R600 per month (for a single individual).

These assumptions treat the effectiveness of anti-poverty policy with generosity, in that they are likely to understate the number of poor. Point estimates in the 1997 OHS allow for the examination of actual distributions in each of the 80 expenditure household 'types' in the two expenditure categories. Almost without exception, mean expenditure levels disclosed by the survey lie well below those predicted by the simple linear distributions that have been assumed.[82] It is possible that the actual distributions of expenditure are log-normal. Given that point estimates are available for 1997, the data for that year, if used in the computations, might bring the results closer to the 'true' values. The complications that arise for the modelling exercise as a consequence of the mixture of actual and assumed distributions are, however, of such a nature as to render the use of assumed distributions for the 1997 figures acceptable. As we shall see, ignorance of the 'true' level of expenditure in each household probably overwhelms any errors introduced by the use of an assumed distribution for 1997.

UNDER-REPORTING OF EXPENDITURE

Surveys have a reputation for under-reporting income and expenditure.[83] Population censuses do not do all that well either. Discovering the extent to which expenditure has been under-reported is no simple matter. A recent paper by Deaton (2003b) points to an almost universal mismatch between survey and national accounts consumption estimates. More acute in some countries than in others, it can reach spectacular proportions, even in the most advanced economies. In the United States, the ratio of survey consumption to national accounts consumption fell from 0.80 in 1984 to 0.64 in 2001 (Deaton 2003b: 15). Deaton claims that, apart from extremes, what we have is

> some combination of underestimation of poverty decline, underestimation of a widening in the distribution of consumption [growing inequality], and overestimation of growth. Quantifying the contribution of each is an urgent task for anyone interested in growth, poverty and inequality. (Deaton 2003b: 17)

Non-response, and the degree of inequality, are shown by Deaton to be important in explaining (part of) the drift between surveys and national accounts figures. Having looked at the weaknesses in both, he comments that

> [w]hen rich households are less likely to cooperate with the survey than poor people, survey-based estimates of consumption will understate mean consumption, and overstate the fraction of people in poverty. The fraction by which consumption is understated will typically be larger the greater is the inequality of consumption. Unless consumption inequality is increasing over time, or the fraction of non-cooperating households is increasing, income-based non-cooperation does not, in and of itself, imply that the ratio of measured to true consumption is increasing over time. (Deaton 2003b: 33)

It is possible that both non-response and the degree of inequality conspire to overstate poverty in South Africa – certainly as far as the most recent IES was concerned, non-compliance among the rich was very high.[84] Although it might be possible to discover whether or not income-based non-cooperation has increased over the period of concern here (1997–2002), it cannot be said with any confidence whether inequality (which, of course, is still high) is increasing or not. In short, it is difficult to say whether the 'ratio of measured to true consumption is increasing over time'.

Instead of trying to discover the possible margins of under-reporting of expenditure by attempted reconciliation of national accounts and survey estimates, the approach adopted in Meth (2004b) was to assume that the ratio of mean survey expenditure levels to national accounts consumption means lay within the range shown in Table 1 in Deaton (2003b). Using the population-weighted figures, and ignoring the anomalous results for sub-Saharan African surveys, the ratio (of survey expenditure to national accounts consumption estimate) ranged from a minimum of 0.569 (for South Asia) to a maximum of 0.867 (Middle East). Ratios of this magnitude would be generated by errors of 70 to 15 per cent respectively.[85] Talk of error is, of course, somewhat misleading; as noted above, national accounts estimates themselves are believed to overstate growth rates.[86] This would have the effect of moderating the ratio furthest away from unity. In other words, it was thought that the error in the South African case was unlikely to be as high as 70 per cent (the ratio as low as 0.569).

Support for this assumption appeared to come from knowledge of rough calculations performed by Professor Charles Simkins of the University of the Witwatersrand which suggested that both the 1996 Census and the 2000 IES captured only about 60 per cent of estimated national accounts income.[87] Professor Servaas van der Berg of Stellenbosch University claimed that the 1995 IES found 90 per cent of national accounts income,[88] while the 2000 IES could find only 80 per cent of it.[89] As long as I worked only with the bottom two expenditure categories, there was little danger of discovering the true extent to which the GHSs (and LFSs) appear to under-report expenditure. Then, in a study on child vulnerability (Meth 2005), I attempted to reconcile the implied consumption estimates in the 2003 GHS with the national accounts figures. The results were highly instructive. The GHS figure obtained using the actual survey results is R22.3 billion per month, whereas reported monthly consumption expenditure in the national accounts is R62.5 billion per month.[90] This suggests that the 70 per cent correction used in Meth (2004b) is too small, and the 15 per cent correction laughably so.

A back-of-envelope calculation confirms that this is indeed the case. From the national accounts data in the Reserve Bank *Quarterly Bulletin* for December 2003 (South African Reserve Bank 2003), we observe that Gross National Disposable Income at current prices amounted to R1 087 billion in 2002 (2003: S-131). According to the *Ten Year Review* (PCAS 2003: 91), the bottom 30 per cent of households received only 3.5 per cent of pre-transfer income in the year 2000. If the distribution of incomes did not change much over the period, it would imply that the bottom three deciles of households would have received about R38 billion per annum (about R3.15 billion per month). In 2002, the bottom expenditure category contained a little under one-third of all households (about 27 per cent). If the people in these households (10.4 million of them) had received the 2.8 per cent of total compensation, monthly per capita incomes would have been in the region of about R242. Since the group contained very few old-age pensioners (that is part of the reason why many of them are so poor), social grant income (mainly child support grants) would hardly have added much more than about R10 per capita per month to the figure of R242. In the expenditure category R0–399 per month, average household size was about 3.32, implying a mean per capita expenditure of R90.4, which is about 37 per cent of the figure implied by the national accounts estimates. The 70 per cent under-reporting error adjustment raises this to 63 per cent.

Further confirmation of the fact that the mean expenditure estimates used in Meth (2004b) are too low comes from the results in the SSA publication that compares estimates of earnings and spending derived from the 1995 and 2000 IESs (Statistics South Africa 2002b). Although problematic, the results are not wholly discredited.[91] They suggest that per capita expenditure in the bottom quintile in 2000 was between R0 and R2 014 per annum, and in the second quintile, between R2 014 and R3 702 (Statistics South Africa 2002b: 29). These translate into monthly means of R126 and R238 respectively. From this we may estimate that the monthly mean expenditure of the bottom three deciles would have been about R151 in 2000. If we allow inflation of about six per cent per annum, the mean expenditure level in the bottom expenditure category in 2002 would have been about R161 per capita. A mean income of this size suggests that the surveys are under-reporting income by something of the order of about 80 per cent. This figure is considerably lower than that suggested by the national accounts calculation above. As a compromise, the poverty estimates have been redone using an upper error level of 120 per cent and a lower level of 80 per cent.[92]

Errors of this magnitude must force us to sit back and ponder the wisdom of attempting to use the GHS and LFS as data sources for poverty studies. As noted above, SSA has issued warnings about the dangers of doing so. The temptation to use the LFSs and GHSs for poverty studies is twofold. In the first place, the surveys collect similar information on an annual basis, household expenditure being an item of particular interest. In the second place, since the surveys use different samples, they are quite independent of each other. Comparison between the results of the surveys conducted in any year should, therefore, be capable of revealing errors. Apropos of which, the odd thing about the expenditure estimates is the consistency with which they are under-reported in different surveys. The results presented here have been compared with those generated by the 2003 GHS and the LFS for September 2003. Not only are the numbers of households and individuals in the bottom two expenditure categories similar, but the differences between the distributions of household 'types' in the various surveys are also slight. In the time before the reconciliation between the survey and national accounts consumption estimates was attempted, this coincidence of results provided the confidence to proceed. That confidence is now thoroughly shaken; there is, however, nothing to do but re-estimate poverty using the new, higher error limits.

Survey reliability (consistency)

More than enough has been said above to raise suspicions about the quality of the data used, at least as far as the poverty analysis part of this chapter is concerned. Expenditure data became available in an OHS for the first time in 1996. Because the survey for that year sampled only 16 000 households (conducting the population census and a full-scale OHS in one year would have placed too great a demand on the resources of SSA), the year 1997 has been used as the starting point. The data are from a full survey (30 000 households). In the early days of the OHS, the sample frame, for a variety of reasons, was regarded as deficient. The 1997 figures appear to be reasonably consistent, but questions have been raised about the 1999 results. By September 2002, SSA seemed reasonably confident that the sample frame was satisfactory. The September 2002 LFS results are, however, weighted by the 1996 Census results. This means that the numbers will probably all change when LFS figures reweighted to the 2001 Census appear.

A paper by Fedderke, Manga and Pirouz (2004) looking at inequality in South Africa in the period 1995–2000, and drawing on all available surveys conducted by SSA in the period to do so, concludes that

> there is much contradictory evidence that emerges from household data on inequality – suggesting that the choice of data set is non-trivial.... (2004: 2)

For what it is worth, the 1997 data seem to behave a lot better than do the corresponding 1999 figures (see their Figure 1 on page 48, and the remarks on the quality of the income estimates on pages 29–31). Tests in the form of comparisons between the household forms (proportions of households containing varying numbers of adults, and adults and children) performed on the basic data do not reveal any wild inconsistencies (Meth 2004b). On those grounds, it seems reasonable to proceed, always with the thought at the back of the mind that the 1999 results are probably a bit suspect.

How bad is poverty in South Africa?

Angus Deaton (2003a: 378) refers to an article[93] which posed the question of whether the MDGs had not already been met. In South Africa's case, the answer must be an unequivocal negative. The question arises because some of the results to be presented below suggest that while the goal has not already been achieved, with a little more effort by the government, it possibly could be. The trick is performed by allowing the poverty line to sink towards the PPP-based dollar-a-day poverty line. This *reductio ad absurdum* (the PPP-based dollar-a-day poverty line is manifestly wrong) illustrates the importance of agreeing on an adequate poverty line to identify the absolutely poor. Allowing the poverty line to move away from a region of utter destitution soon puts paid to the enticing prospect of a goal well on the way to being achieved. It is possible that the goal of halving poverty by 2014 is so ambitious that no reasonable hope of achieving it by the designated date should be entertained. Before looking at poverty at the PPP-based dollar-a-day poverty line, however, a few words about the social wage are in order.

It has been argued above that to consider income poverty without attempting to assess the impact of social spending (loosely described as the 'social wage') on households would be inappropriate. Accordingly, we draw here on the estimates of the impact of the social wage on consumption presented in Meth (2004b). That paper presents a method of valuing the social wage that differs from the two standard approaches described, for example, in Demery (2000). It is not the intention to spell out in any detail the method by which the estimates are obtained. Suffice it to say that if the social wage is to have any impact on income poverty, i.e. for it to be 'bankable', either it must place income directly in the hands of the poor (in the form of transfers) or it must reduce the amounts that households have to spend to achieve a given standard of living. Non-income transfers that have this effect work either directly, by allowing households to reallocate spending after the introduction of a component of the social wage, or indirectly, by making available socially desirable goods and services which households could not previously consume. In effect, this latter process lowers the poverty line. Apart from income transfers (cash grants such as the state old-age pension and the child support grant (CSG)), the social wage in South Africa is defined (pragmatically rather than rigorously) as consisting of half a dozen or so goods and services. Free basic allowances of water and electricity, subsidised transport, health care (including school feeding schemes),[94] education, housing and sanitation make up the list.[95] In the paper from which these results are drawn, the full value of the social wage (with the exception of housing and education) is assumed to accrue to each intended beneficiary, i.e. targeting is assumed to be perfect. This assumption is generous to government's policy measures, overstating considerably the impact of anti-poverty policy.

For the most common adult-and-child household in the bottom expenditure categories (R0–399 and R400–799 per month), namely, those containing two adults and a child (about 12.7 per cent of households in the former category, and 11.0 per cent in the latter), the social wage was estimated to be worth about R86 per month per adult equivalent in 2002. For the next most common households, those containing two adults and two children (about 11.4 and 9.7 per cent respectively of all adult and child households), the social wage was worth about R76 per month per person. With the bottom boundary of the lower expenditure category assuming a value of 50 per cent of the upper boundary, maximum pre-social wage potential consumption at the very bottom end of the expenditure scale for the two-adult, two-child household was a little over R85 per month per person (under-reporting assumed at 80 per cent). This means that the social wage would have raised potential consumption of these households by about 89 per cent. The effect obviously falls as one ascends the expenditure scale. Even so, at the upper boundary of the bottom expenditure category for the two-adult, two-child household the social wage raises potential consumption by a hefty 43 per cent.[96]

There is one more issue to be addressed before we get to the results themselves. For many households, much of the expenditure on which data are captured in the surveys is made possible because households receive income in the form of social grants, chiefly the state old-age pension and the CSG.[97] In earlier versions of the paper, the results referred, somewhat misleadingly, to estimates of poverty before and after the social wage, when, in fact, the pre-social wage estimates included the substantial amounts paid out in the form of grants.[98] An attempt has been made to correct this shortcoming in the present version.[99] The correct way to solve this problem would be to subtract from each household the values of pensions (and disability grants, as well as the CSG in the case of the 2002 figures) received. This would give a 'true' pre-social income position. It is not possible to perform this trick with the simulation model used in the study from which the results are drawn.[100] As a compromise, it has been assumed that pensions in 2002, 1999 and 1997 were equally distributed over all households in the household expenditure categories in which we are interested, R0–399 and R400–799 per month. Child support grants for the year 2002 were treated in a similar way. With a minimum of juggling, the model returns values of social grants roughly equal to administrative-record estimates of total payouts.[101]

Estimating poverty levels by simulation

So much for the social wage – it is time to look at the results of the simulation exercise set out in the paper 'What has happened to poverty in South Africa as unemployment has increased?' (Meth 2004b). Instead of playing with endless outcomes produced by varying all major assumptions, that paper confines itself to estimating two sets of results in which the extent of under-reporting of expenditure and the magnitude of the poverty lines (there are three sets of poverty lines) are allowed to assume different values.[102] Variations in the child cost ratio and the household economies of scales parameters are explored by switching between poverty line sets. Those in poverty line set No. 1 are all of the per capita type, i.e. the child cost ratios and household economies of scale parameters are set equal to unity. A movement away from unity for these two coefficients generates the per adult equivalent poverty lines in sets No. 2 and No. 3.

Three tables numbered 11.3a, 11.3b, and 11.3c present headcounts for each of the poverty lines (five or six) in each of the three poverty line sets. Table 11.3a contains, in addition, estimates of poverty gaps (as does Table 11.4a). Expenditure under-reporting is set at 80 per cent. A similar set of tables numbered 11.4a, 11.4b, and 11.4c gives the corresponding figures for a 120 per cent under-reporting error. The values in Tables 11.3a–c and 11.4a–c are based on the assumption that the value of the social wage has been correctly estimated. Following this is a set of tables (Tables 11.5, 11.6, 11.8 and 11.9) containing somewhat more detailed results for four per capita poverty lines (R214, R344, R387 and R422 per month). Tables 11.5 and 11.9 contain three sets of results for the post-social wage for the year 2002. One of these is based on the assumption that the value of the social wage has been correctly estimated. The other two sets are based on the assumptions that the social wage has been either under- or over-valued in the model. To compensate for this, the five components electricity, water, transport, housing and health either have added to, or subtracted from, them an additional 25 per cent of the estimated value of these components. Squeezed in between Tables 11.6 and 11.8, Table 11.7 presents similar results for the HSL 1 poverty line (R557 per adult equivalent per month). This uses a child cost ratio of 0.5 and a household economies of scale parameter of 0.9. Table 11.10 decomposes the social wage, showing the effects of each component on the poverty headcount. It also gives the approximate values of the transfers attributable to each of the components.

Before commencing the analysis in earnest, let us glance at the tantalising prospect raised in the heading of this section of the chapter, namely the possibility that absolute poverty has already been halved by the social wage. This may be done by referring to Tables 11.3a and 11.4a. These tables illustrate a simple and rather obvious point – the lower the 'official' line demarcating absolute poverty, the greater the likelihood of the 'bankable' component of the social wage enabling the Millennium Declaration poverty reduction goal to be met. At very low expenditure levels, even though the value of the bankable component of the social wage is, itself, quite low (about R76–86 per person for small households), it is capable of lifting large numbers of people above the poverty line. If it were assumed that the PPP $1/day line (R104 per capita per month) were correct, then the post-social wage headcount of people in absolute poverty could have fallen from 2.9 million in 1997 to about 600 000 in 2002 (at the 80 per cent expenditure under-reporting level, see Table 11.3a), or from 1.5 million in 1997 to a mere 200 000 in 2002 (the 120 per cent under-reporting error figures in Table 11.4a).

The results churned out by the model do not seem to be much out of line with the World Bank's figures. According to the 2004 *World Development Indicators*,[103] in 1995, 7.1 per cent of South Africa's population was below the $1/day line, while 23.8 per cent was below the $2/day line (Table 2.5).[104] It is not suggested that the South African authorities will attempt, by sleight of hand, to make poverty disappear through the use of results like those disclosed above. There is, however, some risk that the poverty figures may be misunderstood. The Hoogeveen and Özler (2004) paper describes the Deaton (1997) poverty line of R105 in 1993 (R214 in 2002) as being close to the $2/day poverty line.[105] If someone takes it into their head to make claims about poverty reduction goals based on the $1/day criterion, which is, after all, the poverty line proposed in the MDG, they would have the (mistaken) authority of the World Bank on which to rest their case.

Table 11.3a *Numbers of people (thousands) below various poverty lines*

	Child cost ratio =		1.0	
	Hhold econs of scale parameter =		1.0	
	Error level (%) =		80	
		2002		
2002 Poverty line (R/m in 2002 prices)	Pre-social wage	Post-social wage	Change	Poverty line – short description
R104	10 400	600	9 800	6. PPP $/d
R214	17 000	11 400	5 600	5. Deaton $/d
R344	19 400	17 800	1 600	4. HSL 1pc
R387	19 800	18 500	1 300	3. Official
R422	20 200	19 100	1 100	2. Chen

| | 1999 | | |
	Pre-social wage	Post-social wage	Change
R104	7 100	3 300	3 800
R214	14 100	11 900	2 200
R344	16 800	15 700	1 100
R387	18 000	17 300	700
R422	18 300	17 800	500
	1997		
	Pre-social wage	Post-social wage	Change
R104	6 600	2 900	3 700
R214	14 100	11 700	2 400
R344	17 300	15 900	1 400
R387	18 800	18 200	600
R422	19 300	18 700	600

Poverty gap estimates (R billion/annum in 2002 prices)

| | 2002 | 1999 | 1997 |
	Pre-social wage	Pre-social wage	Pre-social wage
R104	5.8	3.3	2.9
R214	24.6	17.7	16.9
R344	53.6	34.7	33.4
R387	63.6	52.0	52.2
R422	72.0	59.7	60.4
	2002	1999	1997
	Post-social wage	Post-social wage	Post-social wage
R104	0.0	0.8	0.6
R214	7.4	10.9	10.0
R344	31.2	26.1	24.4
R387	40.4	42.4	42.2
R422	48.6	50.0	50.0

Note: The poverty line is in R/month in 2002 per person.

For an 80 per cent under-reporting error, the three other poverty lines above the starvation line of R104 per month (Table 11.3a) and the R214 line, described by Hoogeveen and Özler as an 'extreme' poverty line, generate pre-social wage poverty headcounts for the year 2002 that lie in the range of 19.4 to 20.2 million. From Table 11.3a it would appear that the social wage, if it reached its intended beneficiaries, could have lifted some 5.6 million people above the absolute poverty line of R214 per month in 2002. In general, the smaller the under-reporting error, the smaller the social wage effect – at the 120 per cent error level, the social wage lifts about 6.3 million people above the line of absolute poverty. There can be no doubt that the conditions of people subsisting on as little as R214 per month are bad. It therefore matters a great deal whether there were 8.7 million of them, as one would discover using the 120 per cent under-reporting assumption, or 10.6 million, as would be the case if under-reporting of expenditure were 80 per cent.

To say that it matters greatly how many poor people there are, and what the extent (the depth) is of their poverty, is to state the obvious. Unfortunately, as long as use is made of LFS (or GHS) data there is no way of narrowing the ranges of the estimates like those presented in Tables 11.3a and 11.4a. The absence of point estimates for consumption (or income), in particular for the bottom expenditure category, makes a resort to guesswork unavoidable. The guess (assumption) that expenditure (income) is distributed in linear fashion is almost certainly wrong. Made to ensure that poverty is under- rather than overstated, the comfort it provides would diminish if the true distribution is (or approaches) log-normal. Compounding this is the fact that ignorance of the true extent of under-reporting of expenditure is profound, as is that of the child cost ratios and household economies of scale parameters. Clearly, there can be no easy answer to the question of how many people are located in the various expenditure categories below the absolute poverty line, nor can it be known with any precision how much these numbers have changed over time.

It may be useful, before looking at any more tables, to refresh the memory on the different poverty lines whose short names are listed in the last columns of Tables 11.3 and 11.4 (in their various guises). D$1, 2A + 2C (or 3C) is the Deaton dollar-a-day line of R214 per month per person converted to per adult equivalent form for a two-adult, two- (three-)child household. HSL 1 is the Household Subsistence Level figure used in so many previous studies. HSL 2 uses a child cost ratio of 0.8 instead of the more common 0.5. Off, 2A + 2C is the per adult equivalent version of the line described as the 'Official' poverty line (about R387 per month in per capita terms). Chen, 2A + 2C is the Chen and Ravallion (2001) line. Admittedly arbitrary, it seeks to label as 'poor', all those who do not consume more than some fraction of the mean consumption level for the country as a whole. The fraction selected is one-third. The line represents an attempt to grope towards a measure of the as yet poorly defined concept of 'social exclusion'. The process of allowing for conversion to adult equivalents raises the value of the Chen and Ravallion line of R422 per capita to float somewhere between R533 and R684 per month.

Returning to the Table 11.3a results, we observe, as expected, that the effect of the social wage at very low income levels is substantial. If the fragile[106] estimates of the numbers at the R104 level in 2002 are to be believed, then almost 10 million people would have been lifted above this line if they had all received the social wage at the set of values assumed in the model. The somewhat smaller number moving out of absolute poverty (5.6 million people in Table 11.3a) shows that even after the social wage had been provided, the number of people stuck in the R104–214 region was still very large. A scan of the results for successive years shows two things of interest, the first of them being the substantial increase in the numbers below the R104 and R214 levels; the second of them is the extent to which the social wage could have softened the blow that this implies. Assuming effective delivery, and plausibility of the social wage estimates in the model, the 2002 social wage package has a greater impact (as it should) than its 1999 or 1997 counterparts. Consisting, as it does in the model in those two years, of only the old-age pension, the impact of the social wage in 1997 and 1999 was, however, still substantial.

Table 11.3b *Numbers of people (thousands) below various poverty lines*

	Child cost ratio =		0.5	
	Hhold econs of scale parameter =		0.9	
	Error level (%) =		80	
		2002		
2002 Poverty line (R/m in 2002 prices)	Pre-social wage	Post-social wage	Change	Poverty line – short description
R319	17 000	12 200	4 800	6. D$1, 2A + 2C
R347	17 800	13 700	4 100	5. D$1, 2A + 3C
R557	20 600	19 400	1 200	4. HSL 1
R576	20 700	19 600	1 100	3. Off. 2A + 2C
R628	21 000	20 100	900	2. Chen, 2A + 2C
R684	21 300	20 500	800	1. Chen, 2A + 3C
		1999		
	Pre-social wage	Post-social wage	Change	
R319	13 500	11 700	1 800	
R347	14 400	12 900	1 500	
R557	18 000	17 400	600	
R576	18 600	18 100	500	
R628	19 000	18 700	300	
R684	19 400	19 100	300	
		1997		
	Pre-social wage	Post-social wage	Change	
R319	13 300	11 300	2 000	
R347	14 400	12 600	1 800	
R557	18 600	17 900	700	
R576	19 200	18 600	600	
R628	19 700	19 300	400	
R684	20 100	19 700	400	

Note: The poverty line is in R/month in 2002 per adult equivalent.

Tables 11.3b and 11.3c, whose two lowest poverty lines may be described as scaled dollar-a-day equivalents to the R214 per capita line denoting absolute poverty, both find either equal or slightly larger numbers of poor than the per capita line. There are, however, substantial differences in some of the post-social wage estimates. Instead of the 10.6 million one sees in Table 11.3a, the R319 line in Table 11.3b has 11.2 million. The gap widens when the line goes to R347. The R271 line in Table 11.3c records 11.7 million people below the Deaton dollar-a-day two-adult, two-child line. The differences that result from assuming that the two-adult standard household has in it either two or three children are visible, and are obviously affected by the magnitude of the child cost ratio – the closer that gets to unity, the smaller the difference. There are some quite marked differences for the other two scaled poverty lines, the 'Official' and the Chen and Ravallion. In both cases, assuming that there are either two or three children in the standard household makes some difference. A similar conclusion holds for lines HSL 1 (R557, Table 11.3b) and HSL 2 (R454, Table 11.3c). The lesson to emerge from this is that choosing a per capita line, as opposed to its per adult-equivalent variant, can sometimes make quite a difference to the conclusions one draws.

Table 11.3c *Numbers of people (thousands) below various poverty lines*

Child cost ratio =		0.8		
Hhold econs of scale parameter =		0.9		
Error level (%) =		80		
	2002			
2002 Poverty line (R/m in 2002 prices)	Pre-social wage	Post-social wage	Change	Poverty line – short description
R271	16 900	11 700	5 200	6. D$1, 2A + 2C
R283	17 300	12 500	4 800	5. D$1, 2A + 3C
R454	20 000	18 600	1 400	4. HSL 2
R489	20 300	19 200	1 100	3. Off. 2A + 2C
R533	20 600	19 700	900	2. Chen, 2A + 2C
R556	20 800	19 900	900	1. Chen, 2A + 3C
	1999			
	Pre-social wage	Post-social wage	Change	
R271	13 600	11 600	2 000	
R283	14 100	12 200	1 900	
R454	17 500	16 700	800	
R489	18 300	17 700	600	
R533	18 700	18 300	400	
R556	18 800	18 500	300	

	1997		
	Pre-social wage	Post-social wage	Change
R271	13 500	11 200	2 300
R283	14 000	11 800	2 200
R454	18 100	17 200	900
R489	19 000	18 400	600
R533	19 500	19 000	500
R556	19 700	19 300	400

Note: The poverty line is in R/month in 2002 per adult equivalent.

Halving the proportion of ultra-poor, as noted earlier, is a relatively modest ambition when compared with the Copenhagen goal of 'eradicating absolute poverty'. This modesty is matched by a silence in the Millennium Declaration on the question of targets for reduction of poverty gaps. The absence of a benchmark makes evaluation of progress difficult, so, in a sense, the discussion on poverty gaps that follows takes place in a bit of a vacuum. That does not relieve us, however, of the need to consider the poverty gaps. Doing so serves to highlight the modesty of the MDG targets. Poverty gap estimates are only made for the per capita poverty line estimates in Table 11.3a. As the model currently stands, the poverty gap estimators are not able to cope with a change from a per capita poverty line (from poverty line set No. 1) to per adult equivalent poverty lines (to poverty line sets Nos. 2 and 3). The intuition that poverty gap estimates prepared by the two different methods should not differ by too much has, however, been tested on the pre-social wage figures for the bottom expenditure category (R0–399 per month) for the year 2002 for the R214 poverty line. The test result is satisfactory.[107]

Two aspects of the poverty gap estimates at the foot of Table 11.3a need to be considered: firstly, their absolute size, and secondly, the change in poverty gaps over time. As far as the absolute size is concerned, the pre-social wage gap in 2002 grows from R24.6 billion per annum at the R214 per month level, to R72.0 billion at the R422 level (the Chen and Ravallion line). In absolute terms, the post-social wage figures are similar – a social wage of about R20 billion per annum in 2002 reduces the gap at the R214 level to R7.4 billion per annum, and at the R422 level, to R48.6 billion per annum. As one would expect, with increasing numbers of poor found by higher-level poverty lines, the poverty gaps all rise quite substantially. The post-social wage figures offer one ray of hope amidst a generally gloomy outlook. At the absolute poverty line of R214 per month, the poverty gap falls quite substantially (i.e. the number of post-social wage poor falls at that level, so the severity of poverty decreases). For the R387 and R422 poverty lines, the post-social wage poverty gap in each of the three years is stable.

The 120 per cent error figures in Tables 11.4a, 11.4b and 11.4c paint an altogether more optimistic picture of conditions, especially in the end year, 2002. Focusing on the Table 11.4a results (those obtained using the per capita poverty lines in poverty line set No. 1), and comparing them with the corresponding Table 11.3a results, we observe a huge difference in the estimates of the numbers down in the starvation category of R104 per month.

Instead of 10.4 million of these unfortunates in the pre-social wage setting, we find about 7.6 million people. Post-social wage, both sets of numbers approach zero (200 000 versus 600 000 with an 80 per cent error). At the Deaton dollar-a-day line (R214 per month) there are 15.0 million people[108] as opposed to 17.0 million. The social wage reduces these numbers to 8.7 and 10.6 million respectively. The difference between changes at the 120 per cent error level and those at the 80 per cent level presumably results from the concentration of people not far below the R214 level. Whatever the explanation, the relief of absolute poverty (always assuming benefits are reaching their intended recipients) is almost palpable.

Table 11.4a *Numbers of people (thousands) below various poverty lines*

	Child cost ratio =		1.0	
	Hhold econs of scale parameter =		1.0	
	Error level (%) =		120	
		2002		
2002 Poverty line (R/m in 2002 prices)	Pre-social wage	Post-social wage	Change	Poverty line – short description
R104	7 600	200	7 400	6. PPP $/d
R214	15 000	8 700	6 300	5. Deaton $/d
R344	18 400	16 100	2 300	4. HSL 1pc
R387	19 100	17 300	1 800	3. Official
R422	19 400	18 000	1 400	2. Chen
		1999		
	Pre-social wage	Post-social wage	Change	
R104	4 800	1 900	2 900	
R214	11 700	9 400	2 300	
R344	15 100	13 700	1 400	
R387	16 800	16 000	800	
R422	17 200	16 700	500	
		1997		
	Pre-social wage	Post-social wage	Change	
R104	4 300	1 500	2 800	
R214	11 500	8 800	2 700	
R344	15 200	13 500	1 700	
R387	17 400	16 400	1 000	
R422	18 100	17 200	900	

Poverty gap estimates (R billion/annum in 2002 prices)			
	2002	1999	1997
	Pre-social wage	Pre-social wage	Pre-social wage
R104	3.6	1.9	1.6
R214	18.9	12.7	11.8
R344	45.5	27.5	25.7
R387	55.4	43.3	42.7
R422	63.6	50.5	50.3
	2002	1999	1997
	Post-social wage	Post-social wage	Post-social wage
R104	0.0	0.4	0.2
R214	4.8	7.3	6.4
R344	24.9	19.8	18.1
R387	33.5	34.6	33.6
R422	41.0	41.5	40.7

Note: The poverty line is in R/month in 2002 per person.

With the 120 per cent error assumption, the number of absolutely poor stabilises around the 9 million mark, yielding – as we shall see when we consider the Table 11.5 results – a fairly substantial reduction in the poverty rate. Further up the expenditure scale, the pre-social wage numbers of poor begin to converge. The difference between the numbers of poor at the R344 and R422 lines is only 1 million. Tables 11.3 and 11.4 make visible the intuitively obvious fact of the increasing effectiveness of the social wage at reducing poverty as the poverty line falls. Consider for a moment Table 11.4a. In the column containing the pre-social wage headcounts, we observe that in 2002, the jump from the R214 poverty line to the R344 line (about R130) is associated with an increase in the number in poverty of 3.4 million. The increase in the poverty line from R344 to R422 (R78) is associated with an increase in the number of poor of only 700 000 million. The effect is much more noticeable when the post-social wage figures are considered. In 2002, the social wage, had it been distributed to every eligible beneficiary, would have lifted about 6.3 million people above the absolute poverty line of R214 per month. In contrast, only 2.3 million are pushed by the social wage into the expenditure category R344–387. Given the high degree of inequality in South Africa, and the extreme poverty of some large number of its inhabitants, this is only to be expected.[109]

Deciding how many people lie beneath a line drawn arbitrarily in consumption space is not always a meaningful activity.[110] When, however, one is concerned to measure the impact of policy on a condition as dire as absolute poverty, estimates of the number of poor people have to be made, willy-nilly. Under these conditions, the sensitivity of the poverty line to changes in its level begins to assume some importance. At or near a line whose level is sufficiently 'generous', not only are poverty headcounts relatively insensitive to the social wage; they are also relatively invariant to quite large changes in the assumptions used to construct the poverty lines. Although still responsive to changes in the (assumed) extent of under-reporting of expenditure, they do not display anything like the sensitivity to variation in under-reporting that is visible lower down the expenditure scale. This relationship may be expressed in the familiar terms of an elasticity (I have called it the 'headcount elasticity'). If the percentage change in the number of people (say, for argument's sake, the pre-social wage totals) is divided by the percentage change in the level of the poverty line in each case, one finds that it has a value of 0.59 for the change from R214 to R344, and a value of 0.30 for the change from R344 to R378. For relatively 'high' poverty line levels, the interest in this curiosity lies in the fact that it becomes asymptotic, thus driving home the point that beyond some fairly low level, reducing the number of poor becomes increasingly difficult.

Table 11.4b *Numbers of people (thousands) below various poverty lines*

	Child cost ratio =		0.5		
	Hhold econs of scale parameter =		0.9		
	Error level (%) =		120		
		2002			
2002 Poverty line (R/m in 2002 prices)	Pre-social wage	Post-social wage	Change	Poverty line – short description	
R319	14 600	9 100	5 500	6. D$1, 2A + 2C	
R347	15 600	10 700	4 900	5. D$1, 2A + 3C	
R557	19 600	17 900	1 700	4. HSL 1	
R576	19 700	18 200	1 500	3. Off. 2A + 2C	
R628	20 200	19 000	1 200	2. Chen, 2A + 2C	
R684	20 500	19 600	900	1. Chen, 2A + 3C	
		1999			
	Pre-social wage	Post-social wage	Change		
R319	10 700	8 800	1 900		
R347	11 800	10 100	1 700		
R557	16 300	15 400	900		
R576	17 100	16 500	600		
R628	17 800	17 300	500		
R684	18 300	17 900	400		

| | 1997 | | |
	Pre-social wage	Post-social wage	Change
R319	10 200	8 100	2 100
R347	11 400	9 400	2 000
R557	16 600	15 600	1 000
R576	17 500	16 700	800
R628	18 300	17 600	700
R684	18 900	18 400	500

Note: The poverty line is in R/month in 2002 per adult equivalent.

Reference has been made above to the finding from the sensitivity tests on poverty lines conducted by Woolard and Leibbrandt (2001).[111] At the 'high' poverty line levels with which they worked, they found that headcounts were fairly insensitive to comparatively large changes in poverty line levels. The finding that this is not the case at low levels, such as the absolute poverty line tested in Tables 11.3a and 11.4a, highlights the importance of agreeing on lines, and then maintaining them in good condition during the period for which they are supposed to function as benchmark indicators. Maintenance of the lines (it may be necessary to have several, say, for rural and urban conditions, both with upper and lower bounds) requires that careful attention be paid to selection of deflators.

At the foot of Table 11.4a the poverty gap estimates are presented (as is done in Table 11.3a). Looking once more at the two aspects of the gap that are of concern here, it may be seen that at the R214 level, the pre-social wage gap was R18.9 billion per annum in 2002. This increases to R63.6 billion at the R422 level. As is the case with the Table 11.3a figures, the post-social wage poverty gaps provide some light in the gloom. The social wage pushes the R214 gap to only R4.8 billion per annum. Whereas the pre-social wage poverty gap rises (from R11.8 billion in 1997 to the aforementioned R18.9 billion in 2002), the post-social wage poverty gap appears to fall slightly. Given the apparent fall in the post-social wage headcount over the period, the severity of absolute poverty declines. Although it seems unlikely that the poverty MDG will be met with existing anti-poverty policies, the reduction in the severity of poverty that would ensue if the full package of social wage components reached the intended beneficiaries is still considerable. Once government's ambition extends beyond lifting people above the Deaton dollar-a-day line (R214 per month), the difficulties begin to mount. In both Table 11.3a and Table 11.4a the post-social wage poverty gap is either rising, or static above the line of absolute poverty, despite the billions of rands that have been thrown at poverty.

The need for surveys that are better able to measure expenditure more accurately (and more frequently than at present) is apparent in the differences between the magnitudes of the post-social wage poverty gap in 2002 in Table 11.3a and its

11.4a counterpart (R40.4 billion versus R33.5 billion at the 'official' poverty line). This indicator of the depth of our ignorance of the 'true' conditions of the poor is important. Implications for financing the social wage, should the larger amount have to be found, are obvious.[112]

Poverty gaps estimated here are close enough to those in Bhorat (2001) and Samson (2003) to inspire some confidence in the simulation exercise. Bhorat's (2001: 160) figure for the year 1995 estimates that R12.8 billion (in 1995 prices) would have to reach the poor each year to eradicate poverty. Inflated to 2002 prices, the requisite amount would be R22.2 billion. Bhorat uses the HSL 1 poverty line (R293 per month in 1995, which translates into R557 per month per adult equivalent, or R344 per capita). His estimates would have included expenditure made using the old-age pension, the most important element of the social wage available in 1995. The estimate is neatly bracketed by the simulation figures. The Table 11.3a post-social wage poverty gap at the 80 per cent error level in 1997 is R24.4 billion. The Table 11.4a pre-social wage poverty gap for 1997 (at the 120 per cent error level) is R25.7, while the post-social wage figure is R18.1. Samson (2003: 31), using an HSL poverty line, put the 2000 poverty gap at R44.6 excluding grant income, and R31.8 billion including it. Converted to 2002 prices, these yield poverty gaps of R53.6 and R38.1 billion respectively. Increases in social spending between 2000 and 2002 could have reduced this a little. The Table 11.3a results for 2002 are close to these figures – R53.6 and R31.2 billion respectively. The Table 11.4a 2002 pre-social wage figure is R45.5 billion; that for the post-social wage is R24.9 billion. It does not require much reduction in the under-reporting error assumption level to bring the estimates in the paper roughly into line with those in the Samson piece.

Table 11.4c *Numbers of people (thousands) below various poverty lines*

	Child cost ratio =	0.8		
	Hhold econs of scale parameter =	0.9		
	Error level (%) =	120		
		2002		
2002 Poverty line (R/m in 2002 prices)	Pre-social wage	Post-social wage	Change	Poverty line – short description
R271	14 600	8 700	5 900	6. $1, 2A + 2C
R283	15 100	9 500	5 600	5. $1, 2A + 3C
R454	19 000	17 000	2 000	4. HSL 2
R489	19 400	17 700	1 700	3. Off. 2A + 2C
R533	19 800	18 500	1 300	2. Chen, 2A + 2C
R556	20 000	18 900	1 100	1. Chen, 2A + 3C

	1999		
	Pre-social wage	**Post-social wage**	**Change**
R271	10 900	8 800	2 100
R283	11 500	9 400	2 100
R454	15 800	14 800	1 000
R489	16 900	16 200	700
R533	17 500	16 900	600
R556	17 800	17 300	500
	1997		
	Pre-social wage	**Post-social wage**	**Change**
R271	10 500	8 200	2 300
R283	11 000	8 800	2 200
R454	16 100	14 900	1 200
R489	17 400	16 500	900
R533	18 100	17 400	700
R556	18 400	17 800	600

Note: The poverty line is in R/month in 2002 per adult equivalent.

Comparison of the pre- and post-social wage headcount estimates for the R319 poverty lines in Table 11.4b and the R271 poverty line in Table 11.4c with the R214 poverty line figures in Table 11.4a, shows that sometimes, converting a per capita poverty line into a per adult equivalent line ('scaling' it), has only a small effect on the poverty headcount. The pre- and post-social wage poverty headcounts applying the per capita R214 line are 15.0 and 8.7 million respectively (Table 11.4a), while their counterparts in Table 11.4b and Table 11.4c are 14.6 and 9.1 million, and 14.6 and 8.7 million. Substantial differences start to emerge, however, if the conversion is based on the assumption that the standard household contains three rather than two children. Moving to the HSL 1 line in its two variants, R344 in Table 11.4a and R557 in Table 11.4b, one sees substantial differences emerge (18.4 and 16.1 million for the R344 line versus 19.6 and 17.9 million for the R557 line). These differences are reduced a bit by pushing up the child cost ratio as is done in the HSL 2 line in Table 11.4c. The R454 line suggests that the pre-social wage headcount was 19.0 million and the post-social wage was 17.0 million. The moral of the story is that not only does the level of the poverty line matter, but the line's form (per capita or per adult equivalent) is also important.

Table 11.5 presents the estimates of poverty at the line separating the absolutely poor from the merely poor (R214 per capita per month).[113] It contains three sets of results for the year 2002. This is to facilitate a consideration of the consequences of the value of the social wage not being correctly estimated. The table presents estimates for both the 80 and the 120 per cent expenditure under-reporting errors. As shown in Tables 11.3a and 11.4a, in 2002, the social wage reduces the headcount from 15.0 million to 8.7 million if the under-reporting error is 120 per cent, and from 17.0 million to 11.4 million if it is 80 per cent. If the social wage has been under-valued by 25 per cent, the post-social wage headcounts would fall to 8.0 and 10.6 million respectively. If it had been over-valued by a similar percentage, the post-social wage headcounts would have been 9.5 and 12.2 million respectively.

Pre-social wage estimates, of course, are unaffected by all of this. In the absence of the social wage, the 120 per cent error figures would have the number of poor rising by 3.3 million between 1997 and 2002. The lower error (80 per cent) sees a slightly smaller increase (2.9 million) in the headcount. The smaller increase in the number of poor is more than offset by the higher initial headcounts. The impact of the social wage for both error conditions is similar, with the magnitude of the final change showing considerable sensitivity to the value of the social wage. If a correction is made for an under-valuation of the social wage of 25 per cent, the headcount falls by between 800 000 and 1.1 million in the period between 1997 and 2002. A correction of similar magnitude for over-valuation would disclose that the post-social wage headcount had risen by something in the region of 500 000–700 000. Self-evidently, accurate estimates of the impact of the social wage are indispensable if anything credible is to be said about changes in poverty over time.

Poverty rates, the critical variable for the poverty reduction goal, behave as expected. For zero social wage error, and 120 per cent under-reporting of expenditure error, the post-social wage poverty rate falls slightly (from 21.3 per cent in 1997 to 19.1 per cent in 2002). If the value of the social wage has been under-estimated, the rate falls to 17.6 per cent in 2002. An overestimate of its value would still see the rate falling (but almost imperceptibly), to 20.9 per cent. The 80 per cent expenditure under-reporting error results differ slightly, with falls in the poverty rate, from a higher base, registered in each case. Post-social wage poverty gaps in 2002 are barely affected.

The variability of the numbers notwithstanding, if any of the headcount figures is correct (as ever, the question of whether or not the benefits went to the most deserving hovers over us), then what can only be described as a major catastrophe will have been averted.[114] That much acknowledged, it is sobering to reflect on the magnitude of the task of halving poverty rates. If the vast sums of money poured into poverty alleviation have brought down the poverty rate by between only one and two percentage points over five years, then the goal of halving the rate (starting from high base rates) by 2014 may not be capable of being achieved.

Table 11.5 *Poverty at R214 level in 2002*

Parameters	Child cost ratio	Hhold econs of scale	Bottom bound (%)		
	1.0	1.0	50		
	Poverty headcount (thousands) (z = R214 per month per person in 2002)				
	Sept. 2002			Oct. 1999	Oct. 1997
120 per cent under-reporting of expenditure					
Pre-social wage	15 000	15 000	15 000	11 700	11 500
SW error (%)	+25	0	−25	–	–
Post-social wage	8 000	8 700	9 500	9 400	8 800
80 per cent under-reporting of expenditure					
Pre-social wage	17 000	17 000	17 000	14 100	14 100
SW error (%)	+25	0	−25	–	–
Post-social wage	10 600	11 400	12 200	11 900	11 700
	Changes in numbers of people below z				
		02–99	02–97	99–97	
120 per cent under-reporting of expenditure					
Pre-social wage		3 300	3 500	200	
Post-social wage (+25% error)		−1 400	−800	600	
Post-social wage (0% error)		−700	−100	600	
Post-social wage (−25% error)		100	700	600	
80 per cent under-reporting of expenditure					
Pre-social wage		2 900	2 900	0	
Post-social wage (+25% error)		−1 300	−1 100	200	
Post-social wage (0% error)		−500	−300	200	
Post-social wage (−25% error)		300	500	200	
	Poverty rate (%)				
	Sept. 2002			Oct. 1999	Oct. 1997
120 per cent under-reporting of expenditure					
Pre-social wage	33.0	33.0	33.0	27.2	27.9
SW error (%)	+25	0	−25	–	–
Post-social wage	17.6	19.1	20.9	21.8	21.3
80 per cent under-reporting of expenditure					
Pre-social wage	37.4	37.4	37.4	32.7	34.2
SW error (%)	+25	0	−25	–	–
Post-social wage	23.3	25.1	26.8	27.6	28.4

→

Poverty gap (R billions/per annum)				
	Sept. 2002			Oct. 1999	Oct. 1997
120 per cent under-reporting of expenditure					
Pre-social wage	18.9	18.9	18.9	12.7	11.8
SW error (%)	+25	0	−25	–	–
Post-social wage	4.1	4.8	5.7	7.3	6.4
80 per cent under-reporting of expenditure					
Pre-social wage	24.6	24.6	24.6	17.7	16.9
SW error (%)	+25	0	−25	–	–
Post-social wage	6.4	7.4	8.5	10.9	10.0

Other than reinforcing the common-sense assertion that the social wage, if properly targeted and delivered, would have had a significant impact on the welfare of those below the line demarcating absolute poverty, the Table 11.5 results cannot tell us much more. This forces from us an acknowledgement of the fact that it is not possible to say with any certainty what has happened to absolute poverty – there are just too many 'ifs' for comfort. The zone of ignorance begins to shrink, however, as the level of the poverty line is raised. This may be seen in Table 11.6, where the poverty line is raised to R344 per person per month.

Table 11.6 *Poverty at R344 level in 2002*

Parameters	
Child cost ratio =	1.0
Hhold econs of scale =	1.0
Bottom bound (%) =	50.0

Poverty headcount (thousands) (z = R344 per month per person in 2002)			
	Sept. 2002	Oct. 1999	Oct. 1997
120 per cent under-reporting of expenditure			
Pre-social wage	18 400	15 100	15 200
Post-social wage	16 100	13 700	13 500
80 per cent under-reporting of expenditure			
Pre-social wage	19 400	16 800	17 300
Post-social wage	17 800	15 700	15 900

Changes in numbers of people below z			
	02–99	02–97	99–97
120 per cent under-reporting of expenditure			
Pre-social wage	3 300	3 200	−100
Post-social wage	2 400	2 600	200
80 per cent under-reporting of expenditure			
Pre-social wage	2 600	2 100	−500
Post-social wage	2 100	1 900	−200

Poverty rate (%)			
	Sept. 2002	Oct. 1999	Oct. 1997
120 per cent under-reporting of expenditure			
Pre-social wage	40.5	35.1	36.9
Post-social wage	35.4	31.8	32.7
80 per cent under-reporting of expenditure			
Pre-social wage	42.7	39.0	42.0
Post-social wage	39.2	36.5	38.6
Poverty gap (R billions/per annum)			
	Sept. 2002	Oct. 1999	Oct. 1997
120 per cent under-reporting of expenditure			
Pre-social wage	45.5	27.5	25.7
Post-social wage	24.9	19.8	18.1
80 per cent under-reporting of expenditure			
Pre-social wage	53.6	34.7	33.4
Post-social wage	31.2	26.1	24.4

R344 per person per month is the amount, it may be recalled, required to yield the same level of consumption as the Potgieter HSL 1 poverty line of R557 per adult equivalent per month. To obtain this figure, the 'conventional' child cost ratio and household economies of scale parameter of 0.5 and 0.9 respectively are used. The Table 11.6 figures should be read in conjunction with those in Table 11.7.

Table 11.7 *Poverty at R557 level in 2002*

Parameters			
Child cost ratio =	0.5		
Hhold econs of scale =	0.9		
Bottom bound (%) =	50.0		
Poverty headcount (thousands) (z = R557 per month per adult equivalent in 2002)			
	Sept. 2002	Oct. 1999	Oct. 1997
120 per cent under-reporting of expenditure			
Pre-social wage	19 600	16 300	16 600
Post-social wage	17 900	15 400	15 600
80 per cent under-reporting of expenditure			
Pre-social wage	20 600	18 000	18 600
Post-social wage	19 400	17 400	17 900

Changes in numbers of people below z			
	02–99	02–97	99–97
120 per cent under-reporting of expenditure			
Pre-social wage	3 300	3 000	–300
Post-social wage	2 500	2 300	–200
80 per cent under-reporting of expenditure			
Pre-social wage	2 600	2 000	–600
Post-social wage	2 000	1 500	–500
Poverty rate (%)			
	Sept. 2002	Oct. 1999	Oct. 1997
120 per cent under-reporting of expenditure			
Pre-social wage	43.1	37.9	40.3
Post-social wage	39.4	35.8	37.8
80 per cent under-reporting of expenditure			
Pre-social wage	45.3	41.8	45.1
Post-social wage	42.7	40.4	43.4

A zero social wage error is assumed for both the Table 11.6 and the Table 11.7 results. As pointed out earlier, estimates of the numbers in poverty in 2002, both before and after the social wage, differ substantially for each of the assumed error levels, the HSL figures in Table 11.7 being consistently higher. Without delving deeply into the arithmetic (which we have no intention of doing here), it is not obvious why this should be. In contrast, the differences between the reductions in the pre-and post-social wage changes in numbers of poor are trivial (a few hundred thousand at most). In its per capita form the social wage appears to reduce the poverty headcount by slightly smaller amounts. This is offset by the lower estimates of poverty headcounts yielded by the per capita poverty measures. Despite this, there may be some virtue in using per capita poverty measures, if only because of their simplicity. The political advantage of such a measure is obvious.

Whatever the case, in both sets of figures the by now familiar pattern of larger headcounts, coupled with smaller changes in them as a result of the social wage, appears yet again. Headcounts and poverty rates appear to be approaching plateaux from which the social wage cannot dislodge them. Under the 120 per cent error assumption, the Table 11.6 post-social wage poverty rate rises by about 2.7 percentage points, while the 80 per cent error sees the rate remaining roughly constant. Associated with the larger headcounts are correspondingly large poverty gaps. The 2002 post-social wage gap could be between R25 billion and R31 billion per annum.

The pattern of changes in the Table 11.7 poverty rates is similar to that in the Table 11.6 figures. With the 120 per cent under-reporting error in Table 11.7, the 2002 post-social wage headcount is larger than the 1997 pre-social wage figure. Between those two years, the poverty headcount rises by 2.3 million, the social wage notwithstanding. As before, the 80 per cent error figures show slightly smaller headcount increases. The 2002 post-social wage headcount is slightly larger than the 1997 pre-social wage headcount (by 600 000 or so).

Using the line that might be adopted as the official lower bound of the poverty critical range, R387 per capita per month, the Table 11.8 figures have about 19–20 million people in poverty. Their number, post-social wage, might have increased by between 300 000 and 900 000 between 1997 and 2002. With the 120 per cent error, the poverty rate is high (in the region of 40 per cent), and the rate of decline is low. Part of the explanation for this is that the higher poverty line is beginning to find many more poor people in 1997. All of which raises a further methodological problem, namely, the question of the level at which to set the under-reporting error for the earlier years. In the model, the same error is used for each year. Since error levels in each year can be set independently, there is nothing preventing us from making the level lower (or higher) in earlier years. The consequences of doing so are interesting. As the assumed under-reporting error level falls, the number below the poverty line rises. If under-reporting errors were lower in earlier years, this would result in a more optimistic set of poverty reduction outcomes. One can see this by doing a 'mix-and-match' with the Table 11.8 results. An under-reporting error of 120 per cent in 2002, combined with one of 80 per cent in 1997, would yield roughly constant pre-social wage headcounts (19.1 and 18.8 million). Corresponding to this would be a drop in the pre-social wage poverty rate from 45.6 per cent to 42.0 per cent. The post-social wage headcounts register a fall of 900 000, while rates fall by a whopping 6 percentage points, from 44.1 to 38.1 per cent. This is the point at which to utter the researcher's usual plea for more research. Apart from a reconciliation of the 1997 survey and national accounts figures, one possible direction that research could take is into the (disputed) results for 1995 yielded by the OHS and the IES conducted in that year. In the absence of an ability to demonstrate that errors in the different years differ, the rate of poverty reduction in Table 11.9 looks desultory, with consequent spiralling of poverty gaps. Our ability to judge the efficacy of social security policy requires that the ignorance disclosed above be dispelled.

Table 11.8 *Poverty at R387 level in 2002*

Parameters	
Child cost ratio =	1.0
Hhold econs of scale =	1.0
Bottom bound (%) =	50.0

$\longrightarrow$

→

Poverty headcount (thousands) (z = R387 per month per person in 2002)		
	Sept. 2002	Oct. 1999	Oct. 1997
120 per cent under-reporting of expenditure			
Pre-social wage	19 100	16 800	17 400
Post-social wage	17 300	16 000	16 400

Poverty headcount (thousands) (z = R387 per month per person in 2002)		
	Sept. 2002	Oct. 1999	Oct. 1997
80 per cent under-reporting of expenditure			
Pre-social wage	19 800	18 000	18 800
Post-social wage	18 500	17 300	18 200

Changes in numbers of people below z		
	02–99	02–97	99–97
120 per cent under-reporting of expenditure			
Pre-social wage	2 300	1 700	-600
Post-social wage	1 300	900	-400
80 per cent under-reporting of expenditure			
Pre-social wage	1 800	1 000	-800
Post-social wage	1 200	300	-900

Poverty rate (%)		
	Sept. 2002	Oct. 1999	Oct. 1997
120 per cent under-reporting of expenditure			
Pre-social wage	42.0	39.0	42.2
Post-social wage	38.1	37.2	39.8
80 per cent under-reporting of expenditure			
Pre-social wage	43.6	41.8	45.6
Post-social wage	40.7	40.2	44.1

Poverty gap (R billions/per annum)		
	Sept. 2002	Oct. 1999	Oct. 1997
120 per cent under-reporting of expenditure			
Pre-social wage	55.4	43.3	42.7
Post-social wage	33.5	34.6	33.6
80 per cent under-reporting of expenditure			
Pre-social wage	63.6	52.0	52.2
Post-social wage	40.4	42.4	42.2

Having arrived at the R422 line, below which Chen and Ravallion suggest social exclusion might lie, we investigate once more the impact of assuming that the value of the social wage has not been correctly estimated.

Table 11.9 *Poverty at R422 level in 2002*

Parameters	Child cost ratio	Hhold econs of scale	Bottom bound (%)		
	1.0	1.0	50		
Poverty headcount (thousands) (z = R422 per month per person in 2002)					
		Sept. 2002		Oct. 1999	Oct. 1997
120 per cent under-reporting of expenditure					
Pre-social wage	19 400	19 400	19 400	17 200	18 100
SW error (%)	+25	0	−25	–	–
Post-social wage	17 800	18 000	18 200	16 700	17 200
80 per cent under-reporting of expenditure					
Pre-social wage	20 200	20 200	20 200	18 300	19 300
SW error (%)	+25	0	−25	–	–
Post-social wage	18 900	19 100	19 300	17 800	18 700
Changes in numbers of people below z					
		02–99	02–97	99–97	
120 per cent under-reporting of expenditure					
Pre-social wage		2 200	1 300	−900	
Post-social wage (+25% error)		1 100	600	−500	
Post-social wage (0% error)		1 300	800	−500	
Post-social wage (−25% error)		1 500	1 000	−500	
80 per cent under-reporting of expenditure					
Pre-social wage		1 900	900	−1 000	
Post-social wage (+25% error)		1 100	200	−900	
Post-social wage (0% error)		1 300	400	−900	
Post-social wage (−25% error)		1 500	600	−900	
Poverty rate (%)					
		Sept. 2002		Oct. 1999	Oct. 1997
120 per cent under-reporting of expenditure					
Pre-social wage	42.7	42.7	42.7	39.9	43.9
SW error (%)	+25	0	−25	–	–
Post-social wage	39.2	39.6	40.0	38.8	41.7
80 per cent under-reporting of expenditure					
Pre-social wage	44.4	44.4	44.4	42.5	46.8
SW error (%)	+25	0	−25	–	–
Post-social wage	41.6	42.0	42.5	41.3	45.4

→

Poverty gap (R billions/per annum)					
	Sept. 2002			Oct. 1999	Oct. 1997
120 per cent under-reporting of expenditure					
Pre-social wage	63.6	63.6	63.6	50.5	50.3
SW error (%)	+25	0	−25	–	–
Post-social wage	39.1	41.0	42.9	41.5	40.7
80 per cent under-reporting of expenditure					
Pre-social wage	72.0	72.0	72.0	59.7	60.4
SW error (%)	+25	0	−25	–	–
Post-social wage	46.4	48.6	50.8	50.0	50.0

Comparing the three sets of estimates for the year 2002 in Table 11.9, the first thing to note is that the increase in the post-social wage poverty headcount between 1997 and 2002 does not disappear as the assumed level of under- or over-valuation of the social wage is allowed to vary. If the social wage had been under-valued by 25 per cent, then at the 120 per cent expenditure under-reporting error level, the number below the line would have grown by about 600 000. Over-valuation of the social wage by a similar percentage would be associated with a post-social wage headcount increase of 1.0 million at the 120 per cent error level. Corresponding figures for the 80 per cent expenditure under-reporting error level are 200 000 and 600 000. After taking the social wage (of whatever value) into account, there are between 18.9 and 19.3 million people below the line. Differences between the three estimates in Table 11.9 of the post-social wage poverty rates in 2002 are trivial – a range of 40.0 to 39.2 per cent, or one of 42.5 to 41.6 per cent. The extent of change in the period 1997–2002 is quite sensitive to under-reporting error. In the table, the lower error may be seen to be associated with a satisfyingly large drop in the post-social wage poverty rate (from 45.4 per cent to somewhere in the region of 42 per cent).

Post-social wage poverty gap estimates obviously vary as the assumption about the value of the social wage is changed. The poverty gaps are so large, however, that these variations are comparatively small when expressed in percentage terms. At the 120 per cent expenditure under-reporting level, post-social wage poverty gaps are roughly constant between 1997 and 2002 regardless of whether or not the social wage is assumed to be correctly estimated. At the 80 per cent expenditure under-reporting level they either remain static, fall slightly, or rise slightly. Once more, the variation in percentage terms is quite small.

Unlike those at or near the line of absolute poverty, the results that emerge as the poverty line is raised are starting to look more robust (depending, of course, on the degree of under-reporting of expenditure in the earlier surveys). As a corollary, poverty looks more and more intractable. So, while the simulation exercises that have to be conducted in the face of data deficiencies cannot tell us much about changes in absolute poverty, it looks as though the figures may have something sensible to say about what happens as the goal of anti-poverty policy is elevated above just coping with absolute poverty. That something appears to be the conclusion that the social wage becomes less and less effective as poverty lines rise towards a humane level. To place the R422 per capita poverty line in perspective, it is useful to recall Hoogeveen and Özler's finding that using a basic 'cost-of-needs' approach,

> a reasonable poverty line for South Africa must lie between 322 Rand (lower-bound poverty line) and 593 Rand (upper-bound poverty line) per capita in 2000 prices... . (Hoogeveen and Özler 2004: 9)

Converted to 2002 prices, this yields a poverty range of R387–R713 per capita per month. Working our way up from the line of absolute poverty (where findings are ambiguous), we observe that not long after climbing above the Hoogeveen and Özler lower-bound poverty line (we are nowhere near the upper bound), the results begin to stabilise around the conclusion that the post-social wage headcount has risen, that the declines in poverty rates are relatively small, and that poverty gaps are relatively insensitive to substantial variations in the assumed value of the social wage.[115] This inevitably poses the question of how much more the 'social wage' can do to lift people out of poverty. With the exception of housing (and education), the model has already awarded everyone the full social wage. The only augmentation of the social security system is the proposed extension of the CSG to children under the age of 14 years. Although this will reduce poverty, there are not enough children in the poorest households to raise household consumption enough to lift the adults out of poverty.[116]

It may be worth noting that the results for some variants of the simulations reported on above suggest a slight improvement in conditions between 1997 and 1999. Where it occurs, it is made evident by a reduction in the numbers in poverty. So small, however, are most of the changes, that they (like many other changes reported above) are almost certainly not statistically significant. In any event, the findings are not wildly out of line with the labour market outcomes over the period. Between 1997 and 1999, the number of unemployed appears to have risen by about 700 000, using either the official or the expanded definition. From 1999 to 2002, according to the expanded definition, the increase was probably in the region of two million.[117] Formal employment declined slightly between 1997 and 1999 (by about 160 000 or so), having hit a trough in 1998, out of which it climbed but slowly. Informal-sector employment probably increased.[118]

On the question of statistical significance, it should be noted that none of the changes reported above has been tested for it. Since there are numerous unanswered questions about the methodology used to derive the pre- and post-social wage estimates, there seems little point in carrying out this time-consuming exercise at present. Assuming that the methods are reasonably robust, one would not want to attach too much significance to changes of a few hundred thousand in poverty headcounts. When the numbers climb over the million mark, however, they are possibly hinting at changes of some importance.

The last figures to be aired in this brief presentation of the model's results give a rough indication of the impact of changes in the levels of individual components of the social wage on the numbers of poor. The figures refer to two scenarios: the Deaton dollar-a-day (R214 per month), and the Chen and Ravallion R422 line, both in their 80 per cent under-reporting settings. For convenience, they are collected and presented in Table 11.10.

Table 11.10 *Impact of individual components of social wage on poverty*

Poverty line	Numbers raised above (thousands)		Value of transfer (R billions)	
	R214	R422	R214	R422
Pensions and CSG	2 018	421	8.9	11.1
Electricity	242	74	0.6	0.9
Water	182	56	0.4	0.7
Transport	184	56	0.5	0.7
Housing (subsidy)	860	251	2.0	3.2
Health	800	121	2.4	3.3
Total – listed benefits	5 534	1 033	14.3	17.1

Source: Own calculations in spreadsheet 'SocialWage-4.xls'.

A few words of caution are necessary before looking at the figures in Table 11.10. In the first place, they are extracted from the zero-error social wage estimates. In the second, the method used to estimate the values of the transfers is rough and ready, consisting as it does of estimating the difference between poverty gaps with and without the benefit under consideration. Even so, where it is possible to check them, the results appear to be within striking distance of the social security administrative data. It looks as though a bit more than half of the total payout of the R15 billion on old-age pensions accrued to people in the bottom two expenditure categories. The total amount paid out for child support grants looks as though it would have been in the region of about R3.7 billion. If about two-thirds of this accrued to people in the bottom two expenditure categories, then the figure of R9–11 billion as total pension and CSG payout would be roughly correct.

Having established the pedigree of at least some of the results, we observe that the most striking of them is the huge number of people lifted out of absolute poverty by the two cash grants for which verifiable data are readily available.[119] Next in line, in order of size of impact, are health and housing. Although individually the other components of the social wage do not have much of an effect on the numbers in poverty, taken together they do contribute to the achievement of the substantial impact the social wage has, if only at the R214 per month mark.

There are two possible ways in which the values of the transfers that lift people out of poverty may be increased: one 'real' and the other 'artificial'. The real method entails increases in the value of some or all of the components of the social wage in the social wage model. The artificial method requires corrections in the values of the components of the social wage where these have been under-estimated. The latter method has already been tried (the plus or minus 25 per cent adjustments). It is, of course, possible to make these adjustments even higher.[120] To examine the effect of doing this, anyone so inclined may go back to the model and insert their own values.

As far as the reliability of the social wage estimates is concerned, it is easy to see from this table which components of the social wage are sensitive to measurement error. Pensions and CSGs are, as we have seen, almost fully accounted for. Health and housing, both difficult to value, are the major obstacles to satisfactory measurement. Electricity, water (both relatively easy to measure) and transport (less easy to measure) appear to account for about one-third of the combined value of health and housing. The allowance for health care in the social wage model seems generous, as does that for housing (scaled in proportion to the number of subsidies granted). Since we are dealing with income poverty, the poverty-reducing capacity of any component of the social wage is the extent to which it is 'bankable', i.e. the extent to which it increases potential private consumption.[121]

If the estimates of the numbers of people in the bottom expenditure category are real, and not merely an artefact of the data, then poverty eradication using existing policies is going to become harder. Raising the age of eligibility for the CSG will have a fairly substantial effect. Unfortunately, much of this will bypass households in the bottom expenditure category, where adult:child ratios are low. Pensions will grow as the population ages, but, once again, the poorest households are poor precisely because they do not have a pensioner in the household. Further efforts to distribute more housing subsidies will help, but not by enough to make a sizeable contribution to the achievement of the MDG. Recall now that we are talking here about the absolutely poor – as the poverty line is raised to reflect a more humane standard of living (still leaving people very poor), poverty reduction becomes more difficult.[122] The intensity of poverty (the poverty gap) becomes increasingly important – the greater the gap, the less the impact of the social wage on poverty levels.

The true extent to which South Africa's anti-poverty policies have been able to counter absolute poverty must remain conjectural – data with which to make a more precise assessment are not available. It is possible that the anti-poverty measures have had, as it were, to run simply to stay still.[123] The likelihood of even the lowest of the observed poverty rates being halved by 2014 by social security policy of the existing stripe (the social wage) may be slender.

Conclusion: And now, what?

As political rallying cries, commitments to loosely specified goals such as halving unemployment or halving poverty have a certain appeal. When social scourges reach epidemic proportions, as they have in South Africa, the repeated invocation of the promise to halve one or the other, or both, may be of comfort, if not to those directly affected, then at least to those who worry over such things. Unless given greater precision, however, their value as indicators of what policy is supposed to achieve is negligible. There is an interesting similarity between the setting of goals that are at once too precise and too ambitious and the setting of goals that by their lack of precision altogether are capable of different interpretations. Reflecting on the failure of GEAR to deliver economic growth of 6 per cent per annum and 400 000 jobs a year by 2000, Friedman argues that

> raising expectations which cannot be met is not a cost-free exercise –
> indeed, it risks destroying over time precisely the confidence which the
> over-cheery projections are meant to create. Just as inflation targeting and
> Manuel's precise deficit reduction targets always run the risk of eroding
> confidence by setting an over-ambitious government goal and ensur-
> ing that failure to meet it obscures real progress, so, it could be argued,
> did Gear's growth and job creation targets create unnecessary political
> opposition to government's current macroeconomic strategy by fostering
> unrealistic expectations of what could be achieved by the proposed policy
> path (Friedman 2004: 186).

In the absence of clarity over the meaning of the halving unemployment and halving poverty goals, people are likely to take it into their heads to interpret these goals in particular ways. What the consequences are of a failure to meet these imagined goals is difficult to say – cynicism, frustration and disappointment are some obvious contenders. We have seen Deaton (2003a) arguing in favour of the use of the dollar-a-day poverty line, not because of its accuracy, but because of its rhetorical nature – it is useful because it has come to be accepted as a 'trademark' of poverty. By analogy, there is possibly merit in using catchy slogans as mobilising devices for campaigns such as the attacks on poverty and unemployment. The question is one of what goals should be formulated.

Considering first the unemployment target, this study has shown that as far as can be ascertained, neither the government nor its social partners appear to have given serious consideration to what is entailed in the making of such a commitment. Since a choice has not, apparently, been made (or if it has been, its makers have not made much effort to communicate the choice to those most affected by it) among the possible contenders for halving, no credible estimates of the numbers involved in such an exercise can be made. The three major variables that determine the rate of unemployment are:

- the rate of growth of the potential workforce;
- the participation rates (official and expanded);
- the rate of growth of employment.

Over the first of these variables the government has little control. What little there is resides in the area of policy to deal with AIDS, and in policies that attempt to reduce South Africa's shockingly high infant and child mortality rates. As we have seen, the greater the number of deaths (either of AIDS-infected adults or of children who fail to live beyond the age of five), the smaller the number of jobs that have to be created for given rates of growth of participation rates. Questions need to be raised about this terrifying contribution to the goal of halving unemployment.

Participation rates are affected by social protection policy (the introduction of unemployment benefits, for example, could encourage people to switch their labour market status from 'not economically active' to 'unemployed'). They will probably also be affected by changes in mortality rates, although in what direction it is not yet possible to say. The rate of growth of employment in the private sector can only be influenced indirectly. Speeding up the rate of job creation beyond the meagre achievement of the past decade is, however, no simple task. Over employment creation in the public sector the government has, of course, much greater control. With the exception of the planned EPWP, the government's goal in recent years has been a reduction rather than an increase in public sector employment levels.

Given (a) the confusion shown to exist in the official statistics about participation rates, (b) the difficulties of guessing what these are likely to be in the future, and (c) the problem of guessing, in the face of the AIDS epidemic, the rate of growth of the potential workforce, it is a difficult matter even to hazard a guess at the number of jobs that would have to be created to achieve the halving goal. Simulations performed on the somewhat flaky information available suggest that, at best, halving the official rate of unemployment would require the number of unemployed to fall by at least 1.4–1.5 million. To achieve this might require somewhere between 4 and 7 million jobs to have been created between 2003 and the year 2014. Attempting to halve the number of unemployed according to the expanded definition might demand in excess of 9 million new jobs – a tall order.

The sensible thing to do is to re-open the debate, this time with (a) discussion aimed at reaching agreement on the likely behaviour of the relevant variables and (b) all participants having at their disposal the means by which they can simulate likely outcomes. Only after these have been critically examined should consideration be given to the setting of goals. In all likelihood, once the relevant figures have been scrutinised, the social partners will recognise the futility of attempting to set goals of this type. Once that is acknowledged, backing away from a meaningless promise with good grace will be possible. Enough is known about unemployment and the variables associated with it to make possible the early convening of a meeting of those most concerned (the people and organisations normally referred to by that awful term, the 'stakeholders'). It should not be difficult to persuade them that a sensible approach to the unemployment problem would be to agree on an attainable goal rather than to engage in pipe-dreaming (as should have been done with GEAR).

Although this is not the place to explore 'attainable goals 'at any length, it is worth noting that pointers to the area in which such goals might lie are provided by that part of the analysis above that suggests which of the variables that determine unemployment levels are most susceptible to the levers of policy. Obviously, everything that can be done to foster private-sector employment creation should be done. The prospects for success need, however, to be disciplined by past performance and realistic assessment of future possibilities, rather than by political wishful thinking. As far as public-sector employment creation is concerned, the only growth in jobs is likely to be indirect, resulting from the EPWP.[124] Critical analysis conducted by McCord (2004) suggests that the EPWP, in its present form, is too small to make much of a dent in unemployment.

The insight that participation rates can be influenced by social protection policy should lead directly to a consideration of forms of social protection that would not have significant perverse incentive effects. One form of social protection policy that does not exert such effects springs immediately to mind – the Benefit Transfer Programmes (BTP) promoted for many years by Dennis Snower (1995a, 1995b). The vouchers he suggested as an alternative to unemployment benefits could be used to reduce the costs to employers of providing employment with meaningful training. A South African version of this could commence by introducing a modest social grant for all potentially economically active people. As the cooperation of employers is secured, the grant could be 'cashed in' with participating firms by those seeking employment, who, in addition to receiving the grant and undergoing training, would be paid a wage. Those who choose not to seek employment via this route would continue to receive the grant. Firms taking part, in addition to being able to pay a lower wage (by virtue of the grant system), would also be able to claim credit from the state for the training provided. A scheme such as this would achieve the dual aims of (a) providing social protection to the mass of people who currently drop straight through the large holes in South Africa's social protection system and (b) reducing the cost of all labour by means of a generalised wage subsidy.[125] The requisite social institution within which the suggestions above may be considered already exists in the form of the National Economic Development and Labour Council (Nedlac). All that is required is that the discussion above make its way onto the agenda of that august body.

Poverty is a somewhat different matter. Not only does the government have the capacity to influence the number of poor directly (in particular, through the social grant system),[126] but the poverty headcount, and the severity of their poverty, can, in principle, be determined with some precision. The fact that this has not been done is an indictment of all concerned. Calls for 'more research' may elicit groans, and reasonably so – the appeal being sometimes little more than thinly disguised self-interest at work. That would clearly not be true in the present case. The problem of poverty is of such overwhelming importance that no effort should have been spared in addressing the difficulties raised above. The government is plainly delinquent in having failed to comply with the Copenhagen Programme of Action stipulation of building an appropriate poverty line (that should have been done by 1996). Its efforts to monitor and evaluate its anti-poverty policies are unimpressive. Statistics South Africa deserves strong criticism for failing to design and implement surveys that would enable poverty to be measured with greater precision. The institution is wary of researchers who use social surveys for purposes other than those for which they are designed,[127] yet it has made no effort to introduce a survey specifically tailored to discovering the (changing) extent of poverty (and inequality). The academic community could have made greater efforts to solve the child cost ratio and household economies of scale problems.[128] It could also have devoted more time to addressing the social wage problem.[129] Poverty, as if anyone needed reminding, is public enemy number one – it should be treated as such.

If one played devil's advocate and accepted the most recent World Bank PPP, the absolutely poor (post-social wage) could number as few as 200 000 (Table 11.4a). In contrast, taking the Deaton (1997) dollar-a-day estimate, and assuming that the social wage was perfectly targeted (and that the error level in the social wage estimates was zero), could leave us with 10.6 million below the line that identifies the absolutely poor (Table 11.3a). Even if one did not play games like this, the range of ignorance is still unacceptably high. Table 11.5 does suggest, after all, that the post-social wage headcount in 2002 could have been as low as 8.7 million in 2002 (8.0 million if the social wage is under-valued in the simulation model by 25 per cent). Which, if any, of these figures is correct, is a matter of no little importance. Compounding the difficulties of estimating the extent of the problem is the confusion that exists about the social wage. Once again, the government has been remiss – this time, in its failure to approach the problem of estimating the overall impact of its anti-poverty policies on the poor in a more systematic (and energetic) manner. At least one of the studies it has commissioned so far serves, if anything, only to heighten the confusion. Claims made by the government about the reduction in inequality consequent upon the 'introduction' of the social wage deserve nothing but contempt – they are an insult to the poor.

Where should we go from here? A first step might be to put the MDGs into a proper perspective. Clemens et al. (2004: 1) suggest that for some developing countries, insistence on an ability to meet these goals, when realistic assessment shows this not to be possible, may undermine relations with donors abroad and impede reform at home. Although such a fate is unlikely to befall South Africa, the ignorance of poverty levels at the starting point of the journey to meet the goals, and the demonstrable inability to measure progress towards meeting them, suggest that, as is the case with the poorer developing countries that cannot meet them,

> [t]he MDGs might be better viewed not as realistic targets but as reminders of the stark contrast between the world we want and the world we have, and a call to redouble our search for interventions to close the gap. (Clemens et al. 2004: 1)

Following this advice would permit a focus on the essential questions related to poverty eradication in South Africa. Priorities in this regard, I would submit, are the following:

- A debate about the 'official' poverty lines must commence forthwith. If it is indeed true that SSA is still sitting on a report which contains the proposed future poverty lines (Babita et al. 2003), then this report must be released forthwith for general scrutiny. That scrutiny, it will be recalled, entails the poverty lines meeting the criteria of *scientific integrity* and *community credibility*.
- A critical examination of household surveys must be undertaken (along the lines of that conducted by Fedderke et al. 2004), one of whose (many) aims would be to address the question of under-reporting of expenditure.
- The creation of a new survey instrument (or the re-engineering of an existing instrument like the General Household Survey) must take place that enables reliable estimates of changes in absolute poverty to be made.
- Bound up with this is a need, caused by the growing size of the social wage, and its impact on incomes at the bottom end of the income distribution, to open a debate on the meaning of poverty along the lines proposed in Saunders (1998), and its measurement as suggested in Pyatt (2003).[130]
- Related in turn, is the need for a critical evaluation of the social wage study undertaken for the government by the HSRC (2004). Of such importance is this topic that it merits a heavy concentration of academic firepower on its redoubtable defences.

Unless satisfactory progress is made with these endeavours, credible estimates of progress in the struggle against poverty (at the level of the country as a whole, let alone at the level of the provinces) will continue to be difficult, if not impossible, to make. Strong objections to the use of household surveys to conduct poverty studies along the lines attempted above may be voiced. The absence of any suitable alternative data for tracking poverty, however, more than justifies the effort. If nothing else, the present study has revealed some of the pitfalls of using the surveys. Not all of these constitute insurmountable hurdles. Until such time as adequate poverty surveys are carried out by SSA (the survey must be national and large!), researchers must make the best of what is available.

Acknowledgements

Friends and colleagues and who have contributed in one way or another to this work include Miriam Altman, Johannes Fedderke, Isobel Frye, David Fryer, Anna McCord, Michael Samson, Jeremy Seekings and Michael Thiede. Debbie Budlender, Michael Noble and Gemma Wright leserve special mention for reading and commenting extensively on its forebears. Rosa Dias, my collaborator on early versions of the work on poverty, also deserves special thanks, as does Julian May for his endless encouragement, information and relevant journal articles (not to mention excellent cooking). Vishnu Padayachee provided me with a comfortable and highly collegial intellectual home in the School of Development Studies at the University of KwaZulu-Natal. My post-graduate students, Phil Donnel, Nonthlantha Dlamini and Leanne Sedowski did a large amount of background work for me on unemployment. Needless to say, the errors in the work (and the views expressed therein) are my responsibility.

Notes

1 This chapter was originally published as a paper under the title 'Half measures: The ANC's unemployment and poverty reduction goals' (Meth 2004a). It has been revised and updated to bring it into line with the most recent official statistics on economic activity and research into poverty in South Africa available at the time of writing (August 2005).

2 The Millennium Development Goals (MDG) are spelled out in a resolution called the Millennium Declaration, adopted by the General Assembly of the United Nations (United Nations 2000a). (A goal is defined as an aim or desired result, whereas a target is defined as an objective or result towards which efforts are directed.)

3 Maxwell (2004a: 3) is eloquent on this point, as are many others. One would have to be both blind and deaf to have missed the debate on the inadequacies of a simple money metric of poverty. The same applies to the headcount measures that poverty lines yield. Their weaknesses, if used in isolation, are far too well known to require recitation here.

4 Responding to the release in March 2004 of the then most recent Labour Force Survey (LFS) results, which registered a fall in the official rate of unemployment from 31.2 per cent in March 2003 to 28.4 per cent in September 2003, the Minister of Labour welcomed the development in a press release headed 'The recent employment figures indicates [sic] that the ANC government and its social partners are committed to half [sic] unemployment by 2014'.

The press release, replete with a reference to the (statistically insignificant) 57 000 jobs created over the period, ignores the explanation offered by Statistics South Africa for the decline in the official unemployment rate, namely that the number of not economically active persons increased by almost 1 million; the number of discouraged (non-searching) unemployed rose from 3.17 million in March 2003 to 3.82 million in September 2003 (Statistical Release P0210, 25 March 2004: iii).

The juxtaposition of references to the official rate of unemployment with the Minister's confident assertion that '[t]his government is on track to meeting its stated goal of halving unemployment by 2014' in the press release, makes it seem highly likely that the goal is indeed the official rate of unemployment.

Press Release downloaded from website www.labour.gov.za on 25 October 2004.

5 http://www.info.gov.za/issues/poa/index.html, accessed on 19 September 2004.

6 Downloaded from http://www.epwp.gov.za/ on 8 November 2004. The number of jobs created each year is a matter of lively dispute (discussed further below). If Casale, Muller

and Posel (2004: 16) are to be believed, the total number of jobs created between 1995 and 2003 could have been as low as 1.4 million, or about 175 000 per annum, rather than the 270 000 per annum implied by the figures that Phillips cites.

7   This conference, a joint effort whose main sponsor was the Development Bank of Southern Africa (DBSA), was held in Pretoria on 28–29 October 2004.

8   A request for information on the source of the passage cited above was made to Dr Phillips (pers. comm. 3 November 2004). It has not been supplied.

9   Unemployment rates are from the LFSs (Statistical Release P0210) for the relevant months.

10 Constituencies represented at the GDS committed themselves to a vision that includes *poverty eradication* (Nedlac 2003: paragraph 1.2.3), identifying it as a priority for national collaborative action (paragraph 1.2.4). The GDS document is silent on what targets this goal might imply.

11 A brief account of the emergence of the MDG and its targets may be found in Maxwell (2004b).

12 Although the dollar-a-day poverty line has attracted criticism, cogent reasons for adopting it have been offered by Chen and Ravallion (2001), and Deaton (2003a). Some of these are discussed below.

13 See the Foreword to the *National Report on Social Development, 1995–2000* (Department of Social Development 2000).

14 Unemployment rates are from the LFSs (Statistical Release P0210) for the relevant months.

15 In the absence of an authoritative critique of the 'official' estimates, this debate was 'won' by the former Minister of Trade and Industry, simply by sticking to those official (statistical) 'facts'. He disarmed his opponents by admitting that most of the two million jobs allegedly created (particularly those in the informal sector) were not of the sort desired by government. See the articles 'Doomsayers take liberties with the facts on unemployment', *Sunday Times (Business Report)*, 22 February 2004, and 'Erwin digs in his heels on employment data', *Mercury (Business Report)*, 23 February 2004. Would-be contributors to the debate fumed and fulminated, some disclosing a woeful ignorance of South Africa's labour statistics in the process – the 'facts' were simply not to be controverted. The paper by Casale, Muller and Posel (2004), as noted above, suggests, however, that the true total may be much lower, possibly as low as 1.4 million.

16 These figures are close to those in the recently released United Nations Development Programme estimates (UNDP 2003: 5). They are also similar to those used in the *Ten Year Review* (PCAS 2003). We consider them and their provenance below.

17 *This Day* 29 April 2004. An article by Miriam Altman of the HSRC in *This Day* ('The Employment Equation', 8 July 2004), takes it for granted that it is the official (strict) rate that is to be halved (from 30 to 15 per cent). According to her, this would entail the creation of between 400 000 and 500 000 jobs per annum, a goal that is beyond the reach of the economy. The article is reproduced in the September 2004 *HSRC Review* (Altman 2004).

18 This is not to suggest that Professor Terreblanche's results are necessarily incorrect. It is also not to suggest that assumptions and data sources should be spelt out in detail in a newspaper article designed for popular consumption. It would have helped, though, if a reference to the work from which these results are drawn had been made.

19 This average hides, however, quite a wide range of changes. The number of economically active, according to the strict definition, reportedly fell by 436 000 between September 2000 and September 2001, and rose by 974 000 between October 1998 and October 1999. See spreadsheet 'Unempl_(1996-2001).xls', worksheet 'Unemployment'. Copies of the relevant spreadsheets are obtainable from the author.

20 Once again, there are some large outliers. The October 1998 to October 1999 change was a fall of 5 000, while the October 1997 to October 1998 figure was an increase of 712 000. The LFS figures are better behaved. See spreadsheet 'Participation.xls', worksheet 'Unemployment' obtainable from the author.

21 *The Ten Year Review* claims that there were 11.5 million economically active in 1995, and 15.4 million in 2002. These figures correspond well with the Statistics South Africa estimates of 11.5 million in October 1996 and 15.9 million in September 2002. As we have seen above, the 'true' figure for 1996 should have been larger by at least 1 million (and possibly more) because of the subsistence agricultural workers. The huge increase in the number of officially unemployed between October 1999 and February 2000 casts doubt on the validity of the series for official unemployment. The claimed increase in the number of economically active (almost 4 million, PCAS 2003: 96) is incorrect.

Seizing upon the alleged 'fact' of the substantial massive rise in participation rates, government has wasted no opportunity to advance it as an 'explanation' of rising unemployment. An article in *Business Day* of 14 October 2003 by Alan Hirsch, Chief Director: Economic Sector in the Policy Coordination and Advisory Services (PCAS) in the Presidency, headed 'Unemployment rises even as jobs are created', sees him dissolving the 'Jobs Paradox' by reference to the 'fact' that the economically active population grew at about 5 per cent per annum (the EAP reportedly grew from 11.5 million in 1995 to 16.8 million in 2003), while job growth averaged about 2.5 per cent per annum.

Suitably retreaded, a very similar article, again written by Hirsch, appeared in *This Day* on 21 May 2004, this time under the heading of 'The unemployment paradox'. Once more, the (imaginary) 5 per cent growth in the economically active population is contrasted with the 1.6 per cent growth in the population. The same explanation for the alleged rise as that used on earlier occasions, an increase in participation by African women, was trotted out.

22 We would not expect participation rates to change very much over a six-month period. The modest ratio change between the (non-comparable) September 2002 and March 2003 figures, therefore, gives a hint that ratios may be relied upon, even when, as in this case, the changes in the absolute numbers are large. The September 2002 figures, it may be recalled, are weighted by the 1996 Census, while the March 2003 figures are weighted by its 2001 counterpart.

23 One hopes that, after the re-benchmarking exercise has been completed, the absolute number actively involved does not fall below its February 2000 total as well.

24 Doubts have been expressed as to the reliability of the mid-year estimates currently being used to re-benchmark the LFSs.

25 The article by Miriam Altman in *This Day* (8 July 2004) cited above suggests that the labour force might be growing at about 2.5 per cent per annum. She goes on to argue that 'once Aids starts having a larger impact, we could expect that the labour force might grow on average between 1 per cent and 2 per cent a year over the next 10 years'.

26   These growth rates have been estimated from the spreadsheets 'No_change_scenario.xls' and 'Change_scenario.xls', both of which are available on the ASSA website, www.assa.org. za/default.asp?id=1000000050. Both spreadsheets and the publication 'Actuarial Projection of the Epidemic: Summary Statistics' were downloaded from the site on 18 August 2005.

27   The assumed values may be changed in the spreadsheet 'Unempl_Model.xls', worksheet 'Front page', cells E6:F8 and E11:F13, available on request from the author.

28   See Statistics South Africa 2002c.

29   Absolute numbers, it will be recalled, are unreliable because of the change in weighting from the 1996 to the 2001 Census results.

30   Their numbers rose from 3.2 million in March 2003 to 3.8 million in September 2003, a jump of 590 000. See spreadsheet 'Unempl_(1996-2001).xls', worksheet 'Unemployment'.

31   The model allows either the September 2002 or the September 2003 LFS results to be used.

32   A superficial reading of the figures might ask why a 2.4 per cent growth rate in the size of the working-age population yields 8.9 million people, while a growth in the participation rate of only 0.3 per cent per annum brings forth 6.1 million. The explanation is that the latter growth rate is associated with a growth rate of about 3.4 per cent per annum in the size of the economically active population.

33   From the point of view of the poor, the most beneficial outcome is that which generates the largest number of jobs – the interests of workers and the poor are best served if the number of unemployed is reduced by this means.

34   To understand this apparently counter-intuitive outcome, it is necessary to refer to the worksheets from which the results derive. See worksheets 'Halving-1', 'Halving-2', 'Halving-3' and 'Halving-4' in spreadsheet 'Unempl_Model.xls', available from the author.

35   These are the only references to the expanded unemployment rate in the *Ten Year Review*. The word 'expanded' is not used anywhere else in the text in relation to unemployment.

With the publication of the September 2004 LFS, Statistics South Africa unveiled its new 'thematic' approach to the commentary on the labour market in the LFSs. The publication contains a fairly detailed discussion of the characteristics of the 'discouraged' (Statistics South Africa 2005: xvi–xviii). It is too early to tell whether or not this will result in the predicament of these people being taken more seriously by the government.

36   The problem raised here is similar to that encountered in 'development' circles when poverty rates fall but poverty headcounts rise.

37   The MDG target year, it will be recalled, is 2015. In South Africa it has been brought forward to 2014, the year that marks the 20th anniversary of democratic rule.

38   Saunders (1998: 11) refers to an article by Tony Atkinson (1993) on the value of a poverty line that has some official status. General acceptance of a particular line (or lines) can help to keep debates from wandering away from wider research and policy issues into esoterica.

39   The word 'reliable' is used with some hesitation. Dr Ros Hirschowitz of Statistics South Africa reminded participants at a workshop on measuring poverty in South Africa, hosted jointly by the National Treasury and the World Bank in Pretoria on 28–29 June 2004, that the sample for the 1995 OHS and IES was poor.

40 The figures in the publication *Earning and Spending in South Africa* do not tell a happy story. It is very different from that told by the wildly optimistic figures in the *Ten Year Review* (PCAS 2003), considered below. Little wonder, then, that the state jumped at the opportunity offered by the problems experienced with the 2000 IES to cast doubt on its results. Not long after the 2000 IES results were released, an article in the *Financial Mail* (31 January 2003) drew attention to the President's preference for the figures produced by the SA Advertising Research Foundation (Saarf) over those produced by Statistics South Africa. Ferial Haffajee, author of the piece, comments that the President is happier with Saarf's development index, which paints '…a more glowing record of delivery and a discernible rising tide. It's from this report that Mbeki chose to quote in his annual address to the National Council of Provinces last November and which his aides use to present a prettier picture.'

41 This paper forms the basis of Chapter 2 in the present volume.

42 This blessing was given during the workshop on measuring poverty in South Africa, organised jointly by the National Treasury and the World Bank, held in Pretoria on 28–29 June 2004.

43 This paper forms the basis of Chapter 3 in the present volume.

44 The 2000 sample was not the same as that used in 1995. From a sample of 29 582 households containing 129 000 individuals in the 1995 figures, they were able to match 113 000 individuals in 28 000 households. In the 2000 figures, among 105 000 individuals in 26 600 households, they were able to match 101 000 individuals in 26 000 households (Leibbrandt et al. 2005: 5–6). Nominal sample size for each of the surveys is 30 000 households. The high non-response rate in 2000 has been responsible for much mischief.

45 The indices of multiple deprivation (soon to become available on the Statistics South Africa website), developed by Noble and his co-workers using Census 2001 data, offer some hope of progress in this field. Whether or not comparable indices for 1996 can be estimated remains to be seen.

46 This comes shortly after Everatt has taken a (possibly well-deserved) sideswipe at the 'small craft industry …measuring poverty and deprivation', now grown into a 'major trans-national industry (in inverse proportion to poverty reduction)' (Everatt 2003: 88).

47 Saunders points to the crisis in Australian poverty research caused by the failure of existing poverty lines to meet the criterion of scientific integrity. This weakness is exploited by conservatives keen to deny the persistence of poverty (Saunders 2004: 1).

48 Everatt's prose is so spare and economical, and his argument so persuasive, that I shall not attempt to write a précis of it.

49 Unless one wishes to count GEAR's 400 000 jobs a year that were supposed to be delivered from 2000 onwards (Friedman 2004).

50 A copy of this report came into my possession because I was asked by the Department of Social Development, the commissioner of the research, to act as a reviewer.

51 See especially Section 76 in the main report. The Poverty and Inequality Report's conclusion in the Summary report, in the section on the strategy for the reduction of poverty and inequality, that the '[c]ollection of social, economic and demographic information to

monitor the extent and nature of change is a priority in managing the reduction of poverty and inequality' (see May 1998b: Section 10.8) has not been treated with the urgency that it deserves.

52 Ms Fraser-Moleketi acknowledged that '…much work still needs to be done to develop the appropriate poverty measurement tools by Government' (Fraser-Moleketi 1998: 2).

53 The use of the word 'merely' is not intended to detract from the misery of poverty experienced by many whose expenditure levels exceed the boundary marking them off from the absolutely poor. One is tempted to use the expression 'relatively' poor to describe the condition. This is not appropriate, however, because the concept of 'relative' poverty is already used to mean something quite different.

54 Apparently the Cabinet Social Cluster requested the DSD to take the lead, with Statistics South Africa, in developing the poverty lines. It is not known whether the Babita et al. effort is the outcome. It was also rumoured that the National Treasury had, independently, commissioned an academic study whose goal it would be to construct a set of poverty lines. If this is so, it is much to be deplored. A single, joint effort by the departments concerned would be preferable.

55 Remarks made at the National Treasury/World Bank workshop on poverty in Pretoria, 28–29 June 2004. She stated that the work was to be carried out by the HSRC.

56 The DPLG report is as generous with its praise as it is with its criticisms. The latter are revealing. The report refers to the 'silo culture' (para. 43), and to the 'fragmentation, overlap and lack of communication or co-ordination amongst (and often within) Departments, even those that are ostensibly doing similar types of things …' (para. 45). Further on it is said that '[t]he majority of respondents reported that monitoring was either not going very well or that it was acceptable in places. Less than a third of respondents reported that they were happy with their monitoring system. Again, readers should note the difference between the responses of M&E officials and those of Chief Directors. The latter tended to regard current M&E performance as partially acceptable, compared to M&E officials who felt more strongly that performance was either going well or going badly and avoided the middle ground. This indicates the closer contact which M&E officials have with the practicalities of managing monitoring and evaluation' (para. 59).

57 The 15 February 2005 update of the 'government's programme of action' webpage for the year 2004 notes that a study described as 'Poverty Measures-Research to audit poverty measures used by different departments', commissioned by the Presidency, had been completed. Extracted from www.info.gov.za/issues/poa/index.html. Site visited on 20 August 2005.

58 Information on the programmes of the Governance and Administration Cluster for 2004 and 2005 was extracted from www.info.gov.za/issues/poa/index.html. Site visited on 20 August 2005.

59 The failure of existing poverty studies to do so, as we noted above, added one more problem to the others discussed above (the failure to base measurement on adequate conceptualisation and definition, and the severe data problems). The problem is by no means unique to South Africa. Saunders (1998: 8ff) discusses the challenges posed for the

measurement of poverty in Australia by increases in the value of the social wage. He notes that the practical problems involved in broadening the income concept (as is attempted in the present study) would be considerable.

60   Evidence is not given for the assertion that 'additional income' earners are removed from households in this process. Those removed could well have been unemployed persons whom households could no longer afford to support. The 'social transition' to smaller households is discussed on pp. 95–6 of the *Ten Year Review*. The reasons put forward include declining fertility rates and family sizes, as well as '...the effect of new government policy on how citizens try to access services, encouraging "unbundling"...'. The housing subsidy is rumoured to be the 'service' that most encourages 'unbundling'.

61   The Gini coefficients are said to be respectively for 'Pre-transfer income share' and 'Income share after social spending' (PCAS 2003: 91).

62   When it came to guessing at the value to individuals of the social wage, every effort was made to err in a direction that would maximise this value, thus making it likely that poverty is understated rather than overstated.

63   Rao refers to two of the more prominent works highlighting such problems, those by Deaton (2000) and Reddy and Pogge (2002), then provides a summary of the major weaknesses (Rao 2003: 2). He cites a passage from a response by Ravallion (2000) to the effect that in

> the vast bulk of Bank's analytic and operational work on poverty, the '$/day' line is ignored, and with good reason. When one works on poverty in a given country, or region, one naturally tries to use a definition of poverty appropriate to that setting. Most of the time, the Bank's poverty analysts don't need to know what the local poverty line is worth in international currency at purchasing power parity...

64   It would be naïve to think that the specification of the dollar-a-day poverty line as the international standard in the MDG would enable controversy over the extent of poverty to be avoided. The call for each country to develop its own poverty line is an explicit recognition of the fact that although the dollar-a-day line does have some merit, it will not necessarily be appropriate for every poor country.

65   Hoogeveen and Özler estimate the value of the dollar-a-day line at R87 in the year 2000 (2004: 9). Raised to 2002 prices, this would equal R104.50, reassuringly close to the figure of R103.88 referred to above. They observe that their $2/day line (R174) is close to Deaton's (1997) of R105 in 1993 (R178.46 in 2000). They treat their $2/day line as an 'extreme' poverty line. It corresponds roughly to what is described as absolute poverty ($1/day) above. The difference must be accounted for by the PPP exchange rate conversion.

66   Deaton's estimate of the headcount ratio (P_0) for the year 1993 puts it at 0.25 or 25 per cent of the total population (1997: 157, Table 3.4). The World Bank's estimate for the number of people below the $1/day line in the same year was 11.5 per cent. See World Bank 2001: 281, Table 4.

67   It has not been possible to replicate this figure. An explanation of the method of construction will be sought from the authors.

68   Ravallion, Datt and van de Walle observe that '[w]hen poverty lines are differentiated by family [*sic*] size we have used the per capita value at roughly average family size' (1991: 347).

69 A household budget for an 'average family' of, say, four persons (two adults and two children) would be $4 per day. Rather obviously, scaling this for child costs and household economies of scale yields a number of adult equivalents smaller than the number of persons in the 'family'. Dividing the daily budget by this number yields an adult equivalent poverty line that is larger than the per capita poverty line. In a two-adult, two-child household, for example, to estimate per adult equivalent consumption, instead of dividing the expenditure level by 4.0 as one would to obtain per capita consumption, one divides it by 2.69 if $\alpha = 0.5$ and $\theta = 0.9$.

70 The topic of converting per capita poverty lines to per adult equivalent poverty lines is dealt with in greater length in Meth (2004b).

71 The concept of social exclusion is contested. Arguing against the uncritical transportation of such terms from First World debates into the developing country context, Du Toit (2004) prefers the term 'adverse incorporation' to describe the conditions of many of the working poor whose mean monthly consumption would certainly lie well below the R422 mark.

72 Estimated from the South African Reserve Bank's *Quarterly Bulletin*, March 2004: S-119.

73 Expressed in 2002 prices, Hoogeveen and Özler's lower bound poverty line of R322 in 2000 prices would amount to about R387 per month. This is not all that far from the suggested Chen and Ravallion (2001) figure of R422 per month (in 2002 prices).

74 Alderman et al. (2000: 11n) used a figure of R800 per month in 1995 as a cut-off to identify households in poverty, and a figure of R250 per month for individuals. Their poverty estimates (the 28 per cent of households and 48 per cent of individuals cited in the *Ten Year Review*) are not adjusted for child costs or household economies of scale (2000: 10n). Hirschowitz et al. (2000: 59) describe as 'very poor' households with a total expenditure of less than R600 per month in 1995. Households in which expenditure was between R601 and R1 000 per month were regarded as 'poor'. These are, respectively, households in the bottom and second from bottom quintiles in the distribution. It is not obvious from the studies in question how the problem of varying household composition was treated.

75 The equivalence scale is of the standard form $E = (A + \alpha K)^\theta$, where E = the number of adult equivalents, A = number of adults, α = the child cost ratio, K = number of children, and θ the household economies of scale factor (Leibbrandt, Woolard and Bhorat 2001: 40). Children in this study are treated as those under the age of 18 years. The process by means of which the values of this poverty line are estimated is described in Meth 2004b, in the section of the paper headed 'Defending the chosen poverty line(s)'.

76 See Woolard and Leibbrandt (2001: 50–51) for a discussion on adult equivalents.

77 For want of a better name, I call this phenomenon 'headcount elasticity' (see Meth 2004b).

78 The Chen and Ravallion 'one third of mean consumption figure' is purely arbitrary, so it can be ignored.

79 Between 1997 and 2002, the proportion of households containing a single individual rose from 2.7 to 7.0 per cent, households containing two adults from 4.5 to 5.8 per cent, while the proportion of households containing adults and children fell from 87.1 to 82.5 per cent. Within the last of these households, the ratio of adults to children appears to have risen from about 92.3 to about 96.6 adults per 100 children.

80   The 1999 data (which are suspect) are from the 1999 OHS. The 2002 data are from the September 2002 LFS.

81   This assumption is generous. In other runs of the model, I have assumed a lower bound of 30 per cent. This gives a mean of 65 per cent of the upper bound, a figure that is close to the two-thirds sometimes assumed in poverty and income distribution studies.

82   The finding that means lie below mid-points of linear distributions is in line with those reported by Keswell and Poswell (2002). Most responses in the 1997, 1998 and 1999 OHSs gave categorical (income bracket) estimates. They devised a technique for dealing with the problem caused by the absence of actual income (point) estimates from the OHSs and LFSs, and their (optional) replacement by estimates that lie within specified income brackets. Critical of approaches that use the mid-point of an income bracket, these authors (who prefer to assume a log normal distribution of income) show that the use of the mid-point assumption overstates true means, leading to over-representation of better-off individuals (see their Appendix B: 42–43 and their Figure 1: 50).

83   If the income and expenditure surveys on which poverty estimates depend are of the 'recall' rather than the 'diary' type, error can be introduced by virtue of the use of an inappropriate recall period. Both Chen and Ravallion (2001: 285n) and Deaton (2003a: 367) refer to the Indian experience where changing the recall period for food from 30 to 7 days almost halved the poverty rate (from 36 to 21 per cent).

84   Under-reporting could, and probably does, vary significantly by expenditure category. Whether the poor are more likely than the well-off to understate their expenditure cannot readily be determined.

85   If reported expenditure is, say, R400 per month, a 15 per cent error would mean that actual expenditure is R460 per month. The ratio of reported to actual expenditure is thus 87 per cent.

86   Deaton observes, in making this point, that he knows of no plausible estimate of the size of the bias (Deaton 2003b: 34).

87   Personal communication.

88   Commenting on the poor quality of the 2000 IES, Van der Berg and Louw (2003: 2) observe that about 25 per cent of the records are useless, either because recorded expenditure for food is zero or because total expenditure and total income differ by more than 30 per cent. In contrast, Van der Berg's claims on the reconciliation of the different data sources get some support from Alderman et al. (2000), cited by Hirschowitz et al. as having found the IES consumption estimates to 'aggregate closely' up to the consumption estimates in the national accounts (Hirschowitz et al. 2000: 55).

89   As reported in *This Day*, 25 February 2004.

90   South African Reserve Bank *Quarterly Bulletin*, March 2004: S-118.

91   Using the same data sets, Leibbrandt et al. (2005) conclude that incomes fell across the board between 1995 and 2000. This is consistent with the findings reported in Statistics South Africa 2002b: 29.

92   The calculations used to make these estimates appear in worksheet LFS 2002b in spreadsheet 'SocialWage-4.xls'. An 80 per cent allowance yields a mean in excess of the

Statistics South Africa figure (inflated at 6 per cent per annum). The 120 per cent error raises the mean to 82 per of per capita GNDI.

93   The paper is by Ravallion (2002).

94   The major school feeding scheme is part of the Integrated Nutrition Project, a programme located in the national Department of Health. The programme was split in 2004. Responsibility for the larger part of the programme, Primary School Nutrition (PSN), was shifted to the Department of Education in 2004.

95   The only other estimates of the value of the social wage to individuals and/or households, those made by the HSRC (2004), do not attempt to assess the impact of the social wage on poverty. The authors do, however, give estimates of the cash values of each component. With certain notable exceptions, for example education, the HSRC estimates do not differ much from those in Meth (2004b).

96   The settings that produce these values come from the Deaton (1997) poverty line. The child cost ratio and the household economies of scale parameter are both set at 1.0. Since the nominal value of the social wage does not change with changing assumptions of the level of under-reporting, the impact of the social wage in proportional terms if an 80 per cent under-reporting assumption is used is much larger. See Rows 262–294 in worksheet 'A02-1' in spreadsheet 'SocialWage-4.xls'.

97   The surveys capture more old-age pensioners than the administrative records. Part of the difference consists of private (non-state) pensions. Recipients of child support grants are less well enumerated, so a correction is made when the 'social wage' is added in to accommodate the under-counting of grants of this type. No attempt has been made to check whether the numbers of disability grants (by 2002, the third largest category of cash grant) captured by the surveys match administrative records of grants paid.

98   It is well known that the state old-age pension has a huge impact on poverty. In defence of the calculations in the earlier versions of the paper from which the results come, it needs to be pointed out that growth in the numbers of recipients of pensions over the period under consideration was modest. In April 1997 there were 1.7 million recipients. By July 2001, this had climbed to 1.9 million, a level it appears to have maintained in 2002. As I have shown elsewhere (Meth 2004b: Table 1), the real value of the state old-age pension fell from R694 to R640 per month (in 2002 prices) between 1997 and 2002. Real transfers via pension grants probably fell slightly, because the fall in the real value of the pension more than offset the additional benefits paid out because of the increase in the number of pensioners. It was argued that if the two effects had neutralised each other, pensions could simply have been treated as a constant. As it is, the earlier years probably had a slightly higher social wage component from this source. Ignoring this would have biased the results in a conservative direction, i.e. increases in poverty would have been understated. Child support grant (CSG) rollout commenced in earnest in 1999, the number of recipients in March of that year totalling about 28 000. The CSG replaced the Parent and Child Allowances, of which there were about 350 000 in 1997 (see Statistics South Africa 2001: 6.4). The CSG therefore became salient only for the final year in the calculations, 2002. Disability grants appear not to have increased in number between 1997 and 2002. Like the state pension, their real value probably fell. They too, were ignored.

99   The need to make this correction was pointed out in discussions with Angus Deaton and Francois Bourguignon at the National Treasury/World Bank poverty workshop in Pretoria on 28–29 June 2004.

100 The limitation arises from the fact that the expenditure data are presented in categories rather than as point estimates. This determines the form of the simulation model.

101 In the model, the grants are subtracted by raising the value of the poverty line in the pre-social wage module.

102 If, as is the case in the present chapter, reported expenditure is R400 per month, an error of 80 per cent suggests a 'true' value of R720. An error of 120 per cent suggests a 'true' expenditure level of R880 per month.

103 See http://devdata.worldbank.org/wdi2005/Table2_5.htm for updated figures.

104 In 1997, the post-social wage poverty rate at R104 per capita per month is 3.6 per cent with the 120 per cent under-reporting error, while the pre-social wage poverty rate is 10.4 per cent. Using the R214 poverty line, and an under-reporting error of 120 per cent, the post social-wage poverty rate is 21.3 per cent, while the pre-social wage poverty rate is 27.9 per cent.

105 Hoogeveen and Özler say that '[w]hile [the $2/day] poverty line is significantly lower than our preferred poverty line for South Africa, it is useful for international comparisons, and to describe what has happened to the welfare of those at bottom end of the distribution' (2004: 9).

106 The numbers are fragile because the distribution of expenditure in the bottom expenditure category cannot be known with any certainty.

107 The calculations may be seen in cells O277:AY340 of worksheet 'A-02' in spreadsheet 'SocialWage-4.xls'. See cell P314:315.

108 The population in 2002 was about 45.5 million. If the poverty rate increased slightly between 2000 and 2002, then the figure of 15.0 million absolutely poor, which yields a pre-social wage poverty rate of 33.0 per cent, would accord well with Hoogeveen and Özler's headcount estimate of 0.34 (34 per cent of the population). See their Table 1.

109 The manner in which pensions and child support grants have to be removed from the raw data in order to estimate pre-social wage expenditure levels (dictated by the nature of the data) makes it difficult to estimate the numbers of ultra-poor (those well below the R214 mark) with any precision. At the R104 mark in 1997, for example, the pre-social wage total was estimated at about 4.3 million people. This rises to 7.6 million by 2002. This is with an expenditure under-reporting assumption of 120 per cent. Using the 80 per cent assumption, the figures are 6.6 and 10.4 million respectively. The substantial falls in the 2002 numbers provide a good demonstration of how important even relatively small changes are at low income levels.

110 Concern is often expressed that a poverty line, a construct of some arbitrariness, unrealistically divides the population into those who are poor and those who are not. To a certain extent, poverty headcounts must be arbitrary. There is a tension between, on the one hand, the need for a benchmark against which to measure progress (or the lack

thereof) in the struggle against poverty and, on the other, the knowledge of the unavoidable arbitrariness of such benchmarks.

111 This is after having tested for a wide range of values of α, the child cost ratio, and θ, the household economies of scale factor (Woolard and Leibbrandt 2001: 50–53). Changes in these two, it will be recalled, change the level of the per adult equivalent poverty line.

112 Meeting the MDG of halving poverty by 2015 (2014) may be possible, but if underlying forces in the economy exert the kind of downward pressure of which the 120 per cent error results presented here are the outcome (roughly constant post-social wage headcounts from R387 per month onwards), doing so becomes increasingly unlikely.

113 Note once more that the adjective 'merely', when placed before the word 'poor', is not intended to suggest that the condition is anything other than undesirable.

114 It is not pleasant to contemplate the consequences of targeting and delivery being less than perfect.

115 Similar results are obtained using an 'arbitrary' R600 per capita line in Poverty Line Set No. 1.

116 In the households in expenditure category R0–399 per month in 2002, the adult:child ratio was 1.41:1. In the expenditure category R400–799 it was 1.37:1.

117 Unemployment figures are from Meth (2004b). There are many discontinuities in the series, the worst of them caused by the changeover from the OHS to the LFS. The OHS and LFS figures can, however, be reconciled. In the first LFS, the reconciliation exercise suggests that the differences caused by the discontinuity would not be very large, at least for the estimates of unemployment, if similar definitions were used. It is not clear what this would do to participation rates.

118 A barely plausible increase (given the subsequent behaviour of the series) of almost 800 000 occurs in the number of informal-sector workers between 1997 and 1999. With the exception of a strange spike in the series at February 2001, the employment level is roughly constant, something that is as hard to believe as the sudden leaps in employment levels. The simple truth is that it is not known what has happened to employment in the informal sector.

119 Recall from Table 11.5 that the total number of people raised above the R214 line with a 120 per cent under-reporting error assumption is 6.3 million. At the R422 level (Table 11.9) it is 1.4 million.

120 This is easily done in cell B68 of worksheet 'Front page' in spreadsheet 'SocialWage-4SW.xls'.

121 Unlike the HSRC (2004) approach to valuing the social wage, that used in Meth (2004b) argues that education (one of the largest items of social spending) is not 'bankable', i.e. it does not reduce income poverty in the short run. Indeed, it may exacerbate poverty by obliging poor households to dig deep for money with which to buy school uniforms, pay school fees and pay for transport.

122 For what it is worth, a simulation exercise by Hanmer and Naschold (2003) found it unlikely that the high-inequality sub-Saharan African countries would achieve the poverty-halving goal by 2015. Those among them that switched to a 'broader-based' (more labour-intensive) growth path required real average annual per capita growth in GDP of 3.5 per cent to do so. Countries in which the growth path did not change required a

staggering 10.4 per cent per capita GDP growth to halve poverty (Hanmer and Naschold 2003: 269). Optimism about South Africa's growth prospects is a recurrent refrain in the popular and financial press. It is not obvious that this is justified. Lewis's (2001) paper put feasible GDP growth over a decade at about 4 per cent per annum on average. Even if the population growth rate falls to, say, 1.5 per cent per annum, that would still yield per capita GDP growth of only about 2.5 per cent per annum. Where, for Lewis, skills are a major constraint, for Leftwich (2000), the form of the state itself limits growth possibilities. He describes South Africa (and Venezuela) as '[c]lass-compromise non-developmental democracies' (2000: 182), using the term 'non-developmental' to highlight (exaggerate) the differences in growth possible in such democracies, and the 'dynamic growth achievements of dominant-party and coalition democracies …' (2000: 182). Outlining a number of problems facing class-compromise states, he argues that they illustrate 'why, *ceteris paribus*, [such states] are likely to have slow and limited developmental rates and why the agreements comprising these democracies tend to be so conservative in practice' (2000: 186).

123 Our ignorance about the precise numbers of people in absolute poverty is a serious problem. No effort should be spared to design and implement surveys that reduce this ignorance to a minimum. When official statisticians are caught napping by large errors, they can (and do) take refuge behind the claim that absolute levels do not matter too much as long as trends are accurately captured. This may be the case (in some instances) for the national accounts – it certainly cannot be true for poverty estimates. The precise number of poor, and the depth of their poverty, matters greatly to the poor; it should do to policy-makers as well.

124 There will be a modest increase in the number of jobs in the construction sector because of the switch to more labour-intensive methods. For the rest, if the programme is to have a major impact, it will have to offer more than short-term employment with a genuflection towards training. In general, PWPs will not create significant skills or entrepreneurs. As a means of relieving poverty they will be effective only if the jobs offered are of relatively long duration (years rather than months). Although the private sector may be the nominal employers of those taking part in the programme, they will be indirectly employed by the state, almost as though it were outsourcing certain services. Confusion about what can be achieved by the EPWP, revealed by McCord's work, suggests that a thoroughgoing review of the project is required, and that before the programme has reached its full (limited) potential.

125 The introduction of a benefit transfer programme was suggested by the members of the task team appointed by the Minister of Labour to examine the workings of the Unemployment Insurance Act (Meth, Naidoo and Shipman 1996).

126 Whether it has the will to do so is, however, another matter altogether.

127 Statements to this effect were made more than once by Dr Ros Hirschowitz of Statistics South Africa at the workshop on poverty held in Pretoria on 28–29 June 2004. The point is well taken – as we have seen, there are problems involved in doing time series analysis on cross-section data. When, however, there is nothing else available, one has little choice in the matter. Incidentally, IESs, useful in the past for reweighting the CPI, as well as for

making poverty and inequality estimates, will henceforth be used for the former rather than the latter purpose. In the past, the IES was tied to the OHS (1995) or the LFS (2000). This link will not be maintained in the 2005 IES.

128 The pioneering efforts of the compiler of the Household Subsistence Level estimates, Professor Potgieter, should have stimulated research aimed at the admittedly hard job of pinning down these two variables. It is ironic, but perhaps predictable, that the impetus for the most substantial research into the cost of living in South Africa should have come from the business community. Both the Bureau for Market Research (BMR) at the University of South Africa (UNISA), which used to estimate the value of the 'Minimum Living Level' (MLL) and its more generous cousin, the 'Supplemented Living Level' (SLL), and Professor Potgieter's unit at the University of Port Elizabeth, which publishes the 'Household Subsistence Level' and its more generous counterpart, the 'Household Effective Level', relied heavily on corporate support. The BMR stopped measuring the MLL and the SLL a few years ago, when corporate support dried up.

129 In the magisterial 'Measuring Poverty in South Africa', Woolard and Leibbrandt (2001) steer clear of the social wage. They note that for measuring well-being, '… a person's standard of living is generally taken to depend only on the consumption of *market* goods. While the limitations of this approach are well documented … the problems involved in valuing access to public goods are enormous. It is thus to a large extent for pragmatic reasons that current consumption or current income is used as the indicator of wellbeing' (2001: 42; emphasis in original). Further on they observe that '[t]he choice of private consumption expenditure (PCE) per adult equivalent as an appropriate welfare measure has a strong theoretical as well as [an] intuitive appeal' (2001: 43).

130 Engagement with the work of Noble et al. (2004) is also necessary.

References

African National Congress (2002a) Economic transformation. National Policy Conference Discussion Papers, *Umrabulo* No. 16, August 2002. Accessed online 25 September 2003, www.anc.org.za/ancdocs/pubs/umrabulo/index.html.

African National Congress (2002b) Social transformation: Fighting poverty and building a better life. National Policy Conference Discussion Papers, *Umrabulo* No. 16, August 2002. Accessed online 25 September 2003, www.anc.org.za/ancdocs/pubs/umrabulo/index.html.

African National Congress (2002c) *Resolutions adopted by the 51st National Conference of the African National Congress.* Accessed online 25 September 2003, www.anc.org.za/ancdocs/history/conf/conference51/index.html.

African National Congress (2004) *Manifesto 2004: A people's contract to create work and fight poverty.* Accessed online 15 June 2004, www.anc.org.za/elections/2004/manifesto-f.htm.

Ahmad S (2003) *Historical view of the International Comparison Program.* Washington, DC: World Bank. Accessed online 18 June 2004, web.worldbank.org/wbsite/external/datastatistics/icpext/0.

Alderman H, Babita M, Lanjouw P, Makhata N, Mohamed A, Özler B & Qaba O (2000) Combining census and poverty data to construct a poverty map of South Africa. In R Hirschowitz (ed.) *Measuring poverty in South Africa*. Pretoria: Statistics South Africa.

Altman M (2004) Halving unemployment? *HSRC Review* 2(03) September 2004: 8–9.

ASSA (Actuarial Society of South Africa) *Aids model. Actuarial Projection of the Epidemic: Summary Statistics*. Accessed online 18 August 2005, www.assa.org.za/default.asp?id=1000000050.

Atkinson AB (1993) *The institution of an official poverty line and economic policy*. Discussion Paper WSP/98, Welfare State Programme, London School of Economics. Cited in Saunders 1998.

Babita M, Özler B, Shabalala N & Thema H (2003) Changes in poverty and inequality in South Africa: 1995–2000. Unpublished manuscript, Statistics South Africa, 2003. Cited in Hoogeveen and Özler (2004).

Bhorat H (2001) Public expenditure and poverty alleviation: Simulations for South Africa. In H Bhorat, M Leibbrandt, M Maziya, S van der Berg & I Woolard, *Fighting poverty: Labour markets and inequality in South Africa*. Cape Town: UCT Press.

Bhorat H, Leibbrandt M, Maziya M, van der Berg S & Woolard I (2001) *Fighting poverty: Labour markets and inequality in South Africa*. Cape Town: UCT Press.

Black R & White H (eds) (2004) *Targeting development*. London: Routledge.

Booth A & Mosley P (eds) (2003) *The new poverty strategies: What have they achieved? What have we learned?* Houndmills, Basingstoke: Palgrave MacMillan.

Casale D, Muller C & Posel D (2004) 'Two million net new jobs': A reconsideration of the rise in employment in South Africa, 1995–2003. Unpublished mimeo, University of KwaZulu-Natal.

Chen S, Datt G & Ravallion M (1994) Is poverty increasing or decreasing in the developing world? *Review of Income and Wealth* 40: 359–376.

Chen S & Ravallion M (2001) How did the world's poorest fare in the 1990s? *Review of Income and Wealth* 47(3): 283–300.

Clemens MA, Kenny CJ & Moss TJ (2004) *The trouble with MDGs: Confronting expectations of aid and development success*. Working Paper No. 40, Center for Global Development, Washington, DC.

Cornes R (1995) Measuring the distributional impact of public goods. In D van de Walle & K Nead (eds) *Public spending and the poor: Theory and evidence*. Baltimore, MD: Johns Hopkins University Press.

Daniel J, Southall R & Lutchman J (eds) (2005) *State of the nation: South Africa 2004–2005*. Cape Town: HSRC Press.

Deaton A (1997) *The analysis of household surveys: Microeconometric analysis for development policy*. Washington, DC: World Bank.

Deaton A (2000) Counting the world's poor: Problems and possible solutions. Unpublished mimeo, Princeton University. Cited in Rao, 2003.

Deaton A (2003a) How to monitor poverty for the Millennium Development Goals, *Journal of Human Development* 4(3): 353–378.

Deaton A (2003b) *Measuring poverty in a growing world (or measuring growth in a poor world)*. NBER Working Paper 9822, Cambridge, MA: National Bureau of Economic Research. Accessed online 26 February 2004, www.nber.org/papers/w9822.

Demery L (2000) *Benefit incidence: A practitioner's guide.* World Bank, Poverty and Social Development Group, Africa Region.

DPLG (Department of Provincial and Local Government) (2001) *A national monitoring framework for South Africa.* Pretoria: DPLG.

DSD (Department of Social Development) (2000) *National report on social development, 1995–2000.* Pretoria: DSD.

DSD (2002a) *Strategic plan 2002/03–2004/05.* Pretoria: DSD.

DSD (2002b) Transforming the present – protecting the future: Report of the committee of inquiry into a comprehensive system of social security for South Africa (Consolidated Report). Pretoria: DSD.

Du Toit A (2004) Some objections to the export of 'social exclusion' talk: A case study of chronic poverty in South Africa's deciduous fruit export sector. Unpublished mimeo, Programme for Land and Agrarian Studies (PLAAS), University of the Western Cape.

Everatt D (2003) The politics of poverty, *Development Update* 4(3): 75–99.

Fedderke J, Manga J & Pirouz F (2004) Challenging Cassandra: Household and per capita household income distribution in the October Household Surveys 1995–1999, Income and Expenditure Surveys 1995 and 2000, and the Labour Force Survey 2000. Unpublished paper, University of Cape Town.

Fraser-Moleketi G (1998) Government's response to the poverty and inequality report. Paper presented at the Conference on Poverty and Inequality, Midrand, June.

Friedman S (2004) An act of will: Manuel and the politics of growth. In Parsons R (ed) *Manuel, markets and money: Essays in appraisal.* Cape Town: Double Storey Books.

Hanmer L & Naschold F (2003) Attaining the international development targets: Will growth be enough? In A Booth and P Mosley (eds) *The new poverty strategies: What have they achieved? What have we learned?* Houndmills, Basingstoke: Palgrave MacMillan.

Hirschowitz R (ed.) (2000) *Measuring poverty in South Africa.* Pretoria: Statistics South Africa.

Hirschowitz R, Orkin M & Alberts P (2000) Key baseline statistics for poverty measurement. In R Hirschowitz (ed) *Measuring poverty in South Africa.* Pretoria: Statistics South Africa.

Hoogeveen JG & Özler B (2004) Not separate, not equal: Poverty and inequality in post-apartheid South Africa. Draft paper, World Bank, February.

HSRC (Human Sciences Research Council) (2004) *The social wage in South Africa: Phase 2 report.* Integrated Rural and Regional Development Research Programme, HSRC, Pretoria. Accessed online 27 June 2005, http://www.hsrc.ac.za/research/npa/outputsByGroup.php?group=IRRD.

Kanbur R (2004) *Growth, inequality and poverty: Some hard questions.* Accessed online 1 June 2004, www.people.cornell.edu/pages/sk145.

Keswell M & Poswell L (2002) *How important is education for getting ahead in South Africa?* Centre for Social Science Research, University of Cape Town, CSSR Working Paper No. 22.

Leftwich A (2000) *States of development: On the primacy of politics in development.* Cambridge: Polity Press.

Leibbrandt M, Levinsohn J & McCrary J (2005) *Incomes in South Africa since the fall of apartheid.* National Bureau of Economic Research, Working Paper 11384, Cambridge, MA.

Leibbrandt M, Poswell L, Naidoo P, Welch M & Woolard I (2004) *Measuring recent changes in South African inequality and poverty using 1996 and 2001 Census Data.* CSSR Working Paper No. 84, South African Labour and Development Research Unit (SALDRU), University of Cape Town.

Leibbrandt M, Woolard I & Bhorat H (2001) Understanding contemporary household inequality in South Africa. In H Bhorat, M Leibbrandt, M Maziya, S van der Berg S & I Woolard (eds) *Fighting poverty: Labour markets and inequality in South Africa.* Cape Town: UCT Press.

Lewis JD (2001) *Policies to promote growth and employment in South Africa.* World Bank Southern Africa Department, Discussion Paper No. 16.

Maxwell S (2004a) Lost in Translation? Implementation constraints to results-based management. Unpublished paper, Overseas Development Institute (ODI), London.

Maxwell S (2004b) Heaven or hubris: Reflections on the new 'New Poverty Agenda'. In R Black & H White (eds) *Targeting development.* London: Routledge.

May J (ed.) (1998a) Poverty and inequality in South Africa: Report prepared for the Office of the Executive Deputy President and the Inter-Ministerial Committee for Poverty and Inequality. Final Report, 13 May 1998. Accessed online15 June 2004, www.polity.org.za/govdocs/reports/poverty.html.

May J (ed.) (1998b) Poverty and inequality in South Africa: Report prepared for the Office of the Executive Deputy President and the Inter-Ministerial Committee for Poverty and Inequality. Summary Report, 13 May 1998. Accessed online 15 June 2004, www.polity.org.za/govdocs/reports/poverty.html.

May J, Carter M & Posel D (1995) *The composition and persistence of rural poverty in South Africa: An entitlements approach.* Land and Agricultural Policy Centre Paper No. 15. Land and Agricultural Policy Centre.

Mbeki T (2005) Address of the President of South Africa, Thabo Mbeki, at the second joint sitting of the third democratic parliament, Cape Town, 11 February 2005. Accessed online 12 February 2005, www.info.gov.za/speeches/2005/05021110501001.htm.

McCord A (2004) Policy expectations and programme reality: The poverty reduction and labour market impact of two public works programmes in South Africa. Economics and Statistics Analysis Unit (ESAU) Working Paper No. 8, Overseas Development Institute (ODI), London.

Meth C (2004a) *Half measures: The ANC's unemployment and poverty reduction goals.* DPRU Working Paper No. 04/89, Development Policy Research Unit, University of Cape Town.

Meth C (2004b) What has happened to poverty in South Africa as unemployment has increased? Draft manuscript (version 5), School of Development Studies, University of KwaZulu-Natal.

Meth C (2005) Reflections on the difficulties of identifying and protecting vulnerable children and orphans. Unpublished paper prepared for Save the Children UK, School of Development Studies, University of KwaZulu-Natal.

Meth C, Naidoo R & Shipman B (1996) *Unemployment insurance and related coverage issues.* Report of the Task Team appointed by the Minister of Labour to review the UIF, December.

Mosley P & Booth A (2003) Introduction and Context. In A Booth & P Mosley (eds) *The new poverty strategies: What have they achieved? What have we learned?* Houndmills, Basingstoke: Palgrave MacMillan.

Nedlac (National Economic Development and Labour Council) (2003) Growth and Development Summit Agreement, 7 June. Johannesburg: Nedlac.

Noble M, Ratcliffe A & Wright G (2004) Conceptualizing, defining and measuring poverty in South Africa: An argument for a consensual approach. Unpublished paper, Centre for the Analysis of South African Social Policy, Department of Social Policy and Social Work, University of Oxford.

Parsons R (ed) (2004) *Manuel, markets and money: Essays in appraisal.* Cape Town: Double Storey Books.

Phillips S (2004) The expanded public works programme. Paper presented at the conference Overcoming underdevelopment in South Africa's second economy, Pretoria, 28–29 October.

PCAS (Policy Co-ordination and Advisory Services) The Presidency (2003) *Towards a ten year review: Synthesis report on implementation of government programmes.* Pretoria: Policy Co-ordination and Advisory Services.

Pyatt G (2003) Poverty versus the poor. In A Booth & P Mosley (eds) *The new poverty strategies: What have they achieved? What have we learned?* Houndmills, Basingstoke: Palgrave MacMillan.

Rao DS Prasada (2003) *PPPs for the measurement of global and regional poverty: Issues and options.* Accessed online 18 June 2004, web.worldbank.org/WBSITE/EXTERNAL/DATASTATISTICS/ICPEXT/0.

Ravallion M (2000) Comments on Deaton's 'Counting the world's poor: Problems and possible solutions'. Mimeograph, World Bank. Cited in Rao, 2003.

Ravallion M (2002) Have we already met the Millennium Development Goals? *Economic and Political Weekly,* 16 November. Cited in Deaton (2003a).

Ravallion M & Chen S (1997) What can new survey data tell us about recent changes in distribution and poverty? *World Bank Economic Review* 11(2): 357–382.

Ravallion M, Datt G & van de Walle D (1991) Quantifying absolute poverty in the developing world, *Review of Income and Wealth* 37(4): 345–361.

Ravallion M & Sen B (1996) When method matters: Monitoring poverty in Bangladesh, *Economic Development and Cultural Change* 44(4): 761–792.

Reddy S & Pogge T (2002) How not to count poor. Mimeograph, Columbia University. Cited in Rao (2003).

Roberts B (2005) 'Empty stomachs, empty pockets': Poverty and inequality in post-apartheid South Africa. In J Daniel , R Southall & J Lutchman (eds) *State of the nation: South Africa 2004-2005.* Cape Town: HSRC Press.

Samson M (ed.) (2003) The social and economic impact of South Africa's social security system. Unpublished report prepared for the Department of Social Development by the Economic Policy Research Institute (EPRI), Cape Town.

Saunders P (1998) *Defining poverty and identifying the poor: Reflections on the Australian experience.* Social Policy Research Centre Discussion Paper No. 84.

Saunders P (2004) *Towards a credible poverty framework: From income poverty to deprivation.* Social Policy Research Centre Discussion Paper No. 131.

Skweyiya Z (2004) Budget Vote Speech by Minister of Social Development, Dr Zola Skweyiya, National Assembly, Cape Town, 3 June. Accessed online 20 July, http//:www.info.gov.za/speeches/2004/04060315451004.htm.

Snower D (1995a) Evaluating unemployment policies: What do the underlying theories tell us? *Oxford Review of Economic Policies* Spring 1995 11(1): 110–135.

Snower D (1995b) Unemployment benefits: An assessment of proposals for reform, *International Labour Review* 134(4–5): 625–647.

South African Government (2004) Government's plan of action. Accessed online 19 September 2004, www.info.gov.za/issues/poa/index.html.

South African Reserve Bank (2003) *Quarterly Bulletin*, December, Pretoria.

Statistics South Africa (2000) October Household Survey 1999, Statistical release P0317. Pretoria: Statistics South Africa.

Statistics South Africa (2001) Discussion paper No. 1: Comparative labour statistics. Labour force survey, February 2000. Pretoria: Statistics South Africa.

Statistics South Africa (2002a) *Income and expenditure of households 2000. Statistical release P0111.* Pretoria: Statistics South Africa.

Statistics South Africa (2002b) *Earning and spending in South Africa: Selected findings and comparisons from the income and expenditure surveys of October 1995 and October 2000.* Pretoria: Statistics South Africa.

Statistics South Africa (2002c) *Labour force survey February 2002. Statistical release P0210.* Pretoria: Statistics South Africa.

Statistics South Africa (2003a) *Labour force survey September 2002. Statistical release P0210.* Pretoria: Statistics South Africa.

Statistics South Africa (2003b) *General household survey July 2002, Statistical release P0318.* Pretoria: Statistics South Africa.

Statistics South Africa (2004) *Labour force survey September 2003. Statistical release P0210.* Pretoria: Statistics South Africa.

Statistics South Africa (2005) *Labour force survey September 2004. Statistical release P0210.* Pretoria: Statistics South Africa.

United Nations (2000a) Resolution adopted by the General Assembly: 55/2. United Nations Millennium Declaration, September 2000a. Accessed online 20 September 2004, www.un.org/millennium/declaration/ares552e.pdf.

United Nations (2000b) World summit for social development: Programme of action, August 2000b. Accessed online 20 September 2004, http://www.un.org/esa/socdev/wssd/agreements/index.html.

United Nations (2002) The road from Johannesburg. World summit for sustainable development. What was achieved and the way forward, 2002. Accessed online 20 September 2004, www.un.org/esa/sustdev/media/Brochure.doc.

UNDP (United Nations Development Programme)(2003) South Africa Human Development Report 2003. *The challenge of sustainable development in South Africa: Unlocking people's creativity*. Oxford: Oxford University Press.

Van de Walle D & Nead K (eds) (1995) *Public spending and the poor: Theory and evidence*. Baltimore, MD: Johns Hopkins University Press.

Van der Berg S & Louw M (2003) Changing patterns of South African income distribution: Towards time series estimates of distribution and poverty. Paper presented at the Conference of the Economic Society of South Africa, Stellenbosch, September.

Woolard I (2002) *An overview of poverty and inequality in South Africa*. Working Paper prepared for DFId (South Africa), July.

Woolard I & Leibbrandt M (2001) Measuring poverty in South Africa. In H Bhorat, M Leibbrandt, M Maziya, S van der Berg & I Woolard *Fighting poverty: Labour markets and inequality in South Africa*. Cape Town: UCT Press.

World Bank/The International Bank for Reconstruction and Development (2001) *World Development Report 2000/2001: Attacking Poverty*. New York: Oxford University Press.

List of contributors

Haroon Bhorat is Associate Professor and Director in the Development Policy Research Unit at the University of Cape Town.

Daniela Casale is a lecturer in the School of Economics at the University of KwaZulu-Natal and a research associate with the Child, Youth and Family Development Research Programme, Human Sciences Research Council.

Gabriel Demombynes is an economist in the Latin American and the Caribbean Region, Poverty Sector, The World Bank, Washington, DC.

Lawrence Edwards is a senior lecturer in the School of Economics at the University of Cape Town.

Johannes Fedderke is Professor of Economics in the School of Economics at the University of Cape Town.

Johannes G Hoogeveen is an economist in the Human Development Network, Social Protection Team, The World Bank, Washington, DC.

Ravi Kanbur is the TH Lee Professor of World Affairs, International Professor of Applied Economics and Management Professor of Economics at Cornell University, USA.

Murray Leibbrandt is Professor, and Director of the Southern African Labour and Development Research Unit (SALDRU), in the School of Economics at the University of Cape Town.

Julian May is Associate Professor in the School of Development Studies at the University of KwaZulu-Natal.

Charles Meth is Senior Research Fellow in the School of Development Studies at the University of KwaZulu-Natal and a research associate of SALDRU, in the School of Economics at the University of Cape Town.

Pranushka Naidoo is a researcher in the Development Policy Research Unit at the University of Cape Town.

Morné Oosthuizen is a senior researcher in the Development Policy Research Unit at the University of Cape Town.

Berk Özler is an economist in the Development Research Group, The World Bank, Washington, DC.

Dorrit Posel is Associate Professor in the School of Economics at the University of KwaZulu-Natal.

Laura Poswell is a senior researcher in the Development Policy Research Unit at the University of Cape Town.

Sandrine Rospabe is a lecturer in the Centre for Research in Economics and Management (CREM), Université de Rennes, France.

Harris Selod is a researcher specialising in urban and regional economics with the *Institut National de la Recherche Agronomique* (National Institute for Agricultural Research), Paris, France.

Servaas van der Berg is Professor in the Department of Economics at the University of Stellenbosch.

Matthew Welch is Deputy Director of Data-First and Research Associate in the Southern Africa Labour and Development Research Unit (SALDRU) at the University of Cape Town.

Index

IF